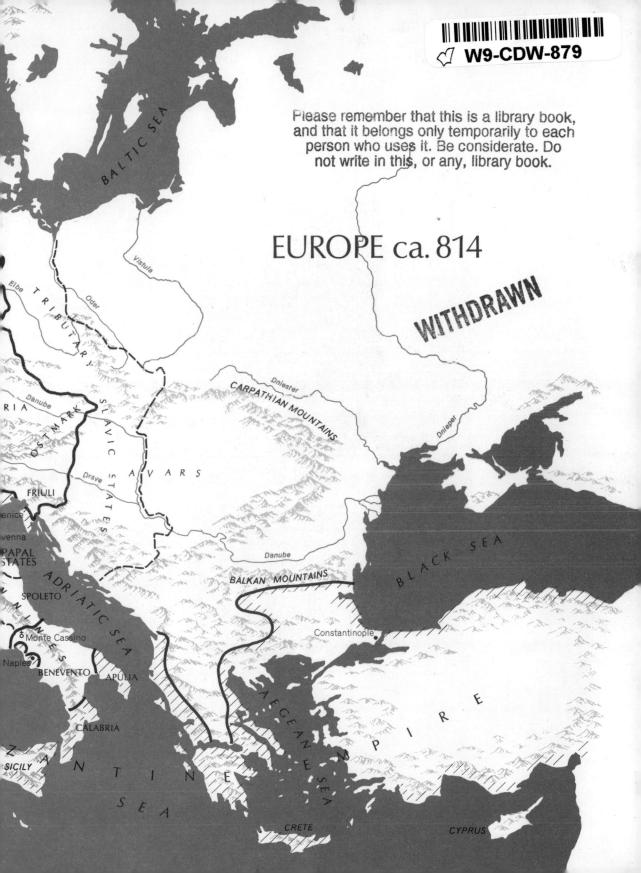

EUROPE ca. 814

BALTIC SEA

Vistula

Elbe

TRIBUTARY

Oder

SLAVIC STATES

OSTMARK

Danube

Drave

AVARS

Dniester

CARPATHIAN MOUNTAINS

Dnieper

FRIULI

RIA

Venice

Ravenna

PAPAL STATES

Danube

Balkan Mountains

BALKAN MOUNTAINS

BLACK SEA

ADRIATIC SEA

SPOLETO

APENNINES

Monte Cassino

Naples

BENEVENTO

APULIA

CALABRIA

EMPIRE

Constantinople

BYZANTINE SEA

AEGEAN SEA

SICILY

CRETE

CYPRUS

# EUROPE IN THE
# MIDDLE AGES

### THIRD EDITION

# EUROPE IN THE MIDDLE AGES

## THIRD EDITION

## Robert S. Hoyt
LATE OF THE UNIVERSITY OF MINNESOTA

## Stanley Chodorow
UNIVERSITY OF CALIFORNIA, SAN DIEGO

HARCOURT BRACE JOVANOVICH, PUBLISHERS

SAN DIEGO  NEW YORK  CHICAGO  ATLANTA  WASHINGTON, D.C.
LONDON  SYDNEY  TORONTO

**For Adam and Eric**

Maps drawn by Marlene Fein and Bill Walker

*Credits and Acknowledgments*

EDWARD ARNOLD LTD for a selection from J. Huizinga, *The Waning of the Middle Ages.* Reprinted by permission of the publisher, Edward Arnold Ltd.
CHATTO & WINDUS LTD for a selection from *The Confessions of Golias* from J. A. Symonds, *Wine, Women, and Song.* Reprinted by permission of the publisher, Chatto & Windus Ltd.
ALFRED A. KNOPF, INC. for a selection from *Dies Irae* from Frederick B. Artz, *The Mind of the Middle Ages.* Third Edition © 1958 by Alfred A. Knopf, Inc. Reprinted by permission of the publisher, Alfred A. Knopf, Inc., a Division of Random House, Inc.
JACK LINDSAY for selections from *Vexilla Regis Prodeunt* and *Hisperica Famina* from Jack Lindsay, *Song of a Falling World.* Reprinted by permission of the translator, Jack Lindsay, and the publisher, Andrew Dakers Ltd.
DAVID MCKAY COMPANY, INC. for a selection from "A Song of Nothing," translated by T. G. Bergin, from *Medieval Literature in Translation,* edited by C. W. Jones. Reprinted by permission of the publisher, David McKay Company, Inc.
THE MEDIAEVAL ACADEMY OF AMERICA for a selection from Peter Charanis, "A Greek Source on the Origin of the First Crusade" in *Speculum* 24 (1949). Reprinted by permission of the editor of *Speculum,* The Mediaeval Academy of America.

Pages 678–79 constitute a continuation of the copyright page.

# Preface

Robert S. Hoyt's *Europe in the Middle Ages* has always had a special importance for me. As a student I studied the first edition, and as an instructor I have used the second. From the beginning of my acquaintance with it, the book has impressed me as an excellent text because it is well organized, comprehensive in its treatment, and moderate in its interpretive approach. Hoyt indicated his own interests and ideas in his emphases, of course, but he did not impose an overall interpretation on the history of medieval Europe. In particular, he did not explain the medieval world in terms of the modern and did not organize his work to treat the rise of Europe as a center of world power. When Hoyt was educated and when he conceived and wrote his book, the scholastic concentration on Western civilization and on European history had not yet been challenged by students and professors demanding equal time for non-Western civilizations, and the interest in decolonization had not yet produced a felt need to explain why the colonization had taken place. In the nineteen years since Hoyt first published his text, the focusing of medieval-history courses on the rise of Europe and the attempt to create all-encompassing interpretations of medieval European history have had their first full bloom. Hoyt's book, while not participating in this trend, has nonetheless remained a mainstay in the field. It has bucked the trend because its range, breadth, and interpretive reticence allow instructors maximum freedom to create firmly grounded courses that respond to their own and to student interests.

In the third edition of *Europe in the Middle Ages,* I have attempted to preserve the quality of the first two editions while updating the treatment of specific subjects. The book is substantially rewritten, and in many respects it is a new book, but it rests firmly on the original conception. I have condensed the work a little and have reorganized it to make it more compatible with available supplementary materials and books. The additional maps and those revised from the earlier editions increase the geographical component in the history, and the more than 150 illustrations with detailed captions add a visual aspect that was almost wholly lacking from the first two editions. I believe that the new book presents a more complete picture of medieval Europe than any now available and that improvements have been made without sacrificing the qualities that made the first two editions of *Europe in the Middle Ages* so excellent and well received. I am especially honored to have been able to continue in the tradition Hoyt established in his first two editions of this work.

A project of this scope could not have been undertaken without the aid of many people. The comments of the reviewers of the second edition played a large role in my revision. Drafts of the third edition received the careful attention of Thomas N. Bisson, University of California, Berkeley; David J. Herlihy, Harvard University; Boyd H. Hill, Jr., University of Colorado; Elizabeth T. Kennan, Catholic University of America; and Gavin I. Langmuir, Stanford University. I want to express my thanks to those reviewers, while exonerating them from association with my errors of judgment in not following their advice on every point. I reserve special thanks to John F. Benton of the California Institute of Technology, who originally planned the revision and reworked several chapters. Professor Benton exhibited his sure hand as a teacher and scholar in reorganizing the book and in the revisions he made. I am deeply indebted to him for his work on the foundations of this edition. To my editor, Irene Pavitt, I owe gratitude for continuing my education as a writer. She saved me from innumerable howlers, and by successfully adapting herself to my style and approach, made working on my prose a pleasant as well as an important experience. The illustrations were tracked down by Carla Hirst Wiltenburg, and to her belongs the credit for the visual excellence of the volume. Her knowledge of the field and her outstanding judgment made the process of choosing pictures an educational experience. All of us who worked on the book owe thanks to Anna Kopczynski, its designer, who created the format for a clear and effective presentation of the text and illustrations. Finally, a host of typists struggled with the manuscript and paste-ups that are inevitably part of a revision like this one. To mention only some of the most active, I wish to thank Dolores Avila, Kitty Morris, and Alexandra Patterson.

STANLEY CHODOROW

# Contents

## The Early Middle Ages

### I The Precursors of Medieval Civilization

# Europe from the Twelfth Through the Fifteenth Century

# Maps

# Introduction

**The Middle Ages in the History
of Western Civilization**

Why are the centuries between A.D. 300 and 1500 treated as a distinct period in the history of Western civilization? In the twelfth century anyone who thought about history considered contemporary civilization the political and cultural continuation of Roman antiquity: the ancient empire lived in the contemporary empire that occupied the vast territories stretching from the North Sea to the lands south of Rome, and ancient culture lived in the schools. Twelfth-century historians considered the periods of history stages in the salvation of mankind, divided by events of spiritual significance; for example, the covenant of Abraham, the handing down of the Mosaic law, and the coming of Christ. Our world view makes a different division, derived from the historical perception of the fifteenth-century Italian Humanists and the leaders of the Protestant Reformation. The Humanists were the first to recognize a meaningful break between antiquity and the period that followed. In the fourteenth century, Petrarch contrasted what he called "ancient histories" and "modern histories," drawing the line between them at the conversion of Constantine. In his admiration for the belles-lettres and political virtue of ancient

1

Rome, he characterized "modern history," which extended down to his own day, as an age of "darkness" in which the grandeur that was Rome had been debilitated and debased by barbarians. Another Humanist, the fifteenth-century writer Flavio Biondo, drew a sharp line between antiquity and the succeeding age, which for him began with the sack of Rome in A.D. 410. Other early Humanists were aware that in the arts and letters there had been a rebirth of the standards and values of antiquity, but they did not apply this idea of a renaissance to general history. Nonetheless, the Humanists did project a tripartite division of history, distinguishing periods of greatness, decline, and revival.

Protestant historians in the sixteenth century widened the concept of a renaissance by portraying the ascendancy of the papacy, in the period following Constantine's conversion, as part of the decline of the Roman Empire. This decline, they contended, did not end until the restoration of the primitive evangelical Church by Luther. Thus, both Humanists and Protestant writers implied, although neither actually stated, a threefold division of history, of whose second stage they did not approve.

Late–seventeenth-century historians were the first to apply the concept of a tripartite periodization to general history. The Renaissance and Reformation lay far enough in the past so that three distinct periods of time could be distinguished. No longer was the intermediate period simply the era separating themselves from antiquity; it was a period that itself had ended in the past. The term *Middle Ages,* in this sense, derives from the title of a textbook published in 1688 by a Dutch teacher of history, Cellarius (Christoph Keller), entitled *History of the Middle Age from the Times of Constantine the Great to the Capture of Constantinople by the Turks.* Cellarius had already published a textbook on ancient history, and his work on the Middle Ages was followed by a textbook on modern history (*historia nova*). The term *Middle Ages* soon became universally accepted, although Cellarius' chronological limits (ca. 330–1453) were not invariably followed, even by him, in later works.

The historians of the eighteenth century reinforced not only the idea that history divided into three periods but also the negative assessment both Humanists and Protestants had given to the Middle Ages. The most eminent historian of his time, Edward Gibbon, summed up the Middle Ages as "the greatest, perhaps, and most awful scene in the history of mankind." Gibbon's view of the period derived from the conviction of the Enlightenment *philosophes* that history constituted the struggle between reason and unreason. Progress toward the triumph of reason had begun in antiquity and had been resumed after the Middle Ages had had a catastrophic effect on, and almost put an end to, man's progress. Thus the Enlightenment historians created a new historiography that ironically shared much with the medieval idea of history as the story of mankind's progress toward salvation but that preserved the periodization of Cellarius and others.

At the end of the eighteenth century, however, events came to undermine the idea that the struggle between reason and unreason determined the course of history. The perspective of the Enlightenment historians led them to associate the triumph of reason with the replacement or destruction of medieval ideas and institutions; their historiography was therefore linked with the revolutionary agitation of eighteenth-century France. To many intellectuals, the triumph of reason in history resulted in the French Revolution; the failure of that revolution weakened the *philosophes'* historiography as well as their political ideals, leaving historians without a sure orientation, without a conceptual framework to guide their pursuit of knowledge about the past. If history did not lead to the triumph of reason, where did it lead? Early nineteenth-century historians found the answer in the history of the modern nation-state, which had emerged apparently undamaged from the French Revolution and its aftermath. They saw the state as the optimal milieu for mankind's cultural life, and, therefore, the growth of the state appeared as the principal end of history. This historiographical view resulted in a reassessment of the Middle Ages, for historians discovered that the origins of the nation-state were to be found in the medieval period.

Once historians began to focus on the growth of the state, why did they not discard the tripartite periodization of history? If the nation-state had been developing since the early Middle Ages, did it make sense to distinguish between the medieval and the modern ages? For several reasons, the latter question, although raised by the work of nineteenth-century historians, has really disturbed only their twentieth-century successors. In the first place, education in Europe and the United States had been based, until very recently, on the value system established by the fifteenth-century Humanists. Historians' work, therefore, traditionally has reflected the biases of Humanist education, including the recognition that the revival of interest in classical civilization during the Renaissance indicated the beginning of a new era. In the second place, while historical scholarship is aware of the continuity of medieval civilization into the early modern period, it has also confirmed that enough significant changes took place in the fourteenth and fifteenth centuries to justify the division between the two ages. The political entities of the modern world, like the cultural life, may have their origins in the Middle Ages, but they differ significantly from their medieval forebears.

The chronological limits of this book, 300–1500, were therefore set by a tradition stemming from the Renaissance Humanists and Protestant reformers, confirmed by recent historical scholarship largely freed from the perspective of those fifteenth- and sixteenth-century scholars. Twentieth-century historians are certainly more aware than their predecessors that the organization of the past depends heavily on the contemporary standpoint and interests, but they still rely on the traditional chronological categories in their work. Does the modern geographical orientation also stand up to the changes in perspective?

## Land, Climate, and People

The European-centered perspective of most historians is hardly acceptable to mid–twentieth-century people aware of the world's political and economic interdependence. Furthermore, the world out of which modern Europe grew was a Mediterranean world in which the Near East and North Africa were integral parts. The first objection, stemming from the perception of the world in the jet age, does not really affect the perspective in considering the medieval period, for although Europe is now only a part of a worldwide community of nations, it was relatively isolated in the Middle Ages. The second objection is more germane. How can the history of medieval Europe be treated in isolation from that of the Mediterranean world as a whole? This book constitutes an examination of and attempts to answer this question.

Recently, one historian described the geographical region of which Europe is part as a sack. The mouth of the sack opens toward the steppes of central Asia, with a subsidiary opening toward India through the Khyber Pass in the Hindu Kush of Afghanistan. The sides of the sack are formed by the Sahara Desert and the Arabian Sea in the south and the Arctic Ocean in the north. The bottom, or western side, borders on the Atlantic Ocean. The Ural Mountains make an extension of the northern side that comes to the south dividing European Russia from central Asia and narrowing the mouth of the sack. The mountains of Pakistan and Afghanistan contract the opening from the south, except where the line is broken by the Bolan and Khyber passes. These passes had made possible the inclusion of northwest Indian territories and states in the Persian and Macedonian empires. During the Middle Ages, however, this opening to India was effectively closed by nomadic peoples who controlled Turkestan, the region immediately northwest of the passes.

The vast area contained in the sack has been subject to outside influence through much of recorded history. The opening to Asia has let in peoples who disrupted the empires and settled populations surrounding the Mediterranean: the Huns, Avars, and other nomadic Altaic peoples in the late Roman period, from the third to the sixth centuries of our era. The various Turkish groups, such as the Seljuks and Osmanli (Ottoman), also passed through Turkestan, headed for the Near East and Persia (or its successor, the Islamic Empire) instead of central Europe. Finally, the Mongols and Tartars used Turkestan as a land bridge across which they extended the borders of their great twelfth- and thirteenth-century empires, centered in eastern Asia. Thus, the history of the whole geographical area that includes Europe concerns the interaction of established political entities with outsiders who funneled through the valleys of the Oxus and Jaxartes rivers.

In following the history of political configurations and their civilizations within the sack, attention is constantly riveted on the Mediterranean. The major ancient civilizations and empires surrounded this great internal sea;

The Geography of Europe and the Mediterranean

the Romans called it *mare nostrum* (our sea). At the beginning of our era
the Romans controlled the whole Mediterranean littoral and in some places
had extended their power far beyond the coasts. One of those places was
Europe, where the empire's northern frontier was established along the
Rhine and Danube rivers in southern Germany. After the break-up of this
great empire, three successors held the Mediterranean basin—the Byzantine
Empire, the Islamic Empire, and the European kingdoms. As heirs to the
Roman Empire, these regions ought perhaps to be considered together. That
they are traditionally treated separately is due partly to the European perspective of modern historical scholars and partly to the relative isolation in
which the areas developed for five or more centuries after the disintegration
of the Roman Empire. The great territorial blocks certainly had contact during the Middle Ages, but each evolved as a separate civilization and political
entity (or group of them) in response much more to internal conditions and

circumstances than to external influences. The geographical standpoint of this book reflects the convictions of historians that to understand the rise of Europe as one of the great centers of world power, it is necessary to focus on the history of the continent itself. And one of the principal questions underlying the study concerns the reasons Europe, geographically only part of the great area described above, became the locus of a distinct civilization.

This civilization occupies a continent divided geographically and climatically by a ridge of mountain chains stretching from the Pyrenees on the western flank to the Transylvanian Alps on the eastern. The Franco-Swiss Alps are at the mid-point. South of these mountain chains, the so-called Mediterranean climate prevails, which has only a two-season variation—winter and summer. It is generally dry, with rainfall during the winter. This climatic pattern determined, even in prehistoric times, the kind of agriculture possible in the region: first, the Mediterranean is a one-crop climate. The crop must be planted in the fall for harvest in late spring or early summer. Second, the farmer must take care not to disturb the soil in ways that will cause moisture loss. Such dry farming is practiced in about one-quarter of the world, where annual rainfall is between ten and thirty inches. It is essential that the land be plowed on the surface (using light, simple plows) and that the stubble be left on the ground after harvest. Deep plowing would expose too much of the soil to the air, thus causing moisture loss; the stubble holds moisture and helps to protect the topsoil from wind erosion during the long dry season.

Agricultural technique is not the only part of rural life affected by the Mediterranean climate. Shepherds and cowherds are forced to organize their husbandry in accord with the wet and dry seasons, going into the mountain pastures during the summer and returning to the lowlands for the winter months. Aside from the extra work these migrations involve, the movement of the herds deprives the tillage of manure fertilizer, the only fertilizer used in the premodern world, for half of each year.

Northern farmers escape all these limitations on productivity. North of the mountain chain that divides Europe climatically, rainfall is plentiful and is dispersed rather evenly over the year. Notwithstanding seasonal variations, no season is dry. In addition, temperature variation is not great—it is the temperate zone—and thus farmers are able to plant two crops per year. The wetness makes the soils of the north richer and more productive than those of the south and permits the kind of deep plowing that increases the yield per acre. To these advantages is added the constant presence of the herds, which did not have to move to the highlands for the summer and therefore participate in the food cycle throughout the year. Northern Europe, characterized by the great forested plain stretching from England and southern Scandinavia to the Urals (the North German Plain), is one of the world's best-suited regions for human habitation. In the Middle Ages it supported a large and growing population, and in the early modern era, it became the center of European world power.

In the Middle Ages, the north had another major advantage over the south. Since the Mediterranean lands surrounded a great sea, commerce in southern Europe was primarily a coastal activity. The sparse, seasonal rainfall made the rivers useless for inland navigation, so it was impossible to bring inland produce into the trade network that crisscrossed the region. Until recently, land transport was too expensive for large-scale commercial use. The economic situation was completely different in northern Europe, where the consistent rainfall and the flat terrain produced wide, slow-moving, year-round rivers ideal for transporting inland goods to the sea. Not only could the products of inland agriculture be transported to the trade network but inland cities could develop as ports and commercial centers. Medieval Paris, London, Hamburg, and even Cologne became shipping centers, and this development brought virtually every region of northern Europe into the long-distance trade system. At the beginning of the Middle Ages, the commercial development of the northern geographical and climatic region was only potential. At the end of the period, it had begun to be realized and was becoming the basis for the modern world economy.

Any attempt to survey prehistoric settlement in Europe would be extremely difficult because archeologists are uncertain about what happened during much of the period before 500 B.C. Recent discoveries indicate that between about 450 and 200 B.C. Celtic peoples migrated throughout Europe and beyond, taking with them an Iron Age culture called La Tène—the archeological site in western Switzerland at which its characteristics were first revealed. This early Celtic culture, whose center was just north of the Alps, developed under the auspices of aristocratic and princely leaders before spreading to the lower classes. In the period of expansion—coinciding with Mediterranean developments like the rise and fall of the Greek city-states, the creation of the Macedonian Empire, and the establishment of the Roman Republic—the Celtic peoples moved west into France, southwest to the Iberian Peninsula, east toward the Hungarian plain, and southeast into the Balkans. They also extended their power into southern Russia, where they engaged in a long struggle with the Greek colonies on the northern littoral of the Black Sea, and they established themselves in central Anatolia (Asia Minor). The Galatians of New Testament times were descendants of the Celtic group that had conquered this region. In addition to the Continental expansion, the Celts entered the British Isles during the fourth and third centuries B.C., first northern Scotland and later the area surrounding York. From these centers, they took control of most of the islands. At the same time, Celtic groups entered northern Italy and attacked the Etruscan cities. They sacked Rome in 386 B.C.

Archeologists cannot yet estimate the degree of unity in this extraordinarily widespread Celtic empire, but they are learning more about the pattern of its settlement. The Celts, who appear to have been an urbanized people, built fortified cities along the trade routes. Julius Caesar wrote of their *oppida* (towns), and archeologists have discovered several of these both in the ancient center of Celtic civilization and in the far-flung regions they conquered. In the course of their expansion, the Celts came under the influence of the Greeks. Greek trade and culture moved west, through the Danube valley, affecting the civilization of the eastern Celts, and north, along the routes from the Greek colony at Massilia (Marseilles), into present-day France. The Celtic culture and its political structure is an important subject for future study by historians because knowledge of this ancient civilization will permit a better understanding of the confrontation between Rome and the Celts in the first century B.C. as well as the ways in which Celtic culture affected the Germanic tribes. The Celts did influence Germanic cultural development both before and during the time when the Germanic tribes were becoming part of the Roman world.

The Germanic peoples occupied the regions just south of the Baltic Sea from at least the fifth century B.C. onward. At about the same time the Celts began to migrate throughout Europe, the Germans began to move south. Archeologists are not yet certain about the relationship between the two movements. Some have suggested that the Germans caused the Celtic expansion by putting pressure on the ancient center of Celtic culture. Others have argued that the Celtic migration was aggressive and was not spurred by external pressures. These scholars think the Germans moved south in the wake of Celtic movement.

Although the Celts had been influencing Germanic civilization for several centuries, the Germans possessed a distinct culture apparently derived from pre-Celtic cultures once spread throughout Eastern Europe but restricted by Celtic power and expansion to northeastern Germany. When Julius Caesar conquered the Celts of Gaul (58–51 B.C.) and crossed the Rhine into Germany, he met peoples he distinguished by both language and customs from the Celts. Caesar's description of these Germanic groups constitutes our earliest historical source of information about them. Caesar's campaign also marked the beginning of a new cultural influence on the Germans. Now the Romans too would participate in the development of the Germanic tribes. This text begins at the point when the interaction between the Germans and the Romans had already had a major impact on the history of both peoples and was beginning a new phase that would produce a European civilization in the course of the Middle Ages.

## Suggestions for Further Reading

**Bibliographies** L. J. Paetow, *Guide to the Study of Medieval History*, rev. ed. (New York, 1931) is the best single-volume, general bibliography. The third edition of this work is presently being prepared. So many more specialized bibliographies exist that a guide to them became necessary: see R. H. Rouse, *Serial Bibliographies for Medieval Studies* (Berkeley and Los Angeles, 1969). In addition, each volume of *The Cambridge Medieval History,* 8 vols. (Cambridge, 1924–67) contains substantial bibliographies. For translations of sources published before 1942, see C. P. Farrar and A. P. Evans, *Bibliography of English Translations from Medieval Sources* (New York, 1946).

**Historical Atlases**   W. R. Shepherd, *Historical Atlas,* 8th ed. rev. (New York, 1956) is standard. Two other good atlases are Colin McEvedy, *The Penguin Atlas of Medieval History* (Baltimore, 1961), and the medieval section of R. R. Palmer, *Atlas of World History* (Chicago, 1957).

**General Medieval History**   The most exhaustive history of the Middle Ages is *The Cambridge Medieval History.* A good four-volume work is M. Deanesly, *A History of Early Medieval Europe, 479–911* (London, 1956); Z. N. Brooke, *A History of Europe from 911 to 1198,* 3rd ed. (London, 1951); C. W. Previté-Orton, *A History of Europe from 1198 to 1378,* 2nd ed. (London, 1948); and W. T. Waugh, *A History of Europe from 1378 to 1494* (London, 1932). The first two volumes on the Middle Ages have been published: C. N. L. Brooke, *Europe in the Central Middle Ages, 962–1154* (London, 1964), and Denys Hay, *Europe in the Fourteenth and Fifteenth Centuries* (London, 1966). A fine survey of late medieval history and society is W. K. Ferguson, *Europe in Transition, 1300–1520* (Boston, 1962).

**Intellectual and Cultural History**   H. O. Taylor, *The Medieval Mind,* 2 vols., 4th ed. (New York, 1925) is still unsurpassed, now supplemented by F. B. Artz, *The Mind of the Middle Ages,* 2nd ed. (New York, 1954). For medieval philosophy, the standard full-length work is M. de Wulf, *History of Medieval Philosophy,* 3 vols. (New York, 1925–53); the two best one-volume works are Étienne Gilson, *History of Christian Philosophy in the Middle Ages* (London, 1955), and David Knowles, *The Evolution of Medieval Thought* (London, 1962); introductory essays in brief compass are Gordon Leff, *Medieval Thought from Saint Augustine to Ockham* (Baltimore, 1958), and F. C. Copleston, *Medieval Philosophy* (London, 1952). The basic work in its field is R. W. Carlyle and A. J. Carlyle, *A History of Medieval Political Theory in the West,* 6 vols. (London, 1903–36), while the best treatment in one volume is C. H. McIlwain, *The Growth of Political Thought in the West* (New York, 1932). For literature and science, good general introductions are E. R. Curtius, *European Literature and the Latin Middle Ages* (New York, 1953), and A. C. Crombie, *Augustine to Galileo,* A.D. *400–1650* (London, 1952). C. R. Morey, *Medieval Art* (New York, 1942), and Nikolaus Pevsner, *An Outline of European Architecture,* 5th ed. (Baltimore, 1957) provide general introductions to art.

**Economic History**   The standard work is *The Cambridge Economic History,* vols. 1–3, ed. M. M. Postan, E. E. Rich, and E. Miller (Cambridge, 1965–66). A good new one-volume survey is G. A. J. Hodgett, *A Social and Economic History of Medieval Europe* (London, 1972).

**General Collections of Translated Sources**   There are many useful volumes. An old and still valuable one is E. F. Henderson, ed., *Select Historical Documents of the Middle Ages* (London, 1896). More recent collections of translations are Norton Downs, ed., *The Medieval Pageant* (New York, 1964); and for the period to 1300, Robert Brentano, ed., *The Early Middle Ages, 500–1000* (New York, 1964); Bryce Lyon, ed., *The High Middle Ages, 1000–1300* (New York, 1964); and D. A. White, ed., *Medieval History: A Source Book* (Homewood, Ill., 1965). The later medieval sources are emphasized in J. B. Ross and M. M. McLaughlin, eds., *The Portable Medieval Reader* (New York, 1949).

# The Early Middle Ages

# I

# THE PRECURSORS
# OF MEDIEVAL
# CIVILIZATION

# 1 | The Late Roman Empire

In nearly every age there are voices becrying the state of society—the decline of morals and the dissipation of public spirit. The Roman Empire, particularly from the third to the fifth centuries, had its share of indigenous critics, but later historians' treatment of the period has given the views of these critics an uncommon weight and durability. During the Middle Ages, historians stressed the continuities rather than the changes that took place during the age of the Germanic invasions, the fourth to the sixth centuries. This emphasis was accompanied by an interest in the growth of the Germanic kingdoms as successors and heirs to the empire, and this interpretation obscured the troubled history of the empire during the years before the Germanic onslaught. Historians' viewpoints and attitudes changed in the fifteenth century. Basing their approach on the Humanists' recognition that there was an unbridgeable gulf between classical civilization and their own, Renaissance historians saw in the Germanic invasions the end of the classical world. Once this view prevailed, the political collapse of the Western Roman Empire took on epochal significance, and historians' attention shifted from the glories of the founders of the Germanic kingdoms to the degeneration of the empire

prior to its dramatic collapse. This view of the period has persisted throughout the first half of the twentieth century and has made the moral judgment
of Rome's critics part of the intellectual baggage of modern historians.

This interpretive construct is not unreasonable because the political
structure of the empire did disappear in the West, and the process of political
disintegration was of great importance in the history of the West from the
third century on. Nonetheless, the interpretation has had unfortunate side
effects in the historiography of the late imperial period. First, historians have
tended to treat virtually all aspects of life in the late Roman Empire as less
excellent than the earlier, classical forms and conditions. This treatment
carries with it a strong moral or aesthetic bias that makes it difficult to
appreciate late antiquity on its own terms. Second, historians writing about
the late imperial world have based their work on the question: Why did the
empire in the West fall? They have proposed many answers to this question.
The great eighteenth-century historian Edward Gibbon thought that the
spread of Christianity created a state within a state in the empire and thus
weakened the political structure and civic spirit of the Roman community.
Others have argued that the empire was destroyed from without, by the onslaught of Germanic invaders from across the northern borders. Many historians have pointed to flaws in the Roman economy, to the barbarization of
the army, and to the decline of slavery, which deprived Roman agriculture of
its primary source of labor. Some historians have attempted to integrate
several causative factors to explain the decline and fall.

This search for an explanation of why the Western empire collapsed has
produced a somewhat eccentric view of the late imperial period because it has
led historians to treat changes as causes that vie with one another. Transition
from one epoch to another should not influence historians' understanding of
the earlier civilization, even though understanding the causes of the transition
is important. Assessing the causes for the change from ancient to medieval
civilization requires a composite picture of the late ancient world. This chapter draws such a picture in very brief compass.

## Roman Government and Society: The Third to the Fifth Century

The Roman Empire was the political manifestation of a Mediterranean civilization that had developed centuries before the Romans succeeded in bringing
it under their governmental control. The Greeks of the fifth century B.C.
recognized that they were part of a civilization that geographically circled
the Mediterranean Sea, with the sea providing the principal means of communication necessary for maintaining this vast cultural community. This
civilization was based on small coastal city-states founded as colonies by the
Phoenicians and Greeks and supported by the agricultural productivity of

small districts immediately surrounding the urban centers. The Phoenicians had colonized the North African and Spanish coasts. The Greeks spread more extensively along the coasts of Italy, Thrace, Asia Minor, North Africa, Gaul (France), and Spain. They even settled colonies in the Black Sea. The Greek cities and colonies of the eastern Mediterranean were not united until Philip II of Macedon and his son Alexander the Great imposed a single government on them in the fourth century B.C.

The Romans, who were in a more central Mediterranean position than the Macedonians, began extending their political power in the third century B.C. Roman expansion proceeded at the expense of Alexander's successors. However, Rome's location also brought it into rivalry with the western Mediterranean power of Carthage, and the Romans won control of the West before extending their power into the East. As the Roman Empire took shape in the last two centuries before Christ, it united East and West in the Mediterranean world for the first time. By A.D. 200, this process of expansion and unification was complete; the Romans had made their last conquests in the second century.

In Europe, the Romans gained control of territory far from the coast. Under Julius Caesar, Roman legions conquered Gaul and southern Germany. Under the emperor Claudius (A.D. 41–54), Britain became a province. This inland expansion did not move the focus of the empire's civilization away from the Mediterranean basin, but it did require a massive military and administrative commitment that became one of the hallmarks of the imperial period. The extensive borders had to be defended; sporadic rebellions had to be put down; and thus the government developed into a large and cumbersome machine that required vast financial resources. Under the Romans, Mediterranean civilization penetrated deep into its hinterland, but its reach turned out to exceed its grasp.

The empire attained its peak prosperity under the Antonine emperors, from 96 to 180. The civilized Mediterranean world enjoyed Pax Romana, universal peace imposed by Roman arms. It was occasionally disturbed by barbarian raids from across the borders or by rebellions like the Jewish revolts of 66 to 70, 115 and 116, and 133 to 135, but it was remarkably pervasive. The Roman genius for good government, just laws, and the applied sciences of engineering made the empire of the period a relatively stable world adorned with excellent roads, harbors, aqueducts, public baths, magnificent temples, and theaters. These monuments of Roman civilization were constructed by both the central, imperial government and local authorities, for while the emperor exercised ultimate power, governance of the empire was still largely decentralized. The imperial government reached into every corner of the empire through its control of the public lands and of the army. A vast bureaucracy developed to administer imperial affairs throughout the empire. But municipalities remained important units of local govern-

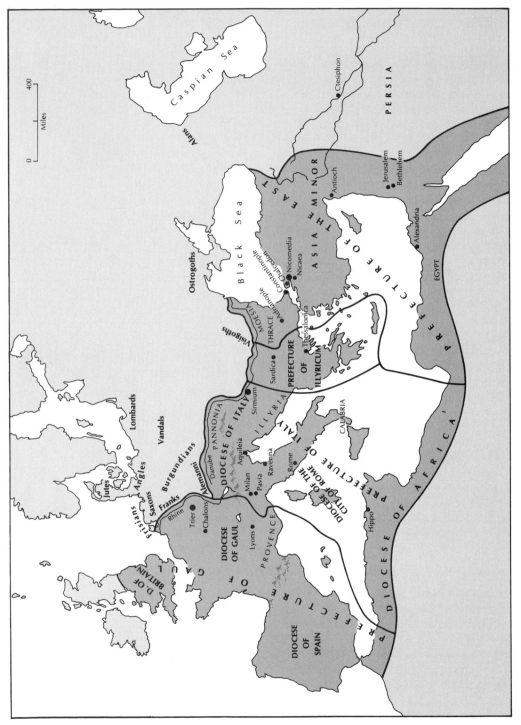

The Roman Empire in the Third and Fourth Centuries

ment, and the imperial authorities delegated many important functions to them. City councils collected taxes, supplied recruits for the army, maintained order in their districts, kept up the imperial road and transport system, and performed myriad other political functions. This is why the early Roman Empire has sometimes been characterized as a "federation of city-states." In the eastern provinces of the empire there were approximately nine hundred municipalities. In the western part there were more, although many western cities would today be considered agricultural towns.

The governing body of each city was the *curia* (council), whose members, called *curiales,* were drawn from the local aristocracy. Under imperial law, anyone who owned a substantial amount of property was automatically a *curialis* and was required to undertake the obligations of government if elected to do so. The imperial government took an avid interest in maintaining the effectiveness of the municipal *curiae* and enforced the rules concerning membership and participation. The central government also had to look out for itself, however, and therefore it exempted all those engaged in its service from local affairs and obligations. Imperial service became a widely used avenue of escape from city government during the third century, when the empire was disrupted by civil wars and border problems. But during the first and second centuries, participation in city government was honorable and valued by the leading citizens of the empire's cities.

The urban aristocracies constituted the largest class of educated people, and their education was remarkably similar throughout the empire. A linguistic and cultural division existed between the Greek East and the Latin West, but it was narrowed by the educational system. Greeks did not study Latin, on the whole, unless they were interested in pursuing military or legal careers. All official documents transmitted to the East were accompanied by a Greek translation. In the first and second centuries, all educated Westerners mastered Greek. In the fourth century many translators were at work on the corpus of Greek philosophy, theology, and science, a sign of the decline of Greek studies among Westerners.

The aristocracy was a thin, homogeneous veneer on an empire of very different peoples. Since Latin and Greek were virtually the only written languages (with the exception of Syriac; Gothic received an alphabet in the late imperial period but could hardly be called a language with a rhetorical tradition comparable to Latin and Greek) and the only ones taught in schools, it is difficult to assess the strength of native languages and cultures in the empire. Celtic languages survived in Gaul and Britain, and several native cultures thrived in Asia Minor. Syriac and Coptic (the Egyptian language) continued to be spoken in the East. Modern Albanian probably derives from the language spoken by the ancient Illyrians, and, at the end of the fourth century, Thracian was still a living language. Thus the culture of the late empire was of a double fabric. On one side, the imperial government and the classes that served it (for the most part identical to the municipal aristocracies) saw a

This stretch of aqueduct, part of a sixty-mile system built by the Romans at Segovia, Spain, is still used to supply water to the city. The water flows in a channel along the top. (Photo by Walter Sanders from Time-Life Great Ages of Man Series, © Time Inc.)

great territorial empire united by the Mediterranean and by a network of roads that provided inland communications for the state services and armies. The policies, institutions, and culture of the governing classes were remarkably homogeneous, and it is this culture that is known as Greco-Roman civilization. On the other side, most of the populations in the empire maintained their pre-Roman customs virtually untouched by the culture of the governing classes, although the imperial system often had a major effect on the lives of these peoples.

To the extent that there was a Roman society, then, it was that of the upper classes; in the population as a whole, there were many societies. Nonetheless, after all free men in the empire became citizens in A.D. 212 (under a law aimed at solving problems of taxation and army recruitment), citizenship became the index of social position. The linguistic and cultural boundaries that in reality fragmented the Roman world were ignored. Romans had a propensity to seize on honorable titles to distinguish their social and governmental positions. In the late third century, the highest class, the senators, bore the title *clarissimi* (most distinguished), while the high judges of imperial courts, the praetorian prefects, were called *eminentissimi* (most eminent) and their immediate subordinates, *perfectissimi* (most perfect). The prestige ascribed to these titles became diminished as people strove for them and as emperors rewarded faithful service with higher status. Thus, in the late third century approximately five hundred senators were called *clarissimi,* but by the middle of the sixth century, several thousand claimed that title. In the same period, the *perfectissimus* was attached to such positions as provincial financial clerks and regimental quartermasters. This inflation in titles resulted in the creation of new titles for those who really were distinguished. In the fifth and sixth centuries, the class of *spectabiles* (notables) included vicars of large administrative districts called dioceses and military commanders of high rank; the title *viri illustres* (illustrious men) was accorded to high officials of the imperial palace. The praetorian prefects had become *viri illustres.* Above these high officials were a very few men who had gained the honor of being consuls for a year, who were relatives of the emperor, or who warranted special imperial favor. They were granted the rank of *patricius* (patrician).

The titles of the aristocracy were defined by the privileges they accorded their bearers. Members of the middle and lower classes also received legal titles, but their positions were defined by the obligations imposed on them. At the top of the middle class stood the *curiales.* The imperial authority was constantly tampering with the laws dealing with this class in order to maintain it at sufficient numerical and economic strength. The *curiales* were personally responsible for the obligations of city government and were held to account for its failures. If a disastrous crop diminished the tax base and prevented the *curiales* from collecting the required revenues, they had to make up the difference from their own funds. In addition, those assigned to oversee the maintenance of roads, bridges, and social services had to finance their duties from their own incomes. Naturally, there was incentive for escaping these burdens, and since imperial service both exempted a man from participation in local government and raised his status, entry into the civil service or the army became the primary goal of the *curiales.* This class dwindled so steadily that in the fifth century the imperial government had to reorganize local government on a new basis.

Merchants had low status and only rarely became *curiales.* On the whole, they were on the same level as craftsmen, although craftsmen had a greater chance of rising into the honorable ranks because a great many of them worked for the government in state factories that produced matériel for the army. The superintendents of these factories were substantial men and received substantial titles. Peasants, who comprised about 90 percent of the population of the empire, were at the bottom of the social scale. A large proportion of the peasants owned their own land, but in the late empire small peasant farmers were forced to grant or sell their lands to the great landowners in return for help during the inevitable bad seasons. In the late

A woman selects a goose in a Roman butcher shop. Like many shops in Rome, this one was managed, and perhaps owned, by a woman.

imperial period a good market in land flourished, since land was the only long-term investment. Most officials and professionals supplemented their incomes with rents, and even small shopkeepers and craftsmen bought plots.

The eagerness of the urban middle class to buy land and to realize the benefits of agricultural production demonstrates the enormous importance of farming in the economy of the empire. As in all periods prior to very recent times, the imperial economy was overwhelmingly agricultural. Another index of the predominance of agriculture can be seen in the imperial tax returns, which show that only about 10 percent of the revenues came from urban and commercial taxes. The two most important crops were wheat and barley, but olives were also grown on a large scale, and wine-making was a major industry. Most of the smaller cities lived off the produce of their local districts, but larger cities like Rome and Antioch had to import almost all the grain their populations required. The principal grain producing areas were in Sicily, North Africa, and Egypt, with production concentrated around rivers and canals that provided transport to the sea. Britain grew the grain that was shipped down the Rhine to the border armies in that district. It is impossible to estimate the number of farmers and the amount of arable land involved in the agricultural supply system, but both were large. It is important, however, to recognize that the agricultural system did not have a commercial basis. A great part of the agricultural surplus was paid in taxes and did not create an income for the farmers. The peasants realized very little from their holdings,

since they paid heavy taxes or, if they were tenants, heavy rents. Most farmers lived at the subsistence level. The great landowners earned large incomes
however, for not only did they often have tax privileges that left them in
control of their estates' production, but they sold their crops in a lucrative
market through which the government supplemented the supplies it had received through the tax system.

The government also dominated other sectors of the economy. Many
goods were manufactured in state factories, including all the weapons and
most of the clothing used by the armies. The goods were sent along an
extensive government transport system that virtually monopolized large-scale
shipping. Since the government organized and subsidized the provisioning of
the major cities, independent merchants were largely restricted to dealing in
a few widely available raw materials like timber, wool, and flax, and in the
tools and implements used in everyday life. Merchants also dealt in luxury
items like spices, jewelry, and fine wines, but this trade was limited and did
not lead to the establishment of great commercial empires. Most of the traders who sold luxury wares in the West were Orientals, such as Syrians and
Jews, who had connections in the eastern Mediterranean cities through which
these goods passed.

The commercial organization of the late empire greatly affected the
economy of the early Middle Ages, after the western part of the empire had
collapsed. Since the imperial government was the major consumer and pro-
ducer of manufactured goods, its disintegration left the main sector of the
commercial economy without a market and without organization. To the
extent that an imperial economy existed, it was a state economy deeply influenced by events that shook the state. The imperial economy successfully
linked the many local economies to the central government and its activities,
and thus any strain put on the imperial system was soon felt in the districts.
During the third century, events did shake the state and disrupted the lives of
the subject peoples.

## Crisis and Recovery: The Third and Fourth Centuries

The empire's magnificent governmental structure was flawed seriously by the
problem of succession to the imperial throne. Theoretically, the Senate and
the people elected the best man in the state to be emperor. In practice, the
army played the main role by proclaiming a candidate who the Senate
and people were constrained to accept. Occasionally, as in A.D. 96 when the
aristocrat Nerva was raised to the purple, the Senate played the principal
role. The people acclaimed the man presented to them. This system, if it can
be called that, resulted in many disputed successions because those involved
in the election of the emperor did not always agree on the kind of man fit for
the throne, much less the individuals proposed at any given time. The army

and the people supported the dynastic principle, but the Senate stoutly resisted hereditary accession because it wanted only men of proven ability and aristocratic sentiment to be chosen, and it desired a large role in the process of elevation. Nonetheless, a few dynasties had maintained themselves during the early imperial period. Adopted descendants of Augustus reigned until A.D. 68, when civil war broke out following the suicide of Nero. Vespasian established a new dynasty in 70. This dynasty ended with Domitian's murder in 96, after which a long line of good emperors succeeded one another. Then Marcus Aurelius (161–180) was followed by his incompetent son Commodus, and when Commodus was murdered in 192, civil war again erupted. In 193 Septimius Severus emerged as victor, and in 211 he was able to pass the imperial power to his son. This dynasty lasted until 238.

The crisis that followed the end of the Severi dynasty coincided with an increase of pressure on the borders of the empire. Before the end of the second century, the Germanic tribes across the Rhine-Danube frontier had become restive and began massive raids inside Roman territory. Up to the late second century, the border armies had been able to police the frontiers, chasing down invading parties and engaging in attacks of their own. Marcus Aurelius had to spend much of his reign fighting the Germans, and the city of Trier, close to the Rhine frontier, began to develop into a major governmental center. Marcus Aurelius succeeded in pacifying the Rhine district, but the peace was short-lived. For reasons that can not be ascertained, the pressure on the Rhine-Danube line increased during the first half of the third century. Along the lower Rhine, in the north, the Germanic tribes formed a confederation called the Franks. To the south another confederation—the Alemans—was established, and on the lower Danube the Gothic federation emerged. These groups broke the empire's border defenses repeatedly and raided deep into Gaul and the Danube provinces.

At about the same time, new disruptions erupted in the East, where the crumbling and quiescent Persian Empire was replaced by a state characterized by religious fanaticism and military aggressiveness. The Persian Empire was one of the heirs of the empire of Alexander the Great, and its culture had been strongly influenced by Hellenistic civilization. Some Persians were of course critical of Hellenism and sought a return to ancient Persian culture. In 224 opponents of the Hellenized regime rebelled in Fars, a southern district, quickly overthrew the central government, and established an imperial dynasty under the Sassanids. This new power reorganized the state, wiping out Hellenistic influence and reestablishing Zoroastrianism, the ancient Persian religion, as the only permissible worship. The Sassanids soon led armies against the Roman territories in the Near East. In 260 Sapor I defeated the army of Emperor Valerian and captured the emperor himself. (Only nine years earlier, the emperor Decius had lost his army and his life against the Germans.)

This carved gem from Persia depicts the capture of the Roman emperor Valerian by Sapor I in 260. Valerian, who is pictured with a vainly brandished sword, never returned to Rome and apparently died as a slave at the Persian court.

These border crises and the wars over succession to the imperial throne combined to make the political history of the late Roman Empire chaotic. It has been estimated that in the half century from 235 to 285 more than fifty men claimed the imperial power. Most were generals who led their armies against other claimants, thus depriving the empire of its border defenses. Wide-scale breaches of the frontiers by the Persians and the Germanic federations increased both the need and the outcry for a reestablished central authority and intensified the competition among the rivals. Approximately twenty of the contenders succeeded in gaining recognition as emperor, but only one reigned longer than seven years. Then in 285 the fortunes of the empire suddenly shifted. Diocletian, proclaimed emperor by his troops in 284, established himself after a year of fighting and reigned without opposition for twenty years. In 305, he resigned, declaring that he had attained his goals. He died in 316.

*comes from Dalmation coast*

Like many of his predecessors, Diocletian, who came from Illyricum, had risen in the ranks. He was a practical and energetic administrator and organizer who intended to reform the state to save the empire from destruction. Diocletian attempted to solve the problems of succession and defense of the frontiers by dividing the imperial authority. The military problem had become too great for one emperor, so he associated Maximian with himself in the imperial dignity. Both assumed the traditional title of the emperor, Augustus. He later designated two assistants, called Caesars, and gave them a share of the military and governmental authority and responsibility. The appointments also provided for the succession to each imperial post, for the Augusti adopted the Caesars as their heirs. When Diocletian retired, he forced his colleague Maximian to retire also; the two Caesars, Galerius for Diocletian and Constantius Chlorus for Maximian, became the Augusti. Two new Caesars were then selected.

In addition to dividing imperial authority, Diocletian reorganized the administrative structure of the empire. He increased the number of provinces from fifty to one hundred and combined the provinces into thirteen dioceses. Each member of the imperial college supervised several diocesan administrations. Of these reforms, the reorganization of the provinces had the greatest impact on the lives of the empire's populations. In the second century, the provincial administrations had been small and had been concerned mainly with supervising the operations of the *curia* and representing the emperor in the district's imperial affairs. The disruptions of the third century put enormous strain on the municipalities. The work of government was hampered by the barbarian raids and the civil wars; taxes were increased to meet the expenses of the constant wars, thus augmenting the burdens of governmental service. Under these circumstances, the *curiales* attempted to escape the obligations of municipal leadership, and the quality of local government declined. The success of the *curiales* in avoiding their responsibilities greatly increased the burdens of the provincial governors, who had to involve themselves actively in municipal affairs. When Diocletian reduced the size of the provinces, he recognized the political situation and tried to make the provincial administrations effective in their new role. At the same time, he and his successors attempted to stabilize and preserve the *curialis* class by closing some of the avenues its members had been using to escape it. Diocletian forbade *curiales* to join the army, but even under Diocletian and in the fourth century, the number of *curiales* obligated to serve in local government continued to diminish. In the early fifth century, the *curiae* were replaced by imperial officials in the West. In the East, this development took place about the end of the same century.

The imperial government attempted to preserve the caste system as a whole. It tied tenant farmers to the land to ensure high agricultural productivity and the all-important taxes based on it. Farmers were to remain in the places they occupied when the great census was taken in the late 290s, and infant sons were to be registered with the census. Other occupations, such as bakers and sailors, were also made hereditary castes. These

Like coins, statuary had propaganda value for the Roman government. This work depicting Diocletian (second from right) and his imperial colleagues emphasizes their military strength (the prominent swords) and their cooperation. It now stands in the Piazza di San Marco in Venice.

were the social effects of Diocletian's fiscal reforms, and the census was the basis for a tax system that effectively marshaled the resources of the empire for the needs of the government. Each year high officials calculated the monetary needs of the empire and used the census data to apportion the levy. It was an efficient system that permitted the government to raise taxes at will. Between 324 and 364, the tax rate doubled.

During the third century, inflation had been rampant. Diocletian tried to halt it by restoring the currency, which had been progressively debased. He reissued gold and silver coins of high quality, but he was unable to circulate enough such coinage to make it an effective currency. He therefore issued copper coins as well. Despite frequent attempts to stabilize the money supply, however, the government found it impossible to stop the inflation, and in 302 Diocletian issued a decree that fixed prices on many goods. The penalty for transgressing the edict was death. This policy failed completely. Many goods disappeared from the market, and the devaluation of the currency continued at a fast pace.

While Diocletian's administrative reforms had a lasting effect, his solution to the problem of succession had the same fate as his monetary policy. When he retired, a serious round of civil wars began, caused by the dynastic aspirations of sons of the men Diocletian had included in his imperial college. From these struggles, Constantine, son of Constantius Chlorus, emerged as sole emperor (324–337). Like Diocletian, Constantine preferred to rule the empire from the East, where he built a new capital at Byzantium, an old Greek trading city on the Bosporus. The city was dedicated in 330 and was later renamed Constantinople. The establishment of the Eastern capital, which removed the center of government from Rome, was not an innovation. Even in the West, Milan had replaced Rome as the imperial headquarters because it was nearer the northern frontier and was thus a better center for directing the defense of the Western empire. The Eastern capital would be able to exploit the empire's richest provinces more effectively and would be a better base for meeting the threat of the Sassanid Empire.

In general Constantine continued the policies of his illustrious predecessor, seeking to stabilize the social and economic structure of the empire and to increase the efficiency of the government. When he died, his three sons divided the imperial power, thus re-creating the collective authority of the imperial college. After more than ten years of intermittent warfare among the co-emperors, interrupted by defensive actions against the barbarians, Constantius emerged as the sole emperor in 350. When he died in 361, he passed his dignity on to his cousin Julian (361–363). Even before he came to power, Julian had engaged in campaigns against the Germans, and he spent most of his brief reign fighting the Persians. He is best known, however, for his effort to revive the worship of the ancient pagan deities. For this, Christian writers excoriated him as "the Apostate." Valentinian I (364–375), raised to the throne by his troops, immediately reestablished the collegiate principle by designating his brother Valens (364–378) co-emperor in the East, and his son Gratian, a brilliant young military commander, co-emperor in the West. The military problems of the empire were too great for one man.

The pressures on the imperial defenses did not abate at the end of the third century, but the relative stability of the central government, as a result of Diocletian's reforms, permitted the Romans to hold off their enemies. To do this, however, the imperial government continued to raise taxes, as noted earlier, and took over more and more governmental functions. The central bureaucracy grew immensely, numbering approximately 30,000 by the end of the fourth century. The size of the army also increased. In the third century, it had numbered about 300,000 men, but under Aurelian (270–275) and Diocletian it had been reformed, reorganized, and placed in permanent fortresses along the borders. The reformed army's fighting units were smaller and more mobile, but the size of the army as a whole increased dramatically. By the end of the fourth century, it numbered approximately 635,000 men. Such an army and the vast supply system it necessitated was a heavy burden on the subject populations of the empire.

**Suggestions for Further Reading**

For a survey of late Roman history, see H. M. D. Parker, *History of the Roman World from* A.D. *138 to 337,* rev. ed. (London, 1969). The two best works on late Roman social and economic history are M. Rostovtzeff, *Social and Economic History of the Roman Empire* (Oxford, 1926), and A. H. M. Jones, *The Later Roman Empire, 284–602,* 3 vols. (Oxford, 1964). P. Brown, *The World of Late Antiquity* (New York, 1971) is a brilliant short essay on the entire transitional period. Also specifically concerned with the transition from Rome to the Middle Ages are Solomon Katz, *The Decline of Rome and the Rise of Mediaeval Europe* (Ithaca, N.Y., 1955), and Mortimer Chambers, ed., *The Fall of Rome: Can It Be Explained?* (New York, 1963). Still useful are S. Dill, *Roman Society in the Last Century of the Empire* (London, 1910) and *Roman Society in Gaul in the Merovingian Age* (London, 1926).

# 2  The Growth of Christianity

Originating as a religious system profoundly antagonistic to many of the values and entrenched interests of antiquity, by the late fourth century Christianity had become the predominant religion in the empire. Its historic role in the period of transition was to absorb many of the best elements of ancient civilization and to transmit them to the Middle Ages.

## The Origins and Early Growth
## of the Christian Movement

Christianity developed from Judaism at a time when that ancient religion was in ferment, broken into sects vying with one another for religious and political leadership in Judea. At the beginning of the Christian era, the Romans took over the governance of Judea, organizing it as a territory under a Roman administrator. It had been a semiautonomous state ruled by its own kings, of whom the most famous was Herod the Great (37–4 B.C.). Even under the native kings, Judea had been seriously troubled by political unrest, in which religious disputes had a large effect. Under Roman administration, the tension increased. The tiny movement led by Jesus between about A.D. 26 and 29 was part of this turbulent situation. At first, the Christians were and seem to have considered themselves Jews, and Jesus suffered the punishment reserved for Jews convicted by the Romans as subversives. Thousands of Jews were crucified from 4 B.C., when the Romans stepped in, until 70, when the future emperor Titus put a bloody end to a great Jewish rebellion, making a desert of Jerusalem.

By the end of this rebellion, Christianity had spread to large cities like Antioch, Alexandria, and Rome, and to many smaller centers in the eastern provinces. The religion was propagated among Hellenized Jews, such as Saint Paul, and gradually attracted adherents from other groups. The literature of the New Testament was written for these Hellenized converts, who needed a translation of Jesus' message and teaching, which had been Aramaic in language and Judaic in content. Thus, the New Testament writings reflected the popular culture of the eastern cities and reformulated the religion.

Christianity was at first just one of a multiplicity of cults in the empire, but it soon acquired a special place among them. The pagan religions originated as civic cults, and most of them remained local in imperial times. Each city had a patron god or goddess with a cult to serve the deity. As the Romans gained control of the Mediterranean world, they gave the names of their gods to those worshiped by their new subjects. For example, the Carthaginians worshiped a Heavenly Goddess; the Romans equated her with Juno, and she is portrayed as Juno in Virgil's *Aeneid*. Since most information about pre-Christian cults comes from Roman sources, historians have been given the false impression that the various cities and peoples worshiped Roman deities.

The civic cults had been closely tied to the political life of the cities in which they arose and therefore declined when the cities lost their independence. During the imperial period, the cities became part of a larger world, and although the aristocratic leadership of the municipalities continued to support the old cults, the commercial population became increasingly involved in the international world prospering under the Pax Romana. It was a world in which faraway events affected the local situation, in which goods traveled long distances and brought large returns in a complex economy, in which there was amazing cultural variety, in which anxiety about how this new world worked was a constant companion. The creation of the empire had broken down the barriers that had confined people's lives, and they grasped for a new understanding that would ease their anxiety. During the chaotic third century, people throughout the empire poured into the religious cults. Particularly successful in gaining new adherents were a group of secret, or mystery, cults in which initiates were introduced step by step to the knowledge that would save them from this world of woes.

Some of the mysteries originated in Greece (such as the Eleusinian mysteries) and some in the East (such as Mithraism or the cult of the Egyptian deity Isis). Like Christianity, they emphasized individual religious experience and a personal, emotional, and intimate contact with the deity. They were exclusive. The participant had to be initiated into their rites. Their main rewards were twofold: communion with the deity during this life through participation in worship, and eternal salvation or union with the deity after death. Specific characteristics found in one or more of the mystery cults included the following: a man-god savior whose intercession on behalf of the faithful guaranteed salvation; sacraments, such as initiatory rites (baptism) or religious ceremonies intended to cleanse and purify the worshiper preparing for communion with the deity; an explanation of the mysteries of life in terms of a divine hero who in dying conquered death, and whose life was a pattern for the faithful to follow in the hope of attaining immortality; miracle-working by this divine hero and by those who were priests of the cult, as an attestation of the truth of their worship and of the power of the divine hero; and a highly developed sense of exclusive membership or brotherhood among the elect that kept their teachings secret and unprofaned.

Christianity developed in the context of this profusion of cults. The reasons for the success of the new religion were manifold. First, Christianity's rich Judaic heritage provided a sound foundation for its development as a separate religion. Even as the new cult became conscious of its independence, after the destruction of Jerusalem and during its mission to the gentiles, it remained rooted in an ancient tradition that delivered it from the disadvantage of being a novelty. Second, from the Jews, the Christians inherited the intense exclusiveness evidenced both in their absolute refusal to accept or honor the gods of the Greco-Roman pantheon or other cults and in the careful relationship the Christian communities maintained with the imperial government. At all times, the demands of the religion were made plain in its refusal to render unto Caesar what was due to God. This attitude made the Christian group more a community than a sect, for joining the group not only imposed a credo on the convert but determined his relationship with the state and with all other political and social groups. In a world in which people were searching for a social focal point to replace those disintegrating under the new imperial system, the communal character of the Christian cult gave it a distinct advantage over its competitors. Christianity provided guidance for living in this world as well as for attaining eternal salvation. Third, Christianity benefited from being a religion of a book. Most of the mystery cults and civic cults were religions of practice that involved people on the ritual level but not on the intellectual level. The Christians inherited and expanded the literate tradition of the Jews, and although educated Greeks and Romans considered that literature unworthy of their attention, it was susceptible to analysis and explication similar to that practiced on Homer and Virgil. The Judeo-Christian tradition was especially

A second-century pagan drew this derisive graffito of a crucified donkey and added the legend "Alexander is worshiping his god."

challenging because unlike other cultic traditions it went beyond cosmological beliefs claiming to be the true interpretation of history. Thus, while the cosmology of most cults could be harmonized with Roman ideas of history, the Christians presented a complete and independent system of their own, setting up a conflict that could engage the attention of educated people. Finally, Christianity evolved partially by responding to the religious ideas of the subject peoples of the empire. Despite its Judaic origins, its Easternness, the religion that emerged in the canon of the New Testament, formed in the second half of the second century, was greatly influenced by Hellenic beliefs and ideas. While the other religions of the period could make claims based on their great antiquity, Christianity had both the advantages of ancientness, derived from its Jewishness, and of flexibility, since its adherents saw themselves as successors, not continuators, of Judaism.

The Christians' effort to distinguish themselves from the Jews had disadvantages as well as advantages. Jews and Christians refused to recognize any god other than their own. The Romans usually tolerated the exclusiveness of the Jews, although they considered it peculiar, because the Jews were following an ancient national cult, and the Romans had always been tolerant of such traditions. Occasionally Roman authorities tried to force Jews to participate in the Caesar cult, but this was the exception rather than the rule. The Christians were a different matter. The Christian communities did not correspond to any ethnic group in the empire and thus seemed to be perversely recalcitrant. Such stubborn defiance was considered a serious matter because the Romans believed that the fortunes of the empire depended on the gods' good will and that all subjects had to work to win divine favor. Even the first generation of Christians came under attack for their refusal to participate in that work. Before the end of the first century, Roman law declared it a capital offense to be Christian. The refusal of Christians to help save the empire from divine wrath, without a credible excuse based on the historical roots of their religion, was the basis for these anti-Christian laws; Christians were suspected of subversion. These suspicions were strengthened by scandalous reports about secret meetings and "love feasts," at which Christians were commonly thought to engage in immoral practices. For these reasons the government occasionally sanctioned minor and local persecutions of Christians on the legal ground that they withheld allegiance to the emperor. Actually such persecutions were more often in response to antagonistic local public opinion, searching for a scapegoat for whatever disasters had recently occurred. Official attitudes were usually rather tolerant, however. At the beginning of the second century, the emperor Trajan advised Pliny, the provincial governor of Bithynia, not to hunt for Christians but only to take action against those whose defiance of imperial law became public. The sporadic and local persecutions produced some martyrs, but not many. The Romans executed people for their religious beliefs only when forced to do so by a resistance that threatened the public order.

The popular and official suspicion of the Christians intensified as the news of military disasters on the borders went from bad to worse during the third century. In 250, the emperor Decius based the first large-scale persecution on the popularly held belief that Christians displeased the gods. To win the support of the gods, the emperor ordered all his subjects to perform the ancient sacrifices and to receive certificates that they had done so. Many Christians tried to ignore the order, hoping the administrators of the sacrifice would not notice them. Where the administrators proved vigilant, some Christians bribed them to issue the certificates. Only a few were executed for public refusal to perform their duty. When Decius was killed the next year, the momentum went out of the empirewide persecution, but the period was still a bad one for Christians; it was precisely disasters like the one that befell Decius for which they were blamed. In 257 Valerian renewed the effort to unite the empire in an appeal to the gods, and the Christians again suffered for their recalcitrance.

After the Persians captured Valerian, official persecution virtually disappeared for forty years. In the second half of the third century, the Christian communities grew significantly and came to exercise a large influence in many towns. Diocletian, whose plans for restoring the empire included the revival of the ancient Roman religion, ended this period of peace for the Christians in 303. Urged by priests and his Caesar Galerius, who blamed the failure of sacrifices on the Christians', refusal to participate in them, Diocletian issued a decree that closed the churches, ordered the confiscation and burning of the Scriptures, prohibited Christians to meet, and deprived Christians of any official rank they might have acquired. The persecution lasted until Galerius' death in 311. It resurged under Maximin (Galerius' Caesar 305–310; Augustus 310–313), who tried to organize the pagan cults as Christianity had become organized. He ordered that each municipality have a high priest and each province, a supervisory priest. Under his authority, Christians were expelled from several provinces in the East. When Maximin lost the struggle for control of the East in 313, he revoked the decrees of persecution, and Licinius, the victor, respected the revocation.

The persecution actually had a surprise ending. During the civil wars that followed Diocletian's retirement in 305, the ultimate victor, Constantine, dramatically changed his attitude toward Christians and Christianity, and his personal convictions eventually became the religious policy of the imperial government. Early in his struggle for control of the West, Constantine became convinced that the pagan god worshiped by his family, the Unconquered Sun, was identical to the Christian god and that he had been taken under the protection of this god. Before the final battle of the war, at the Milvian Bridge near Rome in 312, he ordered his soldiers to paint the labarum, a Christian symbol, on their shields. After Constantine's forces won the battle, Christians suddenly found their religion one of the most favored in the empire. The new emperor in the West, soon to be sole ruler of the empire, took the religion under his protection and showed an avid interest in its growth.

Constantine's motives for his new religious policy will never be fully known. It is clear that personal conversion played an important role at some time between his victory at the Milvian Bridge and his death-bed baptism (337). It is less certain whether this conversion caused or resulted from the pro-Christian policy that he adopted in his struggle for power and in his later effort to consolidate his rule. Constantine's main claim to statesmanship was his recognition that the Church could add strength to the empire far beyond the number of its members. In no part of the empire were Christians in the majority. In the East they averaged about 10 percent of the population, and in the West about 5 percent, but they were concentrated largely in the cities, and their organization made them the most cohesive religious group in the empire. At one stroke Constantine converted the opposition of a persecuted sect into the most effective new source of loyalty and support that any emperor had gained. This was accomplished by an agreement with Licinius, the Eastern Augustus, which is usually referred to as the Edict of Milan

This view of the crypt of Saint Cornelius in the Catacombs of Saint Calixtus gives an impression of the underground passages where pre-Constantinian Christians buried their dead and met for worship. The wall frescoes in the catacombs are among the earliest examples of Christian art.

(313). By its terms Christianity was officially tolerated, property confiscated during the recent persecution was returned to the Church, and the Christian clergy was accorded the same privileges and exemptions from public duties enjoyed by the priesthood of the official pagan cults.

The Christians' problems with private and public opposition and persecution were almost equaled by their problems with one another. Saint Paul's letters indicate that the earliest Christian preachers competed with one another and differed in their teachings. Various groups within the Christian movement developed their own doctrinal positions and charged other factions with straying from the true religion. Many of the splinter groups produced their own literature, for which they claimed divine inspiration, and in the mid-second century, attempts were made to establish a canon of sacred writings. The first of these attempts was made by Marcion, a Christian preacher who carried Paul's strictures against the law of the Old Testament to the extreme and argued that most of the sacred book of the Jews should be expunged from the Christian tradition. The orthodox canon of the New Testament evolved as a reaction to that of Marcion.

The representation of the Madonna and Child derived from Egyptian cults of Isis and Osiris and quickly spread throughout the Christian communities. This third-century example from the Catacomb of Priscilla in Rome shows the influence of contemporary Roman art.

As Christianity spread, many heresies, to look at the variant theologies from the standpoint of those who eventually won out, arose from the desire of new converts to transfer their previous beliefs to the new religion, making the transition from one to the other easier and more comfortable. Some heresies developed from attempts to adapt the new religion to Greek philosophical systems. Another type of heresy arose directly from the persecutions, since the Christians who had held fast to their faith during the time of trouble resented the readmission of those who had compromised or surrendered under the pressure. All these splits in the Christian movement were extremely long-lived and persisted well after the emperors began taking an active interest in the unity of the Church. The Marcionites still existed in the sixth century, as did some other very early heretical groups.

The two most important heresies confronting the Church in the West after the Edict of Milan were Donatism and Arianism. The Donatists (named for Donatus, their bishop of Carthage) were, mainly, survivors of the persecutions in North Africa. They believed that priests who had deserted the Church during persecution should not be allowed to return to their pastoral positions. They went further to declare that the sacraments administered by any unworthy priest were invalid. Although this is primarily a disciplinary rather than doctrinal question, the efficacy of the sacraments—especially baptism and the Eucharist, which were widely considered indispensable for salvation—was a fundamental problem with doctrinal implications. The Donatists claimed that their views were essential to the maintenance of purity and catholicity in the Church; extremists went so far as to exclude from membership all who had committed mortal sin, both clergy and laity. Later reformers, both in the Middle Ages and in the Reformation, tended toward or accepted the Donatist position in their criticism of the sinful clergy and their concept of the Church as a communion of saints.

The African Church was deeply and bitterly divided over these issues. Constantine intervened in the quarrel on the orthodox, or Catholic, side. But more important than the emperor's orthodoxy was his determination to preserve the unity of the organization on which he relied for support. His policy of favoring Christianity led to active intervention in the affairs of the Church. The question of Donatism he referred to two synods of Western bishops at Rome and Arles, in 313 and 314, and he attempted to enforce by governmental decree the decisions of those synods, that the efficacy of the sacraments was independent of the personal character of the priest. By implication, the emperor, who was not yet even a member of the Church, had exercised ecclesiastical leadership over the bishops and had assumed responsibility, as Constantine later wrote, for "a common harmony of sentiment among all the servants of God." The orthodox view prevailed, but common harmony did not. Donatism survived as a major force in the African Church until the Moslem conquests of the seventh century.

Constantine's next intervention in Church affairs was even more impressive. This concerned the heresy of Arianism, which had spread from Alexandria throughout much of the eastern half of the empire. Arianism arose from a dispute between Alexander, bishop of Alexandria, and his priest Arius, concerning the divinity of Christ and the relation between God the Father and God the Son. Arius' view demeaned the Son to a subordinate position: he admitted that Christ was the Word of God incarnate in human flesh, and was thus divine, but he denied that the Son had the same nature as the Father. Alexander insisted that Christ was of the very same nature and substance as God, since salvation depended on being one with the Son, and this oneness would not avail unless Christ's nature was the same as that of the Father. The arguments on either side were very complicated and were altered slightly as the dispute continued, but essentially Arius' view was an effort to adapt Christian theology to philosophical distinctions, while Alexander's arguments represented the traditional Christian view expressed in philosophical language. The controversy reached a crisis when Arius was exiled and his numerous supporters came to his defense.

At this point Constantine intervened by summoning on his own authority a council of over three hundred bishops representing the entire Church, the first ecumenical council, which met at Nicaea in 325. Sitting in his presence and probably influenced by the emperor to reach a unanimous decision, the bishops condemned Arianism as heresy. The council promulgated other canons binding on the whole Church and formulated articles of faith that became the basis of the orthodox doctrine of the Trinity as found in the Nicene Creed (actually enunciated by the Council of Constantinople in 381). The problem of Arianism was by no means settled in 325. The heresy spread to the East German peoples who began to enter the empire in the fourth century. The original problem that Arius had debated was widened to include the nature of the Trinity and other doctrinal problems that continued to plague the Eastern Church with heresy and schism for centuries.

The Council of Nicaea set two important precedents for the development of the Church. First, an ecumenical council of all the bishops was recognized as the supreme authority on doctrinal and disciplinary matters; second, the initiative and leadership of the emperor were tacitly accepted. As long as the emperor was orthodox, no objection to his implied supremacy over the Church was voiced. But Constantine's immediate successors were as often Arian as they were orthodox, or even pagan (as Julian the Apostate), so that the danger of imperial control became obvious to the orthodox bishops. Recognition and support by the state had brought to Christianity difficulties as well as benefits. Persecution by the state now became a weapon used by Arians and Catholics against each other, depending on the persuasion of the emperor in power.

By the end of the fourth century the problem of the relation between spiritual and temporal authority had become acute. It is not quite accurate to speak of this as a struggle between Church and state. The emperors, following ancient Roman tradition that placed all religious affairs under state control, played the leading role in ecclesiastical matters. Thus, imperial favor meant that Christian teachings were incorporated into civil legislation and that episcopal courts, which were originally informal tribunals for settling differences among members of the Christian communities, could issue judgments that would be recognized by imperial authorities. These developments did not result from the growing influence and power of the Christian Church. They were the consequence of Christianity becoming an imperial religion (it was made the official religion by Theodosius I in 390). Christianity was integrated into the structure of the state, taking the place of the ancient cults of Roman civic religion. When looked at from this standpoint, the predicament of the fourth-century bishops can be appreciated. They had to struggle to achieve an independent authority in moral and doctrinal matters. Only then could that which belongs to God be rendered unto God.

The determination of the bishops to be independent of imperial or secular

Caspian Sea

Volga

Don

Dnieper

ARMENIAN CHURCHES

SYRIAN CHURCHES

Tigris

Euphrates

Antioch

Jerusalem

BITHYNIA

GALATIA

Black Sea

Constantinople

Alexandria

COPTIC CHURCH

Nile

KHAZARS

PETCHENEGS (PATZINAKS)

RUSSIANS

BULGARIANS

SERVIANS

MAGYARS

NORTHERN LIMIT OF ISLAM

Mediterranean Sea

LIVONIANS

LITHUANIANS

PRUSSIANS

Niemen

Vistula

DIVIDING LINE BETWEEN GREEK ORTHODOX AND LATIN CHRISTIANITY

POLES

WENDS

Danube

GOTHIA

DANES

SAXONS

FRIESIANS

BAVARIANS

LOMBARDS

Baltic Sea

Rhine

BURGUNDIANS

FRANKS

Rhone

Rome

North Sea

VISIGOTHS

Atlantic Ocean

SUEVES

Tagus

Northern limit of Christianity–325

Extent of Latin Christianity

Extent of Greek Orthodox Christianity

Rome        Patriarchates

Chief Archbishoprics

Bishoprics

Monastaries

0                500   Miles

The Growth of Christianity

control was dramatized by an incident that made a profound impression on contemporaries. Theodosius I had, in 390, put down a minor revolt in the city of Thessalonica by ordering the massacre of some seven thousand citizens trapped by imperial troops in the local circus. For this atrocious deed, Ambrose, the bishop of Milan, forced the emperor to do penance in his cathedral, declaring roundly that "the emperor is within the Church, not above it; in matters of faith and morals bishops judge emperors." This public humiliation of Theodosius did not solve the problem of the relation of temporal and spiritual authority—the problem has never been permanently solved in Western civilization—but it graphically emphasized the attitude of a large majority of the bishops, especially in the Latin West, that in the organization of the Church the emperor was not to be supreme.

## The Growth of Church Institutions

Perhaps the most striking difference between Christianity and other religions in the Roman world was the fact that the early Christians formed not only a collection of the faithful but an *ecclesia,* a Church with a definite (although at first rudimentary) organization whose bonds were only strengthened by hostile public opinion and occasional persecution. By the second century this organization had already taken on the hierarchical form that characterized its later development. The highest official was the bishop, or leader of the local community of Christians. The area of the bishop's jurisdiction or spiritual leadership corresponded from the beginning with the administrative unit of the Roman government, the *civitas.* From a very early date various other officials or specially distinguished members of the original Christian communities were already in evidence. These were the presbyters (or priests, who had spiritual authority), deacons (who were assistants to the bishop, performing nonspiritual functions, such as maintenance of places of worship and distribution of charity), exorcists, readers, and other lesser officials. As a whole, they constituted the clergy as distinguished from the rest of the faithful, who were the laity. This distinction, and the hierarchically arranged functions or dignities of the clergy, provided a nucleus of leadership and a framework of organization. Many laws of persecution in the third century recognized the effectiveness of this organization by attacking Christianity through the clergy. Again and again the clergy were banished or imprisoned. The clergy suffered most in the great persecution of Diocletian and his successors.

The survival and growth of the local churches depended largely on the personal ability of the bishops, whose position was further enhanced by a theoretical justification of episcopal authority. This was the theory of apostolic succession, first enunciated by Irenaeus of Lyons (ca. 180). By Irenaeus' time, it was commonly held as a tenet of faith that the ancient Hebrew Scriptures and the apostolic writings subsequent to the Incarnation contained the authoritative statement of Christianity. And yet questions might arise concerning the correct interpretation of doubtful points in the Scriptures. Irenaeus set forth the view that a true interpretation could only come from the spiritual heirs of the Apostles: the bishops. All bishoprics had been established by the Apostles or representatives of the Apostles, who had conferred on the first leaders of local churches their spiritual authority. This authority had been handed down in an unbroken chain of transference from bishop to bishop, Irenaeus declared, because even though a new bishop was usually designated by election of the local community, he received his spiritual authority, or consecration as bishop, at the hands of other bishops.

The supremacy of the bishop over the Christian community of the *civitas,* or the ecclesiastical diocese, was thus recognized in the unique episcopal power to confer spiritual authority on priests within his diocese or on bishops-elect of other dioceses. Theoretically, it might be argued, each bishop was the equal of every other bishop because all derived authority from the Apostles. But two facts tended toward the elaboration of an episcopal hierarchy in which the superiority of some bishops over others gradually came to be recognized. First, some of the bishoprics had been founded by the Apostles themselves; second, the bishoprics of important cities in the empire were wealthier and more influential than later and lesser foundations. Both facts tended to enhance the prestige of the bishops of such cities as Antioch, Alexandria, Carthage, and Rome. The bishops of these apostolic sees and of the larger cities often took the lead in combating divisive tendencies within the early Church and in resisting sporadic local persecution.

In the third century, every Christian community appears to have raised its own bishop. The bishop of the principal city in each province, the metropolis, often asserted his authority over other bishops, and Diocletian's reform of the provincial administrations, reducing the size of the provinces, also helped consolidate episcopal organization. Most bishops were elected by their communities and consecrated by one or more of the neighboring bishops. In practice, the power to elect devolved on the clergy; the laity simply acclaimed the man presented to it. Occasional conflicts between the electors and the local bishops who consecrated the new bishop arose, and the problem of the relationship between the electors and consecrators remained a sticky one in ecclesiastical law throughout the Middle Ages.

The clergy that assembled around the bishops formed their *familia.* The ecclesiastical organization was largely confined to the *civitates* (the cities and their immediate hinterland), where two types of churches were established. In the cities the churches were directly under episcopal control, supported by episcopal funds, and served by members of the bishop's *familia.* In suburban and country villages churches with independent endowments were founded. On the whole, however, the bishops were able to exert their authority over the latter, parochial churches, although the parochial clergy was often chosen

by leading men of the village. The bishops appointed priests with authority
to supervise the country churches in specified districts. The churches in the
East had reached this rather advanced stage of organization under episcopal
power by the end of the third century.

Recognition by the imperial government increased the responsibilities and
added to the duties of the bishops. There was a great influx of converts into
the Church, many of whom were less drawn by the faith than moved by a
sense of expediency. Instruction and confirmation of laymen, the ordination
of new priests, and the building of new churches to provide for the growing
number of Christians, were the principal concerns of the bishops. The Church
now enjoyed the right to hold property and to receive gifts. As the Church grew
wealthy from pious donations, the bishops had to devote an increasing
amount of time to maintaining and exploiting large holdings of real property
and to distributing the income properly among the various activities or
services that they could now extend to the great majority of the people in
their dioceses. They built hospitals, maintained orphanages, dispensed charity
to the poor, provided inexpensive and equitable justice in their courts, supported the clergy of their cathedrals, preached regularly to their own congre-
gations, visited the churches under their jurisdiction, and provided the moral
leadership to meet local disasters or difficulties, such as plague, fire and flood,
or barbarian invasions. Because he usually rose out of the local diocesan
community, the bishop represented local interests and was concerned for civic
welfare. The emperor Honorius, reorganizing the Western cities under imperial administration in 409, indicated the growth of episcopal power and prestige by ordaining that the *defensores civitatum* (defenders of the cities, who
were to oversee municipal government) should be elected by the bishop,
clergy, and local landowners as well as by the *curiales*.

The tendency for bishops of apostolic and metropolitan sees (episcopal
seats) to assert their leadership continued in the fourth century under the
impetus of the imperial government. The government's stress on the unity
of the Church, under the emperor's authority, encouraged the centralization
of episcopal power. This increased centralization led to the rise of four sees to
quasi-legal preeminence. As sees founded and ruled by Apostles, Jerusalem,
Antioch, Alexandria, and Rome took precedence as preservers of Christian
tradition. In the course of the fourth century, Constantinople, supported by the
imperial government with which it had close connection, asserted an equal
authority with the four major sees. In 381 the Council of Constantinople
affirmed the superiority of the bishop of Constantinople over the bishops of
Antioch and Alexandria and recognized the primacy of the bishop of Rome
over the whole Church. But the patriarch of Constantinople refused to accept
a subordinate position and, with support from the emperor, persuaded the
Council of Chalcedon in 451 to recognize Constantinople as equal in rank
with Rome and supreme over the churches of the East.

The rapid rise of Constantinople intensified the conflicts that already disturbed the relationship among the great sees. Alexandria continued to assert its hegemony in the East and won several battles over specific points during the late fourth and early fifth centuries. The bishops of Rome were also involved in this competition for position. They claimed a primacy in matters of discipline and doctrine on the ground that the Roman Church owed its foundation to the two principal Apostles, Peter and Paul. As successors to these Apostles, the Roman bishops maintained that they were the repositories of the most authoritative apostolic tradition. Papal claims in matters of discipline, principally the right to hear appeals from the judgments of other bishops, rested on the pope's succession to the power of Peter, the prince of the Apostles.

The popes were making their claims at least as early as the mid-third century, when some African bishops objected to the papal demands, but when Constantine and his successors took an active role in the universal organization of the Church, the popes intensified their efforts to have their supremacy recognized. A theoretical justification for papal supremacy, known as the Petrine theory, evolved. The first complete and formal enunciation of the theory was given by Leo I the Great (440–461) in his refutation of the arguments for the equality conferred on the patriarch of Constantinople by the Council of Chalcedon in 451. Leo thought the Church of Rome had held the theory since its foundation.

The Petrine theory was based on Matthew 16:18–19: "You are Peter and upon this rock I will build my Church; and the gates of hell shall not prevail against it. And I will give to you the keys of the kingdom of heaven: and whatsoever you shall bind on earth shall be bound in heaven: and whatsoever you shall loose on earth shall be loosed in heaven." According to the Petrine theory, these words of Christ made Peter the chief Apostle, the ruler of the Church, possessed of unlimited spiritual powers. By apostolic succession, these powers descended to the successors of Peter, the first bishop of Rome. Hence, as successor of Peter the bishop of Rome was supreme over the universal Church.

Opposition to this theory, which later became a doctrine, has usually taken one or more of three lines: first, a different interpretation of the text, for example, by construing *rock* figuratively as Peter's confession of faith rather than as referring to Peter personally; second, a denial of the tradition that Peter founded the Church in Rome (on this point the evidence is late, and the problem is to decide how much weight can be given to early tradition); and third, a denial of the theory of apostolic succession, on which the Petrine theory is dependent.

Whatever might be the merits of the arguments for or against the Petrine doctrine, the rise of the bishop of Rome is clearly recorded in the historical evidence of the fourth and fifth centuries. Several milestones in this rise illustrate the ways in which the pope was recognized as the supreme head of Latin Christianity. The Council of Sardica in 344, attended mainly by Western bishops, ruled that a bishop who had been deposed by a local or provincial council might appeal his case for final decision to the bishop of Rome. This canon was never accepted in the East, but it was acted on frequently in the West. Pope Damasus (366–384), who commissioned Saint Jerome to make a new Latin translation of the Bible, was the first pope to define formally his superiority over all other bishops. His successor, Siricius (384–399), issued the first surviving authentic decretal (385), an authoritative decision in response to questions concerning matters of discipline submitted to him by Spanish bishops. From this time on, the decretals of the popes became important sources of canon law, supplementing the canons of the Church councils, as regulations binding on the whole Latin Church in the West. Leo I, the first of three popes to be called "the Great," brought both the prestige and the power of the papacy to a new height. His reaction to the Council of Chalcedon has already been noted, and the leadership he exercised —in default of the emperor or other civil magistrate—in the defense of Rome against the Huns (452) and Vandals (455) will be discussed in a later chapter. Another of his achievements was to secure from Valentinian III the issuance of an edict (445) recognizing in civil law the superior jurisdiction of the pope over all Western bishops and directing imperial officials to enforce this obedience to Rome.

Most of the popes during the century and a half after Leo the Great found it difficult enough to preserve the prestige already won, without trying to add to papal power. After Leo the only unity left in the West was that of the Church, and that unity was precarious. In Italy, the invasions led to the settlement of the Arian Ostrogoths under their king Theodoric at the end of the fifth century. Theodoric was tolerant of the Catholics and supervised their affairs as well as those of the Arians. He did not scruple to influence papal elections and papal policy. The Byzantine reconquest of Italy in the sixth century did little to improve the position of the papacy, for Justinian firmly controlled the Church. He and his successors enforced the rule that no new pope was to be consecrated without the emperor's consent. On more than one occasion a pope found himself exiled or driven to take refuge from his Ostrogothic or Byzantine opponents. During the turbulent period of the Gothic wars and the Lombard invasion, in the second half of the sixth century, papal authority over the Church in the West was rarely exercised. The popes were too absorbed in local problems of survival. However, while the popes' universal power over the Church waned during the sixth century, the basis was being laid for the later temporal authority of the papacy in Rome. More and more local political power was either assumed by the popes or delegated to them by the Eastern emperors, until the popes became more important in the government of Rome than the imperial officials.

Θειαρ·ετιωορ·θοδοζιασ·ηεκληρωρόμασαρ·δυοθελησεις
Καιδυοόμεργείασ·ωτ·χκηρίττουσαρ·ολεμθαολθωτιS
ωμεζαπαωκαρωσιωσαρ·ότείρθμlε̇ε6λότιποθτι·

This miniature from Saint Basil's Calendar of Saints portrays the majestic Pope Leo I the Great, who enunciated some of the most important arguments for papal supremacy over the Church and who effectively presided over the Church of his time.

The consolidation of papal power over Rome and the development of the papacy's patrimony during the late imperial period is best illustrated by the activities of Pope Gregory I the Great (590–604). Gregory's impact on the medieval Church was enormous because of his exceptional ability in pursuing the policies and programs of the late Roman papacy, his influential theological, ethical, and pastoral writings, and the great body of his official correspondence that survived and inspired popes throughout the Middle Ages. Gregory was born into an ancient senatorial family of great wealth and had all the advantages of his class; he entered the imperial administration at a very high level. In 573 he attained the highest position in the civil administration of Rome, becoming the prefect of the city. His true interests were revealed two years later, however, when, on the death of his father, he dedicated his inheritance of landed property to the foundation of six monasteries in Sicily and one in Rome, and entered the latter as a monk. His retirement from the world, which he later described as the happiest years of his life, ended with his appointment as deacon of one of the seven regions into which the bishopric of Rome was divided for administrative purposes. In 579 he was appointed papal envoy to the court at Constantinople, where he spent the next several years broadening his experience in both secular and ecclesiastical affairs. On his return to Rome he spent three years as abbot of his monastery. When Pope Pelagius was carried off by the plague, Gregory was elected pope.

Several developments are associated with Gregory for which he was not, perhaps, originally responsible. But they appear clearly for the first time during his pontificate, and they were to have an important influence on the medieval Church. The liturgy of the Roman Church, the organization of the diocese, and the administration and expenditure of the revenues of the endowment of landed estates of the apostolic see were all improved by Gregory. Gregory launched the Roman Ordinal (containing the daily services in the Church for the entire year) on its eventful career by sending it with missionaries to England, from where it later spread throughout the West. The Ordinal, while absorbing elements from the Gallican, the Visigothic, the Ambrosian (north Italian), and other Western rites that had grown up semi-independently, later supplanted them. The richness and variety of Christian worship, reflecting the varying temper and spiritual needs of the diversity of peoples embraced within the Church, was never in the Middle Ages crushed beneath any rigid insistence on liturgical uniformity. But there was always a latent danger that differences in liturgical usages might lead to disunity in the Church—for ritual is a symbolic expression of the substance of faith. The historical significance, then, of the Roman rite is that liturgical differences in the West would be variations of one universally accepted rite, rather than fundamentally different rites.

As bishop of Rome, Gregory is best known for his administration of the landed estates of his see, the so-called Patrimony of Saint Peter, consisting of properties located in almost every part of Italy, in the Mediterranean islands, in Gaul, Africa, and the Balkans. The surviving correspondence of Gregory reveals the efficiency of a humane exploitation of papal lands. Their revenues supported the Roman Church, most of the normal functions of the imperial administration in Rome, such as poor relief, support of garrison troops, and maintenance of fortifications, as well as orphanages, schools, and hospitals. In this work Gregory relied on the clergy of his diocese, headed by the deacons of the seven regions of Rome and by the so-called cardinal priests (the priests permitted to celebrate Mass in the twenty-five, later twenty-eight, "titles," or parishes, into which the city was divided).

Finally, Gregory as bishop was a noted preacher. His pontificate was begun during a plague, and nearly every year thereafter was marked by some disaster, famine, or pestilence that set the atmosphere for a series of moving sermons on the theme of the Day of Judgment. The horrors of hellfire and damnation, the eternal bliss of paradise for those who are saved, the rapidly approaching end of the world in which most of his listeners stoutly believed— these subjects were not original with Gregory, but he did much to make them the stock-in-trade of medieval preaching. His graphic descriptions of demons and angels contributed to the general atmosphere of living halfway in the supernatural world that characterized medieval popular religion.

Gregory's activities created a reputation that greatly enhanced papal prestige. He intervened in the doctrinal disputes and ecclesiastical affairs of every Western kingdom. In Africa he continued the fight aganst the Donatists and encouraged appeals from local synods to Rome. His correspondence with the bishops and kings of Frankish Gaul kept alive the tradition of contact between the papacy and the Gallican Church and became the basis for the later deepening of that connection. In Spain he promoted the conversion of the Visigoths, who were Arian Christians, to Catholicism. Far more important for the future, he initiated the conversion of the Anglo-Saxons in England. By establishing this precedent, Gregory was responsible for the tradition of papal leadership in the conversion of heathen peoples in later centuries. Finally, as supreme head of the Church in the West and claimant of supremacy over the Church universal, Gregory firmly but politely rejected the claim of John the Faster, patriarch of Constantinople, to be styled "universal patriarch," pointing out that this sort of talk was more suggestive of Antichrist than of Christian humility. For himself, he preferred to use the style *servus servorum Dei* (servant of the servants of God), a perfect expression of the Benedictine spirit of humility, which has been, since his pontificate, the title by which popes have referred to themselves in decretals and official correspondence.

As temporal ruler of Rome, Gregory, like his predecessors, simply did what had to be done to meet the recurring emergencies of the Lombard invasion. Since the hard-pressed Byzantine emperor was not able to spare enough troops to garrison Rome adequately, Gregory himself raised and provisioned a local militia, supervised the defenses of Rome, conducted negotiations with the Lombard king, and worked out a separate peace—much to the indignation of the emperor—whereby Rome was saved from further attack. Technically this was insubordination or even treason, but the necessities of the case justified Gregory's action. The Byzantine government was unable to give assistance and unwilling to recognize the Lombard conquests. To the people of Rome, Gregory was a hero and a statesman who had brought some security to their lives.

Gregory's work as a theologian and writer will be discussed later, together with other cultural developments of this period. It remains only to add that Gregory as pope represented not only the tradition of imperial Rome united with the vigorous episcopal traditions of Christianity, but also a new and vital element in the Christian world of the future: the monastic ideal. In his person, "monasticism ascended the papal throne" and was given a promotion that helped establish it, in its Benedictine form, in Western society. The history of the monastic form of Christian life will be treated in a later chapter.

## The Age of the Fathers: Ambrose, Jerome, and Augustine

Toward the end of the second century Christianity began to attract an increasing number of intellectuals. This development probably resulted in part from the interest stirred by the ancient literate tradition the Christians inherited from the Jews and by the disputes over the continuation of that tradition in the New Testament writings. At the same time, as noted earlier, educated men were again turning their attention to religion, and Christianity was only one of the beneficiaries of this renewed concern. The reorientation of the educated class is indicated by the decline of the ancient philosophical schools like Stoicism and Epicureanism and by the increasing interest among philosophers in cosmological problems. At the end of the second century Platonic philosophy began to enjoy a new vogue, with greatest attention given to works like the *Timaeus,* in which Plato had expounded his cosmology. As in the heyday of the philosophical schools, the propounders of Neo-Platonic ideas not only developed their own hypotheses, but also attacked others' cosmological theories. In Alexandria, where Neo-Platonism was centered around Celsus, Ammonius Saccas, and, most importantly, Plotinus (205–270), a strong Christian community existed, and therefore Christian cosmology played a part in the debates. Before the end of the second century Celsus wrote an extensive treatise against the Christians, and later writers from among Plotinus' disciples followed suit. In this atmosphere of dispute and challenge, Christians had to respond, at the same time developing their doctrine and making it familiar to all who followed the debates. During the third century, therefore, Christianity became one of the schools of thought to which intellectuals and educated men could adhere; it became both philosophy and cult and thus united in itself the attractions of both these related but different activities.

Educated Christians suffered the disabilities and the intermittent persecutions of their less fortunate co-religionists, but upper-class, educated Christians shared the social and economic position of pagans of their class in most respects. Pagan and Christian received the same education; Origen (d. 254), Plotinus' most brilliant Christian opponent, studied under Ammonius Saccas a few years before Plotinus did. Nonetheless, Christians had a particular problem concerning the classical tradition in which they were raised. Classical education was based on study of the great literary works of preimperial times, and those works contained not only the models of grammar and style but also the ancient mythology. In rejecting the mythological content of their literary tradition Christians recognized a dilemma: either the Christian should shun classical letters and remain uneducated, or the Christian seeking knowledge must run the risk of losing his faith through exposure to the blandishments and beauties of pagan literature. Some, like Tertullian (d. 222), counseled against reading the errors of the pagans, claiming that the Christian could obtain all knowledge from Scripture. Most Christian thinkers, however, agreed with Origen, the greatest of the Greek Fathers, that Christians must be equipped not only to understand the mysteries of the faith but also to refute the pagan philosophers in their own terms and on their own intellectual level. While recognizing the dangers involved, men like Jerome and Augustine advocated the study of the best pagan philosophers because, in the words of the biblical injunction, it was praiseworthy to "spoil the Egyptians," that is, to take from the pagans whatever intellectual weapons might be turned against them in defense of Christianity and whatever knowledge might be useful in understanding Christian revelation. The triumph of this view is not surprising because many of the Fathers were converts to Christianity.

Later antiquity was a great age of schoolbooks in which the learning and literature of the past were condensed and simplified for educational purposes. From these schoolbooks most Christians gained their knowledge of pagan philosophy and enjoyed the dangerous pleasures of pagan literature. Most popular of all the grammar books were two fourth-century treatises by Donatus, the *Ars Minor* and *Ars Maior* (elementary and advanced), which for over twelve centuries were standard textbooks in their field. They treated the parts of speech and syntax, illustrating them by literary extracts. In the Middle Ages the next most popular textbook was Priscian's *Institutes of Grammar* (ca. 500), a more advanced treatise that contained a disorganized storehouse of quotations from ancient literature. In the pursuit of what today is called a "liberal education," grammar (including literature as well as language) was the first discipline or art to be mastered. There were six others: rhetoric, dialectic, arithmetic, music, geometry, and astronomy. These were the seven "liberal arts" that became the standard medieval curriculum. Early in the fifth century Martianus Capella composed an encyclopedic treatise on the seven liberal arts entitled *The Nuptials of Mercury and Philology*. This book preserved the basic instruction of antiquity.

Considering the general educational level of the times and the fact that by the end of the fourth century a knowledge of Greek was a mark of very high erudition in the West, the attainments of the Latin Fathers of the Church are truly remarkable. The greatest influence on the future were the Four Doctors: Saint Ambrose, Saint Jerome, and Saint Augustine, who were contemporaries, and Saint Gregory the Great, who was pope two centuries later.

The general significance of the Latin Fathers for medieval thought was two-fold: they mastered pagan philosophy (notably Neo-Platonism and Stoicism) and incorporated it into their exposition of Christian doctrine and the teaching of the Church; and they transmitted and interpreted for Latin Christians the subtleties and profundities of Eastern Christian dogmatic speculation.

The Greek Fathers had applied Greek philosophical ideas and logical tools to Christian doctrine and had provided the foundation for the exposition, called exegesis, of the Old Testament. Origen had compiled a great biblical text written in six columns, hence called the *Hexapla,* in which the five major translations were compared with the original Hebrew text. Origen had recognized the need for meeting opponents of Christianity on grounds that both sides would accept, and his work of textual scholarship provided the basis for finding those grounds. The *Hexapla* also provided a sound basis for textual commentary, which was becoming increasingly important in the development of a rational explication of Christian revelation. Much of the scholarship of the Latin Fathers followed this methodological line and owed a great deal to men like Origen. The Latin Fathers also took up the doctrinal interests of the Greek Fathers but gave greater emphasis to ethics.

Ambrose (ca. 340–397) was born into an aristocratic Roman family and, after an excellent education, advanced rapidly to the rank of provincial governor. When the death of the bishop of Milan led to a dispute between the Arian and orthodox factions over the election of a successor, Ambrose intervened to maintain the peace. According to a story circulated shortly after his death, when he was called on to address a riotous multitude during the local controversy, a child's voice was heard crying out, "Let Ambrose be bishop!" With one accord the whole city pressed the episcopal office on the reluctant governor, who was not yet a baptized Christian. This deficiency was made good, and within a week he was advanced from minor orders to the priesthood and consecrated bishop. Ambrose now turned to the study of theology and to the administration of his diocese. His greatest influence on the future was his uncompromising assertion of the independence of the Church and of the superiority of the spiritual authority over the secular in matters concerning faith and morals. His most dramatic statement of these principles, during his contest with Theodosius I over the Thessalonican massacre, has already been noted. Ambrose was a distinguished preacher. His sermons were the basis for his most important contributions to biblical exegesis: the *Hexaemeron,* dealing with the Creation, and a shorter commentary on the Gospel of Saint Luke. In these and other theological treatises, Ambrose introduced the ideas of Stoic ethics as expounded in the works of Cicero, especially the concept of duty, although he made it clear that the first object of the Christian's duty is no longer the state but God.

Ambrose and Hilary, bishop of Poitiers (d. 367), were the first Latin Fathers to expound the Scriptures on as high an intellectual level as that of the Greek theologians. In doing so they incorporated the leading Eastern ideas and methods in their work, especially the use of the allegorical method of interpretation (setting forth the hidden meaning behind words whose literal sense implies a higher, but veiled, truth). Hilary was equally interested in the literal, or straightforward, meaning of the Bible; Ambrose was equally interested in expounding Christian ethics. Both were thus typically Western and Latin in balancing the Eastern influence with a common-sense interest in the practical and the useful, in terms of a Christian aspiration for salvation. Finally, Hilary and Ambrose were the two earliest important writers of a new form of poetry set to music and used in the liturgy of the Church. Hymns were the most original Christian contribution to Latin poetry. Rarely surpassed for beauty and religious feeling, Ambrose's hymns were written for antiphonal singing, "after the manner of the eastern churches," that is, in short stanzas to be sung alternately as a response by choir and congregation, which accounts for their extreme simplicity. At least four of Ambrose's hymns whose authenticity is beyond question are still sung and enjoyed today. One of these, *Veni Redemptor Gentium,* inspired the great hymn by Martin Luther, "Now Come, the Heathen's Saviour."

Jerome (ca. 340–419) was born a Christian into a well-to-do provincial family. He completed his early education in Rome, probably under the grammarian Donatus, and later devoted himself to theological studies in Gaul and northern Italy. Endowed with an eager intellectual curiosity and a rather contentious nature, Jerome dedicated himself to two goals: the elevation of Christian scholarship and the propagation of the monastic way of life. Jerome was a reformer. His zeal for scholarship and monasticism was a personal reaction against what he considered to be the low intellectual level and the worldliness of the Church in the Latin West. This attitude, his forceful personality, and rather more than normal vanity gave him the reputation of being a troublemaker. These traits also made him the best-educated and one of the most influential of the Fathers.

Jerome's ardor for asceticism led him to translate the rule of Pachomius and thus make available to the Latin West the basic formula of the Eastern form of monasticism. His theological treatises and commentaries were distinguished by two characteristics found in all his writings: an interest in textual criticism, and a constant use of the best pagan writings to elucidate Christian revelation. His great love of the classics gave him a guilty conscience. In a dream that came to him during an illness, a voice from heaven accused him, "You are a Ciceronian, not a Christian, for where your treasure is, there shall your heart be." Jerome was unable to keep the vow he then took, never again to read a pagan book. But the experience was decisive in his life, for it turned him to a study of biblical exegesis and the writings of the Greek Fathers, which he pursued in Constantinople under the greatest of contemporary Eastern scholars, Saint Gregory of Nazianzus. During this period he also learned Hebrew.

In 382 Jerome accepted the invitation of Pope Damasus to come to

Rome. During the next three years he leveled caustic criticism at the fashionable and indulgent pseudo-Christians who corrupted the Church of his day. He inveighed against the "luxuries of Rome," and against false widows "who remain widows from necessity, not inclination," and whose carefully made-up faces would make one think "they had not lost husbands but were on the hunt for them." He poked fun especially at the wealthy Roman matrons, pampered by flattering priests (with hands extended not to give benediction but to receive gratuities), who "after a seven-course dinner dream of the Apostles" (a barb adapted from Terence), and who "when they give alms blow a full blast on the trumpet, and when they go to mass hire the town crier."

Pope Damasus was able to harness and direct Jerome's inexhaustible intellectual energies, turning him to the monumental task of retranslating the Bible into Latin. A Latin translation, called the *Itala,* already existed. It had been written piecemeal during the preceding centuries. Much of it seems to have come from North Africa, and it appears to have been incomplete. It was also inaccurate, and Damasus, responding to the decline of Greek studies in the West, recognized the need for a new translation. Jerome was the obvious choice for the job, but Rome was uncongenial to this vicious critic of local Christian society, especially after his protector Damasus died in 384.

Jerome therefore retired to Palestine, where he founded a monastery at Bethlehem and spent the rest of his life. He could not resist one final (and, we might say, ecumenical) thrust at Christians whose fervor exceeded their intelligence, observing that "only doctors practice medicine and only carpenters build houses, but searching the meaning of Scripture is the one art that everybody is sure that he possesses; it is bad enough to teach what you do not know, but worse not even to be aware of what you do not know." Jerome knew, as some modern translators of the Bible into English have learned, how strong was the force of religious conservatism against changing, even if change meant making more accurate, the traditional and familiar translation of Scripture. The final result of Jerome's prolonged study, based on the previous textual criticism of Origen but going beyond it, was a text of both the Old and New Testaments translated accurately from the best Hebrew (or Aramaic) and Greek manuscripts then accessible. This translation used the freer idiom and more expressive figures of speech of fourth-century Latin rather than the more formal Latinity of Cicero or Virgil. The final version, the Vulgate Bible, did not gain universal acceptance in the West until the end of the eighth century.

The greatest of all the Latin Fathers was Augustine (354–430), one of the most fascinating personalities in all history as he was one of the most influential. He was born in North Africa and received an excellent classical education in schools in Carthage. The first step in his spiritual odyssey came at the age of nineteen, when he read Cicero's introductory treatise on philosophy, the *Hortensius,* which led him to investigate pagan philosophy, especially Manichaeism and Neo-Platonism. During this period, first as a student and then as a teacher of rhetoric, Augustine lived what later seemed to him a life of vice and wantonness. When his teaching career took him to Milan he came under the influence of Ambrose, whose great sermons finally clarified for him what he had been seeking and the path by which to attain it, the understanding that "all knowledge should direct itself toward knowing God."

Augustine, now intellectually convinced, was enrolled as a catechumen eagerly studying the Christian faith. His real conversion, his attainment of faith, came through an experience that he could only recognize as the operation of divine grace: "instantly, by a light as it were infused into my heart, all darkness of doubt vanished away." Shortly afterward he was baptized by Ambrose and then returned to North Africa, where he was later ordained a priest and then became bishop of Hippo. He died during the siege of his city by Vandals in 430. During the busy years of his episcopate he found time to write on almost all the important issues of Christian doctrine. His theological treatises and his controversial writings against the heresies of his day constitute the greatest patristic achievement and the most profound influence on Western religious thought exercised by one mind. His influence dominated medieval philosophy and theology and lives on not only in modern Catholic thought but also, mainly through Calvin and Luther, in Protestant thought.

Augustine's earlier interest in pagan philosophies is apparent throughout his works. Many of these were undertaken to refute pagan errors and Christian heresies. In his treatises against Manichaeism, Augustine dealt with the problem of evil. The Manichaeans had argued in their dualistic system that good and evil were two irreconcilable principles, the one spiritual and the other material. For Augustine the created material world could not in itself be evil nor could evil be anything positive; evil was simply the absence of good, or the turning away from God, the Supreme Good. Neo-Platonic metaphysics helped him define good as whatever serves or tends toward God, to the degree that it achieves union with God. Intimately connected with this view was Augustine's concept of free will in human nature. Pelagius, a layman from the British Isles, had been teaching in the schools of Spain and Italy that men did not inherit original sin and that human free will was sufficient to attain salvation, thus rendering divine grace and the sacraments of the Church superfluous. Pelagius' optimism did not appeal to a man like Augustine, who had suffered the torments of a will that sought but could not find truth without grace. For Augustine human will could only turn toward God if fortified by divine grace because original sin turned man from God. Psychologically Augustine was on sounder ground. But his enthusiasm in refuting Pelagianism led him to emphasize so strongly the omnipotence of God and the insignificance of human good works that he also seemed to imply, logically, that the sacraments (the normal means of receiving grace, according to the teaching of the Church) were superfluous. In its extreme form this position was simply a belief in predestination. On this point the teaching of the medieval Church did not follow Augustine, taking rather a middle position between him and Pelagius, and emphasizing both the necessity of grace and the necessity of good works for the Christian life that leads to salvation.

Augustine's two best known works are the *Confessions,* an intimate personal revelation of his own spiritual quest and final attainment of faith, and *The City of God,* the greatest apologetic (defense of the faith) in all Christian literature. *The City of God* was written to answer the pagan accusation (brought to the fore again by the sack of Rome in 410) that Christianity was responsible for the misfortunes of the empire. Its twenty-two books were published separately as he wrote them from 413 to 426. The work as a whole was never revised, and although its length and complexity make it difficult to follow at times, it is still the most challenging and all-embracing statement of a Christian philosophy of history, an interpretation on the grandest scale of the ultimate meaning of human existence in terms of Christian theology. Briefly, Augustine's argument is that history accords with a divine plan whose central theme is the continuing struggle between the City of God, whose triumph is assured, and the Earthly City. The City of God is the community of all those, living and dead, who have turned to God and seek him before all else. The Earthly City contains all who have turned their energies toward worldly pursuits. These two communities were therefore not real—they were not to be confused with states or nations existing at any time in history—but were constructs based on the community of purpose among individuals of any state in any age. Later, the Church was commonly referred to as the City of God and the secular polities as Earthly Cities, but this "political Augustinianism" was not faithful to the master's ideas. The crucial issue for him was the relationship of the soul with God. Through its striving, the soul perfected that relationship, grew closer to God, and shed its earthly concerns. The tragedy was that not all souls devoted themselves to this striving, and, in fact, those that did not were locked in conflict with the souls that did. Thus for Augustine, all history is a preparation for the final event, the Last Judgment, when citizens of the City of God will find salvation while those of the Earthly City, including nominal Christians who turn away from God although they are members of the Church, will be damned.

This argument had a twofold impact: first, the attack on Christianity was turned aside, since the Christian community could not be accused of being subversive. It was otherworldly. Success in the world was not the test of the success of the Church. Second, the argument formulated the Christian view of the universe. Augustine set the values of the physical world against those of the spiritual and made the spiritual values the ones toward which all self-perfecting souls turn themselves. But in turning away from the world of the flesh toward the world of the spirit, a denial of the value of the flesh is implied. The spiritual values are the only real ones; physical reality may seem real, but it is not. Here was a doctrine that tended toward Manicheanism. The Christian could not deny that the created world was real—that is, that it had real value —because it was God's own creation, and Augustine did not deny his Christianity on this point. But he did put the created world on the verge of unreality, suspended between being a quagmire that could entrap the soul and the realization of a divine act. His work thus presented the central paradox of Christian life: If one should seek God, who is pure spirit, and turn away from the material world, how can he give proper honor to God's work? And how far should this denial of the material world go?

The work of Ambrose, Jerome, Augustine, and the other Latin Fathers of the Church had two general results. First, many of the doctrinal and philosophical ideas of the Greek Fathers were brought permanently within the range of Western intellectual life, to form part of the heritage of Christian antiquity on which medieval culture could be built. Second, the intellectual opposition of a waning paganism had not only been met, but many of its philosophical concepts, especially Stoic ethics and Neo-Platonic metaphysics, had been assimilated into Christian thought. The Church was heir to Rome not only in ecclesiastical organization; the Fathers of the Church incorporated the intellectual heritage of Rome into Christian thought.

### Suggestions for Further Reading

**Secondary Works**    The best works on early Christianity and the growth of the Christian Church are H. Jedin and J. Dolan, eds., *Handbook of Church History,* vol. 1 (New York, 1965); H. Chadwick, *The Early Church* (Harmondsworth, 1967); and the classic L. Duchesne, *The Early History of the Christian Church,* 3 vols. (London, 1914–22). In addition, see E. R. Goodenough, *The Church in the Roman Empire* (New York, 1931) for a preliminary sketch. For an introduction to the intellectual culture of the Church Fathers, see C. N. Cochrane, *Christianity and Classical Culture,* 2nd ed. (New York, 1944). E. K. Rand's lectures, *Founders of the Middle Ages* (Cambridge, Mass., 1928) are still an outstanding introduction to the character and influence of the Latin Fathers. Augustine, the most important Western thinker, is the subject of an excellent biography by Peter Brown, *Augustine of Hippo* (Berkeley, Calif., 1967).

**Sources**    For general collections of sources for Church history, see H. Bettenson, ed., *Documents of the Christian Church* (New York, 1947), and C. J. Barry, ed., *Readings in Church History,* vol. 1, *From Pentecost to the Protestant Revolt* (Westminster, Md., 1960). Two large compilations of English translations of the patristic texts are now in progress: J. Quasten and J. C. Plumpe, eds., *Ancient Christian Writers* (Westminster, Md., 1946–), and R. J. Deferrari et al., eds., *The Fathers of the Church* (New York, 1947–). Good translations of Augustine's *City of God* and *Confessions* are by Marcus Dods and by E. B. Pusey, respectively, in several editions. The most important early history of the Church is Eusebius, *The History of the Church,* trans. G. A. Williamson (Harmondsworth, 1965).

# 3   The Foundations of the Germanic Kingdoms

Late Roman government and social and economic life formed one foundation stone for the development of medieval civilization, the growth of Christianity another. The third foundation stone, the Germanic contribution, is the most difficult to assess. The invasions of the Germans added a new element to the cultural mix of the empire's European population and probably accelerated the changes taking place in the Western empire. The Germans did not constitute a large portion of the total population, but they were rulers, and thus their culture had an impact disproportionate with their numbers. Nonetheless, most of the German peoples who established themselves on Roman territory had had long contact with the Romans, and they tried to preserve Roman administration. The invading Germans entered Western Roman society at the top, but they were integrated into that society. The effect they had in shifting the direction or hastening the changes taking place within the late Roman empire was exercised from within rather than from without.

Germanic penetration into the empire had been going on steadily for several centuries, and it was not entirely the result of conflict or warfare between Germans and Romans. Peaceful infiltration of individuals or small

The disorganized attack of barbarians was bound to create a chaotic battle scene
even when the Germans fought the disciplined Roman legions. Here the sculptor of the
Ludovisi Battle Sarcophagus (ca. 250) captures the chaos as well as the defeat
of the barbarians.

groups of barbarians dates back to before the Christian era. The "invasions"
were in many cases so unmilitary in nature as to deserve the German historians' term, *Völkerwanderung* (the wandering of the peoples). Large numbers of Germans, Iranians, and Asian-Altaic peoples were constantly on the
move during the third, fourth, and fifth centuries. The later emperors often
settled them within the empire to defend the frontier against other wandering
groups. By the end of the fourth century, more than half of the Roman army
was actually Germanic, and Germans occupied many of the highest positions
of command.

   As noted, the German kings who invaded the Western empire with
armies came to conquer and rule, but not to destroy. Most of them sought
and many gained recognition from the emperors so that their rule might be
buttressed by legitimacy. This is why, even in the West, it is impossible to fix
a date for the end of the empire. The German kings in fact ruled independently; in theory they ruled in the name of the emperor and by his appointment. This theory was expressed in the Roman titles by which they were

distinguished. Theodoric, king of the Ostrogoths, bore the dignity and rank of *patricius;* others sought similar legitimization of their *de facto* power. But none of the Germanic kings dared assume the title of emperor. This fact is a striking illustration of the spell that Rome, the idea of universal sovereignty over the civilized world, cast on men's minds. The German king might rule a mixed Romano-Germanic population; he might even possess Roman citizenship and the highest Roman dignity, but he did not aspire to the purple.

## Early Germanic Society

Writing a history of early Germanic society is difficult. Few literary and archeological artifacts remain; the historian must fill the interstices with speculation. In the historiographical tradition, the speculation and therefore the picture presented have been deeply affected by ideology. The first important attempt to make sense out of the remains of the early Germanic period (the first to the fifth centuries) was consciously based on Rousseau's portrayal of the noble savage. The Germans were pictured in communities of free yeoman farmers who gathered in assemblies to carry out their common business but who normally lived in total and splendid freedom. Of course, there was hardly any crime or deviancy in such a community. The character of the German peoples was the ideal of purity and wholesomeness. During the nineteenth century, historians of English constitutional development held up the Germanic tribes as the source of the political ideas contained in the great reform legislation of their own time. The ideology of political egalitarianism underlying the extension of the franchise and making a constitutional monarchy into a democracy came, they said, from the original Germanic genius for democracy, a genius once realized in those jewel-like communities that existed before the Germans migrated into the corrupting cultural atmosphere of the autocratic Roman Empire. It did not bother such historians that it had taken more than fifteen centuries for the genius of Germanic popular government to reassert itself, and of course they assumed that the governmental development had ended in their own time.

Recent historians of the distant German past have reanalyzed the sources and have added to the corpus of source material both by searching the libraries and by intensifying archeological investigation. The picture that emerges from this new work discards the idea that the Germans lived in a classless, democratic society and has largely freed itself from racial theories.

The Germans originated in Scandinavia and northern Continental Europe. They constituted a large group of related peoples who spoke similar, although by no means identical, languages and who shared some gross cultural characteristics while differing from one another in many cultural details. The peoples seem to have had a hierarchical organization, both socially and politically. Over the centuries groups of Germans had migrated south and east, but their life was not nomadic. There were long periods of settlement, lasting generations. The early biography of the Visigothic Saint Sabas indicates that before the Visigoths moved into the empire, they were united under a kind of council of chieftains. It is obvious from the story of the martyrdom of Saint Sabas that the council could not often exercise effective authority over the villages. It might be best to characterize large-scale political organization as potential rather than real. Petty kings united in themselves the authority of both war leader and charismatic tribal ruler, but the power of these men rarely extended over wide areas or great numbers of people. Large confederations only formed to meet temporary threats or to take advantage of temporary opportunities, and they collapsed when some major element in the situation changed.

Villages were apparently united in tribal units, although these may have been nothing more than temporary conglomerations. In any case, the villages were clearly the primary unit of social organization among the various Germanic groups. Village communities were governed by councils of chieftains and other great men. The principal difference between chieftains and other aristocratic persons seems to have consisted in the chieftains' religious and judicial duties. The chieftain families claimed an ancient right and maintained their position from generation to generation. By the time the Germans became known to the Romans in the first century, families with chieftainships justified their special position by claiming divine origin, and according to the Romans, the units based on chieftain power were stable elements in German political organization.

The aristocratic families were wealthier than their neighbors, although the differences in wealth were not great by later, medieval or modern, standards. The other families generally formed a loose clientele structure around the aristocratic families. The relationship between patron and client was between freemen who possessed substantially the same rights and obligations before the law. The patron helped his clients with financial and legal problems and with marriages and other social acts that affected a family's status, while clients owed allegiance to the patron. The allegiance became the basis for action whenever the great man went to court or to war or when there was need for common activity on some problem that arose in the district. In addition, servants and slaves were attached to the households of many families. These unfree people were either captives taken in war or members of the tribe forced to subject themselves because of financial or legal disaster.

Status was important in Germanic society. For example, law suits that dealt with injuries appear to have concerned the loss of status that resulted from the fact of being injured rather than the actual physical damage done. Status was also the factor that brought kin groups into dispute, for the loss of status by a member of a kin group constituted a loss to the whole clan. Communal law provided the means for resolving conflicts without having to resort to blood feuds. In fact, however, disputes were normally brought to law after a vendetta had begun, and the law did not provide remedies for injuries but only procedures for arriving at a resolution of the conflict. The purpose of the resolution was to reestablish the original relationship between the parties. This is not to say that every change in the status relationships led to conflict and a law suit but that some actions that effected a change were considered inappropriate or unacceptable. It was action of this sort that lay behind the law suits.

It is difficult to ascertain the state of the Germanic legal systems at the time of the invasions, but in Scandinavia they later developed into very complex and sophisticated systems. Medieval Scandinavian law was founded on an intricate procedural law designed to protect the parties to a law suit from each other. The irony of this system was that the extraordinary complexity of the law—the profusion of technicalities meant to insure that substantial justice prevailed between the parties—could also be used, as similar rules are used today, to prevent justice from being done.

Law designed to provide an alternative to fighting touched only that part of the community that might turn to violence in the pursuit of its interests. Women, children, and old people were excluded from the consideration of the law and could not be parties, either plaintiff or defendant, to a suit. This exclusion did not mean that women played no role in early Germanic society. They were important figures in the kinship system, and it is clear that their desires often could affect the outcome of marriage negotiations carried out exclusively by the men. In addition, women could generate the kind of activities that led to vendettas and law suits, although they themselves could not be physically harmed, since they were noncombatants. They also could not suffer legal penalty. These advantages were limited, however, because a woman's husband had virtually a life and death authority over her and could put a violent end to her troublemaking proclivities. It can not be known how often men exercised such power—which a man had over his children also—but it should be pointed out that the kinship system tempered a husband's legal right to harm his wife. A man had to consider the reaction of his wife's kin to any injury he did her and the effect the injury would have on his status and his own kin relations. Women's legal subjection, therefore, did not reflect their actual strength or position in the community, and the law's failure to take cognizance of women's acts seriously weakened its effectiveness as an organizing factor in Germanic society.

Contact with Roman civilization transformed the German societies. When the imperial government found itself incapable of organizing the forces necessary to protect all the borders from the constant pressure of raiding groups, it resorted to two devices. In the Near East, where there were relatively stable

This model of the Roman fortress at Deutz, across the Rhine from Cologne, shows how much Roman military building influenced that of the Middle Ages. Forts like this one were effective salients in barbarian territories across the frontiers.

political entities like Judea and Armenia, the imperial government established buffer kingdoms commissioned to protect the borders in return for local autonomy. On the Rhine-Danube frontier, where there were no preexisting kingdoms, the imperial government apparently encouraged the development of royal power. The kings could organize multitribal political units useful to the Romans, and they became figures with whom the imperial government could deal. Under the kings, groups of Germans, called *foederati* (allied or confederate peoples), were settled on Roman soil to perform the same function as the buffer states in the East. By the fourth century they formed the bulk of the Roman army, especially in the West. Thus German military leaders became generals in the Roman army, and a large body of Germans, related culturally and historically to those across the borders, were Romanized. The process of Romanization affected the tribes across the frontiers because during periods of peace considerable intercourse among all Germanic peoples existed. German social organization benefited from this contact with the Romans because the *foederati* were not only trained in Roman military and administrative systems, but also exposed to other aspects of the empire's civilization. When the invasions began in the late fourth century, German society had changed significantly, and this transformation made the social amalgamation of Germans and Romanized Gauls easier than it might have been.

During the last quarter of the fourth century, conditions in the West deteriorated rapidly. Gratian (375–383), son of, and since 367 co-emperor with, Valentinian I, kept the frontier defenses intact, but it augured ill for the future when on his father's death in 375 Gratian accepted his half brother, Valentinian II (383–392), as junior co-emperor. Valentinian II was a pawn in the court intrigues and the politics of the empire. These were reminiscent of the third century before Diocletian: Gratian was assassinated by agents of a Spanish usurper, and a struggle for power ensued between several German generals of the Roman army. Arbogast the Frank emerged supreme. When Valentinian II made the mistake of trying to rule as well as reign, Arbogast had him strangled and set up a puppet emperor, Eugenius.

In the West, these political conditions were not new, but in the East, the successors of Constantine were confronted with an unprecedented crisis, precipitated by the movements of the German tribes. Deflected from the empire by the Rhine-Danube frontier, one group of Germans had, at an early date, moved south and southeastward. These were the Goths. Impelled by overpopulation, wars, or hunger, they wandered into the plains of southern Russia, where they split into two branches. In the fourth century, the Ostrogoths settled in the fertile region north of the Black Sea, while the Visigoths occupied the region extending westward to Dacia, just north of the lower Danube. About 375, the Goths were struck by the sudden impact of the Asiatic Huns. The appearance of the Huns in Europe was the end result of obscure movements of Ural-Altaian tribes in central Asia whose original impulse was a combination of overpopulation, the effect of climatic changes on an essentially pastoral existence, and the endless struggle for power among the nomadic tribes north of the Himalaya Mountains. The plains of southern Russia were ideally suited to the military tactics of these horse-riding nomads, and the Ostrogoths were crushed and dispersed.

The terrified Visigoths, whose turn was next, begged permission to settle within the empire in the depopulated province of Moesia just south of the natural barrier of the lower Danube. The Eastern emperor Valens (364–378) allowed them to cross the Danube on the condition that they become *foederati* responsible for the defense of the frontier in return for provisions supplied by Roman officials. The provisions were not forthcoming, however, and the Visigoths suffered indignities and oppression, which provoked them to abandon the frontier, renounce their alliance with the empire, and begin a systematic plundering of the province of Thrace. To Valens this was desertion of duty and treason. As the Visigoths moved southward, threatening Constantinople itself, the emperor met them in a pitched battle near Adrianople in 378. Here the hitherto supreme Roman infantry was decisively defeated by the Gothic cavalry. Valens was killed and his army dispersed, but the Goths had no program or goal and spent the next year aimlessly pillaging Greece and the provinces to the north.

To meet this crisis, Gratian appointed as co-emperor in the East Theodosius I (379–395), a Spanish general who had been retired in disgrace only a few years earlier. Skillfully combining force and diplomacy, Theodosius settled the Visigoths once more in Moesia as *foederati*. Meanwhile, the remnants of the shattered Ostrogoths drifted westward and were settled with the same status in the province of Pannonia, farther up the Danube. After Gratian's assassination, Theodosius divided his energies between restoring the empire and attempting to bring it all under his authority. In 394 he dethroned the puppet emperor Eugenius and destroyed his creator, Arbogast. For the last five months of his reign, Theodosius I ruled alone, the last to unite East and West under one emperor. He was also the first to declare Christianity the state religion in the empire, and for these achievements in the service of both the empire and Christianity, he received the cognomen "the Great."

Far more significant than these achievements themselves was Theodosius' accomplishment of all this by diplomacy and by the skillful use of German generals for his own ends. The "Roman" army that defeated Arbogast included Visigothic forces commanded by Alaric, a contingent under Stilicho the Vandal, and even an auxiliary troop of Huns. When Theodosius died and was succeeded by two sons, one a mere youth and the other a child, the tables were turned: German generals used the emperors for their ends as Theodosius had used them for his. Theodosius was the last of the Roman emperors to be appointed on the basis of ability and experience. Thereafter the dynastic principle triumphed at the expense of the empire. The successors of Theodosius in the West were either incompetents whose claims to the throne were based on heredity, or puppets set up and pulled down by the generals of the Roman army to whom real power had now passed.

## The Invasions: Alaric, Theodoric, and Clovis

The recovery under Theodosius was short-lived. Within a half-century the Western frontiers had been permanently breached, and the various German tribes, confederacies, and "nations" had begun to establish barbarian kingdoms on Roman soil. The Germanic peoples at this time may be distinguished as East Germans and West Germans. The East Germans (whose origins were east of the Elbe river) were more migratory; they experienced earlier and more intimate contact with the civilized world; they adopted Christianity earlier; and they established their kingdoms in Roman provinces that touched the Mediterranean. The most important East German tribes were the Visigoths, Ostrogoths, Vandals, and Burgundians. The Visigoths were the first to play an important role within the empire, but the Ostrogoths and lesser East German tribes had even earlier pushed their raids as far as the Caucasus and into Asia Minor.

This commemorative silver plate was almost ruined by the peasants who found it and sawed it in half so that each would have his share. It was made around 390 and depicts Emperor Theodosius I and his two sons.

It was during such a Gothic marauding expedition that a Roman provincial family of Greek-speaking Christians were carried off as captives from their home in Cappadocia. Two generations later, a child from this family—doubtless part Gothic by now—was sent as a hostage to Constantinople. This was Ulfilas (ca. 310–383), who was consecrated a bishop there in 341, and who became the apostle to the Goths. Unfortunately for the Germans, he was an Arian Christian. Thus the Romanizing influence of his missionary efforts among the Visigoths, and through them among all the East German peoples, created for these conquerors their most difficult single problem when they later forced their rule on the Roman and orthodox population of the Western provinces. Within twenty years of Ulfilas' death, all the East Germans were at least formally Arian Christian. The rapidity of their conversion is partly explained by Ulfilas' translation of the Bible into Gothic (for which he adapted and expanded the Greek alphabet), the earliest surviving literary monument of a Germanic language.

After the death of Theodosius, the Visigoths had become restive once more. Their new king, the ambitious Alaric, saw the opportunity to expand his rule. The phlegmatic Arcadius (395–408) reigned in Constantinople and was himself ruled by whatever faction was currently supreme in the endless rounds of court intrigue. The Western throne was occupied by the mentally retarded child Honorius (395–423), whose early years were dominated by the able Vandal general Stilicho, a former lieutenant of Theodosius. The Eastern court and Stilicho maneuvered for control of western North Africa (on which Rome and Italy depended for food) and of Illyricum (roughly, modern Yugoslavia and northwestern Greece), which Theodosius had, with faulty prevision, split between the Eastern and Western halves of the empire. Alaric, occupying the province of Moesia (in northern Illyricum), played one side against the other.

Alaric's policy did not succeed. He ravaged the southern Balkan Peninsula and Greece, but he could not conquer the fortified towns. As long as Stilicho lived, Alaric was unable to penetrate into Italy with more than temporary success. To defend Italy, Stilicho withdrew the Roman garrisons along the Rhine, leaving its defense to Frankish *foederati* who conspicuously failed to hold the line. He practically ignored an insubordinate general who crossed the Channel into Gaul in 407 with the bulk of the Roman troops stationed in Britain, leaving that province to its own defense against the raids of Picts, Scots, and Germans. What ultimate ambition Stilicho harbored will never be known, but its nature is suggested by two facts. First, he could have destroyed Alaric and his army, but instead he came to terms and courted the support of the Visigoths. Second, shortly after the death of Arcadius, Stilicho's enemies accused him of seeking the Eastern throne for his son. Stilicho was arrested and executed for treason with the connivance of Honorius, whose jealousy of the general was the only passion that could rouse his energy.

The execution of Stilicho in 408 was the beginning of the debacle in the West. Alaric moved into Italy with his people. Negotiations with Honorius were abortive—the emperor, safe with his court in impregnable Ravenna, hardly wished to replace the Vandal Stilicho with the Visigoth Alaric. For two years the barbarians ravaged the peninsula. The climax of this Italian campaign came when Alaric took Rome in 410. The fall of the Eternal City shocked contemporaries from one end of the civilized world to the other. The physical destruction was negligible, but the incident made a more memorable impression than any other event of the late imperial period. In his cell in distant Bethlehem, Saint Jerome exclaimed, "All humanity is included in her ruins," a sentiment with which pagan and Christian alike could agree.

Alaric's next move reveals the weakness, as it does the motivation, of the Visigothic invaders. Alaric sought not the splendor of empire, nor the luxury of Rome, but food. For centuries, however, Italy had not produced enough food for its own needs—great quantities of grain were imported from Sicily and North Africa—and therefore it could not support the Visigothic hordes that had now descended on it. After three days of pillaging Rome, Alaric marched south to collect ships in southern Italy to transport his people to North Africa. These plans were ruined by a storm that destroyed the fleet and by the death of Alaric shortly thereafter. The first great German king to invade the empire was buried with barbaric pomp in the bed of a temporarily diverted river in Calabria. The slaves who did the work were killed so that "no man knoweth his sepulcher unto this day."

Alaric's successor, Ataulf, led his people northward out of Italy and into southern Gaul. Meanwhile the Vandals, with the lesser tribes of Alans and Suevi, had plundered their way across Gaul and into Spain, and the general confusion was compounded by dissension and conflict among three Roman generals, each of whom sought the help of Germanic tribes in furthering his own ambitions. One of these generals was Constantius, successor to Stilicho as the power behind Honorius' throne. The Western provinces were all but reduced to chaos. Ataulf's Visigoths found that they could not live off the ravaged country. Their newly revived status of *foederati* could not be honored by the imperial government because it depended on delivery of African food, which rebellion in that quarter, too, had now cut off.

The exasperated Ataulf now played his trump card. By a stroke of luck, Alaric had captured and passed on to his successor a precious spoil of victory: Galla Placidia, daughter of Theodosius I, half-sister of Honorius and Arcadius, and nearest in hereditary line of succession to the throne in the West. During the years of her captivity and travels in the wagon train of the Visigothic army, Placidia was honorably treated, and she and Ataulf fell in love. This is not inconceivable, and it was during this period that Ataulf (according to a story carried to Palestine during these years by a Christian pilgrim) renounced his earlier ambition to displace Rome by a Gothic empire and declared, "the unbridled barbarism of the Goths is incompatible with law, and without law there can be no state. Therefore, since I cannot supplant her, I hope to be known to posterity as the restorer of Rome." Whether or not this was related to a tender passion for Placidia, Ataulf showed every sign of wanting to imitate Stilicho, who had strengthened his position by marrying a niece of the emperor Theodosius. In 414 Ataulf, attired in the garb of a Roman senator, married his imperial hostage. Constantius, who coveted (and later won) the hand of Placidia for himself as a means to succeed the childless Honorius as emperor, then drove the Visigoths out of Gaul into Spain, where Ataulf was assassinated shortly thereafter.

The new Visigothic king, Wallia, finally achieved for his people by diplomacy what his predecessors had failed to obtain by force: political autonomy within the empire and settlement in Aquitaine (southern Gaul) with the status of *foederati*. The price for this was the return of Galla Placidia, for whom Honorius also agreed to pay the flattering ransom of nineteen thousand quarters of grain. The hand of Constantius can be seen in this final settlement, for he married Placidia in 417 and was appointed co-emperor in the West in 421, the same year in which he died. A better future was in store for Wallia and his successors. The Visigothic kingdom in southern Gaul was consolidated and expanded during the fifth century until it reached its height under Euric (466–484), who also began a new Visigothic expansion into Spain.

Meanwhile, Honorius dawdled out the last years of his reign and died in 423. He was succeeded briefly by a usurper, whom the Eastern emperor, Theodosius II (408–450), displaced with Valentinian III (425–455), the child of Placidia and Constantius. Real power was exercised by Placidia, who was given the title Augusta, and by the general Aëtius, "the last of the Romans." The greatest strength of Aëtius lay in his influence over the Huns settled on the upper Danube, whom he used as mercenaries against the German enemies of the empire. Placidia and Aëtius cooperated in a policy of containment and stabilization, yielding territory where the Germanic pressure was too great, but repulsing the barbarians where they could assemble enough Huns and other troops. Although Aëtius won several victories, success did not on the whole attend either his military or diplomatic efforts.

During the reign of Valentinian III the West lost most of its provinces outside of Italy. The Vandals in Spain crossed over to North Africa in 429, under their king Gaiseric (428–477), the ablest general of his age. The establishment of a powerful Vandal kingdom in Africa was a double blow to the empire. It cut off the most important grain supply for the West (or gave the Vandal king a priceless diplomatic weapon), and it accelerated the declining security of commerce and travel on the Mediterranean. In Spain the departure of the Vandals did not restore much territory to Roman rule. The country was torn by peasant revolts, and the relatively weak tribe of the Suevi gained possession of about half of the peninsula. Britain, stripped of troops, was thrown back on her own resources to ward off the growing raids of the Picts and Scots. After a vain appeal to Aëtius in 446—the so-called Groans of the Britons—the British leaders hired German mercenaries. These troops came from the North Sea coast and included Angles, Saxons, and Jutes. The German mercenaries soon became self-employed, and by the 450s were establishing permanent settlements in England.

In Gaul, Aëtius was successful. He prevented the Visigoths from enlarging their kingdom. He threw back Frankish incursions along the lower Rhine. He suppressed peasant revolts. Aëtius was most successful, however, against the Burgundians, who had settled as *foederati* west of the middle Rhine, but who were pushing southward. In 436 catastrophe almost obliterated the tribe. This was the work of Aëtius' mercenaries, the Huns. The tragedy gave rise to the legends enshrined in later German epics, such as the *Nibelungenlied*. A second Burgundian kingdom was established by the survivors in the area around Lake Geneva. This kingdom slowly expanded southward along the Rhone River until it included (for a few years) Provence on the Mediterranean, reaching both its greatest extent and its height of Romano-Germanic culture under the legislator-king Gundobad (474–516).

Between their first appearance in southern Russia, when they shattered the Ostrogoths (ca. 375), and the near-annihilation of the Burgundians, the Huns had slowly built up a loosely knit empire of Germans, Slavs, and other Altaic peoples like themselves stretching from the Rhine to the Caspian. Their Asiatic ferocity had almost wholly been expended against those outside the empire, except when Roman rulers like Theodosius or Aëtius had used them inside the frontiers as mercenaries. In the fifth century the center of their power was in the plains of modern Hungary. In the 430s this great empire was unified under the leadership of Attila (433–453), the rude splendor of whose court made a profound impression on envoys sent from Rome and Constantinople. In their capacity as mercenaries the Huns had been in the pay of both Eastern and Western emperors; when Attila chose to look on this arrangement as simply another tribute exacted from a dependent people, relations between the empire and the Huns became rather strained. When Attila demanded more tribute, a plot to assassinate him was hatched at the court of Constantinople, but it was forestalled at the last moment. Attila referred contemptuously to "his slave, Theodosius [II], who paid him tribute but dared to plot the murder of his master."

Attila turned his Hunnish hordes from the subjugation of Germans and Slavs to the plundering of the empire. The Huns' behavior during these campaigns contributed to the reputation for slaughter and rapine they had earned in their first raids in Continental Europe. The wealthier East attracted Attila first, and he pillaged the Balkans as far as Constantinople. But Constantinople held out, and the Huns turned to the West. By this time Attila had earned his nickname, "the scourge of God" (the punishment visited by God's wrath on a sinful people). The terror struck into the hearts of his intended victims by this sort of propaganda was a potent weapon. Attila gathered together all his forces, including a motley array of subject German tribes, and swept through Gaul. Aëtius hurriedly assembled a coalition of Roman provincials and armies of the Germanic kingdoms of the West. Attila avoided a pitched battle as long as he could, since speed and terror rather than tactical skill were his main strength, but he was finally caught early in 451 retreating eastward from Gaul, on the Catalaunian Plains in the vicinity of Châlons (the engagement is sometimes called the Battle of Châlons). Here a "battle of the nations" took place. Attila's army included, in addition to his Hunnish cavalry, such German, Altaic, and Iranian auxiliaries as the Gepids, Ostrogoths, Thuringians, Rugians, Sciri, Heruli, northern Burgundians, and Ripuarian Franks. Aëtius' allied forces included Gallo-Roman provincials, Visigoths, Alans, Armoricans, southern Burgundians, and Salian Franks. Aëtius' generalship and the stubborn valor of the Visigoths (whose king was slain) brought the day-long struggle to a bloody close with the Western forces undefeated if not victorious. The Huns withdrew eastward, never to recover from the carnage.

Attila, denied the plunder of Gaul, next turned to Italy. In 452 he sacked Aquileia, whose refugees fled to the swamps at the head of the Adriatic and founded villages that later grew into the city of Venice, and he pillaged Milan and Pavia. But famine and pestilence, Italy's best defense, decimated the Hunnish army. At this critical moment, an embassy from Rome, headed by Pope Leo I the Great, arrived in Attila's camp. As the result of negotiations of which no record remains, Attila decided to withdraw his forces to Hungary. Popular credulity ascribed the Huns' withdrawal to divine intervention summoned by the successor of Saint Peter. Whether this can be believed or not, the important result of the interview was an enormous enhancement of the prestige of the papacy in the secular affairs of the West. There is some reason to believe that Attila was a sick man at this time. Within a few months he died of a broken blood vessel, which he suffered on the night of his wedding to the German princess Kriemhild, as she is called in the *Nibelungenlied*. The empire of Attila rapidly disintegrated after his death.

Aëtius did not long survive the Hunnish collapse. Like Stilicho with the Visigoths a half-century earlier, Aëtius had nothing to gain from the destruction of an enemy whose existence had guaranteed him supremacy in the empire's defense. His position was further weakened by the death of Galla Placidia, his long-time collaborator, in 450. To compensate for this loss of influence, Aëtius forced Valentinian III to betroth a daughter to his son, but this indignity roused the sluggish emperor to assassinate Aëtius in 454. Valentinian in turn was murdered the next year. In the confusion that followed these assassinations, Gaiseric with his Vandals seized the opportunity to descend on Rome from the sea and to plunder the city of its movable wealth, sparing only the Christian churches and works of art that could not be readily sold for money. In addition, selected hostages were carried off, including the late emperor's widow and children. This stripping of the city's wealth was well-planned, almost systematic, in contrast with Gaiseric's opportunistic and disorganized leadership of his forces. His pirating activities had disrupted but not seriously threatened the empire's commercial network across the Mediterranean.

After Valentinian III's thirty-year reign, the next twenty-one years saw nine men raised to the purple in the West, most of them puppets set up by the German general Ricimer, who controlled the army in Italy. Beyond the Alps imperial authority almost completely lapsed during this period (455–476). Roman generals in Gaul and elsewhere ignored the emperors who ruled momentarily in the court at Ravenna. Syagrius, the last Roman governor in Gaul who could claim an imperial mandate for his power, was in fact simply the ruler of an autonomous district, the evanescent "kingdom of Soissons." After Ricimer's death, another general of the troops in Italy,

Orestes, deposed the emperor and established his young son, Romulus Augustulus (475–476), as heir of the founders of Rome and the empire. Orestes was then overthrown by a new revolt of the troops led by Odoacer, who did not bother to choose an emperor. Odoacer had been elected king by his German army, and now he petitioned the Eastern emperor, Zeno, for appointment as patrician with authority to rule in the emperor's name. To gain time, since nothing could be done about the situation at the moment, Zeno granted his request. Thus the forms of imperial rule were maintained. The date 476 has been traditionally assigned to the "end of the Roman Empire of the West." In theory, however, it would be more accurate to say that 476 marked the restoration of the unity of the empire under one emperor, for the legal basis of Odoacer's rule was explicit recognition by Zeno. Like the other Germanic kings, Odoacer was desirous of legitimizing his power through an imperial delegation of authority.

The weakness of Odoacer's position was that what had been granted could be revoked. In a few years it became obvious to the emperor that the solution of one of his most vexing problems, the revival of Ostrogothic power, lay in making a new arrangement for Italy. Now settled on the southern bank of the middle Danube, the Ostrogoths had begun to ravage the Balkan Peninsula. Their king, Theodoric, had spent several years as a hostage in Constantinople, where he had acquired some knowledge of Roman government and a high respect for Roman culture. Zeno bought off the Ostrogoths from further ravaging in the East by granting Theodoric the title of patrician and delegating to him the rule of Italy. In 489 Theodoric led his people into Italy. After four years of fierce resistance, Odoacer finally submitted on terms, only to be treacherously murdered at a banquet given by Theodoric himself.

The Ostrogothic kingdom of Theodoric (493–526) was in many ways the most brilliant and successful of all the barbarian realms in the West. Theodoric was a Roman citizen and had even held the office of consul in the East. The essence of his policy was to preserve the civilization of Rome. Odoacer had pursued the same policy, but Theodoric brought it to fruition, and under his rule, Italy achieved a revival of prosperity and of culture. After a century of turbulence, Theodoric brought peace to Italy. Even his Arian Christian faith proved no great obstacle to a stable reign, as long as his orthodox subjects were estranged from Eastern emperors who supported heretical creeds. His religious policy was official toleration, and his patronage of arts and letters benefited Arian and Catholic alike. Public works were subsidized, bringing employment to town-dwelling artisans; agriculture prospered under a new security enforced by Ostrogothic arms. Theodoric also followed a "foreign policy," not new with him but pursued now on a large scale. Once settled in Italy, the Ostrogoths launched no further wars of conquest (although Provence, in southeastern France, was occupied for strategic reasons). Instead, Theodoric spread his influence throughout the Germanic kingdoms of the West by a system of marriage alliances. His purpose was to preserve peace by uniting the interests of the ruling houses. He was married to a Frankish princess; he married his sister to the king of the Vandals, his two daughters to the Visigothic and Burgundian kings, and a niece to a Thuringian king.

Theodoric's kingdom in Italy was short-lived, although his achievement was impressive. Other East German peoples established more lasting political structures, such as the Visigothic kingdom of Spain and the Burgundian kingdom in eastern Gaul and the western Alps. The West German groups achieved less at first, but their kingdoms were more enduring. They did not migrate but expanded without losing contact with their homelands. They were less Romanized, in some cases remaining almost wholly beyond the influence of Mediterranean civilization, and they became Christian much later, usually as Catholics rather than Arians. The most important West German peoples were confederations of lesser tribes, such as the Franks, the Alemanni (from whose name eventually arose the French word for Germany, l'Allemagne), the Frisians, the other north German tribes of Angles, Saxons, Jutes, and, finally, the Lombards. The Lombards and Frisians had no significant contact with lands of the Western empire before the sixth century. Before the end of the fifth century the Angles, Saxons, and Jutes were hardly beyond the stage of hit-and-run raids on the derelict province of Britain. Only the Franks invaded the empire and established a kingdom in the fifth century.

The Franks appear first during the chaotic mid-third century, when they penetrated into Gaul and as far south as northeastern Spain on extensive plundering raids. During the fourth century the Franks were always a potential danger but were kept back beyond the frontier. Constantine won his spurs against them on the Rhine before he was proclaimed emperor. After Stilicho recalled the Roman garrisons from the Rhine, the Franks were given the status of *foederati* with the duty of holding the line. Instead, they occupied most of northern Gaul while Vandals, Alans, and Suevi swept across the frontier. As a loosely knit confederation, the Franks were vulnerable to internal dissension, and at the time of Attila's invasion two main groups (Salians and Ripuarians) were actually at war with each other and fought on opposing sides. Each group of Franks was itself split into several tribes, each with its own king.

One center of Frankish strength in northern Gaul was at Tournai (near the border of modern France and Belgium), where, five years after Romulus Augustulus was deposed and eight years before Theodoric invaded Italy, a youth of fifteen succeeded to the throne. This was Chlodovech, better known as Clovis (481–511), whose career of conquest culminated in the establishment of the Frankish kingdom of Merovingian Gaul, so called after Merovech, the semimythical founder of the Frankish royal house. Clovis' success

Germanic Migrations, ca. 375–550

Black Sea

Baltic Sea

North Sea

Mediterranean Sea

CRETE

HUNS 375
OSTROGOTHS
ALANS 400
GOTHS after 100
VANDALS
BURGUNDIANS 250
GOTHS
150
VISIGOTHS
378
Adrianople
Constantinople
Athens
Sparta
ATTILA 443
486
443
401–403
HUNS 441
SUEVI 250
LOMBARDS 450
SUEVI 403
ATTILA 451
568
Ravenna
Beneveno
410  568
406  Florence
412
Rome
455
Milan
401–402
LOMBARDS
ALEMANNI
FRANKS
BURGUNDIANS 433–534
Lyon
358
406
258
413
406–409
409
Paris
Toulouse
CORSICA
SARDINIA
BALEARICS
JUTES
ANGLES
SAXONS
425–450
ANGLES
London
SAXONS
SUEVI from 411
VANDALS 411–421
ALANS 411–418
Toledo
422
VANDALS 411–418
ALANS to 429
415
430–431
Carthage
VANDALS 439–534

Angles, Saxons, Jutes
Vandals and Alans
Suevi
Lombards
Huns
Visigoths
Ostrogoths
Franks
Burgundians
Roman Empire

0       200
Miles

was the slowly won result of years of fighting, but three military victories may be singled out as important stages in Frankish expansion. The last stronghold of Gallo-Roman rule in northern Gaul, Syagrius' "kingdom of Soissons," was destroyed in 486. The Alemanni were annihilated in a great battle near Strasbourg in 496. This allowed the Franks to expand eastward back into Germany and ensured that the Frankish kingdom, of all the barbarian kingdoms on Roman soil, would be the most Germanic in character and would be best able to replenish its manpower among Germanic peoples. The third and crowning victory of Clovis' career was the defeat of the Visigoths at Vouillé in 507 (in west-central France, near Poitiers), which led to the conquest of all of southern Gaul to the Pyrenees. The only reverse suffered by Frankish arms was at the hands of Theodoric, who prevented Clovis from reaching the Mediterranean by occupying Provence and by helping the Visigoths to retain Septimania (a coastal province stretching from Provence to the Pyrenees).

Clovis' success cannot be explained on military grounds alone. Although motivated primarily by lust for power, Clovis displayed a consistency of attitude and an ability beyond simple shrewdness sufficient to warrant considering him, with Theodoric, as capable of statesmanship. It was a statesmanship in which calculated self-interest, brutality, and a rough sense of justice were about equal ingredients. His grasp of political realities was unsurpassed by any Western ruler before Charlemagne. Toward the conquered Gallo-Romans he could afford to be lenient, since most of his Frankish followers could be settled in depopulated districts in the north, without need to expropriate landowners. Consequently the Gallo-Roman people offered little resistance. Frankish expansion into Gaul was an invasion only in the sense of a military campaign against the armies, not the people, of its previous rulers. Finally Clovis' authority was given an aura of legitimacy. After Clovis' defeat of the Visigoths, the Eastern emperor bestowed on him the insignia of an honorary consul, although Clovis never became, like most of the East German kings, an actual official of the empire bearing the title of patrician.

Far more important was Clovis' policy toward the Church in Gaul. He had an inestimable advantage of being, with the rest of the Franks, merely a heathen rather than a hated Arian heretic. The bishops conceived the hope, which Clovis was careful not to abate, that he might be converted to the Catholic faith and thus become the champion of orthodoxy. The Catholic bishops of Gaul formed the most powerful single political group in the country. They were allied with the Gallo-Roman nobility, from whose ranks most of them were chosen; they controlled the greatest concentration of wealth; and they exercised the greatest influence over the population. The support of the bishops, and thus of the bulk of the population, was strong enough reason for a barbarian king who contemplated conversion to turn to the Catholic faith. It is not known whether such realistic considerations motivated Clovis. Perhaps it was the persuasion of the Burgundian princess Clotilda, whom he married in 493 (a Catholic, although her people were still Arian), or the miracles that Clovis is said to have witnessed at the tomb of Saint Martin of Tours. Or was it the vow, which according to later tradition he made in the heat of battle against the Alemanni, that he would adopt his wife's faith if Christ would give him victory? It seems probable that it was a combination of realistic politics and personal inclination that prompted Clovis to be baptized along with three thousand other Franks. The conversion of Clovis was a decisive moment in the history of the West: he became the only Catholic ruler among the German kings. At a single stroke he called into being an effective "fifth column," the episcopate, within any territory on which he had designs. Further expansion took on the character of a religious war to extirpate heresy: "It grieves me," he is said to have told his troops on the eve of the campaign against the Visigoths, "that Arians should hold any part of Gaul."

Toward his Frankish followers, Clovis' policy was simple and effective. On the one hand, he provided the opportunity for fighting, which appealed to their bellicose nature, together with the rewards of conquest in booty, land, and participation in the government of the conquered. On the other hand, he pursued a remorseless policy of unification of the several Frankish tribes. From being simply a Frankish king, Clovis became king of the Franks by methodically liquidating all other chieftains or kings who were potential competitors for the supremacy that he had won. Clovis employed all the techniques of treachery and assassination known in the violent world of the politically ambitious. Some of his rivals (and blood relatives) he caused to be murdered by hired assassins; others he tricked into an unarmed meeting and laid low with his own battle-ax. "Thus did God daily deliver the enemies of Clovis into his hand," wrote Gregory, bishop of Tours, toward the end of the sixth century, "because he walked before Him with an upright heart, and did what was pleasing in His eyes."

## The Germanic "Successor States" in the West

Clovis had begun his career of conquest as a petty kinglet in 481 and ended it as the most powerful Germanic king ruling the largest territory. On his death in 511, the kingdom was divided among his four sons in accordance with the Germanic custom making all sons heirs and treating kingship as personal property. The sons of Clovis cooperated against external enemies, so that the Frankish kingdoms continued to expand. Burgundy was conquered in 534. Two years later Provence was occupied, bringing the Franks for the first time to the Mediterranean and into direct contact with the Eastern empire. One of Clovis' sons even invaded Italy, as an ally of Justinian who was then fighting the Ostrogoths, but the expedition gained nothing for the Merovingians. East of the Rhine the Franks fought their way farther into central Germany, conquering the Thuringians in 531.

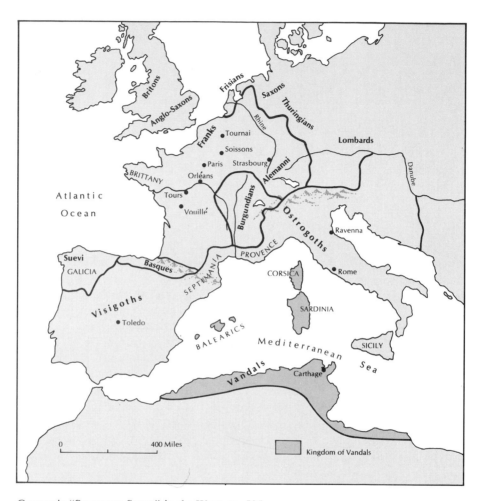

Germanic "Successor States" in the West, ca. 525

Within Gaul, the sons of Clovis showed no such cooperation. Each coveted the others' shares of the kingdom, and when not conquering foreign soil they spent their time fighting one another, using the techniques of treachery and subversion that Clovis had taught them. By 558 all but one of the brothers and their heirs had been eliminated, most of them by violent deaths. The survivor, Chlotar I, briefly reunited the kingdom (558–561). On his death the Merovingian realm was again divided among his four sons, and the civil wars were resumed on an even more savage and violent scale. The degeneracy, faithlessness, and congenital criminality of the sons of Chlotar I and of their queens and concubines are all vividly portrayed by Gregory, bishop of Tours, in his contemporary *History of the Franks*. This generation had almost exterminated itself when the sole survivor, Chlotar II, was put on the throne of a united kingdom in 613 through machinations and murders by a group of nobles and bishops.

The only significance of the single rule of Chlotar II is that his reign marks the definitive shift of power from the Frankish monarchy to the landed aristocracy. By an edict of 614 Chlotar relinquished certain royal rights over the Church and extended privileges to both the ecclesiastical and the lay nobility. Under Dagobert (629–639), "the Merovingian monarchy shone for the last time, but with a false splendor." The revival was brief, and Dagobert also made concessions to the local interests of the landed aristocracy. After Dagobert, the Merovingian kingdom owed nothing to the policies or the efforts of its kings.

And yet the future lay with the Franks. The seeming decadence of the Merovingian kingdom arises only from the misleading habit of identifying the history of a kingdom with its kings. The Merovingian realm as a whole was in a healthy, if turbulent, condition, when compared with the other Germanic kingdoms of the West. The kingdom of Burgundy, conquered by the Merovingians, became—with Austrasia, Neustria, and Aquitaine—one of the four main constituent parts of the Merovingian kingdom. The Vandal kingdom of North Africa and the western Mediterranean islands declined after the death of Gaiseric in 477, losing territory to Moorish tribes south of the coastal area. The weaknesses of the Vandal state were insuperable. Religious differences between Arian Vandals and Catholic provincials led to persecution by the kings and the estrangement of their subjects. The Vandal conquerors failed to become assimilated economically or socially with the provincial population. They simply confiscated the property of the Roman nobility and like that nobility exploited the bulk of the people.

Meanwhile, the Eastern emperor Justinian (527–565) sent an expeditionary force under Belisarius, the ablest general of the sixth century, to reconquer North Africa. Several reasons lay behind Justinian's policy of reconquest, of which the recovery of the Vandal kingdom was only the first step. North Africa was still an important food-producing area. Vandal control of the western Mediterranean was a handicap to trade with the West. The disaffected population of the Vandal kingdom seemed to be a potential source of manpower for the Byzantine army. Finally, North Africa and Sicily could provide advance bases for further reconquest of the other lost provinces in the West. Belisarius arrived in North Africa in 533 and broke the main resistance by taking the Vandal capital at Carthage the same year. Insurrections and raids by the Moors were not quelled until 548, however, when the former Vandal kingdom, with its Mediterranean islands, was reincorporated into the empire.

Having achieved command of the Mediterranean, Belisarius turned to Ostrogothic Italy. Here the situation after the death of Theodoric in 526 seemed even more ripe for easy reconquest. During the last years of Theodoric's reign, disaffection already had begun among the Catholic population. The advent of an orthodox emperor (Justin) in Constantinople was sufficient to produce plots and rumors of plots against the Arian Theodoric, whose policy of religious toleration was not appreciated by his less enlightened Italian subjects. Theodoric struck back at all whom he suspected of treason with the same fury that had inaugurated his reign. Among the victims were several nobles of ancient senatorial families, including Boethius, the leading intellect of his age. After Theodoric's death, a minor heir, the regency of Theodoric's daughter, and the conflicting interests of the nobles all combined to weaken the Ostrogothic state. Belisarius took Sicily in 535 and within the next year had occupied Rome. Then the Goths swept away all hereditary claimants to Theodoric's throne and elected Witigis, a military leader, king.

Witigis launched a bitter war of resistance that continued under him and his successor, the popular Totila, for more than twenty years. In the Gothic wars the population suffered more from plundering, pestilence, and famine than during any previous generation. Italy never fully recovered from the devastation, which was mainly the work of imperial mercenaries brought in from the East. The Ostrogoths, having some stake in the country, generally spared captured cities and thereby gained substantial popular support. Thus the reconquest was not, as the orthodox Justinian had hoped, welcomed as a liberation from the Arian Ostrogoths. But by 556 all Italy, except for isolated Gothic strongholds, was ruled again from Ravenna, where the viceroy, or exarch, attempted without much success to raise taxes and troops for the Byzantine armies fighting on the Persian frontier. The Exarchate of Ravenna, as the imperial government in Italy was called, endured for another two hundred years, and Byzantine control of parts of southern Italy was not extinguished until the eleventh century. But a reunited Byzantine Italy lasted only a dozen years.

The last German people to invade the empire—for such, once more, Italy must now be considered—were the Lombards, who first appeared around 552, typically, as auxiliaries in the Byzantine armies fighting against the Ostrogoths. Of all the East German peoples who entered the Mediterranean world, the Lombards were the least touched by Romanizing influence, although by the sixth century their religion was formally Arian Christian. They returned to Italy as invaders in 568. The impoverished country offered little resistance outside the fortified cities, where imperial garrisons sometimes held out. Under the Lombard king Alboin, the early stages of the invasion were successful. Some northern cities fell, including Pavia, which became the Lombard capital. But after Alboin's death in 572 (when his wife had him assassinated for making her drink out of her late father's skull), the Lombard dukes refused to elect a new king, and the conquest of Italy proceeded piecemeal. Each of the thirty dukes captured various towns or districts and established small principalities. The most important of these were the duchies of Spoleto in central Italy and Benevento in the south.

Even the Lombard king, whose people resisted Romanization more than others, had himself represented in the traditional rite of the imperial triumph. This segment from the crown of King Agilulf (early seventh century) shows the king being greeted in the cities he conquered, symbolized by the towers on the sides. The banners are carried by winged Victories, and new subjects bring tribute to the conquerer.

Most of Italy was thus overrun when, in 584, the Byzantine emperor sent in troops and enlisted the aid of the Catholic Merovingians against the Arian Lombards, an effort sufficient to reunite the Lombard dukes, who elected a king in order to meet the threat. The situation was finally stabilized, and the Lombard monarchy firmly established under Agilulf (591–616), who completed most of the conquest that the Lombards were to make in Italy. The most important districts still in Byzantine hands were Ravenna and the surrounding countryside (including Venice); Apulia and Calabria (the "heel" and "toe" of the peninsula); Sicily; Naples and Rome, with the surrounding countryside; and Genoa and its hinterland. Even in these nominally Byzantine areas, however, imperial control was not always effective. In the "duchy of Rome," for example, the popes acknowledged the sovereignty of the empire but exercised almost complete control of the local government.

The Visigoths were pushed south of the Pyrenees by Clovis (507), except for the coastal province of Septimania, which Theodoric's intervention had saved for them. Their kingdom included the whole Iberian Peninsula except the northwestern corner (Galicia, occupied by the Suevi) and part of the Pyrenees (held by the Basques). The Visigothic kings had difficulty maintaining order. The Catholic population would neither cooperate when their Arian rulers were lenient nor were they made submissive by persecution. The Visigothic aristocracy was jealous of royal power, and the Franks menaced Septimania. After the Byzantine reconquest of Italy, Justinian's troops found it easy to win back southern Spain for the empire. But royal power was restored—perhaps more dramatically than effectively—by Recared I (586–601), who became a Catholic and under whose aegis a national council of bishops and nobles at Toledo in 589 proclaimed Catholicism the official faith. This ensured Recared the support of the Catholic hierarchy and the majority of his subjects. Ecclesiastical support of the monarchy was graphically emphasized in the solemn anointing and consecration of Recared as king. This was a religious sanction for his rule reminiscent of the sacred character of kingship in the Old Testament.

In the former Roman province of Britain, developments took a radically different course from those in Gaul, Africa, Italy, and Spain. Britain, on the fringe of the civilized world, had a small Romanized community confined to the southeastern part of the island. The province was in a precarious position. To the north lived Picts and Scots (the former in Scotland, the latter in Ireland), who threatened the border and coasts and against whom Hadrian had built a defensive wall just north of Durham (A.D. 122). Antoninus had constructed another fortification across the island north of Hadrian's Wall between the Forth of Clyde and Forth of Firth (A.D. 140). When Roman troops abandoned Britain around 410, the northern peoples found it easy to raid deep into the Romanized regions. The Britons, settled in Roman villas and towns, found their relatively new civilization threatened with destruction, and as noted earlier they invited German mercenaries to come across the Channel to protect them. Of course the Germans found the wealth and culture of the Romanized communities, and of the island, just as enticing as the Picts and Scots did, and soon there were numerous German settlements, expanding and coalescing but still divided by forest and fen from other groups. By the end of the sixth century several tribal kingdoms had been established. In the southeast was the Jutish kingdom of the Cantwara, or Kent, with its capital at Canterbury. The Saxons formed several petty kingdoms in southern Britain: the South Saxons in Sussex; the East Saxons in Essex; and the West Saxons in the region farther west along the Thames and along the southern coast, which, with its hinterland, became the later Wessex. In the Midlands and in the region north of the Humber River other districts were settled under tribal kings by the Angles: Mercia, a frontier region in the Midlands; Deira, centered at York; and Bernicia farther north. Other Angles had won the area known as East Anglia, divided into a northern and a southern kingdom, Norfolk and Suffolk.

Compared with Merovingian Gaul, Visigothic Spain, or Ostrogothic Italy, none of these Anglo-Saxon kingdoms was important. None of their kings was able to unite the tribes settled in Britain. The nearest to political unity that any king achieved was a vague recognition, under the title of *Bretwalda,* of personal supremacy over the other kings and kinglets. The conquest of Britain was in several ways unique. It was achieved piecemeal by many small groups; no single leader dominated the movement; the culture of the con-

Germanic "Successor States" and Byzantine Areas in the West, ca. 575

querors obliterated the Romanized culture of the conquered province, since
the Celtic-Christian population retreated to the west, leaving their former
territory to the Germans. As a result, few traces of Roman civilization remained in England. At the same time, the western movement of the Britons
into Cornwall, Wales, and, ultimately, Ireland forced the migration of the
Scots to present-day Scotland, where they mixed with the native Pictish
population. Some Britons even left the island altogether and settled in Gallic
Amorica, which later became known as Brittany and where an ancient Celtic tongue is still spoken by segments of the rural population. The
Britons did not leave their ancient homes without offering resistance, however.
Beginning about the end of the fifth century, they mounted a stout but ulti-

mately unsuccessful defense of their Celtic-Christian civilization. A great victory (ca. 500) over the heathen Anglo-Saxons was won by a military leader whose name was perhaps Artorius, the historical personage behind the later King Arthur legends. This bitter resistance, together with the wars of aggression among the Anglo-Saxons, led to the strengthening of tribal kingship and the consolidation of several tribes into larger political units. Deira and Bernicia were united into one kingdom of Northumbria by Ethelfrith (593–617), who drove a wedge between the northern and southern Britons by expanding westward all the way to the Irish Sea. In the south Ethelbert of Kent (560–616) established a hegemony over the Saxon kingdoms similar to the predominance of Northumbria in the north. This period brings to a close the heathen and heroic age of Anglo-Saxon conquest and inaugurates a second stage whose two main features characterize the rest of the seventh century: the struggle between kingdoms for predominance and the conversion of the Anglo-Saxons to Christianity.

Throughout the barbarian West, conquest transformed the nature of Germanic political institutions, particularly kingship. Old German kingship was tied to war and had no stability as a form of government. When the Germanic tribes settled in the imperial territories their concept of kingship changed because the Germans were brought into direct contact with the Roman bureaucracy and its political ideas and were in control of areas in which landholding patterns accorded with a highly stratified political and social culture. Since the conquerors usually tried to preserve the Roman society and recognized the advantages of taking over the relatively efficient governmental machinery of the former political system, their own political institutions were transformed. The Roman administration necessitated, both in theory and in practice, a stable authority to whom the bureaucracy could be responsible. Since Germanic political ideas did not justify the maintenance of royal power, the kings borrowed ideology from the Romans to create a kingship that symbolized the process of cultural change that produced medieval civilization. The kings stepped into the old German legal systems and took upon themselves the maintenance of peace within their communities. Thus coercive power was slowly concentrated in the hands of the monarch. The conversion of the Germans to Christianity also increased the authority of the kings. The kings stemmed from the chieftain class and thus claimed a sacred authority tied to the mythical foundations on which all chieftains justified their position. The brutal process by which kings like Clovis established their exclusive claim to power reduced the number of individuals and families that could claim a sacredness appropriate to royal authority. When the pagan priestly kingship became Christian, the Church recognized the king's sacred character, but did not recognize the sacredness of the entire chieftain class. The Church thus became one of the principal supports of the new monarchies.

The invasions produced neither great social upheaval nor abrupt economic change. In some kingdoms, as in Vandal Africa, the barbarians appear to have replaced the provincial aristocracy by confiscating and redistributing among themselves the great estates. In other kingdoms the barbarians followed old Roman rules for rewarding the army. For centuries the soldiers had been compensated with land, and where that land was expropriated for the purpose, it amounted to one-third of each estate in the region affected. *Foederati* had been settled in this way on the borders, and when they began to settle in the heart of the Western provinces, they continued the old system. The great majority of the population hardly felt the change: their status as peasant proprietors or as *coloni* on the great *latifundia* was unaltered, regardless of who collected their rents and supervised their labor services. There was no change in agricultural methods, and the tendency toward local economic self-sufficiency continued. In the towns, where few Germans were inclined to settle, the provincial urban populations were relatively undisturbed, except when they suffered from the ravages of war. What economic decline occurred was caused by the disruption of the old imperial commercial network that had tied the Mediterranean world together and stimulated the local societies.

The dislocation of the Roman system in the West was, as already pointed out, countered by the new rulers' attempts to maintain it. The Roman *civitas* (city or town with its surrounding countryside) continued to be the unit of administration. It was governed by a barbarian count or duke appointed by the king and theoretically removable at the king's will. The count or duke exercised almost all the powers of government within the area of his jurisdiction. He collected taxes, led the local contingent of the army, presided in person or by deputy over the courts, kept roads in repair, and maintained some semblance of peace and order. Local government was far more important to the people than was the authority of the central government. The local counts and dukes were in a position to work together among themselves and, with the provincial Roman or Germanic nobility, against the interests of the royal government. In Merovingian Gaul and Lombard Italy the counties and duchies were more important and enduring political units than the kingdom as a whole. The tendency was toward political as well as economic localism.

The kings relied less on the total resources of their kingdoms than on the lands they had won by right of conquest. These lands became the royal fisc, and their revenue supported the royal government. The Merovingian kings granted away large sections of the royal fisc in Gaul to the Church, in the form of pious gifts, and to the nobility in return for support during the many civil wars. This further diminished the resources of the central government and accelerated the tendency toward localism.

To facilitate the work of the law courts of barbarian counts unfamiliar with Roman law, and to clarify the legal provisions applying in disputes between two parties of different races (thus involving both Roman and Germanic law), the kings issued legal codes. These codes were not exhaustive or complete statements of all the laws in force. They were official and binding instructions to judges, or clarifications of doubtful points that probably arose from particular cases in the courts and were referred to the king for final decision. The barbarian codes of Roman law (*leges romanae*) were based on the Theodosian Code and on various legal writings of the later Roman jurists. These commentaries on the edicts and laws were accepted by the courts as authoritative interpretations of the application of laws to particular cases. The codes of Germanic customary law (*leges barbarorum*) were statements of custom governing relations between the barbarians and between barbarian and Roman peoples. The attempt to preserve each legal system as distinct ultimately led to the assimilation of the two systems. The barbarian codes were written in Latin (except in England where they were in Anglo-Saxon— the earliest surviving monuments of the English language). The necessity of expressing in Latin the legal concepts of the Teutonic world Romanized the Germanic jurisprudence, or basic legal concepts, of barbarian law even though the specific legal provisions remained non-Roman. Equally important was the influence of the teachings of the Church, which also tended to Romanize Germanic custom. This was true even of the Anglo-Saxon codes.

The most important codes issued by the Germanic kings were compiled in the late fifth and early sixth centuries. The earliest was the *Lex Visigothorum* promulgated by the Visigothic king Euric about 483. His successor, Alaric II, issued a Roman law code, the so-called *Breviarium Alaricianum,* in 506, on the eve of the attack on the Visigoths by Clovis. It was a last-minute effort to win over, or neutralize the antagonism of, his Gallo-Roman and Catholic subjects. In Burgundy Gundobad promulgated the *Lex Burgundionum* or *Lex Gundobada* shortly after 484. Both he and his successor, Sigismund (516–524), made additions to this code. Gundobad also approved a code for his Roman subjects, the *Lex Romana Burgundionum.* After the Frankish conquest of Burgundy in 534 this was displaced by the *Breviarium Alaricianum,* which, because of Frankish sponsorship, became a kind of common law for all non-Germanic peoples under Frankish rule. This benefited the Church and the Gallo-Roman population because Alaric's "Breviary" contained concessions intended to appease his hostile subjects.

The Germans preserved much of their own culture and influenced the Roman civilization as much as the Roman culture influenced theirs. Later medieval society was built on a Germanic as well as on a Roman foundation. Examples may be seen in the transformation of the ancient tribal assemblies mentioned by Tacitus at the end of the first century into assemblies of the nobility and free people of territorial areas. The importance of the relationship between a war leader and the companions of his *comitatus* (as Tacitus described it) did not disappear after the conquests. It was rather transformed into a more stable relationship between lord and dependent that was in some cases associated with the tenure of land, or with nonmilitary service.

The one great obstacle to assimilation, and the greatest political problem for the German kings, was the religious antagonism between the Arian Germans (except the heathen Anglo-Saxons and the Catholic Franks) and their orthodox or Catholic Roman subjects. This antagonism was an element of weakness at crucial points in the history of the kingdoms of the Vandals, Visigoths, Ostrogoths, Burgundians, and Lombards. Arianism was a divisive force in the Germanic kingdoms for a long time. It became an insignificant factor only toward the end of the seventh century.

Thus in religion, law, and government, as well as in social, political, and economic institutions, the period of the establishment of the Germanic kingdoms in the West (ca. 450–700) was one of both gradual transformation and gradual assimilation of diverse elements, a process that led to and helped produce the basic unity of medieval society. The same may be said of intellectual and literary developments in the period but with the significant difference that the Germanic element was far less prominent in this part of the process of assimilation. The Germans became the students of Roman intellectual culture, and the Church functioned as the teacher of the Western empire's new residents and rulers.

### Suggestions for Further Reading

**Secondary Works**  On the Germanic invasions, see Ferdinand Lot, *The End of the Ancient World and the Beginnings of the Middle Ages* (New York, 1931); K. F. Drew, ed., *The Barbarian Invasions: Catalyst of a New Order* (New York, 1970); and the monumental work by Thomas Hodgkin, *Italy and Her Invaders,* 8 vols. (Oxford, 1892–1916). On early Germanic society and culture, see E. A. Thompson, *The Early Germans* (Oxford, 1965) and *The Goths in Spain* (Oxford, 1969). More specialized but important is J. M. Wallace-Hadrill, *Early Germanic Kingship in England and on the Continent* (Oxford, 1971). Wallace-Hadrill provides a good brief study of European history after the invasions in *The Barbarian West, 400–1000* (London, 1952). See H. St. L. B. Moss, *The Birth of the Middle Ages* (Oxford, 1935) for a similar survey.

**Sources**  A convenient translation of Tacitus is H. Mattingly, *Tacitus on Britain and Germany* (West Drayton, Middlesex, 1948). The only complete translation of Gregory of Tours' *History of the Franks* is a two-volume work by O. M. Dalton (Oxford, 1927); selections are available in a one-volume edition by E. Brehaut, ed. and trans., *History of the Franks* (New York, 1969). Thomas Hodgkin, *Italy and Her Invaders* contains much translated primary material, such as letters of Cassiodorus and selections from Paul the Deacon's *History of the Lombards*. Paul's work was translated by W. D. Foulke, *History of the Langobards* (Philadelphia, 1907). For barbarian law, see K. Fischer (Drew), trans., *The Burgundian Code* (Philadelphia, 1949), and K. F. Drew, trans., *The Lombard Laws* (Philadelphia, 1973).

# II THE ORIGINS OF THE MEDIEVAL WORLD

# 4 The Emergence of Early Medieval Culture

The transformation of the late Roman world resulted from institutional and cultural changes in the empire and from the interaction of Germans and Romans. In the social history of Europe, these changes are evident only as evolving over a long period of time because social change tends to be slow and diffuse, depending on the peculiar conditions prevailing in small and semi-isolated districts and on the passing of generations. However, the process of cultural change can be seen over the shorter term in a study of the high culture—the intellectual and artistic life of the elite—and the institutions through which it occurred, since the interpenetration of styles and ideas can be traced in works that can be placed, reasonably well, in time and locality.

## The Spread of Christianity and the Rise of Monasticism

After Constantine placed Christians under the protection of the imperial government, the religion spread rapidly throughout the empire. From the fourth century on, Christianity remained a movement centered on *civitates,* but its adherents began to undertake the arduous task of converting the rural people, who constituted by far the largest part of the empire's population. The countryside was the most conservative area in the empire, the region where paganism was most strongly entrenched. The word *pagan* comes from the Latin *pagani* (dwellers in the country). The struggle of Christianity against local cults, against survivals of pagan mythology, and against sheer superstitious ignorance in the rural districts of the empire was a far longer and more difficult struggle than was the conflict with pagan philosophies, the officially supported Roman pantheon, or the Greco-Oriental mystery cults, whose devotees were educated city-dwellers. By the end of the fourth century imperial law banned all these competing religions, and the government persecuted their followers just as it had persecuted Christians a century earlier. But the Mediterranean world was still far from being Christianized outside of the cities, where the churches were strongest and the government's support was effective. Laws and persecution could not reach the masses of country-dwelling peasants.

The Church attempted to penetrate the farther reaches of the countryside by promoting the construction of parish churches. Progress was slow and unspectacular, but the steady success of the missionaries made their spirit and activities a main part of Church life and ideology for centuries. The expansion of Christianity also brought important changes in its nature and character. Development of the full implications of the originally simple doctrines of the religion provided Christianity with a rich, and especially in the East a controversial, theology able to meet the criticism of pagan philosophers on their own terms. Doctrinal controversies led to heresy and schism. The unity of the Church was broken, but such controversial discussion was clear evidence of a healthy and growing interest among Christians in the ultimate meaning of all they believed. Other changes, equally far reaching but on a lower intellectual level, resulted from contact between Christianity and the popular religious customs and beliefs of the people who were converted in large numbers during the fourth century and later. New ideas and practices were incorporated that certainly enriched the spirit and the forms of worship of the religion, although conservative Christians of the time complained that there was danger of altering its substance.

Formal conversion did not always mean, for ordinary people, the complete abandonment of older and familiar religious ideas. The bishops who were directly responsible for the early expansion of Christianity found that some adaptation of Christian practices to the polytheism of the Roman official religion and to the multitude of local cults speeded their work of conversion. Augustine, for example, described how his predecessors in Africa had of course forbidden the often ribald celebration of festivals in honor of local deities, but as a "temporary concession" had allowed festivals in honor of the holy martyrs of the Christian Church in Africa to be celebrated on the same occasions and with the same revelry. How enduring such temporary concessions might be is illustrated by the revelry still associated with Christmas and Halloween (the evening before the festival of All Saints); both festivals originated in pre-Christian pagan rites. By the time of Gregory the Great it had become an official policy, in his words, "not to interfere with any traditional belief or religious observance of the heathen which can be harmonized with Christianity."

The essential problem created by this policy was to preserve the distinction between the deity to whom worship was due and the less-than-divine angels or human heroes of the faith (the Virgin Mary, saints, martyrs, and confessors) to whom veneration only was to be accorded. Educated Christians did not find the distinction difficult, but the ordinary convert tended to confuse the Christian heavenly hierarchy with the multiplicity of greater and lesser gods of the hierarchical pagan pantheon. Furthermore, the religious atmosphere of pagan antiquity was full of portents, supernatural forces, and miraculous events. Ordinary Christians shared many of these superstitions, and the Church leadership condoned most of them while giving many new interpretations. They attributed the magical and miraculous happenings that were part of popular religious life to demons working for the Devil. Even as late as the eleventh and twelfth centuries, the Church was still trying to destroy the remnants of underground paganism, and just before the French Revolution, priests were observed leading villagers across the fields and streams in the pagan springtime blessing of the land that would bring forth the coming year's harvest.

In the fourth century contemporaries were fully aware of the problem of converting the rural population, but they were more concerned with the growing corruption and worldliness among both clergy and laity, a danger that hardly existed in earlier times when Christianity was a proscribed religion attracting only those who were willing to risk losing the rewards of this world to gain the kingdom of heaven. After Constantine's conversion, Christianity had become something of a fashion and had begun to attract people who entered the Church simply because it offered a road to preferment and wealth. Devout Christians, such as Saint Jerome, inveighed against the worldliness of priests who behaved more like dandies than ministers of the Gospel or who pursued wealthy widows in the hope of obtaining pious gifts or legacies for their own use. Women were especially drawn to the new religion because, unlike pagan worship or the mystery cults, Christianity recognized the dignity and equality before God of both sexes. Many of the earliest martyrs had been women whose virtues were for Christians as important as those of men. But after the triumph of Christianity there arose criticism of Christian women who were more interested in coiffures and cosmetics than in true religion.

This criticism was part of a broad and important theme in Christian attitudes during the late imperial period. Christian preachers set incredibly high moral standards for members of the Church. People engaged in normal employments could not hope to avoid sin and damnation, so the moralists said. This attitude stemmed in part from the early doctrine of penitence, which admitted the possibility of remission of sin only once in a person's life. Thus the businessman who fell twice into sin after his baptism was doomed, and churchmen made it plain that they saw little chance that a businessman could avoid the double fall. The result of this attitude was twofold. First, few people were baptized before they retired from the active life. Many Christians thus lived the bulk of their lives as catechumens and waited to wash away their sins only when they were certain that the chances of sinning again were minimal. There were many deathbed baptisms, like that of the emperor Constantine and his son Constantius. When Ambrose became the popular choice to be bishop of Milan, he was not yet baptized. This tendency to wait for baptism until one was about to enter a morally safe profession or time of life led to the second result of the Christian moral attitude, the development of a profession that could be a substitute for all others. Monasticism—withdrawal from the world and devotion to the conquest of sin—became an alternative for simple Christians who could not or did not want to enter the clergy.

Monasticism was not peculiar to Christianity but was an expression of the ascetic tendencies that are found in every religion. Some men have always and everywhere believed they could attain a higher ideal of moral and spiritual excellence by the self-denial of bodily pleasures and by the cultivation of a contemplative life. The earliest Christian ascetics engaged in such practices as prolonged fasting, a simple diet and little sleep, the wearing of rough and irritating clothes, a deliberate avoidance of personal cleanliness (they associated bathing with the immoralities of the Roman public baths), and of course celibacy. It was believed that the individual could achieve purity of soul and could strengthen his hope for salvation by conquering the sins of the flesh and by fortifying his faith through contemplation of the sublime. This program was the manifestation of the theology of value espoused in Augustine's works. The ascetics denied the values of the material world in order to pursue those of the spiritual. The soul's progress toward God was made easier, they thought, by reducing the needs and desires of the body.

The earliest movement toward this way of life was spontaneous and without encouragement from the Church, although the New Testament contains passages that encourage such withdrawal (for example, Mark 10:21–25, Romans 13:14, 1 Corinthians 6:13–20). In the mid-third century certain devout Christians fled from the temptations of the world to the more congenial solitude of the desert in Egypt. Perhaps the climate and the economic difficulties that afflicted this area encouraged some of them. The persecutions in Egypt during the period drove others to leave their cities and escape to the desert. Here they lived in caves or huts, assembling occasionally for worship. The leading figure among these "desert fathers" was Saint Anthony (251–356), whose personal sanctity and austerity attracted many followers. These monks were hermits. Each monk lived alone without any formal organization to regulate his religious life, even though he might have several hermits as neighbors. The relaxation of discipline and the vagaries of these hermit monks led one of Saint Anthony's disciples to formulate a common way of life. This was Pachomius (fl. 318), the founder of cenobitic monasticism (life in a *cenobium,* or community, as opposed to eremitic monasticism, or the monastic life as practiced by a hermit or recluse). He drew up the first rule for a monastic community. Pachomius' chief concern was to provide common worship, thus combining asceticism with the sacramental system of the Church. This could only be realized by bringing the monastic community under the supervision of the local bishop, who could ordain priests to care for the monks' souls. Episcopal control was thus a feature of the earliest cenobitic monasticism.

Pachomius' rule was rather disorganized, a collection of precepts and anecdotes that provided a guide to the monastic life. In order for his ideas to have lasting effect, other monastic leaders had to systematize them. In the East, Saint Basil (329–379), who rose out of monasticism to become patriarch of Constantinople, brought Pachomius' vision into a carefully constructed rule. He provided a balanced regimen of worship and work for his monks. To the accepted monastic virtues of poverty and chastity, he added obedience to the abbot (father) in charge of the community. The three virtues became special vows that new monks took before they were accepted permanently in the monastery. Basil's ideal was a rigorous but not excessive asceticism. His main concern was to avoid the wayward individualism and extreme austerities of the desert fathers of Egypt and the self-torturing mortification of the flesh of the spiritual athletes of Syria, whose greatest hero, Saint Simeon Stylites (395–461) lived atop a pillar for forty years with a monthly diet, it is said, of a handful of millet seeds.

The ascetic life spread throughout the West during the fourth and fifth centuries, although its progress was much faster in the East. Where monasticism did establish itself in the West, it was, like its Eastern counterpart, influenced by Pachomius' model. Athanasius, patriarch of Alexandria and the author of the first life of Saint Anthony, spent several years as an exile in Italy around 340. His presence in the peninsula promoted monastic ideas there. In Gaul, Saint Martin, a soldier, became one of the earliest Western monks and, as bishop of Tours, later founded a monastic community of the Pachomian type (ca. 360). The most important early Western monastery, however, was established on the island of Lerins, near Marseilles, toward the end of the fourth century. The greatest abbot of Lerins was John Cassian (d. 429), who had lived in Egypt for many years and who organized Lerins on the Pachomian model. He also wrote two important works through which

This gold plaque from a sixth-century Syrian reliquary shows Saint Simeon Stylites, the "athlete of God," who lived atop a pillar outside Antioch for forty years. His defeat of Satan, here symbolized by a snake, made him counselor to thousands of Christians who climbed the ladder to his platform. Representations like this one spread his fame throughout the Roman world.

the traditions of Eastern monasticism were transmitted to the West. The first, the *Institutes,* presented the Pachomian rules, while the second, the *Collations,* contained sayings of the desert fathers that Cassian thought would inspire his monks to maintain their profession. Lerins was therefore a fount of monastic ideology, although it is not clear what part it played in the spread of monasticism in the West.

In the East, the monks were drawn into Church politics and became troops in episcopal struggles first against the pagans and then against heretics. A good deal of street fighting and destruction occurred during these struggles. In the West, monasticism and missionary work were joined early by Saint Martin of Tours and his followers. Thus as the monks became involved in the life of the Western Church, their role was on the whole more constructive than that of their Eastern counterparts. The missionary effort of the monks was soon carried to the British Isles by monks like Saint Ninian, who began the conversion of the Picts of Galloway in southwestern Scotland (ca. 397) and Saint Patrick, who reinvigorated the anemic Christianity that had filtered into Ireland and thus became the true founder of the Irish Church (ca. 440–461). Ninian prepared for his work at Rome and at Tours; Patrick's background is unknown. The Romano-British Church had survived in western Britain (especially in Wales), but it was isolated from Continental developments. The extreme asceticism of Eastern monasticism was congenial to the temperament of the newly converted Irish. Within the Celtic Christian world generally the monastery under the abbot, rather than the bishop's diocese, gradually became the unit of ecclesiastical organization. Each monastery served the spiritual needs of a single tribe, and the abbot was a tribal leader. The bishop, whose duties were wholly spiritual, was a subordinate official in the monastery. Celtic monasticism was the expression of a tribal society, just as the diocese was the expression of the society based on the *civitas*.

The vigor of Celtic Christianity was best displayed in its combination of monasticism and missionary work. By 565 Saint Columba, an Irish monk, had established a monastery at Iona, from which the conversion of the Picts

Excavations of pre-Roman and Roman Celtic villages in Britain show that they were made up of small round huts. After the Anglo-Saxon invasions, this form of building was confined to Cornwall, Wales, and other Celtic regions. Celtic-Irish monks were responsible for its importation to other areas, including the islands of the North Atlantic —the Hebrides, the Orkneys, Iceland, and even the Faroes. It appears here as a stone beehive cell of the monastery at Inishmurray in Ireland (probably early seventh century).

in northern Scotland and of the Angles of Northumbria was begun. The leaders and heroes of this movement equaled the ascetic extremes of the desert fathers. To quell their bodily desires, they stood for long periods of time immersed to the head in an icy stream, and they collected long lists of sins, with their appropriate penances, to help them regulate their lives. These works, called penitentials, had a profound impact on European ideas about sin and atonement. Their zeal for self-punishment was equaled by their zeal for missionary work. This activity, carried on by wandering monks, took them to the Continent, where they were instrumental in the spread of Christianity into the thickets of rural culture. Saint Columbanus (585–615) introduced new life into the Merovingian Church and founded the monasteries of Luxeuil (in Gaul) and Bobbio (in northern Italy). Luxeuil, with its six hundred monks, became the monastic metropolis of the new Frankish kingdom. The great age of Celtic monasticism lasted from around 550 to 650. It was not an enduring element in Western Christianity, nor was the Pachomian rule on which it was ultimately based. Western monks and ecclesiastical leaders were creating a new form of cenobitic monasticism destined to become the dominant form in the West.

In southern Gaul, Caesarius of Arles had composed a short rule for a community of nuns. His rule was relatively well organized, exhibiting the ancient Roman capacity for communal governance. But while it was in some respects better than Cassian's guides, it was too short to be comprehensive enough for monasteries not subject to the personal guidance of such men as Caesarius. The need for a monastic constitution sufficient to the requirements of isolated and independent communities was filled by Saint Benedict of Nursia (ca. 480–543), much of whose adult life was spent in Italy during the chaotic years that succeeded the death of Theodoric the Ostrogoth (526). Benedict did not consider himself a reformer or leader, except for his own community of monks, and he had no program for other monasteries to follow. He thought of his rule as "the least of beginnings" to help the monk get started on the ascetic life. His ideal was the life of the hermit or of the desert fathers of Egypt, and he was deeply influenced by John Cassian, whose work he cited at least ninety times. However, the rule he wrote for his monks at Monte Cassino (founded ca. 520) became the model for all later monastic life in the West, and Benedict has justly been called "the Father of Western Monasticism."

The central feature of the Benedictine rule, like all other monastic rules, was the *opus Dei* (work of God; that is, worship by the monks in common at set intervals throughout the day), but the success of the rule was due to four new elements that Benedict introduced. First, his rule was a constitution that consisted of general regulations rather than a set of specific bylaws, so that it was supremely adaptable to local conditions. Second, Benedict enhanced the authority of the abbot, who was to appoint all officials of the monastery, control monastic finances, and exercise wide discretionary powers over the

Early Monastic Centers and Cultural Outposts in Western Europe

organization and discipline of the community. Although the abbot was elected by vote of the community, he was to be installed by the bishop of his diocese. Thus episcopal control was provided for in the rule itself. Third, in addition to the usual vows of poverty, chastity, and obedience to the abbot, a fourth was added, the vow of stability. This was a promise not to leave the monastery except at the command of the abbot. It enhanced the abbot's disciplinary control of the community, as it increased the sense of solidarity among the monks. Finally, the Benedictine rule confirmed the old principle that monks should do manual labor. Benedict founded his monastery in the disruptive environment of the Gothic wars, and he wanted it to be isolated and self-sufficient.

Moderation is a striking feature of Benedictine monasticism. It consists of an asceticism proper to the pursuit of spiritual values and goals without making it impossible for persons weak in body to meet its demands. Benedict made no specific provision for intellectual activity beyond public and private reading of the Scriptures and the works of the Fathers, and he referred only casually to the instruments of writing. Benedictine monasteries, however, normally included a school for novices, a library, and a scriptorium (writing room), and they therefore were ideally suited for the preservation of the pagan and Christian culture of antiquity. This was ultimately one of the greatest contributions of Benedictine monasticism, but its immediate contribution was, ironically for a movement designed to escape the world, within the life of the Church as an institution. The rules of Benedictine monasticism were taken to Rome by the monks of Monte Cassino in the early 580s after the Lombards had destroyed their monastery. The initial contact between the first Benedictines and the Romans had far-reaching results because one of those attracted to Benedict's followers and his ideas was the young Gregory I the Great. As pope, Gregory wrote a work called the *Dialogues,* in which he recounted the life of Saint Benedict. It is not clear if Gregory played a direct role in the dissemination of Benedictine monasticism, but he did much to spread Benedict's fame and to make the Benedictine rule attractive to those who came under papal influence. Nonetheless, like papal power, Benedictine monasticism grew very slowly. The Benedictine rule did not supplant the other guides until the ninth century.

## Art and Literature to the End of the Sixth Century: Cassiodorus, Boethius, and Gregory the Great

The invasions produced a hiatus in the cultural activity of the Western empire. In Britain, the cultural outpost in the southeast was wiped out as the Germans overran the province. In Gaul, the aristocracy lost some of its wealth to the German lords but became involved in the governance of the new kingdoms. Education continued but obviously at a reduced level, and the schools produced no great authors, as they had in the fourth and fifth centuries. In Italy, the events of the late fifth and early sixth centuries induced perceptive intellectuals to take action to save what they could of their classical heritage. Nonetheless, in the mid-fifth century, after the Byzantine conquest had apparently succeeded, there was a revival that found expression in architecture and related arts. The Byzantine authorities rebuilt the cities in which they located their new administrative centers. Ravenna in particular became a showplace for contemporary Byzantine architecture, and many of its buildings became models for medieval architects.

The earliest Christian churches were simply an adaptation of the public building, the basilica, used by the Roman government. The early Christian basilica was a rectangular building with the altar at one end and the entrance at the other. The exterior was unadorned, but the interior was often decorated elaborately with mosaics and colored marble on the floors, walls, and the semidome over the apse (the projecting end of the building where the altar was located). The interior space of the larger basilicas was broken into three main parts, the central nave and two aisles separated from the nave by a row of columns supporting arches that in turn bore the weight of the central roof. The effect was to produce a nave arcade whose horizontal rhythms converged on the focal point of the structure, the altar. The largest basilicas, such as Old Saint Peter's (built between 324 and 336 and demolished in the sixteenth century) or Saint Paul's Outside the Walls, sometimes had two aisles on either side of the nave and also two other features th⁀t were lacking in

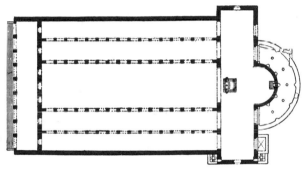

Floor Plan of Basilica

the ordinary church: an atrium, or open courtyard in front of the church, surrounded by covered galleries and serving to seclude the church proper from the noise and distractions of the street; and an interior space called the transept, whose axis was at right angles to the rest of the basilica and which separated the apse from the nave and aisles. The transept sometimes projected beyond the walls of the aisles; enlargement of the transept and extension of the apse, in later centuries, produced the conventional cruciform ground plan of the medieval church. The bishop's *cathedra,* or throne, was placed in the apse behind the altar (hence a bishop's church is called a cathedral). The straight lines and wooden construction of the ceiling and the sloping roofs over nave and aisles set practical limits to the size of the basilica, as well as handicapping basilica churches with a built-in fire hazard. These were two difficulties confronting medieval architects when they began to improve on the basilica.

In northern Italy during the sixth century, both under Theodoric and during the Byzantine occupation, an architectural revival took place. Examples at Ravenna are the church of Sant' Apollinare in Classe, a basilica with highly ornate Byzantine interior decoration, and San Vitale, which was an example of another Byzantine type of floor plan and construction. San Vitale is a central-space church, octagonal in shape, whose walls support a dome covering the interior. The effect is static, and the vertical dimension is emphasized, compared with the horizontal movement suggested by the nave arcade of the basilica. This type of church is Syrian in origin. Its construction is a development of the arch, vault, and dome system common in Roman architecture.

A vault is simply an arch extended for the desired length in a third dimension; two vaults of the same size intersecting at right angles will enclose a square space if the length of each vault is equal to the width. But the resulting structure will not be strong in relation to its weight, and its height is limited by the width of each vault. A dome is simply an arch rotated in a complete circle; its height is limited by its diameter, and it cannot enclose a square space. In order to enclose a square space and achieve greater height, the Byzantine architects, in effect, mounted one dome on top of another "dome." The first dome was constructed so that its circumference touched the four corners of the square space to be enclosed, and then the portions of the dome projecting beyond the square were cut off vertically; then the top of this dome was cut off horizontally just above the top of the four arches formed by the previous vertical trimming. The resulting horizontal circle was then used as the base for the second true dome, which was thus raised to a greater height than would be possible by intersecting vaults. The total result is called a dome on pendentives (pendentives are the masonry left from the first "dome": the triangular sections of a hemisphere whose diameter is equal

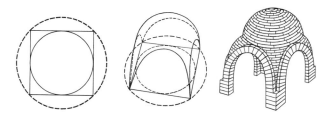

Dome on Pendentives

to the diagonal of a square inscribed within its largest section). If all this is clear, the reader will appreciate the engineering problem and its greatest architectural solution, Justinian's great church, Hagia Sophia (Holy Philosophy), in Constantinople, whose dome soars 180 feet above the interior pavement and covers (together with two half-domes built up on opposite sides) an interior space of 100 feet by 250 feet. Because the lateral thrust is so great in such a structure, buttresses of such size had to be added that the exterior resembles a massive pile of masonry. The interior effect was what interested the architects. They introduced enough light and provided the spherical interior surfaces with such colorful decoration to overawe and astonish all who saw it before 1453, when the Moslems whitewashed (and thus, fortunately, preserved for the modern archeologist to restore) the beautiful mosaics. This Byzantine architectural achievement was so much greater than anything accomplished by contemporaries in the West that it affords an indication of the relative ability of the governments in the two areas to collect funds from their respective territories. In the sixth century, only the Byzantine bureaucracy could gather the resources for a project the size of Hagia Sophia. In the West, the principles involved in building this great church had been introduced earlier, but they received their greatest application in the church of San Vitale in Ravenna. Some of these principles underlie future medieval architectural development, although the central-space church was to play a minor role.

In painting, sculpture, and the decorative arts, early Christian art developed from pagan prototypes in style and even in subject matter. Thus in the fourth century a Christian bridal casket was decorated with representations of Venus and cherubs, or a sarcophagus (stone coffin) in the catacombs with pagan nymphs, tritons, and mermaids. The entry of Jesus into Jerusalem was portrayed after the manner of an emperor's triumphal entry into Rome. The earliest representations of Christ (third century) show him clean-shaven and modeled on figures of Apollo, while in the fourth century Christ was portrayed as an austere and bearded figure resembling pagan representations of Jupiter or the ancient philosophers who, artistically, symbolized Wisdom. Christianity adopted the artistic style that, in the later empire, was "modern." Itself of provincial origin, Christianity took over the art forms and style that had been developing in the provinces as a reaction against the "official" Greco-Roman style as illustrated in the realistic portraiture of the early empire, or in the copies of naturalistic art of Hellenistic Greece.

This provincial reaction led to the transformation of classical style into a transcendental and abstract style. The provincial pagan artists who rejected the traditional realism and naturalism of Roman art were not interested in lifelike, three-dimensional, "photographic" reproduction of nature or the outside world. Rather, they were concerned with portraying a reality that transcended sense experience, a higher reality (as they conceived it) beyond time and space, and therefore to be represented as an expression of spirit rather than of material form. Thus individuality gave way to abstraction. Realistic details, which portray the merely physical and therefore changing exterior, were subordinated to a portrayal of the inner essence of the subject. For example, a typically Roman portrait-bust suggests the flesh-and-blood reality of an individual human being whose existence has been caught and reproduced at a particular moment. The "modern art" of the later empire would instead portray the subject's soul by exaggerating the eyes and one or two details of the facial expression. The Roman bust lives here and now; the provincial style represents the eternal and unchanging essence of the subject.

In popular literature, as contrasted with patristic theology and philosophy or pagan belles-lettres, an analogous development of new values and standards took place in the transition from ancient to early medieval culture. The pagan literature of entertainment was the Greek romance or a Latin version of it, such as the *Golden Ass* of Apuleius or the *Satyricon* of Petronius, often full of classical mythology and ribald episodes that were not considered fit for good Christians to read. To replace these worldly adventure stories, a Christian popular literature of spiritual adventure evolved whose heroes were the martyrs or saints who had renounced the world and its vices. The earliest accounts of these heroes concerned the desert fathers of Egypt. From these were developed the later *Vitae Sanctorum* (Lives of the Saints), semibiographical stories about hermits and monks who were, preeminently, the models after whom the good Christian should pattern his life.

The compelling purpose behind the writing of *Vitae Sanctorum* was edification of the faithful, the inculcation of Christian ideals and conduct among simple folk who could neither read nor understand the metaphysical or mystical writings of the Fathers. Many of these "lives" grew directly from sermons preached on the festival days of the various saints. To attract and hold attention, to emphasize the virtue of the saint, and to exemplify various points of Christian ethics, the *Vitae Sanctorum* were replete with tense situations, hairbreadth escapes, miraculous events (that is, inexplicable in terms of ordinary human experience), and happy endings, just like some popular modern short stories. In this literature for popular consumption there rapidly arose a huge number of legends, some of them taken over from Greco-Roman mythology and some of them attached to more than one saint. A Christian mythology replaced the pagan mythology. Historians can reconstruct Christian thought on the highest level from the serious writings of the Fathers; their only glimpse of the popular religious culture of the early Middle Ages is afforded by the Lives of the Saints.

In the West, the outstanding early life of a saint was Sulpicius Severus' *Life of Saint Martin of Tours* (ca. 400), on which many later authors (or compilers) of saints' lives based their accounts. Hagiographical literature, like the modern detective story, is dominated by conventions, and Sulpicius Severus was responsible for many of the conventions that reappear in saints' lives during the next eight centuries. The typical saint is born amid miraculous events. As an infant he performs some prodigy, such as uttering a prediction at the age of two or three days, and as a child he confounds his elders with his precocious wisdom. Late childhood and adolescence are usually treated very briefly or left unrecorded, but the saint's mature years are full of miracles that he performs as proof of his virtue (virtue being conceived primarily in terms of supernatural power). After an ascetic life of renunciation and humility, his death is attended by appropriately miraculous events (such as being seen by eyewitnesses to ascend into heaven in the company of angels, or up a ladder). The resemblance between the conventional pattern of a saint's life and the life of Christ according to the Gospels is obvious. But this similarity did not surprise contemporaries who believed that a holy man should naturally model his life on the life of the Lord.

The popularity of the *Vitae Sanctorum* and the fashionable cult of saints in the West were intimately connected, the one reinforcing the other. Both were also associated with the monastic life, which produced so many saints. In addition to Scripture, novices in the monasteries were encouraged to read the Lives of the Saints as part of their spiritual and intellectual program. The Benedictine rule specifically recommended the reading of sacred literature, including the writings and lives of the Fathers. The Benedictine monastery thus required a library together with a scriptorium where copies of books could be made and new books occasionally written. Enough education to teach all monks to read and the further education of one or two monks preparing for ordination to the priesthood were a normal part of monastic life. In such an environment natural intellectual curiosity often led to the cultivation of reading and study far beyond the minimum requirements. Without the monastic scriptoria of the early Middle Ages the physical preservation of pagan and patristic classical literature would not have been possible.

Benedict's attitude toward learning, with true Benedictine moderation, was tolerant and permissive; his service to Western culture was incidental to his main purpose. In contrast, Benedict's younger contemporary Cassiodorus (ca. 490–580) was a man with a program. He rose high in the government of the Ostrogothic kingdom, in which he rendered valuable service to Theodoric and his successors as the author of their official correspondence. Cassiodorus made a collection of these letters and state papers, the *Variae,* a fascinating record of Ostrogothic policy and of contemporary interests and values.

This work also reflects the increasingly difficult time intellectuals were having during the wars that beset Italy after Theodoric's death in 526. Men of the senatorial class, such as Cassiodorus, were particularly affected by the struggle between the orthodox Byzantines, who subscribed to the Greco-Roman culture so dear to upper-class intellectuals, and the Arian Goths, who in general did not support or respect the high culture. Theodoric himself had valued the civilization of Cassiodorus and his confreres and had inculcated that respect in his daughter Amalasuntha, who ruled as regent for her son after the great king's death. But the Gothic aristocracy, at war with the Byzantines, did not look kindly on the cultivation of the enemy's civilization, especially since there appeared to be a conflict between Romano-Byzantine and Gothic values. The encouragement of Roman culture thus became an important issue in the 530s, intensifying the predicament of Cassiodorus' class. During this period, Cassiodorus' political loyalties changed back and forth, and around 540 he fled to Constantinople. When he returned to Italy a few years later the political situation made it impossible for him to realize his plan to establish a Christian center of higher studies in Rome, perhaps on the model of the Academy in Athens founded by Plato at the beginning of the fourth century B.C. and closed by Justinian in A.D. 529. Instead, Cassiodorus established a monastery dedicated to his educational and cultural projects on his private estate at Squillace in southern Italy.

In his most important work, *An Introduction to Divine and Human Readings,* Cassiodorus outlined a curriculum of study and his educational philosophy, which can be briefly stated in his words as "using the methods of the liberal arts to aid the study of sacred works." This involved a conscious effort to preserve and to master all the literature of antiquity for the service of Christian education. He also provided his monks with a reading list of the best books in each field, together with instruction on textual emendation, copying, and binding manuscripts. Cassiodorus' work is an embodiment of the cultural situation in Ostrogothic and Byzantine Italy in the sixth century. By drawing that culture together, making it coherent and comprehensible, Cassiodorus contributed much to the preservation of the civilization he loved. The *Divine and Human Readings* was a popular handbook or guide to literature, surviving in an impressive number of manuscripts.

Another representative of Cassiodorus' class was Boethius (ca. 480–524), whose work exhibits the same duality as that of his contemporary. Boethius was a wealthy, highly educated man with a deep interest in philosophy and theology. He spent considerable time at Theodoric's court, but aside from achieving the high position of consul, he does not seem to have been an active participant in the Ostrogothic administration. Toward the end of his reign, Theodoric became uneasy about the tension between himself, an Arian and foreign ruler, and the orthodox Roman population, especially the senatorial aristocracy that had most to gain from the reestablishment of imperial government in Italy. Boethius fell victim to the king's suspicions, and although he protested his innocence, Theodoric had him executed for treasonous dealings with Byzantium. Only a small number of Westerners had been directly conversant with Greek philosophical thought during the long history of the empire, and Boethius, living in a time when men were aware that even this small number might be diminishing, was a member of the select company. When this fact is comprehended, his importance and the tragedy of his premature death can be appreciated. Acting on the same impulse as Cassiodorus, Boethius planned to make both Plato and Aristotle available to the Latin West in translation. Unfortunately, he got no further than a selection of Aristotle's logical treatises, and translations of only two elementary treatises survived (plus a translation of, and commentary on, Porphyry's *Isagoge,* an introduction to Aristotle's logic). Limited as it was, Boethius' work provided the West with its technical philosophical vocabulary and its only knowledge of Greek logic until the twelfth century. Boethius also wrote five important theological *Tractates,* all of them staunchly orthodox. One was a systematic application of Aristotelian logic to a problem of Christian theology—an anticipation of later achievements that has earned Boethius the title, "First of the Scholastics." As he himself put it, in a letter to a friend, his purpose was to "reconcile faith and reason."

When imprisonment cut short his brilliant career, Boethius found it inexpedient to continue writing on theological subjects. Separation from his books precluded further philosophical studies. Instead he wrote the literary work for which he has always been best known, *The Consolation of Philosophy,* a dialogue half in verse and half in prose between himself and Philosophia, who gently leads him from black despair over his lot to "that true contentment which reason allied with virtue alone can give." The *Consolation* is one of the great masterpieces of prison-literature and has given the West a profound summary of Christian-classical psychology and of Augustine's value theory. The *Consolation* represented an achievement of escape from the prison of material existence, in which psychology and philosophy met. In bringing together Christianity and classical culture, the *Consolation* was a fitting end to Boethius' life work. Neither Christ nor the Bible is mentioned in the *Consolation,* and the ideas expressed in it are classical. The work, however, can be regarded as thoroughly Christian because Boethius organized and presented the classical themes in a way that was becoming traditional among Christians. It is therefore a symbol and a demonstration of Christianity's assimilation of classical culture.

The chaotic wartime conditions that impelled Cassiodorus and Boethius had not disappeared during Gregory the Great's life (540–604). In fact, the Lombard invasion had prolonged and deepened the disruption. Gregory was a product of the declining educational system his predecessors had tried to preserve. In his writings, therefore, he represented the midpoint along the downward curve of intellectual life that continued until the late eighth century. Gregory is considered the last of the Four Doctors of the Latin Church (with Ambrose, Jerome, and Augustine), but in some ways he was the most important of the four because he stood between the sophisticated and difficult ideas and doctrines of his predecessors and the elementary understanding of those who came after him. He dealt with the esoteric theological tradition of the classical period on a level that could be understood by men without a classical education. He also enshrined many of his contemporaries' beliefs and superstitions in his works, giving his writings a popular appeal. Some scholars have criticized him for propagating superstition, but perhaps it is fairer to Gregory to see him not as Augustine's equal in sophistication, using superstition as a manipulative tool in order to influence his audience, but as a man of his time who saw the world in much the same way as his contemporaries.

Gregory wrote a great deal, and nearly all of his works had an important impact on medieval civilization. As pope, he wrote letters to ecclesiastical and lay figures throughout Europe (over eight hundred letters have survived), and these still influence Church law and political ideas. In addition, he wrote sermons that have had a continuing influence on the Christian pulpit. As a theologian Gregory was thoroughly Augustinian. In his longest work, the *Moralia in Job,* he developed a highly allegorical interpretation of the Old Testament book, demonstrating the richness of his imagination and intellectual resourcefulness in the context of a work devoted to the Judeo-Christian ethical teachings. This work exerted a great influence on medieval biblical exegesis, ethics, political ideas, and literary symbolism. A related work was his *Pastoral Rule,* in which he discussed the character, qualifications, and work of the good bishop. This book too became a standard reference during the Middle Ages, when it was used as a guide to pastoral work. Finally, Gregory wrote a work on Christian life called the *Dialogues,* one part of which recounted the life of Saint Benedict and did much to popularize the saint and his monastic ideal. The *Dialogues* also encouraged the cult of saints, the veneration of relics, and popular beliefs about demons, angels, and supernatural phenomena, giving these superstitions and practices a foundation in the patristic tradition. Until the intellectual revival of the eleventh and twelfth centuries, Gregory was medieval Christianity's most prominent and most effective schoolmaster.

## The Survival of Classical Culture: Spain, Ireland, and the Northumbria of Bede

In sixth-century Italy classical education, and thus culture, weakened progressively as men like Boethius and Cassiodorus had foreseen. In other parts of the empire, the decline had occurred earlier. Augustine died just a few days before Gaiseric and his Vandals conquered his episcopal city of Hippo in 430, and no other great intellectual figures appeared in the former North African province after the Vandals established themselves. As noted earlier, Gaul suffered a decline but not a complete collapse of intellectual culture during and after the invasions. The excellent schools of rhetoric situated there during the later empire disappeared, but education continued on a lower level and more haphazardly. One of the Merovingian kings, Chilperic (561–584), fancied himself a patron of arts and letters. Fortunatus (535–605), the best poet of the sixth century, wandered about Gaul visiting courts and monasteries, exchanging his pleasant, lightweight verses for room and board. The fact that his poetry should be appreciated is surprising, but it is far more surprising that Fortunatus was able to compose two really good Christian hymns, *Pange Lingua Gloriosi* and *Vexilla Regis Prodeunt.* The first stanza of the latter follows:

*Vexilla regis prodeunt.*
*Fulget crucis mysterium,*
*Quo carne carnis conditor*
*Suspensus est patibulo.*

[The King's advancing banners wave!
The Cross gleams out its Mystery
Where He that made the body gave
His body to the gallows-tree.][1]

The most important writer in Merovingian Gaul was Fortunatus' friend and occasional benefactor, Gregory, bishop of Tours (538–594), a member of the Gallo-Roman aristocracy. Gregory's contribution to hagiographical literature is next in importance only to that of Sulpicius Severus and to that of his namesake and contemporary, Gregory the Great. What made Gregory of Tours unique in his age was his remarkable *History of the Franks,* which for the period of his own episcopate (after 573) was detailed, dramatic, and generally accurate narrative. Gregory was not particularly well educated; he probably knew the classical authors (except for Virgil) only through Martianus Capella's textbook. He reveals all the prejudices and predilections of his age (antagonism toward heretics and an unquestioning acceptance of miracles, which he loves to enlarge on), and his viewpoint is strictly that of the high churchman, betraying no dislike of the Franks on racial or cultural grounds but judging them solely on the basis of their attitude toward the Church. His language and style are vigorously uncouth, but they make a better medium for his vivid portrayal of Frankish life than the bombastic and artificial affectations of contemporary rhetorical usage.

After the death of Gregory of Tours, the Frankish kingdoms produced nothing of intellectual interest. As in Italy, the seventh and the first half of the eighth centuries constitute a dark age in Gaul. There are only a few wretchedly inadequate annals, the "grammatical" works of an author who assumed the name of Virgilius Maro, and the geographical lore collected by a certain Aethicus the Cosmographer. Their efforts often read more like elaborate practical jokes than anything to be taken seriously.

The Visigothic conquest of Spain certainly weakened the Roman culture of the Iberian Peninsula, but under Visigothic rule Spain did eventually produce a cultural activity of Europeanwide significance. The conversion of the Visigothic King Recared I (586–601) from Arian to Catholic Christianity stimulated doctrinal disputes and organizational activity. Recared held a series of Church councils designed to bring the Spanish Church into the orbit of Roman Christianity. These ecclesiastical assemblies also became forums in which doctrinal issues were discussed and thus vehicles for the dissemination

[1] Jack Lindsay, *Song of a Falling World* (London: Andrew Dakers, 1948), p. 271.

of patristic ideas, creating an intellectual community among Spanish church-men. Coincidentally, the conversion occurred during the pontificate of Greg-ory the Great, whose attempts to extend papal influence throughout the Church deeply affected Spain.

The greatest intellectual in the Spanish renaissance of the seventh century was Bishop Isidore of Seville (ca. 570–636). Isidore was a man of enormous learning who had obtained a classical education and was thus prepared to perform a task like that of Cassiodorus. He produced an encyclopedia of classical knowledge called the *Etymologies,* which became the basis of learn-ing up to the thirteenth century. The whole range of human knowledge then available was organized, in this work, according to the unifying principle of the origin and meaning of words. It is easy to poke fun at the fanciful expla-nations that Isidore drew from chance similarity of spelling or sound rather than from real linguistic knowledge. For example, a friend is one whose main concern is for the soul's welfare, because, according to Isidore, *amicus* is derived from *animi custos* (guardian of the soul); or again, a man cries more easily when kneeling in prayer because the knees and eyes of an unborn infant are close together in the womb. But the absurdities of Isidore's "ety-mological" method should not be allowed to obscure his substantial achieve-ment in accumulating so huge a body of organized knowledge—most of it accurate by the standards of classical antiquity. The *Etymologies* was a kind of ultimate epitome to end all further epitomes, but it was much more than a mere storehouse of facts. Just as Gregory the Great had applied an allegorical method to the Book of Job, so Isidore applied it to all of the knowledge he had acquired. He sought the hidden meaning in objective facts about the world and tried to integrate the corpus of classical learning into the moral and spiritual teachings of Christianity. Later theologians and poets con-sulted the *Etymologies* as well as Gregory's writings as a rich source of Christian symbolism.

Isidore wrote other important works on theology, history, and cosmology that were known throughout Europe during the Middle Ages. One of the most important early collections of canon law was also attributed to him. The culture that produced Isidore did not die with him, but Spain never became a major cultural center in the Visigothic period. Nonetheless, the modest tradi-tion of learning and poetry that continued in Spain had an effect on European intellectual life in the eighth century. When the Moslems destroyed the Visigothic kingdom in the early decades of that century, cultured Spanish churchmen took refuge in the Frankish kingdom and contributed to the great cultural revival called the Carolingian renaissance. That revival will be dis-cussed in a later chapter.

Strangely, it was in the British Isles that classical civilization had its latest flowering, and the source of this amazing cultural continuity was Ire-land, an area that had never been part of the Roman Empire. The Romanized Britons had been pushed westward by the Anglo-Saxon invasions and had suffered cultural as well as political decline. The expiring gasps of their community are recorded in the little work of moral exhortation by Gildas (ca. 500–570), ineptly entitled *On the Annihilation and Conquest of Britain,* in which the tantalizingly scanty historical information is overwhelmed by tedious moralizing about the dreary times. Another, related work is the weird collection of anonymous schoolboy verses called *Hisperica Famina,* which read like the work of a conscientious idiot, although some critics have found in them "artistic feeling" and a commendable "directness and freedom in expression." In translation, some of the verses may even suggest the mode and feeling of some twentieth-century poetry, as in the lines:

> Roaring Westwind downbows
> > oaks with strong-cherishing boughs
> old knotty holmoaks harrows
> > flat to the furrows
> stoutly snorting harms
> > crested thatch of farms
> cracks
> > topmost tiles on the chimney-stacks
> raves
> > thrashing earth with blue waves
> and carries high
> > foamdrops on the starry sky.[2]

One of the fascinating problems of European history is to explain how the flourishing of arts and letters in Ireland and England came about in the seventh century, when Continental Europe had reached its lowest level. A cultural flourishing in the British Isles could not take the form of a renaissance of classical culture, since in Ireland there was none to revive and in western England the British Church, cut off from Europe by the Anglo-Saxons, lacked the educational resources or intellectual traditions to survive the post-Roman collapse. British Christians, moreover, were conspicuous failures in the work of converting the heathen Irish and Anglo-Saxons. When Christianity was reintroduced from the Continent, by the mission of Saint Patrick to Ireland and the later arrival of Saint Augustine of Canterbury in Kent, it came as a new movement with the enthusiasm and dedication characteristic of evangelical work. Conversion established contact in the fifth century between Ireland and southern and southwestern Gaul, where some of the best provincial schools of the later empire were located and where the earliest missionaries had received their training. Thus the explanation seems to be that conversion provided the initial motivation, and contact with the surviving classical culture in southern Gaul provided the materials for the

[2] Ibid., p. 260.

cultivation of arts and letters in Ireland. The monasteries that dominated the Celtic Church became sheltered centers for the study of both sacred and secular learning, and the later competition between Irish missionary monks and the Benedictines of the Roman mission during the conversion of the Anglo-Saxons stimulated debate over theological issues in the seventh century. Further nourishment of both Irish and Anglo-Saxon cultural development came from Visigothic Spain, for the works of Isidore of Seville and other Spanish writers were known in Ireland and England before the end of the seventh century.

In England the initial cultural stimulus of conversion was as modest as Augustine's limited success in his missionary efforts among the Anglo-Saxons. But a beginning was made, and it produced a fascinating byproduct whose consequences were significant for the future. The Anglo-Saxons were the first people in the early Middle Ages to feel the full impact of the spell of Rome, the Eternal City, the symbol of man's highest achievements. Leaders of the Celtic Church found in Roman Christianity an alien if not hostile spirit. Contemporary Romans could see only a collapsing world about them, "a straitened age . . . a failing world," as Pope John III referred to his own times. In contrast, the many Anglo-Saxons who made pilgrimages to Rome were profoundly impressed with the superiority of Mediterranean civilization to their own, rather than with the decay of antiquity felt by Mediterranean people, for whom a sense of continuity with the past still existed. Thus what depressed the Roman elated and stimulated the Anglo-Saxon. Pilgrims from England eagerly collected the books, jewels and objects of art, and the knowledge of architecture with which they might adorn and improve their own material and intellectual life.

Irish monasteries were already centers of learning in the sixth century, but from this early period only a penitential and some hymns survive as examples of creative work rather than the assimilation of Latin culture. In the seventh century, the most interesting and original treatise on a secular subject produced in all of Europe was the work of an anonymous Irish author. Entitled *On the Twelve Abuses of the World* (ca. 660–700), it is a lively critique of contemporary social, political, intellectual, and religious life. The author was obviously well educated, wrote excellent Latin, drew on a wide range of patristic literature, and was capable of independent and original thinking. Typically Irish in genius and temper is the contentious spirit pervading the treatise, as well as the specific injunction to kings "to give no countenance to the superstitions of wizards, soothsayers, and witches."

The most distinguished representative of Irish religious culture in the seventh century was Adamnan, abbot of Iona (679–704), whose best-known works are the *Life of Saint Columba* (founder of the monastery), a commentary on Virgil, and a descriptive essay entitled *On Holy Places.* The last work was drawn from an oral account of the Holy Land by a contemporary

Frankish bishop who had recently returned from a pilgrimage to Jerusalem, then under Moslem control. The far-flung cultural interconnections illustrated by this treatise (embracing Moslem Palestine, Byzantine and Orthodox Constantinople, Merovingian and Catholic Gaul, and a Celtic monastery off the northwestern coast of Anglo-Saxon England) emphasize how inaccurate it is to think of the Dark Ages as a period of isolated provincialism.

The entrance of England into the cultural life of Western Europe resulted from the interaction between Irish learning (emanating from the monastery of Lindisfarne in the north, founded around 634) and the classical tradition of the Mediterranean world brought to England by Theodore of Tarsus, archbishop of Canterbury (668–690), and his companion Hadrian. Theodore and Hadrian established a school at Canterbury (ca. 670), from which the Roman influence spread northward to such centers as the monasteries of Wearmouth and Jarrow in Northumbria, founded in 674 and 682 by Benedict Biscop, who was one of the most assiduous book collectors of the age. Canterbury was the only school north of the Alps in the early Middle Ages where students could learn Greek and study Roman law as well as pursue the several disciplines of the liberal arts.

The Irish and Roman traditions were combined in the West Saxon Aldhelm, abbot of Malmesbury (675–709), of whom it has been said that "no country in western Europe during the seventh century could show his equal in intellectual achievement." His early training was at Malmesbury, the only important monastery in southern England founded by Celtic missionaries; later he studied at Canterbury under Theodore and Hadrian; and, like so many of his Anglo-Saxon contemporaries, he made a pilgrimage to Rome. Few men before the twelfth century had read as much—and, it must be added, to so little purpose. He wrote poems, a tract in praise of virginity, and some letters that are valuable evidence for the cultural interests of his period. Like his Irish contemporary Adamnan, he loved the artificial language and esoteric style of Celtic scholarship; it has been questioned whether Aldhelm was capable of writing a readily intelligible sentence. But the mannerisms of his Latinity must be recognized as a cultivated art rather than an inability to compose more straightforward prose.

Northumbria, the battleground between Celtic and Roman Christianity (ca. 634–663), produced the greatest scholar and literary figure of the early Middle Ages. Bede (ca. 672–735) was brought up at Jarrow, where Benedict Biscop had assembled a magnificent library, the product of his book-collecting travels in Gaul and Italy over many years. Bede was even more widely read than his elder contemporary, Aldhelm. Several Irish and Anglo-Saxon scholars were acquainted with Greek in the seventh and eighth centuries, but Bede alone applied his knowledge to a useful end. He drew at first hand on the work of some of the Greek Fathers, and he corrected some errors of translation in Saint Jerome's Vulgate Bible. In scholarship, if not in pro-

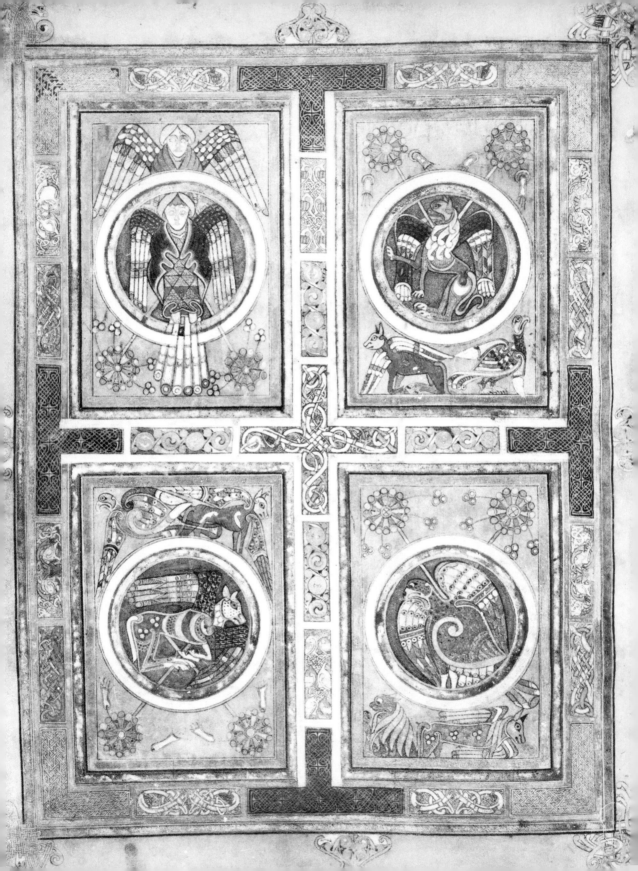

fundity of thought, Bede was the intellectual equal of the Latin Fathers. His own age knew and valued him primarily as a teacher and writer of didactic treatises on the Old and New Testaments and on astronomy and chronology. Bede introduced into the West the dating system of Dionysius Exiguus; that is, the modern reckoning of dates in terms of the birth of Christ (B.C. and A.D.), which later became standard. His most important work was the *Ecclesiastical History of the English People,* written in a style and language unsurpassed since the age of Augustine and for the period from 597 to 731 (when it ends), a work of sustained interest and remarkable accuracy. Even in the *History* Bede was primarily a teacher. He believed that the value of history lay in its lessons for posterity, a view shared by ancient and patristic writers. He grasped the significance of early English history as being a part of the larger whole of Western Europe and of the expansion of Christianity and civilization among the Germanic peoples.

Anglo-Saxon art, like learning and literature, developed under a twofold Roman and Celtic influence. The Irish influence dominated handwriting so completely that it is impossible to determine whether many of the manuscripts of the seventh and early eighth centuries were written in Ireland or England. The Irish were particularly brilliant as manuscript illuminators and created some of the most precious examples of early European art. The Book of Kells (early eighth century) was recognized throughout the Middle Ages as an extraordinary work. Many writers mention seeing it or hearing about it; they were as impressed by it as we are. The book is a deluxe copy of the Gospels and originally was bound in gold. It was stolen in 1006, lost for about six weeks, but found buried in a peat bog, its cover missing but miraculously undamaged otherwise.

The style of the Book of Kells and contemporary works of art was basically decorative, related to the early and exceptional metalworking art common to the Celtic and Germanic peoples. The designs might be representative, but even if they were—and some were pure design—the figures were extremely abstract. Monastic missionaries carried this style with them to England and the Continent, deeply influencing the arts there. Outside Ireland, the Irish artistic tradition combined with the Roman to produce a composite style of intricate decoration and realistic figure representation. In

This carpet page from the Book of Kells, illuminated in Iona or Ireland in the eighth century, shows the symbols of the Evangelists. Matthew is represented by the winged man because he begins his Gospel with the human genealogy of Christ. Mark by the lion because he speaks first of John the Baptist, "the voice crying in the wilderness." Luke by the ox because he speaks first of the sacrifice of Zachariah, and the ox was the animal of sacrifice. John by the eagle because he speaks immediately of the divinity of Christ, and, as the eagle, he flies higher than the others. Medieval bestiaries claimed that the eagle could look directly into the sun; John had performed a similar feat by looking directly at the divinity of Christ.

HHIACOLEOHII

The lion of Mark as represented by the illuminator of the Echternach Gospels (ca. 690). Echternach was founded by the Anglo-Saxon missionary Willibrord, one of the successors of Saint Columbanus, the great Irish missionary. This Gospel shares much with contemporary works of Irish and Anglo-Irish monasteries and is thus one of the precursors of the Book of Kells.

beautiful presentation copies of the Gospels, such as the Lindisfarne Gospels (ca. 700) and the *Codex Amiatinus* (ca. 689–716), the oldest surviving complete copy of Saint Jerome's translation of the Bible, made at Wearmouth and sent to the pope, the cultural amalgamation of Roman and Irish-German stands out. The Irish Continental monasteries produced similar works.

In this context, it is appropriate to mention the Germanic contribution to the artistic tradition of the seventh and eighth centuries. In early Germanic literature, the practice of gift-giving, common in nearly all societies in every age, is often mentioned, and it is suggested that the gifts—bracelets, belt buckles, helmets, magnificent inlaid swords with carved handles—were artistically impressive. How impressive became clear when a large collection of such articles was discovered at Sutton Hoo in East Anglia in a barrow, or burial mound, that had probably been a ship-burial cenotaph for a fallen king. The grave dates from the 650s and is a memorial to an Angle king,

Aethelhere (d. 654), whose followers, in tense struggle with Christians in their community, used the elaborate pagan burial rites to demonstrate the magnificence of the ancient tradition they supported. The intricate enameled and worked designs on the articles provide evidence of the capability of the best German artists and incidently indicate that cultural connections existed between the Angles and the Swedes, who practiced ship-burial and whose armor was of the same type as that found at Sutton Hoo. Continental coins in the purse provided for the dead man's journey in the afterlife show that the Angles of East Anglia were also in contact with the Franks and other Continental groups. The general similarity of the Sutton Hoo artistic style and Irish works like the Book of Kells points to the cultural ties between Celts and Germans in the seventh and eighth centuries. The fusion of Germanic, Celtic, and Roman art styles produced the foundations of Western art, another product of cultural amalgamation, facilitated by the spread of Christianity, in the early Middle Ages.

The treasure trove of Sutton Hoo is the principal existing monument to the struggle between the pagans and Christians in East Anglia and other Germanic communities in England and on the Continent. The ceremonial equipment of the Germanic warrior-king was placed in the ship burial. This purse contained almost fifty coins, many from the Frankish kingdom, which indicates there was trade between England and the Continent. The coins were one of the principal means by which the find was dated.

## Suggestions for Further Reading

**Secondary Works**   On the spread of Christianity and the growth of the Church, see the works cited at the end of Chapter 2. The origins of monasticism are treated in David Knowles, *Christian Monasticism* (New York, 1969). A more complete study of the early hermits is Hippolyte Delehaye, *The Legends of the Saints,* trans. D. Attwater (New York, 1962), and E. S. Duckett, *The Wandering Saints of the Early Middle Ages* (New York, 1959). See also A. J. McCann, *Saint Benedict,* rev. ed. (New York, 1958). The best survey of European intellectual culture in the sixth and seventh centuries is M. L. W. Laistner, *Thought and Letters in Western Europe,* A.D. *500 to 900,* 2nd ed. (Ithaca, N.Y., 1957).

**Sources**   H. Waddell, trans., *The Desert Fathers* (London, 1936) contains the earliest lives of Egyptian monks. The sources for the early history of Western monasticism are in Sulpicius Severus et al., *The Western Fathers,* ed. and trans. F. R. Hoare (New York, 1954). The Benedictine rule is translated in several of the general collections cited at the end of the Introduction and Chapter 2; see especially Henderson, Brentano, and Bettenson. Cassiodorus, *Introduction to Divine and Human Readings,* ed. and trans. L. W. Jones (New York, 1946), and Boethius, *The Consolation of Philosophy,* trans. R. Green (New York, 1962) are the most important literary works of the sixth century. The principal history of the Gothic wars is Procopius, *The History of the Wars,* trans. H. B. Dewing, 5 vols. (London, 1914–28).

# 5  Europe's Neighbors: The Byzantine Empire and the Rise of the Islamic Empire

During Roman times, Europe had been divided between the civilized area centered on the Mediterranean Basin and the territories controlled by tribal societies. The European Continent was considered from the standpoint of the empire. The most important political, economic, and cultural assessments of Europe were made in judging the impact of Roman government, economy, and culture on a particular region. By the eighth century this perspective had changed, or was in the process of changing. People began to recognize that Europe was a political, economic, and cultural entity founded on the amalgamation of Roman and Germanic elements. In their attempts to determine why a distinct civilization arose in Europe, historians have focused their attention on the early Middle Ages.

Historical explanations of the rise of Europe vary according to the interests of the historians who have proposed them. Political historians like Gibbon have argued that the disintegration of Roman political power in the West created a vacuum into which the Germanic tribes were drawn. Intellectual and cultural historians have traced the transformation of Roman civilization in the West and have suggested that the invasions broke the cultural links between northern Europe and the Mediterranean world of Rome. Economic historians have emphasized the dissolution of the Roman commercial network, which, during its heyday, included Europe. It was only when Europe was cut off from the Roman economy, they argue, that it became independent of the empire. Some historians believe that Europe did not come into being until Europeans had developed a consciousness of themselves as a people: the coronation of Charlemagne on Christmas Day 800, which will be considered in the next chapter, marked the formation of that consciousness.

Most of these views concern themselves with the breakup of the Mediterranean world brought about by the transformation of the Eastern Roman Empire to an Eastern state and by the rise of the Islamic Empire, which removed half the Mediterranean Basin from the political universe of Rome and its successors. The great Belgian historian Henri Pirenne tried to integrate the economic approach to the process of Europe's cultural definition with an assessment of the impact of Islamic imperialism. His controversial interpretation, now called the Pirenne Thesis, brought the history of the non-European Mediterranean world permanently into the purview of European historians.

## The Byzantine Empire
## from Constantine to Leo the Isaurian

Within the Roman Empire, there had always been a variety of languages and cultures as well as regional differences in economic and military conditions. Despite these differences, the empire had been one both in theory and practice. The government was Latin and military, an elaborate superstructure that held the empire together. Students in Asia Minor, the Near East, and Egypt learned Latin, and from the evidence of lesson books discovered in Egypt, containing translations of Virgil into the native language, it would seem that study of the language has not changed since ancient times. The spread of artistic motifs also demonstrates the unity of the empire. Near Eastern Christians created the icon, the simple representation of holy figures on which the worshiper could concentrate as he prayed. Soon such images were found throughout the empire. The portrayal of the Madonna and Child common in Christian art derived from the pre-Christian Egyptian practice of representing the goddess Isis and her son Horus on medallions and in sculpture.

Many examples of the internationalization of local ideas and cultural motifs could be drawn from the period after Constantine established his capital at Byzantium (renamed Constantinople soon after Constantine's death). The decision to set up a new center at this old Greek trading city was not an attempt to move the empire to, or even to refocus it in, the East. Throughout the third century, emperors had established capitals in the cities from which they could most efficiently organize the defense and government of the empire. At one time or another Rome, Milan, Treves (Trier), Sirmium, and Nicomedia had all been capitals. Throughout the fourth century, Latin remained the official language of the empire, and the governing classes continued to see the empire as the great state of earlier times.

The limiting of the imperial system and the transformation of the world empire into an Eastern one resulted from events that took place during the fifth century. The progressive isolation of Europe from the rest of the Mediterranean world is usually considered a consequence of the rise of the Byzantine and Islamic empires, but it might be more fruitful to see the Byzantine state as a product of its isolation from the West. By the late fifth century, the Ostrogoths, Visigoths, Franks, Vandals, and other tribes had destroyed the unity of the empire and had made Constantinople the capital of the East. Separated from the West and the ancient sources of armed might organized under a Latin or Latinized hierarchy, the Eastern part of the empire began to use its own resources for governing its rich provinces. This process has been characterized as the change from a military, Latin government and bureaucracy to a civilian, Greek and Near Eastern one. In the fifth century, increasing numbers of Egyptians and Syrians, long excluded from the institutions of the central authority by the Western heritage and cultural bias of the government, made their way to Constantinople and into the imperial administration. Under the emperor Anastasius (491–518), the civilianization of imperial government was accelerated, and the great officials of his government—the financial wizards, advisors, and lesser administrators—were intelligent careerists from the Eastern provinces. As Constantinople and its government attracted educated men and gained control of the sinews of the Eastern part of the empire now cut off from the Western part, it ceased being the capital and became the "ruling city." Constantinople was no longer just the hub of government; it was the mistress of the empire.

The fifth century was a period of renewed trouble on the eastern borders. Persia, under revived Sassanid leadership, successfully attacked the empire. To meet this threat, the emperors had to organize a military machine of considerable proportions, and the way in which they did it demonstrates the shifting governmental and cultural focus of the empire. Zeno I (479–491) deflected the threat from the Ostrogoths by sending them westward to conquer Italy instead of trying to incorporate them into his army as mercenaries. He relied on Isaurian troops from eastern Asia Minor in his struggle against the Persians. Anastasius reduced Isaurian influence in the court and army, but he too relied on Eastern troops to defend the empire's eastern border.

Anastasius' Eastern-oriented policy also led him to take a firm role in religious affairs and to refuse to heed papal, orthodox commands to destroy heresies that rested on deeply ingrained modes of thought. Monophysitism, a Christology that emphasized the unity of Christ's nature (*monos,* single; *physis,* nature) and the divineness of that nature, had been condemned by the Council of Chalcedon (451), but Anastasius resisted Roman appeals that he wipe out Monophysitism because he recognized that toleration of deep-seated beliefs in the Greek and Eastern churches formed the basis for the peace of the Church under Constantinople's leadership. Westerners and consequently modern historians have emphasized the doctrinal leanings of emperors during this period, but the emperors themselves rarely took doctrinal differences very seriously. Anastasius, who died leaving a large surplus in the imperial treasury and a bureaucracy filled with intelligent, well-educated, and able men, looked on religious differences primarily as a political problem.

Anastasius was succeeded by a soldier from the Balkans, Justin I (518–527). Justin was a traditional Latin soldier-emperor, and his reign might have led to the reestablishment of the military form of imperial government had it not been for his nephew and heir Justinian, who played a large role in Justin's court. Educated in Constantinople, Justian married Theodora, a courtesan from a family connected with the racing stables in the Hippodrome, the city stadium, and he studied with the highly educated bureaucrats gathered by his uncle's predecessor. When he succeeded his uncle to the throne in 527, Justinian inaugurated a decade of exuberant cultural and political revival that has left its mark on all subsequent history, in the West as well as in the East.

At the beginning of his reign, Justinian (527–565), strengthened the bureaucratic machinery left by his predecessors and sought to consolidate imperial life under its authority. He commissioned a council of great lawyers, under the leadership of Tribonian, a major court official, to organize and restate the whole corpus of Roman law. This project was begun in 527, and its product, the *Corpus Juris Civilis* (Corpus of Civil Law), was ready for circulation in 531. A second, augmented edition (the version that has been preserved) was issued in 534. In the *Corpus,* Justinian's officials achieved what earlier codifiers, like those commissioned by Theodosius II (ca. 438), had failed to accomplish. They brought the enormous, confused body of classical Roman law and jurisprudence into a coherent and comprehensive scheme. Like the contemporary works of Cassiodorus, Boethius, and others, this work preserved the core of the Roman legal tradition but did not include many riches of that tradition. The project manifested Justinian's vision of a restored empire made possible by the successful administrative efforts of his predecessors.

Justinian's leadership faced one grave threat in these early years, the Nika riots of 532. This mob violence (named for the cry used by the mobs—*Nika,* vanquish) erupted in response to government fiscal measures and quickly became a general attack against hated ministers in Justinian's administration. The seriousness of the uprising stemmed from its foundation in the circus factions of the city, the Blues and Greens. These groups had originated as clubs that organized the games in the circus and put up rival teams. The rivalry had become tense and had often led to street violence. In the 480s the emperor Zeno had taken the extraordinary step of arming the factions as an *ad hoc* militia against the threat posed by the Ostrogoths. As a result, the mobs were truly dangerous by the time Justinian came to power. In rising against the government, they joined forces and burned and looted the city. Very little was left standing in the center of the imperial capital. At a crucial point in the rebellion, Justinian was ready to flee, but Theodora convinced him to resist the threat, arguing, it was said, that the purple made a fine burial shroud. In fact, she obviously recognized that to leave the city was to lose the empire, since someone would step in to restore order. A new emperor would hunt down Justinian; it was better to take a chance with the mobs.

The gamble paid off. Within a short time the rebellion collapsed; Justinian's troops effected a blood bath. The experience of the rebellion had a cathartic influence on Justinian and impelled him to renewed creative activity. In 533 he sent an army to North Africa under the brilliant general Belisarius, who had participated in the government's suppression of the Nika riots. Thus began the conquests that reestablished Byzantine rule in North Africa, Sicily, and parts of Italy. The wars engendered by Justinian's effort to reassert Roman authority in Italy have already been discussed.

The destruction of much of the city during the riots gave Justinian the opportunity to enter on a great building program. He did it on a scale befitting his conception of Rome's majesty and his recognition that Constantinople was the seat of that majesty. Hagia Sophia had been built first by Constantine and had been destroyed and rebuilt once before around 400. Justinian commissioned two Greeks, Anthemius of Tralles and Isidore of Miletus, to construct a completely new type of church on a magnificent scale. The church, described in the last chapter, was completed in just under six years. In addition, the emperor dedicated twenty-five other churches in the city and its suburbs. He also built new baths, aqueducts, cisterns, and numerous buildings elsewhere in the empire. Such an extensive program required great financial outlays, and throughout his reign, Justinian experimented with new forms of taxation and new ways to create a stable income for the government. About 541 silk manufacture became a government monopoly, and during the 540s Justinian showed himself to be not only a first-rate spender but also an excellent cost-cutter. He reduced the upkeep of roads and ended the old, and expensive, system of government-supported transport. Such measures became necessary when the flamboyant spirit of the 530s was ended by the revival of conflict with the Persians in 540.

Although Belisarius led the army that defeated the Vandals in 535, this commemorative coin portrays the emperor Justinian as the victor. Coins were one of the principal means for disseminating propaganda in the Roman Empire, and the imperial government kept close control of minting.

In the late sixth century, Ravenna became the showcase, as well as the administrative center, of renewed Roman (Byzantine) power in Italy. The new basilica church of Sant' Apollinare Nuovo was decorated with Byzantine mosaics.

This rare survival of early medieval textile art proves that the textual evidence indicating that Carolingian weavers excelled is not misleading. This fragment of silk from the mid-eighth century shows two hunters attacking lions.

Under Shah Khusro I, the Persians moved against the eastern provinces and took Antioch, the second city of the empire. The shah offered to sell the city back to Justinian. At about the same time, the Slavs moved into the Balkans and destroyed Byzantine authority there. The military disasters occurred against the backdrop of a plague that ravaged between 541 and 543. (The epidemic recurred in various places throughout the Mediterranean until the 570s.) Justinian was forced to take extreme measures: he reduced the campaign in the West to a holding operation; he cut the costs and programs of the imperial government; he started an assiduous search for new sources of revenue. Under his aegis, Justinian's military leaders began to experiment with new technology—leading a century later to the development of "Greek fire,"[1] which made Byzantine fleets a permanent threat—and with

---

[1] Greek fire was an incendiary material—apparently based on petroleum—that burned on the surface of water. It was therefore very effective against ships.

new tactics designed for small armies. In 552 the new studies proved their value when a well-planned and well-executed campaign broke Gothic resistance in Italy. On the eastern frontier, Justinian compensated for the lack of men by constructing a string of fortifications, and on all fronts he replaced military operations with diplomatic ones whenever he could. By the 560s, the imperial government, under an emperor popularly thought never to sleep, had defeated the Goths, held off Khusro I, pacified North Africa, establishing a strong, fortified frontier there, and built an elaborate system of alliances on the Danube border.

However these activities had severely strained the empire. The former state transport system, for example, had been not only an important link among the far-flung regions of the empire but of crucial economic importance in many areas. When the network was destroyed in the southwestern part of Asia Minor, the farmers of the region went bankrupt. They were too far from the coast to ship their produce to the Mediterranean and had earned their income by selling fodder to the state transport system. This is only one example of what happened to the empire under Justinian's regime. He inherited a full treasury and left an empty one.

Justinian had also reduced the size of the government and taken increasing power into his own hands. On the one hand, this was just another way to save money. On the other hand, it was a natural result of the recurrent crises that required the kind of decisive, centralized power the vast bureaucracy could not exercise. In the end, it meant that even the most capable emperor had too much to do.

The emperor Maurice (582–602) was an able man, but he could not cope effectively with the simultaneous breakdown of Justinian's constructions. Pressure on the Danube border increased; the Lombards invaded Italy; the Persians became aggressive again. After Maurice, the succession of the incompetent Phocas caused the empire to reach its nadir. By the time Phocas died in 610, the empire consisted of the city of Constantinople. Asia Minor had been overrun by the Persians and had become a satrapy of the Persian Empire. The Balkans and Greece had been conquered and settled by Slavs and Altaic peoples, such as the Bulgars and Avars. Byzantine authority in Italy was confined to the malaria-ridden marshes around Ravenna and some areas of Apulia and Calabria. Heraclius, who succeeded Phocas in 610, can be excused for his doubts about the possibility of reconstructing Justinian's edifice.

Heraclius (610–641) was the scion of the family that ruled North Africa for the empire. When he arrived in Constantinople, he judged the situation hopeless. Loading the remains of the imperial treasury on a ship, Heraclius planned to transfer the government to Carthage and to rebuild from there. But the ship was wrecked and sunk in a storm, and the new emperor found himself wholly without the means to govern. At this point, the patriarch of Constantinople promised to furnish Heraclius with the Church's wealth if he

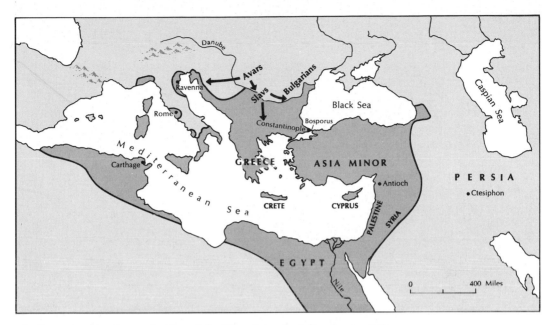

The Byzantine Empire on the Eve of the Rise of the Arab Empire, ca. 630

would try to drive the Persians out of Asia Minor. The emperor decided to make the effort.

During the next twelve years, Heraclius rebuilt the army and prepared for a long campaign. In 622 he shipped his small, highly trained army down the coast of Asia Minor to Miletus and put all his resources into a campaign against the Persians. This war took on the aspect of a crusade. Heraclius burned the fire-temples built shortly before by the Persian governors and colonists sent to make Persian rule over Asia Minor and the Near East permanent. He also forced all conquered people to convert to Christianity. The campaign was bitter and bloody. Heraclius met several large Persian armies, and when he had finally driven the Persians out of his territory in 626, Persian military strength was permanently broken. In 627 the emperor was able to raid deep into Persia, destroying towns, temples, estates, and even the shah's great palace at Dastgerd. The shock turned the Persian nobility against their once successful and popular ruler, Khusro II, and they murdered him in 628. By that time, Heraclius had reestablished Byzantine rule in Syria, Palestine, and Egypt. The empire had recovered—on the surface. The wars had destroyed the prosperity of the Eastern provinces and left them crucially weakened. They became a drain on the imperial fisc and energies rather than an income-producing region on which renewed imperial fortunes could be based. When the Arabs, united and inspired by the new Islamic religion, began to expand their power in the 630s, neither the Byzan tine nor the Persian empires could resist them. The Persian Empire was in chaos following the death of Khusro II, and Heraclius' government could not muster the wherewithal to meet the new threat.

Nevertheless, Heraclius had recaptured the eastern Mediterranean in time to preserve its Christian culture, and the area remained the center of Christianity during the seventh century. The first great archbishop of Canterbury, Theodore (669–690), came from Tarsus in Asia Minor, and a significant commerce in goods and ideas still existed between East and West. Heraclius established a dynasty and therefore stabilized the succession to the throne, but his successors steadily lost control of the territories he had recaptured. Arab expansion, the increasing settlement of Slavs within the empire in the southern Balkans and in Greece, and the establishment of a Bulgarian kingdom just north of the Danube stymied any attempt by the emperors to rebuild the empire. Byzantine control of the seas was challenged by the Arabs, and Constantinople was repeatedly brought under direct attack (ca. 669–677). The mighty fortress stood firm—mainly because of superior Byzantine defensive tactics and the use of "Greek fire." Although the southern and eastern provinces were lost to Islam, Asia Minor and the other predominantly Greek areas of the empire remained. Thus the decline in territorial extent was partially offset by an increasing homogeneity in language and culture.

The last fifteen years of the Heraclian dynasty were troubled by palace revolutions of exceptional ferocity, culminating in the deposition and murder of the emperor in 711. The next six years of anarchy were brought to an end by the successful bid for power by an Anatolian general, Leo, founder of the Isaurian dynasty (717–802), under which the empire was restored once more to a flourishing condition. The accession of Leo III the Isaurian (717–741) came at one of the most critical moments in Byzantine history, the great siege of Constantinople by the Arabs in 717 and 718, on both land and sea. By using "Greek fire," by employing a great underwater chain to bar the entrance into the Golden Horn (the harbor of Constantinople), and by gaining the timely alliance of Bulgarians who attacked the Arabs on land, Leo successfully defended the capital. He was the hero of the empire, the savior of Constantinople, and he followed up this victory by a series of campaigns in Asia Minor that halted the first stage of Arab expansion (ca. 630–730) at the expense of Byzantine territory.

Equally significant, Leo symbolized in the internal politics of the empire the triumph of the landed aristocracy of Asia Minor over the imperial court and bureaucracy, whose interests were represented by the last rulers of the Heraclian dynasty. Although he has been given credit for more than he actually accomplished, Leo the Isaurian was responsible for the most important legal and administrative reforms since the age of Justinian. Several new codes in Greek are usually associated with Leo. The most important was the *Ecloga* (selection), issued around 726, an official condensation in Greek of parts of the *Corpus Juris Civilis* together with amendments to bring the law up to date. In governmental reform, Leo and his successors regularized the system of administrative units, called themes, of the empire. The most important change was the reduction of the size of the themes, which like Diocletian's earlier reform of the provincial administration made the government more effective. None of these developments impressed contemporaries as much as the new religious policy of Leo the Isaurian, which will be discussed later in connection with the rise of Islam and relations between the Byzantine Empire and the Latin West.

From the end of the fifth to the middle of the eighth century, no state in the civilized East or in the barbarian world, either East or West, achieved more against greater odds or preserved its own heritage more tenaciously and successfully than did the Byzantine Empire. Nor, it must be added, was any state less appreciated for what it was or what it accomplished. Byzantium was in fact a bastion of defense against the westward expansion of the Avars, Persia, and Islam. But to the Germanic kingdoms of the West the Eastern Empire was an aggressor state that had tried under Justinian to reconquer the lost Roman provinces of the western Mediterranean. The failure of this aggression left Byzantine power in the West very restricted, although it took another five centuries for it to be destroyed altogether. The empire had often demonstrated its tenaciousness, its ability to retreat into strongholds from which it might sally forth when conditions permitted. The Western strongholds demonstrated this ability as well as any, but conditions never permitted the sally.

## Islam and the Rise of the Arab Empire

A great deal more is known about the development of Christianity than about the formation of Islam. This is true not only because more time has been spent studying the origins of Christianity but also because Christianity arose out of an articulate, literate civilization, while Islam grew out of a largely illiterate, disorganized, nomadic culture. No substantial body of pre-Islamic Arabic literature exists in which the seminal ideas of the new religion are apparent. The rise of Islam was the principal catalyst in the growth of an Arabic civilization.

The seat of Islam, the Arabian Peninsula, had been bounded by great imperial civilizations for millennia. The ancient civilizations of Egypt and Mesopotamia had once flourished to the north, northeast, and west. In more recent times, the Persian Empire stretched its power into the northeastern sector of the peninsula, the Roman (later Byzantine) Empire into the northern and northwestern sector. To the south, the Yemenite kingdom controlled the midpoint of the great trading network between the Mediterranean and the Far East. This kingdom was very ancient and very rich, and kingdoms established in the central portion of the Arabian Peninsula in the early centuries of the Christian era were most often organized and ruled by an aristocracy from the south. The Yemenites competed with the Abyssinians, who lived on the African side of the Red Sea, for control of the mouth of the Red Sea. Since the Romans traded by way of the Red Sea and the peninsula on a land route to Yemen, it was essential for the Romans to maintain good relations with these kingdoms. This policy was complicated by the rivalry between Yemen and Abyssinia and by the slow decline of the Yemenite kingdom; by the first half of the fourth century, Yemen was dominated by Abyssinia.

Religion cannot be excluded from this political picture. Ancient Arabic religion, in Yemen as well as to the north, was pagan—a bewildering variety of deities and cults. By the fifth century missionaries from Egypt had converted the Abyssinians to Monophysite Christianity. When the Abyssinians conquered Yemen, they forced the Yemenites to convert too. This religious element of the Abyssinian domination gave Persia, locked in conflict with Rome, a means of countering the new, pro-Roman aristocracy in southern Arabia. They sent their forces into the southern kingdom under the banner of Nestorian Christianity, whose sectaries had taken refuge in Persia (the Persian religion Zoroastrianism was too parochial to serve the purpose). In this way, Yemenite resistance to the Abyssinians became involved in the international struggle between Rome and Persia and in the religious controversies of Eastern Christianity. The struggle in Yemen continued through the sixth century and issued in Persian victory in the 590s, when Persian armies were engaged in a general attack on the Byzantine Empire. The struggle affected the interior of the peninsula only intermittently, however. A succession of kingdoms was established in the desert by southerners, Yemenite and Abyssinian, to control the Arab-Bedouin tribes, which was necessary to protect the land routes across the peninsula. But the kingdoms were artificial constructs that never lasted very long, and the nomadic tribes generally retained their independence and their ancient culture, unaffected by developments on the borders of their desert world. Only the Monophysite churches attempted to convert the Bedouins, and at the beginning of the sixth and seventh centuries bishops were appointed for the largest camps. The influence of these Christian missionaries may have been a factor in the formation of a federation of Bedouin tribes that fought and defeated the Persians in 611 (perhaps 604), at the height of Persian power elsewhere in the Mediterranean world. This battle was not very important from the Persian standpoint, but it provided the Arabs with a symbol of their strength in national unity and of the possibility for national expansion.

The Monophysite bishops had little impact on the desert world of the peninsula. In the early seventh century, most of the nomads were pagans not, it seems, because they were self-conscious conservatives but because the organized religions did not maintain a sufficient presence in their midst to convert them. The south was Nestorian Christian, the north Monophysite, and many Jews had migrated to the peninsula, along the caravan routes, after the rebellions of 66 to 70 and 135 in Judea. These Jewish immigrants organized themselves in tribes, as did the Arabs. Not all Arab tribes were nomadic; some had settled in cities along the trade routes. Medina and Mecca were tribal cities engaged in the international trade and trying to extend their influence over the Bedouins living in their vicinity. Commerce was a communal effort; in each town, the tribes cooperated in sending large caravans north and south twice a year. This independent Arab participation in the trading network, like the confederacy that had fought the Persians in the first decade of the seventh century, gave the peoples and cities of the peninsula a sense of their own power and potential. These nationalist, or potentially nationalist, feelings became evident in the last decades of the sixth and the first decade of the seventh centuries. Mohammed, born about 570, became a major figure in this development.

Mohammed was born into the leading tribe in Mecca, but he was orphaned at an early age. He was, therefore, raised by relatives and remained on the fringes of the city's wealth and power throughout his youth. Although he did not inherit any significant fortune or position, his kinship connections gave him the opportunity to enter the commercial life of the community, and as a young man, he apparently traveled with the caravans to Syria and perhaps to Yemen. Mohammed appears to have had an abiding interest in religion, but he had little time for it before the 590s, when he married a rich widow. From then on, he devoted himself entirely to religious study. He received his first call, in an inchoate vision later identified as the archangel Gabriel, sometime before 610, and after a period of confusion about his mission, he began to preach a new religion, claiming to be the prophet of the one God. He preached his message in private for about three years before widening the circle of his audience to include the Meccan public. Mohammed's following grew, but he also met considerable opposition among members of his own as well as other tribes, which became intense as the political implications of his movement became clear. In the loose, tribal framework of Meccan government, any person who attracted a following became a political figure and could not ignore the political potential of his movement. Thus while Mohammed indicated no desire to take control of the government of Mecca, many merchants and tribal leaders considered his movement a political threat. The tension created by Mohammed's preaching did not erupt in violence only because the opposition was incapable of organizing itself and because, ironically, the tribal system that he undermined with his movement protected him from his opponents. The two principal protectors were his uncle and his wife. His uncle, leader of the clan from which Mohammed himself stemmed, honored the tie of kinship and supported him, while remaining a pagan. His wife was able to neutralize her clan. When both these people died in 619, Mohammed lost even more than might have been expected. His wife's clan was no longer tied to him, but neither was his own. The new leader of his clan refused to honor the ties of blood, no doubt because Mohammed claimed that his dead uncle, having remained a pagan, had gone to hell. In this new situation, Mohammed recognized that a community based on spiritual fellowship rather than on blood ties would have little chance to grow in the homogeneous tribal environment of Mecca.

The spiritual basis of Mohammed's movement limited its development in Mecca, but other communities were more receptive to its message and more conducive to its growth. To the north was Medina, an oasis that took its name from the Aramaic word for "legal district," a name that reflected the character of the city. Medina was a heterogeneous settlement of village communities that included three large Jewish as well as a variety of Arab tribes. In the early 620s, the district was disrupted by internal strife, and in 622 the tribal leaders appealed to Mohammed, as a spiritual and charismatic leader, to come north and save the city. In the summer of that year Mohammed sent about seventy followers to the oasis; he arrived there about September 4. Sixteen years later, this migration, called the Hegira and reckoned as having occurred on July 16, 622, was established as the beginning of the Islamic era. This interpretation of the importance of the migration was not unreasonable, since the invitation extended by the leaders of Medina implied their recognition of Mohammed's position as the prophet of God.

Soon after he settled in Medina, Mohammed began raiding Meccan caravans. At first, the raids seem to have been necessitated by the Islamic community's need for some means of support, but the Meccan response, and Mohammed's success in uniting the Medinan tribes under his leadership, turned the raiding activities into a war between the two cities. The struggle reached a stalemate by 628, but in that year Mohammed made a move that led to his victory, by a very circuitous route. Mecca was an ancient cult center focused on the Ka'ba (Cube), a shrine to which pagan Arabs paid special homage and to which many came as pilgrims each year. In 628 Mohammed and about fifteen hundred followers joined the annual pilgrimage. When Mohammed reached the outskirts of the city, the Meccans barred him, and negotiations began that led to the postponement of the pilgrimage until the next year, when the Meccans would evacuate the town and permit Mohammed to remain there for three days. The Islamic community was disappointed and humiliated, but Mohammed stood by his compromise because it not only implied recognition of his community as a political entity in a basically tribal society, but it gave him the freedom to proselytize among the Bedouins living near Mecca. By the next year, Mohammed had brought most of those tribes into alliance with Medina, now reorganized as an Islamic state, and the Meccan leadership recognized the futility of resistance and submitted to Mohammed. The Meccan aristocracy had more experience in government and warfare than the Medinans, and they were related to the Prophet. In the early Islamic period, many of these men, such as the military genius Khalid ibn al-Walid, exercised leadership in the growing Arab state, even though Medina remained its administrative center.

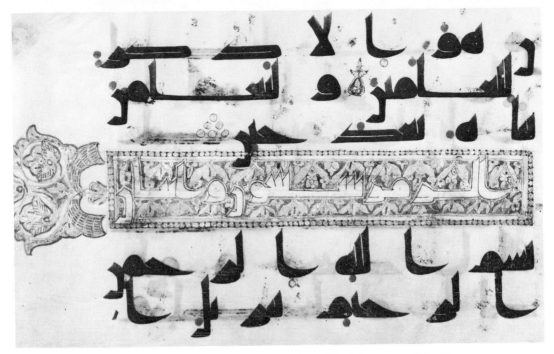

Europeans were not the only ones to illuminate manuscripts. This deluxe copy of the Koran, illuminated in Egypt in the eighth or ninth century, shows the same interest in beautiful books.

In 630 the Prophet led an army north against the Byzantine territories. He also condoned attacks on the Persian Empire, thrown into disorder by the successes of Heraclius and by the murder of Khusro II in 628, and extended his influence south to the Yemenite kingdom. When he died on June 8, 632, after a brief illness, Mohammed left a state that included most of the Arabian Peninsula and was expanding to the north and northeast at the expense of the Byzantine and Persian empires. But military ventures did not occupy the center of Mohammed's attention during his last years. After he incorporated Mecca into his state, he reformulated his religious ideas, bringing the ancient cults centered on the Ka'ba into conformity with the basic tenets of his teaching and thus smoothing the transition from paganism to Islam. At the same time, he sharpened the distinction between Islam and the religions of the Bible, Judaism and Christianity. Earlier he had spoken well of Jews and Christians, now he turned against them. From this period dates the Koranic revelation "Fight those to whom the Book was given, who believe not in Allah and in the Last Judgement, and who forbid not what Allah and his apostle have forbidden and who do not practice the true religion" (Koran 9:29). From this late period also stem many of the characteristic prohibitions of Islam: against the eating of pork and the drinking of alcoholic beverages, against marrying non-Moslems, and against the participation of non-Moslems in the pilgrimages taken over from pagan religion. All these prohibitions helped define the Moslem and to distinguish him from infidels.

Mohammed's achievement was to unite Arabia under a single approach to the divine that derived not from outside but from the culture and traditions of the peninsula. In this respect, Islam was analogous to Christianity—a religion formed by a cultural milieu that later became a cohesive force in that milieu. Only the creation of a spiritual community that embodied the common elements of Arabia's tribal society made it possible for the peninsula's people to break the bonds of tribalism and achieve a political union that could become a force in world history. Islam literally created the Arab Empire.

Before turning to the growth of the Arab Empire after Mohammed's death, something should be said of his religious ideas. They were an original formulation of age-old Semitic and Near Eastern conceptions of the divine and of ethics and are striking for their great simplicity. Mohammed had a slight knowledge of Christianity, and although he was more knowledgeable about Judaism—since Jews constituted a significant part of the population of the Arabian Peninsula—he did not rely much on Jewish thought. His teaching can be divided into two parts, the doctrinal and the social or ethical. The tenets of faith and the obligations imposed on the faithful were extremely simple and only five in number; much of the success of Islam as a religion has been due to its straightforward and easily intelligible doctrine. First, the Moslem must profess belief in only one God, Allah, and in Mohammed as his Prophet. Second, he must pray regularly, according to a simple ritual (later such prayer was prescribed at set intervals, five times a day, kneeling and facing toward Mecca). Third, the faithful must give charity to the poor of the Moslem community. Fourth, the holy month of Ramadan must be observed by fasting and a prohibition of all pleasures between sunrise and sundown. Fifth, the Moslem must, if at all possible, make at least one pilgrimage to the Ka'ba at Mecca.

The ethical teaching of Mohammed, while it embodies the highest moral principles, is even more impressive in its simplicity. Essentially, Mohammed preached peace, love of one's fellow men, and self-control. The Prophet's goal was to elevate his people's tribal notions of right and wrong, to substitute forgiveness for vengeance, and to abolish certain primitive customs that degraded the dignity and worth of human life. Thus, infanticide (by burying alive) was prohibited, the number of wives legally allowed to a man was reduced to four, and dietary prohibitions were imposed. The central tendency of Mohammed's religious and ethical teaching was against the polytheism and materialism of the Arab world. By achieving a higher spiritual life and obeying Mohammed's injunctions, the Moslem was promised an eternal paradise that would bring all the materialistic pleasures that the believer was asked to forego in this life. Although this concept of heaven was quite different from the Christian, the idea of hell was similar, and the celestial hierarchy of angels and demons (genii) was common to both religions.

No provision had been made for carrying on the work of Mohammed or for continuing the position of leadership that he had built for himself as founder of Islam. The crisis caused by his unexpected death was met by the election of one of the Prophet's intimate circle of early converts as his caliph (representative or vicar). This was Abu Bakr, Mohammed's father-in-law, whose caliphate (632–634) was spent largely in retaining the precarious allegiance of Bedouin tribes and preserving the movement intact. The fighting of this period was directed almost entirely against dissident Moslems or non-Moslem Arabs. At the end of Abu Bakr's brief reign, all Arabia had been at least nominally subjugated to Islam. From these campaigns in the desert emerged the great general, already mentioned, Khalid, "the Sword of God."

During the pre-Islamic period, the Arabs had occupied important territory in the world trading network that linked the Mediterranean and Near East with the Far East. As previously mentioned, the Romans and their Byzantine successors took an active interest in Arabian affairs because of the peninsula's strategic importance, and the Persians, who had other routes to the East, interfered in Arabian matters as part of their conflict with the Romans and Byzantines. The great powers that had influenced the peninsula and kept the Arabs disunified for so long became targets of Arab attack when Mohammed had succeeded in uniting the tribal societies. This new Arab expansionism had, of course, religious as well as political motives. The Moslem sought to glorify Mohammed's deeds as the seal of his faith, and thus there was great pressure within Islam to maintain the momentum of the Prophet's conquests.

Abu Bakr was succeeded as caliph by the Prophet's son-in-law Omar, who had contested the succession with Abu Bakr when Mohammed died in 632. During the ten years of Omar's caliphate, all of Palestine, Syria, and the Persian Empire was conquered, except for mopping-up operations in the interior. Damascus fell in 635. Jerusalem was taken in 638 at the end of a long siege and after the patriarch of the city secured a promise from the Arabs to respect Christian churches and worship. Jerusalem became (with Mecca and Medina) the third holy city of the Moslems. In 637 the Persian capital, Ctesiphon, had fallen. The Arabs sent border raids into India by 643. On the western front, Egypt was quickly reduced (640–642), although the Byzantine naval base at Alexandria was not permanently in Arab possession until 646. Arab columns pushed farther westward through the desert into the Byzantine North African provinces as far as Tripoli. Meanwhile, from the coastal cities of Syria and from Alexandria, the Arabs began to challenge Byzantine naval supremacy. By the middle of the seventh century they had defeated an imperial fleet off the coast of Asia Minor and occupied Cyprus.

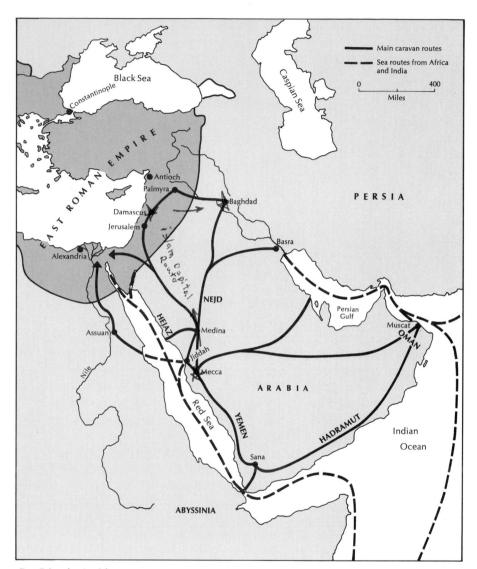

Pre-Islamic Arabia

The growing empire was organized from the center, although many factors militated against effective centralization. The caliph encouraged tribes, officially abolished by Mohammed but in actuality still a vital force in Arabic society, to settle as insulated, governing communities in administrative and military districts of the new provinces. A governor was appointed to each center, and toward the end of the seventh century, the governors delegated some of their jurisdictional power to judges, the *qadi*. The imperial government was a theocracy. Like Mohammed, the caliphs held both spiritual and temporal authority and recognized no distinction between them. Strikingly, this theocratic government did not enforce conversion to Islam in the conquered territories. Non-Moslems had to pay a heavy land tax and of course could not become government servants, but they were otherwise left to themselves.

After the middle of the century Arab expansion slowed almost to a halt. Internal dissension among the Arabs had broken out over the administration and exploitation of the conquered provinces and over the succession to the caliphate. A brief civil war, from 656 to 661, ended with the murder of the last Orthodox caliph, Ali, nephew and son-in-law of the Prophet. His successor, Muawiyah (661–680), abolished the elective principle of succession to the caliphate and founded the Omayyad dynasty, moving the capital of Islam to Damascus. The Omayyad caliphate (661–750) represented the triumph of the imperialistic Arab aristocracy, which was more interested in conquest than in religion, over the traditions of Mohammed's theocracy of Medina as represented by the Orthodox caliphate. It was also a triumph over the disorderly desert Arabs, who had participated in the expansion primarily for booty and were impatient of restraint or organization from a central government. Another reason for the slowing down of Arab expansion after the 650s was that on all fronts the Arabs began to meet real resistance. The phenomenal rapidity of the first conquests was due less to Arab military ability than to the exhaustion of Byzantine and Persian military resources, the collapse of the Persian monarchy, and the general disaffection of the conquered peoples for their Byzantine and Persian rulers. The Byzantine provincials were everywhere oppressed by efficient taxation, and in Palestine and Syria they felt a closer cultural and ethnic affinity to the Semitic Arabs than they did to their Greek rulers. The predominantly Greek and Orthodox provinces of Asia Minor, however, put up a stiff resistance, and in western North Africa the Berbers were a non-Semitic people who allied with the Byzantines to resist the Arab advance.

Under the Omayyad caliphate expansion was resumed but at a slower pace. Notable successes were achieved at sea, where Arab fleets secured naval supremacy in the eastern Mediterranean by the end of the seventh century. In the East, Moslem armies crossed the Indus River, pushed north as far as Samarkand, and reached the Caucasus Mountains from the Black Sea to the Caspian Sea. Slight progress was made on the Asia Minor front, and repeated attacks by sea on Constantinople (ca. 669–677) failed by a narrow margin. These developments cut off most of the Byzantine trade routes to the Far East and imperiled communications by sea between Constantinople and the West. Byzantine commerce suffered, and Byzantine control of the Western provinces of Italy and North Africa was in jeopardy.

After a generation of fighting in western North Africa, Carthage finally fell in 698, when an Arab victory at sea over an imperial fleet bringing reinforcements finally broke Byzantine resistance. Meanwhile, the campaign against the Berbers slowly turned in favor of the Arabs, who gained not only the territories of Algeria and Morocco but also the military assistance of the conquered Berbers, whose conversion to the new faith brought to Islam a religious fanaticism previously unknown in the Moslem expansion.

The Moslem conquest of the Visigothic kingdom of Spain began in 711, when the Berber leader Tarik led a band of his men across the straits between Africa and Spain, landing on the great rock that bears Tarik's name (gib-al-Tarik, or Gibraltar). Divisions within the Visigothic kingdom made conquest of the Iberian Peninsula easy. Within a couple of months, Toledo, the capital city, fell as the Moslem Berber forces swept north. The Berber raiders avoided most of the walled cities, such as Seville. Arab reinforcements soon followed the Berbers to the peninsula, and they slowly reduced the cities. Together the Berbers and Arabs conquered the entire peninsula except the mountainous northwest corner, where the Christian state of Asturias was able to maintain a precarious independence. After a brief period of consolidation, the Moslems crossed the Pyrenees into Septimania, which had remained under Visigothic domination protected from Frankish aggression by alliance with the Ostrogoths and later the Lombards. In 720 the Moslems conquered the province, establishing the ancient city of Narbonne as their capital, and raided Merovingian Aquitaine, where for about ten years they met stiff resistance from Eudes, the duke of Aquitaine, who had maintained *de facto* autonomy from the Frankish royal government. The further history of this Moslem presence in southern Gaul will be discussed in the next chapter. In Spain, considerable disunity was caused by conflict between the Berbers and Arabs.

Under the Omayyad caliphate, the governmental structure of the new empire evolved its basic form. The rapidity of the conquests made the Arabic administrative organization founded by Omar ineffectual, and most governmental functions remained in the hands of provincials, under Arab military authority. In the late seventh century, the caliphate's system took over and replaced the previous administrations. Arabic became the official language of law and government, and new Arabic coinage (in gold, silver, and copper) began to circulate in the 690s. At first all Moslems had been exempt from the land taxes paid by the conquered provincials who refused to convert. The progress of conversion in the empire, however, with the consequent loss of revenues, finally forced the caliphate to cancel the Moslems' exemption. To distinguish between Moslem and non-Moslem, the government created a new head tax, paid only by non-Moslems. In addition to these political changes, the Moslems began to absorb elements of Byzantine and Persian culture, laying the foundation for a magnificent Arabic civilization in later cen-

Islam and the West, ca. 750

turies. The Omayyad period produced little in this regard except in architecture, of which several fine examples survive in Damascus and Jerusalem.

The imperial system of the Omayyads was based on the Bedouin tribes of the Arabian Peninsula. The extreme cohesiveness of the Bedouin aristocracy preserved it from being assimilated into the great mass of newly converted Moslems among the conquered peoples. But it also isolated it from the subject populations of the empire. The Bedouin armies swept over the provinces and established themselves on the borders, leaving the provincial peoples to continue in their traditional sociopolitical framework, "a garden protected by our spears." This kind of laissez-faire imperialism had many advantages, since it did not impose heavy burdens or try to force major changes on the subject populations. But the Bedouin aristocracy had organized the empire according to the values of the desert, which did not fit the settled life and cultural traditions of populations long accustomed to an imperial system based on an educated bureaucracy. Furthermore, the Bedouins were isolated from the core of Islam. The new religion had been grafted onto their ancient value system and tribal society, and the tension of differing values increased as a literate piety, based on the Koran, became the mainstream in Islam.

The growing opposition in the empire to the Arab supremacy led to a rebellion in 750. The Omayyad caliphate at Damascus had committed its prestige and resources to the conquest of the Byzantine Empire but had repeatedly failed to break its resistance. Between 669 and 717, Arab fleets attacked Constantinople several times but never succeeded in taking the city. In the early eighth century, the Byzantine forces, under the new Isaurian emperors, began a successful counterattack. The caliphs' setbacks in the Mediterranean permitted an opposition group to form around the converted aristocracy of Moslem Persia. The Omayyad caliphate, engaged in the creation of a new Mediterranean empire, had established itself in Damascus in the buffer zone between the two great empires it sought to replace. But the heart of imperial organization in the Near East, the source of imperial civilization and government, had been in Iran and Mesopotamia, and the progress of Islam there shifted the political as well as cultural focus of the new empire to those centers. The rebellion of 750 began in Iran and resulted in the fall of the Omayyads. The new Persian dynasty, the Abbasids, consolidated their imperial power by founding Baghdad in 762. The Persians did not simply replace the Bedouin aristocracy in the imperial administration;

The wealth of the caliphate of Córdoba is demonstrated by the mosque built there in the ninth century. The building, one of the largest in Europe during the Middle Ages, shows the influence of Byzantine styles in its elaborate decoration, but it was done by local craftsmen. It has been preserved because it was transformed into a church after the reconquest.

they really created the imperial administration in the garden protected by Bedouin spears. By the end of the eighth century, imperial power was in Persian hands, and the empire was being unified culturally under Persian leadership. The new center of Islam was only thirty-five miles from the ancient Persian capital of Ctesiphon; the Abbasids and their supporters sought to re-create the prosperous, cultured world of Khusro I and Khusro II. The move from Damascus to Baghdad was, in effect, a symbol of the transformation of the Islamic Empire from an expansionist, frontier society into an established empire.

### Suggestions for Further Reading

**Secondary Works**    Two excellent histories of Byzantium are A. A. Vasiliev, *History of the Byzantine Empire, 324–1453,* 2nd ed. (Madison, Wis., 1952), and G. Ostrogorsky, *History of the Byzantine State* (Oxford, 1956). Also valuable and interesting is C. Diehl, *Byzantium: Greatness and Decline* (New Brunswick, N.J., 1957). The most recent treatment is in *The Cambridge Medieval History,* vol. 4, 2nd ed. (Cambridge, 1966). An excellent short survey of the Moslems is G. E. von Grunebaum, *Classical Islam: A History, 600–1258* (Chicago, 1970). Another good examination is B. Lewis, *The Arabs in History,* 4th ed. (London, 1958). P. K. Hitti, *History of the Arabs,* 6th ed. (London, 1958), and G. E. von Grunebaum, *Medieval Islam,* 2nd ed. (Chicago, 1954) are more detailed studies.

**Sources**    Procopius, *Secret History,* trans. R. Atwater (Ann Arbor, Mich., 1961) is an important source for the history of Justinian's reign. Constantine VII Porphyrogenitus' treatise on government is translated by R. Jenkins (with G. Moravcsik), *Constantine Porphyrogenitus, De administrando imperio* (London, 1962).

# 6 Europe in Transition: The Eighth Century

Certain periods in history stand out as times of great change, in which something ends and something begins, however difficult it might be to define precisely what the somethings are. The eighth century was one of those periods. By the beginning of that century, the Arab Empire controlled more than half of the Mediterranean littoral and had penetrated into Western Europe, and the Byzantine Empire had turned its back on Europe to face the permanent threat of the Arabs from the Near East. The Byzantine emperors continued sporadically to insinuate their influence into Eastern Europe, but substantially the empire had evolved into an Eastern power, both politically and culturally. Thus during the eighth century, Europe was set apart from the Mediterranean world it had once been part of, and by the end of the century Europeans had developed a consciousness of their separateness.

Within Europe, the Frankish kingdom became an enormous conglomerate of peoples and territories, which covered nearly the whole of what is now called Western Europe. This growth reached its peak under Charlemagne, whose forty-five year reign is a landmark in the history of Europe.

## The Rise of the Carolingians and the Crisis
## of the Eighth Century

From about 640 to 751, the Merovingian dynasty became almost an appendage of royal government in the Frankish kingdom. Dagobert (629–639), great-great-grandson of Clovis, was the last Merovingian king to exercise effective leadership in the realm; his successors reigned without ruling. Few of them had the physical strength to survive into manhood. Dagobert himself lived to a respectable old age of thirty-eight, but his two sons died at eighteen and twenty. The next king lived out a full span of thirty-eight years, but his sons reached only thirteen and eighteen. Under such circumstances it is remarkable that the royal race of the Merovingians was able to continue supplying kings at all. Obviously these kings were ineffective rulers. French historians have called them *rois fainéants* (do-nothing kings). Ascending their thrones as children or striplings, they were little more than figureheads in whose names their officials ruled. The maintenance of a *roi fainéant* by the Germanic kingdom demonstrates the amalgamation of Roman and Germanic society and ideas during the sixth century. To understand the significance and character of the development, the social and political structure of the Frankish kingdom must be studied.

Recent prosopographical studies (studies of the history of individuals and families) of the nobility of Roman and Frankish Gaul show that the Gallo-Roman aristocracy continued to function in its traditional bureaucratic and political roles, continued to control the churches, and only very slowly lost its social and cultural identity. The lineage of the Gallo-Roman families can still be traced into the eighth, even the ninth, century. The mastership of the Franks consisted in their monopoly of military power, which they had possessed for decades. By the late fifth century, the Franks and other Germanic peoples had become the main element in the "Roman" armies. The invasion of Gaul by the Franks might just as well be considered a military *coup d'état* that left the old bureaucracy intact.

This perspective on the invasions, partially engendered by new knowledge about the durability of Gallo-Roman society under Frankish rule, conforms to what is known about the history of Frankish settlement. Surprisingly, the invasions produced little outcry from the Romanized Gauls, which suggests that there occurred little disruption and a minimum of the sort of injustice and outrage usually associated with the invasions. The new rulers took control of an old, established, wealthy society. They controlled the army and dictated policy for the government, but the historic pattern of government in the province limited royal power, or at least the freedom of the kings to act as they wished. Furthermore, the kings had to contend with the Frankish nobility. Clovis was one of many kinglets, as the French historian Ferdinand Lot called them, and while he ruthlessly suppressed rival leaders, he could not destroy the whole noble class. Thus the Merovingian kings ruled with the support of their Roman and Frankish nobles, who were bound to them by personal and family ties. The other side of this political equation was, however, that the kings' power was limited by the wishes and ambitions of the aristocracy.

The early Germanic kings were little more than war leaders. Clovis and his successors maintained this ancient tradition, but their new position added attributes to their authority. The maintenance of minors and weaklings in a position of power marked the change. No such person could have maintained himself in the sixth century because the conception of the king as war leader meant that only the able and the forceful could reign. By the mid-seventh century, Roman ideas of permanent, bureaucratic, almost corporate, government had taken hold among the Germans. Contemporary chroniclers relate that only a Merovingian, descendant of Merovech and Clovis, could sit on the throne; it did not matter that government was actually carried on by others. The Roman tradition of government run by the aristocracy under the aegis of an autocratic ruler, whose authority had to be legally recognized but did not have to be real, had become established in Frankish Gaul.

Another sign of the changes that had taken place in Frankish political culture was the role played by an office, rather than an individual, in the government in which the *rois fainéants* were figureheads. The mayor of the palace (*major domus*) became the focal point of Frankish government and the prize for the leading noble families. The mayor of the palace was a household official originally responsible for the material well-being of the royal entourage. The position was honorable, however, and the king usually awarded it to a nobleman who was his companion. As a result, the man who held the mayoralty stepped naturally into a *de facto* regency when the king failed to meet his obligations. Throughout the Middle Ages, men found offices of royal households a strong base for the exercise of power.

Clovis had divided his kingdom among his four sons, but during the civil wars of the sixth and early seventh centuries, two of the subkingdoms, Neustria (in northern and western Gaul) and Austrasia (in northeastern Gaul and the Rhineland), emerged as the most important centers of power. After the Merovingian line degenerated, the mayors of the palaces in these kingdoms sought to gain control of the whole ancient *regnum Francorum* (kingdom of the Franks). In Austrasia, the union of the two most important noble families, the Arnulfings (who controlled the central bishopric of Metz) and the Pippinids (who had intermittently controlled the mayoralty), produced a powerful family that gained permanent control of the mayoralty under Pepin of Heristal. In Neustria, the contest for the mayoralty was more involved, but it did not weaken the office or the kingdom very significantly. In the 680s, the struggle for control of the whole realm intensified, leading in 687 to the Battle of Testry, in which Pepin won a decisive victory. After that, he was able to unite the royal courts under the mayor of Austrasia. Pepin then turned his energies to the task of restoring the central authority

and gaining control of outlying lands once ruled by the kings but now only nominally subject to Frankish power. Aquitaine in the southwest, Burgundy in the southeast, the Thuringians and Bavarians to the east, and the Bretons in the northwest were all ruled by local nobles who paid little attention to the central authority. The tendency of Pepin's activities was to reassert the Gallo-Roman tradition of centralized government. This did not mean that he sought to suppress the nobility but only that he forced the aristocratic rulers to recognize royal authority. The Frankish kingdom was still an aristocratic community, although Pepin did much to enhance the role and importance of the royal court.

Pepin died in 714 and was succeeded by two sons, who were minors. The principle that an office could be occupied by someone incapable of exercising it had spread from the kingship to the mayoralty. The weakness of the royal court, now again split in two and ostensibly governed by boys, encouraged widespread aristocratic rebellions, and Charles, an adult, although illegitimate, son of Pepin stepped in to save the situation. He of course saved it for himself rather than for his half brothers, who disappeared from the pages of history in short order. By 719 Charles was master of the Frankish kingdom and was ready to continue his father's work. At first, this work consisted of putting down rebellions, but it soon acquired a more positive aspect. For more than a century, Irish and Anglo-Saxon monks had been

This wood relief from a
Frankish casket (probably
early seventh century)
shows that the Franks used
the same round shields as
the Anglo-Saxons and that
their weapons were bows
and arrows and swords.
They were already using
chain mail at this early date;
it is represented by the
knobby upper clothing on
two of the attackers.

undertaking missionary work among the north German peoples. These monks
occasionally received support from the Frankish monarchy, although normally
they were left to their own devices. Charles made it his policy to support the
monks and became associated with the greatest missionary of his century, the
Anglo-Saxon Wynfrith, who took the Latin name Boniface. During the early
years of his reign, Charles found valuable support among the churchmen, but
in his last years, he obtained a reputation for harsh treatment of the churches
because he had carried out an extensive confiscation of their lands. This
program was part of Charles' royal (it is unnecessary to say mayoral) policy, but it would be wrong to see it as an attempt to strengthen the monarchy
at the expense of the aristocracy. The Frankish monarchy cannot be described in late medieval or early modern terms, by emphasizing its majesty
or self-conscious loftiness. The Frankish king stood above his people because
he had a sacred character. He was supposed to be able to heal those he
touched, to be the living link between his people and God. But this intermediary position also made him a man of the people, responsible for their
well-being. In early days this responsibility had been expressed in the idea
that the king was guarantor of the people's luck; when things went wrong,
the king was deposed. In the seventh century such ideas coalesced in the
notion that kingship was a trust rather than a power. Under the influence of
the Church, kings began to be compared to David and other divinely or-

dained Old Testament kings. Perhaps it is best to understand Charles' confiscations of Church property in light of his obligation to build up his people, but before turning to the explanations that have been offered for the confiscations, the history of Charles' governance as a whole must be understood.

In 720 the Moslems established themselves in Septimania and began raiding the southern regions of the Frankish kingdom. These incursions were resisted by the duke of Aquitaine, Eudes, who had maintained a large degree of autonomy from the palace government, but in 732 or 733 the Moslems sent a large force north toward Tours, where the greatest pilgrimage center in the kingdom was focused on the wealthy church of Saint Martin of Tours. Eudes could not resist this attack, which, because of its object, constituted a direct assault on the kingdom itself. In mustering an army to meet the threat, Charles not only protected the ancient church of Tours but also forced Eudes and his duchy into closer relationship with the royal court. Charles' army met the Moslem force in the region between Poitiers and Tours and defeated it. The battle probably involved a relatively few men, and while it must have appeared significant to contemporaries because it prevented the Moslems from reaching the great shrine at Tours, historians have endowed it with an importance that would have surprised Charles and his army. Although the battle was only the beginning of active royal participation in the task of ridding Gaul of the Islamic forces, accomplished by Charles' son Pepin in 759 but still of concern to his grandson Charlemagne, historians have made it the most important event of Charles' reign. During the Middle Ages, chroniclers considered the defeat of the Moslems the climax of the conflict between Christianity and Islam, and some textbooks still describe Charles Martel (he earned the sobriquet Martel—the hammer—in the course of his later campaigns against the Moslems) as the man who saved Europe from becoming another province of the Arab Empire. A lesser known tradition has had an important effect on scholarship and teaching about the Middle Ages. Historians have linked the battle with Charles' confiscations of ecclesiastical property and have explained his program in terms of the clash of Frankish foot soldiers and Moslem cavalry at Tours. When Charles recognized the superiority of cavalry troops, it is argued, he sought to create his own army of heavily armed horsemen. The development of a cavalry required enormous resources, since the heavy war horses (ancestors of the modern workhorses) and the armor were expensive, and the soldiers had to be thorough professionals who spent their youth learning how to handle the new arms and strengthening themselves for the task and their adulthood in constant training. Since the only resources in the kingdom were landed estates, Charles needed huge amounts of land to distribute to his cavalrymen. Some of this land came from the royal fisc, but the exclusive use of royal lands would leave the monarchy crucially weakened and would not be sufficient. Thus Charles turned to the churches, taking some of their extensive landholdings outright and forcing bishops to relinquish some of them directly to the new warrior aristocrats. Recent studies have undermined this interpretation, however, by showing that the confiscations began before the defeat of the Moslems, that the Moslem army was overwhelmingly an infantry force, and that the Moslems, like the Franks, did not develop a predominantly cavalry force until the late eighth or nearly ninth century at the earliest. Furthermore, the Moslem threat was not as great as once imagined. The Moslem army was a raiding army, not a great force sent to conquer the Frankish kingdom. If any such ideas existed in the minds of Moslem leaders in Spain or Septimania, Charles' campaigns in the 730s kept them from being realized. From 732 or 733 on, the Franks seem to have had the Moslems on the defensive in southern Gaul.

The new studies on the power and role of the Frankish and Gallo-Roman aristocracy in his kingdom hold the key to understanding Charles' program of confiscating Church lands. Charles saw the aristocratic class as the strength of his people, and he sought therefore to strengthen that class, as an integral element of the realm under royal power. The churches were the most formidable obstacle to this policy because over the centuries more and more of the kingdom's landed resources had come into their possession. Since churches did not die, since they tended to be controlled by great families, and since these families could by virtue of that control suppress rivals and compete with the king for power, Charles moved to reduce and redistribute the wealth of the churches. It was a paradoxical program in which Charles followed an aristocratic policy to defeat the leading aristocrats. He wanted to broaden the aristocratic class. It is attractive to see this policy as an attempt to establish the monarchy by crushing its major rivals, but this view may overemphasize Charles' desire to raise the monarchy above the nobility, to gather authority into his hands. Surely some such desire was part of Charles' intention, but it can also be argued that he wanted to strengthen the kingdom by reforming the landholding pattern on which its military strength rested. Without denying Charles' self-interest, his policies can perhaps be better understood by recognizing his concern for the kingdom's welfare, for in the kingdom's strength resided his own. This view emphasizes the aristocratic as against the monarchist structure of Frankish society and government in the eighth century and prepares the way for understanding the historic significance of events taking place toward mid-century.

The work of the missionary Boniface formed a link between the papacy and the Frankish kingdom because Boniface had traveled to Rome, received papal blessing and authority for his work, and kept in contact with the popes. The papacy attempted to make the connection an effective working relationship in 739, when Pope Gregory III appealed to Charles Martel for aid against the Lombards. This appeal was a symbol of something new in the history of the papacy and of Europe. For centuries the popes had considered themselves subjects of the Roman Empire. After the collapse of the empire in the West, they continued to recognize the emperor at Constantinople as the legitimate sovereign of the Roman Empire of which Rome and much of Italy continued to be part. The historic and natural ties of the papacy were with the East, and these ties continued to be strong despite the hazards and upheavals of the sixth and seventh centuries. In some ways these ties grew closer. After the year 550 official papal documents were dated in the name and regnal year of the emperor. Beginning with the reign of Justinian, imperial ratification of a papal election was necessary before the consecration of a new pope, and in some instances this imperial control had gone so far as direct appointment of a new pope by the emperor. Such direct intervention in papal affairs ceased after the reign of Heraclius (610–641), but Byzantine influence in Rome continued to grow. Between 678 and 752 only two of thirteen popes were Roman by birth—the others were Syrian, Greek, or Sicilian (Sicily was Byzantine at this time). This Greek leadership in the papal see did not necessarily reflect subservience to the emperor, but it showed that the papacy was still part of a universal Church whose center of gravity was in the East. The leaders of the Roman clergy were Easterners, and at the beginning of the eighth century the Western-oriented tradition established by Gregory the Great a century earlier appeared to be dead.

From the standpoint of the Byzantine court, however, Italy was a backwater province in which conditions made it unwise to commit forces sufficient to pacify and control it. The troubles of the sixth and seventh centuries made it impossible as well as unwise for the imperial government to commit troops to oppose the new Lombard invaders, and, in fact, the expansion of the Arabs in the 630s caused Heraclius to strip Italy of the garrisons left there by his predecessors. Throughout the seventh century, however, the Lombard kingdom centered at Pavia posed only a moderate threat to the exercise of papal power in central Italy. The reason for this relative weakness was not that the Lombard king had no power over his dukes in general, as has often been supposed, but that he had to deal with the exarchate of Ravenna, who represented the Byzantine power and with the dukes of Spoleto and Benevento, whose lands lay closest to papal territory and who succeeded in maintaining their independence, often with papal aid. This situation changed in the early eighth century. In the 720s King Luitprand (712–744) finally led a successful assault on Ravenna and then secured the obedience of his southern dukes. By 739, then, the Lombards posed a serious threat to papal independence as rulers of Rome and its environs. It does not seem that Luitprand wanted to disturb papal spiritual functions—the Lombards were Christians by then—but he obviously recognized Rome as the key to symbolic as well as actual power over the Italian peninsula. The reaction of the papacy, which first appealed in vain for aid from Constantinople and then turned to Charles Martel, stemmed not only from its desire to hold the power it had obtained over the past century or more but also from its long association with the East and the imperial government. The turn to the Western, Frankish power was both sudden and a sharp break with this tradition, and it cannot be explained by reference simply to Luitprand's threat. A doctrinal dispute lay behind it—the debate over cultic images, commonly called the Iconoclastic Struggle.

The icon developed in Egypt, and the spread of monasticism from Egypt diffused the icon culture throughout the empire. Like the wall paintings in churches, the icons were part of the Church's attempt to reach out to the uneducated masses, presenting its message in an easily intelligible, nonliterary form. In addition, the Christians had adopted the old belief that holy persons could intercede with God for individuals who prayed to them for aid and that intercession was particularly effective when the saintly soul rose to heaven. The icon helped to concentrate the worshiper's attention on the saint, or on Christ, and to intensify his prayer or raise his level of spiritual awareness. The problems created by these practices and doctrines were twofold. First, the common people, and not only they, tended to identify the image and saint, so they slipped into the pagan mode of worshiping the image instead of what it represented. Second, the Second Commandment (Exodus 20:4) forbade the representation of God: "You shall not make for yourself a graven image, or any likeness of anything that is in heaven above. . . ." This prohibition had naturally become part of Christianity, and from early times, many Christians opposed the use of images. This opposition occasionally became part of heretical sects' hostility toward orthodox theology. The Monophysites, for example, opposed the use of images because they believed Christ had a simple, that is, divine nature and, according to the Second Commandment, should not be represented in art. As the use of icons spread throughout the empire and as Christianity became the majority religion in the empire, during the sixth and seventh centuries, the conflict between iconodules (icon worshipers) and iconoclasts (icon breakers) intensified. For reasons that are not clear, a few bishops of Asia Minor became the leaders of the iconoclasts, and in the 720s they appealed to the emperor Leo the Isaurian (717–741) for support. Leo has generally been considered the initiator of the iconoclastic movement. However, Leo did not initiate the movement and did not even take a firm stance in the first stages of the dispute. The bishops who approached him had already tried unsuccessfully to enlist the support of the patriarch Germanus I. Leo was more sympathetic, but he issued only an exhortation urging Christians to give up the use of images. It was not until 730 that the emperor actually prohibited their use, and by that time the bishops had embarked on their own program of cleansing the churches, and the movement was gaining widespread support. Whatever iconoclastic proclivities Leo had were enhanced by the political implications of the movement, which had become clear by the beginning of the year 730.

Leo's decree split the Church and stimulated a fervent theological debate over the role of images in Christian worship. The arguments against images were based on the Old Testament tradition. The arguments for the use of icons were summed up by John of Damascus (d. before 754), whose family had served as officials in the Omayyad caliphate for three generations. John is called the Eastern Aquinas because he summarized the whole corpus of Greek patristic thought in his works. With respect to image worship, he maintained that the incarnation of Christ qualified the prohibition of the Second Commandment because God had taken human form himself. Thus the commandment given to the Jews could not be taken literally unless it were argued that God himself had transgressed it. Christians are prohibited, John said, from worshiping images but not from using images in their worship of God. As Gregory the Great had said in guiding his flock of Western Christians, "To adore a picture is wrong; to learn through the picture what is to be adored is praiseworthy."

Iconoclasm was stoutly opposed by large segments of the Eastern Church and by the Western churches under papal leadership. In the West, where image worship was not as widespread as in the East, the papacy hewed to the line set by Gregory the Great. Pope Gregory II (715–731) considered the imperial position theologically unacceptable and also an intolerable invasion of the religious sphere by a secular ruler. When Leo informed Gregory, "I am emperor and priest," compromise was out of the question. At a synod in Rome in 731 the new pope, Gregory III (731–741), denounced iconoclasm and excommunicated the subservient patriarch of Constantinople who had approved Leo's decree against images. In retaliation, Leo ordered the transfer of all the dioceses of Illyria, southern Italy, and Sicily to the jurisdiction of the patriarch of Constantinople, together with the expropriation of the Patrimony of Saint Peter situated in those dioceses. This heavy blow at the resources and jurisdiction of the papacy helps explain why Gregory III made his appeal for help to Charles Martel in 739 and supported so strongly the missionary efforts of Boniface in Germany. The expansion of Christianity under papal auspices north of the Alps made up, in part, for papal losses in the Mediterranean. Then, there was a temporary respite from the Lombard peril when, following Liutprand's death in 744, a struggle began among the Lombard dukes over succession to the monarchy.

The pope foresaw that the breaking point in papal–imperial relations would come as soon as the Lombards resumed their aggression. The Byzantine emperor, whose historic and proper role was that of ruler and protector of the Christian Empire, had not only failed to protect Italy against aggression but also had become a heretic who persecuted the supreme spiritual authority. On Gregory III's death the new pope, Zacharias (741–752), did not bother to obtain imperial ratification of his election from the emperor Leo's son and successor, Constantine V Coprynomous (an epithet given to him by

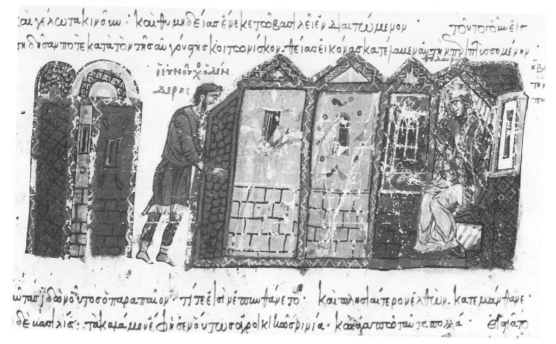

Even for members of the imperial family, icon worship sometimes had to be secret. In this manuscript illumination, the empress Theodora (wife of Theophilus) is caught kissing an icon. When she came to power as regent for her son Michael, Theodora gradually drove the iconoclasts from the imperial court.

the iconodules that might delicately be translated "dung name"). Under Constantine, imperial support of the iconoclasts reached a peak. During his thirty-four year reign (741–765), Constantine pursued a relentless policy of destroying images and driving his opponents into exile or submission. The iconodule monks suffered most. Constantine forced them to cleanse their churches, to give up their profession, to marry nuns. He even drafted them into the army.

The 740s were also years of change in the Frankish kingdom. Charles Martel died in 741, leaving the mayoralty to his two sons, Pepin the Short and Carloman. Both these men had a personal relationship with Boniface, who had had an influence in their upbringing. The change of government in the royal court stimulated rebellions among the nobility and the urge for autonomy in outlying regions like Aquitaine and Bavaria. In suppressing the rebellions and forcing recognition of their authority, the brothers relied on the churches, holding provincial councils for the purpose of both reforming the churches and making churchmen loyal to the royal court and its mayors. These councils were organized and presided over by Boniface under the joint aegis of the papacy and the mayors, thus strengthening the bond between the papal see and the Frankish kingdom. The reform movement had another effect. In the eighth century it would have been impossible to speak of the

Frankish Church as though an overall organization held together the churches in the kingdom. Boniface's activities did not create a national Church, but they introduced the idea into the kingdom. The royal court and a leading, papally authorized churchman had undertaken to reform the churches, making them relatively uniform in their discipline and ritual and enhancing the monarchy's role in ecclesiastical affairs. Henceforth, at least one force, the royal one, and often two, royal and papal, were active in ecclesiastical life throughout the realm.

Charles Martel had kept the throne vacant for the last four years of his life because the existence of a puppet king had been the excuse for a revolt by some nobles who claimed to be fighting for the king against the mayor. When Pepin and Carloman became mayors, the same nobles rebelled again, alleging that they were fighting for a royalist restoration. So the brothers decided to legitimize their rule by establishing another puppet king in whose name they could rule. A search throughout the kingdom produced a distant relative of the last Merovingian king, and in 743 he was installed on the throne as Childeric III, the last of his family to wear the Frankish crown. By 747 the brothers completed the work of consolidating their power, and while Pepin continued to rule, Carloman retired to the monastery of Monte Cassino—one of several instances when an early medieval ruler retired from the world for no apparent purpose other than a sincere preference for the contemplative life.

Once Pepin was in firm control of the kingdom, he sought to transform his position by means of a radical change. By 751 he was ready to transfer the kingship, whose authority he held by hereditary right to the mayoralty, to himself, thereby ending the Merovingian dynasty. Pepin's assumption of the throne was in at least one respect conservative, since it appeared to be a rejection of "modern" ideas according to which the kingship was an office to which a member of the royal family had a right notwithstanding his incompetence to function as king. This idea had permitted the existence of the *rois fainéants* and of the mayors of the palace who had ruled in their place. Pepin sought to push the kingship back along the path it had taken from its Germanic roots. He argued that the king ought to rule as well as reign and that he who could not rule could not be king.

The dynastic change, however, amounted to a revolution, or at least the manifestation of a revolution, in Frankish politics. First, Frankish history contained many precedents for the establishment of a king but none for the exchange of one king for another. Second, kingship was a sacred position held by a man endowed with spiritual power in virtue of his genealogy. The king-right belonged to a family thought to be endowed with supernatural power because it had divine origins. Pepin's family was great but not divine, and it was not clear that it had the king-right. A change like the one carried out by Pepin brought the old, half-remembered traditions to the fore, so it was important to verify his right to the sacred office. Pepin succeeded in winning the support of the Frankish nobility and then turned to the pope for help in making a claim to the indwelling spirit that characterized a true king.

Pepin did not ask the pope to depose Childeric III and make him king; that had already been done. He asked for both recognition and a judgment of his new spiritual condition. He asked "whether it were good that those who were of the royal race and were called kings, but had no power in the kingdom, should continue to be called kings." Pope Zacharias answered that they should not be so called. It all seems to have been a game, but it was not. Pepin was questioning whether kingliness was tied to function or to kinship, whether the attributes of a king were possessed by Childeric because he was of the Merovingian line or by Pepin because he functioned as a real king. In his answer, Zacharias confirmed Pepin's possession of the name and attributes of the king, in particular of the indwelling spirit that of course now came from the Christian God instead of one of the gods of the Germanic pantheon. Zacharias then commanded Boniface to anoint the new king after the manner of the Old Testament kings, a practice already followed in Visigothic Spain and perhaps introduced to the Franks by Visigothic refugees, some of whom played important roles in the court and churches of their adopted kingdom. In the short run, the papal participation in Pepin's rise to power stemmed from his weakness, his need to make himself appear qualitatively adequate to be a German king. In the long run, the new association of king and Church strengthened the monarchy by making it possible for the king to claim extensive powers in virtue of his divine ordination. The Carolingian king (the dynasty was named for Pepin's son Charlemagne) was created in the image of David. He was divinely ordained as a minister of God, and thus of an order wholly different from his people.

Three years after Pepin became king, the alliance between the Franks and the papacy was sealed. When he ascended the papal throne, Stephen II (752–757) found the Lombard army of Aistulf (who had succeeded to the throne in 749) besieging Rome. As if by habit, or perhaps to justify the appeal to Frankish arms, which was now inevitable, Stephen II made a last, futile request for protection from the emperor. Then he set forth across the Alps in the winter of 753/54, as Aistulf's army waited for spring to renew the campaign, and implored Pepin to save Rome and Italy from the Lombards. Pepin did not refuse, and, in fact, he promised to restore the Lombard conquests not to the rightful sovereign, the Byzantine emperor, but to the pope himself. In return, Stephen consecrated Pepin king of the Franks once more and by his apostolic authority prohibited the Franks, on penalty of excommunication, from ever choosing a king who was not descended from Pepin. Finally, Stephen conferred on Pepin and his two sons the title of *Patricius Romanorum,* the traditional title of the exarch of Ravenna.

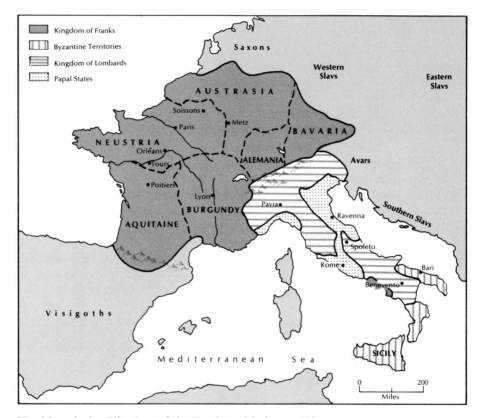

The Merovingian Kingdom of the Franks and Italy, ca. 700

The crisis of the eighth century was thus a papal crisis caused primarily by the unification and success of the Lombards. On a secondary level, this crisis was deepened by a new split between the Roman see and the imperial court in Constantinople at a time when the Byzantine Empire became permanently engaged in holding off the Arabs to the east. In the tenth century, the empire rose again and even turned west, but it never again played a significant role in Western Europe. And the papacy had been forced to look elsewhere for support and protection. In a sense, the papal alliance with the Franks was analogous to Pepin's *coup d'état* because it legitimized the *de facto* power to replace the recognized but ineffectual authority of the emperor.

The events of the eighth century were thus of extraordinary importance in European history. East and West became almost permanently estranged. The papacy found itself in a dilemma that forced it to develop a new political policy and to take a Western perspective on its position and role. The changes effected in Frankish political institutions, especially the kingship, by the amalgamation of Germanic and Gallo-Roman culture were settled on a permanent foundation by Pepin's takeover, and while this new kingship developed independently of the events taking place in Rome, the two transformations were soon brought into relationship with one another.

## The Politics of a New European Consciousness: The Reign of Charlemagne

Pepin the Short only slowly strengthened his position as monarch during the years following his dramatic *coup d'état*. Opposition to his seizure of the throne and to his active support of the pope continued. In 739 Pepin's father had refused to aid the papacy because he was involved in campaigns to drive the Moslems out of Septimania, and to this end he had allied himself with the Lombard king, whose kingdom was always a threat to Frankish activities in the south. Pepin broke with that policy. He too was involved in a war of attrition against the Moslems, but he owed a debt to the papacy and recognized in the papacy a support for his not yet secure kingship. Many Frankish nobles believed that involvement in Italian affairs would seriously hinder efforts to drive back the Moslems, the project they thought was most important.

Following Pope Stephen II's visit, Pepin negotiated with the Lombard king, Aistulf, but to no avail. In 756 the Frankish king invaded Italy and defeated the Lombards. Ignoring the protests of Byzantine envoys, he gave most of the former Byzantine Exarchate to the papacy in fulfillment of promises made to Stephen II just before his second coronation. By this so-called Donation of Pepin, the Papal States were founded. For over a century the popes had been temporal rulers of the duchy of Rome, in the name of the Byzantine emperor. For eleven more centuries the papacy continued to exercise temporal authority over territory that had never been part of the duchy.

Pepin himself sought no territorial gains in Italy because he was fully occupied in the southwestern regions of his kingdom. By 759 he had reconquered Septimania and pushed the Moslems south of the Pyrenees. Then, during the years 760 to 768, he reduced the semi-independent duchy of Aquitaine to obedience. Pepin's reign was epoch-making, but its importance has been overshadowed by that of his son, who was so worthy of his father that historians have tended to see the father as worthy of the son.

When Pepin died in 768, he left the kingship to his two sons, Charles, who was about twenty-six years old, and Carloman, who was in his early twenties. Pepin and his brother Carloman had cooperated well during the six years they shared the position of mayor. Charles and Carloman were not on friendly terms. Charles had received a belt of territory stretching from Aquitaine to the southwestern part of Austrasia. Carloman held the rest of Austrasia and the eastern part of the kingdom. When Carloman died suddenly in 771, Charles seized his brother's half of the kingdom; Carloman's widow wisely sought refuge for herself and her two sons with the Lombard king Desiderius (756–774), who had succeeded Aistulf. During the next two years, Charles (who earned the epithet "the Great" and is called by the French derivative, Charlemagne, of his Latin name, Carolus Magnus) consolidated his control over the kingdom. He then reaffirmed the alliance between himself and the papacy, demonstrating fidelity to his father's policy, which continued to set the monarchy at odds with the nobility. The Frankish nobles still favored an alliance with the Lombards as the conventional way to protect the southern flank of the kingdom and permit unhampered campaigns against the Moslems. Charlemagne had pursued the more traditional policy of alignment with the Lombards during the years he shared the kingdom with Carloman. He had been betrothed to Desiderius' daughter, to the great dismay of Pope Stephen III (768–771), who wrote to Charlemagne describing the marriage as "the invention of the devil, a mere illicit union . . . a folly by which the illustrous Frankish blood would be defiled by the stinking, faithless race of the Lombards, from whom the race of lepers is well known to have sprung." Stephen III had dramatic flair, but the events following Carloman's death rather than papal fulmination caused Charlemagne to repudiate his bride soon after the marriage was celebrated. A rebellion in Aquitaine showed that the danger in the south was more internal than external and induced the king to rely on the churchmen there for support against the rebels. These churchmen were in close alliance with the papacy, and thus Charlemagne's reliance on them drew him in the direction of Pepin's controversial propapal policy. Furthermore, Desiderius had received Carloman's widow and sons and thus possessed the means to undermine Charlemagne's position by supporting them as claimants to the throne. Charlemagne's repudiation of his marriage did not endear him to Desiderius, and it appears that the Lombard king did agitate in the Frankish kingdom on behalf of Carloman's sons. Charlemagne therefore took the opportunity provided by Desiderius' renewed attacks on territories donated to the papacy by Pepin, but of course claimed by the Lombard king, to reassert his alliance with the pope by answering a papal appeal for aid. He invaded Italy in 773.

The campaign ended the Lombard threat. Charlemagne defeated the Lombards, confirmed the Donation of Pepin, and restored Desiderius' recent encroachments on papal territory, and then assumed the title of king of the Lombards himself, thus incorporating northern Italy in a personal union with the Frankish kingdom. As king of the Lombards Charlemagne adopted many of the aims of the earlier Lombard rulers. Like them, he tried to unite all of Italy under his rule, but also like them he was able to subdue neither the

ET SYRIAM SOBAL · ET CONVERTIT
IOAB · ET PERCYSSIT EDOM IN VAL
LE SALINARYM · XII MILIA ·

The knights pictured in this ninth-century manuscript illumination represent an intermediary stage in the development of the medieval mounted warrior. They are using stirrups, but their spears are not yet the heavy lances used in shock tactics. These soldiers rode into battle, but they threw their spears before making contact with the enemy and then fought with swords when they did close.

independent Lombard duchy of Benevento nor the Byzantine provinces in Sicily and southern Italy. Carolingian control of northern and central Italy was strengthened by the substitution of new counties under Frankish counts for the older Lombard duchies, and by political and administrative supervision over the Papal States, ruled directly by the pope. The pope's temporal rule now differed only in two respects from the earlier situation: first, the area under his immediate control was much larger than the old duchy of Rome;

and second, instead of a distant and ineffectual Byzantine emperor for suzerain he enjoyed the protection, but was under the effective supervision, of Charlemagne as *Patricius Romanorum*.

The strength of Charlemagne's hold on his kingdom and ultimately on his empire resulted from his successful combination of the military power of the ancient war leader and the sacred image of the Germanic king. As an exceptionally successful warrior-king, Charlemagne became the living embodiment of the Davidic king who waged campaign after campaign in God's name. This identification gave Charlemagne's military activities a momentum and an ideological importance rarely matched in the Middle Ages.

By far the longest and most arduous of Charlemagne's wars was the series of almost annual campaigns against the Saxons, lasting thirty-two years (772–804). Settled on the northeastern frontier of the Carolingian kingdom, the Saxons were fiercely heathen, independent, and predatory. Their continual raids posed a threat best reduced by conquest, conversion, and annexation. By contrast, Charlemagne's strategy of his several campaigns in the southwest against the Moslems, between 778 and 801, was primarily defensive. He succeeded in establishing a military district, the Spanish March, centered on Barcelona. An incident in the campaign of 778 later gave rise to the first and greatest French epic poem, the *Song of Roland* (written down ca. 1100). On the eastern frontier, Charlemagne moved to end Bavarian independence. In 787 he took the opportunity offered by a rebellion in the duchy to depose Duke Tassilo and replace him with Frankish royal officials. In the eastern district of the duchy, he designated a territory as another march to act as a buffer between his kingdom and the Slavic tribes settled, rather restlessly, in Eastern Europe. This march was called the Ostmark (East March) and formed the core of what later became Austria.

In all these activities, Charlemagne realized the mixed traditions of eighth-century Frankish kingship. He was the exemplary war leader whose generalship greatly impressed his contemporaries. At the same time, Charlemagne was the embodiment of the Roman part of his royal tradition. His policy was aristocratic to be sure, but he also extended royal power in a direct way. Throughout his reign he sought to establish and maintain control over local royal officials, called counts. The countships derived in a vague, almost forgotten way from the Roman administration of the territories over which Charlemagne now ruled, but they had long ago ceased being closely tied to a central, Roman-type government. Carolingian aristocrats who still retained the title of count considered it an ornament of their prestige and nothing more. Their loyalties and interests were focused on themselves and their local affairs. Charlemagne revived the office and succeeded to a remarkable extent in making the counts responsible to him. Charlemagne also instituted the *missi dominici* (those sent by the lord), special representatives of the monarch who traveled throughout the kingdom. These officials possessed royal power

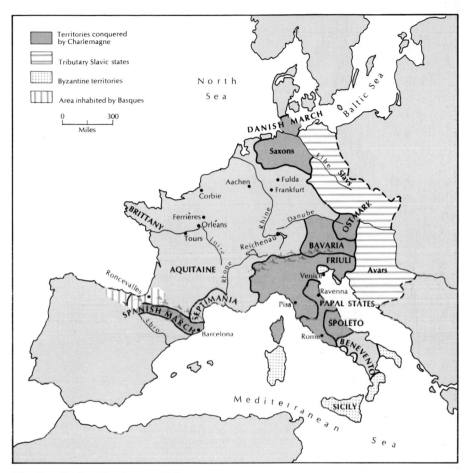

The Carolingian Empire, ca. 814

by delegation, a thoroughly Roman idea, and could bring recalcitrant counts to justice. As long as the threat of Charlemagne's armed force lurked behind the *missi,* they were an effective instrument of royal control over the kingdom. The aristocracy still had considerable power, but in the world of eighth-century Gaul and Germany, what was striking was that the power was limited.

Another aspect of Charlemagne's kingship that stemmed from Roman rather than Germanic sources was his legislative power, exercised most actively in the second half of his reign. Germanic law was founded on custom, which was thought to have existed from time immemorial and to be unalterable. The Germanic warrior-king had had no power to make law; he was under the law. After the invasions, the kings, maintained in their posi-

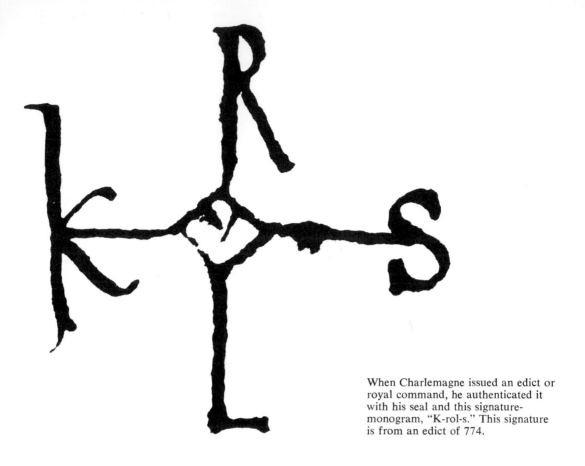

When Charlemagne issued an edict or royal command, he authenticated it with his seal and this signature-monogram, "K-rol-s." This signature is from an edict of 774.

tion by their peacekeeping activities, began to function as law speakers who preserved the legal traditions of their peoples. The Romanization of kingship transformed the lawfinding king into a lawmaking one, and Charlemagne's legislative activities established this new function as a permanent and important part of the medieval concept of kingship. Charlemagne most often legislated in council with the great men of his realm and issued his laws as capitularies, so called because they were divided into *capitula,* or chapters, in the documents containing them. The capitularies were binding on all persons in the kingdom, and they covered the whole range of subjects on which the king wanted his will felt. Most capitularies contained simple administrative regulations concerning the duties of governmental officials or the functions of local institutions. Others dealt extensively with such matters as organization of royal estates, regulations for the clergy, and recruitment of the army. Only rarely did the capitularies affect the legal rights of subjects, and then usually by adding certain provisions to existing laws in order to meet new conditions not covered by tribal customs. The content of the laws reflected the place of legislative authority in the political life of the kingdom. The king did not interfere much with the private law that primarily derived from ancient customs, which governed the status and freedom of freemen, although he might consider the legal problems raised by a specific case. In administrative and ecclesiastical matters, the situation was entirely different. The anointment of Pepin and his sons had constituted the Church's recognition that the new kings possessed the sacred character of the old, but the Old Testament imagery used to describe the Carolingian monarchs implied that they held a special position in the Christian community. Even before the theoretical justification of royal participation in ecclesiastical affairs was enunciated, Pepin and Carloman had become involved in the reform activities of Boniface. Thus the implications of the new ecclesiastical language of kingship were quickly realized, and many of Charlemagne's capitularies embodied ecclesiastical legislation of a disciplinary and doctrinal nature.

A combination of this ecclesiastical element of Charlemagne's kingship and his policy of alliance with the papacy induced him to become involved in the internal affairs of the papal see in 800. This involvement resulted in the imperial coronation of Charlemagne as the *Imperator Romanorum* (Emperor of the Romans), and while Charlemagne's involvement in papal affairs might be explained by reference to his position as *Patricius Romanorum*, or to the implications of his Christianized kingship, the coronation cannot be understood without taking a longer and wider view of his position in eighth-century Europe.

Eulogistic portrayals of Charlemagne produced during his reign changed his image from that of a German war leader in the 770s and 780s to that of an emperorlike head of all Europe in the later 790s. Charlemagne had assembled a court of scholars from all over Europe during the 790s, and while it is unlikely that he patronized the intellectuals of his court with the intention of creating a new image for himself, that was the result of bringing scholars educated in the traditions of Roman history and literature into contact with a man who was almost universally successful in extending his power and influence. The king consciously established a "second Rome" at Aachen and constructed there a great palace and church modeled on the Byzantine buildings in which the exarch of Ravenna had once resided. Charlemagne was in active contact with kings throughout Europe, and many of them, such as Offa of Mercia in England, who had established his hegemony over the entire southern part of the island, appear to have looked to the Frankish king as a model. Charlemagne's greatness made him the natural leader of all Christendom.

This inchoate feeling of superiority to other kings in Europe colored Charlemagne's attitude toward and relations with the empire in the East. In the 790s, the Frankish king became involved in the Iconoclastic Struggle when Pope Adrian I (772–795) approved the decrees of the Council of Nicaea (787), where a compromise settlement of the dispute had been

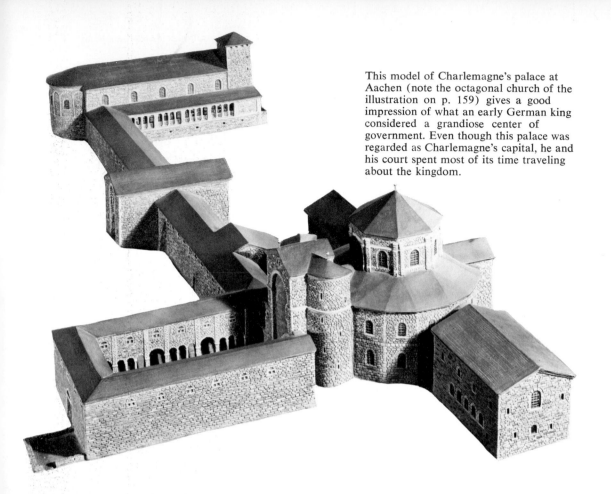

This model of Charlemagne's palace at Aachen (note the octagonal church of the illustration on p. 159) gives a good impression of what an early German king considered a grandiose center of government. Even though this palace was regarded as Charlemagne's capital, he and his court spent most of its time traveling about the kingdom.

worked out. In 794 Charlemagne summoned the clergy of his realm, including churchmen from the kingdom of the Lombards, to Frankfort and from this council issued a series of doctrinal decisions—the *Libri Carolini* (Caroline Books)—that took to task both the pope and the Eastern court. Charlemagne's assertion of his position as the *rector populi christiani* (rector of the Christian people), so that he could even try his hand at doctrinal formulation, had significant effects. From the standpoint of the Frankish court, only the kingdom of Charlemagne was orthodox; thus in the course of the next few years, court scholars developed the view that the *populi christiani* was coextensive with the kingdoms that recognized Charlemagne's suzerainty. In 797 the king's schoolmaster, Alcuin, began to use the word *imperium* (empire, or imperial authority) to describe Charlemagne's power over these peoples. Certainly the building of Aachen, accomplished in this period, contributed to the imperial image of Charlemagne's kingship. The palace in that city became the scene of ceremonial receptions of embassies from, among others, Pope Leo III in 796, and the great caliph Harun al-

Rashid (of Baghdad) and the emir of Córdoba in Spain in 797. The spoils of great conquests, like the immense treasure captured from the Avars in 796, were presented to the king and kingdom in the palace.

In the midst of the celebration of the victory over the Avars, a letter arrived from the court in Constantinople. This was the first letter to Charlemagne in more than ten years, and it made overtures for the establishment of friendly relations. It also confirmed the rumors concerning the condition of the Eastern court. The Westerners had already learned that Irene, widow of Leo VI and for several years regent for her young son, had blinded and deposed him in 797 and now ruled on her own authority. In 798 she approached Charlemagne in hopes that peace between them might help her maintain her position in the face of both legal and political threats. The news of Irene's usurpation of the imperial throne led some people in the West to argue that the empire had no legitimate ruler, but the imperialist ideology of

The classicism seen in the illuminations on pp. 170 and 171 is also evident in the church Charlemagne built for his palace at Aachen. Just as his scholars and artists looked to Italy for models of language and form, so his architects looked to Byzantine Ravenna for their exemplars. The German craftsmen even brought prefabricated columns and other masonry from Italy, so that they could reproduce the model as exactly as possible. This building is one of the indications that Charlemagne took his imperial title seriously and sought to re-create "Rome" north of the Alps.

Charlemagne's advisors did not evolve into a campaign for the imperial crown for him until Pope Leo III arrived at the court in Paderborn in late 799.

In contrast with Adrian, Leo had been elected pope against the opposition of the Roman aristocracy, whose hostility Leo was unable either to placate or suppress. In April 799, a faction of Roman nobles (led by two relatives of the late pope Adrian) seized the person of the pope, assaulted and kidnaped him, and held him prisoner in a monastery. But Leo was able to escape, and in the company of a Carolingian official he made his way north of the Alps to Charlemagne. Leo appealed for protection from his enemies, whom he denounced as traitors, but at the same time, letters arrived from Rome accusing Leo of a variety of crimes, including perjury and adultery. Leo was sent back to Rome with the security of a Frankish guard, and Charlemagne decided to go to Rome himself to settle the dispute.

The king reached Rome in December 800 and summoned a council of bishops and magnates to hear the charges leveled against Leo. But once the council met, many bishops argued that since the pope was the highest priest, he could not be judged by the assembly; the hierarchical structure of Church government did not allow inferiors to judge their superiors. On December 23, the problem was resolved by Leo's volunteering to take an oath purging himself of the charges. The acceptance of this proposal indicates that Charlemagne was also troubled by the problems raised by a trial of the pope.

Some contemporary sources relate that the council also discussed the coronation of Charlemagne as emperor, and historians might have accepted those statements without question if it were not that the king's principal biographer, Einhard, later wrote that Charlemagne "never would have gone to mass that day, even though it was Christmas, had he known what the pope intended to do." If Einhard was right about the king's attitude, then the coronation plans must have derived from a source outside the royal court. But if Charlemagne did not know that Leo would place the imperial crown on his head as he came forth for communion that day, the great mass of Frankish and Roman clergy and nobles assembled in Saint Peter's apparently did. As Charlemagne rose with the crown on his head, the throng acclaimed him in a version of the ancient ritual phrases, "To Charles, the most pious Augustus, crowned by God, the great and peace-giving Emperor, life and victory."

These events have been a crux for historians of Charlemagne's reign and of the early Middle Ages. The great late–nineteenth-century English historian John Bury considered the coronation of Charlemagne to be the most important single act in the early medieval history of Western Europe. For Bury, the coronation completed the development of the postinvasion West by re-creating the Roman Empire. Henri Pirenne worked on a scale not much smaller than Bury's when he argued that the growth of the Islamic Empire

If this dalmatic (coronation robe) is really the one worn by Charlemagne on Christmas Day 800, as scholars think, then what should one make of Einhard's story that the king did not know he would be crowned emperor that day?

isolated Europe and forced on educated men like those at Charlemagne's court a consciousness of their distinctness. The coronation was therefore a self-conscious act by which Charlemagne and his court set their empire against its Islamic counterpart. More recently, historians have sought to get closer to the events and to explain them in terms of specific circumstances and personalities. Some have argued that the pope conceived the plan to assert his role in the establishment, in this case the transference, of the empire. Thus Pope Leo sought to set a precedent with far-reaching theoretical implications that would give the papacy a legal superiority over the emperor, since the authority that crowned the emperor could depose him. Others have looked to the specific legal problems of Pope Leo, who needed a definitive authority capable of dealing with his enemies. Once Charlemagne was emperor, there could be no appeal from his judgment. Perhaps it is best to see the coronation as the result of Charlemagne's greatness, a way of symbolizing that he was Europe's most powerful king. It signified not the restoration of the empire but the fact that like the Roman emperors Charlemagne ruled over many peoples.

## Suggestions for Further Reading

**Secondary Works**   J. M. Wallace-Hadrill, *The Barbarian West, 400–1000* (London, 1952) provides a good introduction to the history of the eighth century. For the economic life of the period, see R. Latouche, *The Birth of the Western Economy,* trans. E. Wilkinson (London, 1961), and the classic work by A. Dopsch, *The Economic and Social Foundations of European Civilization* (New York, 1937). Dopsch's study represents the scholarly tradition that Henri Pirenne challenged in *Mohammed and Charlemagne* (New York, 1939). The controversy is surveyed in A. F. Havighurst, ed., *The Pirenne Thesis: Analysis, Criticism, and Revision* (Boston, 1958). The importance of technological advance is analyzed in L. White, Jr., *Medieval Technology and Social Change* (Oxford, 1962). Heinrich Fichtenau, *The Carolingian Empire,* trans. Peter Munz (Oxford, 1957), and D. Bullough, *The Age of Charlemagne* (New York, 1966) are excellent general studies. Bullough's book is profusely illustrated. An outstanding introduction to a fascinating historical problem is R. E. Sullivan, ed., *The Coronation of Charlemagne: What Did It Signify?* (Boston, 1959).

**Sources**   For the work of Saint Boniface, see *The Letters of Saint Boniface,* trans. E. Emerton (New York, 1940), and *The Life of Saint Boniface by Willibald,* trans. G. W. Robinson (Cambridge, Mass., 1916). For Charlemagne, see *Einhard and Notker the Stammerer, Two Lives of Charlemagne,* trans. L. Thorpe (Harmondsworth, 1969), and, more generally, S. C. Easton and Helene Wieruszowski, *The Era of Charlemagne: Frankish State and Society* (Princeton, N.J., 1961).

# 7 Society and Culture in Charlemagne's Europe

The political and military successes of Charlemagne's reign were paralleled by developments in the intellectual and artistic culture. Charlemagne reinvigorated the old court school, making it the center of a significant intellectual revival. In the best tradition of royal prosperity, he patronized intellectual and artistic activities in order to spread his reputation for magnificence and munificence throughout the world. The work of the scholars, poets, historians, and artists supported by Charlemagne, was on the whole imitative, but it was also often excellent, and it assured the survival of Western Europe's classical heritage.

What role did Charlemagne himself play in the activities he supported? His biographer Einhard was at pains to show that the king made an effort to participate in the intellectual work of his scholars. It is clear that the king did not have much education—he probably could read a little—but he was an active participant in the discourse of his intellectuals and spent considerable time arguing theological points, listening to histories and poetry, and discussing scholarly enterprises. He apparently liked to visit the court school to see how it was functioning. He had a keen and wide-ranging mind and the personality for the give and take a good patron must engage in with his intellectual and artistic clients. The quality of the men who came to his court demonstrates the excellence of his taste and judgment.

The Carolingian renaissance was a veneer on a changing society, for Charlemagne's reign was a time of social flux, of the spread of the influence of the Church into the countryside through the agency of the great landlords, of agricultural expansion within and on the borders of the kingdom. The distinctions between Frank and Gallo-Roman were just disappearing, and important technology, not new but not much used, was coming into wide use in monastic communities and on the estates of the king and his aristocratic associates.

## European Society
## During the Reign of Charlemagne

Once settled in the heart of the old Roman province of Gaul the Germans slowly assimilated the social patterns of the native population; German aristocrats tended to rise to the social and economic level of the Gallo-Roman aristocracy, while the German freemen tended to sink to the level of the indigenous peasantry. The reason for this social change among the Germans is not difficult to understand. The relative equality in preinvasion Germanic tribal society rested on the economic conditions of migratory life. While it would be an exaggeration to describe the Germans as nomads, they did move often enough to prevent wide economic differences from developing among the families of the tribes and villages. In addition, the small scale of social organization, based on the agricultural village, gave the community considerable strength, and part of the communal instinct for self-preservation expressed itself in the maintenance ⌐f substantial equality among the kin groups. In these status-oriented societies, significant changes in relationships usually led to violence, and thus the community used what strength it had to minimize such changes. These social conditions produced an ideology of freedom and equality expressed most conspicuously in the name the Franks took for themselves. The word *Frank* meant "free"; all Franks were freemen.

In Charlemagne's time, the ideology still prevailed, but the reality had changed. Settlement in a well-organized, hierarchical society encouraged detribalization and created a milieu in which wide social and economic distinctions could and did develop. Clovis' success realized the potential for centralized government and broke down tribal barriers among the Franks by suppressing, which normally meant killing, the chieftains who embodied tribal institutions and consciousness. By Charlemagne's time, little was left of the old Frankish society.

The amalgamation of the Frankish and the Gallo-Roman societies produced a fluid situation in the eighth century. Any economic setback threatened small farmers with disaster, forcing them to appeal to the aristocracy for help. The nobles supported them in exchange for the tenure to their land. Thus the Frankish freemen were progressively reduced to the economic status of the Roman *coloni* (tenant farmers), who had cultivated large portions of the great estates of Roman aristocrats since imperial times. The legal status of the Frankish freeman was not identical to that of the *coloni* however. Franks who held their land by a subject tenure—at the will of their lords, or, as the English would say, in villeinage—retained their free status in law. They therefore held an anomalous position in which their economic condition prevented them from meeting their legal responsibilities, especially their obligations to fight in the king's army and to serve in the law courts.

But the process by which small farmers were forced to subject themselves to great landlords was not the only one going on during the Merovingian and Carolingian periods. Small farmers of exceptional ability were able to profit from the economic problems of their peers, and many such prosperous peasant farmers were among those who benefited from Charles Martel's program of redistributing Church lands. As Charles moved to the offensive against his enemies, he recognized the need for larger armed forces than the aristocratic class could provide. The changes that had taken place in Frankish society since the invasions had reduced the population of freemen obligated to and capable of serving in the army, and Charles' reforms were intended to rectify this situation. His program is therefore one indication of what had happened and was happening to the Franks. Pepin the Short and Charlemagne continued Charles Martel's policy of maintaining the kingdom's fighting force by protecting the economic status of its common soldiers.

The general prosperity under the firm rules of Charles Martel, Pepin, and Charlemagne manifested itself in the expansion of the acreage of arable land, which began during the eighth century and continued, with occasional setbacks, for centuries afterward. Enterprising peasants could obtain permission from lords to clear new land, and those who made the effort and took the risks usually received a less onerous tenure on reclaimed land than those who remained in the ancient villages. At the same time, the lords developed their own farms and estates and took on many peasants as servants who functioned as administrators. Entrance into the service of a great landlord required intelligence and some rudimentary education for handling the problems of estate management. Exceptional talent could find reward in exceptional careers. In Charlemagne's time, a few high churchmen and royal officials had risen out of the peasantry on the basis of their ability. Ebbo, archbishop of Reims, was the son of a serf on a royal estate, and Walafrid Strabo, who became tutor to Charlemagne's grandson, came from a humble family. A very talented young peasant could attend Charlemagne's court school, while many not quite so lucky could obtain the education necessary for a good career, and a rise in social status, in monastery and cathedral schools. Charlemagne decreed that such schools be established throughout his realm.

Poverty was widespread in Carolingian society, however. Contemporary sources often refer to runaways, both serfs and suppressed freemen. These citations indicate several things. First, many among the poor suffered burdens heavy enough to impel them to flee the small and relatively secure world of the villages to seek freedom, however uncertain. Second, the world outside the village offered some hope to give runaways an inducement to flight. If runaway peasants became involved in the reclamation of land, they could obtain a better situation, a chance for relative prosperity. Third, the governing classes obviously considered the escapees a problem. The landlords lost tenants and service when their peasants ran away, and the runaways apparently created a problem of vagrancy. Charlemagne issued capitularies that required masters to supervise their poor dependents and to keep them at work. These laws refer to crowds of vagrants as if they were a common sight throughout the kingdom, although the travelers on the roads included pilgrims as well as the oppressed and criminals. Charlemagne gave great quantities of alms to the wayfarers because in their wandering they spread the fame of their generous king. This informal poor relief, practiced by religious houses and aristocrats as well as the king, was one of the few sources of aid for the poor who took to the roads and faced a multitude of dangers every day. Highwaymen, famished wayfarers, slave traders (who had a reputation for seizing their merchandise on lonely stretches of road), and disease and other natural disasters threatened travelers.

Among the poor were the lower clergy. While the bishops and their clerical helpers were born into or rose to the aristocratic class and considered themselves nobles, the lower priests were part of the peasant class they served. On the whole, they were illiterate and unprepared for the religious functions they were supposed to fulfill. Most lower clergymen were appointed by the aristocratic landlord who owned the church in which they served. According to Germanic law, the lords held all buildings on their land as private property, including the churches. It was customary in Charlemagne's time for every lord to have his own priest to serve the spiritual needs of his family and household and of the flock in the local village. The lords appointed men from among their own serfs as priests, and although Church law decreed that all priests in a diocese were under the authority of the bishop, in actuality the lower clergy were controlled by their lords. They did not escape from serfdom by becoming priests and did not even receive the revenue produced by ecclesiastical taxes—tithes (one-tenth of all produce) and first fruits. The lord collected the revenue for himself and paid his priest a pittance. Many priests farmed small holdings to supplement their incomes. Higher churchmen who were concerned about the sorry state of the lower churches realized that no poor man was as poor or as insecure as the priest, who aside from his normal penury was subject to dismissal by his master. Some priests had even "risen" to their status against their will. A lord could not make another lord's serf a priest without the consent of that serf's master, but the serf was not able to decline the honor. The wayfaring mobs in Charlemagne's kingdom included runaway priests who were trying to escape their pastoral experience. The clerical profession was so low on the social scale that it was an object of contempt. Freemen refused to enter the priesthood because so many priests were serfs and because ecclesiastical law forbade them from bearing arms or attending the law courts, both of which duties distinguished a freeman.

Thus, like society at large, the Church was a double fabric, but with a difference. While a legal and social gulf existed between lord and serf, there was no legal gap between priest and bishop. The bishop had some sacramental power not given to the priest, and he was a member of a different social class, but the spiritual and legal equality of priest and bishop was much greater than their differences. In addition, the Church was a closed and hierarchically organized institution in which higher clergy had complete responsibility for the work of their inferiors. If the bishops took their obligation seriously, which they did occasionally in the eighth and ninth centuries but which became characteristic of them later, they became a powerful force for ecclesiastical reform, since they were part of the noble class and were in control of great wealth. This potential for reform was realized during the eleventh century.

Charlemagne's society was rural. The peasant class constituted the overwhelming majority of the population. The towns were a mere shadow of what they had been in Roman times. They continued to be ecclesiastical administrative centers, but Church administration was not as active or pervasive as Roman administration had been. The bishops controlled the towns and were virtually the only aristocratic element in the urban population. While the Roman nobility had been an urban class until the late empire, the disruptions of the fifth century and the increasing pressure of the imperial government on the municipalities had driven the aristocracy to country estates. When the Germans invaded the Roman territories, they used the towns as fortresses but focused their attention on farms and estates. The size of the towns, walled in during the fifth century to protect them against the migratory tribes, was consistent with their use as fortresses. Most were only a few acres, the largest perhaps twenty or thirty acres. Paris, confined to the Île-de-la-Cité in the Seine, comprised seven acres. Those who remained in the urban centers worked as craftsmen or laborers for the episcopal administrative class, and since that class was small and could not sustain the town economy by itself, the townspeople grazed flocks and raised crops both within and just outside the city walls. Even the urban population, therefore, was ruralized. Urban land tenure was often different from its rural counterpart, and although urban people did not fit into the regular structure of Carolingian society, they were so few in number and their economic impact was so small that they did not create any disturbance in the general social pattern.

Carolingian society was fluid and complex. It provided opportunity for social advancement in a situation fraught with natural and man-made dangers. The principal vehicles for advancement were economic prosperity and education. In education, Charlemagne's sure hand could be seen at work.

## The Carolingian Renaissance

Charlemagne's European empire required a larger and more expert bureaucratic establishment than any previous Frankish kingdom. Charlemagne organized the aristocracy to govern effectively under his aegis and increased the role of royal officials, such as the *missi dominici,* to oversee the governors. He also continued his father's policy of maintaining close relations with the papacy and of supporting ecclesiastical reform in his domains. Charlemagne's interest in ecclesiastical affairs grew in the 780s as his kingdom became prosperous. Contemporaries noted that for the first twenty years of Charlemagne's reign, the kingdom and its royal court were poor; the king and his people struggled with each famine or poor harvest and could not support the kind of intellectual and artistic life later associated with them. When the economic situation began to improve, Charlemagne offered preferment to intellectuals and artists throughout Europe and began to build his capital city; these activities contributed to the momentum that eventually took Charlemagne to Saint Peter's on Christmas Day 800. If the territorial product of Charlemagne's court did not survive its founder by more than two generations, its cultural achievement maintained its impetus until the late ninth century.

In the prosperity of the 780s, perhaps as a direct result of it, Charlemagne began to realize the potential of his position as the greatest Christian king in Europe. As God's vicar, he assumed responsibility for the churches in his realm, and under the posthumous influence of Boniface, martyred in Frisia in 754, he understood this to mean the obligation to reform those churches. As in Boniface's time, reform was undertaken in close cooperation with the papacy, but it was a royal program emanating from the royal household. Charlemagne thus sought a man who could organize the movement, and it is a sign of the way the king thought of the policy that he chose Alcuin of York (735?–804), a monk who never took sacred orders, rather than a bishop or an archbishop. Alcuin had a reputation for learning and an educational pedigree that included the great Bede. He was educated at York by Aelbert, a student of Egbert who had studied under Bede. Aelbert succeeded his teacher as archbishop of York in 767 and took Alcuin, his favorite pupil, to Rome, where Aelbert received the *pallium* (a circular, white wool band worn over the shoulders that signified an archbishop's metropolitan authority in his province). Aelbert maintained control of the cathedral library, which he had largely built, but he made Alcuin the master of the cathedral school at York. When Aelbert retired from his see in 780, the new archbishop, Eanbald, sent Alcuin to Rome to get the *pallium* for him. The schoolmaster had met Charlemagne on his previous trip, and he visited him this time at Parma, where the king was attending to affairs in his Lombard kingdom. At this meeting, in the spring of 781, Charlemagne urged Alcuin to stay with him in order to administer the palace school. After receiving permission from the king of Northumbria and from his archbishop, Alcuin accepted the offer.

Alcuin was a prolific writer and a man capable of attracting others to the enterprise he now undertook. At Charlemagne's behest, the English monk, supported by several abbacies in the Frankish kingdom, attempted to provide the instruments for a reform and standardization of liturgical practices throughout the realm. The source of his standards was Rome, where Pope Adrian I provided the Frankish court with an official copy of the collection of ecclesiastical law that governed Church discipline. The original was kept in the king's library, and all duplicates were certified as authentic. The same procedure was followed for other basic works. The pope could not provide a good copy of the Gregorian Sacramentary—which governed the order, form, and content of the Mass—but he sent the best he could find. Alcuin then undertook to edit the work, correcting its errors and placing the perfected version in the royal library, where it too became the basis for certified transcriptions. Fifteen of those copies, with their certificates of authenticity, are still extant.

Alcuin's other major editing project was of the Bible itself. Jerome's translation had not triumphed absolutely in the West and was used along with other versions. In the course of the centuries it had been corrupted by these other texts and by copyists' errors, so that it was in sorry shape by Charlemagne's time. Alcuin recognized its excellence and sought to refurbish it for the Frankish churches. He never completed the project himself—it was completed by his students—but when finished, the new edition of Jerome's translation was declared the official one. Although other versions of the Bible continued to be used throughout the Middle Ages, the one edited by Alcuin and his successors soon became the Vulgate (common) text. But the churches needed more than these basic works for their reformation. During the same period, scholars at the court produced a standard edition of Gregory the Great's works (much of which dealt with the work of pastors) and of Vitruvius' great treatise on architecture (one supposes for the rebuilding of the reinvigorated churches). The king also requested a perfect copy of the Benedictine rule for monks from the abbot of Monte Cassino, whom he visited during one of his trips to his Lombard kingdom. This version is probably the one preserved at the famous monastery of Saint Gall in Switzerland (on the south shore of Lake Constance), and it became, like the other books, the exemplar for authentic copies circulated throughout the realm. Under Charlemagne's son, Louis the Pious, the Benedictine rule was decreed the only one to be recognized in the kingdom.

The library of Saint Gall also preserves the earliest manuscripts with musical notation, and this too represents an important interest of Charlemagne and his successors. The manuscripts date from the ninth century, but Charlemagne himself had requested that Adrian send singers from the Roman *schola cantorum* (school of singers) to aid in the liturgical reforms being carried out under his aegis. Until the ninth century, chant was regional, divided into four main branches with many subvarieties. The main groups were Roman (that of the *schola*), Ambrosian (peculiar to Milan and its dependencies), Gallic (used in most of the Frankish territories), and Mozarabic (used in Spain and heavily influenced by Arabic music). The *schola* itself was very old and had been reformed or reorganized many times, once probably by Gregory the Great, who was later thought to be its founder. As the Roman singers established themselves in the Frankish kingdom, especially

The work of the Carolingian court school shows the influence of the classical revival led by Alcuin and his contemporaries as well as that of the Irish style (see p. 108). This realistic portrait of Saint Matthew replaces the symbolic representations of Anglo-Irish tradition.

The style of the Reims school, which became the basis for Charles the Bald's court school in the later ninth century, is exemplified by another depiction of Saint Matthew in which body movement is emphasized.

at the royal court, a process of musical development began that produced, a few generations later, the style of chant known as Gregorian. Over the centuries this form spread throughout Europe and supplanted the regional chants. Alcuin himself was active in the musical reform of the Frankish churches, and he wrote a treatise on music that continued to exert an influence on liturgical music for many centuries. Another aspect of this liturgical reform was the standardization of sermons used by churchmen. Sometime between 786 and 800, Charlemagne circulated a letter in which he complained that the churches lacked good sermons and good texts of sermons. The king, or his scholar-advisers, found a man at Monte Cassino capable of assembling a collection of such works; Paul the Deacon undertook the project in the early years of the ninth century and produced a collection that contained excellent homilies suitable to all the great feasts and the annual cycle of Masses.

The main thrust of the reform was twofold. It sought to standardize and, in standardizing, to ensure the quality of ecclesiastical discipline and practices. The reformers hoped to overcome provincialism by attacking its very basis—local liturgical practices and clerical customs. A second part of this program consisted in the training of a new clergy at the revitalized court school. The centralization of clerical education, at least for the highest grades of the clergy, went far toward rooting out the localism that had prevailed in the Frankish churches. It also made the churches more amenable than before to royal influence and authority. Thus the reform program was a realization of Charlemagne's authority in and responsibility for, as God's vicar on earth, his kingdom's churches.

Notwithstanding the rather specific focus of the court's activities, their importance went far beyond reform of the churches. Alcuin restructured the educational system, basing it on the seven liberal arts organized by the textbook writers of late antiquity. He divided these subjects into two curricula— the *trivium* and the *quadrivium*. The *trivium* comprised grammar, dialectic, and rhetoric; the *quadrivium* included arithmetic, geometry, astronomy, and music. Grammar (that is, Latin grammar) was the primary subject and embraced not only morphology and syntax but also literature. In connection with this study, the court commissioned Europe's leading grammarian, Peter of Pisa, to prepare a standard edition of the grammatical handbooks written in the fifth century. Dialectic consisted of rudimentary studies in logic based on the few treatises of Aristotle that had been translated by Boethius. The principal part of the *trivium* was rhetoric, the central subject of education in antiquity. Along with that of grammar, the study of rhetoric was especially relevant for the scholars engaged in the great editing projects of the age. The second curriculum, the *quadrivium,* was important for the king's officials, who needed the intellectual tools for administering the royal estates and for other royal business. The relevance of arithmetic and geometry for their work is obvious. Astronomy held the key to calculating dates, an important function for Church life and estate management, and music had been closely connected with cosmology ever since Pythagoras had speculated on the reflection of the structure of the universe in the intervals between musical tones. Study of music was particularly appropriate for future churchmen.

Charlemagne's school brought together several old educational traditions. It became the training ground for bishops and royal officials, who once studied at cathedral and monastic schools. These schools continued to function throughout the Carolingian period, however, and remained the backbone of the educational system. Alcuin's reforms soon spread to them. The court school itself had of course undergone important changes. That school had been maintained to serve the sons of noblemen sent to the court for their education, or, more generally, their formation, since custom dictated that families sent their sons to be raised at the households of their superiors. During Charlemagne's reign, some of these young men obtained a fine education and even caused their families chagrin by choosing to enter the Church in order to pursue their intellectual interests free of the obligations and life style of the Carolingian aristocracy. Charlemagne himself lost a young relative to the ecclesiastical, intellectual profession.

An important byproduct of the royal program of educational and ecclesiastical reform was the transformation of script, which resulted in the creation of Carolingian Minuscule. This is the script in which this book is printed. It may have been developed as a conscious effort to make the newly standardized texts easy to read. The Romans used a majuscule script for copying books, in which all letters fit between two lines and in which there was no separation between words and no punctuation. They also employed a cursive script for private correspondence and documents, characterized by complex letter forms and connected letters called ligatures. The Merovingians used ligatures extensively and separated words in their scripts, which were not standardized, but they did not make consistent letter forms. This made their hands difficult to read and contributed to the textual corruptions of the Bible and liturgical works. The cursive script used in their charters and correspondence was a form of torture original with the Merovingians. Reading any of these texts has always required education and practice; even the scribes of the seventh and eighth centuries did not have an easy time with such scripts.

The new script developed in monastic scriptoria connected with Alcuin and his associates. By the early ninth century, monastic copyists, notably at Saint Martin of Tours, where Alcuin himself was abbot, were producing beautifully written manuscripts in Carolingian Minuscule. That hand continued to be used until the thirteenth century, when it developed into an increasingly angular and complex style called Gothic. When the Humanists of the Italian Renaissance sought the earliest texts of the classical works they esteemed, they found them in the beautifully clear hand of the Carolingian monks, which they contrasted derisively with the awkward, difficult to read, and overly ornate Gothic of late medieval scribes. The Humanists thought they had found the beloved works in the script of their authors, and they revived the script along with the literature. It has come to us from them.

The finds of the fifteenth- and sixteenth-century Humanists indicate the wide-ranging interests and activities of the Carolingian intellectuals. Although their principal concerns were ecclesiastical and liturgical, in pursuit of these interests they founded their work on the widest possible education. Thus they searched libraries for classical works that became models for their literary styles and sources for the subjects of their works. There were several fine Latin poets, such as the Visigothic refugee Theodulf, who became bishop of Orléans under Charlemagne and who was a frequent visitor at the king's court. Many scholars imitated the ancients' passion for history. Paul the Deacon wrote a great *History of the Lombards* on the model of the histories

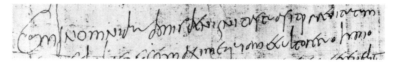

Roman Book Script. Virgil, *Georgics* IV, 170 (fourth century).
*Ac veluti lenti Cyclopes fulmina massis*

Late Roman Cursive. Private letter (fourth century).
*Cum in omnibus bonis benignitas tua sit praedita, tum*

Merovingian Book Script. Luxeuil Lectionary (seventh century).
*Et uidet lenteamina posita, et sudarium, quod fu-*

Merovingian Book Script. Saint Gregory, *Dialogues* II, 28 (eighth century).
*In vitreo vase remaneret. Tunc quidam subdiaconus Agapitus nomine*

Merovingian Charter Script. Childebert III (A.D. 695).
*Cum nos, in D(e)i nom(ine) Compendium in palacio nostro una cum nostris fedelebus resederem(us)* (Letters in parentheses are abbreviated in text.)

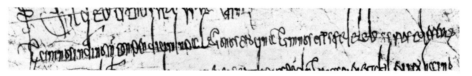

Carolingian Minuscule. Zurich Alcuin Bible, Genesis 1:3 (ca. A.D. 800).
*Dixit vero D(eu)s congregentur aque quae* (Letters in parentheses are abbreviated in text.)

Carolingian Minuscule. Psalter (A.D. 872–883).
*ditabitur institiam tuam quia*

of Rome by the ancients, and through him and others the works of earlier historians like Eusebius, Jerome, and Orosius were brought back into circulation. Einhard, Charlemagne's principal biographer, demonstrated the same classical influence when he constructed his biography following the pattern of Suetonius' *Lives of the Twelve Caesars.* Peter of Pisa's work on ancient grammar has already been mentioned.

The court scholars naturally became deeply involved in their king's theological disputes and policies. At Charlemagne's request, a group of them composed the *Libri Carolini,* which reaffirmed the position of Gregory the Great on the use of icons. Since Pope Adrian was constrained to accept the doctrine contained in these books, it became the definitive orthodox statement on images in the West. Another instance in which Charlemagne asserted his leadership of the Western Church in doctrinal matters was the endorsement by a synod, held in 808 at Aachen, of the doctrine, defined a few years earlier by Alcuin, concerning the relations between the Holy Spirit and the First and Second Persons of the Trinity. According to Byzantine theologians, the Holy Spirit should be understood to proceed "from the Father *through* the Son," a concept repugnant to theologians who agreed with Alcuin's statement of the traditional Western definition of the Holy Spirit as proceeding "from the Father *and* the Son." From the crucial words of the Latin formula, this dispute is known as the *filioque* (and the Son) controversy. The popes did not oppose the Carolingian view, which was derived from both Augustine and Gregory I and minimized any distinction between the Father and the Son in theology. But they were reluctant to press so fine a distinction at the risk of further alienating the Eastern from the Western half of Christendom. Under pressure from the Carolingian theologians supported by Charlemagne and his successors, however, the Frankish definition was allowed as an acceptable addition to the Creed, and in the twelfth century it was incorporated into the orthodox Latin statement of the Creed.

One other important theological controversy during Charlemagne's reign arose in the reconquered portion of Spain, where the last vestiges of Visigothic Arianism found expression in the heresy of Adoptionism. Adoptionists held that Christ was the Son of God, in his human nature, only by divine grace or adoption. Charlemagne's theologians roundly condemned the doctrine, as did the synod held at Frankfort in 794, where the monarch presided and engaged in the debates.

Apart from their importance in Church history, these theological disputes have a significance for intellectual history because they show that the Carolingian scholars had mastered the Latin Fathers. Alcuin and his associates restored patristic studies to the level achieved by Bede. During the reign of Charles the Bald (840–877) further advances were made when the earliest formal treatises on the problem of the Real Presence in the Eucharist were written by Ratramnus and Radbertus, two monks of the abbey of Corbie in northern Gaul. Although both based their arguments on the writings of

Augustine, they came to irreconcilably different conclusions. It is usual to emphasize that no controversy ensued on this abstruse subject, the implication being that settlement of the dispute was beyond the intellectual reach of contemporaries. From another point of view, it is just as important that for the first time since Augustine a mystery of the faith was treated in philosophical terms and with some originality.

Metaphysical problems did not interest Western theologians as much as questions bearing directly on Christian ethics and salvation. Thus the problem of predestination and human free will, revived because of the new mastery of Augustine's writings, stirred up the greatest number of controversial treatises of the whole period, although this problem is no less philosophically difficult than the Eucharistic question. The leading figure in this controversy was a Saxon, Gottschalk (d. 869), the first man to apprehend the full logical consequences of Augustine's writings on grace, free will, and predestination. Gottschalk's treatises on these subjects contained several unorthodox views and some statements explicitly rejected by earlier Church councils. His most extreme doctrine was that of a twofold predestination (that is, that God not only predestines the good to salvation but also the evil to damnation). It follows, according to Gottschalk, that the sacraments of the Church cannot save the wicked, that Christ did not die for all men but only for those predestined to salvation, and that human free will is totally inadequate to assist in attaining salvation. Most of Gottschalk's opponents concentrated on vindicating the efficacy of free will and the sacraments. Others launched a bitter persecution of Gottschalk himself, whose independent temper and rather strident personality had involved him in breaches of clerical discipline.

The theological interests of the Carolingian age were not exhausted by doctrinal controversies. Less well known but equally constructive were the continuing efforts to provide adequate commentaries on the books of the Bible, a work in which Bede and Alcuin at the beginning and end of the eighth century had excelled. A culmination of this kind of literature was reached in the compilations of two German scholars, Hrabanus Maurus (d. 856), abbot of the great monastery at Fulda, and Walafrid Strabo (d. 849), his pupil and abbot of Reichenau. These works became an important part of the exegetical tradition eventually embodied in the *Glossa Ordinaria* (Ordinary Gloss) on the Bible compiled in the twelfth century.

The greatest thinker of the ninth century was an Irish refugee who enjoyed the patronage of the emperor Charles the Bald. This was John Scotus Erigena (d. 877). John took part in the controversy over predestination, although contemporaries understood just enough of what he wrote to condemn it as unorthodox and to dismiss his contribution as "Scot's porridge." He was acquainted with pagan philosophy, and his knowledge of Greek was sufficient to enable him to translate the treatise attributed to Dionysius the Areopagite, *On the Celestial Hierarchy*. The work was actually by an anonymous late–fifth-century writer who attempted to harmonize Neo-Platonic metaphysics and Christian theology. The influence of Neo-Platonism, as well as of both the Greek and Latin Fathers, is evident in John's most ambitious work, a philosophical discourse entitled *On the Division of the Universe*. John's learning, his preference for reason over authority, his effort to combine theology and philosophy, and his originality have made him the most interesting personality of the Carolingian period to modern historians. More important in terms of the cultural development of Western Europe is the fact that no thinker of equal ability had less influence on contemporaries or on the future, partly because few people could understand him and partly because contemporaries had little interest in speculative philosophy. When later philosophers turned to his work it was not difficult to see the pantheistic tendencies of his treatise, and it was condemned as heretical in 1225.

Even John Scotus Erigena was not wholly exempt from the dependence on tradition and authority that characterized Carolingian thought and letters as a whole. In education, theology, and philosophy the sources of knowledge, the criteria of truth, and the range of intellectual interests were all dictated by the past. Where some independence or originality was achieved, it was usually accomplished only in the sense of applying the heritage of the past to new conditions or problems. This is also true of correspondence. The personal letters that have survived from the period reveal an imitative character. But of necessity they dealt with contemporary events and interests and are therefore more interesting than most of the other writing. More than one hundred letters are extant from the pen of Lupus of Ferrières (d. 862), the greatest classical scholar of the period. These and other letters reveal much about the eager search for manuscripts, the care in copying and preserving them, the emendation and correction of texts, and the other activities of ninth-century humanists.

The most significant advance was made in textural criticism. Lupus was not content simply with accurate copies of literary works, but by collating (systematically comparing, word for word) all the available manuscripts of the same work he sought to improve the existing texts. Part of this work included systematic glossing of the texts by insertion, between the lines or in the margin, of words or brief notes to explain the meaning of difficult terms and phrases. A glossary is thus a collection of such terms and phrases with explanatory notes, extracted from the text and arranged alphabetically. Lupus' classical studies did not absorb all his energies. He was a theologian of the first rank, the abbot of his monastery at Ferrières, an active adviser and emissary of Charles the Bald, and he even found time to accompany the army on more than one campaign. Despite these heavy drains on his time, Lupus' knowledge of classical literature and his literary style were unsurpassed in the whole period from the death of Bede until the twelfth century.

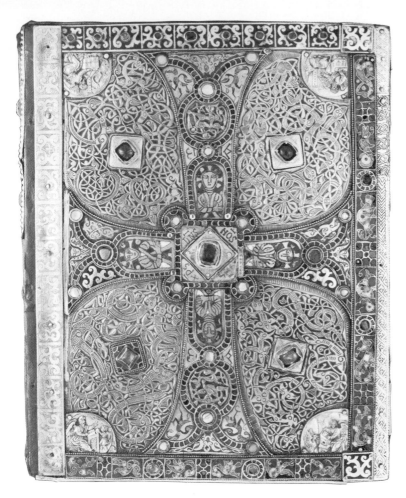

Carolingian scribes and illuminators produced magnificent books for use on special court occasions. After they prepared more than one hundred folios of vellum (each one made from the skin of an unborn lamb), dyed them purple, wrote them in gold ink, and filled them with masterpieces of illumination, they took great care with the binding, as is evident from the cover of the Lindau Gospels.

Carolingian historians produced more than the works by Einhard and Paul the Deacon mentioned earlier. Carolingian annals were on the whole more complete than the chronicles of the Merovingian age, and more of them were written. The annalists displayed their interest in contemporary history, of course, and some historians wrote about their own times. Nithard, an illegitimate grandson of Charlemagne, produced an excellent contemporary history entitled the *History of the Sons of Louis the Pious*. Written in an unassuming style, his *History* combines the interest in dramatic events reminiscent of Gregory of Tours with the clear prose and remarkable accuracy associated with Bede. Nithard preserved "the oldest extant specimen of a Romance language," the version of the Strasbourg Oath (842), which he copied down in the *lingua Romana* of his day. In the following extract the original Strasbourg Oath in Romance is on the left and a modern French translation on the right:

| | |
|---|---|
| *Pro Deo amur et pro christian poblo et nostro commun salvament, d'ist di in avant, in quant Deus savir et podir me dunat, si salvarai eo cist meon fradre Karlo et in aiudha et in cadhuna cosa, si cum om per dreit son fradra salvar dift. . . .* | *Pour l'amour de Dieu et pour le peuple chrétien et notre salut commun, à partir d'aujourd'hui, en tant que Dieu me donnera savoir et pouvoir, je secourrai ce mien frère Charles par mon aide et en toute chose, comme on doit secourir son frère, selon l'équité. . . .* |

Carolingian interest in the Germanic past is illustrated by Charlemagne's unsuccessful attempt to preserve in writing the old Teutonic myths and by his order that the customary laws of the Germanic tribes within his empire be written down. If this project was ever completed, the results have not survived, but it is known that the Salic Law of the Franks was reedited and published in an official version at this time.

As Charlemagne's court attained greatness, it required a grand artistic production for its adornment. Monastic scriptoria produced magnificent presentation copies of the Bible and a few other works. These texts were sometimes made on the finest parchment, dyed purple and written with gold ink. They were illuminated and often were bound in covers of carved ivory or worked gold or silver, often with inlaid gems. Some of these bindings still exist; many, such as the one that once bound the famed Book of Kells, were stolen and melted down. The art of these works and of altar pieces, reliquaries, and utensils displays such a rich diversity of traditions and influences in interrelations so complex that generalizations are hazardous. Celtic motifs, the abstract style of the north, Mediterranean models, late Roman naturalistic style, contemporary Byzantine neo-Hellenistic narrative representation, and Greco-Oriental ornamentalism are all intermixed. In architecture, monumental sculpture, wall paintings, and mosaics, nothing of interest or value was accomplished in the period. Charlemagne's palace church at Aachen, the only surviving architectural monument, is a slavish copy of the Byzantine central-space church of San Vitale in Ravenna. The Carolingian builders were not only dependent on San Vitale for their design, they even had to transport the columns and mosaics adorning the walls of their new church from Italy.

### Suggestions for Further Reading

For a general introduction to the culture of Charlemagne's Europe, see the works by Fichtenau and Bullough cited at the end of Chapter 6. The second part of M. L. W. Laistner, *Thought and Letters in Western Europe*, A.D. *500 to 900*, 2nd ed. (Ithaca, N.Y., 1957) is an excellent survey of the Carolingian renaissance. On Alcuin, see E. S. Duckett, *Alcuin, Friend of Charlemagne* (New York, 1951). The history of Carolingian arts is surveyed in K. J. Conant, *Carolingian and Romanesque Architecture* (Harmondsworth, 1959), and A. Grabar and C. Nordenfalk, *Early Medieval Painting: From the Fourth to the Eleventh Century*, trans. S. Gilbert (New York, 1957).

# THE REORGANIZATION
# OF MEDIEVAL EUROPE

# 8 Disintegration and Recovery in the West

When Charlemagne took the imperial title, he became the personification of his far-flung kingdoms. But the unity he represented as emperor was an illusion, and the collection of kingdoms he ruled could hardly be called an empire. The political fabric of this great conglomerate began to disintegrate almost immediately after his death in 814. The breakdown of central government had many causes—rivalry among royal contenders; new invasions from the north, east, and south; and the cultural and historical differences among the peoples of the empire.

## The Collapse of the Carolingian Empire: Civil Wars and New Invasions

Except for the three years (768–771) when Charlemagne shared the kingship with his brother Carloman, that authority was held by one ruler for three generations, from 751 to 840. This concentration of power was fortuitous, for throughout the period succession continued to be controlled by the ancient principle of equal division among the sons of the late king. Charlemagne had followed the tradition in 806, when he divided his realm among his three sons, Pepin, Carloman, and Louis. The great king's power prevented these men from engaging in a struggle like the one Charlemagne had had with his brother, and only Louis lived to succeed his father. But what Charlemagne's power and the deaths of his sons prevented in the years from 806 to 814, occurred under Louis.

Louis the Pious (814–840), so-called because of his association with monks and churchmen, succeeded to the throne in 814. He was not the only claimant, but he rushed to Aachen as soon as he received the news of his father's death, and his nephews soon disappeared. In the Middle Ages, piety often accompanied a sound grasp of political realities. Louis has been treated poorly by historians because he has always been compared with his father, but he was intelligent and well educated. Louis was a zealous supporter of the ecclesiastical reform program begun by Charlemagne, and one of his first acts was to rid the royal court of his father's close associates, who had a reputation for riotous licentiousness. Louis' intention may have been to consolidate his own power in the court by placing his own trusted companions in the royal entourage, but by his action he earned the reputation for moral righteousness and gave weight to his sobriquet. Under the influence of ecclesiastical advisers, Louis promoted reforms in the discipline of monastic communities and cathedral clergy. He supported the monastic reformer Benedict of Aniane (751–821), called the second Saint Benedict, and in 817 he imposed the Benedictine rule on all monastic communities in the empire. Louis also supported episcopal reformers who tried to impose a regular life —that is, a life according to a rule—on the cathedral clergy. The success of this reform effort was only temporary, but it established an important precedent.

Louis also followed Charlemagne's political and military policies. He succeeded in keeping Bavaria and Aquitaine under his authority and even extended the sway of his monarchy to Brittany, which had remained outside Charlemagne's power. He continued to support the war of attrition against the Moslems in the south, and in the north, he tried to maintain the frontiers against the Scandinavians. In almost every instance, however, Louis' activities were defensive, whereas his father's had been offensive. Charlemagne had seized the momentum of expansion and centralization passed on by his father and grandfather and had mustered his kingdom for a great round of conquest. By the early ninth century, the resources of the Frankish kingdom precluded any further expansion in Europe. Louis was left to hold the extended borders, and he did a reasonably good job, especially considering his domestic problems.

Louis became emperor in 814 at the age of forty. The previous year Charlemagne had crowned him co-emperor to ensure succession to the title

An acrostic poem covers this portrait of Louis the Pious made around 840. The letters making up the cross and the halo, which are part of the main poem, form poems of their own.

(the imperial title was not mentioned in the division of 806). In so doing, Charlemagne ignored the papal role in the imperial coronation; the *imperium* came from God through its holder. The pope's participation, if at all necessary, had only given impetus to the transmission of the dignity from emperor to successor. Louis followed this precedent in 817. Since his sons had already reached their majority when he became emperor, Louis divided the kingdom among his three sons—Lothair, Pepin, and Louis—only three years after he assumed power. Lothair received a great stretch of territory from the North Sea to Rome, including Burgundy and Provence. With this middle kingdom went the imperial title; Lothair was designated co-augustus and would actually receive the *imperium* when his father died. He would then hold a higher authority than his brothers and thus be able to hold the kingdom together. Pepin acquired the kingdom of Aquitaine and territories

This manuscript illumination portrays the emperor Charles the Bald with his councilors. It captures the majesty of imperial authority by placing Charles on a high throne, but it has a more subtle, symbolic meaning as well. The shroud hanging above the emperor separates him from the divine power he represents on earth. This power is given to him through the hand that stretches forth from heaven above his head, which is higher than the heads of his councilors. Charles holds a special position relative to God; he is closest to the firmament that separates the world of the spirit from that of the flesh, over which Charles rules. During the Ottonian period, this image of the emperor as minister of God on earth was enhanced in similar portraits by lowering the shroud, so the emperor's head and shoulders were within the realm of God.

including the Neustrian kingdom centered on Paris and Orléans. He also had suzerainty over Brittany. When Pepin died, he was succeeded by Charles, later called "the Bald," who was the issue of Louis the Pious' second marriage. Louis received the eastern, German section of the realm with suzerainty over Bavaria; he consequently became known as Louis the German.

It is doubtful that Charlemagne could have made this arrangement work; Louis certainly could not. Within a few years, the young kings began a series of civil wars that often had them aligned against their father. At one point in 832 Louis was practically imprisoned in Aachen. These wars did extensive damage to the royal house. First, they allowed independent-minded Frankish aristocrats to strengthen their own positions by playing members of the royal house against one another. As a result, the emperor and his sons granted or promised estates and benefices to their supporters, thereby diminishing their own wealth and position. In doing this, Louis the Pious ignored his own decrees. Second, the wars forced Louis to recognize papal rights to bestow the imperial title. In 817 he permitted himself to be crowned by Pope Stephen IV but crowned his son Lothair himself. In 823 he allowed Pope Paschal I to recrown Lothair in order to shore up Lothair's claim to the imperial title in the face of his brothers' challenges. This coronation confirmed the principle that "no one was emperor who had not received the crown in Rome at the pope's hand." It weakened the empire and placed the papacy in a central position within the political framework of Europe. Finally, in a surprising action, Louis the Pious was deposed by the episcopacy of the Frankish kingdom. In 833 the bishops allied themselves with the emperor's sons and judged Louis unfit to exercise the royal power. They excommunicated him and forced him to do penance. When Louis had satisfied their demands, his power was gone, and for the remaining seven years of his reign, he was little more than a pawn in the struggle among his sons. When he died in 840, he left a realm confused by almost twenty years of rebellions, shifting alliances, and the progressive diminution of royal authority.

Lothair (840–855) succeeded without opposition to the title of emperor, but here agreement among the surviving sons ended. Lothair's goal was to relegate his brothers to the subordinate position intended in the settlement of 817. He was supported by most of the magnates of Austrasia, Burgundy, and Italy, and also by the papacy and the ecclesiastical lords who adhered to the ideal of imperial unity. His brother, Louis the German (840–876), was king of the East Franks. His half brother, Charles the Bald (840–877), was king of the West Franks. They combined forces to reduce Lothair to an equality with them, leaving him only the superior titular dignity of emperor, while they sought full independence for their respective kingdoms.

Another round of warfare was inevitable. In a bloody but inconclusive slaughter known as the Battle of Fontenay (841), Lothair's brothers checked his ambitions. They then met at Strasbourg the following year and sealed their alliance by the famous Strasbourg Oath, whose significance in cultural history was noted in Chapter 7. Charles took the oath of alliance in the contemporary German vernacular, so that his half brother's troops might understand him, while Louis for the same reason swore his oath in the Romance tongue then spoken by the West Franks.

Confronted by this alliance, Lothair submitted. By the Treaty of Verdun (843), the Carolingian empire was divided into three independent kingdoms; Lothair retained the imperial dignity. Historians have sometimes referred to this partition as the remote origin of modern France and Germany. In a very elementary geographical sense this is partly true: most of the lands of Charles the Bald's kingdom have been, in modern times, part of France, and most of the lands assigned to Louis the German have been part of (or claimed by) modern Germany. But it would be a mistake to assume that the three brothers were motivated by protonationalistic considerations. The boundaries drawn in 843 ignored linguistic, natural, and strategic frontiers (and, of course, there were no cultural or economic differences that could be distinguished by a line on a map). The strangely zigzagging boundaries were drawn, primarily, so that each brother would receive an approximately equal share of the Carolingian crown lands (the resources at the immediate disposal of each ruler). There may also have been some concern with the placement of the bishoprics and the landed estates of the ecclesiastical and lay nobles who supported each of the three brothers. Of the three realms, Lothair's middle kingdom exhibited the greatest diversity of language, culture, and economic life, and from a military point of view it was the least defensible. The significance of the partition of Verdun can be summed up as the final disappearance of the actual political unity of Western Christendom, although the ideal of unity survived as a basic concept in the political ideology of the West.

The next stage in the disintegration of the Carolingian empire followed the death of Lothair, who as emperor had championed the principle of unity, but who still adhered to Frankish ideas of succession. In 855 his kingdom was divided equally among his three sons. Louis, his eldest son, took Italy and the imperial title. Charles reigned, but hardly could be said to have ruled, in the kingdom of Provence (between the Alps on the east and the Rhone on the west, from Arles in the south to Basel in the north). Lothair II received the northern third, "Lothair's Kingdom," or Lotharingia (*Lotharii regnum*), as it was called, comprising modern Lorraine and the Netherlands. After Lothair II died in 870, Lotharingia was split between Charles the Bald and Louis the German by the Treaty of Mersen. The cooperation between Charles the Bald and Louis the German, which had long been to the detriment of Lothair and his heirs, ended when the emperor Louis died in 875. His two uncles went to war over the succession to the imperial dignity, and after a brief struggle, Charles won. He received the imperial crown in Rome and reigned as emperor for the last two years of his life.

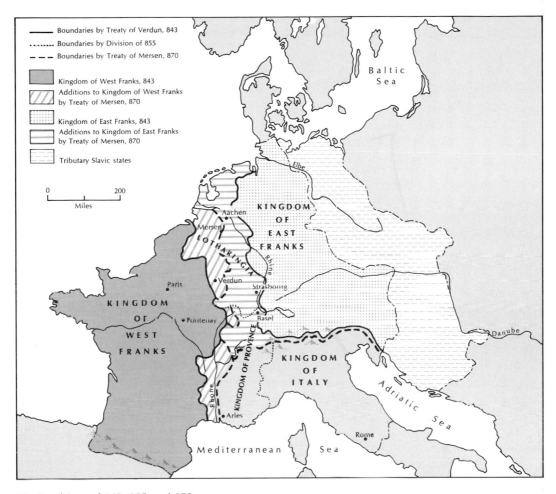

Boundaries by Treaty of Verdun, 843
Boundaries by Division of 855
Boundaries by Treaty of Mersen, 870

Kingdom of West Franks, 843
Additions to Kingdom of West Franks by Treaty of Mersen, 870

Kingdom of East Franks, 843
Additions to Kingdom of East Franks by Treaty of Mersen, 870

Tributary Slavic states

The Partitions of 843, 855, and 870

When Louis the German died in 876, he was succeeded by three sons. Of these sons, the most important was Charles the Fat, who became emperor in 884 but was deposed for incompetence in 887. Charles was succeeded as king of the East Franks by his nephew Arnulf (887–899), who also won the imperial crown three years before he died. There were hiatuses in the series of imperial titleholders: the successors of Charles the Bald in the kingdom of the West Franks never obtained the imperial title, but Charles' dynasty lasted longer than did that of Louis the German. In 877 Charles was succeeded by a single son, Louis the Stammerer, but Louis died two years later, and his two eldest sons succeeded him. Louis III, although only in his late teens, showed promise of becoming an effective leader against the Vikings, but after achieving an impressive victory against them in 882, he was killed in a peculiar but characteristic accident. Returning home from the battle, Louis galloped off in pursuit of a woman who had taken his fancy. She ducked beneath an archway, but Louis, in his haste, did not. After his brother died in 884, the West Frankish branch of the Carolingian house was excluded for a time from the kingship. During this period the Robertian counts of Paris began to contest the royal power with the successors of Charles the Bald, a conflict that continued for a century before issuing in the establishment of Hugh Capet, count of Paris, as king in 987.

After the deaths of Charles the Bald and Louis the German, the Carolingian dynasty rapidly declined. The sobriquets of the various successors almost tell the story—"the Stammerer," "the Fat," "the Child," "the Simple." Continued adherence to the principle of divided succession certainly played a role in the weakening of both branches of the royal house, but other factors also made themselves felt. The civil wars during the ninth century had crucially weakened the family, since the various kings were forced to grant away huge amounts of royal lands in order to keep the loyalty of their supporters. Under the weakened and competing kings, the particularistic tendencies of feudalism were realized. By the end of the ninth century, the kings remained suzerains but not sovereigns. Governmental authority was exercised by feudal lords who had extorted or usurped jurisdictional rights and who recognized the royal authority as the source of their own legitimacy but ignored it otherwise. This development of political particularism was accelerated by the arrival of new invaders, whose attacks tended to be localized and swift, thereby requiring the quick reaction of aristocratic leaders in the endangered district.

The most serious problems were caused by the Viking raids, which had begun before the turn of the ninth century and increased in number and seriousness during the reigns of Louis the Pious and his sons. Toward the end of the eighth century, Northmen appeared in Western Europe as traders, part of the commercial network of the North and Baltic seas. But these traders were always strongly inclined toward piracy, and they made numerous minor raids on shrines and monasteries, whose gold and silver objects proved a great attraction. The monarchs paid little attention to these attacks until the Vikings sacked and destroyed the great monastic center at Lindisfarne in England (793). Lindisfarne was one of Europe's greatest intellectual and artistic centers, whose loss Europeans felt deeply; its destruction made them recognize their own vulnerability. The Vikings had demonstrated a capacity for undertaking major military operations. It became clear that royal governments would have to take action against such dangers.

Who were the new barbarians? Called Northmen by the Europeans, they came fom Norway, Sweden, and Denmark. Culturally, they were closely related to the Germanic peoples who had migrated into the Roman Empire

Before the Germans learned the Latin alphabet, they wrote in Runes, an alphabet based on Greek but modified for ease of carving into wood and stone. The earliest examples are from the second and third centuries A.D. The German Runic alphabet was of twenty-four characters; the Anglo-Saxon, thirty; and the Norse (pictured on the Rune stone here), only sixteen. Since almost all the Runic inscriptions now extant are poems, the word *Rune* is sometimes used to mean "old Germanic poem." The Latin alphabet replaced Runes when the Germans, and eventually the Norse, came into contact with the Europeans and were Christianized.

centuries earlier, but the northerners had maintained the social structures and institutions of early Germanic society. Agriculture was carried out on homesteads rather than in villages because the land was not suited to the intense cultivation characteristic of the village economy. A loose district organization was represented in assembly meetings, where law suits and trading activities were pursued, but the districts were not defined, and the concept that the districts formed some sort of political entity would not have occurred to their inhabitants. The development of the northern trade brought the Northmen into contact with the Europeans. Increasingly, aristocratic clansmen gathered their clients, manned their long ships (*keels*), and took furs and other northern products to the wealthy markets of the Frankish and English kingdoms. The name *Viking,* by which these trader-warriors were often called, emphasized their freewheeling activities. The word meant simply "those who go away," and those who went away engaged in a great variety of activities: they fought as mercenaries; they traded; they raided; and after a few seasons they returned home and resumed their roles as local aristocrats

The timbers and nails of the Sutton Hoo ship burial left only their patterns and odd fragments in the soil of the barrow, but this ship burial at Oseberg, Sweden, was well preserved by the clay soil in which it rested. Although jewelry and metal work had been stolen, excavators still found kitchen utensils, the remains of cloths, several sleds, and a beautifully carved cart.

and farmers. As raiders, the Vikings were particularly difficult to deal with. They usually traveled by boat, so their victims had no early warning of their coming. They sailed their long ships up the rivers or along the coasts, attacked, and swept back out to sea. The royal government, even in the moments when it was not engaged in internecine warfare, could not muster its resources to meet such raids, nor was it expected to do so. The Frankish aristocrats had always been participants in government, and it was precisely in meeting local emergencies, such as the Viking attacks, that aristocratic responsibility rested. But the progressive weakening of royal government and the rapid increase in the number of raids resulted in the nobility's assumption of all effective governmental power.

The Vikings focused their raiding activities in accordance with their own geographical positions. The Norwegians attacked and settled in the Hebrides and Shetland Islands, in Scotland and Ireland, and in northern England. The Swedes moved eastward and established themselves in the Baltic, in Finland, and later in Russia, where they founded or conquered the Kievan state on the Dnieper. On the whole, the Swedes engaged in fewer attacks than their confreres, probably because they were the first to be brought under the authority of a central government. The king exerted some control over his aristocratic associates and organized their foreign activities. Finally, the Danes moved against Norway and Sweden to the north and against the Franks to the south. In the early ninth century, Gorm the Old succeeded in imposing his rule on the Danes, and he, like the Swedish kings, exercised his power by organizing foreign campaigns. In 810 a large Danish seaborne force swept over the Frisian coast and destroyed Charlemagne's defenses. The old Frankish king made immediate plans to lead an expedition against the invaders, but the confrontation never took place because Gorm was assassinated shortly after the invasion. For the next several years, his sons struggled with one another and with other forces for control of Denmark. Charlemagne and Louis the Pious tried to keep the factions at odds and used the respite to build a strong line of fortresses along the Frisian coast.

The emergence of Gorm the Old's son Horik as victor in Denmark and the breakdown of centralized government in the Frankish kingdom coincided in the 830s. Beginning in 834 Danish raids became a yearly feature of northern European life. Horik sent a force of two hundred long ships up the Seine to sack Paris in 834 and another huge force up the Elbe to destroy Hamburg, a northern bastion of Frankish power and an ecclesiastical center for missionary activities in Saxony, Frisia, and Denmark itself. About the same time, Danish forces invaded the Netherlands, destroying a number of major towns and fortresses. Throughout the ninth century, Viking armies—small and often independent of any Scandinavian royal power—established themselves in Brittany and raided up and down the Atlantic coast. From this base, they also attacked Moslem Spain, even achieving the amazing feat of sacking Seville in the heart of the powerful caliphate of Córdoba. The Moslem state was able to organize its defenses, however, and the Vikings were forced to find other victims. In the 850s, Viking leaders took their ships through the Straits of Gibraltar and attacked southern France, North Africa, and northern Italy. For a time, the Vikings settled on islands, from which they launched yearly raids along the Mediterranean; being seized by pirates became a common danger for merchants.

The raids changed character shortly after the middle of the ninth century.

About 860 Harald Finehair established central rule in Norway, and a large-scale migration from the country was led by aristocrats firmly opposed to royal power but not able to withstand Harald. Some of these clans went to Iceland, where they established a vital, antimonarchical community destined to have a long history and an impressive culture during the Middle Ages. Others emigrated to England, where a large disorganized force settled in Kent and East Anglia (Norfolk and Suffolk). Over the years this force grew as new contingents joined it, and it became known as the Great Army. In battling the Great Army, the royal house of Wessex, under Alfred the Great (871–899), established itself as the royal house of all the English. In the 870s Alfred defeated the Great Army and forced its contingents to settle in eastern England, in the area called the Danelaw during the Middle Ages because its inhabitants lived under the law of the Danes, or Scandinavians. In the tenth century Alfred's successors brought the Danelaw under their control.

Alfred's victory had a direct impact on the Continent. In the late 870s contingents bound for England and the Great Army went instead to north-western France, where they were joined by remnants of the Great Army not willing to settle in the Danelaw. For the next twenty or more years, northern Europe was under the constant threat of devastation by this large force. Louis III defeated a part of this army in 882 before succumbing to his libidinous drives. Out of this army the permanent settlement of Normandy ensued in the first years of the tenth century. Charles the Simple (898–922), who had attained the West Frankish throne after an interlude in which Count Robert of Paris held power, recognized Rollo, leader of the Norman settlers, by naming him duke of Normany in 911, thus legitimizing his rule and allying him to the West Frankish crown.

The Viking invasions were coming to an end at the turn of the tenth century. But as the settlement of the Vikings occurred, new invaders appeared from the south and the east. In the early ninth century, Moslem expansion in the Mediterranean had begun again. The principal target was Byzantine Sicily, attacked in 827 and conquered piecemeal in the course of the ninth century. From Sicilian bases, the Moslems launched raids on the coastal towns of southern Italy. In 840 they captured the strategic port of Bari, and in 846 they raided Rome. Unable to breach the Wall of Aurelian, they pillaged the suburbs, including the basilicas of Saint Paul's Outside the Walls and Saint Peter's (also, at that time, outside the perimeter of the walls of Rome). Two years later, Leo IV (847–855) strengthened the defense of his city by repairing the main walls and enlarging fifteen towers as strong points. Finally, he enclosed the Vatican suburb (which included Saint Peter's) with a new wall, thus adding the so-called Leonine city to the fortified city of Rome. Meanwhile the Moslems had launched attacks on southern France, plundering Marseilles in 848. At about this time they began to occupy coastal strips permanently, either as Moslem principalities or simply as bases for

About the time the Vikings penetrated deep into northern Europe, the Moors of Africa renewed their expansion. They established bases in southern Europe, devastated large districts of Italy and southern France, and conquered Sicily. This miniature from a Spanish manuscript shows the Moorish cavalry with its drums and trumpets.

more extended pillage. Of the latter, the two most important strongholds were Fraxinetum, on the coast of Provence between Marseilles and Nice, and a fortress on the Garigliano River on the west coast of Italy between Rome and Naples. From the former base the Moslem "mountain goats," as they were called, ranged inland into the Alpine passes, plundering traders and travelers and pillaging as far north as southern Germany. From their base on the Garigliano, the Moslems destroyed the monastery of Monte Cassino, in 881, and plundered the Papal States. The most effective check on these Moslem raiders was their own internecine strife. Their leaders were often rebels against the North African rulers and were thus cut off from reinforce-

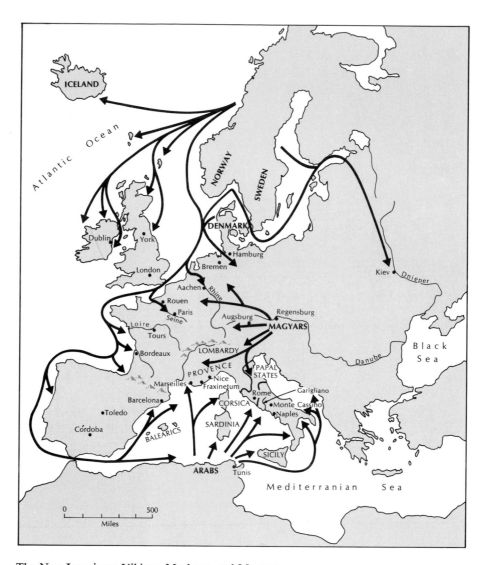

The New Invasions: Vikings, Moslems, and Magyars

ments. This was fortunate for Italy and southern Europe, whose Christian
defenders were no less internally divided than were the Moslems.

Before the close of the ninth century a third wave of invasions had begun,
this time from the east. The Magyars arrived in the upper Danube plains,
taking over the area formerly controlled by the Avars, modern Hungary. In
899 they poured into northern Italy and left Lombardy a shambles. In the
following year they began a series of almost annual raids deep into Germany.

## The Foundation of the Medieval Empire

In the late ninth century, the East Frankish kingdom was more stable than any other part of the Carolingian empire. Germany had suffered less because there was less wealth to attract raiders, because the nobility was powerful locally although fewer immunities and privileges existed to exclude the central power, and because the local tribal districts were kept under Carolingian control by assigning them to sons of the monarch. In 876 one son succeeded as king of Bavaria, another as king of Saxony; Charles the Fat became king of Swabia. By 882 the older sons were dead, and for five years Charles reunited the whole East Frankish kingdom. This generation of Carolingians was not very prolific. Only one of the three brothers had a son who survived to manhood, and his birth was illegitimate. This was Arnulf, who was given the duchy of Carinthia in the southeast and assigned the task of defending the frontier against the Slavs. For lack of sons or nephews, Charles the Fat had no other recourse than to allow the several tribal districts to revert to their previous status as duchies ruled by dukes appointed by the king.

These dukes were great magnates who represented local landed interests as much as the central government. The growth of localism in Germany centered around five great duchies: Saxony in the north, Franconia in the center, Swabia in the south, Bavaria in the southeast, and Lorraine west of the Rhine. In political and social development, Lorraine resembled the West Frankish realm: feudalism was developing as the basis for a new organization of society. The slower growth of feudalism in the other four duchies, where tribal society persisted, has given rise to the expression *stem duchies* (*Stamm,* or tribal, duchies), but tribal unity was not as important as the simple dynastic ambition of the dukes. The German dukes of the late ninth and the tenth centuries behaved much like the dukes of Aquitaine and of Bavaria during the reigns of Pepin the Short and Charlemagne, and their greater success in achieving local predominance is the measure of the decline of Carolingian central authority.

When Charles the Fat's incompetence led to his deposition in 887, the German magnates ignored the claims of the grandson of Charles the Bald, a mere boy, and instead chose as king the illegitimate grandson of Louis the German, Arnulf, duke of Carinthia. He was the only adult Carolingian who had proven himself a capable ruler. Arnulf (887–899) devoted most of his time to border warfare against the Slavs on the eastern frontier, but against the Northmen he won a great victory in 891 on the Dyle River in modern north-central Belgium. Germany was no longer troubled by invasion from that quarter after this battle. Following this and other victories, the pope appealed to him for protection against the factions in Italy whose quarrels and ambitions threatened not only the Papal States but the independence of the papacy. Arnulf made two expeditions into Italy, but he was unable to enforce his authority there even after he was crowned emperor in 896.

Arnulf was succeeded by his son, Louis the Child (899–911); he was six years old when he succeeded. Louis' reign brought the central power in Germany to its nadir. Except when they had joined forces against the Magyars, the dukes, counts, and other magnates of the kingdom fought incessantly against one another, jockeying for position and power in a kaleidoscopic political situation. When Louis died in 911, the magnates again had to cast about for a Carolingian to succeed him, but Louis had been the last German Carolingian, legitimate or illegitimate. The nobles again refused Charles the Bald's grandson, whom they had rejected in 887—Charles the Simple, king of the West Franks since 898. Instead they elevated Conrad, duke of Franconia, to the kingship, and as Conrad I (911–918), he spent the seven years of his rule vainly trying to assert royal authority over the magnates. Conrad was hemmed in by a kingship that was little more than the title but that made him divert his energies into pursuit of its interests. One sign of the disunity in the East Frankish kingdom and of the ineffectiveness of Conrad's monarchy was that Charles the Simple, no great king himself, succeeded in gaining control of the duchy of Lorraine. Conrad also lost the allegiance of upper Burgundy and was not able to muster the necessary forces to meet the Magyar campaigns that penetrated into the Rhineland and as far west as Burgundy and Lorraine. Louis the Child had been too weak to try, and Conrad I tried and failed to maintain the traditional leadership of the king over the German duchies.

On his deathbed, Conrad designated the duke of Saxony, Henry I the Fowler (918–936), as his successor. The nobles of Franconia and Saxony confirmed this choice by acclaiming Henry king after Conrad died. Henry spent the first few years of his reign forcing the dukes of Lorraine, Bavaria, and Swabia to recognize his kingship. He then concentrated on strengthening his own duchy of Saxony. This policy did not reflect Henry's lack of interest in the monarchy but rather his recognition that the foundation of his kingship lay in a strong power base in the kingdom. When Henry came to power in 918, the landed wealth of the East Frankish royal house had been reduced to 180 estates sprinkled about the realm. The dukes and lesser magnates had extorted or simply assumed control of most of the land that once had supported Carolingian government. The dukes and counts had even extended their power over many of the 180 royal estates, since they controlled the bailiffs on them. Henry knew all about this process of encroachment; he had been one of its most successful practitioners. Only five royal estates were left in Saxony in 918, and when Henry added his family lands to those of the royal house, the total number of estates held by the East Frankish king jumped to about six hundred.

Henry did not ignore his kingdom's interests in other respects either. He repulsed the northern Slavs and began a deliberate policy of eastern expansion called the _Drang nach Osten_ (push to the east). The essence of this policy was the colonization of frontier regions from which the Slavs and other peoples were pushed back. The border towns were fortified as burgs, such as Magdeburg, Oldenburg, and Lüneburg. Henry also built fortifications against the Magyars and raised a cavalry force that inflicted the first defeat on the fast-moving Magyar raiders in 933. In the course of his attempts to win recognition from the duchies, Henry brought Swabia into close relationship with his monarchy by successfully imposing a Saxon as duke after the death of Duke Burkhard without heir, and he connected Lorraine with his house by arranging a marriage alliance. He also began the arduous task of regaining direct control over royal estates throughout the realm. At the same time, it seems, he initiated a policy to bring the German episcopate and the great abbeys under the patronage of the monarchy. Control of the churches was the principal support of royal power in Germany for the next two hundred years. Henry the Fowler was the greatest German king since Louis the German. He strengthened the German monarchy, and he founded the Saxon dynasty, which lasted until 1024.

Henry's son, Otto I the Great (936–973), became king by what was in fact hereditary succession, although a formal election was held in accordance with custom. The dukes were quite willing to accept the son of a father who had left them largely independent. Otto continued his father's efforts to strengthen his duchy of Saxony, and he pressed forward the wars against the Slavs to the east. Otto also pursued his father's policies aimed at strengthening royal power, but whereas Henry had followed the royalist policies with moderation, Otto became an aggressive centralizer. He intended to enforce his authority over the dukes and magnates and to bind his realm into a united German kingdom. He was met by a series of rebellions centered in the duchies and spent the first five years of his reign suppressing them. He slowly gained control of the ducal power in Bavaria, Swabia, and Lorraine, and after 939, annexed Franconia to Saxony. To consolidate his power, Otto established his sons and other relatives as rulers of the duchies, but soon his sons had become leaders of local rebellions against him. The failure of nepotism forced Otto to adopt Henry's idea of controlling the churches and abbeys as the foundation of his power, and he pursued that policy energetically throughout his reign. To be successful, Otto's ecclesiastical policy depended on the king's ability to obtain the exclusive privilege to appoint archbishops and bishops throughout the kingdom. Otto successfully reasserted the Carolingian rights over ecclesiastical appointments, wresting from the dukes whatever influence over the Church they had usurped. In frontier districts, he established new bishoprics, such as Magdeburg and Prague, and tended to the ecclesiastical organization of conquered territories as carefully as to their military defense. He revived the Carolingian program of supporting missionaries in border areas, and as he gained control of the churches, he strengthened them by granting them land. From the ecclesiastical support he received, Otto gained three main advantages. First, he came into close contact with the best educated and ablest class of men in his kingdom and recruited them into his government. Second, the rule of celibacy was enforced among the higher clergy, if not among the lower, and thus ecclesiastical positions never became hereditary. Royal control over the churches was therefore much firmer than it was over even the most loyal feudatories. Third, Otto could rely on the bishops to be not only a counterbalance to rebellious or potentially rebellious magnates in their dioceses but also direct supporters of royal government. Otto accelerated the already ongoing process of feudalizing the Church and increasingly relied on armies provided by episcopal instead of lay vassals. The success of this program was demonstrated in 982 when Otto II went to Italy at the head of an army in which 76 percent of the troops were supplied by ecclesiastical vassals. In addition, Otto I delegated the exercise of royal power to bishops. When the duke of Lorraine rebelled, Otto suppressed the rebellion and then entrusted the archbishop of Cologne, who was Otto's brother Bruno, with ducal power. In the same way, the bishops of Bamberg and Würzburg became counts during Otto's reign.

Thus Otto the Great had become the most powerful ruler in Europe by the middle of the century. In many respects his reign was a revival of the Carolingian system, or an adaptation of the means employed by Charlemagne to secure results that, under new conditions, were not dissimilar to the goals achieved by Charlemagne. And like his Carolingian predecessors, Otto became involved in Italy. The German court had been a refuge for political exiles from Italy as early as 945. Otto's intervention could swing the balance in the confused struggles for the Italian kingship. In 951 an opportunity presented itself that was too tempting to turn down. Adelaide, the widow of one of the contestants, appealed for succor from the marriage her archenemy plotted to force on her in order to secure the crown for himself. Otto solved her problem by invading Italy, marrying Adelaide himself, and assuming the title of king of Italy. Contemporaries were delighted; they saw in these events a romantic episode in which the hero, Otto, rescued the lady in distress from the clutches of the evil suitor. Actually, Otto had sound political reasons for responding to this opportune appeal. Only by intervening himself could he prevent the king of Burgundy and his own overmighty subjects, the dukes of Swabia and of Bavaria, from rescuing Adelaide in order to win the throne. Control of the wealth of Italy would augment his meager revenues from the German crown lands and regalian rights. And finally, Otto was already planning to revive the imperial title, vacant since 924. As it turned out, a hostile pope and rebellion at home forced Otto to abandon these plans temporarily and to return to Germany.

An aftermath of the rebellion at home was a renewal of the Magyar raids into Germany. Some of Otto's rebellious magnates may even have appealed

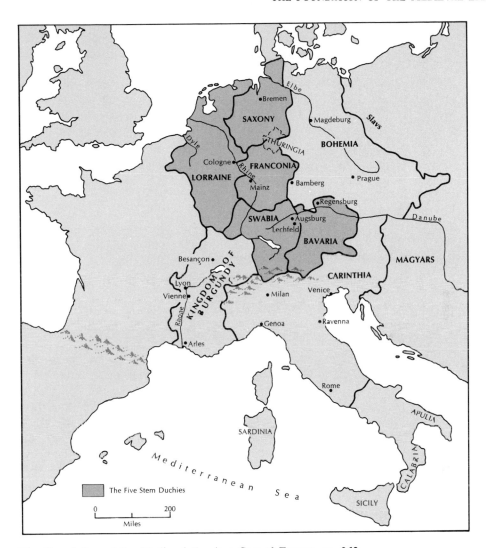

The Foundation of the Medieval Empire: Central Europe, ca. 960

to the Magyars for help against their king. Otto dealt the Magyars a crushing defeat in the Battle of Lechfeld, near Augsburg, in 955, after which they never again harassed Germany. Equally important, by this victory Otto secured his lines of communication with Italy and was now ready to revive his Italian plans. His second intervention south of the Alps came in response to an appeal from Pope John XII for protection against Berengar, marquis of Friuli, who had recently won general recognition as king of Italy in defiance of Otto's assumption of that title. Otto crossed the Alps in 961, put Berengar's forces to flight, and early in 962 received his promised reward by being crowned emperor by John XII.

This imperial coronation, so reminiscent of the coronation of Charlemagne, formed the real foundation of the medieval empire. However, both in geographical extent and in the powers exercised by Otto and his successors, the revived empire fell short of the Carolingian model. The most obvious difference was that Otto depended on the support of the Church. Otto's control of the Church gave him power, whereas Charlemagne's power gave him control of the Church. Also, the relations between the new emperor and the pope were by no means clear in 962, as they had been in 800. Otto thought his imperial authority gave him the right to control the pope just as his royal authority gave him power over his bishops. The growing connection of king and bishops in Germany had produced an ideology to justify royal power. As God's vicar, Otto administered his whole kingdom, lay and ecclesiastical, and while he did not have sacramental power, he did stand above common laymen and could claim authority in ecclesiastical affairs by virtue of his divine ordination. Many of the ideas used to justify this ideology of royal authority over ecclesiastics derived from theological writings of the Carolingian period, but they began to coalesce into a powerful doctrine of royal theocracy during Otto's reign. By the mid-eleventh century, they were fully developed. Otto's claims, however, were met by the countervailing ideas of Pope John XII. In John's view, the emperor was only the defender of the Holy See, and, in fact, the special meaning of the imperial title, at least as far as the Church was concerned, was that its holder was obligated to protect the Roman Church. Before the end of 962 Otto and John became definitively estranged when Otto demanded that no pope be consecrated until he or his son had approved the election. This demand was consistent with German practice, but John refused to accept it. Otto drove John from Rome and then presided over a synod that deposed the pope. On two subsequent occasions, Otto forced the election of his own candidate to the papal throne, thus setting a firm precedent for imperial control of the papacy.

Until the year before his death, Otto spent most of his time in Italy consolidating his control of the north and trying unsuccessfully to extend his power over the south. He also secured recognition of his new status from the Byzantine emperor, confirmed by the marriage of his son to a Byzantine princess, Theophano. After the substantial achievements of Otto the Great, the reign of his son, Otto II (973–983), was anticlimactic. Most of his time and energy was devoted to Germany, where he was on the defensive. He was able to suppress revolts among the dukes and magnates and to repel attacks by the Danes and the French, but the Slavs recovered the northern part of the territory conquered by his father. Toward the end of his reign, Otto II was finally free to pursue his personal ambition, the conquest of southern

The Germans were interested in pedigree, since the claim of a man to be king largely depended on his ability to claim membership in one of the many royal families that traced their genealogies to one of the gods. Thus one of the most important sources for the history of the early Germanic kingdoms is genealogies. The concern for family continued after Christianity had made descent from Woden irrelevant, and this genealogy of the Saxon dynasty preserves the ancient tradition. At the top is Liudolf, duke of Saxony, whose son Otto refused the throne after the death of Louis the Child (911). Under this Otto is Henry the Fowler, who accepted the throne eight years later. The influence of Rome and its Church is demonstrated not only by the absence of Woden but also by the use of realistic portraiture.

Italy. His attempt ended in a disastrous defeat in 982, and he died a year later, leaving an infant heir, Otto III (983–1002), under the regency of Theophano and Adelaide.

The succession of Otto III was unopposed in Italy, but in Germany the regency was accepted only after lengthy and tortuous diplomacy. After he came of age, Otto III succeeded in winning recognition in Germany at the price of allowing the dukes and magnates a larger measure of autonomy than they had enjoyed under Otto the Great and Otto II. The young king had been raised primarily in Italy under the tutelage of his cultivated mother and teachers she had chosen for him. He was well-educated and imbued with the traditions of Roman history, which induced him to see himself as the renewer of the Christian Roman Empire who would restore the imperial power of his father and grandfather to what it had been under Constantine. When Otto's former tutor, Gerbert of Reims, was elected pope in 999, he took the name Sylvester II to symbolize the rebirth of Constantine's empire. Otto III and Sylvester II wished to complete the work of Constantine and his pope, Sylvester I. It was a chimerical dream of two of Europe's best educated men. For Gerbert, who had traveled to Spain in search of knowledge, and Otto, raised in the cultured, cosmopolitan milieu created by his Byzantine mother, the world was one, and Roma, the ancient matron who personified Rome when the city and its culture were the center of the world, could again seize men's loyalties. But the great work of renovation failed. Otto III died childless in 1002, and the differences between the main centers of his empire, Italy and Germany, were more glaring than ever.

## The Feudal States of Europe

The contrast between Germany and France in the tenth century is striking. In Germany the kings, and after 962 the emperors, reestablished political order and led the defense against the Northmen, Slavs, and Magyars. Recovery followed the fortunes of the central authority. In France the power of the kings of the West Franks dwindled steadily until the end of the tenth century and did not begin to increase until toward the end of the eleventh. Recovery of some measure of political stability and defense against barbarian invaders was accomplished on the local level. The role of the king in this recovery scarcely differed from the parts played by a dozen great lords who were his nominal vassals but who in many instances were far more powerful than he. In Germany the authority of Otto the Great far exceeded that of Louis the German a century earlier; in France the authority of Charles the Bald was not equaled by any of his successors until the twelfth century.

This weakness of the central authority in France was due partly to a contest for the throne between the Carolingians and the Robertians. The latter descended from Robert the Strong (d. 866), count of the march of Neustria, which stretched across the territory roughly between the Seine and Loire rivers. After the inglorious reign of Charles the Fat and his deposition in 887, the French magnates, like the German dukes and counts, ignored the claims of the next in line of the Carolingian family. They chose instead Robert's son, Odo (887–898), who rose to prominence through his heroic defense of Paris against the Northmen in 885. During the century following the accession of Odo, three Robertians occupied the throne at different times for a total of twenty-five years, while four members of the Carolingian family were kings for a total of seventy-five years. In their efforts to retain the crown, the Carolingians progressively weakened the central authority by granting away most of the crown lands and much of their jurisdiction over duchies and counties to the local lords in return for often worthless promises of support against the Robertians. The Robertians did the same in parts of the kingdom, especially in Flanders and Lorraine, where their Carolingian opponent Charles the Simple had established himself. In those periods when a Carolingian wore the crown, the counts of Paris, as the Robertians were often called, attempted to control the monarchy in much the same way the Carolingians had done in the seventh and eighth centuries. Hugh the Great of Paris (d. 956) involved himself so deeply in royal politics that he weakened his family's position in the Île-de-France (the region surrounding Paris) where its power base lay. Hugh satisfied his royal ambitions with the title duke of *Francia*. His son Hugh Capet rejected his father's royal policy and devoted himself to strengthening his control over his rich county. For thirty years, the Carolingian king Lothair (954–986) enjoyed a peace unknown to his father and grandfather, both of whom had been in constant conflict with the Robertians. When Lothair's son died only a few months after he succeeded to the throne, the magnates elected Hugh Capet king. Hugh reigned for nine years (987–996) and founded the Capetian dynasty, which lasted in a direct line for more than three centuries.

The achievements of Hugh Capet and his early successors were very modest, but they kept the monarchy alive as a political force, and they arrested any further decline. The Capetians could not continue the Carolingian practice of granting away crown lands in the hope of gaining supporters, for there was practically none left to grant. Nor did the Capetians follow the vain policy of the later Carolingian kings, who dissipated their energies trying to assert their authority over the whole of France and to extend it over Lorraine. With few exceptions the early Capetians were realistic enough to pursue what has been called a "domainal policy." They restricted their efforts to enforcing obedience and maintaining order within the royal domain, which had shrunk until it included only the cities of Paris and Orléans and a strip of territory connecting the two. In this area Hugh Capet, his son Robert II the Pious (996–1031), and his grandson Henry I (1031–1060) pursued much the same policy as most other territorial magnates of the times. They contracted advantageous marriage alliances for their children; they waged endless petty wars against unruly lesser barons ensconced in hilltop forts; and they were always ready to seize a town or occupy a fief on the slightest pretext, thus adding bit by bit to the meager royal domain. As long as the early Capetians were content to behave like any other feudal lord, and made no real attempt to enforce their obedience, the greater dukes and counts were willing to give a nominal allegiance to the king. It is a striking sign of the character of Capetian kingship that none of these first successors of Hugh faced rebellions like those confronted by the German kings. The French monarchy was no threat to the interests and ambitions of the great feudal lords.

Luck, combined with the Capetians' competence, tenacity, and longevity, played a role in the family's successful maintenance of the kingship. From 987 to 1223, the average Capetian reigned for thirty-four years. Since rebellions normally accompanied successions, the long reigns gave fewer opportunities for rebellion than in other kingdoms, and this relative peace contributed to the monarchy's stability. In addition, although the Capetians had remarkably long reigns, nearly all of them succeeded to the throne as adults capable of meeting the obligations of government. Hugh Capet had taken the precaution to ensure his son's succession by having him crowned and associated with him as co-ruler. Later Capetians followed this precedent of crowning the designated successor before the death of the father until the second half of the twelfth century, when the dynasty was firmly established on a hereditary basis. The elective principle, which seemed about to triumph in the tenth century, did not survive under such circumstances.

The early Capetians inherited certain advantages that, no matter how slight their real power, provided a basis for future growth. The monarchy gave them prestige. They were the heirs of Charlemagne; they were kings anointed of God; they were the vassals of no other lord; and their moral authority was supported by the teachings of the Church. Also, they inherited from their Carolingian predecessors certain regalian rights that no duke or other feudal lord could assert. Most of these rights were ecclesiastical and derived from Charlemagne's control of the Church. The Capetian kings could nominate new abbots and bishops in monasteries and bishoprics founded by earlier kings or under royal protection. They could collect revenues arising from the lands or the ecclesiastical courts of vacant abbeys and bishoprics, after the death of the old and before the election of the new abbot or bishop. These, with other rights extended over two dozen bishoprics and three dozen monasteries both within and without the royal domain. Finally, feudalism, so far advanced in France, paradoxically both protected and weakened royal power. The great feudatories repeatedly recognized the suzerainty of the king because the king permitted them to govern their territories independently. Furthermore, the sanctity of the feudal bond was very important to the great lords as the foundation for their control over their own vassals.

The great feudatories of the kingdom had been created at the same time and in the same way as the Capetian royal domain. Many of the lords were descendants of Carolingian counts who had converted their offices into hereditary titles and their counties into hereditary fiefs. Others were magnates who had carved out spheres of power during the chaotic years of the Viking invasions and had expanded and consolidated that power during succeeding generations. The process by which the greater lords had acquiesced in the usurpations of lesser lords, legitimizing their authority by granting them fiefs over lands the lesser nobles already held, now began to work in favor of centralization. The feudal relationship gave lords an excuse and a right to demand loyalty from their less powerful neighbors and to obtain control over the lands of those who died without male heirs. In those areas where the great lords stemmed from Carolingian counts or had succeeded to the power of the counts, the title *count* lived on, although the office differed from the countship under Charlemagne. In those areas, such as Normandy and Aquitaine, where the ruler had achieved his position outside royal government, the higher title *duke* was used. The Viking leader Rollo received only legitimization of his power from Charles the Simple; he was called the duke of Normandy. The territorial authority in Aquitaine went back to Merovingian times and even when the Carolingians were able to assert their superiority over the dukes of Aquitaine, the relationship was one of reciprocity rather than one of subordination.

By the first half of the eleventh century, the duchies and counties of France exhibited cultural and linguistic, as well as political, diversity. In Normandy, the Northmen had occupied the area around Rouen on the lower Seine. Some regions of the county were still Norse-speaking in the twelfth century, but on the whole, the Normans quickly assimilated the north French culture. By the mid-eleventh century, most inhabitants of the region spoke the Norman French dialect, which was created by the intercourse between the conquerors and the native population. Because it recently had been founded by a war band, this duchy was the best organized in the kingdom. The duke had to control his unruly vassals but did not have to confront subordinates who had developed their positions of power independently of him.

To the west and south of Normandy was the county of Brittany, whose half-Celtic people were no less independent of the French king but were much less assimilated into the culture of Carolingian and Capetian France. East of Brittany and south of Normandy in the valley of the lower Loire River was the county of Anjou, whose counts were descended from leaders in the resistance against Viking raids. In the eleventh century they were absorbed in quelling the violence of their vassals or expanding their domain by a singular display of ferocity.

South of Anjou and stretching across much of south-central France toward the Rhone lay the former Carolingian kingdom of Aquitaine. Its ducal title had been a prize of the competition among the region's great families. At first it was held by the counts of Auvergne, in the eastern part, and then it was contested between the counts of Poitiers in the north and of Toulouse in the south. By the middle of the tenth century the counts of Poitiers had won control of Aquitaine, and within a century they had annexed the duchy of Gascony to the south. Meanwhile the counts of Toulouse pushed eastward to the Mediterranean by conquering Septimania, now known as the march of Gothia because of its earlier Visigothic rulers. These southern provinces—Aquitaine, Gascony, Toulouse, and their dependent counties—differed from the north both culturally and in the slower growth of feudal institutions. Collectively they came to be distinguished as the land of the Languedoc (from *oc,* or late Latin *hoc,* yes) in contrast with the northern regions of the Languedoïl (from *oïl,* or late Latin *hoc ille,* the modern French *oui,* yes).

East of the duchy of Aquitaine were Provence and Burgundy—the coastal region to the south, the Rhone valley, and the mountainous regions of eastern France, western Switzerland, and the border between France and Italy. Carolingian control in this area lapsed after the death of Lothair I in 855. Lothair's son Charles (d. 863) tried vainly to curb the unruly and volatile local nobles, while conditions steadily deteriorated with the advent of Moslem raiders. Then one of the nobles, Boso, organized resistance in Provence and subdued the Rhone valley as far north as Lyons. During a colorful career Boso had married the daughter of the emperor, Louis II of Italy (855–875), acquired such titles as count of Vienne and duke of Lyons, and had acted briefly as regent in Italy for Charles the Bald after the latter became emperor (875–877). In 879 Boso assumed the title of king of Provence with the acquiescence of enough of the bishops and counts to be able to defy the efforts of the Carolingians to oust him. On Boso's death in 887 the southern half of his realm passed to his son as king of Provence, while in 888 an adventurer named Rudolph made good his claim to be king of Trans-Jurane Burgundy in the north. The two kingdoms of Provence and Trans-Jurane Burgundy remained separate until about the middle of the tenth century when Otto the Great made the united kingdom of Burgundy an imperial protectorate under the rule of his protégé, Conrad, a descendant of Rudolph.

The successors of Boso in both kingdoms were able to maintain enough order at home to indulge in desperate gambles for a foothold in Italy. One of them gained the imperial title for a few years, and another won a precarious recognition as king of Italy. These ventures weakened the hold of the kings on Provence and Burgundy, so that the tendency toward localism, which Boso had temporarily checked, continued. The local counts were practically autonomous. Their combined efforts finally routed the Moslems from their stronghold at Fraxinetum in 972, thus permanently freeing the Alpine passes into Italy and Germany.

During the ninth and tenth centuries the whole Italian peninsula suffered

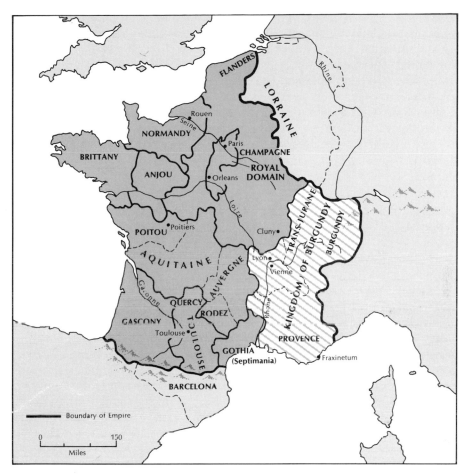

The Feudal States of Western Europe, ca. 1030

from civil strife, incessant struggles for the crown, and the raids of plundering Moslems on the coasts and Magyars in the northern plains. Recovery from the worst phase of these difficulties began when, under the leadership of Pope John X (914–928), a combined force of north Italian, papal, and Byzantine troops from the south, cooperating with a Byzantine fleet, annihilated the Moslems in their stronghold on the Garigliano River (915). Moslem raids continued throughout the tenth century, and the Moslem conquest of Sicily was completed in 917, but conditions in Italy never again were as hopeless as during the period from 880 to 915. Petty wars between rival principalities continued until intervention by Otto the Great restored some order in Lombardy and the Papal States, but Otto and his successors all failed to dislodge the Lombard, Moslem, and Byzantine rulers in the south.

The situation changed at the beginning of the eleventh century, when two new forces appeared in Italy. The first was Italian sea power, developed by great port cities like Venice and Genoa. The Venetians defeated the Moslems in a defensive engagement near Bari in 1002, and the Genoese did the same at Reggio in 1005. Both cities soon went on the offensive: Venetian fleets slowly cleared the Adriatic and gained control of its coasts, and on the opposite side of the peninsula the Genoese occupied Sardinia in 1016. The second new element in the Italian situation was the arrival of Norman adventurers in the second decade of the century. The Normans had been hired as mercenaries against the Moslems in the first years of the century, and they soon settled in southern Italy and Sicily. The formation of this kingdom, finally established in the twelfth century, began a new age of Mediterranean history.

As Europeans took the offensive against the aggressors who had for centuries disrupted their political, economic, and social stability, centralized governments began to develop their power at the expense of local aristocratic families. Most of the outward motion on the borders began as local offensives by independent adventurers or magnates. The Norman advances in southern Italy, the German *Drang nach Osten,* and the war of attrition against the Moslems in Spain all follow this pattern. But success had two effects. First, it freed the interior from the invaders and permitted the development of more stable and larger political units. Second, it gave the new powers a positive goal that could become a device for enhancing political cohesion. In the tenth and eleventh centuries, kings and great feudal lords increasingly became involved in the outward push and took over its leadership. Thus the new strength of the Europeans contributed to a slow but perceptible trend toward centralization that began in the tenth century and continued throughout the Middle Ages. For a long time, the focus of the centripedal forces was the great feudatories, but eventually the kings gained the greater benefit.

### Suggestions for Further Reading

**Secondary Works**   The work of J. M. Wallace-Hadrill cited at the end of Chapter 6 provides an excellent introduction to the history of the later Carolingians. The best account of the Vikings is Peter Sawyer, *The Age of the Vikings* (London, 1962); see also Johannes Brønsted, *The Vikings* (Harmondsworth, 1960), and, especially good on Scandinavian art and archeology, Holger Arbman, *The Vikings* (New York, 1961). On the foundation of the medieval empire, see G. Barraclough, *The Origins of Modern Germany* (London, 1947), and the materials collected in Boyd H. Hill, Jr., ed., *The Rise of the First Reich: Germany in the Tenth Century* (New York, 1969). On the origins and growth of the feudal states from the tenth to the thirteenth century, see Charles Petit-Dutaillis, *The Feudal Monarchy in France and England* (London, 1936). Also useful is Robert Fawtier, *The Capetian Kings of France: Monarchy & Nation (987–1328)*, trans. Lionel Butler and R. J. Adam (London, 1960), and the readings edited by John Bell Henneman, *The Medieval French Monarchy* (Hinsdale, Ill., 1973).

**Sources** A general view of the tenth century from the sources is provided by R. S. Lopez, *The Tenth Century* (New York, 1959); *Saint Odo of Cluny,* ed. and trans. G. Sitwell (London, 1958); and *The Letters of Gerbert,* trans. H. P. Lattin (New York, 1961). A selection of sources is included in the work edited by Boyd H. Hill, Jr., cited above.

# 9 The Feudal Organization of Medieval Society

Medievalists once practically equated medieval society and feudalism, making the study of medieval social and political history the study of the history of feudalism. Modern historians no longer consider either the society or the political institutions of medieval Europe in so narrow a focus, but an understanding of the growth and character of feudalism remains essential for a proper appreciation of medieval society and politics. At the outset, a historiographical aside will be helpful. The term *feudalism* was coined in the eighteenth century to describe the society based on fiefs (Latin, *feudum*). The fief was an estate in land held by military tenure, which meant that the possessor of the estate owed military service to the owner of the land. As conceived in the eighteenth century, the system of fiefs was arranged in hierarchical order leading to the king, who owned all the land held in military tenure. The neat arrangement of the feudal system and the fact that it characterized the social, economic, and political institutions of the aristocratic classes made it easy for historians to slip into the practice of describing the whole of medieval society as feudal. The peasants fit into the pattern as holders of tenures in villeinage, which gave their lord prior right to their land.

The urban landholders did not fit into the feudal system, but the character of their society and social situation was analyzed by comparing it with the dominant feudal system. Thus *feudalism* became the descriptive term not only for the military tenure characteristic of part of medieval society but for the society as a whole. It was an all-purpose word that oversimplified the complex and multivarious social structures of the medieval period. Recent historians have recognized that the feudal model has only limited descriptive applicability and have studied the peasant and urban populations of medieval Europe without reference to it. A growing body of historical work corrects the distortions of earlier historians and expands the understanding of social institutions and conditions that existed at the same time as feudalism, that were affected by and in turn affected feudalism, but that cannot be properly described by looking at them through the medium of aristocratic society. Only a small percentage of the population actually participated in feudal society.

Two other caveats may help put the study of feudalism in the proper perspective. First, feudal *institutions* should not be confused with feudal *society*. Feudal institutions are specific ways in which men have solved certain personal, proprietary, and governmental problems. A feudal society is one in which these feudal institutions are so important and useful that they dominate the social and political organization of that society. Feudal institutions may appear earlier and linger on later than the society that is properly termed feudal. Some feudal institutions survived into modern times, when they were anachronistic and thus proper objects of severe criticism. But in the tenth, eleventh, and twelfth centuries the growth of feudal institutions was the most convincing sign that European society was achieving stability and was capable of further development. It is grossly unhistorical to criticize medieval feudalism simply because feudal institutions that met the needs of medieval society survived as useless remnants in modern society.

Second, no "feudal system" was common to all Europe. Feudal institutions varied from area to area, affected by economic and historical factors. In describing feudalism a single type, that of northern France, which was the most thoroughly feudalized region in Europe, will be used as the model for understanding regional variations. In the eleventh century, this type spread to other areas as Norman knights carried it to Spain, England, southern Italy and Sicily, and the Levant. Regional differences consisted not only in the character of specific feudal institutions and life styles but also in the relative impact of feudal organization on the life of the aristocracy. In Germany, for example, feudalism never displaced older forms of proprietary rights among the nobility and thus could never be used as an effective instrument for unifying the kingdom under the monarchy. Where feudalism was dominant in aristocratic society, as in France and England, strong, unified national states emerged at the end of the Middle Ages; where the aristocratic class owed only a part of its position to feudal institutions, as in Germany and Italy, particularism resulted.

## The Origins and Growth of Feudal Institutions:
## Vassalage, the Fief, and Private Jurisdiction

Medieval feudalism consisted of three closely related elements—the personal, the proprietary, and the governmental. In feudal terminology these were vassalage, the fief, and "justice," or private jurisdiction. Each of these elements had a distinct and separate origin. In the Carolingian period they began to merge, and by the tenth century feudal institutions became so closely and coherently interlocking that a feudal society may properly be considered to have evolved.

Vassalage arose on both Germanic and Roman foundations. The Germans had an institution that the Romans called the *comitatus,* in which "followers," or "companions," were attached by strong ties of personal loyalty to a war leader. This institution existed throughout the Germanic world after the migrations. Among the Anglo-Saxons the king or leader was sometimes called *hlaford,* whence our word *lord,* and his companions were *gesiths,* or in Latin *comites,* reminiscent of the *comitatus.* Merovingian kings had companions called *antrustiones* because they constituted a personal retinue or bodyguard called the *trustis.* In addition to such armed companions there were other dependent royal retainers whose service was not military. They were under the king's special protection and were maintained in his household, where they performed either honorable or menial tasks. Such dependents also swelled the households of the Frankish and other Germanic nobility. The Roman provincial aristocracy were familiar with the personal dependence of the weak on the strong and with conditions under which the strong protected themselves by acquiring retinues. Their armed retainers were called *buccellarii,* and like the German nobles they also had dependents whose service was not military and might range from the menial tasks of the household servant to the support and assistance of a near-equal. In Roman law the relationship was recognized as patronage or clientage, whereby the client or retainer was under the protection of his patron before the law. A person who placed himself under the protection of another was said to commend himself, and the act establishing the client–patron relationship was called *commendatio.*

The turbulence of the Merovingian period, the social and economic disruption caused by the establishment of a new aristocracy and frequent wars, induced large numbers of men to seek the protection of great men in their neighborhoods. Most of those who commended themselves were not qualified for the status of armed companion and had to accept a more humble relationship of dependence, neither military nor honorable in nature.

Both lord and man found commendation advantageous. The dependent preserved his free status and secured both personal maintenance, including food and clothing, and protection. The lord increased his own security and power by gaining the service of another retainer. The mutual benefits of commendation are illustrated by a legal document of the eighth century in which the man commending himself is represented as saying to his new lord, "as long as I live, I shall give you service and obedience, befitting my free status, and will not have the power to withdraw from your authority and protection." The act of commendation was in theory voluntary. It was binding on both lord and man until one or the other died. Men who had commended themselves were described by terms reflecting their social status or the service they performed. The *fidelis* (faithful man) was a member of the upper classes who had taken an oath of fidelity to his lord. Armed retainers of the lesser sort were variously described as *pueri* (boys), *viri fortissimi* (strong-arm men), *satellites* (henchmen), and *custodes* (guards). The commended man of humble status, whose service was menial, might be called a vassal.

In the eighth and ninth centuries, the term *vassus,* or vassal, gradually came to denote a man who served his lord in a military or honorable capacity. The Carolingian rulers, as mayors of the palace, kings, and finally emperors, were responsible for this transformation of the character of vassalage and for a tremendous increase in the number of vassals. In their rise to power, the Carolingians needed a loyal and efficient army that could move swiftly against local rebellions or enemies on the frontiers. They also needed a large force of reliable officials to govern their realm. They secured both by requiring their supporters to become their vassals, thus tying to their own rising fortunes men who hoped to gain new power and position for themselves. The result was twofold: first, the social status of vassalage rose because royal vassals were closely linked to the king; second, the growth of the class of vassals exalted the status of the king. The great aristocrats were companions and friends of the king, but vassalage emphasized the personal subordination of the vassal to his lord, and since at first only the king created vassals, the growth of this class enhanced the superiority of royal authority.

Vassalage was thus unattractive to the great Frankish nobles. Until well into the eighth century great men—dukes, counts, bishops, and abbots—did not willingly demean themselves by becoming vassals. If they commended themselves to the king or emperor, the act was essentially no more than a pledge of loyalty, making them his *fideles,* or faithful men. But the Carolingians gradually broke down this attitude. In 757 Tassilo, duke of Bavaria, was caught in a net of political intrigue that placed him in the position of being a rebel and traitor, and he was forced to commend himself to Pepin the Short as a vassal. Again in 787 Charlemagne forced Tassilo to acknowledge his status as a royal vassal. By these submissions the Carolingian rulers intended to solve a troublesome political problem, that is, forcing their overmighty subjects to recognize the unity of the kingdom under royal government. But the personal form of this recognition made it an acknowledgment of the personal superiority of the king over the duke. Contemporaries were shocked to witness the formal commendation of a duke not as a *fidelis* but as a mere vassal. But the significance of the intended degradation of Tassilo was just the reverse. By degrading the duke to the status of a vassal, Pepin and Charlemagne gave the institution of vassalage a higher social position and respectability. If a duke could be a royal vassal, who else could shun that status?

The proprietary element in feudalism derived wholly from Roman origins. Estates granted by the king to his vassals and other supporters were granted in use, not in ownership. Such an estate was a benefice, a landed property held on very favorable terms or even gratuitously. The benefice was much like the earlier Roman form of tenure called a *precaria* and was sometimes called by that name. In Roman law a precarial grant conveyed to the grantee for a specified period of time the use and occupation of the property granted, while ownership remained with the grantor. By the seventh century, the tenure was normally the lifetime of the grantee. During the eighth century, lords frequently used this kind of grant to provide the maintenance they owed to their men under the terms of commendation, or vassalage. Such an arrangement was often more convenient than maintaining vassals in the lord's household.

In the eighth century, not all vassals held benefices, but the practice of bringing the two institutions together had begun. Charles Martel and Pepin the Short forced churches and monasteries to grant benefices to royal vassals. Such grants were called *precariae verbo regis* (precarial grants at the king's command). The recipient of the benefice paid a nominal rent to the church or monastery but was a vassal of the king. This situation was confusing and unsatisfactory for all parties, and by the end of the ninth century most of these benefices were held either by royal vassals as benefices of the king or by church vassals as benefices of a church. This tendency to unite the institutions of vassalage and benefice-holding increased during the period when the Carolingian empire was disintegrating. In the tenth century it was the general rule that if a vassal held a benefice he held it of the lord to whom he had commended himself.

When this point was reached, the benefice was recognized as the reward, the *quid pro quo,* for becoming a vassal. By becoming a vassal, a man could increase his wealth. The original purpose of the benefice had thus been reversed. At first benefices were granted because vassals performed services; now services were performed by vassals because they received benefices. Men were no longer willing to become vassals unless they were granted a sufficient benefice. As the personal and proprietary elements were bound more closely together, the bargaining power of vassals increased because lords could no longer secure supporters without granting benefices. Thus the later Carolingian rulers granted away most of their crown lands in a futile effort to retain support or gain new support. Other great lords did the same. The more powerful vassals of kings and dukes granted benefices to their vassals. By the end of the ninth century, the feudal hierarchy was beginning to emerge clearly. At about the same time, the term *benefice* was giving way to a new term—*feudum,* or fief.

The development of fiefs and vassalage rested on assumptions underlying Frankish ideas about government and government service, and these ideas must be understood in order to understand the origins of feudal society and institutions. It is usually said that the king used vassals in the governance of the realm, but this statement is misleading. The king's power had a double foundation. On the one hand, he and his family held enormous tracts of land, which made him the wealthiest member of the community. These lands were supposed to support his activities. All freemen had an obligation to participate in public activities, such as road building, but the king could not appropriate for his own, or even his official, use the products of others' property. The counts who were established throughout the kingdom to administer royal affairs therefore had as their principal duty the administration of royal estates. On the other hand, the king acquired certain responsibility for keeping the peace in the kingdom. In this capacity, he acted as the highest judge and as the executor of judgments, thereby replacing in the first instance the old courts of chieftains and in the second the self-help traditions of early Germanic society. These royal functions were ultimately of greater importance than the enjoyment of great wealth, but in Merovingian and Carolingian times, the main support for royal power was wealth. The counts also functioned as delegates of royal authority in these judicial and police matters. The estate management and peacekeeping activities are the ones to which the term royal government is applied and for which the king granted fiefs.

Frankish ideology of service and of delegation of power presented some difficulties. The king granted a fief for the life of the recipient. Such a grant was a judgment of the suitability of the recipient's character for governmental service and rested on the assumption that character did not change. Thus both personal and official rights were involved in the holding of governmental positions and the resources assigned to support them. The royal appointment endowed an individual with personal royal power, not just as holder of a royal office. Offices and benefices eventually became hereditary because of the implication that the power and right of office inhered in the very character of the appointee. Heritability was not a feature of the original grants or enfeoffments, but the lords gradually had to recognize the right as part of the contract, and when this stage had been reached, the lord could not regain the fief as long as the service due from the vassal was performed and as long as there continued to be heirs. Heritability of fiefs first developed in northern France and was recognized as a widespread custom among the higher nobility in a capitulary of Charles the Bald in 877. It took almost two centuries for the hereditary principle to spread throughout feudalized Europe and to be extended down to the lowest levels of the feudal hierarchy.

The early medieval king based his authority on military and judicial power. He led the nation in war and gave justice. To perform these functions, he relied on a council of great men, some of them his relatives, others important figures in the aristocracy and the Church. This manuscript illumination from Anglo-Saxon England portrays the king with his council (Anglo-Saxon *Witangemot*) and shows his principal functions: he is the judge who has just condemned the man being hanged and the war leader with his sword.

The third element in feudalism was "justice," or private jurisdiction. It had two roots, one in Roman culture and one in the chaotic conditions of the disintegrating Carolingian empire during the late ninth and the tenth centuries. During the later Roman Empire, estates of the imperial fisc often enjoyed a privileged position called immunity, which excluded the imperial government and most of its activities from the lands. The government collected no taxes there; imperial officials could not enter the estates to enforce the laws; and inhabitants were exempted from the normal duties of Roman citizens. The Merovingian kings preserved such immunities and extended the privilege to lands owned by certain favored churches and monasteries. The Carolingians confirmed the grants and made some of their own. Moreover, the kings sometimes granted immunity directly to laymen or transferred it from churches and monasteries, the original grantees, to royal vassals who held benefices on lands once owned by churches. Those who held immune benefices exercised within their lands the authority usually exercised by the king. During the late ninth century and increasingly in the tenth, vassals extorted benefices with immunity as the price for their support. In addition, vassals who held some fiefs with immunity usurped the same privilege on estates they held without immunity.

This last development was accelerated and extended by the collapse of the Carolingian empire. The kings tried to ensure the loyalty of dukes and counts by making them royal vassals. Estates traditionally set aside for the support of Carolingian officials were assimilated to the benefices these officials held as vassals. Finally, the heritability of fiefs was assimilated to the heritability of offices now associated with those fiefs. The office of duke or count thus became itself a fief; or more accurately, the office itself, the lands associated with the office, and the benefices held as vassal rather than as official, all merged into one hereditary fief. There was no distinction between office and landed endowment. This development was not necessarily authorized, or acquiesced in, by the kings. It grew out of the brutal necessities of the times, when strong men rose to power on a local scale, usurping powers that under Charlemagne had been controlled by the central authority. The existence of immunity provided, in some cases, the starting point of usurpation. Conversely, usurpation of private jurisdiction was often given a specious legality by later grants of immunity or of hereditary governmental authority. These grants preserved, in law, the superior authority of the king, even though they only legitimized usurpations. A future king might claim real authority over the fiefs and fiefholders because he could point to the grant made by his predecessor. By that time, it no longer mattered that the grant had been subsequent to the exercise of the power it granted. The significance of these developments was that while European government became localized, the tradition and theory of centralized authority was preserved. Feudalism was thus a highly flexible form of social organization that permitted the community to meet its needs for centralized or decentralized authority.

It has been generally agreed that Charles Martel took the steps that if not a conscious effort to create the new feudal society, at least led directly to its creation. Most historians argue that Charles and his successors fashioned readily available institutions, vassalage and the benefice in particular, into the new system because they wanted to create an armed force based on the heavily armed cavalryman. This explanation of the origins of feudalism is bound up with the interpretation of Charles' confiscation of Church lands, but recently some historians have attacked this theory, as discussed in Chapter 5. The debate about the origins of feudalism ultimately turns on disagreement about which feature characterized the system. If it was a military system, then the creation of a heavily armed cavalry marked its beginning. If it was a set of political institutions, then the spread of private jurisdiction was crucial. If it was a set of social or landholding institutions, then the spread of fiefs made the difference. In northern France all these elements were present by the second half of the tenth century.

## The Political, Economic, and Social Consequences of Feudalism:
## A Comparison of England and the Continent

Although feudal institutions grew more slowly in southern France, Italy, and Germany than in northern France, by the middle of the eleventh century an essentially feudal society had emerged throughout Western Continental Europe. England before the Norman Conquest presents a great contrast to this Continental development. To understand the impact of feudalism, it may be useful first to examine briefly what happened in a country where a feudal society failed to evolve.

England during the seventh and eighth centuries suffered the same turbulence that afflicted the Continent before the rise of the Carolingians. The Anglo-Saxon invaders had established seven separate, small kingdoms on the island. These kingdoms formed what historians call the Heptarchy—Wessex, Sussex, Essex, and Kent in the south; East Anglia and Mercia in the Midlands; and Northumbria in the north.

During the seventh and eighth centuries, the various kings struggled with one another for hegemony, and the focus of power shifted from kingdom to kingdom. By the middle of the ninth century, only Northumbria, Mercia, East Anglia, and Wessex remained independent. Then the Vikings invaded England, and in the struggle with them, the king of Wessex (Alfred the Great, 871–899) emerged as the leader of all the English.

Royal leadership of the war against the Vikings harked back to an earlier age when the tribal kings had led their peoples into the Roman Empire. In the ninth and tenth centuries, England was a frontier kingdom in which the armed hordes were again establishing themselves in settled communities. Thus royal authority still depended on the king's war-leader role, and the king did not have to establish a class of royal vassals specifically faithful to him or to grant fiefs to buy the loyalty of settled aristocrats who had become political opponents because of their localized interests. In military tactics the kings relied on piecemeal conquest consolidated by frontier fortifications much like those used by their contemporaries Henry the Fowler and Otto the Great in Germany. For garrisons and field armies they relied on the obligation of all free men to serve in the royal army, while lightening this burden of universal military service by requiring only half the entire force to be active at any given time. Since neither the Danes nor the Anglo-Saxons fought on horseback (horses were employed only for rapid movement of infantry troops), the English kings were not dependent on the mounted knight, the typical vassal of the Continent. The rudimentary lease-hold tenure, or benefice-holding, used by the Anglo-Saxons was never directly associated with the performance of military service by the tenant, as the Continental fief normally was.

The strength and prestige of the West Saxon monarchy were so great that grants of private jurisdiction were a rare privilege, limited almost wholly to monasteries and churches. The normal machinery of local government re-

The Heptarchy, ca. 800

mained under the authority of the king, and the reconquest of the Danelaw
provided the opportunity to introduce reforms that made local government
more effective and more amenable to royal control. The king put his representatives, called reeves, in charge of new local districts into which old
Wessex and the newly reconquered Danelaw were divided. Larger districts
called shires were governed by shire-reeves, or sheriffs. The shires were
composed of smaller territorial units called hundreds or, in the Danelaw,
wapentakes. The novelty of this system and the need for constant vigilance
over the recently reconquered and potentially rebellious Danish areas led to

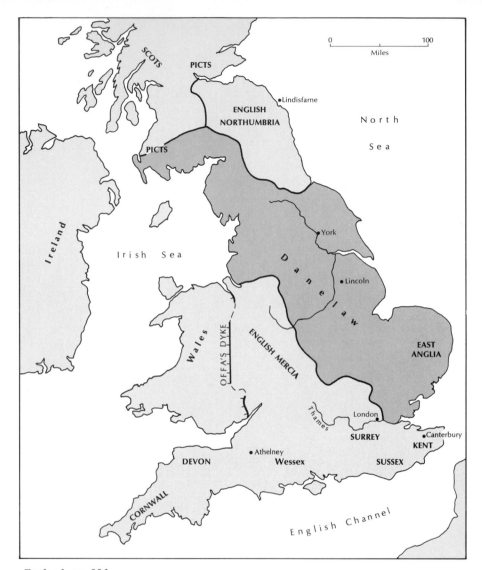

England, ca. 886

such close royal supervision that ambitious local aristocrats had little chance to usurp the functions of local government. Commendation and lordship were common enough in English society at this time, but this was primarily an economic and social relationship that the kings were able to keep from interfering with a person's allegiance to the crown. The kings not only accepted lordship but also found it useful as a political device by which they could enforce their subjects' appearance in court and their fulfillment of legal obligations by holding their lords responsible. Finally, the reconquest of the Danelaw extended English rule over a people who had preserved kin-based society once common to all the Germanic peoples. This type of society, destroyed on the Continent by assimilation into the more structured Gallo-Roman society, was not at all congenial with the growth of feudal institutions based on ties of personal dependence. Most important of all, however, was that in England the elements of feudalism—the institutions of commendation, benefice tenure, and private jurisdiction—were not combined into a coherently organized feudal society. The ordinary subject in England might be under the lordship of one person, hold his land either freely or by paying rent and performing services to a second person, and owe suit to a public court or to one in the hands of a third person. Compared with the mergence of feudal institutions on the Continent, which concentrated men's interests in a closely knit set of relationships, the obligations of society in England were diffused, and the political, economic, and legal interests of an individual might easily conflict.

The development of royal power in Scandinavia in the ninth century eventually affected England and its aristocratic society. In 1013 King Swein of Denmark annexed England after one decisive campaign. Shortly thereafter,

When raiding troops came across country, word could precede them, and defenses could be prepared. But when the raiders came from the sea and rushed up the rivers in swift long ships, there was little hope of organizing for defense. The element of surprise was one of the principal reasons for the success of the Vikings, pictured here landing on the English shore, against the settled communities of Europe. When they operated like more traditional land forces, as the Great Army did in England and on the Continent, the Vikings could be defeated, as they were by Alfred and Louis III.

Swein was succeeded by the greatest Scandinavian ruler of the age, Cnut (or Canute), who united the kingdoms of England, Denmark (1019), and Norway (1028) in one great northern empire. Cnut's reign (1016–1035) inaugurated the spread of Latin Christian culture into the Scandinavian world, for he allied himself with the Church in return for its support. He was the first king of England since Alfred to make a pilgrimage to Rome, in 1027.

Cnut's kingship strengthened the unity of the Old English kingdom for two reasons. First, Cnut and his retainers came from a north German culture that, as in the Danelaw, had continued in the older Germanic social forms. Thus Cnut did not follow the feudalizing policies pursued by the Carolingians and their successors on the Continent. Second, as a foreign conqueror Cnut was not influenced by regional interests. His alliance with the Church strengthened the central government, which was already strong enough to assess and collect the only national tax on land being levied in Western Europe at the time. The Danegeld (originally paid to keep the Northmen

The Empire of Cnut, ca. 1025

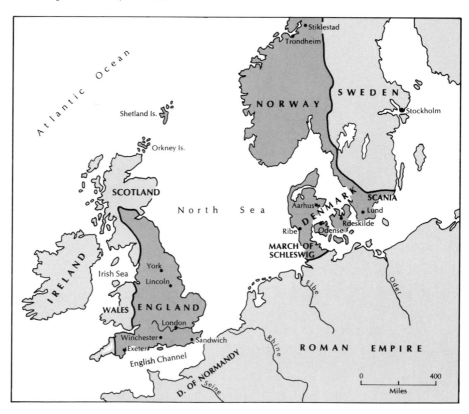

The introduction of Christianity transformed but did not destroy the Germanic culture. Pagan practices, with a veneer of Christian interpretation, continued for centuries in many of the kingdoms founded after the invasions. The quality of the religious shift is implied in these two objects. A traditional amulet, Thor's Hammer (left) was reworked into a crucifix that shows the same design characteristics and was undoubtedly used for the same purposes. This crucifix is the earliest one yet found in Scandinavia.

from overrunning English settlements) was continued, in all essentials, as a tax for the support of Cnut's standing army of personal retainers, the house-carls. The earliest unequivocal evidence of a royal treasury and chancery comes from this period, but probably Cnut created nothing new and merely preserved the institutions of government as he found them. Cnut's conquest was an essentially military operation, not a migration of people as in the earlier colonization of the Danelaw. Old English society remained largely unchanged until its superstructure was swept aside by the Norman Conquest later in the century.

On the Continent, in contrast, the growth of feudalism continued to transform society. The most notable feature of this development was the concentration of political, economic, and social power in the hands of a comparatively small nobility of lords and vassals. The most feudalized region was the land stretching north from the Loire and east to the Rhine. In this region direct local government was in the hands of the lord (seigneur, viscount, castellan) of each district. The typical seigneur was the vassal of a count, marquis, or duke, and was thus a subvassal of the king. He himself might have a half-dozen or more vassals. It is easy to describe this hierarchical system of society and government in a way that contrasts sharply with the conditions of diffused relationships and obligations of individuals in the English kingdom, but this description is misleading. Certainly, the merger of vassalage, fiefholding, and private jurisdiction simplified the social position of individuals, but it must be kept in mind that feudal society developed within the context of older forms of social relationships and thus complicated rather than simplified the general social fabric. In reality, English society, complex as it was, was simpler than Continental society. Continental society during the sixth and seventh centuries was an aristocratic community in which many families owned lands, in which the churches owned lands, in which many families held lands by a lesser tenure patterned on the colonate and precaria of late Roman times, and in which the king owned estates throughout the realm. Sixth and seventh century Continental society was therefore similar to tenth and eleventh century English society. In the course of the sixth and seventh centuries, in the Frankish kingdom, the aristocrats got richer and the small farmers got poorer, while the landed wealth of the churches grew steadily due to the accumulation of donations and grants. The kings' estates were more or less under royal control depending on political circumstances and on the ability of royal administrators, the counts, to establish *de facto* autonomy. The growth of feudalism did not transform as much as add a new element to this social situation.

Charles Martel brought much of the accumulated Church lands back into circulation by using them for benefices granted to royal vassals. He also used royal estates for the same purpose but could not grant away too much of the royal demesne without seriously undermining the finances of the royal government. As said earlier, the existing aristocracy did not become royal vassals in the early years of feudalism, since vassalage was an institution of subservience. As aristocrats changed their attitudes toward vassalage, during the late eighth and the ninth centuries, they accepted benefices that were joined to but did not subsume their other patrimonies. Thus the expansion of the feudal system created a dualism in the proprietary rights of the upper classes. Most aristocrats held both benefices and privately owned lands (later called allodial lands). From a governmental point of view, this dualistic situation meant that the king's relationship with his aristocratic associates and supporters was twofold. He was their feudal suzerain, and he was their king in the older sacred, war leader, keeper-of-the-peace image. Any landowner could enfeoff his lands, and many royal vassals enfeoffed the estates or part of the estates they had received as benefices. Thus the feudal tenure system could reach down into the community for several levels, and each man could hold benefices from several lords (even from those who held benefices from him and were his vassals), as well as allodial lands. With the addition of a few generations of well-planned marriage alliances, this complex system assumed an almost infinite capacity for becoming more complex.

In the public sphere feudalism had a more transformational effect than in the private sphere. The assimilation of the aristocratic class into the feudal system changed the older forms of government into feudal institutions. The local court, center of both judicial and administrative activities, became a feudal court in which the suitors (attendance at the lord's court was called suit of court; those who attended were called suitors) were the seigneur's vassals. The court handled the same kinds of business it had always handled, but the seigneur presided, while his vassals acted as the judges. It was the seigneur's duty to enforce the judgment that they delivered. Vassals who were litigants before the court did not, of course, participate in the collective judgment of their co-vassals or peers. Also, this collective judgment by peers had nothing to do with the origins and nature of trial by jury. Judgment by peers was essentially a feudal principle, while the jury originated as a royal administrative device and developed much later.

The feudal court was also a meeting place for deliberation, when the lord took counsel with his vassals about questions of policy, and for ceremonial occasions, such as the performance of homage to a new lord or by a new vassal. By this act the feudal bond between lord and vassal was publicly acknowledged. The vassals were also required to attend the court because the lord could be sure of their loyalty only as long as they were willing to take part in the work of the court and thus bind themselves to its decisions, the most important of which concerned the waging of war. Suit of court was thus the counterpart of the most important obligation of all, military service, on which each seigneur relied, not only to serve his own lord but also to promote his own ambitions.

The amount of military service owed by a vassal varied from region to region, and within the same region it would often vary in accordance with the size or value of the fief. In each individual case there was an understanding between lord and vassal concerning the service due, and sometimes the terms and conditions of this service were strictly defined—including a stipulated number of days in the field, so many days spent in the garrison of the lord's castle, or the right of the lord to additional service at the lord's expense. Failure on the part of the vassal to perform the required military service was punished by forfeiture of his fief. Thus the vassal's material interests were united with his fidelity to his lord, and the development of feudalism produced results the Carolingians had not foreseen. They had hoped to enhance the coherence of aristocratic government under the royal authority by adding the personal loyalty of vassals to the traditional ties between people and their king. But the growth of feudalism actually introduced a new bond between secondary lords and their vassals that interfered with the allegiance men owed to the king.

The importance of military service due from each vassal meant that women and children could not be vassals. When fiefs became hereditary it became conceivable for minor heirs and women to come into the feudal relationship with a lord. To reconcile heritability and the necessity for military service, it became customary for the lord to recognize the right of women and children to inherit while resuming control of the fief during the minority of the heir or, in the case of a widow or heiress, by controlling the marriage to ensure that the new husband was loyal and capable of performing military service as the vassal. Other feudal customs developed defining the rules of inheritance, transfer of fiefs, and certain rights of the lord called the incidents of feudal tenure. These latter included the right of the lord to hospitality (or to be lodged by his vassal during his travels) and to financial aid on such occasions as the knighting of his eldest son or the marriage of his eldest daughter, or for a ransom to redeem him should he be captured in war. These customs varied in their details from region to region and from barony to barony. Feudal custom was not legislated by the state. It evolved slowly from the necessities of the everyday relations between the lords and vassals.

Feudalism reestablished political order on a local basis following the collapse of the Carolingian effort to stabilize Europe on a universal basis. And yet the "blood and iron" character of tenth-century feudalism was chaotic. Contemporary chronicles are filled with accounts of petty wars. Each lord sought to enlarge his territory and increase his power, and each vassal sought to climb higher in the feudal world by defying his lord at an opportune moment and acquiring more vassals for himself. It has been said that feudalism "would have been a very excellent device if it had been administered by archangels," but feudal strife should not be exaggerated. Armies were small, wars were local, and fighting rarely extended beyond the summer months. The feudal age knew no total war, no genocide, no mass destruction of life or property—all characteristic of a more modern civilization.

There is much to say about the impact of feudalism on the Church and on economic life. The churches became partially feudalized because of the Carolingians' policies. After Charles Martel, the kings did not confiscate Church lands, but they forced the churches to grant fiefs to their vassals and in time bishops and abbots became vassals of the crown and used some of their lands to create their own vassals. The feudalization of the episcopate made bishoprics attractive to men who had little aptitude for spiritual work but who saw in the Church a road to secular power. Tenth- and eleventh-century chroniclers tell of many bishops and abbots who fought in military campaigns, both the king's and their own. At the parish level of the Church, the proprietary churches built by lords on fiefs and allodial lands were easily assimilated into the new social structure. The pastors of these churches were akin to serfs and therefore part of the underpinning of aristocratic life. Strictly speaking, the parish churches were not feudalized, but the lords acquired their proprietary and patronage rights to them as appurtenances of their fiefs. Of course, spiritual aptitude and capacity had little to do with the appointment of lower priests just as such qualities were often missing in the elevation of their superiors. The condition of the Church in this period will be discussed in a later chapter.

In economic life, feudalism meant specialization of a rudimentary sort. The noble and fighting class did not produce, and the producing class for the first time since the late Roman Empire was not expected to divert its energies into making war. Because the peasants and the lower ranks of the freemen constituted the overwhelming majority of the population, a much greater labor force was, under feudal conditions, available for production. But under feudalism, commerce, or the movement of goods, was impeded by the numerous local tolls imposed by seigneurs. Merchants who needed freedom of movement had no place in feudal society. Security and social position could only be obtained in the local hierarchy of lords and vassals.

In the opinion of the feudal nobility merchants were no better than peasants, for they neither waged war nor governed people. The social values of the early feudal world were restricted wholly to the relations between lord and vassal, and they served to rationalize the relationship in terms that emphasized the lord's rights and the vassal's obligations. Loyalty was the highest social ideal. The further development of medieval civilization depended in part on the eventual triumph of this ideal over the actuality that was so often characterized by ambition, treachery, and violence. Already in the ninth century, when Carolingian vassals were bargaining their loyalty to the highest bidder, the ideal is expressed in a letter written by a noble lady to her son: "May the madness of infidelity be ever far from you; may evil never find such a place in your heart as to render you unfaithful to your lord in any matter whatsoever."

## Suggestions for Further Reading

**Secondary Works**   On the origins of feudalism, see F. L. Ganshof, *Feudalism* (London, 1952), and C. Stephenson, *Mediaeval Feudalism* (Ithaca, N.Y., 1942). The classic work is Marc Bloch, *Feudal Society,* trans. L. A. Manyon (London, 1961). The first chapter of Lynn White, Jr., *Medieval Technology and Social Change* (Oxford, 1962) presents an interesting thesis on the origins of feudalism. R. W. Southern, *The Making of the Middle Ages* (London, 1953) discusses feudalism in the larger context of medieval society and culture. On English feudalism and society, see Dorothy Whitelock, *The Beginnings of English Society* (Harmondsworth, 1952); D. M. Stenton, *English Society in the Early Middle Ages, 1066–1307* (Harmondsworth, 1951); and F. M. Stenton, *The First Century of English Feudalism* (Oxford, 1932).

**Sources**   For feudal documents with commentary, see R. S. Hoyt, *Feudal Institutions* (New York, 1961), and, for the Carolingian and Ottonian period, the earlier part of J. R. Strayer, *Feudalism* (Princeton, N.J., 1965), and D. Herlihy, *The History of Feudalism* (New York, 1970).

# 10 The World of Feudal Europe

In the late Roman Empire and under the early Germanic monarchies the nobility had been distinguished by their wealth rather than by their military capability. Roman senators throughout the empire sought lives of peaceful and refined luxury, while in the Germanic armed tribes the freemen participated fully in warfare along with their aristocratic leaders. As mentioned before, feudalization resulted in specialization of function. Power shifted from the armed levy of freemen to the mounted warriors bound by feudal contracts.

Form soon followed function; by the late twelfth century a small group of hereditary warriors had constituted itself as a noble class, spread like a thin veneer across the whole of Europe. In thirteenth-century England, with a population of more than 2 million people, there were only about fifteen hundred landed knights. Even if the unlanded knights are included in the feudal nobility, the men, women, and children of the most privileged class probably constituted less than 1 percent of the population. Wealth still made a difference, of course, and a lowly knight lived quite differently from a great lord. A minor vassal who owed a fraction of one knight's military service and who held his small fief of a lord who was the vassal of a higher lord who was in turn the vassal of a count or duke, possessed resources more nearly comparable with those of a prosperous peasant than with the wealth and power of a count or duke. Yet by the beginning of the thirteenth century, each was a member of the nobility; their common code of honor, their military way of life, and the mutual benefits they derived from feudal arrangements gave members of the military elite a sense of group identity.

Although generalizations about the medieval nobility have to cover a wide range of the sorts and conditions of men and cannot be accurate for all of them, in this brief survey the diversity of regional practice will be submerged and the chronological development of feudalism in different parts of Europe will be subordinated to the treatment of feudalism as a stage in European history, a stage of localized military and political power between the early medieval monarchies of the Carolingian type and the "national" monarchies that emerged in the later Middle Ages.

How did the feudal aristocracy live? What did they think about their world? What ideals did they hold? The answers to these and related questions vary according to time and place and the section of the feudal class being considered. Feudalism was created by powerful Carolingian kings, and the first members of the feudal aristocracy reflected their origins as royal servants. Their interests were potentially local in focus, and their positions tended to become settled and hereditary. Their own models were the older aristocratic classes of Frankish society. But in the first few generations, the king kept a tight rein on the vassals' activities and loyalties, the hereditary tendency was held in abeyance, and the older aristocrats shunned the upstart nobility of royal service. By the mid-tenth century, however, the realization of the hereditary tendency and the assimilation of older aristocratic classes into the feudal system had affected the life style and point of view of the whole feudal class. If the original vassals had considered themselves royal servants, tenth-century vassals had assimilated the aristocratic consciousness of being royal companions and participants in the governance of the realm. And the amelioration of social and political life in the later eleventh and the twelfth centuries affected the lives and views of the feudal class as much as, perhaps more than, it did those of other classes. In addition, feudal law was primarily customary law and thus varied from one region to another. It could even differ from fief to fief, and the variations could be large enough to affect the answers to the questions posed above.

### The Social and Political Ideas of the Feudal World: Lordship and Kingship

The earliest treatises about feudalism, written in the twelfth and thirteenth centuries, deal with only one aspect of the feudal world, the legal system. These works concentrated on tenurial relationships, which had become so complex that the first problem of any legal writer was to simplify and systematize, a process that inevitably distorted reality. And, of course, the legal treatises provide only a glimpse of feudal life and values in the thirteenth century, when the system was already in decline. They say nothing useful about the life of the feudal aristocracy in the tenth, eleventh, and twelfth centuries, when feudalism was flourishing. In order to reconstruct the life and ideals of the first feudal age, the tenth and eleventh centuries, historians have to rely on chance remarks or stories in contemporary or later chronicles, theoretical works, charters in which the feudal nobility recorded its legal transactions, and literary works, written by learned and ecclesiastical men who did not have much in common with the unlettered warrior-aristocrats of the feudal class. The importance of charters in early feudalism derived from the close relationship between law and politics; many political conflicts were resolved by a legal act that established a new relationship between the disputants.

Before the thirteenth century noble status derived from function, not birth. In lay society there were two criteria of nobility: feudal tenure of property and knighthood. Each was acquired by a formal and public act: homage and being knighted. The act of homage created a relationship between superior and inferior, or lord and vassal. Initiation into knighthood placed a man within the military fraternity of the nobility. Knighthood was a bond between equals who shared the same privileges and duties, the same training, experience, and code of the mounted warrior. Feudalism was both hierarchical and crudely equalitarian. The noble had inferiors who were his vassals (unless he was at the bottom of the hierarchy); he had his equals who were his co-vassals or peers holding fiefs of the same lord or who occupied the same rank in the hierarchy; and he had his superiors, his lord (or lords) from whom he held his fief (or fiefs) and their lords. As a knight, however, the feudal noble was the equal of all other nobles, whether emperor or king or the lowliest knight who had little more than his horse and his hauberk (coat of mail).

The institution of knighthood, important as it was, did not influence political and social ideas very much. The great virtues of the knight were originally valor and prowess (brute courage in battle and skill in fighting) and loyalty to his lord and comrades-in-arms. These virtues were primarily individualistic rather than social in their bearing; their value lay in nourishing the spirit of fraternity, the *esprit de corps* or consciousness of kind that tended to bind the knighthood of Europe together as a military elite. By the middle of the twelfth century this class consciousness had developed into a code of behavior that conventionally governed relations between knights. Most important among these conventions was the notion that a knight did not take advantage of another knight, an idea that lay within the larger concept— honor—to which other conventions made their contribution. A knight was expected to fight fairly, not by stealth or ambush or when his opponent was not in a position to defend himself. The vanquished knight was not to be

Chain mail was the principal armor used from late Roman times until the fifteenth century. Mail shirts weighed about twenty-five to thirty pounds and allowed the warrior considerable freedom of movement. The fully clothed knight of the twelfth century wore underclothing, then a quilted shirt, then the chain mail, and then a leather shirt. Sometimes a cloak was also worn. Most chain-mail shirts had hoods, under which a cloth hood was worn for protection from chafing, and over which a plate-metal helm was placed. Altogether, the knight's armor, which also included several layers of leg coverings, weighed between fifty and sixty pounds, not very different from the weight carried by modern soldiers bearing packs. The makers of chain-mail shirts often signed them, thus guaranteeing quality, by inserting a special ring inscribed with their names or by dropping hot lead onto it and pressing the lead with a seal. The one pictured here was made by the Armorers' Guild of Nuremburg.

butchered like a soldier (who fought for wages rather than because he owed his lord military service); his life was to be spared so that his person might be ransomed.

This code was prescriptive rather than descriptive, and it arose slowly during the first feudal age. In the tenth century, prominent local men established predominance in their neighborhoods. They then sought to regularize their positions by placing themselves under a recognized feudal lord who "granted" them "fiefs." Some families, usually those already established in the aristocracy, extended their sway over relatively large districts by conferring such "fiefs" on local magnates. Most of the great families of the twelfth century, including the Capetians in France and the Plantagenets in England, achieved their status in the tenth century. In the early period, these families had the limited interests and horizons of local, relatively isolated clans. They were prominent branches of families in which some members still farmed small plots, and they remained immersed in the daily life of the district.

Until the end of the twelfth century feudal society remained relatively fluid. Noble families could rise or fall several levels in the feudal hierarchy within two or three generations. Where primogeniture was the rule of inheritance, and this was the general rule in feudal society, the younger sons of the lesser noble families were likely to slip down the social scale, perhaps even to become free but dependent peasants. This was one reason why so many of the Norman nobility left their homes to seek their fortunes in Spain, Sicily, and England. Not all the children of noble parents could be provided for by marriage to an heiress, by enfeoffment from a different lord, or by entering the ranks of the ecclesiastical hierarchy.

The invasions and civil wars that destroyed centralized government in the old Frankish kingdom and produced regional centers of power ended about the middle of the tenth century, and the process of enfeoffment that had placed the local magnates under the nominal authority of the great families began to take effect. The greater lords used their legal superiority to justify the imposition of actual authority. The success of this recentralization depended on the conditions that prevailed in the various districts and on the relative strength of the families at different levels of the feudal hierarchy. In Normandy, for example, Rollo and his heirs were able to establish a firm central power. The count of Anjou was never able to impose his rule on his vassals as effectively as the Norman duke, but his grasp on his county was relatively firm. In Aquitaine, the duke held sway over a very large and wealthy territory, but he never really succeeded in establishing a powerful central government. The petty nobility of Aquitaine was famous for its independence and unruliness, and the duke rarely tried to control his vassals. In the late tenth and early eleventh centuries the power of the great feudal lords was rather narrow, at least by modern standards, and very insecure. The succession of a weak duke or count resulted in the immediate decline of the central power in his territory; the rise of a strong petty magnate could create a shift of authority to the detriment of the great feudatory no matter how able he was. On the whole, however, the end of the invasions brought stability to European politics and produced a climate in which powerful individuals and families could use the feudal system to gain control of substantial territories.

During the eleventh century a new element was added to the value system of the noble class. Defense against the invasions had required the services of many knights who were not enfeoffed but were supported as household retainers, such as the housecarls in England, in the entourages of the greater barons. Most of these men were younger sons of feudal nobles who shared the mores of knightly society but had little hope of ever gaining a foothold in the feudal hierarchy. Others rose out of the peasantry as serf knights, or sergeants, who functioned as household officers. They, of course, imitated the life style and values of their noble masters. This large group of warriors was left at loose ends by the reduction in warfare toward the end of the tenth century, and many probably entered the upper ranks of the peasantry. In the early eleventh century, however, some of these soldiers moved to the frontiers of Europe to fight against the Wends and the Slavs in the east and northeast, the Moslems in Spain, and the Moslems and Byzantines in southern Italy. The Normans played an important role in this movement, but knights from all over Europe were involved. Since this border warfare was waged against infidels for the most part, it interested ecclesiastical leaders. The reconquest of Spain and southern Italy and the *Drang nach Osten* in Germany brought educated churchmen into close contact with the roughest, least stable element in the noble class. The ecclesiastics were properly horrified by the values and life style of these men and began the slow process of reforming their character. The rules of behavior developed by the feudal nobility were first articulated by churchmen, and it may be assumed that in formulating these rules, the ecclesiastical writers often refined them significantly. Already in the late tenth century, the Church in Aquitaine had tried to impart a sense of obligation to the feudal lords. There and in Burgundy, diocesan and provincial synods had anathematized military operations on the lands of the Church and of the poor. The decrees of these councils also solemnly pronounced that non-combatants (clergy, women, children, and peasants) should be inviolate in time of war. Local rulers endorsed these statutes, collectively called the Peace of God, in the interests of their own control over their districts. By the early eleventh century, these decrees had been promulgated throughout Europe and were reinforced by what was called the Truce of God, according to which military activities were prohibited on Sunday and other Church festivals. Gradually, the Truce of God was extended from Thursday evening until Monday morning of each week. These laws were surprisingly effective, and they gave greater lords an excuse for limiting the feuds among their vassals. The Peace of God and the Truce of God formed the foundation for the new attitude of churchmen toward the feudal warriors that is evident in the propaganda connected with the launching of the First Crusade: the highest purpose of knighthood is the service of God, acquitted by the good knight in protecting the poor, punishing the wicked, and defending the Church.

The influence of religion can be traced in the solemn and ceremonial act of initiation into knighthood. The earliest accounts of knighting, in the mid-eleventh century, describe a simple and secular rite by which the young noble entered the ranks of the mounted warriors. By the early twelfth century the ceremony had become more elaborate but was still secular. For example, just before Henry I of England married his daughter Matilda to Geoffrey of

The essential element of the ceremony of knighting was the girding of the new knight with his sword. These fourteenth-century illuminations focus on this central act, even though by that time the ceremony was encrusted with vigils in church, prayers, a Mass, and other symbols of the Church's entry into the world of the medieval knightly class. This ecclesiastical participation began about the time of the First Crusade (1096–1100) and increased in succeeding centuries.

Anjou in 1128, the young count was made a knight by his prospective father-in-law. The ceremony took a whole day. First Geoffrey took a bath; then he was dressed in fine clothes and paraded in public with companions who were to be knighted with him that day. Finally he and his companions received horses and arms and engaged in military exercises. The essence of being knighted was to be dubbed—that is, to be given a sound but ceremonial thwack with the broadside of a sword—and to receive arms from a man already a knight. In the next generation, initiation into knighthood began to assume the form familiar to modern readers of historical romances. Knighthood became sanctified. The new knight was expected to confess his sins, keep an all-night vigil of fasting and prayer, lay his sword on the altar as a symbol of his service to God, hear Mass, be dubbed while kneeling before the altar, and finally be girt with the sword. All this could obviously take place only in a church, and it usually was done on an important feast day.

By the end of the twelfth century knighthood had been Christianized and thus transformed from a military fraternity into an institution whose highest purpose was service to Christian society. But knighthood never became as important as homage and the relationships that homage established, as far as social and political ideas were concerned. Originally, homage created a relationship of total subordination of vassal to lord. The ceremonial act of homage was, and remained, wholly secular except for the vassal's oath, which necessarily implied religious sanctions. Kneeling, the vassal placed his hands within the hands of his lord and declared himself to be his man, solemnly swearing that he would be faithful to his lord "against all men" or "against all creatures that can live and die." The greatest virtue of a vassal was loyalty, understood in a very individualistic and concrete sense as the fealty of a man to his lord. Abstract conceptions, such as the "state" or the "government," did not have a place in feudal political ideas. Society and politics were understood in terms of the relationships between individuals, between vassal and lord. The public functions of government were completely merged with the private rights and duties of vassal and lord, whose personal relations were created by the bond of homage.

The most important forces that influenced feudal institutions fall under three heads: custom, contract, and Christianity. The feudal world, far from being chaotic or unregulated, was organized according to specific rules that arose from custom. The essential idea governing the relations between inferior and superior in the feudal hierarchy was contract. The ideals, or ultimate sanctions, serving to explain and justify the organization of feudal society were derived from the teaching of the Church—that is, the ethics as well as the doctrine of Christianity.

The law that the feudal court administered was custom. A rule that had survived "from the time whence the memory of man runneth not to the contrary" impressed feudal lords as a good rule, not simply because feudal lords were conservative by nature, which they were, but for two other reasons. A rule must be good to stand the test of time, and a custom of long standing must be well known by everyone. It was accepted by usage, and through usage it was public. No one made or legislated law; law was above human will. Theorists who knew Roman law or canon law might talk about law being something that is reasonable, or something enacted by the ruler, but feudal nobles rarely came close to such ideas in their own interpretation of law. New conditions or a crisis might force the clarification or even the modification of law, but that happened rarely and was not to be done without the consent of those living under the law. Just as every member of the feudal hierarchy, including the lord king (*dominus rex*) was subject to the conditions of the feudal contract, so all were subject to the law. There was no room for absolutist theories of government in the political ideas of the feudal world. The most important function of the feudal ruler, whether he was a petty lord or a great king, was to do justice. Judicial administration was accomplished by the judgment of the lord's court—the vassals who were obligated to attend the court. When Henry II of England forced his archbishop Thomas à Becket into exile, it was the legal result of a court action, a judgment rendered not by Henry but by Becket's co-vassals or peers in the *curia regis,* and the same is true of Frederick Barbarossa's treatment of Henry the Lion in Germany two decades later.

Homage created a contractual relationship between lord and vassal, and the terms of the contract bound both superior and inferior. In the year 1020 a French bishop expressed this concept when, after describing the vassal's duties, he wrote, "the lord must also in all things do similarly to his vassal." According to Glanvill, author of the treatise *On the Laws and Customs of the Realm of England* (ca. 1190), the vassal owes no more to the lord, by his homage, than the lord owes to the vassal, "reverence alone excepted." Loyalty and service by the vassal were conditional on the lord's fulfilling his duties of protecting his vassal and providing justice. If the vassal broke the contract by failure to perform his service, or by disloyalty, the lord could not punish him without first securing the judgment of the vassal's peers in the lord's court. If the lord broke the contract by depriving the vassal of his rights, the vassal could not rebel until he had formally and publicly defied his lord—that is, withdrawn his homage and fealty by a ceremonial act called *diffidatio*. The concept that government involves an agreement between ruler and subject, together with the corollary that the subject has an inherent right of resistance against an arbitrary ruler, is the most important contribution feudalism made to Western political theory.

Many vassals held fiefs of more than one lord, and this created a problem of plural allegiance, a particularly vexatious problem when two lords of the same vassal were at war. At first, the vassal had to choose between them at the risk of losing the fief held of one of his lords. The solution of this problem came with the notion of liegeancy, according to which the vassal served one of his lords, his liege lord, without reservation, and gave service to his other lords only to the extent that it did not prevent him from fulfilling his duties to his liege lord. For example, if his liege lord and another of his lords were at war, the vassal might serve the former in person and send hired knights to serve his other lord. Since these relationships could become quite complicated, it became the custom in the twelfth century for a vassal with several lords to stipulate the service owed to each under various possible conditions, "saving his fealty" to his liege lord. In England the kings were powerful enough to enforce the rule that the king was the liege lord of all freemen. The vassals of his barons were required to take an oath of fealty to the king. Elsewhere, except in Normandy, rulers were not powerful enough to require an oath of fealty from the vassals of their own vassals until Frederick Barbarossa tried to enforce the rule, without much success, in his effort to maintain peace in Germany. Thus the feudal system produced a solution to the problems created by its own complexity and, in the process, made a great theoretical advance in European ideas of government. The special relationship between a lord and his liegeman rested on a distinction between personal, political relationships on the one hand and property rights and obligations on the other. Liegeancy therefore moved the feudal system back toward the older Germanic and Roman ideas of political allegiance unrelated to tenure in land. These ideas underlie the development of modern theories of citizenship. This is not to say that liegeancy was the basis for the theory of citizenship but that the institution made the feudal class more amenable than they might have been to the growth of such ideas. In political development, a psychological twist can make all the difference.

Just as the Church formulated the ideals of knighthood, the social teachings of the Church influenced the feudal concept of society and of lordship and kingship. The amalgamation of Christianized ideas of sacred kingship and the feudal suzerainty of the king gave feudal monarchy a strong religious aura. At first, the religious enhancement of the king's position as the anointed vicar of God, the divinely ordained peacekeeper and giver of justice, simply solidified his position of feudal superiority. During the darkest days of kingship, when great feudatories achieved an independence that rendered royal authority virtually without substance, the religious position of the king proved a firm foundation for his continued existence. In the eleventh century, it became one of the principal assets in the rebuilding of royal power, together with the religious sanctions underlying the oaths by which feudal relationships were created. Yet the union of feudal and sacred kingship was paradoxical because the two ideas of royal power were theoretically opposed. The authority derived from feudal relationships, limited both by the terms of the contract and by its personal, one-to-one nature, contrasted sharply with the overwhelming power derived from God's vicarate. Against an arbitrary lord or one who failed to fulfill his obligations, the contractual partner could rebel; against God's vicar, he could not.

## The Life of the Feudal Nobility

In the tenth century, the families that entered the feudal nobility did not rise very far above the economic level of most members of the local community and counted heavily on that community for support. They lived in wooden houses larger than those of their neighbors and perhaps fortified with an earthwork, but they were not very much more comfortable than the prosperous peasants. Because of their prominence, the petty nobility shared their houses and their provisions with their clients; the price of prominence was a large household of servants, retainers, and friends. In time of famine, the entire community, including the lord, suffered privation.

The size, shape, and construction of a castle depended on the resources of the lord and on the advantages or possibilities offered by the terrain. Castles of the period from about 950 to 1150 bore only the slightest resemblance to the massive piles of masonry, complete with turrets and mechanical devices, described in almost all modern historical romances or shown in almost all motion pictures that deal with the Middle Ages. Parts of the feudal castle might, rarely, have been constructed of stone, but ordinarily it was entirely an earth-and-timber fortification.

Because of the general similarity of arrangement or plan, most of these fortifications are called "motte and bailey" castles. The motte was a large mound (from one to a half-dozen acres in area) surrounded by a wooden palisade; the bailey was an adjacent courtyard or open space usually much larger in area, also enclosed by a palisade. Depending on the terrain, either the motte or bailey or both were surrounded by a ditch, called a moat, just outside the palisade. If the location of the castle allowed, the moat was connected with a stream by which it could be kept filled with water as an additional obstacle to the entry of an attacking force. Where the land was very flat, the motte was built by using the earth excavated in digging the moat, but usually it was possible to take advantage of a rise in the ground or some natural feature, such as a cliff or bank at the bend of a stream, so that less human labor was needed to build up the elevated area for the motte. A source of water within the fortified area was indispensable, and castles were often built near streams or in hilly country where natural springs were plentiful or wells could be sunk.

In the center of the motte the largest structure, dominating the whole castle, was built—a wooden tower called the donjon, or keep. On the ground floor of the tower, and sometimes in cellars below ground level, were storerooms for food and supplies. At this level there was no means of entry, and the thick walls were unbroken by any windows or openings. (The modern notion that a dungeon is a dark, underground prison derives from the medieval practice of keeping prisoners in one of the lower rooms of the donjon.) Entrance to the tower was gained at the level of the second story, by means of a narrow and steep and thus easily defended gangway that led up to a small door. When under attack, the defenders could easily destroy this gangway and seal up the door. Other openings in the walls of the tower were rarely larger than slits through which arrows could be shot. Inside at this level were the lord's hall and residential quarters, which in a large tower might occupy two stories. Above were the battlements from which the defenders could hurl stones, boiling tar or pitch, logs, and other missiles intended to discourage attack.

Except in the largest castles, the tower was the only building within the palisade enclosing the motte. The bailey contained all the buildings necessary for the normal life of the castle: barracks for the garrison, storehouses for food and supplies, the stable, a smithy and other workshops, and a chapel or church that usually served as the parish church for the neighboring village. The castle was more than a fortified residence for the security of the lord; it also served to defend a whole district. When invasion threatened, the villagers and people from the surrounding countryside took refuge at the castle, driving their cattle and carrying their movable goods within the shelter of the bailey. The long walls of the bailey were probably manned by peasants integrated into the military system for the purpose.

The greater proportion of military operations in the eleventh and twelfth

The motte and bailey castle predominated in Europe during most of the Middle Ages, even after the great lords and kings began constructing stone castles. Most feudal nobles could only afford the motte and bailey structures, although many improved on the ancient works by adding stone walls and buildings. In this castle, located at Great Berkhampstead, England, the original eleventh-century wooden palisade on the earthwork surrounding the bailey was replaced by a stone wall.

centuries consisted of the humdrum business of siege warfare. Pitched battles involving large numbers of cavalry, such as the battles of Hastings (1066) and Legnano (1176), were infrequent, although when they did occur they were often decisive. Normal warfare was on a smaller scale and consisted mainly of besieging the enemy's castles. No territory could be conquered until the castle that dominated and protected it was taken. Almost any garrison could defend its castle successfully against a frontal assault, unless overwhelmed by the greatly superior numbers of an enemy willing to accept enormous casualties. Rarely could so large an attacking force be assembled, so the more usual and economical method was to blockade the castle and starve the garrison into submission. This was not easy to do. A well-provisioned castle could withstand months of siege, and the besieger had to have considerable resources to invest a fortification that long. When a knightly army laid siege to a castle, the limits of service set by custom and agreement made the likelihood of success small. In addition, knights were not trained for siege warfare and did not consider it a particularly honorable form of fighting. As a consequence, besieging armies were usually made up of nonnoble mercenary soldiers, which cost money, and since liquidity was not a characteristic of the wealth held by the feudal lords, such armies could not be kept in the field very long. Even the king, who had considerable resources of fluid wealth, could not expend his funds frivolously on long sieges.

Chepstow, at the mouth of the Wye, was built in the eleventh century as a base for the conquest of southern Wales. Its wooden palisade around a stone keep (tower), much like the keeps built by William the Conqueror in London (Tower of London) and elsewhere to control his newly won lands, was replaced by stone walls in the thirteenth century. This castle could be provisioned from the river and was thus almost impossible to reduce.

Rules that often went into operation as a siege began might dictate its result without too much pain and trouble. Many castles were held by castellans, usually petty nobles, for great lords. The castellan had to defend the castle against his lord's enemies and would be dishonored if he surrendered it. But if the defenders were surprised by an armed force, so that they did not have the necessary supplies for withstanding a lengthy siege, the castellan could receive a three-day truce to inform his superior. The lord of the castle could bring an army to relieve it, but the castellan and lord could not use the truce to provision the castle. If the lord could not provide relief, the castellan could surrender the castle without dishonor.

The stakes in this type of warfare were often high. Around 1150, for example, a petty English noble named John Marshal held some castles for Matilda of Anjou, the daughter of Henry I. During the civil wars between Matilda and Stephen of Blois, who had seized the English throne when Henry died in 1135, Stephen invested one of John's castles. John got his truce and an extension because of the time it took to inform Matilda or her representative. He was not permitted to provision the castle, of course, and to guarantee that he would not do so, he gave his fourth son, William, then about five years old, to Stephen as a hostage. If John provisioned the castle, Stephen would hang William. John provisioned his castle. His breach of the rules was followed by another committed by Stephen. The king did not hang his hostage, and the child eventually was returned to his father. That sort of softness weakened Stephen's hold on his men; there was little place for such romanticism in the world of the medieval noble.

William's career is an excellent vehicle for explaining the life pattern of the knight in the twelfth century. His father had been Henry I's marshal and took his name, John Marshal, from his office. The office had once been a lowly one, concerned with keeping the royal stables—lesser lords also had marshals—but it had become an honorable position, a title rather than a job. John had overseen the provisioning of the royal household. After Henry's death, John had been placed in charge of the castles just mentioned. He proved a faithful liegeman of the countess Matilda in more than the one instance that involved the sacrifice of his son. He probably reasoned that William would have a small future anyway. As John's fourth son, William could not hope to inherit his father's position as marshal and would have to make his way as a landless knight or choose another career. It is apparent that the boy showed some athletic ability at a young age, and William began his training for knighthood when he was about eight years old.

William had already learned to ride, and he now began the arduous training in the control of the enormous, powerful war horses and in the use of knightly weapons. For this instruction, he was sent to the household of his Norman cousin, the great landed baron William of Tancarville. The son destined for the knighthood, whether he would inherit land or not, was customarily sent to the household of his father's lord or of a relative in a higher position. Most of the youth's time was spent in long hours of riding practice and learning to use the lance, sword, and other weapons. Targets were set up in a field, and the boys rode at them under the instruction of a knight. The targets often had spiked balls hanging off arms stretched out from the center and would spin if hit off center. The boy who missed had to learn quickly how to contort himself so that the swinging ball did not hit him in the back as he rode by. The apparatus was designed to true one's aim and to develop the litheness and moves necessary for avoiding an enemy's blows. In a modern army, soldiers are trained for combat duty in the infantry in a period varying from fourteen weeks to six months. The training of an eleventh- or twelfth-century knight took about twelve or thirteen years, and of course the knights had to stay fit and practice throughout their careers. A young boy like William functioned as a servant while he trained. He served at table and helped with the chores of the household, consistent with his status as a noble youth.

When he reached his teens and if he were able, he moved into the ranks of the squires attached to a knight of the household; if he were lucky, he would serve the lord himself. He continued to serve at table but in addition was responsible for maintaining the arms and armor in good order, keeping the horses, and accompanying the knight into battle. In battle, the squire provided weapon replacements, helped fix bridles and saddles, brought in new horses, and, in the pinch, might protect his lord from capture when he had been knocked down, injured, or otherwise placed in jeopardy. The knights of the household taught the boys and squires the rules of knightly behavior on and off the battlefield and instilled in them the values of the class they would enter. The instruction filled all a young man's time. It gave no place to book learning, and, in fact, turned the future knight away from intellectual life. It was the concentrated training of an athlete and usually produced a powerfully built, anti-intellectual man.

William finally became a knight on the eve of a battle; William of Tancarville needed men. The young knight was twenty-one and had waited thirteen years since coming to Tancarville to become a knight. In his first battle, William justified his cousin's faith in him and his training. He began the second stage of his career with a great success, but his biographer records a mistake William made that day, one he must have remembered for the rest of his life. He had defeated many knights in one-to-one combat, but he had not paused to capture any horses or men, even after his own horse was killed. At the end of the day, he had glory but was left with badly battered equipment and no horse. He had to equip himself for the next campaign by selling the costly cloak in which he had been knighted. He never again ignored the exigencies of knightly economics, even in the heat of battle. These economics now became William's support for fifteen years in the world of the *juventes* (youths), or knights-errant.

A knight charges a target that will spin around when hit and send the mace hanging opposite on the arm swinging after the knight as he passes. He will therefore learn to aim his blow and to avoid the counter.

A squire leads horses to a resting place as knights join in a tournament. The unhorsed knight would lose his armor and horse and have to ransom them back if he could, but here it is evident that the lance has penetrated.

The knights-errant drifted through the feudal world. In the twelfth century, they were the main body of those who participated in tournaments, fought in wars, and went on the crusades. Some were attached to the households of great barons, but even household knights were often on their own. As they traveled about from tournament to war, they made trouble for villagers and townspeople. Idleness and a rather rough sense of privilege contributed to their style. The principal source of income for many knights-errant was the round of tournaments. Tournaments were probably as old as feudalism, but they became common toward the end of the eleventh century, when political conditions left many trained knights idle. They originated as mock battles between teams of knights often organized and led by the wealthy heirs of the great feudatories. Teams of as many as one hundred knights clashed in a battle that looked, smelled, and sounded real and that caused many injuries and deaths. Some knights even captured men and material worth a fine ransom. A tournament might attract several teams of varying sizes, and it usually degenerated into a melee in which each team and knight fought for itself or himself. There was usually a time limit, dawn to dusk of a single day, and a safe area where knights could retire to rest or to repair their armor. It might have been a great spectator sport, but there were no spectators. The image of the tournament as a display of refined one-to-one jousting, with "fair damsels" in the stands, passed on by romantic literature, was a creature of the postfeudal age; by then the competition had become a game, and, to the horror of purists, the combatants used fake weapons and did not tie themselves to their saddles. The Church repeatedly prohibited tournaments, but without effect. For the knights, the tournaments were good sources of fun and profit, and they saw no reason why the churchmen should be so concerned about them. Rules devoid of obvious moral or spiritual content were not likely to make much impression on the knights' consciences.

William became rich. He was a man of extraordinary athletic ability, strength, and skill, and he emerged from melee after melee with a substantial reputation and income. The price paid for such success was physical punishment. After one tournament, William was found in the smithy's quarters with his head on the anvil; his helmet had been battered so badly he could not get it off. As a result of his success, William became a permanent member of the knightly entourage of young King Henry of England, oldest son and heir of Henry II, and eventually rose to the position of the young king's mentor in knighthood. When Henry was knighted in 1181, William had the honor of dubbing him.

This honor was substantial, but it had limited value. William was still a landless knight and was not part of the feudal hierarchy. The favor he had won might lead to the king's giving him a fief or an heiress of a fief in marriage, but of course Henry had to succeed to the throne to do this, and he died in 1183. William had thus progressed very little in the fifteen years since his knighting. Although he was rich by virtue of his success as a fighter, he had no steady income, and he was getting old. After his lord's death, William went to the Holy Land as a crusader because he had vowed to do so with young Henry and now hoped to fulfill both his own and his dead lord's obligation. When he returned to France in 1185, his reputation for ability and faithfulness induced Henry II to include him in his own entourage. The king did not, of course, make the rounds of tournaments, as his son had done, and William's new position therefore involved him in the important business of governing Henry's extensive realms. Henry rewarded his service by giving him guardianship over a young heiress of some fiefs, and William thus enjoyed the income from a feudal tenure for the first time in his life; he was in his late forties. During the civil wars between Henry II and his remaining sons—Richard, Geoffrey, and John—William faithfully supported Henry, and at the end of his life the old king promised him the hand of the heiress of one of the great feudatories of England, the earldom of Pembroke. But Henry died in 1189 without having fulfilled his promise, and William again stood on the edge of oblivion. His former enemy, Richard, recognized his value, however, and gave William what Henry II had promised. In 1190 William Marshal—who succeeded to his father's title by outliving his brothers—became the earl of Pembroke, one of the most powerful lords in England, responsible for the defense of the Welsh frontier. William's later career will be touched on in a succeeding chapter. He died in 1219 after spending thirty years at the heart of English politics.

William's career was extraordinary, but it followed a common pattern of the feudal world, in which some men inherited their wealth and position, and some won it by their own merit. Few knights-errant rose as high as William Marshal, but many obtained a position in the feudal hierarchy by the favor of great lords. It is difficult to estimate the length of the career of knights-

In the high and later Middle Ages, wealthy nobles in England had their graves, placed in the pavements of churches, covered with elaborately sculpted brass. Most of these were melted down for cannon during the Civil Wars of the seventeenth century, but some survive. *Left* Brass over the grave of Robert de Bures, buried in 1302. *Right* Brass over the grave of Robert de Trumpington, buried in 1289.

errant, but they probably could participate in the round of wars, both mock and real, for fifteen to twenty years. In his later years, William Marshal continued to fight and obviously stayed in good physical health, but he functioned more as a general than as a front-line soldier. Those nameless men who did not achieve a position disappeared from the sources and probably became estate administrators or prosperous peasants.

Superbly trained for individual combat, knights were also capable of simple tactical maneuvers either as unsupported cavalry or in combined operations with supporting infantry and archers. At the Battle of Hastings in 1066 the Norman cavalry coordinated their attack with the covering "artillery" fire of archers. In the climax of that battle the cavalry were well enough disciplined to feign a retreat and to improvise a counterattack that turned the tide of battle in favor of the Norman host. The crusaders in the Holy Land often suffered heavy casualties when confronted with the superior tactical ability of the Turks, however. Actually, the knight was at his best when man-to-man. The massed charge of one cavalry force against another, resulting in a great crash of horses, human beings, and metal, could rapidly degenerate into a multitude of individual fights—some still astride a mount, others on foot. In hand-to-hand combat, the foot soldier was at a serious disadvantage, and the development of tactics in medieval warfare is associated with the infantry rather than the cavalry. When forced to meet cavalry in the open, foot soldiers could survive only if they exploited all the possibilities of field fortifications, the element of surprise, maneuver and deployment, concealment, and fighting in small groups.

Military leaders understood the need for planning a campaign, but by modern standards their grasp of strategy was deficient. They paid little heed to the problem of supply because their armies lived off the country through which they passed. This meant that an effective scorched-earth policy could usually defeat any large-scale invasion. Armies were often committed to battle with inadequate information concerning the strength, disposition, and probable intentions of the enemy. In Western Europe these deficiencies were shared by both sides and the result was not fatal, but against the Moslems in Italy and in the Holy Land the results were sometimes disastrous.

A chronicler reported of King John of England (1199–1216) that he bathed once a year, whether he needed it or not. The chronicler was speaking in admiration, and his statement probably conforms to the modern stereotype of the way people, even those at the top of the social, economic, and political scale, lived in the Middle Ages. It is very misleading, however. Throughout the premodern period, sanitation and cleanliness were not of great concern to the human population, but at least in the Middle Ages, there was some awareness of the need to keep clean. Medieval nobles usually cleaned their hands before and after meals, and literary sources show that knights washed off the rust and grime after climbing out of their armor. Baths were not common, but they were a part of upper-class existence and are pictured in manuscript illuminations, especially those of the later Middle Ages, when illuminators found their subjects in scenes from everyday life. In the warm months, swimming helped clear away the encrustations, and in Germany, people could take advantage of the many hot springs. Aachen had such springs, used frequently by Charlemagne's court. Nonetheless, medieval individuals suffered from skin disorders commonly associated with a lack of hygiene. There was also a high incidence of infectious disease, not only because people did not keep clean but also because they lived in close quarters. The households of both lord and peasant allowed for very little privacy. In the houses of the feudal aristocracy the lords' families, servants, retainers, and others lived and slept in a few rooms. Only the great lords had houses in which the lord and lady occupied a private room, but even then, all the others lived together. The houses were practically unheated, badly ventilated, leaky, and dirty. It was a difficult life, although not as difficult as that of the peasants who, in their cottages and hovels, had less to eat and drink and fewer layers of clothing to keep them warm.

Perhaps the most striking impression twentieth-century Americans would receive, were they by some means transported back to a feudal castle of the eleventh century, would be a shock to their sense of smell. The odor of decaying food, filthy and mildewed clothing, rotting teeth, and foul breath would confront such visitors at every turn. But the medieval noble enjoyed a much better material life than that of his peasants. The most obvious difference was that the peasants' existence was reduced almost to the same level as that of the animals with which they, literally, shared their daily lives. In the winter the animals in their huts helped keep the peasants warm. Nobles, who lived at one remove from animals, in the winter wrapped themselves in furs. In some parts of northern Europe the wearing of furs was as much a distinguishing mark of the noble as the bearing of arms.

Diversion from the monotony and restrictions of peacetime life in the castle consisted mainly of activities that provided some of the experience and pleasure of fighting. The tournament has been described.

The hunt was closer to the modern conception of leisure activity than the tournament. Hunters might spend a few days in the forest, but they remained close to home and considered hunting a sport rather than a business. Nonetheless, hunting large animals could be very dangerous. When brought to bay the wild boar was likely to charge into his tormentor with such speed and force that unless struck down with a single accurate blow his tusks might leave the hunter permanently maimed with a vicious wound in the leg. Killing wild boars, bears, and wolves served the practical purpose of ridding the forests of dangerous animals. Shooting deer with the crossbow provided the lord's table with venison, far more palatable than the scrawny beef and tough mutton that was occasionally available. Falconry was an art popular with both lords and their ladies. The falcon was trained to kill wild fowl in the air and return with the prey to its master or mistress. Most great lords employed professional foresters, huntsmen, or wardens to patrol their forests and enforce the local customs against encroachment and poaching, so that the lord's game might be preserved for his own hunting and consumption. In the eleventh and twelfth centuries, nobles were criticized for indulging their passion for hunting rather than going to church. Even some churchmen, often raised in an aristocratic milieu, enjoyed the hunt, to the chagrin of monks and high-minded men who considered it a dangerous distraction from the work of God.

Castle life provided little indoor diversion, aside from infrequent great occasions, such as the marriage of the lord's oldest daughter or the knighting of his oldest son. At such times it was appropriate to invite many guests and to entertain them with a banquet, where quantity exceeded quality both in food and drink. Festivities might be prolonged for a week or more. During inclement weather and after dark the nobles had little to do. Very few of the lay nobility were literate, but they did enjoy listening to stories told by wandering minstrels, or jongleurs. Charlemagne ordered the collection of old

In the twelfth and thirteenth centuries, great nobles and kings could afford elaborate entertainment. This illumination from the *Psalter of Saint Elizabeth* (thirteenth century) shows a precursor of the court orchestra of early modern Europe.

Chess was a popular gambling game in the Middle Ages, played by relaxing knights and by erring churchmen. These pieces, dating from around 1200, come from exquisite sets carved from walrus ivory in northern England or Scandinavia.

tales and legends. Another form of amusement was provided by entertainers who often accompanied the minstrels from castle to castle, where they put on acts featuring juggling and tumbling. These entertainers and other travelers were usually welcome to stay at castles because they were a link with the outside world, the purveyors of news and gossip. Without them the daily life of the feudal noble would have been even more isolated than it was, for his castle was often many miles from the nearest other castle, and he took no part in the activities of the village community of peasants, in whose midst the castle was situated. In addition, some indoor games like chess were popular. Many of these games were played for money, and in the twelfth century, most people associated chess with gambling. When Henry II of England chose Thomas à Becket to be archbishop of Canterbury in 1162, the candidate's enemies alleged, among other things, that he had played chess when he was a student.

The foregoing description, like that of feudal institutions, is necessarily schematic, for the habits of life and the resources of the nobility varied greatly. The lowliest knight in the feudal scale possessed no castle but lived in the household of a great noble who might have a standard of living somewhat better than suggested. Next above the household knights were the petty nobles who had been enfeoffed with a fief of no more than a manor or two. Such a noble lived in a fortified residence that was little more than a small manor house surrounded by a simple wooden stockade. The vassal who was lord of several manors spent much of his time traveling from manor to manor, since it was easier for his family and household to move to the source of supplies than it was to transport the produce of his manors to a central location. One of these manors was the lord's principal residence, where he held his feudal court. It was fortified as well as the lord's resources would allow, usually in the form of a small motte and bailey castle. The greatest feudal nobles (kings, dukes, counts, barons) possessed far-flung fiefs consisting of from a dozen to several hundred manors. Such a great lord might have several or many castles strategically located for the defense and administration of his barony. The castle was not so much a residence of the lord (who would visit it occasionally) as it was of his officials who held court for him and stored his revenues there.

Life styles among the feudal nobility changed over time as well as varying from region to region. Economic fluctuations affected the lords more than their peasants because the nobles controlled and spent the liquid wealth of the community. In a period of rising prices, their incomes, based principally on rents, were fixed by custom and did not vary as much as the price index. In addition, the cultural revival of the twelfth century, considered in a later chapter, affected the nobles by creating new forms of literature that reflected the life style and values of the feudal world as it shaped and transformed that world.

### Suggestions for Further Reading

**Secondary Works**   The studies cited at the end of Chapter 9, especially the work by Marc Bloch, are an excellent introduction to the social and political ideas of the feudal world. In addition, see the articles collected in Frederic L. Cheyette, ed., *Lordship and Community in Medieval Europe* (New York, 1968). For a general introduction to the culture of the feudal nobility, see Sidney Painter, *French Chivalry* (Ithaca, N.Y., 1957) and *William Marshal* (Baltimore, 1933).

**Sources**   The collections cited at the end of Chapter 9 are useful. See also Andreas Capellanus, *The Art of Courtly Love,* trans. J. J. Parry (New York, 1941), which was written around 1180 at the court of Marie de Champagne, daughter of Eleanor of Aquitaine and Louis VII of France. This court was also the patron of the greatest writer of chivalric romances, Chrétien de Troyes. Most of his works have been translated into English, and they exhibit the ideals of knightly behavior in the late twelfth century. The best source for the religious view of knighthood can be found in the late–thirteenth-century work by the Catalan theologian Raymond Lull, *The Book of the Order of Chivalry, translated and printed by William Caxton,* ed. Alfred T. P. Byles (London, 1926).

# II The Early Medieval Economy

The great bulk of the medieval European population were peasants whose agricultural labor supported the military and clerical classes. The primary social and economic unit of the medieval peasant population was the village, although in regions where the land was not very fertile the pattern of settlement usually took the form of scattered homesteads or small hamlets.

The village society predated the Roman conquest of Western Europe. Caesar noted that the Gauls, most of them of Celtic origin, lived in agricultural village communities (*vici*) and in cities (*oppida*). The Roman conquerors took up residence in the cities and transformed them into *municipia*. The agricultural villages were left to themselves, except in the areas immediately surrounding the cities. In the late Roman period, the senatorial families became great landholders, establishing huge estates in the countryside. This development did not disrupt the life of the peasant villages, however. From a legal standpoint, the foundation of the estates reduced the status of villagers to subject tenure and made their lives more precarious because they now faced the danger of losing their right to farm their plots. From a social and economic standpoint, the legal change meant little. It was in the interests of

**251**

the senatorial landlords to keep the villages in a sound condition, and, in fact, the process by which the villages declined into tenurial servitude was usually connected with an aristocratic family's willingness to help the villagers financially and otherwise. In return for the aid, the landlord received a right to the lands of the community or of individual families in the village. By the time the Germans established themselves in the old Roman provinces, this process had gone far toward bringing the majority of villages under the control of the great landlords. The conquerors did not simply replace the old Gallo-Roman aristocracy but rather took a portion of their estates and in remote regions established their own estates. The invasions of the fifth and sixth centuries did not destroy the ancient pattern of village society and economy.

The development of feudalism also did not significantly disrupt this society. Fiefs were based on manors, which comprised, typically, a single village, although sometimes a village was divided among two or more manors. A single manor might also include more than one village or a collection of homesteads and hamlets. The word *village* derives from the one village = one manor equation: the Latin term *villa* designated the estate of a Roman senatorial family, and in the Middle Ages came to mean a manor. There were some important differences between the ancient and medieval village, however. The Roman villas had been based on villages within the commercial sphere of towns and had thus been part of the international economy of the Roman Empire. Outside of these municipal spheres, the *vicus* (ancient village community) tended to continue as a self-sufficient, subsistence level economic and social unit, but inside the spheres, the villages produced money crops to supply the towns and the commercial interests of the great families. The transformation of the Roman world in the early medieval period substantially weakened international trade and forced the villages to retreat to a self-sufficient economy similar to that of the communities in outlying districts. At the same time, the rural character of Germanic society led to the incorporation of those outlying villages into the power sphere of the ruling aristocracy. The surplus production of the villages was consumed by the families and households of the upper classes. In some instances, this change may have caused a drop in the productivity of the villages no longer a part of the trading network, but usually it only resulted in the redistribution of the surplus production. Even though the medieval aristocracy—the feudal aristocracy, the upper levels of the ecclesiastical hierarchy, and their extended households —was a thin veneer on the medieval population, it was substantially larger than the old Roman aristocracy. And its geographical distribution differed from that of its Roman counterpart. The Roman aristocracy had been concentrated in the cities, and even when it moved onto its great estates in the fourth and fifth centuries, it did not go so far out into the countryside that it lost touch with the urban centers.

The agricultural surplus that, in Roman times, had flowed into the cities to support the aristocracy and the urban population stayed, after the invasions, in the countryside to support the new ruling aristocracy. The effect of this change was increased by the fact that the same movements that dispersed the Germans throughout the provinces as a new ruling class dissolved the border armies, which they had comprised and which had been one of the principal terminals of Roman agricultural commerce. The resulting isolation of village societies contributed to the tendency of medieval village societies to develop local variations in the general pattern of peasant social life.

## The Early Medieval Agrarian Economy: The Village

Early medieval society was relatively far more rural and agricultural than modern American society is urban and industrial. Before the twelfth century perhaps 95 percent of the population lived outside towns. Trade and industry had declined, and the economy was overwhelmingly agrarian. Villages were of various sizes, ranging from a population of less than a score of families to several hundred families, and the agricultural pursuits of the peasantry varied from region to region depending on the fertility of the soil and the natural resources available. In mountainous, forested, or marshland areas the methods of husbandry, as well as organization and size of population centers, had to be adapted to exceptional conditions. Any brief description of the medieval village must ignore these many differences and deal with what was typical or normal in the districts where the soil was rich and the population was dense.

The predominant physical feature of the typical village was the arable land surrounding the cluster of huts and cottages where the peasants lived. In northern Europe this land was ordinarily divided into open fields whose size might vary from less than one hundred to more than one thousand acres. The fields were "open," that is, not divided by fences or hedges into separate plots or tenements, since husbandry was necessarily a cooperative effort. No single peasant was wealthy enough to own a whole plow team of eight oxen, and few peasants owned plows, but by combining their oxen and plows the villagers could cultivate large fields jointly with greater efficiency than they could farm small plots with their individual resources.

The open fields were divided into blocks whose shape was dictated partly by the contour and drainage of the land and partly by the further division of the blocks into a number of strips. The length and breadth of the strips were determined by the requirements of plowing with a large team of oxen. Ordinarily, a strip was as long as the team could continue a sustained effort in pulling the plow without rest. This varied with the strength of the oxen and the condition of the soil. In northern Europe it averaged about 220 yards (the length of a furrow, or furlong). The width of a strip was ordinarily about sixteen and one-half feet (a rod), the distance dictated by efficiency in turning the plow at the end of a furlong under the customary system of plowing successive furrows alternately on either side and outward from the center of each strip. A greater width would have required too much time and effort in turning the team to resume plowing on the other side of the strip. Four such strips made up approximately one acre: four rods in width and a furlong, or forty rods, in length. The modern acre is derived from this measure, the approximate area that a team could plow in a normal day's work. Years of plowing in this fashion pushed the soil toward the center of the field, creating a sloping mound. These mounds are visible in aerial photographs of European farm lands and can be used to determine the size, location, and pattern of the fields in various medieval villages.

The arable land of the village was divided into two or more portions so that fertility could be preserved by field rotation. In a two-field system the section in use was planted with autumn-sown winter wheat, to be harvested early in the following summer. The other half was allowed to lie fallow until it was planted with autumn-sown winter wheat in the following year. The fallow field was plowed to help it recover fertility, and when not being plowed it was used as additional pasture for animals, thus providing feed for the animals and fertilizer for the soil. In the more efficient three-field system the arable land was divided into three portions, one planted in winter wheat, one planted in a grain sown in the spring and harvested in the fall, and one left fallow. The great advantage of this system is easy to calculate. Two-thirds instead of one-half of the arable land was always in production, and because two types of crops were grown, the work load and the yield of the community was more evenly distributed throughout the year than it was in the two-field system. In both systems, the peasant families owned strips in each of the sections, so all had both cultivated and fallow fields at the same time, and all shared in the good and poor land farmed by the village. The need for common plowing forced collective decisions and work, but each family was responsible for harvesting its strips. In villages where the three-field system was used, the collective activities were more important than in two-field villages because the common effort was required twice instead of once a year. In such communities, constant communal activities and institutions usually developed.

The yield from peasant agriculture was very small, whether it is measured against the amount of labor or the proportion of seed to harvested grain. Weather conditions and other variable factors caused great variations in the yield, but on the average in northern Europe about two bushels of seed were sown to produce approximately eight to ten bushels of wheat per acre. An average sowing of about one bushel of seed produces approximately twenty-five bushels of wheat on a modern Midwestern American farm. One of the many reasons for the low yield was that the medieval peasant scattered his seed by hand. Every planting was thus a race between the soil and the birds to germinate or devour the broadcast seeds. The medieval yield was on a par with that of antiquity or of early modern times. Not until the eighteenth century did the adoption of more scientific methods substantially increase the ratio of two-to-ten from seed to harvest.

Other methods of increasing the total production of grain did not depend on improving the yield as measured against the amount of seed planted. During the ninth, tenth, and eleventh centuries three improvements in agricultural technique appeared in northern Europe that mark a permanent advance over Roman methods of cultivation. The Romans had used the scratch plow, which in its simplest form consisted of a stick that bit into the ground attached to a pole pulled by an ox or oxen. The scratch plow did not bite very deeply and did not turn over the soil. In order to get the desired result, Roman farmers often had to plow their fields in a grid, which required plowing the field twice, producing square fields. Since the plow could be pulled by a single ox; the need for cooperation among the farmers in a village was almost eliminated. The scratch plow could be used fairly effectively, with the limits noted, in the dry soils of the south, but it was virtually useless in the rich, loamy soils of the northern plains and river valleys. In the ninth century, the heavy, wheeled plow (known earlier in some regions) came into wide use. The wheels permitted a tremendous increase in the weight of the plow, which allowed a deeper bite, removed the need to replow, and produced the strip fields described above. The greater weight and bite of the plow required more power to pull it, which resulted in the use of eight-oxen teams common in northern medieval villages. The basic heavy plow was later improved by the addition of such refinements as an iron plowshare to increase its cutting power and durability and a moldboard to turn over the sod. The utilization of the heavy plow spread relatively quickly in northern Europe, where it became a feature of new villages settled on reclaimed lands and of villages reestablished after the disruptions of the invasions and wars of the sixth and seventh centuries. The German farmers seem to have brought it into the old Roman territories, and it traveled with them. In the south, the innovation was slow to take hold, since villages were not disrupted as they were in the north, and they already possessed implements that had served them reasonably well for centuries. In addition, the landholding patterns in these villages were well established and were the foundation for the village society. As always in such stable communities, innovation was resisted because it threatened the whole fabric of the society, and the social fabric was more important to the villagers than the increased efficiency that might result from the new tool. Furthermore, the heavy plow was not as effective in the dry soils of the south as it was in the north, where it was almost a necessity.

A second innovation appeared first in northern France and spread slowly wherever conditions permitted. This was the division, already mentioned, of the arable land into a three-field rotation. However, the two-field system remained the most widespread in medieval Europe, supplanted by three-field rotation only in the most fertile districts. Three-field rotation tended to exhaust all but the best soil, it afforded less grazing area on the fallow field, and it could not be used effectively in the drier climates of southern Europe, where the growing season was shorter. The three-field system also necessitated a change in the landholding pattern and thus a reorganization of the village economy and, potentially, its social structure. Most village communities resisted such changes.

The third improvement over ancient agricultural practice, the use of horses instead of oxen in plow teams, was closely associated with the three-field system. Horses had to be fed grain as well as the hay and fodder on which oxen lived, but horses did not need so much pasture. As draft animals their advantage was in their greater speed. Fewer teams were needed to plow the same area, and the same number of teams could plow far more rapidly, so changing weather conditions were less hazardous. Horses could not be used for plowing, however, until three technological improvements made their appearance. In antiquity horses were harnessed as draft animals by a thick leather strap passing around the neck, an arrangement that threatened the

The two types of plow used in the Middle Ages, and still used in some parts of Europe, were the scratch plow and the heavy, wheeled plow. The scratch plow could become relatively sturdy, with an iron blade and stout timber, but it remained much lighter and less cumbersome than its more sophisticated competitor.

The wheeled plow required much more power than the scratch plow, and unlike the scratch plow, it turned over the clods of earth, creating the rough effect the artist tried to capture in this illustration.

horse with strangulation when it tried to use its full strength. By the ninth century the modern horse collar, by which all of the horse's power was exerted against a stiff padded collar resting well down on its shoulders, had been adopted in some parts of Western Europe. This innovation had been developed in China and had passed along the trade routes or had been carried by Altaic peoples into Western Europe. Its transmission is a striking case of cultural and technological diffusion. The second improvement was the use of horseshoes, which increased traction and prevented the hoof breakage common with horses, especially on stony soils. Such soils also injured the feet of oxen, and thus the horseshoe made it possible to cultivate stony areas. The third improvement was the development of tandem harnessing, so any number of horses, one before the other, could be used to pull the plow. In antiquity horses were harnessed side by side, which decreased efficiency with the addition of each horse to the team. Horses never wholly supplanted oxen. They could be used economically only in conjunction with three-field rotation, which produced a spring crop of oats. They were not as strong as oxen and could not be used on the heavy clay soils. And they were more liable to disease. But use of horses and of the other new agricultural technology was widespread by the eleventh century.

Since each peasant held a number of strips scattered throughout the fields, the yield from the total holding was roughly constant from year to year. In addition to his strips, each peasant possessed a small plot of ground surrounding his hut, usually planted with vegetables to supplement his basic diet. The yard was also used to keep a few chickens or to cultivate fruit-bearing shrubs and trees.

Keeping the plow beasts and other animals alive was essential to the survival of the human population. Every village had to have a meadow from which sufficient hay could be mowed to feed the oxen during the winter. In the spring and summer, animals grazed on wasteland and pasture held in common by all the villagers. After the harvest and haymaking, the fields and meadow were opened to the oxen so they could forage from stubble and scattered bits of grain. These sources of feed were not always adequate, especially during a bad year. When it appeared that because of a shortage of fodder the oxen or cows could not survive the winter and be strong enough for spring plowing, the villagers enriched their diet by slaughtering the animals in the fall. The regular meat supplement for the human diet was pork from the half-wild pigs that roamed in the woodland of the village, where they eked out a tough and stringy existence on acorns and beechnuts. If larger pastures were available, herds of sheep were kept to provide milk, cheese, and wool. Sheep were not eaten unless their survival over the winter was in doubt. The medieval peasants' meat diet of pork and occasional beef and mutton was incredibly unpalatable by modern standards. But it was an important source of fats in northern Europe, where butter was scarce and vegetable fats, like the olive oil of the Mediterranean area, were unobtainable.

Woodland was also important as the main source of both fuel and building materials. Each villager could gather dead wood and undergrowth, but trees were felled only for special purposes and at a rate that did not exceed normal growth unless the village was in a region of abundant forests. In that case the forest might be systematically cleared in order to add to the arable land of the village. Other assets common to most villages were a pond or stream in which fish (a major source of protein) were raised, a mill for the grinding of grain, roads and paths, and a common oven for baking bread. Grain was consumed in liquid form as ale or beer, the standard beverage except in winemaking regions. Water was considered—quite correctly, considering the lack of sanitation—to be unhealthful. Although thin and weak, medieval beer had a sufficient alcoholic content to be far safer for human consumption than milk or water.

Almost every village had a church or chapel, and the parish normally coincided with the village. The church was endowed, for the use of the priest, with a holding, or glebe, consisting of strips scattered throughout the open fields and a share in the meadow, pasture, and woods just like any other peasant tenement. The priest was thus a member of the village community and usually participated in the husbandry of the village.

A village of any consequence would, finally, have a more substantial house set apart from the peasants' huts. This was the residence of the lord— or if more than one lord had possession of part of the village, there might be more than one lord's residence. This house was called, originally, a manor. Because the village was thought of as belonging to the lord's residence and under the jurisdiction of the court held in his hall, the term *manor* was extended to embrace the village over which the lord had proprietary and jurisdictional rights. It then became usual to refer to the lord's residence as his manor house, or hall, and to the village as his manor.

## Organization and Control of the Agrarian Economy: The Manor

The manorial organizations of medieval villages resulted from a slow evolution that brought together two quite distinct institutions, the Roman *villa* and the *vicus*. The evolutionary process proceeded at different rates in various regions. In the ninth century the manor had already developed many of its typically medieval characteristics in parts of Italy, eastern France, the Rhineland, and southern Germany. Manorialization proceeded much more slowly in other regions, appearing in England as a fully developed institution only after the Norman Conquest of 1066 and in Denmark later still. Some parts of north-central Germany and southwestern France were still incompletely manorialized in the later Middle Ages, and the manor never developed at all in parts of the Netherlands and Scandinavia. Even in the countries where the manor developed completely, there were marked differences between the manors of different regions. An introductory sketch of the manor, like that of the village, must ignore these differences and emphasize characteristic features commonly found in the most thoroughly manorialized parts of Europe.

The essence of manorialism was the subordination to the lord of peasants who supported themselves on land held from the lord in return for labor services or rents usually paid in kind. It was thus a tenant-farm economy similar to the sharecropping system that developed in the southeastern United States after the Civil War. The medieval system stemmed mainly from late Roman agriculture, mostly carried on by tenants on the great estates, but it was enlarged by the tendency of free peasant farmers to put themselves under the protection of a great landowner by giving up title to their land and receiving it back as economic and legal dependents of their new lords. These dependent cultivators, whether they were themselves formerly slaves or freemen—or whether descended from slaves or freemen—began to be referred to as serfs (from the Latin *servus,* slave) in documents of the Carolingian period. Different degrees of hereditary dependence could exist side by side, and generalization about the status of medieval serfs can be misleading. What can be said is that on great estates, mass chattel slavery of the ancient—or nineteenth-century American—type did not exist, but that all peasants were to some degree dependent on their lord and could be treated as property.

The starting point for the evolution of the village was not the economic power of a landlord but the political authority of the local village chieftain, whose position was recognized by the customary gifts from the free villagers. The village community was originally independent in its agricultural life, which was entirely communal and ruled by custom rather than directed by the chieftain. Although slaves and half-slave freedmen were known in Gallic and Germanic society from the earliest times, the typical members of the village were free peasants. The most important development after the invasions of the fifth century was the depression of freemen to the status of dependent peasants, tied to the soil and subject to the authority of a local lord who protected them in return for their economic support.

By the ninth century the Roman *villa* and the Germanic village community had merged into the manor. The legal ideas underlying the Roman development and the role of the peasant community in the village development had become assimilated, in greater or lesser degree from region to region, until throughout most of the central part of the Carolingian empire the manor had become the typical unit of economic administration. Then with the disintegration of central government in the ninth and tenth centuries, the economic control of the manorial lord was enhanced by the addition of jurisdiction, or political authority, exercised over the peasants of the manor. By the eleventh century every lord of a manor had his court, which was the heart of the manor.

The most prominent feature of the manor was the division of the open fields of the village, or of the part of the village that comprised the manor, between the lord's demesne and the tenements of the peasants. The lord's manorial demesne was the part reserved for himself, not occupied by the peasants but worked by their labor. In extent, this demesne of the manor commonly averaged about one-quarter to one-third of the arable land, although it might vary from nothing to more than one-half in exceptional cases. The demesne was usually intermixed with peasant tenements, scattered like them in strips throughout the two or three open fields. The basic obligation of the peasants was to plow, plant, and harvest the demesne for the lord. The ordinary peasant—the serf or villein of the eleventh century—fulfilled this duty by what was called week work and boon work; that is, during most of the year he devoted three days a week to cultivation of the demesne, and during the harvest season he gave all of his labor to the demesne before harvesting the crops from his own strips. This rule applied to all ordinary serfs or villeins who held uniform tenements in the open fields.

On many manors there were peasants who were freemen although they held tenements within the manor. From these free tenants lighter services were required, and, in some instances, they owed no labor on the demesne. Other peasants possessed smaller tenements than those of the ordinary serfs and villeins, and they were lower in personal status. In England such peasants can be classified into three different groups: slaves, still to be found on some manors, spent all their time and labor on the lord's demesne; cottars, or cottagers, also held no strips in the open fields but worked on the demesne in return for their huts and gardens; finally, some peasants held less than the ordinary tenement in the open fields—when they held half the number of strips of the ordinary peasant, they were called half-villeins. In return for their tenements they performed half the service of the ordinary villein on the lord's demesne. Peasants of this last group often hired out their services either to the lord or to other peasants, and with the profits of their labor were sometimes able to rise to the status of a full villein.

Except for the free tenants, none of the peasants—villeins, half-villeins, cottagers, and slaves—had any legal rights against the lord of the manor. To the modern mind it seems reasonable to ask why such varied classes of peasants were not all subjected to as many labor services as it might please the manorial lord to exact. The only answer supported by contemporary evidence and opinion is that the force of custom balanced the will of the lord. All medieval social relations were governed by appeal to custom, and the strength of this appeal was impressive because the lords lacked the means of modern governments. They relied on their own resources for economic and political position and thus had to make compromises with their dependents, serf and vassal, in order to protect and maintain their own well-being. This was almost as true of the king as it was of his vassals, and when medieval political power is considered in this way, the importance, and the dangers, of the taxing power become clear.

The demesne of the manor included more than merely the lord's share of the open fields. Part of the meadow, for example, was in the demesne—but not necessarily a physical part, like the lord's strips in the open fields. The demesne of the meadow usually consisted of a certain fraction of the hay produced and an equivalent proportion of the grazing rights after haymaking was finished, these rights being measured in terms of the number of the lord's animals allowed to graze. In like fashion, the demesne extended over the pasture, the woodland, the waste, the stream or pond, and other so-called appurtenances of the manor, such as the mill, the oven, and the roads. The demesne right of the lord varied from a proportionate share to full ownership, subject to the customary use of the peasants.

In return for such customary right of use, the peasants, again according to their personal status or according to the size of their tenement, owed to the lord certain services or payments. They had to make hay for the lord and carry it to the lord's barn. The lord's oxen or other animals had entry to the pasture freely, but the peasants were often required to pay small sums for their use of the pasture or provide a shepherd to keep the animals. Peasants who had use of the woodland paid an annual sum in proportion to the number of pigs they were allowed to have rooting about therein. They were required to produce the lord's proportionate share of dead wood and undergrowth and to fell timber for the lord's use. Various fees or services or proportionate shares of the product were exacted from the peasants for their use of the waste land and the stream or pond. Ordinarily, the mill and the oven of the manor were owned completely by the lord. Peasants were required to render a proportion of the flour ground and the bread baked, and they were prohibited from using any other mill or oven but the lord's. In northern France, such monopolies were called banalities, a term derived from the *bannum* of the Carolingian rulers, a command that could not be disobeyed. This is evidence of the local assumption of public authority by the lord of the manor over his peasants.

The list of peasant payments and services is not yet complete. For example, villeins or serfs on many manors owed a dozen eggs to the lord on Easter (the origin of the modern Easter egg). At Christmas on some manors each peasant owed his lord one goose, on other manors some other payment in kind, such as beeswax (for candles) or honey or feathers (for arrows) or cheese. In addition to such payments, the peasantry of most manors owed to their lords a variety of services like carrying or carting crops and timber when required and those called *corvées,* such as maintenance of roads, paths, and bridges and cleaning or digging of drainage ditches.

All the foregoing services and payments have a direct relationship to the lord's control of the economic activities of the manor. In addition, the lord's rights over the peasants as subject to his will were represented by a variety of other payments, which constituted a substantial part of his manorial revenues. The most important were a customary fee exacted by the lord on the death of a serf or other unfree peasant (called heriot in England), and a payment for permission for the daughter of a serf or villein to marry a man who was not the lord's peasant. In some places failure to pay the marriage fee entitled the

This thirteenth-century bronze kettle was used to keep the tithes of grain brought to church by the peasants. It stands on legs in the form of dragon heads and is decorated with scenes of peasants dancing in a festival (top) and nobles hunting with falcons (center). The Church collected a regular tithe (one-tenth) from the produce of almost all communities, and thus its income grew with the increase in production during the Middle Ages.

lord to sleep with the bride on her wedding night. This unusual penalty gave rise to the belief—denounced with vehemence on the eve of the French Revolution—that lords could normally claim this *droit de seigneur* (right of the first night) from female serfs. On all peasants—including the freemen in many instances—fell the arbitrary manorial tax called tallage, or *taille* (cut), which the lord theoretically could exact at will and in any amount. In practice tallage was often restricted to a customary payment taken at more or less regular intervals, and assessed in proportion to the extent of the tenement or the amount of movable wealth of the individual peasant.

Since the typical lord of a manor was a vassal who spent much of his time serving his own lord or hunting or otherwise amusing himself, and since many manorial lords were great men—kings, dukes, counts, viscounts—whose interests and duties hardly allowed time for attention to their manors—manorial administration and enforcement of the lord's complex and diverse rights were ordinarily entrusted to an official representing the lord and residing permanently in the manor. In Carolingian times this official was called the *villicus* or *maior* (mayor) of the manor. Later he was more commonly known as the bailiff or steward.

Enforcement of the lord's jurisdiction over the peasants rested ultimately on the force that the lord, as a member of the military and feudal aristocracy, could bring to bear on his peasants. But for all ordinary disputes among peasants, questions of obligations and duties to the lord, and maintenance of the tranquillity and productivity of the manor, the court held in the hall of the manor house was the normal resort. Over this court the bailiff, as representative of the lord, presided and gave judgment. But the law enforced in such a court was the custom of the manor, the local rules and regulations handed down from generation to generation within the village community. Thus the arbitrary aspect of manorial lordship was tempered by a recognition of the communal life of the peasants. The medieval manor proved to be stable because it maintained a balance between the proprietary and jurisdictional rights of the lord and the customs of the village community.

## The Growth of Towns and Trade

In the ninth century a Carolingian bishop wrote that society was divided into three classes, "those who pray, those who fight, and those who labor"—the clergy, the feudal nobles, and the peasantry, since labor primarily meant plowing. By the end of the eleventh century this analysis was no longer an adequate description of Western society. A fourth class had emerged: the bourgeoisie, who dwelt in towns rather than in the countryside. The appearance of the bourgeoisie was part of a profound transformation that affected all social classes. This transformation was primarily economic in nature, and it is important to understand the way historians have treated it.

The histories of medieval economic life once reflected Renaissance ideas just as much as the histories of cultural and intellectual life. The medieval period was treated as dead economically as it was culturally or intellectually. As modern historians freed themselves from the legacy of Renaissance prejudices about other aspects of medieval civilization, they began to reassess the economic history of the period. The pendulum of opinion soon swung to the other extreme. Every indication of economic well-being was hailed as a boom, and the upswing of economic activities evidenced in the rise of towns was characterized as a "commercial revolution." For example, historians have ascribed great significance to the growth of the population between 1000 and 1340 from approximately 12 to approximately 36 million, which amounts to significantly less than 1 percent per year. It might be more appropriate for medievalists to ask why the growth was so slow rather than why it was so fast. Careful analysis of the economic situation in early medieval Europe has shown that it did not decline as far or as fast as once thought and that international commerce continued throughout the period even medievalists call the Dark Ages.

Part of the historiographical problem was undoubtedly caused by the fact that historians have usually considered some regions to the exclusion of others when studying the history of Europe from the seventh to the eleventh centuries. After the chaos of the Gothic wars and the Lombard conquests in Italy, the focus of political power seemed to shift to the Frankish kingdom, which appeared to hold the future of Western Europe in its borders, culture, politics, and economy. A study of the Frankish kingdom rather than of Italy produced the impression that the Western economy declined after the sixth century; returning to a consideration of Italy in the eleventh century produced the impression that the economy had revived. In Italy, towns continued to function as active commercial centers throughout the early medieval period, and until the late Middle Ages, northern Europe did not compare economically with southern Europe, as long as the measure of comparison is commercial activity. The north had been more agriculturally productive than the south for centuries, and the introduction of new technology widened the gap in that regard. Recent studies of early medieval economic history demonstrate that it is dangerous to permit political history to determine the focus and inform the conclusions of economic history. The political rise of the Carolingian empire did not make it the center of European commercial life.

The Carolingian kings themselves recognized this and tried to remedy the situation. In 875, when Charles the Bald went to Rome for the imperial coronation he had won from his brother Louis the German, he made contact with a community of Jews in Lucca. When he returned home, the Jews went with him. He settled them in his kingdom, and soon Jewish communities were established in Mainz, Worms, Cologne, Trier, Troyes, and other cities of the empire. This movement of Jews to northern Europe under imperial auspices formed the basis of Ashkenazic Jewry, the community of Jews of northern Europe (from the medieval Hebrew *Ashkenazim,* Germans), set apart from the Sephardic Jews of the Mediterranean. From the late ninth century on, these northern Jews functioned as the merchants of Western and central Europe. Their activities are known from a few narrative sources and from collections of law cases decided by rabbinical courts in the tenth and eleventh centuries.

The Jews engaged in extensive trade and formed a commercial link between the North and the Baltic seas trading area and the Mediterranean. With this development, the Frankish kingdom became one of the links between northern Europe and the eastern Mediterranean. The other route was through the Swedish settlements founded at Kiev in Russia (the word *Russia* derives from the Russ, Swedish people who founded or conquered the Kievan state). It is possible that Charles the Bald invited the commercially sophisticated Jews to his kingdom in order to compete with the Russians. The Jews brought wood, beeswax, slaves, and furs from the north and traded them for a variety of goods produced in Europe. The Vikings and other Scandinavians prized German weapons, especially swords, because of the relatively high quality steel produced in the Ruhr. Charlemagne and his successors repeatedly prohibited the sale of such items to the Northmen for the obvious reason that they were frequently used against the Franks themselves. Presumably the swords were traded in the commercial network of the north European Jewish communities. Although some goods, such as spices, silks, slaves, and furs, were carried long distances over the trade routes, most of the trade items did not go far. Typically the traders bought goods in order to sell them just down the river or road, and then with their capital and profits, they would buy a new commodity to sell still farther along. Thus they literally worked their way along the trade routes. If their destiny was the East, as it often was with Jewish merchants, they might come back with a high value, low bulk commodity like spice or silk, or they might work their way back along the route they had come, buying and selling a different series of goods. The communities of the Rhineland tended to do business with other Jewish communities situated along the trade routes. A merchant was often gone for years, and many rabbinical decisions concerned the disposition of property and the right of a wife to remarry when her husband had been gone for an extended period of time. It is an indication of how long even normal trips could take that the law assumed a man was dead after seven years of utter silence about his whereabouts. Of course, the cases often arose because the merchant in question had returned after the seven-year term.

Several elements of Jewish life stand out as evidence of the level and character of commercial life in Western Europe from the ninth through the eleventh centuries. First, whereas in the twelfth and thirteenth centuries, the Jewish businessman traded with his Christian counterpart, in the earlier period, such dealings were rare. It would seem, therefore, that at least in the Frankish kingdom, the Jewish communities stood virtually alone in the commercial sphere. Jewish merchants had extensive dealings with non-Jewish companies (especially carters), but their partners and competitors were primarily Jews. Second, while it is common to suppose that one of the restraints on trade in the tenth and eleventh centuries was the lawlessness of petty nobles and highwaymen, Jewish records show a remarkable degree of safety on the roads. Profits were extraordinarily high, as much as 200 to 300 percent, because of the dangers, but Jews traveled alone and without escort on a regular basis. Furthermore, when robberies did occur, the merchants often got most if not all of the stolen goods back, since it was almost impossible to fence a stolen shipment because of the small number of merchants and the small volume of trade. Third, a principal reason for the surprising safety of travelers and their shipments was that they had the protection of the great lords and kings. Throughout the Middle Ages, the Jews enjoyed a special relationship with the authorities, both lay and ecclesiastical, and this relationship was based on the importance of Jewish merchants for the movement of goods desired by those at the top of the social hierarchy.

Trade, using very sophisticated forms of business organization and banking, continued during the darkest period of medieval history with the active support of the ruling class. The cities, where the Jewish communities were established, were engaged in commerce and remained more active than is often thought. In northern Europe, the cities did stand outside the mainstream of society and culture, and the fact that the wealthiest part of the urban population was Jewish did not make the urban setting very relevant or appealing to many Christians of the period. Even though they declined, therefore, the cities remained commercially viable, and in Italy, the decline was much less than in the north. By the late eleventh century, the towns everywhere were in a rapid upswing. The political settlement that created chivalry in the upper classes and permitted the peasantry to achieve a new prosperity, also affected the towns. The expansion of Europe gave European merchant communities new advantages in Spain, southern Italy, Eastern Europe, and the Levant. The Jews shared in this new commercial prosperity, but they quickly lost their dominant position. By the mid-eleventh century, Christian merchants had become the principal figures in the trade network.

The long-distance trade affected very few lives during the early Middle Ages. It overlaid an extensive system of local markets that served the commercial activity of the peasants and lesser nobility. The number of local markets increased impressively in the Carolingian period. These markets, usually held for a day or two every few weeks, were part of the process of localization of the agricultural economy that followed the decline of the late Roman commerce in agricultural products. Peasants produced a small surplus that they traded at the local markets for goods not available in the district—salt, fish, wine, linen textiles, and perhaps cattle. Peddlers with specialty household items also traveled the roads and visited the markets. This localized, low-value commerce was not particularly impressive when compared with the long-distance trade, but it could be extremely important and could be a vehicle for the accumulation of considerable amounts of capital. Medieval agriculture was more vulnerable than modern agriculture to the vicissitudes of weather and disease. A good season usually produced a surplus of grain, while a bad season almost inevitably brought famine. The earliest significant revival of trade in the West resulted from the sale of grain and other basic commodities in famine-struck areas. The goods were bought at low prices in the markets of a district where conditions had been favorable to a good harvest and sold at high prices in the markets of regions hard hit by weather or pestilence. Peasants could become prosperous in this system, but its greatest beneficiaries were the lords. A striking result of this economic situation was that in the pre-Crusade period, the pattern of money lending went from lord to Jewish merchant instead of from Jew to lord. The Jews and the increasing number of Christians who engaged in trade could utilize the liquid wealth produced by surplus agriculture. The lords used some of their funds to buy luxury goods, thus increasing the demand for such items, but consumption could not account for all their wealth, and the merchants were willing to buy money for their growing enterprises.

The earliest centers of commerce were in areas where population growth outstripped agricultural production. Venice led in the southern revival of trade, closely followed by other Italian and southern French seaports that could not feed themselves. Cities like Venice, Pisa, and Marseilles traded salt for food and later branched out into other commodities obtained by their shipping. Venice had two great advantages: a favorable geographical location, assuring protection from enemies on the mainland and a sheltered trade route along the Adriatic coast to the Levant; and a favorable relationship with the Byzantine Empire—the city had a semiautonomous position that allowed its merchants freedom of enterprise and gave them trading privileges within the empire. In the eleventh century other Italian seaports made aggressive efforts to win trading privileges in Byzantine and Moslem lands. Sometimes by peaceful negotiation, and sometimes by a show of armed force, Genoa, Pisa, Amalfi, and Gaeta won favorable treatment in various North African and Levantine commercial centers. In the twelfth century Venetian supremacy in trade with the East was no longer secure. Mediterranean commerce came to be dominated by several Italian cities, all intermediaries between the economically advanced Levant and the Western European markets.

In the north, the commercial revival was most marked in Flanders, which was located at the center of trade routes radiating by land and sea toward the Baltic, the Rhineland, northern France, and the British Isles. Flanders was well suited for raising sheep, and the Flemish woolen industry

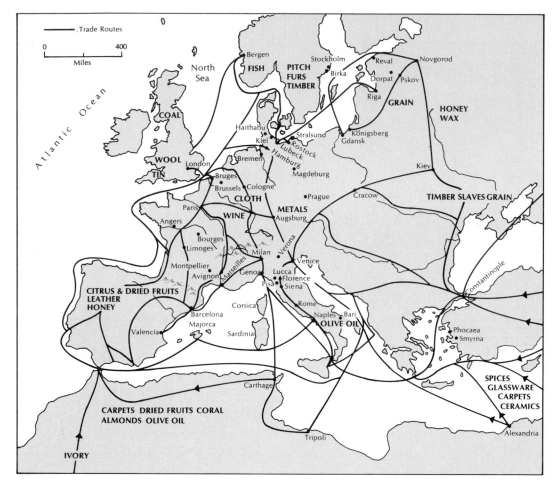

Medieval Trade Routes

was the earliest northern commercial enterprise to grow beyond the stage of handicraft output for local consumption. Inexpensive, high quality Flemish cloth was exported in the eleventh century in exchange for food from nearby regions with richer soil or for lumber, furs, and metals from the north. By the twelfth century, Flanders was the most densely populated and one of the richest areas in northern Europe. Other, lesser centers also developed. In the eleventh century considerable commercial activity existed in the Rhineland, the Île-de-France, and the ports of the North and Baltic seas.

The luxury trade had much less impact on the northern commerce than it did on the Mediterranean, but the northerners maintained contact with the East through the Swedish settlements and their successors on the Dnieper

River. This route was hazardous, running from the Gulf of Finland down the Dnieper to the Black or the Caspian seas. Toward the end of the eleventh century Italian merchants began to cross the Alps with commodities from the Levant. One transalpine route crossed the western Alps into the Rhone Valley, whence goods were carried northward into the populous river valleys of the Loire, Seine, Meuse, and Moselle with their tributaries. Another transalpine route lay over the eastern passes and into the upper Danube and Rhine valleys, from which commodities were transported to western and central Germany by way of the lower Rhine, the Main, and the Elbe rivers and their tributaries.

The expansion of commerce was the direct cause of the growth and, in some respects, the revival of towns. The development of a Christian merchant class not only expanded the towns but also revived them by bringing them once more into the mainstream of European society and culture. The great distance between the interests of the merchant-urban and farmer-rural elements of the population made assimilation between them difficult. Merchants needed three conditions for success. First, they required a base of operations strategically located along trade routes, near local markets, and favorably situated for warehousing and the transportation or transshipment of goods. Second, they needed security in the form of protection by a strong local power against the dangers of war or violent seizure of property by lawless elements in the feudal world. The tradition of such protection was already long established by the eleventh century. Third, they needed freedom of movement and freedom from the restrictions and routine of the manorial peasantry. Wherever merchants found these three prerequisites for successful commercial activity—favorable location, security, and freedom—towns grew and flourished.

These plans show the main types of village settlements found in medieval Europe. The development of the various types depended not on the ethnic origin of the population as much as on the lay of the land. The densely populated round village could only exist in fertile, open country. The street village grew up along main thoroughfares and sometimes expanded into substantial trading centers. The round hamlet was characteristic of small forest settlements in clearings.

ROUND VILLAGE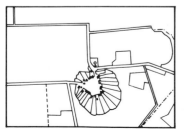

STREET VILLAGE

ROUND HAMLET

The requirements for the survival of a medieval city largely intact include poverty and stagnation, since a bustling trade was usually accompanied by constant urban renewal. The city of Carcassonne, in Septimania, remains much as it was in the twelfth century. It was protected by placement on a hill and by two rings of walls about a mile in circumference. The city commanded the whole plain surrounding it. In the twelfth century the population within the walls was not as dense as it is today, and most of the buildings were of wood—an extreme fire hazard. The suburb to the right is also very old, and its inhabitants took shelter in the city during times of trouble. The town got its food from the surrounding countryside.

Some of the important medieval towns, such as London, Paris, and Cologne, had been cities under the Roman Empire. Other towns grew up where a ruler or great feudal lord had built a castle or fortified strong point, such as those of Alfred and his successors in England, called *burhs,* and those of the tenth-century kings in Germany, called *burgen* (French *bourg*). Originally, the inhabitants of these fortifications were members of a permanent garrison, but the revival of trade transformed some of the "boroughs" from military installations into business and urban centers. Almost without exception, former Roman cities and tenth-century boroughs that remained merely military forts were not located along important trade routes. And almost without exception, those favorably located did grow into towns whose inhabitants—the burgesses of England, the burghers of Germany, and the bourgeoisie of France—lived by trade and industry rather than by husbandry or bearing arms.

The earliest mercantile settlements were not within the fortified area, or inside the walls, of the borough, but adjacent to it. Paradoxically, the revival of urban life took place in the suburbs, clusters of houses and buildings outside the original walled enclosure. During the eleventh and twelfth centuries the growing towns built new walls to surround these enlarged areas. The same pattern of growth is characteristic of towns that had their origin in a mercantile settlement next to a great monastery or a royal manor. The protection afforded by the abbot or king, plus favorable location, provided the incentive for settlement, and as the nascent town grew it eventually enveloped the original monastic or manorial center. This happened most frequently where the king or abbot or other lord was enlightened enough to see that encouragement of trade was profitable even if it was not a traditional activity of his class, and where lords were willing to grant freedom to the urban inhabitants from the labor services and burdens of the peasantry.

### Suggestions for Further Reading

**Secondary Works**  For an excellent introduction, see N. Neilson, *Medieval Agrarian Economy* (New York, 1936), and the classic work by Marc Bloch, *French Rural Society,* trans. J. Sondheimer (Berkeley and Los Angeles, 1966). In addition, see the outstanding work by G. Duby, *Rural Economy and Country Life in the Medieval West* (London, 1968); R. Lennard, *Rural England, 1086–1135* (Oxford, 1959); P. Boissonade, *Life and Work in Medieval Europe* (New York, 1927); and A. Lewis, *The Development of Southern French and Catalan Society, 718–1050* (Austin, Tex., 1965). The second part of Lynn White's work on medieval technology, cited at the end of Chapter 9, is also important. On the towns, see H. Pirenne, *Medieval Cities* (Princeton, N.J., 1925); R. Rörig, *The Medieval Town* (Berkeley and Los Angeles, 1967), which focuses on German towns; and J. Tait, *The Medieval English Borough* (Manchester, 1936). The question of what caused the revival of towns in the eleventh century is treated in John Benton, ed., *Town Origins* (Boston, 1968).

**Sources**  Benton's work contains a selection of the evidence used by historians of the medieval cities. See also J. H. Mundy and Peter Riesenberg, *The Medieval Town* (Princeton, N.J., 1958), and, for materials on the southern European trading sphere, R. S. Lopez and I. W. Raymond, eds., *Medieval Trade in the Mediterranean World* (New York, 1955). On rural life, see C. H. Bell, trans., *Peasant Life in Old German Epics* (New York, 1931).

# 12 The Medieval Empire, the Reform of the Church, and the First Conflict Between Secular and Ecclesiastical Authority

Christianity advanced steadily during the early Middle Ages. It took hold in the rural districts as well as the urban centers. It developed a complex and effective institutional structure. It was woven into the social, intellectual, and cultural fabric of early medieval civilization, which was to partake of both the good and the bad of the society. A strong strain in Christianity urged the faithful, especially their leaders, to stand back and take an outsider's view of society and politics. The religion had originated in a non-Christian milieu in which this standoffish perspective had been natural, and many of the most important patristic writings, which formed the basis of the Christians' world view, started from this perspective. One example was Saint Augustine's *City of God,* which portrayed the decline of the Roman Empire as the result of its spiritual misdirection and placed true reality outside the apparent reality of worldly life. Thus as Christianity increasingly became a part of the world, the tension between its role and its ideology grew more acute. The eleventh-century reform movement realized the ideology and transformed the role of the Church and its community. In so doing, the reform movement revolutionized European society by creating a new foundation on which European social and political institutions would rest. This revolution lies behind the First Amendment to the Constitution of the United States: "Congress shall make no law respecting an establishment of religion," the separation of church and state. After the eleventh century, religious authority in Europe was largely independent of secular authority, and every person had to divide his loyalty and his obedience between two powerful superiors. Some of Europe's most characteristic institutions and ideas derive from the conflicts inherent in this situation, and thus the eleventh-century movement stands as one of the great revolutions in Western history.

Paradoxically, the independence of the Church from secular authority arose from the extension of the secular power into religious affairs. In asserting their authority over ecclesiastical matters, the medieval emperors created the force that would ultimately limit their authority over those affairs.

### The Medieval Empire at Its Height

The eleventh-century emperors were confronted with four major problems: the problem of succession to the throne, the need for strengthening the imperial government, the effort to achieve a territorial stabilization of the empire, and relations with the spiritual authority in the several parts of the empire (and later, relations with the papacy).

The first problem arose with the unexpected death in 1002 of Otto III, a youth of twenty-two years, without a direct heir. An election was now necessary, but the influence of the hereditary principle can be seen in the choice of the nearest kinsman of the Saxon line, the duke of Bavaria, Henry II (1002–1024). The election placed Henry in a difficult position. As duke of Bavaria he had pursued a moderate policy of independence from the monarchy. As king, Henry alienated the southern magnates by placing them more directly under the royal government than they had been. The nobility of Saxony also did not like the election of Henry because they had traditionally supported the Saxon kings against the southerners, and now the king was a southerner. The German nobility as a whole had no enthusiasm for a king whose interests and attention were focused on Germany. After twenty years of rule by absentee emperors in Italy, the German magnates knew that Henry would bring royal government home again. He spent the first years of his reign quelling rebellions among the disgruntled nobility of the kingdom, and he was forced by magnate opposition to rely even more heavily than his predecessors on the churches. Fifty bishops were elevated during Henry's reign; he personally invested forty-nine of them. Most of these men were selected from the royal court, where they had been chaplains. At the same time, Henry completed the work of bringing the great abbeys of the realm, which like the bishoprics were institutions of extraordinary wealth and power, under royal control. By the end of his reign, eighty-five abbeys were recognized as royal foundations and thus received royal protection and patronage. Henry even became a member of the clergy, in an honorary but highly symbolic way, as a canon of several episcopal churches in the kingdom. One result of his reign was therefore an intensifying of the spiritual element in royal ideology, the enhancing of ideas that led to a doctrine of royal theocracy. Ironically, Henry's deep involvement with and reliance on the churches moved the monarchy toward a sharp clash with them because Christian doctrine and tradition placed an inviolable authority over spiritual matters in the ecclesiastical hierarchy.

The problem of succession came up again when Henry II died without an heir. The successful candidate this time was a descendant of Otto I, Conrad II (1024–1039), duke of Swabia and founder of the Salian dynasty. Like his predecessor, Conrad II devoted several years to stamping out rebellion and consolidating his control of Germany. Henry had established a close relationship between the churchmen and the monarchy, but Conrad disturbed this connection. Conrad did not support, as Henry had, the reform movement that was spreading through the higher echelons of the Church, and the churchmen who had been loyal to Henry naturally did not have the same feelings about or commitment to Conrad. Thus Conrad sought to develop a new support for the monarchy. He became the first German king to attempt to found the kingship on the feudal hierarchy of the realm. The great nobles had secured a hereditary position in their offices and for their estates but had opposed the tendency toward hereditary fiefs among the lesser nobility, their vassals. Conrad became the champion of the hereditary principle and thus of the lesser nobility, whom he hoped to make loyal to himself at the expense of his ducal opponents. Further, Conrad succeeded in gaining direct control of most of the duchies. Whenever a duchy became vacant by failure of heirs, the king granted it to his own heir to hold by hereditary right. Every duchy except Saxony and Lorraine had come into the hands of Conrad's heir by the end of the reign. As a final precaution, Conrad within his own lifetime secured the election of his son as king of Germany. Thus the hereditary principle was once more established.

Conrad's successor was Henry III (1039–1056), the first emperor to succeed to the throne without having to devote the early years of his reign to suppressing rebellion. The Salian emperors succeeded each other, from father to son, until the death of Henry V in 1125. The hereditary principle was so strongly established that it survived a regency of ten years (1056–1066) during the minority of Henry IV.

Conrad had solved the problem of succession, but his feudal policy failed. None of the eleventh-century emperors succeeded in building a strong imperial government. Partly this was because the limited resources of the government were spread over too great an area, stretching from Lorraine to the Slavic frontier and from the Baltic to central Italy. The cultural, economic, and political diversity of these vast territories militated against the creation of a strong centralized government. In addition, the emperors did not pursue a consistent policy, and thus the efforts of each succeeding emperor cancelled out the work of his predecessors. Henry II almost ignored Italy, thus reversing the policies of his predecessors. He spent his reign consolidating his position in Germany, as the nobles had feared. He also created an ecclesiastical administration by appointing churchmen to most of the important administrative positions. Ecclesiastics made up a large portion of his court. This policy improved the quality of the government and had the advantage of giving the king increased control over his counselors and aides because the churchmen did not pass on their offices to heirs. But since the policy was an expression of Henry's piety as well as his governmental plans, it led him to give away a large portion of his government's resources as landed endowments for churches and monasteries. He was also generous with grants of various revenue-producing royal rights, such as market tolls and jurisdictions. Thus by 1024, the size of the royal domain had shrunk significantly, royal revenues had declined, and the administrative system was in the hands of churchmen. As a candidate of an antireform party, Conrad II was hardly inclined to continue Henry's policies and was antipathetic to his predecessor's administration. Instead he constructed the feudal policy described above and made a surprisingly successful effort to recover alienated royal lands and regalian rights. In addition, Conrad built another administrative system, patterned on the Carolingian model, managed by low-born but proven men of the servant, or *ministerialis,* class. In doing this, Conrad imitated the Church, which had established an effective bureaucracy administered by serfs who were able to work their way up the administrative hierarchy. The *ministeriales* depended wholly on the emperor's patronage and were a loyal and able body of administrators. Later in the century, the group played an important role in German politics.

Henry III pursued the policies of both his predecessors. He supported the reform movement in the Church and used clerics extensively in his administration, but by doing so, he alienated much of his domain. He also continued and even increased the use of *ministeriales,* but he reversed his father's policy of supporting the lesser nobility against their superiors. First, the increasing use of *ministeriales* put a wedge between the king and the lesser nobility, who felt challenged by the new class. Second, the great nobles were incensed by the king's reliance on the low-born officials, and Henry apparently decided that he could not alienate the most powerful men in the kingdom both by challenging their control over their vassals and by excluding them from the government. Finally, feudalism was not far enough advanced in Germany to make a feudal policy look promising, and the development of the *ministeriales* did look promising.

Henry III's policy seemed to work during his lifetime. The imperial government was never as strong as during his reign. But his success stemmed from neither his artful combination of policies nor his personal ability—both of which can be granted to have been superior—but from a happy coincidence of events and from his impressive inheritance. When he came to power, Henry personally controlled all but two duchies and a few other large fiefs. He also inherited a well-trained corps of royal servants. But perhaps of greater importance was the conjunction between Henry's reign and the reform movement developing in the German Church. Adherents of the reform had achieved ecclesiastical hegemony by the time of Henry's reign. The tension between king and magnates was tempered and held in check by the close relationship between Henry and the churches.

The territorial problem of the empire had two interrelated aspects: the imperial title gave the emperor rule over a vast territory, and the concept of "empire" influenced relations between the emperor and other European rulers. On the eastern frontiers Poland and Bohemia and the Magyar state of Hungary had, toward the end of the tenth century, been consolidated under rulers ambitious to be recognized as kings, to be wholly independent, and to recapture lands occupied by Germans east of the Elbe and in the upper Danube valley. Henry II maintained friendly relations with his royal brother-in-law, Saint Stephen (997–1038), who ruled Hungary and had received his crown from Pope Sylvester II in 1001. Bohemia was in anarchy and presented no threat. But Boleslav the Brave (992–1025), duke of Poland, aimed at the union of all the western Slavs under his rule. Henry II fought a long series of campaigns, finally driving Boleslav from Bohemia, but elsewhere Boleslav's conquests were so impressive that he was able to obtain the title of king in the last year of his long reign.

Conrad II was neither related to Stephen of Hungary nor sympathetic with the saintly king's religious policy. In 1030 Conrad peremptorily demanded that Stephen do homage to him, and when Stephen refused, the German emperor invaded Hungary. Stephen led a successful resistance. Next, Conrad intervened in Poland. After Boleslav's death, his kingdom had been whittled down by his neighbors: Hungary had seized Slovakia; Bohemia took Moravia; Denmark won Pomerania; and Russia got Ruthenia. This "partition of Poland" was finally ended when the Polish ruler did homage to Conrad (1031–1032).

Henry III finally brought all three of the eastern states under the suzerainty of the emperor. Poland, divided by civil war, was reduced to the status of a duchy held by its ruler as an imperial fief. Bretislav I, duke of Bohemia (1034–1055), had set out to conquer the Slavic lands, so that Bohemia would be recognized as a kingdom. Henry crushed these ambitions by forcing Bretislav to relinquish his conquests and do homage for his duchy as an imperial fief. Hungary, after the death of Stephen, was the prize of several claimants whose struggles invited German intervention. Henry was able to place a pro-German contender on the throne, and the new king did homage to the emperor. The eastern frontier was now stablized. The duchies of Poland and Bohemia and the kingdom of Hungary were all imperial fiefs held by rulers who had done homage to Henry III.

On the western borders of the empire an even more impressive territorial settlement resulted in the acquisition of the kingdom of Burgundy, consisting of the older kingdoms of Provence and Trans-Jurane Burgundy now reunited under Rudolph III (993–1032). Being childless, Rudolph had provided for the inheritance of his kingdom by his nephew, the emperor Henry II, but Henry predeceased Rudolph. Conrad II then urged his own claims, both as successor to Henry II and because his wife was a niece of Rudolph. The unruly nobility preferred another nephew of Rudolph, the count of Blois and Champagne, under whom they could anticipate a mild and ineffective rule, but Conrad II took possession of the kingdom and in two years had defeated the count's bid for the succession.

The significance of the union of Burgundy with the empire was twofold. By securing the western passes of the Alps, it protected Italy from French intervention, a danger brought home to Conrad in 1024, when the anti-German Italian nobles had offered the imperial crown first to Robert II, king of France, and then to the duke of Aquitaine. In a more general sense the union marked the transition of the concept of "empire" from that of a dignity to that of a territorial bloc. The earliest medieval document in which the phrase *Roman Empire* occurs in a territorial sense, meaning the three kingdoms of Germany, Italy, and Burgundy, rather than in the Carolingian or Ottonian sense of the highest secular authority, is dated 1034. Hitherto, *empire* had been a word that could be dissociated from any particular territories, as exemplified by the recent appeal to the king of France and the duke of Aquitaine. Henceforth, *empire* was to be a territorial concept meaning the kingdoms that were united as one political unit under the emperor and passed as one bloc by hereditary succession to the new emperor. This territorial stabilization was given further expression when Conrad, during his own lifetime, had his son Henry consecrated "king of the Romans," a title that from then on designated the heir who, as co-ruler of the kingdoms of Germany, Italy, and Burgundy, was the emperor-elect.

Henry II and Conrad II devoted most of their time to problems north of the Alps. Henry had visited Italy briefly three times, and Conrad spent two years there climaxed by his imperial coronation on Easter Sunday 1027, a memorable event attended by two royal pilgrims, King Rudolph of Burgundy and King Cnut of England and Denmark. Except for one more visit late in his reign Conrad neglected Italy, so the Italian nobles regained much of the autonomy they had enjoyed before the intervention of Otto I. After the deaths of Pope Sylvester II and Emperor Otto III, the papacy had once more become the prize of Roman aristocratic factions. The Roman aristocrats considered the papacy a vehicle for enhancing their political power and financial well-being. Since the pope governed Rome and held claims to the Papal States, the family that controlled the papacy ruled the city and might expand its power over outlying districts. Between 1003 and 1012, the Crescentii, a family from the Sabine territory to the west of Rome, dominated Rome and installed three popes. In 1012 the count of Tusculum forced his way into the city and ousted the Crescentii. He gave the papal tiara to his brother, Benedict VIII (1012–1024). Benedict proved an able and not altogether evil man. He cooperated with Henry II in ecclesiastical reforms and took his position as ruler of central Italy seriously. He spent considerable time leading armies against the Moslems in southern Italy. He was followed by two more Tusculan popes, his brother, John XIX (1024–1032) and his nephew, Benedict IX (1032–1048). Under Benedict IX the papacy once more declined amidst charges of scandal and corruption, and in 1044 the Crescentii drove Benedict from Rome. They installed a member of their family as Sylvester III in 1045, but after a few months, he was forced by Benedict and the Tusculans to retire to his original position as bishop of Sabina. Benedict recognized, however, that he would not be able to maintain his position, and he sold the papacy to yet a third family faction that placed one of its own scions, Gregory VI (1045–1046), on the papal throne. Gregory was actually intent on reforming the papacy, but he took a bad step when he paid for his new position. He came from a family that had converted from Judaism only about ten years before and that had established itself in the city, moving from the traditional Jewish quarter in the Trastevere across the river from the center of Crescentii power. This family, later called the Pierleoni, was destined to play a large role in Roman and papal politics during the next century, but its first step into the arena was rather ill-conceived. When Benedict and Sylvester reasserted their claims in 1046, the city was reduced to chaos. Benedict held the Lateran palace and thus the administrative and religious center of the bishopric of Rome. Gregory turned the basilica of Santa Maria Maggiore into a fortress. Sylvester held Saint Peter's across the river. The mobs held the streets.

At this point Henry III arrived for the imperial coronation. In his entourage were a group of German reformers, and the impression the papacy made on these men and their king must have been difficult to describe in decent language. Henry summoned the three claimants to a synod at Sutri just north of Rome in December 1046. Under the king's presidency, the synod deposed all three popes and prohibited simony, the buying and selling of ecclesiastical offices, throughout the empire. On Christmas Day, the bishop of Bamberg, a relative of the emperor, was elevated to the papal throne at Henry's behest. He took the name Clement II (1046–1047) to signify the reestablishment of the papacy as it had been, so the reformers believed, in its beginnings. According to legend, Clement I was Saint Peter's successor.

Clement was the first of four German popes nominated by Henry, and they personified the extension of the close connection between the German monarchy and the German churches to the imperial authority and the Roman Church. Clement II and his successor, Damasus II (1048), died after only a few months in office—some suspected that they were poisoned by locals— but the third in the line, Leo IX (1048–1054), successfully established the reform movement in the papal see. This was a momentous development.

## The Reform of the Papacy and of the Church

In order to understand the eleventh-century reform movement, its ninth- and tenth-century background must be considered. To the eleventh-century reformers, the condition of the Church in this period was a corruption of the pristine institution and community that had existed in patristic times. This view distorted reality. After Constantine, the emperors asserted their traditional rights as the *pontifex maximus* (greatest priest) and presided over the organization and disciplinary functions of the Church. Until the late fifth century, emperors respected the independence of churchmen in doctrinal matters, an independence nonetheless exercised under imperial authority, but beginning in the reign of Zeno (474–491), the secular rulers claimed a voice in this sphere. As Christian ideas on the divine ordination of secular government became influential, the emperors began to see themselves as being above ordinary laymen and as capable of participating in all aspects of the Church's functions.

Throughout the early Middle Ages, the ideology of Caesaropapism (royal theocracy) prevailed, although the actual power in ecclesiastical affairs exercised by kings and emperors depended on political and personal factors. With the rise of the Saxon kings and the foundation of the medieval empire, the fluctuating relationship between king and higher clergy became fixed in the constitutional fabric of the German monarchy and imperial government. The German emperors did not assert the right to expound doctrinal positions, but they controlled the ecclesiastical hierarchy by choosing its membership. This situation produced the ideology of royal theocracy and the explication of the relationship between king and bishops that played a large role in the eleventh century.

Under the Carolingian kings and in early feudal Europe, the parish churches were in dismal condition. The nobility had absolute control over the churches that they or their predecessors had built on their fiefs and allodial estates. The lord owned the church; he received its revenues from tithes and first fruits; he appointed the pastor. The parish clergy were thus almost invariably unfit for the clerical profession by modern or even medieval standards. They rarely could read or write and were just barely able to mumble through the Mass. They were usually married, since they rarely felt a commitment to their profession strong enough to remain celibate, and villagers often would not trust a priest with their wives or daughters unless the priest was ensconced in family life. The parish churches were as much a part of the manorial economy as of the Church, and thus the lords paid the parish priests a pittance that made the churches income-producing properties. The parish clergy were therefore very poor, deriving most of their income from their peasant landholdings in the village. The spiritual impact of such men was at best small, but the establishment of parish churches and clergy in the villages was important because it symbolized the Christianization of Europe and offered hope for the true Christianization of the peasantry.

If in practice, the secular lords controlled the parishes, in theory, the bishops held authority over all churches in their dioceses, including the exclusive right to appoint and ordain priests. During the ninth century, the growth of the Church as a powerful institution, after the decline caused by Charles Martel's policies a century earlier, was accompanied by an attempt at all levels to bring the supposed subordinates under the control of their superiors. On the episcopal level, the bishops tried to extend their real authority over the parish priests, but their efforts met resistance from two groups. First, the secular lords would not relinquish their rights, and the bishops, who came from the noble class and shared its ideas, often acquiesced in this opposition. This conflict resulted in a compromise expressed in the doctrine of ecclesiastical law that the secular lord could choose his pastor but only the bishop could ordain and establish him in his church. The doctrine acknowledged the bishop's right to examine the candidate for his fitness to serve the Church and to reject the lord's choice, but in the ninth century, such conflicts rarely arose. Second, the bishops were opposed by ecclesiastics who had taken up a position between the urban and rural clergy. During the early Middle Ages, bishops had remained urban powers and had had little contact with the rural clergy of their dioceses. To shorten the physical and cultural distance between the two clerical groups, bishops appointed rural core-bishops (*corepiscopi*), who were supposed to oversee the country churches. By the ninth century, the core-bishops had extended their virtually independent control over the outlying areas of many dioceses, especially in France, and sought to exclude episcopal authority from their districts. A long struggle between the independent core-bishops and the bishops ensued, complicated by the relationship between bishops and their legal superiors, the archbishops.

Archbishops generally held a metropolitan authority over a province containing several dioceses. Cases could be appealed from episcopal to archiepiscopal courts, and bishops could be judged by a court of provincial bishops presided over by the archbishop. The archbishop also had the right to consecrate bishops in his province, and as in the bishops' power to ordain priests, this privilege of consecration implied a right of examination. In the ninth century, powerful archbishops, such as Hincmar of Reims (845–882), asserted the panoply of archiepiscopal rights, supported by the kings who used the archbishops as a means to control the churches. The bishops were thus caught between the archbishops and the core-bishops. The measure of the squeeze is its literary product. Toward the middle of the ninth century, in Hincmar's province, members of the episcopal group compiled an enormous collection of forgeries. The main body of this work was composed of papal letters brilliantly produced from snippets of authentic and newly written material. These letters were attributed to such popes as Clement I, Anacletus I, Evaristus I, Sixtus I, Telesphorus I, some of them real persons, others legendary. The collection, known as the Pseudo-Isidorian Decretals, was ascribed to Isidore Mercatus, to whom the most important ancient compilation of conciliar legislation was attributed. Until the Renaissance, the letters were considered authentic. The thrust of the legal doctrines contained in the forgery was twofold. The authors denied the claims of core-bishops to jurisdiction in the dioceses and, in fact, went so far as to deny completely the legitimacy of that jurisdiction. Against the archbishops, the authors directed a traditional device for escaping the authority of an immediate superior; they claimed archiepiscopal authority was subordinate to papal power and that bishops were subject primarily to the pope and secondarily to the archbishop. Only the pope could judge episcopal cases. Only the pope could authorize councils, and if the papal commission was lacking, the decrees of a council had only provincial import. Of course, decrees of such councils found to be in contradiction to papal decrees or conciliar decrees validated by papal authority were null and void. The Pseudo-Isidorian Decretals therefore contained the most extensive and most powerful exposition of the doctrines of papal supremacy produced up to that time. It consolidated and enhanced a tradition of papal ideology only intermittently expounded in earlier centuries and always resisted by great ecclesiastical lords, such as archbishops. Pope Nicholas I (858–867) immediately accepted the letters as genuine. Even Hincmar was forced to recognize their authenticity, and was reduced to arguing an interpretation of injurious passages that would minimize their effect. Everyone had to admit that the men who circulated the collection had found a marvellous instrument.

During the tenth century, one part of the episcopal group's goals was achieved. The development of episcopal power under the aegis of the Saxon kings made it possible for the bishops to virtually destroy the authority of the core-bishops, and by the mid-eleventh century, these intermediaries between the bishops and the rural clergy no longer played a significant role. The realization of the papal authority expounded by the forgers took longer. During the period when the Carolingian empire was breaking up, Nicholas I established important precedents for later medieval popes by successfully asserting his independence of imperial influence, his right to judge all secular rulers in matters of morality, and his universal authority over the Church.

Nicholas found it easier, however, to overawe the shadow-emperor Louis

II (855–875) and to force king Lothair (855–869) to give up his mistress and take back his wife, than to control the higher clergy of the kingdoms north of the Alps. Supremacy over the Church depended on the support of a strong emperor, but a strong emperor would subordinate the papacy to the role assigned it by Charlemagne. Nicholas saw an escape from this dilemma in an alliance with the Frankish bishops against the growing claims of the archbishops, or metropolitans. His treatment of the Pseudo-Isidorian Decretals was one element of this policy. But actual conditions in the late ninth century were no better suited for the survival of central authority in the spiritual than in the secular sphere. Nicholas I had little more than his personal ability and an ideological justification to support his wide claims. As the power of the emperors declined, imperial protection against the vicissitudes of local Roman politics disappeared, and the papacy became once more the prize of party strife in Rome. To survive at all, the popes had to become leaders of factions and incur the risks of factional struggle. The turning point was the pontificate of John VIII, after whose murder in 882 fifteen popes came and went during the next thirty-two years. Most of them gained the pontifical throne through crime or intrigue and vacated it by deposition, exile, or assassination.

Some stability was recovered under John X (914–928), the ablest pope of the period. A man of many talents, he distinguished himself by leading the army that drove the Moslems from their stronghold on the Garigliano River in 915. He was the only pope during the first third of the tenth century who could match the influence and circumvent the plots of the ambitious and quarrelsome local Roman nobility, led by an unscrupulous magnate named Theophylact, who assumed the title Senator of the Romans. After Theophylact's death under doubtful circumstances, power passed to his widow, the notorious Theodora, and her daughter Marozia. Current scandal connected each of them with a half-dozen popes in the capacity of mistress, or mother, or murderess. In this period, its nadir of corruption and degradation, the papacy was little more than the spiritual puppet of the local tyrant Alberic, son of Marozia, who controlled Rome for twenty-two years (932–954). Secularization of the papacy was completed when Alberic's son and successor as tyrant became pope himself, as John XII (955–963). His misbehavior and difficulties finally led to intervention by Otto the Great in 962, with consequences that have already been noted in Chapter 9.

The reform of the papacy and of the ecclesiastical hierarchy was not generated in the hierarchy itself but in monasticism. In the Carolingian period, monasteries suffered the same treatment as churches through the actions of the nobility. Lords built and endowed monastic houses on their land for several purposes, principally pietistic and financial. The monks were the lord's agents before God and prayed for the souls of the lord and his family. In an age in which every noble did things he should not have done—and knew it—the monks of the family monastery provided a kind of insurance; the lord's support of the house was partial payment of his debt to God. The idea that the prayers of holy men on behalf of someone other than themselves were efficacious derived from this system of atonement. A monastic house also gathered in a portion of the local economy just as parish churches did. Men entering the house had to provide an endowment, similar to the dowry a woman brought to a marriage, and if the house obtained a reputation for holiness, it became the recipient of pious gifts. Thus the monastery became another device for a lord's enjoyment of the income produced by his district, and he exercised the same rights over it as he did over parish churches under his control. He appointed the abbot, received the majority of the revenues, and generally treated the house as his property. Since few monks were priests, the houses and their inhabitants were outside the ecclesiastical hierarchy and not quite as subject as the churches to the tensions between bishops and proprietors. In many places, the close relationship between monastic houses and secular lords resulted in a discrepancy between the monastic rule and the life of the house. Few lords had much appreciation for the refined spirituality of Saint Benedict's ideal.

At the same time that the reality of monastic life in the Carolingian kingdom was becoming increasingly dismal, monks in the imperial entourage enunciated anew the rule of Saint Benedict. Supported by Louis the Pious, Benedict of Aniane (751–821) provided the Frankish kingdom with an explication of the original rule, and by means of the royal capitularies, he successfully imposed the rule and his gloss on all monastic houses in the realm. Medieval monks considered him the second Saint Benedict, and his expanded version of the original Benedictine rule predominated in medieval Europe. Benedict restricted the manual labor requirement to domestic chores and household crafts, thereby encouraging the further development of intellectual work, already under way because of monastic participation in the Carolingian renaissance. In addition, monks devoted themselves to copying, illuminating, and binding books. Benedict also expanded the daily prayer services and required that each monk pray daily before every alter in the monastic church. This provision widened the liturgical experience of the community and of the individual monks. In monasteries where it was taken seriously, monks spent most of their day in church and became interested in the artistic culture associated with the liturgy. The new Benedictine monasteries produced a vast number of hymns and chants. In order to isolate the monks from the world and prevent the houses from becoming educational institutions for the society at large, in a reaction to the involvement of monasticism in the royal renaissance, Benedict forbade monasteries to educate anyone other than their oblates (young boys given to monasteries by their parents).

Benedict's ideas had only moderate success against the tendency of monastic houses to be secularized by the lords who founded or inherited them. At the beginning of the tenth century, the spiritual condition of monastic communities was generally poor. A turning point came when Duke William V of Aquitaine founded a monastery on his Burgundian lands at Cluny in 910. William apparently had much to atone for and sought to establish a house that would fulfill the highest ideals of the new Benedictine spirituality. He chose a well-known reform abbot named Berno to govern the monastery and then acquiesced in the new abbot's demands. Berno would not take the position unless William gave Cluny a charter granting the community autonomy from his control. The house would elect its abbots, as prescribed in the Benedictine rule, and the duke would not enjoy its revenues or take any of the other perquisites commonly demanded by secular founders. Since neither Berno nor William trusted the duke's heirs to honor the arrangement, the charter provided that after William's death, the papacy would become the protector of the Cluniac community. This proviso was influenced by a contemporary pietistic fad in Europe that equated holiness with the number of pilgrimages a person made to Rome. In the face of the degeneracy of the Roman Church in the late ninth and the tenth centuries, songs such as this were commonly heard:

> *O Roma nobilis, orbis et domina,*
> *Cunctarum urbium excellentissima,*
> *Roseo martyrum sanguine rubea,*
> *Albis et virginum liliis candida. . . .*

> [Oh noble Rome, mistress of the world,
> Of all earthly cities most excellent,
> Resplendent in red with blood of the martyrs,
> Shining lily-white with the virtue of virgins. . . .]

William V himself demonstrated extraordinary piety by making an annual pilgrimage to Rome. It is not surprising, therefore, that he embodied his ideals in the provision of his charter giving the pope the protectorate over his monastery, but it is doubtful that he really thought the clause was meaningful.

It became meaningful during the next century. Cluny was blessed by extraordinary abbots, extraordinary in their ability and in their longevity. Berno ruled the house until 927 and established it as a viable institution. His successor, Odo, governed until 948. Odo had a lively appreciation of the sorry state of monasticism in Europe, and he sent out reformers from his community. During his reign, the reforms of Cluny, basically those expounded by Benedict of Aniane with the added provision for the freedom and isolation of the community, became established in monasteries throughout Europe. The reformation continued to spread during the second half of the tenth century, aided powerfully by the popular idea that the holy men of Cluny could help sinners escape their burdens. Hundreds of houses were founded, and under Odilo (999–1048) all the reformed abbeys were affiliated with the house at Cluny. The abbot of Cluny exercised direct control over dependent priories (which had priors appointed by the abbot of Cluny), and over dependent abbeys (which had abbots appointed by the abbot of Cluny). He exercised indirect control over a large number of abbeys that elected their own abbots subject to the approval of the abbot of Cluny. Finally, many completely autonomous abbeys were associated with Cluny because they had been reformed in accordance with Cluniac observances. This was a new development. Monastic communities had always been independent, local institutions; now many of them became associated in an international organization. As such, the houses became quite independent of local ecclesiastical and secular powers, and, conversely, by the late eleventh century, the abbot of Cluny's influence was felt in almost every diocese in Europe.

The whole association of monastic houses, inhabited by thousands of monks, was under the protection of the papacy, which was controlled by such men as the Crescentii and Tusculan popes. As the Cluniac movement grew and gained influence in Europe, its attachment to the papacy created a striking contrast between its own spirituality and the condition of the papacy, which was supposed to be its guide in Christ. Furthermore, by the mid-eleventh century, Cluny had stimulated other reform movements in Europe. Tenth-century England had experienced an important ecclesiastical revival based on a monasticism stimulated by and related to Cluniacism. Late–tenth- and early–eleventh century Germany was the scene of another related but independent reform movement that began in the monasteries of Lorraine and Swabia, adjacent to the heartland of the Cluniac movement, and spread slowly but steadily to the episcopate as Henry II and Henry III elevated monks to the episcopal sees. Among the elements of the Cluniac ideology adopted by these other reform groups, an interest in Rome and the condition of the Holy See loomed large. The reform movements reflected the increased spiritualness of the European community, manifested in the large number of pilgrimages to Rome and other shrines, in the building of churches and monasteries, in the Church-supported wars against Europe's non-Christian border enemies, and in the movement within the Church to improve its moral condition by introducing elements of the monastic rule into the life of the hierarchy. The Roman Church stood at the vortex of this great movement. It was the Apostolic See of the West. It was the protector of Cluny and other monastic associations. It had an impressive history, in which such figures as Leo I the Great, Gregory I the Great, Nicholas I the Great, stood out. It was the vessel through which God's ordination of Christian emperors passed. And in the early eleventh century, it was devoid of those spiritual qualities that would have made it an acceptable symbol of Christian unity and government, an acceptable vehicle of divine power. In 1046, even to describe the Holy See as lacking spiritual leadership would have been insufficient to describe its condition. Henry III's installation of German reformers in the Apostolic See finally brought the accumulated pressure for reform of the Roman Church to fruition.

After the death of Damasus II in 1048, Henry elevated his cousin, Bruno of Toul, an able and loyal reform bishop in the imperial entourage, to the Holy See. Bruno was in Germany at the time. He took the name Leo IX (1049–1054), gathered together a small group of reform associates, and made the journey to Rome. The city was held by the local factions, and Leo found it difficult to maintain himself at Saint Peter's. The Lateran, center of Roman city government and of the administration of the Holy See, was controlled by the Tusculans. With the help of Beneventan nobility, who came to Leo's aid with a large gift of money in the hope that he would help them against the Normans encroaching on their duchy, the pope was able to continue in Rome. But Leo and his associates did not want to become involved in local affairs; they intended to free the papacy from such involvement. In mid-1049, Leo and his entourage left Rome for Germany and northern France. He held a synod at Reims and promulgated the basic platform for the reform of the Church that was now to be organized and led by the papacy. The synod banned clerical marriage and concubinage, two moral problems of the lower clergy and the cathedral canons. It condemned simony. Finally, the pope heard the cases of bishops accused of violating the decrees promulgated. The French episcopacy was stunned by this completely new extension of papal power. The legal doctrines expounded in the Pseudo-Isidorian Decretals had meant little during the two centuries when the papacy had been enmeshed in the factional disputes of the Roman aristocrats; now Leo brought the law to bear on the Church at large. Bishops who had been appealing to Rome in order to escape judgment by their metropolitans could not deny the pope's right to judge them. The case of the archbishop of Narbonne demonstrates how far many great French clerics were from understanding the import of the situation. The archbishop arrived at Reims to complain that he had paid much money for his dignity, and the count of Toulouse, who sold it to him, was interfering with his enjoyment of the revenues and perquisites of his see. Leo deposed him for simony. In case after case, bishops and abbots were suspended or deposed for similar transgressions. Reims established the papal reform of the Church in a single, masterful stroke.

Leo moved between Rome and the north several times during his reign, but gradually, he was drawn into local Roman affairs. The Beneventans still hoped for his aid against the Normans, and he began to recognize that his reform of the papacy could only succeed if he took positive action to suppress the Roman factions and to establish the Roman Church on a firm political

Pope Leo IX and Warinus, abbot of Saint Arnulf's Abbey in Metz. The illuminator of this late–eleventh-century manuscript portrayed the majesty of the pope through size difference. This is a pictorial representation of a common papal activity from the reform period on, the granting of papal privileges and confirmation of property holdings of monasteries throughout Europe.

and financial footing. The architect of the local policy was Hildebrand, a Roman closely associated with, and perhaps distantly related to, Gregory VI. Henry III had taken Gregory to Germany in 1046 because he considered the former pope too powerful to leave in Rome. Hildebrand had gone with Gregory and apparently made contact with the German reformers. He joined Leo IX's entourage between 1048 and 1050, and soon emerged as the archdeacon of the Holy See, a position specifically concerned with the administration of the diocese. During the next two decades, Hildebrand established the Roman pontiff as the master of Rome and of the old Patrimony of Saint Peter, carved into small, autonomous principalities during the long period when the papacy was a dynastic prize. Leo's end demonstrates the degree to which he became involved in the restoration of the papacy as governor of central Italy. In 1053 he led an army, provided by Henry III, against the Normans. He was defeated and captured, and although the Normans did not hold him very long, he died shortly after this terrible experience.

Leo's successor, Victor II (1055–1057), continued the policy of fighting the Normans, but a number of men in the papal entourage saw many flaws in this policy. First, the papacy had become an agent of local and imperial interests by fighting the Normans. This was a direct contradiction of the ideals underlying the reform movement. Second, Henry III died in 1056, and his heir, Henry IV, was six years old. The regency that governed for young Henry was proreform but was not strong enough to continue helping the popes against the powerful Normans. Third, some men in the papal entourage were not well disposed toward the regency and sought to free the papacy from its close association with the imperial government. In 1057 the anti-imperial group succeeded in electing Stephen IX (1057–1058), brother of Duke Godfrey of Lorraine. Stephen and Godfrey were long-time opponents of the imperial government. Also about this time, a doctrinal dispute erupted in the papal court that reflected growing disenchantment with the connection the reformers had had with the imperial government. The essence of the reform was the moral regeneration of the Church. Now the foundation for this regeneration became an object of conflicting opinion. On one side were men like Saint Peter Damien, a northern Italian monastic reformer who had been drawn into the entourage of Leo IX and had become cardinal bishop of Ostia. Peter thought that the achievement of the reform goals depended on the placement of good men in the ecclesiastical hierarchy and that as long as the emperor or other laymen aided in this effort, a close relationship between the secular and ecclesiastical governments was acceptable. On the other side was Humbert of Silva-Candida, also a monk who had become a cardinal bishop. Humbert was one of those men who fearlessly follow the logic of their positions to the end. According to Humbert, the Christian vision of the order of the universe, in which the material world was subordinate to the spiritual, implied the subordination of the secular government, ordained for the governance of the material world, to the Church, ordained for the spiritual guidance of mankind. Thus lay participation in ecclesiastical government was anathema: the emperor must be excluded from participation in the elevation of bishops and the pope; all laymen must be excluded from the establishment of any ecclesiastical authority of whatever rank. But Humbert did not stop there. He concluded that any priest or bishop who had been elevated by a layman had not received sacerdotal power and was not a member of the true hierarchy. Considering the condition of the eleventh-century Church, Humbert's doctrine would have affected almost every member of the hierarchy.

Except for the last point, Humbert's ideas were accepted in 1059. When Stephen IX died in 1058, he was succeeded by an Italian bishop who took the name Nicholas II (1059–1061). The choice of name was emblematic of Nicholas' stand. Nicholas I had been a major figure in the tradition of papal independence and power, especially relative to the imperial government. Nicholas II followed his lead. At the Lenten Synod held in Rome in 1059, the pope promulgated new reform legislation. Aside from the now standard decrees against clerical incontinence and simony, Nicholas prohibited lay investiture, the practice by which kings and other lay officials gave the insignia of office to those elevated to the ecclesiastical hierarchy. The ceremony symbolized the fact that the layman had chosen the ecclesiastic for the position; it was not an innocent act. Henceforth, bishops were to be elevated only after being elected by the clergy and people (in practice, the clergy). The investiture was to be performed by the metropolitan. To place the Holy See in the same position as the episcopal churches, Nicholas and the synod issued an electoral decree for the papacy: popes were to be chosen by the cardinals acting as an electoral college. This decree was the origin of the College of Cardinals and of the electoral procedure still followed today. The cardinals included bishops, priests, and deacons incardinated in the Roman diocese. Only they could hold Masses in the churches of the diocese. Under the reform popes, this formerly honorary position was used as the means to establish reformers in the Roman Church. By the end of the eleventh century, the cardinals had become regular participants in both local and international papal government.

One of Nicholas II's first acts was to reverse his predecessors' policy of enmity toward the Normans. The conflict between the papacy and the imperial court demanded that the pope make a new arrangement with Italian powers. Deprived of imperial aid against the Normans and foreseeing the day when the papacy might need assistance against attack by the imperial government, Nicholas made successful overtures to the Norman leader Robert Guiscard, recognizing him as duke of Apulia and Calabria "by grace of God and Saint Peter," duke of Sicily hereafter (when Robert conquered it). The Norman duke became a vassal of the Holy See and promised military aid should the need arise. In addition, the papacy began to rebuild the southern Italian Church, which had previously been part of the Eastern Orthodox Church because the region had been subject to Byzantine authority. The work of reconstruction was connected with the breakdown of relations between the Orthodox and Catholic churches, which had taken place in 1054. Leo IX had sent an embassy headed by Cardinal Humbert to Constantinople to negotiate with the patriarch concerning both several outstanding doctrinal issues and the assertion of papal authority engendered by the reform movement. The doctrinal issues were not considered insuperable. Indicative of their character was the disagreement over the use of unleavened bread in the Eucharist. But Humbert was not the man to send in search of compromise, especially with regard to papal claims. The meetings ended with Humbert excommunicating the patriarch Michael Cerularius in the name of the pope and the patriarch excommunicating Leo. Contemporaries did not consider the breach final, but a few years later Nicholas II was constructing a Church loyal to the papacy in southern Italy.

On the death of Nicholas II in 1061, the cardinals elected Bishop Anselm I of Lucca as Alexander II (1061–1073). The imperial government was ignored, and it reacted by attempting to appoint its own pope, as in the days of Henry III. After a few years, this pope and his supporters gave up the struggle against the reform candidate.

Under Alexander matters that the papacy had formerly left to local prelates or simply ignored were more and more frequently dealt with by papal legates. No Christian, regardless of rank or station, was immune from the spiritual jurisdiction of the papacy. This fact was brought home vigorously to secular rulers whose private lives had in some notorious instances fallen below the moral standards of the Church. Young Henry IV, the boy emperor, felt the new papal authority even before his youthful intentions could become licentious deeds. At the age of fifteen he had been married to Bertha, daughter of the count of Turin, a woman several years his senior whom he had never met. When he did meet her, he found her so repulsive that he declared publicly that he would not live with her and would seek an annulment. To deal with this scandal, Peter Damien, fresh from a victorious campaign against married clergy in northern Italy, was sent to Germany in 1069 as papal legate. Henry was compelled to yield. Bertha ultimately won the emperor's affections and became not only the mother of his four sons but his steadfast supporter and comforter in the long trials and tribulations of his reign.

The leading personalities in the papal court during the first decades of the reform had been Peter Damien, Humbert, and Hildebrand. Humbert died in the early 1060s, Peter in 1072. Hildebrand now emerged as the undisputed leader of the court. He had spent his career building the papacy into a powerful force in central Italy by gaining control of Benevento, the Sabina, and other areas of the Papal States. Unable to break the power of

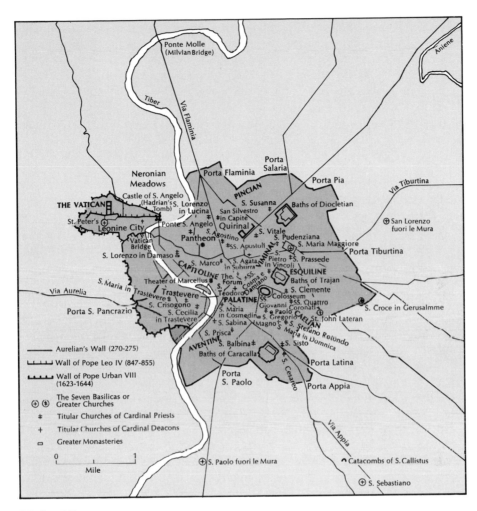

Medieval Rome

the Crescentii in the center of the city, Hildebrand established papal power in a wide belt of territory stretching from the Vatican to the Lateran. This territory was held for the papacy by the Pierleoni (the family of Gregory VI) and the Frangipani. The Frangipani had built a fortress in the Colosseum, which is why the great amphitheater still stands today. When Alexander II died, the Roman population dragged the architect of the papacy's city administration to Saint Peter's and enthroned him as pope. The cardinals acquiesced in the mob's desires and elected Hildebrand, who took the name Gregory VII (1073–1085) in order to affirm the validity of Gregory VI as a reform pope. This was also a tribute to the Pierleoni family, which had

become the most powerful support of papal government in Rome. As archdeacon, Hildebrand had used his considerable talents in the development of
papal political policy at best distasteful to idealistic reformers. He had a
reputation for hardheadedness that made him remarkably successful in city
politics, but he never lost sight of the ideals of the reform movement. This
complex mixture of saintliness and worldliness induced Peter Damien to
characterize Hildebrand as a "holy Satan." He was the man to force the issues
raised by the reformers, and he did so in the course of his pontificate.

## The Investiture Controversy

Cooperation between the German monarchy and the German reformers
brought about the reform of the regular hierarchy of the Church, including
the papacy, but the ideology of the reform contained tenets that endangered,
perhaps made impossible, the permanent cooperation of secular and ecclesiastical authority. Humbert of Silva-Candida had pointed out the problem
when he analyzed the Christian valuation of the two powers. The tradition
that the king held a divinely ordained authority and that he was responsible
for protecting the Church, as Henry III and his predecessors had done, was
a counterargument to Humbert's logic. Thus, in the 1050s, the reformers did
not seek superior authority but rather independence from royal authority.
They believed that the inception of the reform gave the Church the wherewithal to accomplish its own regeneration, and since there was the danger,
as Humbert pointed out, that secular rulers might be less inspired than Henry
III, it was necessary to exclude secular power from participation in ecclesiastical affairs, especially the appointment to ecclesiastical positions. The
regency that was established for Henry IV in 1056 was neither able nor
trustworthy in the matter of reform. By the middle of Alexander II's reign,
the papacy was becoming involved in a struggle with the German court over
measures the regency took to ensure its control of the German episcopate
and the great abbeys. Henry IV continued these antireform practices, mostly
simony, after he came of age in 1066. The remonstrances that Alexander and
his associates made against the regency and the king rested on a doctrine
once forcefully asserted by Saint Ambrose against the emperor Theodosius
the Great: the Church held an independent and superior authority in matters
of morals and doctrine and could judge any layman, including kings and
emperors, on those matters. The new element in the eleventh-century debate
was the assertion, implied in Ambrose's argument but not explicitly stated or
acted on, that the hierarchy endowed with moral authority must be wholly
and independently responsible for its own establishment and continuation.
During the 1060s Alexander II found it necessary to defend both the moral
and the constitutional authority of the reformed Church.

The constitutional issue was joined when the great see of Milan became vacant. Like other imperial bishops, the archbishop had been an appointee of the emperor and had acted on the emperor's behalf in governing the city and its territory. In the 1050s, a communal movement began to develop in Milan that sought to gain control of municipal affairs. The archbishop stood in the way, and thus the struggle revolved around control of the archbishopric. When it became vacant, the German regency and the commune battled over the successor, causing riots in the city. The papacy backed the commune, claiming that its candidate had the support of the clergy and people of the diocese and therefore was canonically established. The young king took up the battle but was soon forced to concede victory to the papal-communal contingent because he could not pursue the Milan question while facing rebellions at home. However, the issue had been raised.

Henry's efforts to rebuild the monarchy led to rebellions during the second half of the 1060s, but in 1073 he faced his most serious threat. All of Saxony rebelled, and for a time the Saxons seemed able to destroy the monarchy. The crisis coincided with Gregory VII's election. The pope had been elevated in an irregular manner and had been careful to await election by the cardinals before calling himself pope-elect. He then took the surprising step of asking Henry IV for confirmation of his elevation before permitting himself to be consecrated. The king did not refuse. He faced the crisis in Saxony and could not risk enmity with the reformers, who might ally themselves with dissidents in southern Germany or Italy while he was fighting the rebels in the north. Also, the pope's request reaffirmed the principle that the emperor, in this case the emperor-designate, had some influence in the establishment of the pope. That the first reason for Henry to confirm Gregory's election predominated is evident in the correspondence between the king and the pope. Henry humbly acknowledged, "not only have I encroached upon the property of the Church, but I have sold churches themselves to unworthy persons poisoned with the gall of simony," admitting that "somewhat repentant and remorseful, we turn to your fatherly indulgence, accusing ourselves and trusting in you. Your direction shall be scrupulously followed . . . and I humbly beseech your fatherly support." Henry wanted Gregory to reestablish the old relationship between the reformers and the monarchy. The king wanted to and would support the reform program if he could ensure his own security and interests while doing so.

Gregory followed a conciliatory policy toward Henry for two years, trying all the time to pursue the reform program without attacking the king or his authority. But the king was unable or unwilling to reform his court and to force antireform prelates to obey the pope. At the Lenten Synod of 1075 (Lenten Synods had become a regular feature of the reform papacy's activities), Gregory reaffirmed the reform program and put forward again the decree against lay investiture issued by the synod of 1059. If Gregory had been hesitant to follow the logic of Humbert's constitutional analysis of the reform

The first eleven assertions of the *dictatus papae* of Gregory VII, which was entered in his register of letters. It has the appearance of a table of contents for a legal collection, and scholars have argued that it was exactly that. Why it should have been entered into the register remains a mystery.

program, he now accepted the late cardinal's ideas. Henry could do nothing about this direct attack on his power because the situation in Saxony had deteriorated dangerously in the spring of 1075. Then Henry defeated the rebels decisively in June 1075 and gained a freer hand in dealing with the reformers. He also had a special need to use his power over the churches in order to reestablish his authority in the defeated duchy. For the rest of the year, Henry was occupied with gaining effective control of the Saxon Church, and he invested two of his favorites with Italian sees under his authority as emperor-designate. He ignored the promises he had made to Gregory two years earlier; the future of the monarchy was at stake, and the reformers would have to understand, and trust, him. Gregory was no longer willing to compromise, however, and the relations between the king and the pope rapidly worsened in 1075. A sign of the pope's new attitude is the document entered in his register called the *dictatus papae* (dictates of the pope), which comprise twenty-seven assertions, probably designed as guides for papal lawyers re-searching the legal foundations of papal doctrine. Some of these assertions were: "That he [the pope] alone may use the imperial insignia." "That he may depose emperors." "That he himself may be judged by no one." "That the Pope may absolve subjects of unjust men from their fealty."

At the end of 1075, Gregory sent Henry a letter of stern admonition, giving him "apostolic benediction on the understanding that he obey the Apostolic See as becomes a Christian king." This letter was borne by legates who privately and orally threatened the emperor with excommunication as the penalty for continued disobedience.

Henry's reaction was to summon a synod at Worms early in 1076. Here his loyal German bishops drew up a letter to Gregory addressing him as "Brother Hildebrand" and renouncing their obedience to him as pope. The emperor sent a covering letter that began, "Henry, king not through usurpation but through the holy ordination of God, to Hildebrand now not pope but false monk," and ending with Gregory's deposition: "I, Henry, king by grace of God, do say unto thee, together with all our bishops, descend, descend, to be damned throughout the ages."

The letters reached Rome during the Lenten Synod of 1076, which promptly excommunicated the archbishop of Mainz, chief author of the bishops' letter, and deprived of their offices all imperial bishops "who voluntarily joined his schism and still persist in their evil deeds." Gregory then put the *dictatus papae* into operation. He deposed Henry, released his subjects from their allegiance, and excommunicated him.

This action was the signal for general rebellion in Germany. The nobility, uneasy about the rise in royal fortunes after the defeat of the Saxons, eagerly supported the pope. Many bishops, while supporters of the king, were afraid to disobey the pope's sentence of excommunication because they had always been allied with the reform movement, and they owed a higher obedience to the pope. At the same time, papal legates were active in Germany stirring up the nobility, bringing pressure on ecclesiastical leaders, rallying the abbots against recalcitrant bishops, and rekindling the smouldering resentment of the Saxons. Success attended these efforts when the German nobles demanded that Henry cease to exercise his royal authority. They then decided that unless he could obtain absolution from the pope at a council to be held the following February at Augsburg, where Gregory had agreed to preside, Henry was to be considered deposed and a new emperor would be elected— formally elected by the nobles, presumably, but certainly not without guidance and influence from the presiding pope. It appeared that the events of Sutri under Henry III were about to be reversed at Augsburg under Gregory VII.

This was the low point in Henry's fortunes. If the council were allowed to meet, deposition appeared inevitable. He therefore set off for Italy hoping to force a meeting with Gregory before the pope could cross the Alps. Gregory, on his way northward, had reached Canossa, a castle of the countess

R ex ROGat ABBATEO. MAThILDIOSupplicAT ATQ ;

Gregory VII's first excommunication of Henry IV (1176) put the king in a difficult position, and before undertaking the extraordinary pilgrimage to Canossa, Henry asked Abbot Hugh of Cluny and Countess Matilda of Tuscany to intercede with Gregory on his behalf. This illumination, with a caption reading "The king asks the abbot and Matilda to intercede . . . ," illustrates a twelfth-century Life of Matilda.

Matilda of Tuscany. Here, in January 1077, occurred the dramatic episode that became for later generations a symbol of the submission of the secular to the spiritual power. Henry presented himself before the castle gate accompanied by only a few intimates, having laid aside all royal insignia in favor of a humble penitent's coarse attire. Standing three days barefooted (in the falling snow, according to later legend) he tearfully besought forgiveness and absolution—until, as Gregory later complained, "some even cried out that we were showing not the seriousness of apostolic authority, but the cruelty of a savage tyrant." The pope's reluctance is understandable, but he could do nothing. Gregory as a priest could not deny absolution to a penitent Christian. Henry, on the surface, had submitted to a public humiliation. But to Gregory and Henry and their contemporaries, the king had won a resounding diplomatic victory. Gregory could claim from the incident no more than he had claimed before: the right to judge and to excommunicate any sinner, even the emperor-designate himself. Henry had never denied that right, even while denying Gregory's authority to act as pope. Now, by recognizing Gregory as pope, Henry had prevented his own deposition by securing absolution before the scheduled council could meet at Augsburg.

Civil war continued in Germany. Despite Henry's absolution the German nobility elected a new king, and the military conflict was prolonged without decisive result. Gregory then put forth the novel claim that he as pope had the right to judge between the two rivals. It was a foregone conclusion when, in 1080, he decided against Henry's claims and, because Henry refused to recognize the papal judgment, excommunicated the emperor for a second time. By the following year, however, Henry was strong enough to defeat his rival, proclaim the deposition of Gregory once more, and arrange for the election of an antipope—Guibert, archbishop of Ravenna, formerly a friend of Hildebrand but loyal to Henry during the struggle. Henry now invaded Italy. Brushing aside the forces of Matilda of Tuscany, he took possession of Rome in 1084 and went through the formalities of receiving the imperial crown from his antipope. Gregory called on his vassal Robert Guiscard for help, and Henry withdrew before the superior military force of the Normans. The Normans then proceeded to subject Rome to such pillaging as the Eternal City had never before suffered. When they finally withdrew, Gregory had no choice but to seek refuge with them from the resentment of the outraged Roman populace. The pope retired to Salerno where, in 1085, he fell sick and died.

The elevation of Guibert brought the conflict between the reformers and Henry IV to central Italy, where the reform papacy had made steady progress toward realizing the claims of papal governance. The forces that had opposed papal authority rallied to Guibert's cause, and for long periods of time the antipope was able to control much of the city of Rome and the Sabina, receiving the support of the Crescentii in both places. The schism split the reformers. Guibert had been a reformer but had not allied himself with Gregory in opposition to Henry and the monarchy. Other reformers who had rejected Gregory's policies and claims or had been uneasy about them joined Guibert. Two groups of cardinals and two papal organizations evolved, and the conflict forced the popes to rely heavily on their supporters. As a result, the tendency for the cardinals to become involved in papal government was realized, and a process of institutionalization began that by the late Middle Ages led to the development of an enormous papal bureaucracy headed by the cardinals. In the years following Gregory VII's death, Guibert moved between Rome and his see of Ravenna, while Gregory's successors spent most of their time in the south, unable to gain a firm position in Rome. Victor III (1086–1087) retired to Monte Cassino, where he had been abbot before being elected pope. Urban II (1088–1099) tried to make some progress against Guibert's followers in Rome but was usually confined to the fortresses of his supporters, the Frangipani and the Pierleoni. Things began to look up for the reform popes when Henry IV made the mistake of renewing his involvement in Italian affairs.

In the late 1080s Henry had consolidated his position in Germany by winning the support of reform bishops who became reconciled to him but refused to recognize his antipope. As long as the king remained in Germany, the conflict inherent in these bishops' position was not made plain, but when Henry decided to lead another army into Italy in 1092, the bishops were forced to choose between their king and the reform papacy. Henry made the decision because his enemies in Germany and Italy were trying to organize a new and dangerous alliance. In 1089 Countess Matilda of Tuscany, the reformers' staunch and very able supporter in northern Italy, had married the son of Welf IV of Bavaria, Germany's most powerful duke. The union between Welf V and Matilda created a territorial principality far more powerful than any Henry had in Germany. In addition, the union of Bavaria and Tuscany cut off the king from his Italian supporters, especially Guibert. Henry's attempt to prevent the realization of his enemies' plans brought all the tensions in the political situation of his empire to a critical point. The German reform bishops renewed their opposition to him. Matilda held out in her mountain fortresses in northern Tuscany. Urban II returned to Rome in order to pressure the supporters of Guibert and the king. Then Henry's eldest son and heir, Conrad, rebelled and joined the reformers. Henry was trapped in northern Italy between Welf of Bavaria and other German magnates, who joined the rebellion and closed the Alpine passes on one side, and Matilda and the papal forces on the other side. Urban was able to reassert his control over Rome and to move north, where he held a great council at Piacenza in 1095, repromulgating the reform decrees against lay investiture and again excommunicating Henry and Guibert. As the reformers seemed on the verge of success in bringing the king to his knees at Piacenza, an important event drew papal attention away from the civil strife in Germany. Ambassadors from Constantinople arrived at Piacenza to ask Urban for aid against the Seljuk Turks, who had conquered the East and were moving toward the capital of the Byzantine Empire. The pope was seized by the desire to send aid for the Christians of the East and to send Westerners, under papal aegis, to rescue the holy places in Palestine, thus asserting papal leadership of Christendom. In the following months, Urban went to France to preach the First Crusade at Clermont and elsewhere, and his preoccupation gave Henry IV the chance to recover his position. As Urban moved through France, the marriage between Welf and Matilda was annulled, and by 1097 Henry had returned to Germany and was reestablishing his power.

Henry was not able to recover his position of 1092, however. The greatest bishops were arrayed against him, and his relationship with the nobility remained uncertain. Welf had retreated but not given up, and most other

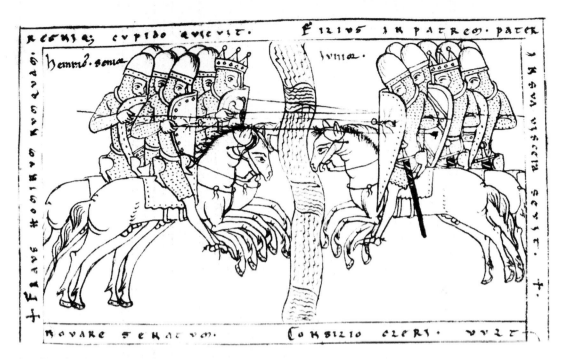

An illumination from a chronicle that recounts the civil war (1104–1106) between
Henry IV (left, crowned and with the imperial eagle on his shield) and his son Henry
V (right, crowned but without the eagle). Many people in Germany supported Henry
IV, or at least favored him, even if they did not participate in the wars. This illuminator
seems to have favored Henry the "Elder": not only did he emphasize the majesty of
Henry IV by adorning him with the eagle emblem, but, more subtly, he placed Henry IV
at the head of his troops while placing Henry V in the midst of his. Supporters of the old
king argued that young Henry had been misled by his friends into rebelling.

magnates shared his attitude. Henry had to rely on the *ministeriales,* but as
they increased their power, they antagonized both the nobility and the
bishops. Thus Henry was forced into a policy that increased the likelihood
of another rebellion, and in late 1104 his second son and heir, Henry V, led
a successful rebellion. Henry V justified his rebellion on the grounds that his
father was an excommunicate and even said that if Henry IV became reconciled to the Church, he would submit to his authority. He put together a
powerful ecclesiastical party and allied the magnates to his cause. Henry IV of
course tried to repeat the coup of Canossa, but the papal representatives in
Germany blocked his efforts. Nonetheless, when Henry IV died in October
1106, he was rebuilding his party in western Germany, and it is obvious that
Henry V was saved from considerable trouble and danger by his father's
death. The old king was fifty-six and had reigned fifty years.

Henry V (1106–1125) assumed power as a reformer; he had contacted Urban II's successor, Paschal II (1099–1118), early in his rebellion. Paschal had given the young king his blessing and had sent papal legates into action on his behalf. The pope and the king tried to negotiate an end to the Investiture Controversy. The negotiations were drawn out over the next five years because many powerful nobles and ecclesiastics in Germany could not permit a compromise that would deprive them of their influence. Chief among them were the reform bishops, whose power derived from their close association with the monarchy. Their obstructionism made it impossible for the pope and the king to achieve even the compromise Paschal had arranged with the kings of France and England in 1106, by which bishops were to be elected freely by the clergy and people of their dioceses, but before they were consecrated by their metropolitans, the kings were to invest them with their regalian rights. Thus in theory the bishops were elevated without royal participation, while in practice the royal will was felt, and the bishop would be obligated to the king because of the investiture and oath. This arrangement was based on a distinction between the secular and spiritual parts of the bishopric. The king was recognized to be responsible for investing with the former, and the Church was acknowledged to control the latter.

The frustrations of the negotiating process between Henry V and Paschal led them to make a secret agreement in Rome in early 1111. Henry later claimed it was Paschal's idea. According to the agreement, Paschal would force the imperial bishops to relinquish the regalian rights (lands, jurisdiction, and financial rights held by the bishop as a representative of the king) they had received since the reign of Charlemagne. In return, Henry would renounce the right of investiture. After the compromise was announced, Paschal would crown Henry emperor. The ceremonial reading of the agreement and the coronation were to be held on February 11, but when it was read to the assembled German bishops and magnates and to members of the Roman Church and community, the reaction was violent. The bishops would not surrender the foundation of their power. The German magnates supported them because they held many fiefs from the churches and because Henry would be overwhelmingly powerful if he received back all the *regalia*. A riot ensued, and the king seized the pope and held him captive in the vicinity of Rome until April 11, when Paschal conceded the right of investiture without reservation to Henry. Two days later, Henry was crowned emperor and soon left Italy for Germany. The pope was left to face an uproar among the reformers; he was threatened with deposition, and churchmen throughout Europe tried to force him to abdicate. Henry V was subsequently excommunicated by great ecclesiastics in France and Germany, although Paschal never confirmed the sentences. In March 1112, the pope was compelled to retract the privilege he had given Henry, and the Investiture Controversy was renewed.

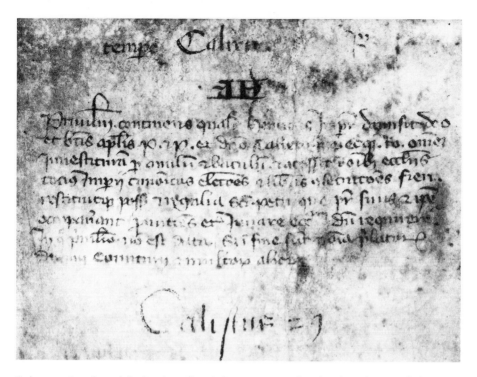

It is rare that the originals of medieval documents survive, but here is one of the most important, the Concordat of Worms (1122). At the bottom is the signature of Pope Calixtus II; in addition, the pope and the emperor would have affixed their seals to the agreement.

Paschal remained in power until his death in 1118. After the brief pontificate of Gelasius II (1118–1119), the cardinals elected Guy, archbishop of Vienne, as Calixtus II (1119–1124). Guy was an able ecclesiastical statesman who had been one of the most vociferous opponents of Paschal's concessions in 1111. He was the first pope since Alexander II who had not been a monk and the first since the beginning of the reform who had not been a member of the reform papal court. As an outsider, he was able to negotiate a compromise settlement with Henry V in 1122 contained in the Concordat of Worms. The agreement was based on the earlier understanding between the pope and the kings of France and England. The essential provisions of the Concordat were: (1) elections were to be "canonical," that is, by the clergy in a positive sense rather than simply as a rubber-stamp approval of the choice of the emperor or lay noble; but in Germany elections were to take place in the presence of the emperor, and in a disputed election the emperor's decision was to be final; (2) in Germany the bishop- or abbot-elect was first to be invested by the emperor with the *regalia* of his office and only then was he to be consecrated and invested by his ecclesiastical superior with his *spiritualia* (the spiritual authority and property of the church or abbey not held of a secular lord) by the ring and staff; and (3) in Italy and Burgundy the bishop- or abbot-elect was to be invested by his ecclesiastical superior with the ring and staff immediately, and investiture with the *regalia* by the emperor or his representative was to follow automatically within six months.

With the Concordat of Worms, the Investiture Controversy ended in a realistic compromise that, although it did not satisfy extremists in either camp, recognized what had, since 1075, come to be the actual situation. The emperor's control of the German Church was conceded, but the emperor agreed to give up lay investiture of spiritual functions and to exercise his authority within the canonical regulations of the Church. Outside Germany, the pope's control of the Church in Burgundy and Italy was conceded by the emperor, although temporalities were to be held as imperial vassals. If the provisions of the Concordat of Worms are compared with the old Ottonian system of domination of both Church and state by the emperor, the outcome of the Investiture Controversy must be considered essentially a papal victory. No longer could the emperor appoint and invest whom he pleased. The papacy had imposed canonical regulations on the form of elections and had taken from the emperor control over approximately one-half of the prelates of the empire. As a peace treaty, the Concordat was an admirable attempt to render to Caesar the things that are Caesar's, and to God the things that are God's. As in all such attempts, spokesmen for Caesar and spokesmen for God differed in their definitions of what was to be rendered. The contest between empire and papacy would no longer revolve around investiture; but the struggle for supremacy was soon to be renewed with even greater violence.

## Suggestions for Further Reading

**Secondary Works**    On the medieval empire, see the works by G. Barraclough and Boyd H. Hill, Jr., cited at the end of Chapter 8. See also J. W. Thompson, *Feudal Germany* (Chicago, 1928), and the important articles translated in G. Barraclough, ed., *Medieval Germany*, vol. 2 (Oxford, 1938). On the reform movement in the Church, see G. Tellenbach, *Church, State, and Christian Society at the Time of the Investiture Contest* (Oxford, 1940), and S. Williams, ed., *The Gregorian Epoch: Reformation, Revolution, Reaction?* (Boston, 1964).

**Sources**    Sources for the history of the medieval empire are cited at the end of Chapter 8. For the history of the Investiture Controversy, see B. Tierney, *The Crisis of Church and State, 1050–1300* (Englewood Cliffs, N.J., 1964). See also *The Correspondence of Gregory VII*, trans. E. Emerton (New York, 1932); *Imperial Lives and Letters of the Eleventh Century*, trans. T. E. Mommsen and K. F. Morrison (New York, 1962); and Otto of Freising, *The Two Cities*, trans. C. C. Mierow (New York, 1928). Otto's work is a nearly contemporary account from the German point of view.

# 13 The First Expansion of Europe: Conquest and Crusade

Europe has experienced two great ages of expansion, when its people and political powers pushed out beyond its borders and conquered or colonized great regions of the outside world. The second is the well-known period of exploration and expansion that began in the late fifteenth century. The first was the eleventh century, when the peoples of the Frankish empire took the offensive against the frontier marauders, who had been plundering their lands for generations. During the eleventh century, this push against the borders became the basis for an attempt by the Europeans to extend their power into the eastern Mediterranean and to conquer territories outside their immediate geographical sphere. This outward movement became a major factor in the history of Europe, as its antecedents in earlier centuries had not been. From the middle of the eighth until the middle of the eleventh century, European history was dominated by developments in the Frankish-Germanic center of Western Continental Europe: the rise and collapse of the Carolingian empire, the feudal reorganization of society, the evolution of a manorial economy, the Cluniac reform movement, the foundation of the medieval empire. Events on the periphery of Europe—the Mediterranean basin and the Iberian, Celtic, Scandinavian, and Slavic regions of Latin Christendom—did not significantly affect the affairs and developments of the heartland. Contact with the Byzantine East and the Arabic world was also historically insignificant: the reports of the tenth-century diplomat Luitprand of Cremona concerning his missions to Constantinople on behalf of Otto the Great are historically significant only for the differences between East and West revealed in them. Luitprand accomplished little of importance as diplomat.

The new aggressiveness of the Europeans was reflected on all the borders of their community. In the west, north, and east, the expansion resulted in the Norman Conquest of England, the penetration of Latin Christianity into Scandinavia and Poland, and the pressure exerted by the Germans along the Slavic frontier. In the south, the Carolingian campaigns against the Moslems in Spain were revived and military activity was initiated against the Moslem and Byzantine communities in southern Italy and elsewhere in the western Mediterranean. The Crusades to the eastern Mediterranean were the most striking result of this expansionism. They were the military and political phase of the reestablishment of contact with the Byzantine and the Arabic East, but they were only one phase of a general expansion that was even more important in several other aspects: the economic revival, the growth of population, and the widening horizon of intellectual and cultural interests, which had all begun well before the First Crusade. Contact with the East served, in turn, to quicken some of the Western developments of the twelfth century, but the Crusades themselves were not the *cause* of any significant advance or achievement in the West.

Far more important than the role played by the Crusades is the fact that Western Europe in the eleventh century was no longer simply struggling for survival. The wealth and energies of the European communities were now available for enterprises beyond merely local needs or military protection against external enemies. Indicative of these changed conditions is the fact that, in each decade of the eleventh century, hundreds of peaceful pilgrims preceded the first crusading army on the route to the Holy Land.

## Spain and Southern Italy: The Beginning of Western Expansion

The expansion of Europe began in Spain and southern Italy. Although the First Crusade was the most dramatic and best publicized chapter in European expansion, conquest and colonization on every other medieval frontier either began earlier or produced more conclusive results than any of the Crusades. Expeditions to the Levant were essentially overseas campaigns that involved greater problems of supply, transport, and reinforcement than were met on the periphery of feudal Europe, where the more enduring expansion took place.

In Spain, conquest at the expense of the Moors (Spanish Moslems) did not begin in earnest until the decline of the Omayyad dynasty. The Moors rejected the Abbasid revolution of 750 and were ruled by an Omayyad emir, or governor, after 756. The emirate of Córdoba recognized the caliph in Baghdad in religious matters but was politically independent. For a century the Omayyad emirs spent most of their time suppressing local revolts and consolidating their authority. Part of their difficulties sprang from the diversity of their subject population. The Arab aristocracy, concentrated in towns, slowly fused with native converts to Islam. The majority of immigrant Berbers from Africa lived in the countryside and led a pastoral and agricultural life. Spanish Christians and Jews were protected by the tolerant Omayyads. Many of them converted to Islam, but throughout the period, Arabic-speaking Christians, the Mozarabs, continued their worship without molestation. In the middle of the ninth century the bishop of Seville, after a century and a half of Moorish rule, felt it necessary to translate the Bible into Arabic for the benefit of his flock. During the tenth century the height of Moorish civilization, measured in terms of both cultural achievement and political stability, was reached under Abd ar Rahman III (912–961), who proclaimed his complete independence of Baghdad by assuming the title of caliph in 929. The caliphate of Córdoba lasted until 1031, when Moorish Spain disintegrated into about a dozen petty principalities (1031–1086).

During the ninth and tenth centuries two Christian territories survived in the Iberian Peninsula: the kingdom of the Asturias in the northwest and the county of Barcelona (the old Spanish March of Charlemagne, now independent) in the northeast. They had taken advantage of occasional periods of civil strife among the Moors to increase their size, and by the end of the tenth century the Asturias had grown into the kingdom of León and the county of Castile, and the country of the Basques at the western end of the Pyrenees had become the kingdom of Navarre. The rulers of these petty Christian states spent most of their energies in wars of territorial conquest, sometimes against each other in alliance with Moorish principalities, sometimes in shifting alliances with each other against the Moors. No single Christian state developed to the point where it could unite the various regions and control the conquests.

The collapse of the caliphate of Córdoba in 1031 coincided with political developments in the Christian states that made possible the beginning of a new period of Christian expansion. The conquests of Sancho the Great of Navarre (1000–1035) and the subsequent division of these territories among his sons resulted in the establishment of the kingdom of Castile (1033) and its union with León (1037), and the establishment of the kingdom of Aragón south of the middle Pyrenees (1035). At this time each of the Christian states —the kingdom of Castile and León, the kingdom of Navarre, the kingdom of Aragón, and the county of Barcelona—was more powerful than any of the bordering Moorish principalities. The momentum of the early–eleventh-century conquests resulted in unifying the efforts of the Christian kingdoms and counties, and the *Reconquista* (reconquest) became a national venture of all the Christian states. The papacy had kept in close touch with Spanish Christians and encouraged volunteers from Normandy, Burgundy, and other areas to join the "perpetual Crusade" against the infidel. During the eleventh century landless younger sons of feudal lords emigrated to Spain to make their fortunes in the wars. The first great expansion was a cooperative effort by Castile and Aragón, ending with the conquest of Toledo in 1085.

The fall of Toledo so alarmed the Moors that they appealed for aid to the Almoravides, a new Berber power that had risen in North Africa. The Almoravides invaded Spain and in a single year brought Christian expansion to a sudden halt. Then they turned to the conquest of the Moors, incorporating all of Moorish Spain except the emirate of Saragossa in the northeast into their African empire. The last decade of the eleventh century and the early years of the twelfth were a confused period in which Castile and León were torn by civil wars, the Almoravides pushed the frontier northward, and Aragón slowly expanded at the expense of Saragossa. It was during this period that adventurers rose to power by exploiting the weaknesses of both Moslem and Christian rulers. The most famous of these men was a Castilian noble, Rodrigo Díaz de Vivar, better known in legend as the Cid, who spent thirty years fighting both for and against a half-dozen Christian and Moorish rulers. He ended his career as the ruler of Valencia (1094–1099), withstanding the Almoravides' repeated assaults. For later generations, the Cid became a national hero and the symbol of the Christian *Reconquista;* in history he was only the most able and successful of the many opportunists on both sides.

In the twelfth century the Almoravides lost control of their far-flung and disparate empire, and the Christian kingdoms resumed their expansion. Aragón conquered Saragossa by 1118 and in 1140 was united with Barcelona in an enlarged kingdom whose further expansion was to be eastward into the Mediterranean islands. Castile pushed southward into the center of the peninsula. But internal struggles for power in Castile provided the opportunity for the count of Portugal to assume the title of king of Portugal in 1139, a rank that he justified by the conquest of Lisbon eight years later. This was the farthest penetration southward made by any of the Christian rulers. By the middle of the twelfth century, about one-half of Spain was in Christian hands.

The expansion of Latin Christendom in the central Mediterranean area was even more impressive than in Spain. In southern Italy, the Lombard, Byzantine, and Moslem states had for more than a century jostled each other until by the beginning of the eleventh century the Moslems had been expelled from the mainland and retained only the island of Sicily. The heel and toe of the peninsula, Apulia and Calabria, were Byzantine. The rest of the south was split into more than a dozen petty duchies, counties, and marches under local rulers who shifted their allegiance as occasion demanded

Spain and Italy, ca. 1100

or allowed. This anarchic situation might have lasted indefinitely, were it not that political and social developments in the distant duchy of Normandy were ultimately responsible for introducing a new element into southern Italy that was to be decisive for the future.

While the Norman nobility probably did not produce more sons than other medieval European aristocrats, political conditions in the duchy made it difficult for landless knights to earn a living or win a place in the feudal hierarchy. By the beginning of the eleventh century, the duke had imposed a relatively secure peace in Normandy and had thus succeeded in preventing the private wars in which landless knights were employed elsewhere in Europe. The same phenomenon was occurring in other counties and duchies where the central authority was becoming stronger, but Normandy was the best organized and most firmly governed area, at least of those under the suzerainty of the French king. At the same time, the Normans had only recently been Christianized and thus experienced the intense piety of the newly converted. Many of them participated in the pilgrimages; William the Conqueror's father, Duke Robert, went on a pilgrimage to the Holy Land in 1034. Thus the conjunction of good government and contact with the outside world produced an emigration from Normandy that made the Normans far more important in the history of eleventh-century Europe than might be expected considering their numbers.

A small band of wandering adventurers from Normandy reached Rome in 1017, seeking employment as mercenaries. From Pope Benedict VIII they learned that they might be of use to a noble named Melo, who conspired to overthrow the Byzantine provincial government in Apulia. That same year Melo and his rebel army, including the Norman mercenaries, were badly beaten in pitched battle with the Byzantines, whose troops were stiffened by a contingent of Russian mercenaries. Despite this inauspicious beginning, groups of Norman knights continued to emigrate to southern Italy and hire themselves out to local rulers, whether Lombard or Byzantine. In 1029 one of the Norman leaders was given the county of Aversa as a reward for services to the duke of Naples, thus making it the first Norman principality in southern Italy. The prospects of such advancement attracted more Norman adventurers, including several of the sons of Tancred of Hauteville. Tancred had twelve sons, only one of whom would inherit his fief in western Normandy. He himself was a vassal of middle rank, but his sons, emigrating to southern Italy, founded a powerful state that became a kingdom in the twelfth century. The first of the Hauteville brothers, William of the Iron Arm and Drogo, joined in a new Apulian revolt against Byzantine rule and by 1046 had carved out an independent Norman county in northern Apulia that was recognized by the Western emperor, Henry III. The several Norman leaders rapidly extended their holdings, while at the same time they engaged in fierce rivalry among themselves. However, they were capable of uniting solidly against a common enemy, as they did when Leo IX tried to intervene in the south and was defeated in the Battle of Civitate in 1053.

Meanwhile, yet another of the sons of Tancred of Hauteville, Robert Guiscard (the "wary" or "cunning"), had arrived from Normandy and established himself in the mountains of Calabria. He began his Italian career by preying on the cattle and sheep of Calabrian peasants and ended it as "the most gifted soldier and statesman of his age." After the death of his oldest brother in 1057, Robert Guiscard took over Apulia and forced the other Norman lords to recognize his leadership. In 1059 he secured from Pope Nicholas II the legitimization of his rule in return for a treaty of alliance. Henceforth, Robert was recognized as duke of Apulia and Calabria, and of Sicily whenever he could reconquer it from the Moslems. He became the pope's vassal and held these territories as fiefs of the papacy. It took Robert twelve more years to complete the conquest of the southern mainland, ending in 1071 with the capture of Bari, the last Byzantine stronghold. In 1061 Robert had helped his brother Roger initiate the conquest of Sicily. With the fall of the main port, Palermo, in 1072, Roger was granted Sicily as a fief to be held with the title of count from his brother Duke Robert. Roger's conquest of the island was completed in 1091.

The success of the Normans, where Charlemagne and his successors and Otto the Great and his successors had failed, is an impressive example of their adaptation to a new environment. The Normans were exceptional fighters, as their contemporary reputation attests, but more than that, they were able to surpass the local rulers in guile, brutality, and treachery. The rise of Norman power in southern Italy and Sicily appalled even the Byzantine catapans and the Moslem emirs, who were well schooled in the arts of ambush, assassination, and betrayal. Finally, the Norman conquest of southern Italy and Sicily was made easier, if not inevitable, by the division and weakness of the enemy. The Moslems of Sicily could not unite in a common defense, and the Byzantine Empire had fallen into serious difficulties in the third quarter of the century, climaxed by the catastrophe at Manzikert (discussed in the next section) in the same year that Bari fell to Robert Guiscard.

Also, the development of Italian sea power constituted a second front for both the Moslems and the Byzantine Empire. Pisa and Genoa began the offensive against Moslem control of the Mediterranean in 1016 by an attack on Sardinia, leading to its conquest in 1022. This was followed by a series of attacks on Moslem ports in North Africa. By the end of the century the Italian sea powers had contributed to the success of the First Crusade and had swept Moslem shipping from the Mediterranean. The year 1100 is a milestone in the growth of Italian maritime power. In that year a Venetian squadron attacked and defeated a Pisan fleet on its return from delivering reinforcements to Jerusalem. Having made the Mediterranean a Christian sea, maritime rivalry between the Italian towns continued for the rest of the Middle Ages.

The Normans in southern Italy and Sicily were unable at first to compete in the development of sea power. Amalfi, once the maritime rival of Genoa and Pisa, declined after it fell to the Normans in 1077. When Robert Guiscard and his son Bohemond of Taranto attempted to extend their conquests of Byzantine territory into northern Greece, the Venetian fleet cut their communications and caused the Norman campaign to collapse (1081–1083). In return for this service, the Byzantine emperor, Alexius, granted Venice such favorable trading privileges that the city's merchants dominated commerce in the Levant for more than a century. From this unsuccessful venture Robert returned to Italy in time to deliver his lord and ally, Gregory VII, from his imperial enemies and to put Rome to the sack in 1084. A year later both Robert and Gregory were dead.

Bohemond of Taranto, born of Robert's first marriage, was passed over in the succession to the duchy of Apulia in favor of Roger Borsa (1085–1111), the eldest son of Robert's union with the sister of the last independent prince of Salerno. Robert's brother Roger I (1061–1101) continued to hold Sicily as count and vassal of his nephew. Under this division, Sicily flourished, and the duchy of Apulia with its dependent principalities declined. In 1127 Roger Borsa's son and successor, William, died, and Roger II of Sicily united the two Norman states of Apulia and Sicily. In 1130 Roger II the Great (1130–1154) assumed the title of king of Sicily.

The Norman kingdom of Sicily was an exotic compound of feudal, Byzantine, Moslem, and Lombard elements. The king maintained a harem in Moslem style; he exercised the authority of papal legate and thus controlled the Church more completely than any other ruler in Latin Christendom; his government issued commands in Latin, Greek, and Arabic to officials who were variously styled justiciars, constables, logothetes, catapans, and emirs. The kingdom possessed the strongest political institutions of any realm in the first half of the twelfth century. Its subjects lived under feudal customs and a mixture of Roman-Byzantine-Moslem laws, but the will of the king and the justice of the royal courts overrode the confusion of divergent local laws and customs. The king of Sicily was more nearly an autocrat than any other ruler in Latin Christendom.

The prosperity of the kingdom grew under the enlightened and benevolent despotism of Roger II. His policy was aimed primarily at developing the sea power that his predecessors had lacked and at promoting trade and industry. Control of the western Mediterranean was ensured by conquest of Almoravid ports in North Africa opposite Sicily. During the last years of Roger's reign the kingdom of Sicily was the strongest maritime power in Italy, an achievement that united Genoa, Pisa, and Venice against Sicily until they had, in the second half of the century, regained mastery of the central Mediterranean.

## The Byzantine Empire Before the Crusades

The Byzantine Empire has puzzled and fascinated historians because, although it seemed for centuries to be tottering on the brink, it never fell. In the East, however, there was no period as dark as the seventh century in the West nor any collapse as complete as the Carolingian disintegration of the ninth century.

The fundamental reason for the difference between Eastern and Western development was the balanced economy in Byzantine lands, which preserved both industry and commerce in the cities and a flourishing agriculture in the country districts. The political history of the empire is alternately dull and dramatic, punctuated by palace revolutions and intrigues, but the vagaries of court politics were a superficial blemish on a highly developed government that maintained its power throughout crisis and catastrophe. The imperial bureaucracy, despite its notorious venality in some periods, for a thousand years—from the fourth to the fourteenth century—served the Byzantine state more efficiently than any other government of that period. Equally impressive was the record of the Byzantine army. No army, not even the Roman army of antiquity, had a finer record of victorious campaigns and of recovery from defeats in the field. It was almost always outnumbered and confronted with enemies on all sides of the empire, but, founding its strategy and tactics on the innovations introduced under Justinian, it did remarkably well. Part of this success stemmed from the cohesiveness of the empire—its tradition and sense of continuity with the past. To its subjects, the empire was still *Romania,* and perhaps the greatest contrast between Byzantium and the West was this sense of being "at home with its past." For centuries the Byzantine Empire was a bulwark against Eastern enemies and made possible the very survival of Western Europe. Latin Christendom did not appreciate the service.

The imperial government was the prize of contending interests within the empire. The Isaurian dynasty (717–802) was based on an alliance between the landed aristocracy and the army against the court or bureaucracy and the Church. The aims of Isaurian policy were territorial expansion, protection of the frontiers, agricultural prosperity, and taxation of commerce for the support of military operations. The Isaurian dynasty came to an end with Irene (797–802), whose pathological craving for power led her to mutilate her own son, in whose name she ruled as regent, and to assume the title of empress.

The period of the Amorian emperors (802–867) began with a palace revolution against Irene and brought the bureaucracy back into power. It also initiated an imperial policy of encouraging commerce and of reestablishing religious peace. The Iconoclastic Struggle had degenerated into a contest for power that had weakened both Church and state. Although there were iconoclasts among the early Amorian emperors, images were restored by a Church council in 843, and the controversy was finally closed. During the Amorian period social and economic discontent in Asia Minor led to an abortive rebellion and to the increasing subordination of the free peasantry to the landed aristocracy.

In literature, learning, and art the age of the Isaurian and Amorian dynasties was dominated by the Iconoclastic Struggle. The greatest theologian was John of Damascus (d. 750), a staunch defender of images. The works of the iconoclasts were entirely destroyed by their enemies, and their arguments have to be reconstructed from the polemics of their opponents. Iconoclasm obviously created an uncongenial environment for religious art, but Hellenistic naturalism revived in secular painting and sculpture. The Amorians also patronized the educational system that produced the bureaucracy on which the dynasty depended. Photius (d. 891), a teacher in the palace school, was elevated to the patriarchate of Constantinople. During his stormy career, Photius produced the most notable literary work of the period, the *Myriobiblon* (*Thousands of Books*), an enormous compilation of extracts from and commentaries on classical Greek authors. The emperors also supported the brothers Cyril and Methodius, the "apostles of the Slavs," who not only converted much of Eastern Europe to Orthodox Christianity but also perfected the Slavic alphabet, first developed by earlier missionaries, so that they could introduce the Scriptures to their converts. Cyril had also been a teacher in the upper levels of the Byzantine educational system.

In the ninth century, missionary rivalry in the Slavic world between the

Greek and Latin churches produced as much antagonism as the earlier icono-clastic schism. The first notable success of the Eastern missionaries was the conversion of the Bulgarian ruler, Boris, in 865, an event that led to sharp competition between the Orthodox and Catholic missionaries for the ec-clesiastical allegiance of the western Slavs. Embittered relations between Constantinople and Rome reached the breaking point when the emperor deposed a patriarch for high treason and appointed Photius in his place. The pope at this time was Nicholas I, whose vigorous assertion of papal su-premacy has already been discussed. It surprised no one when Nicholas promptly excommunicated Photius as a usurper. Photius, in turn, held a great council in 867 that condemned as heretical all points of doctrine and li-turgical usage in which Latin Christianity differed from the Orthodox faith. Then the patriarch excommunicated Nicholas. This Photian schism did not last long. Photius was deprived of his patriarchate in a palace revolution, and although he regained it a few years later, he was deposed once again in 886. The schism was not a cause but a symptom of the widening breach between the two communions. The real issue was papal supremacy. Only when this issue arose were the several doctrinal differences rehearsed and debated and made the basis on which the patriarch and the pope mutually excommuni-cated each other, as they did again in 1054.

In reality, Photius' or any other patriarch's attitude toward papal claims depended on the Byzantine emperor's relations with Rome. Once the Bul-garians had been brought into the Byzantine sphere of influence, it was more important for the emperor to be on good terms with the pope than to pro-mote the ambitions of his patriarch. The emperor needed help in meeting the Moslem attack on the western Byzantine provinces. Sicily was almost wholly lost by the end of the ninth century, and the Moslems were beginning to occupy parts of Byzantine Italy. The pope and a Byzantine fleet cooperated against the Moslem stronghold on the Garigliano River in 915. On the eastern frontiers the Moslem danger had subsided after 833 because of internal strife, but the island of Crete had been lost to Moslem adventurers. A new enemy appeared in 860, when the Russians made a surprise attack by sea on Con-stantinople—the first recorded event in Russian history. The unsuccessful raiders were probably from the newly organized principality of Kiev founded (or conquered) by Scandinavians earlier in the ninth century.

The greatest menace to Byzantine security during the period of the Mace-donian emperors (867–1057) was on the northern frontier, where the Bulgar people had become thoroughly intermixed with native Slavs and had built up a well-organized kingdom after the Byzantine model. Under Simeon (893–927), the first ruler to assume the title tsar (Caesar), Bulgaria included most of the Balkan Peninsula, stretching from the Adriatic to the Black seas. The Byzantine emperor allied with the Magyars against Simeon, who countered by employing another Asiatic people, the Patzinaks, with whose help he drove the Magyars up the Danube to the plain east of present-day Vienna, where they later founded the kingdom of Hungary. Simeon then attacked the Byzantine Empire and forced on the emperor the humiliation of paying an annual tribute.

In the tenth century the empire recovered. Border warfare against the Moslems turned slowly in favor of the Byzantines, and on the sea Nicephorus Phocas (963–969) recovered naval supremacy in the eastern Mediterranean. He reconquered Crete in 961 and Cyprus four years later. The empire attained its greatest prosperity, military strength, and political stability under Basil II (976–1025), who employed arms and diplomacy with equal skill. Although Bulgaria had declined after the death of Simeon, a new Bulgarian dynasty renewed the war with the empire late in the tenth century. Basil's war on the Bulgarians resembled Charlemagne's Saxon wars in length and brutality. At one point, Basil returned to the Bulgarian tsar fourteen thousand prisoners, all of them blinded except for one in every hundred to serve as guide. The tsar is said to have died of shock when he saw them. A few years after this incident the conquered "empire" of Bulgaria became a Byzantine province, and the triumphant Basil was acclaimed with the appropriate title *Bulgaroctonos* (Bulgar Slayer).

During the reign of Basil II relations with Russia became important. At one critical moment, when confronted with a large-scale rebellion in Asia Minor and invasion by the Bulgarians, Basil saved the situation only with the assistance of six thousand Varangian (Scandinavian Russian) troops supplied by Prince Vladimir of Kiev. The outcome of this crisis was a treaty of alliance (ca. 989), by which Vladimir accepted Christianity and married a Byzantine princess. Thus began the expansion of Byzantine and Orthodox culture into an area almost as large as Latin Christendom. Peaceful relations between the courts of Constantinople and Kiev rested on a mutually profitable commerce.

A social revolution in the tenth century weakened the Byzantine state and set the stage for decline in the eleventh century. Most of the Macedonian emperors were military men whose first concern was the strength and dependability of the army. The best troops were recruited from the free peasantry of Asia Minor, where the continuing tendency toward larger estates increased the subordination of the peasants to the great landowners. This transformation of the free peasantry into dependent cultivators undermined both troop recruitment—only the free owed military service—and tax collection. For most of the tenth century the government was beset with rebellions in the provinces of Asia Minor, and several of the best emperors of the period were themselves successful aristocratic rebels. But most of the Macedonian emperors waged a relentless war of legislation against the economic power of the aristocracy, a policy designed to protect and benefit the free peasant class and thus shore up the social foundations of the army.

Manuscript illumination showing Basil II the Bulgar Slayer in court. His military position is emphasized as he stands in armor with his sword, and the obeisance here shown the Eastern emperor differs from the attitude shown by attendants toward the Western emperor in the picture on p. 184.

Under strong rulers this paternalistic protection of the peasants was successful, but ultimately the economic power of the aristocrats triumphed. After Basil II an uneasy balance of power developed between the local authority of great landowners and the weakened imperial authority at Constantinople. The turning point came when the central government gave up the struggle to collect taxes directly. Instead, taxes were farmed to local nobles who paid into the treasury a fixed sum and then recouped themselves with all they could extort from the peasants of their districts. This system further depressed the peasantry and created widespread unrest.

The decline of the Byzantine Empire in the eleventh century did not affect cultural achievement as it did political stability and social welfare. The Macedonian era was brilliant in arts and letters. Scholarship, building, and the decorative arts flourished under imperial patronage. There was a renewed interest in the literature of antiquity, although learning in this field tended to be arid and encyclopedic. The outstanding figure was Michael

Psellus (d. 1078), a teacher of philosophy and rhetoric whose interests were similar to those of Photius in the ninth century. Several good histories were written in the tenth and eleventh centuries, but Byzantine authors particularly excelled in writing technical monographs and treatises on political and military administration. One of the best was *On the Administration of the Empire* by Constantine VII Porphyrogenitus (913–959), the most able scholar at his own court.

The decline under the last Macedonian emperors (1025–1057) was accelerated in the subsequent "time of troubles" (1057–1081). External enemies made inroads on Byzantine territory. In the west the Norman conquest of southern Italy had begun, and in the north the Patzinaks threatened the Danubian frontier. Far more serious, the Seljuk Turks moved into the eastern provinces of both the Byzantine Empire and the caliphate. In 1071 at Manzikert the Byzantine army suffered its worst disaster since the Battle of Adrianople (378). The Seljuk Turks destroyed the forces raised by Romanus IV and captured the emperor. In the same year Byzantine rule in Italy was brought to an end with the fall of Bari. Subsequently the Turks conquered most of Asia Minor, while the Serbs and Bulgarians overran most of the Balkan provinces. Palace intrigues and rebellions by ambitious generals reduced the empire to a state of anarchy. But a new military hero appeared to revive the empire. This was Alexius Comnenus (1081–1118), whose careful husbanding of his military resources and whose astute diplomacy once again restored the empire to a sound although circumscribed basis.

## Islam and the First Crusade

In the Moslem world, the period from the mid-eighth to the mid-eleventh century was one of a great flowering in cultural and economic life. Under the Abbasid caliphate (750–1055) the Islamic Empire was transformed "from a Byzantine successor state to a Middle Eastern empire" whose civilization was Oriental, cosmopolitan, and conservative. The Abbasids moved the capital eastward from Damascus in Syria to Baghdad on the Tigris, in Iraq, at the center of the far-flung trade routes. There the Abbasid caliphs assumed all the splendor and trappings of Oriental despotism. The caliph ruled by divine right, his power was absolute, he was "the Shadow of God on earth." But even Harun al Rashid (786–809), contemporary of Charlemagne and the greatest of the Abbasid caliphs, did not command the allegiance of all of Islam. Political decentralization began early, although it was neither as chaotic nor as complete as the disintegration of the Carolingian empire in the Christian West. Spain refused to recognize the new dynasty and continued to be ruled by the Omayyads after 756. Morocco was an autonomous province under a local dynasty after 788, Tunisia after 800, and Egypt after 868. Persia was divided among local dynasties during the ninth century, and by the middle of the tenth century the caliph at Baghdad ruled little more than Iraq.

By then, however, the caliphs had become simply figureheads dominated by the chief official of the government, the grand vizier, who was himself often merely the puppet of the palace guards. Most of the local dynasties were founded by provincial army commanders whose nominal recognition of the caliph's position took the form of occasional tribute, inscription of the caliph's name on provincial coinage, and the mention of his name during prayers on Friday.

Political decentralization did not affect the prosperity of Islam. The provincial rulers promoted industry and trade and preferred the profits of peace to the risks of war. The honest and successful merchant occupied an esteemed position in society. In the bazaars of Baghdad and other cities, commodities from China, the East Indies, India and Ceylon, central Asia, Russia, Scandinavia, east-central Africa, and Spain were bought and sold. Not all of this commerce was in Moslem hands. Moslem coins have been found in Sweden, for example, brought back from Islamic lands by Swedish traders who had sold such exports from the Baltic area as furs, wax, birch bark, arrows, fish glue, horsehides, honey, nuts, falcons, cattle and—most expensive of all—slaves and amber. In the trade with China, however, Moslem shipping predominated as early as the eighth century. Imports from China were primarily high-priced luxury goods, such as spices, silks, paper, gold and silver utensils, drugs, and jewelry. From Africa the most valuable imports were gold and slaves. The Moslems not only traded but also produced. The most important Moslem industry was in textiles, especially cotton goods (originally imported from India), silks, and carpets. Manufacture of paper became important in the reign of Harun al Rashid and had spread throughout the empire by the tenth century. The flourishing economy was just as important as a universal religion and a universal language in uniting Islam into one cosmopolitan civilization.

Baghdad, the fabulous city of the *Arabian Nights,* was the capital and center of Moslem culture, as it was of commerce, long after its political significance had disappeared. The cultural achievements of the Abbasid period were more impressive and more enduring than anything attained in the West before the twelfth century. Like Western culture, Moslem learning, literature, and art were largely built on the heritage of antiquity. But the Moslems exploited Greek and Persian rather than Latin sources, and Moslem interests were primarily scientific in contrast with the contemporary Byzantine revival of classical literature. Men from all parts of the Islamic Empire contributed to intellectual and cultural activities through Arabic, the language common to all educated people.

Arabic scholars excelled in mathematics, medicine, and geography. "Arabic" numerals were known in the middle of the eighth century by Moslem mathematicians, who called them "Hindu" numerals after the country from which they borrowed them. With these numerals and with the addition of the zero, Moslems developed the science of algebra (*al-jabr*) a century later.

Arabic physicians studied diseases empirically and were especially successful in the diagnosis of rare maladies and of those whose symptoms were superficially similar to other ailments. An advanced system of hospitals aided the practice of medicine, but religious injunctions prohibited dissection, thus preventing any advance in surgery. Arabic medicine was clinical rather than experimental. For theory it was dependent on classical Greek medical works. Arabic geography was descriptive and highly practical; its main contribution was a great accumulation of new facts based on travelers' reports and commercial contacts beyond the boundaries of Islam. Finally, ancient Greek philosophical treatises were an important interest of Arabic scholars. The earlier work consisted of translations into Arabic. Later scholars wrote elaborate commentaries on Aristotle and other Greek philosophers, in which the main effort was to reconcile Greek philosophy with the revealed truth of Mohammed.

The political and military decentralization of this brilliant civilization made it fall rapidly before the assaults of the Seljuk Turks. Appearing first in the tenth century in the region around Samarkand, this Asiatic tribe adopted the Mohammedan faith and with the zeal of new converts swept westward to restore religious orthodoxy and political unity to the Islamic Empire. By 1055 they had captured Baghdad and the person of the caliph, in whose name the Seljuk leader ruled with the title of sultan. At its height following the great victory at Manzikert in 1071, the Seljuk empire included Persia, Iraq, Syria, and most of Asia Minor. The center of Seljuk power was in Persia, and the sultan relied on a Persian bureaucracy to hold together the several conquered provinces. After 1094, however, the same decentralization that had afflicted the Abbasid caliphate set in throughout the Seljuk dominions.

When the Byzantine emperor, Alexius I Comnenus (1081–1118), turned to the task of reconquering the provinces lost to the Turks, it was therefore not a united Seljuk empire that he faced but the semi-independent Seljuk state that the Turks called Rum (that is, Romania, consisting of the former Byzantine provinces of Asia Minor).

Alexius lacked manpower—he hoped to win back that part of the empire that had been the principal recruiting ground of the imperial army. This was a problem that Alexius' predecessors had recognized, and within a year or two after Manzikert they had entered into fruitless negotiations with the Normans of southern Italy and with Pope Gregory VII to raise an army of Western mercenary troops. The Normans were traditional enemies of the Byzantines in southern Italy and looked on the empire's western provinces as their next target. Robert Guiscard led campaigns against the Byzantine provinces in Greece during the early 1080s. Gregory had been excited about the possibility of organizing a Crusade against the Turks, but his involvement with Henry IV of Germany prevented him from undertaking the project. Nonetheless, this history of papal interest made Urban II eager to assist Alexius when the emperor appealed to him at Piacenza in 1095. The

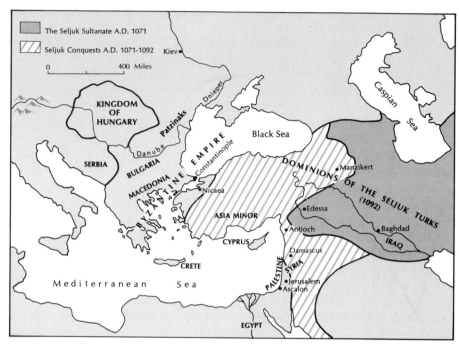

Islam, the Byzantine Empire, and the First Crusade, ca. 1100

emperor had requested help from the pope and from some secular rulers like the count of Flanders in 1090, but at that time the papacy was under such pressure from Guibert of Ravenna and Henry IV that Urban could do nothing. By 1095 the reform papacy had gained the advantage over Henry and his antipope. At the same time, negotiations were resumed between representatives of the patriarch and those of the pope with a view toward healing the schism of 1054 between the Latin and Greek communions.

A later Greek chronicler, who had access to information now lost, summed up the situation as follows:

> Considering it impossible to defeat the Turks alone, Alexius saw that he would have to call in the Italians as allies, which he did with cunning, adroitness, and deep-laid planning. Realizing that westerners found unbearable the domination of Jerusalem by the Turks, he managed by dispatching ambassadors to the bishop of Old Rome and to kings and rulers of the western parts, by the use of appropriate arguments, to prevail over not a few of them to leave their own countries, and he succeeded in directing them to the task which he had in mind.[1]

[1] Abridged and paraphrased from Peter Charanis, "A Greek Source on the Origin of the First Crusade," *Speculum* 24 (1949): 93.

The "appropriate arguments" by which the emperor secured military help are unknown. Most historians agree today that Alexius proposed to Urban II that the Orthodox and Catholic branches of Christendom be reunited under the supremacy of the pope in return for papal sponsorship of an army to help Alexius reconquer the lost provinces of the Byzantine Empire. The times were propitious for such a proposal. Urban, with a broader vision of the world situation than Alexius could have appreciated, saw in the emperor's appeal an opportunity to realize several of the objectives of the Hildebrandine reform program.

Alexius had asked for some mercenary troops; what Urban II gave him was the First Crusade. The Crusade was preached by Urban at the Council of Clermont, in 1095, in one of the greatest orations of all time. Urban confirmed papal leadership of the reform and tied the reform program in with the grand new project of marshaling the forces of Latin Christendom to succor the Oriental Christians and to recapture Jerusalem and the Holy Sepulcher from the infidel. The Crusade would divert the restless military energies of the West to the service of the Church, thus giving the papacy universal leadership in maintaining peace at home (the Peace of God) and in directing a counterassault on the Islamic Empire that would reunite "the churches of God in the eastern parts" with the Western Church under papal supremacy. In preaching the First Crusade, Urban II gave Europe an ideology of expansion.

Public opinion was prepared for Urban's idealistic appeal to arms, and the nobles and clergy who were assembled at Clermont responded to Urban with a zeal approaching frenzy. Shouting "Deus volt" (God wills it), hundreds of Urban's listeners took the cross. In the ensuing months preachers traversed Western Europe enlisting men from all social classes in the Crusade. The most effective response came from the lesser nobility, among whom the crusading spirit consisted in varying parts of religious zeal, zest for fighting, and materialistic ambitions—"younger sons in search of principalities and sinners in search of profitable penance." No king responded to the call. The military commanders included great nobles like Raymond, count of Toulouse; Godfrey of Bouillon, duke of Lorraine, and his brother, Baldwin; and Bohemond of Taranto, son of Robert Guiscard. Bishop Adhemar of Le Puy, the papal legate on the Crusade, was the nominal leader. He was charged with guiding the Crusaders' efforts toward the goals outlined by Urban at Clermont. In addition, Adhemar was to ensure that the lay leaders of the Crusade honored the pledge, confirmed by an oath they took when they reached Constantinople, to return to Byzantine rule captured provinces formerly belonging to the empire.

The crusading fervor did not affect only the aristocratic classes. It spread quickly among peasants and townspeople. Itinerant preachers like Peter the Hermit gathered together increasing numbers of poor people fired by the desire to step from their cramped lives into the world promised by a war for Christ. Such preachers played on the eschatological beliefs of the people and presented the Crusade as the final battle between the followers of Christ and the armies of Antichrist that would precede the Second Coming and the Last Judgment. It was popularly believed that either Constantine or Charlemagne would rise again, returning from a mountain where he had been waiting to lead the Christians against the Turks. Even before the knightly armies were ready to depart, hordes of *pauperes* (poor people) moved through Europe toward the East. The Crusade was the answer to many dreams and the escape from many troubles. The ten years previous to 1095 had been a period of widespread climatic disasters in northern Europe, and from 1089 on, a plague swept through the Continent. Furthermore, poor peoples' pilgrimages to the Holy Land had already become a tradition. In 1033 and 1064, thousands of people had gone to Jerusalem with no intention of returning to Europe.

The eschatological fervor of the People's Crusade led to the first great slaughter of the north European Jews. In popular eschatology, the community of Christians destined to fight the armies of Antichrist had to be purified before it could be victorious. As they traveled eastward, the mobs attacked Jews, destroying their houses and synagogues. Where they could, the bishops and other aristocratic authorities protected the Jewish communities, with which they had long had a close connection. But thousands of Jews died, and the pogroms of 1096 are considered the end of the golden age of north European Jewry. Every succeeding Crusade produced another series of pogroms and kept the Jewish communities in a permanent state of isolation and fear.

The peasant Crusaders pillaged all along the route. Some probably joined the mob because it had destroyed their livelihoods and left them no choice. Eventually the Crusaders, many of whom were killed by Christian authorities in order to save their regions from depredation, arrived at Constantinople. Alexius was appalled but soon found a simple solution to the problem posed by the mass of underfed, undisciplined, militarily useless people. He transported them across the Dardanelles to fight the infidel, and within a short time, virtually nothing was left of the People's Crusade. Nonetheless, some Crusaders apparently did reach the Holy Land and became an effective force against the Turks. This army of poor soldiers, called Tafurs, was led by a "king" said to be a Norman knight who had given up his armor to take the garb of the simple pilgrims. The Turks feared the Tafurs almost as much as they feared the regular crusading army because the poor fought with a religious fervor that made them difficult to defeat. The Tafurs pillaged every town they captured, raped the women, and killed the children. Even the Christian forces avoided the Tafurs for fear of being attacked for lack of spiritual fervor.

Alexius was not much more impressed by the regular crusading army

Many who joined the People's Crusade in 1096 at the urging of Peter the Hermit believed that Christ had appeared to Peter in a dream while he was in Jerusalem and commanded him to preach the Crusade. Peter, a man who apparently spoke several languages eloquently, traveled throughout Europe preaching to the peasants and urban lower classes. A manuscript illuminator here depicted the divine visitation that supposedly stimulated the popular Crusade.

than he had been by the poor Crusaders. He was dismayed by the army's motley appearance and lack of unified leadership. He had appealed for disciplined mercenary troops to bolster his own army; he received a force led by men unwilling to subject themselves to his leadership. Almost immediately, the Western leaders quarreled with him and fell to bickering among themselves. From Alexius' point of view the only constructive achievement of the Crusade was the capture of Nicaea, across the straits from Constantinople, and its return to the empire in 1097. After this victory the crusading armies struck south-eastward toward the Holy Land, leaving Alexius to attempt the reconquest of Asia Minor alone. Before the Crusaders reached Jerusalem, however, Baldwin detached his own troops from the main body and seized Edessa in 1098, thus establishing the first of the Latin "Crusader states" of Syria. Under Baldwin and his successors, the county of Edessa was a strategic salient thrust into Moslem territory that protected the northern flank of the Christian states in Palestine. This military advantage was counterbalanced by Alexius' alienation. He considered the state of Edessa to be an illegal seizure of former Byzantine territory. Eventually, Byzantine antagonism was as great a threat to the Crusaders as Moslem enmity.

While Baldwin was conquering Edessa, the Crusaders besieged Antioch, whose capture would open Syria to invasion. After a prolonged struggle, the city fell in 1098. By that time the leaders of the Crusade were bitterly divided over who should rule there. Some favored returning the city to Alexius, while Bohemond of Taranto and Raymond of Toulouse vied with one another to follow the example of Baldwin in Edessa. Finally Bohemond, who had played the major role in its conquest, was recognized as lord of Antioch by his fellow Crusaders. By now all the leaders were more interested in capturing principalities than in completing the Crusade. Adhemar, the papal legate, had died, leaving the Crusaders without the unified ecclesiastical leadership Urban had envisaged. Adhemar's death permitted the Crusaders to conveniently forget their oath to Alexius to return reconquered Byzantine territory. As the First Crusade was about to degenerate into a series of petty land-grabbing campaigns, Godfrey of Bouillon emerged as the leader and spokesman for the rank and file who demanded that the army press on to the Holy Sepulcher in Jerusalem.

Under Godfrey's leadership the Crusaders reached Jerusalem in June 1099, and after a month's siege they took the Holy City. Then the Christian conquerors got out of control. Although leaders like Godfrey of Bouillon and Raymond of Toulouse spared the defenders who surrendered to them personally, almost the whole of the population—soldiers, noncombatants, the aged, women, and children—were indiscriminately slaughtered. After this brutal carnage, a Moslem army tried to reconquer the city, but in August 1099, the Crusaders decisively defeated the Moslems at the Battle of Ascalon, near Jerusalem.

Founded in the 1120s, the Poor Knights of Christ and of the Temple of Solomon was an order of religious knights who vowed to remain celibate and to relinquish worldly possessions so that they could devote themselves to fighting the infidel in the Holy Land and to protecting pilgrims traveling there. By the late thirteenth century, however, these functions had become largely obsolete by treaties between the Crusaders and the Moslems that permitted free pilgrimage, and the Templars, as the order came to be called, had become financial agents in Europe. They controlled the finances of the French monarchy until 1312, when they were suppressed at the instigation of the French king, who wanted to repudiate his debts to them. This seal of the order is from the mid-thirteenth century, when the Templars were becoming major figures in European finance, although it emphasizes their original vow of poverty by depicting two knights on one horse.

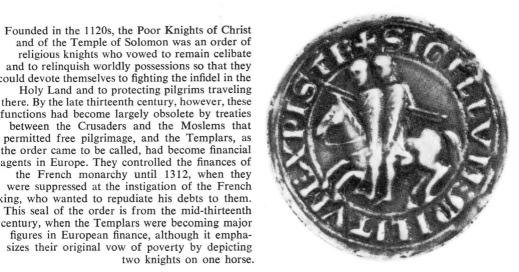

Alexius Comnenus restored the Eastern empire after the disasters of the mid-eleventh century. He succeeded in finding Western support that resulted in the First Crusade; he held the Normans, Patzinaks, and Turks at bay. But in this portrait, his saintliness and his scholarliness are emphasized. Unlike Basil II the Bulgar Slayer, Alexius apparently recognized his position of predominance over a brilliant Byzantine civilization and considered that one of his chief glories.

The First Crusade was now completed, and the organization of the conquered territory began. Godfrey of Bouillon, who had the fewest personal enemies among the strife-ridden leaders, was elected king of Jerusalem, but the pious Godfrey declined that title (refusing to wear a royal diadem in the city where Jesus had worn a crown of thorns). Instead, he became ruler of Jerusalem and the surrounding country with the title Defender of the Holy Sepulcher. The implication was that his secular authority was subordinate to that of the new Latin patriarch of Jerusalem, whose obedience was to Rome rather than Constantinople. But before the year had passed, Godfrey died and was replaced by his brother, Baldwin of Edessa, who had no such pious scruples. Baldwin took the royal title and established the Latin kingdom of Jerusalem in 1100.

Baldwin and his successors were competent, but the problems and perils confronting the Crusaders' kingdom were greater than they could overcome permanently. The initial problem, survival in a hostile world, was partly solved by the establishment of two military orders whose members took religious vows and dedicated themselves to protecting pilgrims and fighting the infidel: the Knights of the Hospital of Saint John of Jerusalem (ca. 1099), and the Poor Knights of Christ and of the Temple of Solomon (ca. 1119). These orders, the Hospitallers and the Knights Templar, recruited members and received economic support throughout Western Europe. Their history became entangled with the growth of the Western monarchies, and thus their power was felt long after their service in the Holy Land had become only nominal.

## Suggestions for Further Reading

**Secondary Works**    On the beginnings of the reconquest of Spain, see R. Altamira, *A History of Spain,* trans. M. Lee (New York, 1949), and H. J. Chaytor, *A History of Aragon and Catalonia* (London, 1933). The works cited at the end of Chapter 5 treat the history of Byzantium and Islam prior to the First Crusade. The second edition of the *Cambridge Medieval History,* vol. 4 (Cambridge, 1966) is especially important on these subjects. On the Crusades, see S. Runciman, *A History of the Crusades,* 3 vols. (Cambridge, 1951–54). A five-volume *History of the Crusades,* ed. K. M. Setton, is in preparation; the first two volumes have been published: *The First Hundred Years,* ed. M. W. Baldwin (Philadelphia, 1955), and *The Later Crusades, 1189–1311,* ed. R. L. Wolff and H. W. Hazard (Philadelphia, 1962). An excellent short survey is H. E. Mayer, *The Crusades,* trans. J. Gillingham (Oxford, 1972), which contains an up-to-date bibliography. More specialized works of interest are R. C. Smail, *Crusading Warfare* (Cambridge, 1956); D. C. Munro, *The Kingdom of the Crusaders* (New York, 1935); and J. L. LaMonte, *Feudal Monarchy in the Latin Kingdom of Jerusalem* (Cambridge, Mass., 1932). See also A. S. Atiya, *Crusade, Commerce and Culture* (Bloomington, Ind., 1962) and *The Crusade: Historiography and Bibliography* (Bloomington, Ind., 1962).

**Sources**   A. C. Krey, *The First Crusade* (Princeton, N. J., 1921) is the best introduction to the sources. A complete account of the First Crusade from one of the three most important sources may be found in *Fulcher of Chartres: Chronicle of the First Crusade,* trans. M. E. McGinty (Philadelphia, 1941). For an ample selection of sources and a good commentary on them, see J. A. Brundage, *The Crusades: A Documentary Survey* (Milwaukee, Wis., 1962). The Islamic point of view can be found in *Arab Historians of the Crusades,* ed. F. Gabrieli (Berkeley and Los Angeles, 1969).

# Europe from the Twelfth Through the Fifteenth Century

# IV THE TWELFTH CENTURY

# 14 The Development of Royal Government in the Twelfth Century

The first result of the process of political consolidation and centralization begun in the late tenth century was the formation of strong duchies and counties virtually independent of royal authority. In Germany the monarchs made significant strides toward establishing an effective central government in the tenth and early eleventh centuries, but the Investiture Controversy and rebellions associated with it set back the monarchy and created obstacles to further progress toward centralization. In England and France the process of consolidation under royal government began later than in Germany, but it continued throughout the rest of the Middle Ages. At the end of the Middle Ages, the royal governments in England and France were the most powerful authorities in their respective nations, while in Germany the great princes held the majority of power. The foundations of these differences in development were the events of the eleventh and twelfth centuries. The political evolution of Western Europe in these centuries may be divided chronologically into three major periods. Development in the eleventh century climaxed during the 1070s and 1080s in the Investiture Controversy between the empire and the papacy, the *Reconquista* in Spain, and the establishment of a Norman state in southern Italy and Sicily. The century was brought to a close with the First Crusade and the foundation of the Latin kingdom of Jerusalem. In France and England during the eleventh century only one event of equal magnitude took place, the Norman Conquest of England in 1066, followed by a rapid development of the Anglo-Norman government into the strongest feudal monarchy in Europe except perhaps for the Norman kingdom of Sicily.

The second phase of political revival corresponds roughly with the first half of the twelfth century. It was a period marked by no great events. The contest between the popes and the emperors subsided, and the settlement at Worms in 1122 was followed, after the death of Henry V, by a disputed succession in Germany and a period of anarchy and localism on both sides of the Alps. The most important new development was the struggle for local autonomy by the communes of northern Italy. In France this was a period of political consolidation rather than expansion, under the stalwart and able Louis VI and his successor, the tenacious although less fortunate, Louis VII. In England the strong rule of Henry I, last of William the Conqueror's sons, was followed by a disputed succession and a period known in English history as "the Anarchy," corresponding chronologically with the anarchy in Germany. Throughout Western and central Europe, the constructive energies of the feudal governments seemed to have been exhausted.

The third period began just after the middle of the twelfth century. In 1152 Frederick I Barbarossa succeeded to the imperial throne, and in 1154 Henry II became king of England. Each ruler energetically set about restoring the rights and powers of his crown, and each sought to expand and increase his control of the lands under his suzerainty. Both Frederick and Henry put together huge, conglomerate empires, and it was in response to the threats posed by these powers that the papacy and the French monarchy found the strength to defend their traditional claims and to develop their own authority. Under Philip II Augustus (1180–1223), the French monarchy successfully challenged the power of the Plantagenet successors of Henry II, and under Pope Alexander III (1159–1181), the papacy organized the opposition to Frederick's Italian plans.

## Anglo-Norman England
## and Capetian France

Cnut (1016–1035) brought peace and order, but he did not preserve the unity of the Old English kingdom. The older county system of local government was subordinated to a new Anglo-Danish system of combining several counties into a few great provincial governments under powerful earls, who did not at first represent any local or landed interest within their earldoms. Cnut effectively controlled the earls, but between his death and the Norman

Conquest, the kingdom was periodically disturbed by the ambitions and intrigues of four or five great provincial magnates led by Earl Godwin of Wessex and his sons.

Following the brief reigns of Cnut's two sons, the house of Alfred the Great was restored to the throne in the person of Edward the Confessor (1042–1066), son of Ethelred the Ill-Counseled and the Norman princess Emma, who had later become Cnut's wife. Edward grew up in Normandy and brought with him Norman advisers and ecclesiastical officials as a counterbalance to the powerful Anglo-Danish earls. Edward's Normanization of the royal court produced a tense political competition between his Norman associates and the established earls and their followers. Led by Godwin and later by Godwin's son Harold, the earls conspired to drive the Normans from England and to assume their traditional role as counselors of the king. Edward himself was popular and had a reputation for piety, but he was not a strong leader, and the conflict for control of his government reduced him to a figurehead.

Edward produced no heir, and thus the succession became part of the conflict between the Anglo-Danish (allied with Anglo-Saxon interests) and Norman aristocrats in his court. In the early years of his reign, Edward had promised the kingship to his cousin William of Normandy (1035–1087), who was a bastard son of Duke Robert the Magnificent, Emma's brother. During Edward's reign, however, a severe anti-Norman reaction in England resulted in the replacement of the Norman archbishop of Canterbury by the Anglo-Saxon Stigand, nominated by Earl Godwin, and in Edward's marriage to Godwin's daughter. Godwin's son Harold consequently made a claim to the succession because he was the king's brother-in-law and because he had the support of the Anglo-Saxon *witangemot* (royal council of great aristocrats). This body still maintained the right to elect the king, even though it usually just acknowledged the hereditary claimant to the crown. This time, however, it would exercise a substantive power. In addition to the competition between Harold Godwinson and William of Normandy, Harold Hardrada, king of Norway, asserted his right to the English crown through his relationship with Cnut. On his deathbed, Edward named Earl Harold as his successor, and the *witangemot* quickly added its voice in support of the powerful Anglo-Saxon leader who might save the country from the threats of both the Norwegians and the Normans.

Duke William considered Harold a usurper and a traitor to himself. The duke had a prior claim to the crown through his relationship with Edward, and he also maintained that Harold had recently sworn an oath recognizing William's bid for the kingship. This obscure incident apparently took place after Harold, shipwrecked on the Norman coast during a fishing expedition, was delivered to William's court. The duke treated the earl honorably and eventually released him. Now, William, who had only recently emerged from twenty-five years of almost constant warfare against rebellious barons in his duchy, prepared to invade England. His succession in 1035, as a minor, had been accompanied by a widespread reaction against the strength of the ducal government. William's bastardy did not help his cause. Once he came of age, the young duke faced an extensive and tenacious rebellion. From 1047 to 1054 he fought for his life and power and only slowly gained the advantage. A few years later a new rebellion threatened William's authority, and in 1058 King Henry I of France (1031–1060) gave his support to the rebels. In defeating the combined forces of the rebels and the French king, William finally crushed all opposition in the duchy; Henry's policy broke the long alliance between the French crown and the Norman duchy, to the eventual despair of the monarchy. In 1066, then, William was powerful enough to organize a great expedition and, in fact, used the invasion to further solidify his control over his duchy. The knightly army he recruited in the late spring was composed primarily of scions of Norman feudal families, but it also included knights from elsewhere on the Continent. A fleet of ships was ready to sail in August, but medieval sailors could not tack against the wind, and the winds were blowing in the wrong direction. For six weeks William sat on the coast with his army, demonstrating his generalship in the mere fact that he held the feudal contingents together through the weeks of idleness.

William's ultimate success depended on more than his generalship, however. In England, events beyond his control created a situation that helped his cause immensely. King Harold's brother, Tostig, had been convicted of a crime, and Harold had banished him from the kingdom. Tostig fled to Norway, where he stirred up the Norwegian king's interest in the English crown. In early September 1066, Harold Hardrada and Tostig invaded Northumbria and crushed the English forces led by the earl of Northumbria. King Harold had been waiting for William's attack on the southeast coast, but now he led his army on forced marches to the north, catching the Norwegians by surprise at Stamford Bridge outside York. The battle was decisive. Harold Hardrada and Tostig were killed, and the Norwegian force, which had come in two hundred ships, retreated in eleven. Two days later, the wind changed, and William landed on the English coast. On the news of William's landing, Harold and his housecarls immediately set off for London where the king ordered the local militia to gather. Harold's courage was in the best Anglo-Scandinavian military tradition, but his decision at this point altered the course of English history. His weary housecarls had not rested after two forced marches and a great battle, all within three weeks, and the levies from the southern shires were only half-assembled, when Harold decided to push on from London in order to fight the mounted knights of the Norman host on high ground of his own choosing. This would favor the tactics of the housecarls, the backbone of his army.

As it turned out, the Battle of Hastings was almost Harold's victory. The day-long struggle was slowly turning in favor of the English, whose defense

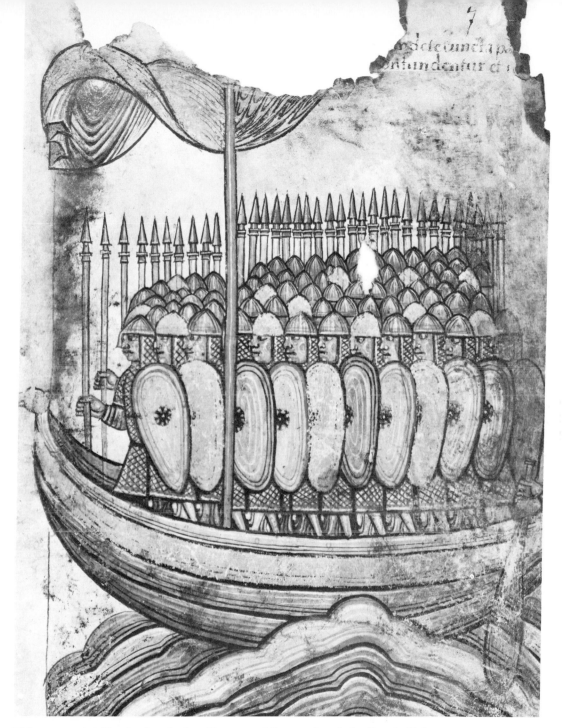

This manuscript illumination depicts Norman soldiers on board the fleet built by William the Conqueror to ferry his troops and their mounts across the Channel to England. The troops bear the arms of foot soldiers rather than those of cavalry. The large shields were used to form a shield wall, a maneuver usually associated with the English and not the Normans.

The Bayeux Tapestry is one of the most important sources for the history of the Norman Conquest. It was woven by order of William the Conqueror's brother Odo, bishop of Bayeux, in the period after the invasion and thus presents the Norman account. Two hundred thirty-one feet long by twenty inches high and containing a running commentary on the action it depicts, the tapestry leaves little to the imagination of the viewer. *Above* Norman knights charge the Anglo-Saxon shield wall. Failing to break it, they use subterfuge to induce the troops to break their lines and chase them. *Below* After their feigned retreat, the Normans turn on their Anglo-Saxon pursuers and cut them down with swords. *Opposite page* Harold takes an arrow in his eye and dies. The divestment of dead knights and thegns is portrayed in the bottom border of the tapestry.

was based on the wall of shields behind which stood the housecarls and against which the Norman cavalry charged in vain. Finally the Norman knights fell back in a disorderly retreat that seemed to augur victory for Harold but in fact sealed his defeat. Some of the English infantry broke ranks and rushed down the hill in pursuit, from the flanks of the defense line. The Normans then cut to pieces the separated elements of the defending forces. The housecarls never moved from their prepared position, but with their flanks exposed they slowly succumbed and perished to a man, Harold with them.

William proceeded throughout the country building stone keeps, of which the Tower of London is one, and repressing rebellions. The keeps were garrisoned, and the soldiers effectively controlled the surrounding region. Surprisingly, the resistance was slight, which indicates how effectively the Old English kings had unified the kingdom, destroying the independent local lords, who were so powerful in other European kingdoms. Once the king and the earls had been defeated, William stepped into the established royal system by almost completely feudalizing the kingdom, so that even bishops and abbeys henceforth would hold their lands by feudal tenure from the king. The degree to which the Norman Conquest created feudalism or only perfected it in England has been disputed among historians since the late nineteenth century. Whatever the answer, historians agree that England was the most thoroughly feudalized kingdom in Europe by the end of William's reign. William did not destroy the old political framework however. He claimed to be the legitimate successor of the Anglo-Saxon kings and sought to become king of England in their image. Thus he preserved the English military system based on the *fyrd* (universal military draft of freemen), and he even used the *fyrd* in campaigns in Normandy later in his reign.

William the Conqueror (1066–1087) had a tripartite plan for establishing his kingship. First, he feudalized the landed estates of the kingdom, while consolidating the approximately two thousand estates into about two hundred fiefs held by vassals who had participated in the invasion. These two hundred vassals, tenants-in-chief of the crown, began immediately to subenfeoff their lands. Second, William moved to gain control over the English Church. Stigand and other Anglo-Saxon bishops were obvious targets for the new king's attack, but William proceeded cautiously. He could not antagonize the powerful episcopate too much for fear of its wealth and its ability to organize an effective resistance. Stigand and other Anglo-Saxon bishops were not deposed until 1070 at a synod presided over by papal legates. The grounds for deposition were purely ecclesiastical. Stigand had succeeded to the see while the previous archbishop, a Norman, was still alive. The other deposed bishops had also violated ecclesiastical law. As the new archbishop of Canterbury, William appointed a great abbot from his duchy, Lanfranc of Bec, who undertook the reconstruction of the English Church as a Norman institution. In addition, the Conqueror supported a very active colonization of England by Norman monks, who founded more than eighty monasteries by the end of the century. Since all the bishops and abbeys held their lands of the king, they were an effective support of William's royal power. Third, William sought to make a detailed investigation of the resources of his realm. By 1086, after crushing a major rebellion the previous year, William was strong enough to undertake the great survey, which was an administrative effort more impressive than anything since the time of Diocletian and Constantine. County by county, and fief by fief, royal officials listed all the manors of England, together with a statement of who held each manor, its assessment for Danegeld, its value, the number of plows and peasants, and other details of manorial resources. Similar information was compiled for each town or borough. The results are still preserved in Domesday Book. It was "an undertaking without precedent, forced upon a reluctant country by the king's will." In its thoroughness and detail, Domesday Book is unmatched for any country until the first United States census in 1790.

In government, the Norman settlement preserved the local institutions of the county court, the hundred court, and the borough court. The personnel who controlled these courts were now French, but the law continued to be the customary laws of the Anglo-Saxons plus such modifications in criminal law as were necessary to maintain order in the newly conquered realm. To stress the legitimacy of his succession, William confirmed the laws and customs of Edward the Confessor and vigorously asserted the rights of the Old English crown. These rights gave him powers exercised by no other feudal ruler at that time, especially the right to collect a national tax on land (the Danegeld) and the transcendent criminal jurisdiction that inhered in the English "king's peace." Under the king's peace, private warfare was outlawed,

Land of the King.          In Woking Hundred.

In Guildford King William has seventy-five
houses in which one hundred and seventy-five men dwell.
In the time of King Edward it rendered eighteen pounds
          and three pence. Now it is valued at thirty
pounds and nevertheless it renders thirty-two pounds.

A passage from Domesday Book (1086) with a translation. This survey of England is one of the principal sources for the history of Anglo-Saxon society, for it provides a comprehensive picture of the state of the land only twenty years after the Norman Conquest.

and all military service by vassals and subvassals was performed only in the king's behalf. Feudalism, grafted onto the rights of the Old English crown, made the Anglo-Norman kings the most powerful monarchs in Western Europe.

The medieval feudal king held a position in which public and private rights were thoroughly mixed. He had obligations, such as keeping the peace and legislating, that are considered part of public law, but his greatest power, the firmest basis of his position, derived from the fidelity and homage due him as an individual from his vassals. As long as this private element of kingship predominated in the power structure of kingdoms, the law of succession reflected the private rather than the public nature of the king's position. Thus William the Conqueror divided his estate, if it may be called that, as any father of three sons might do. Robert, the eldest, inherited the duchy of Normandy. William II Rufus (1087–1100) received England. Henry, the youngest, got no land but received a huge treasure as compensation. Robert could not control the Norman baronage and climaxed his reign by joining the First Crusade, where he could indulge his love for fighting without the responsibilities of government. William Rufus' reign was beset with rebellions and other troubles. The Conqueror had succeeded in establishing a firm control over the English, especially after putting down the great rebellion of 1085.

In the Domesday survey he had taken advantage of his strength and had deprived his vassals and subjects of the comfortable vagueness about the obligations they owed the crown. The lack of precision in the assessment of obligations had made it possible for vassals to hold back from the total fulfillment of their duties and payments. After the Conqueror's death, many lords attempted to reassert some of the privileges and usurped rights the Domesday surveyors had taken from them. William Rufus faced this discontent, which often erupted into open rebellion.

The new king's relationship with the Church differed from that of his father. William the Conqueror had enjoyed the support of the papal reformers and had promised to introduce the reform into England. Like his contemporary in Germany, however, William was an ally of the reformers but not a reformer himself. He and Lanfranc used the program to justify their reconstruction of the English Church, but they had no intention of creating a Church independent of royal power. During the 1070s and 1080s, these attitudes were not challenged by the Roman reformers because William and Lanfranc presented the model of king and Church in cooperation, acting in the interests of reform. The reformers' attitude toward royal participation in ecclesiastical affairs hardened slowly, and it was only in the 1090s, under Urban II, that the papacy became absolutely opposed to such participation and increased the severity of its decrees against lay investiture. William Rufus had to face this new position and found that rights he took to be traditional were being challenged with increasing sharpness. Lanfranc's successor, Saint Anselm, the great philosopher, was not an extremist among the reformers, but he did represent the new views and therefore sought to exclude William from Church affairs. William reacted by exiling Anselm, which pushed the archbishop into closer relationship and agreement with the papal reformers. Like other monarchs of the period, William Rufus considered his right to appoint and invest bishops and abbots as crucial to his ability to withstand baronial opposition. It did not help that William Rufus was a cruel and capricious man who never projected the image of a proper Christian king. Few mourned when he was killed in a hunting accident in 1100.

William II was childless, and thus his sudden death raised serious problems about the succession. Duke Robert was just returning from the Crusade, and many subjects supported his claim to the throne. Henry was in England when his brother died, however, and he rushed to Winchester, seized the royal treasure, and had himself crowned. He then acted quickly to dispel opposition by making concessions. Henry I's (1100–1135) first act was to issue a coronation charter of liberties abolishing the "evil practices with which the realm of England has been unjustly oppressed," an effort designed to assure ecclesiastical and lay aristocrats that he would rule with careful regard to their traditional rights. He then invited Archbishop Anselm to return from exile and in 1106 began negotiations that led in 1107 to a compromise solution of the English Investiture Controversy. Meanwhile, Henry had repelled an invasion by Robert and had invaded Normandy. At the Battle of Tinchebrai in 1106, Henry defeated Robert and reunited Normandy with England. Robert died in prison.

After securing his position, Henry set about developing the central government. He did this by creating institutions, or improving already existing ones, that would increase the efficiency and effectiveness of royal government without presenting a direct threat to the position of his vassals and subjects. He did not survey their holdings or tabulate their obligations but only strengthened his control over those rights recognized to be his own. The constriction of baronial freedom that this might entail could not be easily challenged.

Henry introduced a new department to oversee the financial affairs of his government. It was called the Exchequer after the checkered cloth covering a large table on which accounting was done by means of counters, on the principle of the abacus. Twice each year, sheriffs, the royal officials responsible for carrying out the king's business in the shires (their name comes from a contraction of *shire reeves*), came to the Exchequer to pay the taxes they had collected. The amount presented was set out on the checkered cloth, each square representing a multiple of ten (from one penny up to ten thousand pounds). One part of the cloth was reserved for the total amount collected, another for rendering the accounts of each sheriff in turn. When a sheriff's account had been cleared and accepted by the treasury, the officials of the Exchequer recorded the fact in two ways. First, they notched a tally stick that showed all of the audits the sheriff had undergone and that could be produced to prove that the sheriff had performed his office correctly if a dispute arose or if charges of malfeasance were made. Second, the clerks made a written record of the account on a roll of parchment. The written record was obviously the better one, but both the Exchequer itself and the tally sticks represented the sort of compromises medieval rulers had to make with illiteracy. Only physical acts like placing the counters on the cloth or notching the sticks could represent the transaction completed by those to whom the written records were incomprehensible and thus suspect. Likewise, in the transfer of land, the act symbolizing and recording the transaction was the physical act of the grantor handing a clod of earth from the land to the grantee before witnesses. Until the thirteenth century, the written charter recording the transfer, if one existed, had a limited probative value.

Henry also established a new royal judiciary to hear cases brought before the royal court either because they arose on royal estates or because they involved the breaking of the king's peace. This system was based on circuit judges, justices in eyre, to whom Henry delegated his judicial authority. In addition to doing justice, these men became effective administrative representatives of the royal government, who investigated the activities of sheriffs and other royal officers, such as the bailiffs who managed royal estates. The king was at the top of this hierarchy, but because Henry was often on the Continent attending to Norman affairs, he appointed a chief justiciar to represent him. Typically, these judges were highly trained lawyers who made the English royal judicial system remarkably advanced for its time. Since sources are so fragmentary, it is not known how well established the system was in Henry I's reign, but under Henry's grandson Henry II (1154–1189) it became the basis for the most advanced system of royal justice in Europe. Henry I also adopted the policy of the Salian emperors in Germany by recruiting government officials, such as the justiciars, from the lesser nobility and the nonnoble classes.

Toward the end of Henry's reign a reaction to his growing power developed, and when a disputed succession occurred at his death, the nobility was provided with the opportunity to redress the balance of power in the kingdom. Henry's only legitimate children—he had about twenty-two in all—were William and Matilda. William had died in 1120 in a shipwreck. Matilda had been married in 1114 to Henry V of Germany, and, when he died in 1125, to Count Geoffrey of Anjou. The first marriage reflected Henry's desire to ally himself with the German emperor against the French king Louis VI. The second reflected his desire for an heir whose pedigree might resolve some problems closer to home; Anjou and Normandy were long-time enemies. While the old king lived, he forced his barons to recognize Matilda as his successor, but when he died most of the Norman baronage, traditionally opposed to the Angevins, and many English nobles gave their allegiance to Stephen of Blois (1135–1154), whose claim descended through his mother, a daughter of William the Conqueror. A civil war ensued, and toward the end of the reign Matilda gained the advantage. When his son died in 1151, Stephen came to terms with his rival and recognized Henry of Anjou, son of Matilda and Geoffrey, as his successor. During this period of disputed succession and civil war, "the Anarchy" as English historians call it, central government almost collapsed.

The French kingdom looked very different from England in this period of about one hundred years from 1066 to 1154. Henry I of France (1031–1060) had followed his father's and grandfather's policy of concentrating his attention on securing absolute control over the royal domain, the old county of Paris called the Île-de-France. Henry might have done well to avoid any involvement with other areas in his suzerainty; his interference in Normandy in 1058 was a disaster for the monarchy. Philip I (1060–1108) inherited a royal domain scarcely larger than that of Hugh Capet and no more powerful than the principalities of some other great magnates in the kingdom. Philip's domain had the advantage, however, of being at the center of the kingdom's communications system and of being densely populated and wealthy. Its economy combined a healthy agriculture and the commercial activities of two large and growing towns, Paris and Orléans. But Philip did not have the wealth of the count of Flanders to the north or of the count of Champagne, whose fiefs almost surrounded the royal domain, nor the military power of the count of Anjou to the west and the duke of Normandy to the northwest. Compared with the simple royal household whose officials nominally governed the royal domain, Normandy possessed a relatively advanced administrative system. All Philip I could hope to do was to keep these neighboring vassals divided, concentrate his efforts on controlling the royal domain, and, when opportunity arose, attempt to encroach on the border lands. Philip rivaled the power of the duke of Normandy and excelled that of his other vassals only in his control of Church offices and revenues. However, he was an opponent of reform, and he spent several years under excommunication for moral lapses including a bigamous marital adventure with the wife of the count of Anjou.

These problems might have undermined the French monarchy, as similar disputes between the papacy and the German king had weakened that central power, but Philip was brought into submission to the Church, and gave up his illicit wife, in 1107. The principal figure in this rapprochement between the king and the Church was Philip's son Louis, who had been associated with the old king as co-ruler. Louis VI (1108–1137) inherited his father's corpulence—he was called "the Fat" and had to be hoisted onto his horse in later years—but he was not a lethargic man. He allied himself with the reformers in the Roman and French churches and in that way was able to extend his power. Louis beat the petty barons and vassals of the Île-de-France into submission; he was the first Capetian able to exert his authority over the royal domain with complete effectiveness, and also the first to make royal power felt elsewhere in the realm.

Louis VI spent twenty-five years, with short interruptions, in actual hostilities with Henry I. The French king suffered two major reverses, but at the end of the reign the balance of power abruptly shifted when the duke of Aquitaine entrusted to Louis the marriage of his daughter and heiress, Eleanor. Eleanor of Aquitaine was promptly married to Louis VII, who had already been crowned king in accordance with Capetian policy. The Capetian monarchs became for the first time the greatest feudal lords in the realm, since Eleanor's dowry was the duchy itself, one-third of the territory of medieval France.

Louis VII (1137–1180) had been the second son of the royal family and had been destined for a career in the Church. When his older brother died, he was taken from Saint Denis, the royal monastery near Paris where he was being raised, and crowned king. But Louis was not trained for the kingship. He had neither the physique nor the toughmindedness to face men brutalized from childhood by training in knighthood. His marriage gave him a better position than any of his predecessors, but he was never able to take advantage of its potential. He succeeded his father a few months after the wedding was celebrated and began a reign in which Eleanor's interests were to play a significant role. Although the marriage had been politically motivated, Louis

One of the great sculptors of Chartres Cathedral portrayed King Louis VII and his queen, Eleanor of Aquitaine. This work must have been done around 1150 because it is difficult to imagine the artist having preserved the royal couple in stone after their divorce in 1152.

soon fell passionately in love with his wife. He often seemed to place her interests above his own as king. He engaged in military expeditions in Poitiers and far-off Toulouse. He permitted Eleanor and her sister to bring him into conflict with the count of Champagne and with Abbot Bernard of Clairvaux, then the most powerful monastic leader in Christendom. He even took Eleanor with him on the Second Crusade (1147–1149). The Crusade proved a failure for Louis in more ways than one. Eleanor was rumored to have dallied along the way with her cousin, and the couple separated. Papal intervention on the return trip brought them together for a while, but once back in France, Eleanor and Louis agreed in 1152 to secure an annulment on grounds of consanguinity, which was a flimsy excuse for incompatibility, since they had been married for fifteen years, had two daughters, and had had their marriage blessed by the pope.

If Louis' course of action had been determined by reasons of state rather than by his emotions, he would never have let Eleanor go. With the annulment Louis lost Aquitaine, and within two months Eleanor rushed into matrimony with Henry Plantagenet, count of Anjou, son of the late Count Geoffrey and of Matilda of England. By his father's recent conquest Henry was already duke of Normandy, and by his mother's perseverance he was about to become king of England. Now he became duke of Aquitaine in right of his wife, and the balance of feudal politics once more shifted in favor of the Capetians' hereditary enemy and greatest vassal. For Eleanor, also, it was quite a change. She presented to her new husband not only three daughters but five sons. Louis' second wife bore him two more daughters. His third marriage was more successful both politically and dynastically, for it allied the powerful counts of Blois and Champagne with the Capetian house, and it produced the longed-for heir, Philip II.

In spite of the loss of Aquitaine, Louis VII's long reign was surprisingly successful. At the end of his reign, the monarchy was stronger than ever, which has puzzled some historians, since he was neither a flamboyant empire-builder like Roger of Sicily nor a brilliant administrator like Henry II of England. Louis was a conscientious king, who chose able civil servants, the most distinguished of whom was Suger (d. 1151), abbot of Saint Denis, who was regent during the king's absence on the Second Crusade. Louis protected the Church and encouraged trade and the development of urban liberties, but the growing prosperity of France and its greater tranquility was hardly his personal creation. Conditions during the second half of the twelfth century supported a strong monarchy. The growing towns looked to the king as the guarantor of their freedom to pursue their commercial activities outside the traditional restraints of feudalism. The ecclesiastical reform movement made the king protector of his kingdom's churches and made the churches effective supporters of the monarchy. At the same time that these developments weakened the tendency toward feudal localism and independence, the success of the great dukes and counts in consolidating their own power reduced the number of those with whom the king had to contend. Accidents of succession, marriage, and war could, and eventually did, bring large blocks of territory into the control of the monarchy. The great magnates had done the preliminary work of destroying the resistance of petty nobles against centralized authority and government. Thus even a colorless man like Louis VII could preside over a growing central government.

## Henry II and the "Plantagenet Empire"

Henry Plantagenet was more ruthless than Louis VII: when Eleanor caused him trouble, he captured her and kept her under guard for the last ten years of his life. Politically, he was one of the most astute and effective of the medieval monarchs. A close look at his career shows the limits of what a genius for government could accomplish in the late twelfth century, for he created a monarchy of enduring strength and an empire that crumbled soon after his death.

When he was crowned king of England, at the age of twenty-one, Henry II (1154–1189) issued a coronation charter confirming "to God and to Holy Church, and to all my barons and vassals" the liberties and customs granted by his grandfather Henry I. He omitted any mention of Stephen, indicating that he intended to restore the kingdom to the conditions existing before the Anarchy. His first task was to win full recognition in England, where the civil wars had left the baronage badly divided and largely independent of royal power. The lords had been successful in trading their support for one or the other side for concessions of fiefs and royal rights. Henry spent thirteen months on the island establishing his authority and beginning the arduous task of making it effective. He then returned to the Continent to face the monumental problems of controlling Normandy, Anjou, and Aquitaine while dealing with the French king.

As duke of Normandy Henry also ruled Maine, as count of Anjou he ruled Touraine, and as duke of Aquitaine he was suzerain of the counties of Poitou and Auvergne and had claims, once pursued by Louis VII, to the overlordship of Toulouse. His territories stretched from the Scottish border to the Pyrenees, a congeries of dominions often called the Angevin Empire. The phrase is convenient but misleading, for there was nothing Angevin about these holdings. The designation Plantagenet Empire has the advantage of emphasizing that Henry's realm was a family creation. Although Henry Plantagenet's highest title was king of England, he was above all a French feudal lord. He could not speak English, and he considered England valuable primarily because it gave him the prestige of a royal title to balance against that of his Continental lord, the king of France, and because England provided revenues with which to pursue Continental ambitions. Except for the German emperor, Henry was the greatest ruler in Europe. But the Plantagenet empire was bound together by only one real tie, the personal allegiance of the feudal lords of England, the two duchies, and the several counties to Henry. There was no common government, no common financial or judicial system, and no common linguistic, ethnic, or cultural tradition.

Henry's initial effort in building his "empire" was to make good his claim to the county of Toulouse, in 1159. Louis VII rushed southward to aid the count, his brother-in-law, and entered the city just before Henry's armies could surround it. Henry did not dare to attack his own feudal lord within

The "Plantagenet Empire" and France, ca. 1155

the walls because he could not afford to set such an example to his vassals. The main result of his campaign was to stimulate the French king to make the most effective intervention in southern France since the later Carolingians. Henry's next objective was to annex the Norman Vexin, on the border between the royal domain and Normandy, over which kings and dukes had quarreled for two centuries. The strategic area was then held in trust by three custodians as the prospective dowry of one of Louis' daughters, who had been betrothed to Henry's four-year-old son in 1158. Thwarted at Toulouse, Henry now resorted to diplomatic sharp practice. The two infants were married in 1160, thus delivering the Vexin to Henry's control as his two-year-old daughter-in-law's dowry. Louis protested in vain. Henry further enlarged his empire in 1171, when his son Geoffrey became count of Brittany, thus securing control of the lower Loire and protecting Henry's north–south communications.

Henry's grandiose plans on the Continent will never fully be known because they were not allowed to mature. His influence extended beyond the Pyrenees, into Italy, and east of the Rhine, in each case through marriage alliances involving his daughters and the sons of ruling houses. His relations with the Norman kingdom of Sicily were especially close. Henry's enemies believed he was also trying to purchase the support of the northern Italian communes for some unknown scheme, perhaps for the union of Sicily with his own dominions including northern Italy, or perhaps for nothing less than the imperial crown. Louis VII and Henry's own family were responsible for the failure of his plans. Eleanor's marriages had taken her from one extreme to the other, from the monkish Louis to the profligate Henry, whose only concession to his wife's feelings was to keep his infidelities relatively unpublicized. Eleanor took her revenge by stirring up discontent among their children. Young Henry, crowned king of England in 1170 in imitation of the Capetian practice, did homage to Louis for the Continental possessions he was to inherit (Normandy, Maine, and Anjou), while his brothers Richard and Geoffrey did homage for Aquitaine and Brittany, the lands assigned to them. The grievance of each was that his authority was only nominal. Eleanor and Louis encouraged them into open rebellion. But Eleanor's resentment and Louis' opportunism were only part of the cause for the great rebellion that erupted in 1173.

Henry had persisted through twenty years of conflict to rebuild monarchical power in England and to maintain control of his Continental dominions. In England, he had suppressed the lawlessness of the nobility, forced the destruction of illegal castles, and reactivated royal governmental institutions. The Exchequer resumed its semiannual sessions. The regular revenues from the shires and from the royal courts, plus the extraordinary revenues arising from feudal incidents or special taxes, were again recorded on the tally sticks and parchment rolls. The justices in eyre became a regular feature of royal government and began to develop a law common to all England. At the same time, Henry made slow but steady progress in efforts to gain effective control of the sheriffs, who bore the principal burden of day-to-day royal government and who had become largely autonomous during the reign of Stephen. By 1170 he felt strong enough to react to widespread complaints about extortions and malpractices by the sheriffs and other officials. Henry suspended all the sheriffs from office and instituted a great inquest into the grievances—the so-called Inquest of Sheriffs. This semijudicial investigation even went beyond the Domesday survey in asserting royal control not only over the sheriffs and their bailiffs but also over the barons and their officials. Henry had made himself the champion of the people oppressed by corrupt officials and aristocrats, and he naturally acquired many baronial enemies in the process.

Henry threatened the position and traditional role of the baronage in other ways. From the beginning of his reign, he relied on mercenary troops rather than on the traditional feudal levies. He found the hired troops better in every way: the soldiers would stay in his service for as long as he could pay them, and thus he could plan and execute long campaigns (his vassals were obligated to serve in his army only for good cause and for a limited period); the mercenary soldiers could be welded into a better fighting unit that could be effectively controlled. By the later twelfth century, feudal lords were more interested in developing the economic and political potential of their fiefs than in performing military service for the king, whose interests often were squarely opposed to theirs. Thus Henry encouraged, and the lords appear to have welcomed, the practice of commuting military service by a money payment called scutage. The length and extent of Henry's wars against rebellious nobles in his widespread domains placed a constant strain on his liquid wealth and made him seek ways to increase his revenues. In 1166 he ordered an inquiry into the number of knights enfeoffed by the great barons of England so that he could match the amount of their scutage payment to the number of their subvassals. In addition, the king collected a lucrative tax from the growing towns. Here, as in the matter of scutage, he challenged the position and affected the welfare of the great feudatories, who often considered the towns as part of their fiefs.

All these measures contributed to the tensions that erupted in the rebellion of 1173 to 1174. If the rebellion had been well coordinated, it would have broken the Plantagenet Empire into its constituent parts. Henry was confronted with uprisings in England, Normandy, Brittany, and Aquitaine. But many vassals remained loyal, as did the officials of his several governments, so that Henry was able to crush the rebels separately. The sons were forgiven and treated generously, but Henry was ruthless in destroying the private castles of lords who had supported his sons, while he repaired and strengthened the royal castles. As for Eleanor, she was kept under detention as long as Henry lived.

In an age in which the strongest political bond was still the personal relationship between vassal and lord, Henry's greatest monument was the creation of a central government in England that could operate effectively in the absence of the king. The most important product of this government was the common law of England, which was that part of all the laws and customs of England administered, according to uniform procedures, by the king's courts. Since only the king's courts had jurisdiction throughout the realm, the procedure and the laws recognized by the royal courts became common to the whole of England. Justice administered in the king's courts was less expensive, more rapid, and more equitable than the justice obtainable from courts of local or private jurisdiction. Because royal justice was better justice, the common law grew, and the diverse laws and customs administered by feudal and local courts declined.

The three principal means by which Henry II built the common law were the itinerant justices, the sworn inquest, or jury, and royal writs. None of these was new, but the way Henry employed them together was new and very effective. What had previously been only an occasional use of justices representing the king in the counties became, after 1166, regular and frequent. In that year Henry issued the Assize of Clarendon, instructing his itinerant justices on the administration and enforcement of criminal law. The most important provision concerned the sworn inquest of lawful men of each locality who were commanded to present or state on oath to the itinerant justices whether any person in their neighborhood was suspected of having committed a crime. This new procedure replaced the ancient appeal of felony, according to which a victim or the victim's family brought the malefactor to justice. The appeal had many defects. First, the crime itself often rendered the victim or his family incapable of bringing the criminal to justice. This was particularly true because the appeal of felony often led to trial by battle. The injured party presented himself or herself to the judge, who could be a baronial or royal official, and made formal complaint against the criminal. The accusation was not taken seriously unless the accuser offered to prove the allegation by his body—that is, by battle. Under normal circumstances, therefore, women and minors could not appeal a felony. People incapable of offering proof by battle were forced to rely on the aid of their relatives, who were often reluctant to risk battle, to prosecute the case. Henry's new procedure, called a jury of presentment, resolved this problem by founding the prosecution of crime on the fact of the crime rather than on the capacity of the injured party. Second, the old appeal procedure rested on the idea that crime was a matter of concern primarily, if not exclusively, to the criminal and victim. Henry approached the problem of crime from a different point of view. He saw crime as a breach of the king's peace and as a general threat to the peace and safety of the kingdom. Thus he took steps, embodied in his new procedures, to ensure that criminals were brought to justice whether or not their victims could prosecute them. The problem of doing justice to criminals loomed large in Henry's dispute with Thomas à Becket, to be discussed below.

The essence of the inquest was the oath taken by its members to speak the truth; hence, they are called a jury (*jurati,* those sworn), and their statement is a verdict (*veredictum,* something truly said). The person presented or accused of a crime was required to stand trial. In the twelfth century this usually meant that he was put to the ordeal of cold water, a procedure in which the accused was trussed and lowered into a tub of water that had been solemnly purified by a priest. Because the consecrated water was believed to receive the pure and reject the sinful, if the accused sank, he was innocent (and hauled out before drowned), but if he floated, he was guilty. Henry did not challenge these old forms of judicial proof. His concern was with the identification of those suspected of crime, and his contribution was the creation of the grand jury procedure for accomplishing this task. Like his contemporaries, the king assumed that once the suspect was brought to justice, that is, to court, the old forms of proof by ordeal would ensure that justice was done. Nonetheless, as the number of cases brought before royal courts increased, and as judicial recordkeeping improved, it became clear that the ordeal often did not lead to a proper result. Too many criminals were escaping punishment after passing through the ordeal successfully. Henry himself demonstrated suspicion about the effectiveness of the old procedures by requiring acquitted persons to abjure the realm if they were persons of ill repute. In the thirteenth century, judges began to use the inquest procedure to replace ordeals when it seemed likely a jury of local men might be the best device for finding the truth. This innovation led to the development of the petit jury, which tried cases presented by the grand jury.

Henry himself had already decided to use the petit jury procedure in certain "common pleas," or civil suits, between two individuals concerning property rights. This kind of jury had been used occasionally, but Henry II extended to all freemen what his predecessors had infrequently granted as a favor. The king involved himself in property cases because of their interest to him as the feudal suzerain rather than as the keeper of the peace. His reforms embody some important characteristics of medieval legal institutions. Since property disputes often ended with one party violently seizing the property in question, Henry created jury procedures for determining which party deserved to possess the property. This question could be decided easily and swiftly because the right of possession belonged to the person who had held the land immediately before the dispute commenced. Thus the royal justices were instructed to call a jury of local men, called an assize, to answer the simple question: Did the plaintiff or his father, whose heir he is, possess the land at such and such a time? The jury had to answer either yes or no, without qualification, based on its knowledge of local affairs. Qualifications like "No he did not possess the land because he leased it to the defendant," touched on the right to, as opposed to the possession of, the land. Questions of right were usually tried in feudal courts, although as feudal suzerain the king could entertain appeals from plaintiffs in such courts.

By the end of Henry II's reign the government was issuing the writ of right, whereby any claimant could secure a hearing in his feudal lord's court at the lord's risk of contempt of the royal command to do justice. If this failed to procure justice, another writ was available to transfer the case to a royal court. This development favored the plaintiff, initially, but it created a legal rule that favored the defendant, "no man is compelled to answer for any free tenement except at the command of the king." Judgment of the case always followed a trial, which in a suit involving title to property was normally the judicial combat. The two litigants or their hired champions simply fought out the issue, the victor being adjudged in the right. Judges doubted the real justice of such an appeal to skill and force, and Henry II shared this view. In 1179 he instituted the Grand Assize, by which any freeman could defend his proprietary right on the evidence of a jury of knights rather than submit his case to the uncertain outcome of a duel. The Grand Assize and the possessory assizes were the origin of modern trial by jury, but the medieval jury gave a verdict based on the knowledge of the jurors, while the modern jury's verdict is essentially a judgment of evidence admitted in the trial.

The writ of right was part of the writ system by which litigants entered the royal courts. Henry's legislation established several writs, each designed for one type of litigation. A writ was simply a written command the king addressed to one of his officials directing that the plaintiff be heard. Writs had long been used in administrative matters (they were analogous to memoranda, although they contained a command), and Henry now introduced them into the legal procedure. Their wording was standardized, and they were bought for a nominal fee. The importance of the writs consisted in their flexibility. Once the writs became established as the means of presenting a case before the king's courts, plaintiffs pressed the chancery, which administered the system, to issue writs for cases not covered by the original legislation. With devices like the writ of right and its derivatives, the king extended his control over baronial courts by ensuring that they did justice. To prevent litigious people from using the writs to badger their enemies into submission by instituting suit after suit, the law provided that any plaintiff who lost his case was to be amerced—that is, placed at the king's mercy. If the king or his justice thought the suit honestly pleaded and pursued, the amercement might amount to a small fine. If the suit was a bit of mischief, the plaintiff was in serious trouble. Finally, it is important to recognize that Henry's ingenious innovations simply created a royal procedure for handling cases in which the rights to be protected and the remedies to be given were established by customary law, often local in scope. The king did not interfere with the rights and privileges of his subjects because one of the longest lived legacies of the old Germanic communities was the idea that customary law established a person's rights and obligations. But even with these restrictions, the royal courts became the vehicle for legal development in the realm because they were not absolutely bound by custom and thus were the forum in which conflicting or differing customs could be harmonized and new remedies devised.

By the later years of Henry's reign every freeman could secure protection of his possession of property, or guarantee a hearing of his petition of right. This security affected less than one-half of the male population, however, because villeins and Jews were not considered freemen. Single women could gain entry to the courts, but married women were considered to be united with their husbands in body and soul and thus could not act independently in judicial matters. The converse of this doctrine, which slowly was repudiated during the next few centuries, was that husbands were responsible for bringing their wives into court. Court records of the thirteenth century indicate that many marriages dissolved in medieval England and that husbands often had difficulty finding their wives, much less getting them to go before a royal justice. *De facto* divorce seems to have been common in the Middle Ages, if other societies were similar to England in that respect.

From his first days as king, Henry II planned to recover royal rights over the Church, which had been allowed to lapse under Stephen. During the Anarchy the organization of the Church had been strengthened because of closer relations with the papacy and because of the growth of the canon law. The jurisdiction of the ecclesiastical courts had been enlarged to include the trial of cases earlier restricted to royal courts. Henry waited until the death of the archbishop provided him the opportunity to nominate a man of his own choosing, with whom he could cooperate as William the Conqueror had cooperated with Lanfranc. The king's choice was Thomas à Becket, who had been the royal chancellor for eight years, a faithful and able servant of the crown. "Tom O'London," as his enemies derisively referred to his obscure origins, was a nonnoble professional administrator. Having gained rapid preferment in the household of the late archbishop and then in the royal government, he was still only in minor orders when in 1162 he was ordained priest and consecrated archbishop on the same day. But as primate of England (1162–1170), Becket was transformed. From the stalwart supporter of royal policy he became the ardent champion of the Church. Henry was disillusioned and furious with this unexpected change. In addition to the conflict between royal and ecclesiastical interests, there was a collision between two forceful and antagonistic personalities.

Becket's gratuitously aggressive conduct embarrassed the pope and lost him the support of a majority of the English bishops. Henry took advantage of the situation to draw up a precise statement of the customs governing relations between the Church and the Anglo-Norman kings. This statement, the Constitutions of Clarendon (1164), was approved by all the bishops and barons, including Archbishop Thomas. But then Becket changed his mind. A bitter quarrel led to the archbishop's flight from England and protracted exile. A reconciliation of sorts took place in 1170, but the main points in dispute were unresolved. Most important was the issue of criminous clerks, members of the clergy convicted of crimes in an ecclesiastical court. Henry did not claim the right to try them, for he recognized the exclusive jurisdiction of ecclesiastical courts over the clergy. But he did claim the right to punish criminous clerks after they had been degraded from their clerical status, and he demanded that they be degraded. Henry argued that he could not permit dangerous men to roam free in his kingdom if he was to fulfill his obligation to keep the peace. His claim rested on the old conflict between the king's right to rule and the Church's freedom, and as such, it was a legacy of the liberty the Church had won in the Investiture Controversy. Becket argued that degradation itself was sufficient punishment. He based his stance on theology and canon law, claiming that Henry's formula for doing justice in the cases of criminous clerks violated both the Church's exclusive jurisdiction over clerical persons and the divine prohibition of double punishment for one crime.

Despite the reconciliation, the archbishop's intransigence angered Henry. When news was brought to him that Becket's first act on returning to Canterbury was to excommunicate his enemies, the king flew into a rage. Four of his household knights took Henry's threats literally and hastened to Canterbury, where they murdered the archbishop before the altar of his cathedral. After this martyrdom of Saint Thomas of Canterbury (the archbishop was canonized within three years), Henry had to compromise all the outstanding issues, including that of criminous clerks. Henceforth, the jurisdiction, including punishment, of the ecclesiastical courts was final over all who could successfully plead "benefit of clergy."

Henry's differences with the Church were settled by a general agreement with the pope in 1176, and in the next four years Henry was able to consolidate his position in the British Isles. Scotland had become a fief of the English crown after the Scottish king's unsuccessful participation in the great rebellion of 1173. Henry's relations with the most powerful Welsh princes were cordial. And Ireland, whose conquest was inaugurated by some barons with royal approval in 1169, was now firmly under royal control. Henry had long been interested in Ireland, and in 1155 he had received from Adrian IV (the only English pope) a bull approving his plans for the conquest of the island. Taking advantage of the intervention of English barons in Irish affairs, Henry spent the winter of 1171–72 in Dublin and received the homage of most of the Irish provincial kings and princes. From this point on, the Anglo-Norman baronage was established in Ireland. They were the forbears of a new class of Anglo-Irish, "English to the Irish, and Irish to the English," who were to be at the heart of the continuing conflict between the two islands. In 1177 Henry created his youngest son, John, "lord of Ireland," and John succeeded in establishing an Anglo-Norman administration that lasted until 1333.

The last years of Henry's long reign were beset with difficulties, due to the jealousies that divided his sons and to the ambitions that occasionally united them against their father. In 1183 young King Henry joined Geoffrey in attacking Richard, but young Henry's untimely death ended that threat. Then Geoffrey died "of a surfeit of eels" in 1186, removing another source of discord. Meanwhile Louis VII's successor, Philip II Augustus (1180–1223), was stirring up the sons' hatred for their father. This was not difficult when it became known that Henry was scheming to disinherit Richard and

This twelfth-century illumination is an early, perhaps the earliest, pictorial representation of the murder of Thomas à Becket in his cathedral. It illustrates a letter of John of Salisbury that describes the event.

secure the succession for his favorite son, John. In 1189 Richard led a rebellion supported by Philip Augustus. The king was defeated, but he was already broken, embittered, and dying. The final humiliation of his great career came on his deathbed, when he learned that even John had joined Richard and Philip against him.

## The Rebuilding of the German Monarchy: Frederick Barbarossa, the Papacy, and the Lombard League

Henry V's reign was born in the civil war (1104–1106) that resulted from his rebellion against his father, and it was disturbed by civil war after the crisis of 1111. When Henry returned to Germany after receiving the imperial crown from the defeated Paschal II, he faced opposition in Germany no less impressive than the pope did within the Church. The ecclesiastics who attacked Paschal objected to his concession of the right of investiture to Henry in April 1111. The bishops and magnates who became opponents of Henry in Germany objected to the earlier agreement of February, when Henry had acceded to a compromise that would have disrupted the German political establishment. Just prior to going to Rome in late 1110, Henry had appointed his chancellor, Adalbert of Saarbrücken, to be archbishop of Mainz, the primate of Germany. Henry II of England might have learned from the experience of his mother's first husband. Henry V completed the elevation of Adalbert after returning from Italy in late 1111, hoping thereby to gain strict control over the German Church. Adalbert, like Becket fifty years later, took his new position seriously; he joined his colleagues, and became their leader, against a king who had recently tried to betray the German Church. Thus the period from 1112 to 1122 was a difficult one for Henry, and Germany suffered from almost continuous civil war. Although the civil strife ended after the Concordat of Worms, Henry presided over an uneasy peace because Adalbert and many other ecclesiastics in Germany opposed the compromise it contained. Henry's early death in 1125, without a direct heir, threw the empire into disorder. Some nobles preferred Henry V's nephew, Frederick of Hohenstaufen, duke of Swabia, but many opposed him because he seemed too powerful and too close to his uncle's policies. Led by Adalbert and Archbishop Frederick of Cologne, the magnates elected the devout and popular duke of Saxony, Lothair (1125–1137). Lothair was faced by an immediate rebellion led by Frederick of Swabia and Frederick's brother Conrad of Franconia, and he never firmly established his authority in Germany. The intermittent civil war also prevented him from giving sufficient attention to the imperial territories and affairs in Italy. He visited Italy only twice and did little there except receive his imperial coronation in 1133.

Lothair was a capable man faced by an extremely difficult situation. Recognizing the need for long-term planning to shore up his position, he arranged a marriage between his only child, a daughter, and Henry the Proud, duke of Bavaria, who thus became heir of the duchy of Saxony by right of his wife. As a result of this marriage, Henry became the most powerful lord in the kingdom, as well as becoming Lothair's successor to the kingship. When the king died in 1137, however, the magnates were not interested in adding the royal authority to the power of the one man in the kingdom who might make it effective. They turned their attention back to the Hohenstaufens. Frederick of Swabia had died (succeeded in his duchy by his son Frederick), so the princes elected Conrad of Franconia. The first act of Conrad III (1137–1152) was to attack his great vassal, Henry the Proud, who found himself deprived of his two duchies. Civil war broke out once again. In Germany the two parties were called Welfs (after Henry the Proud's Bavarian ancestors and family name) and Waiblings (after a favorite residence of the Hohenstaufens at Waiblingen). In this early period Welfs generally represented ecclesiastical independence under the papacy plus feudal particularism, while the Waiblings stood for control of the Church and a strong imperial government. The struggle in Germany had its counterpart south of the Alps, among the allies of each party, where the Italian form of the names, Guelph and Ghibelline, has become the English usage. Later, Guelph and Ghibelline were to become merely the names of opposing factions without much reference to the original principles on which the parties were built.

Under Conrad the central authority was almost extinguished in many parts of Germany and most of Italy. He was the first German king since Henry the Fowler not to make at least one visit to Italy to receive the imperial crown. The Guelphs made steady progress, marked by the restoration in 1142 of the duchy of Saxony to Henry the Proud's ten-year-old son, Henry the Lion. Conrad, like his predecessor Lothair, had some success on the eastern frontier, where he reasserted the feudal suzerainty of the German crown over Bohemia and Poland, but the German conquest of the territory of Slavic and other eastern peoples was primarily the work of local lords. This conquest led to colonization by Germans and the building of commercial centers, such as the town of Lubeck on the Baltic, and of new feudal states where the local autonomy of the margrave (marcher lord) was often almost complete. Conrad could not participate effectively in this *Drang nach Osten* because he was tied down by incessant revolts. It was as much to escape these struggles in Germany as it was from a sense of piety or Christian duty that the king joined Louis VII on the Second Crusade (1147–1149), where the two monarchs conspicuously failed to accomplish anything.

When Conrad died in 1152, Henry the Lion was potentially the most powerful man in Germany, but he was too young to exercise royal power. If he succeeded Conrad, the civil wars would continue unabated because the Hohenstaufens had an adult and able claimant in Conrad's nephew, Frederick of Swabia. Thus Frederick Barbarossa (he had a red beard) became the man of choice. Although Henry the Lion was too young to wage a new civil war, he was powerful enough to put a brake on Frederick's ambitions. In addition, although Frederick was a Hohenstaufen, his mother was the sister of Henry the Proud, and it was hoped that this relationship might ameliorate the enmity of the two sides. Thus the political situation at the time of Frederick's election was complex, and his kingship rested on a narrow base.

Frederick I Barbarossa (1152–1190) is a controversial figure. Some German historians have criticized him for neglecting Germany in favor of unrealistic dreams of empire and glory. Actually, Frederick did not neglect Germany; he was its strongest ruler since Henry III. Frederick's policies were apparently well planned and well executed. In Germany, his first efforts were directed toward reconciliation with the Guelphs. He confirmed the duchies of Saxony and Bavaria to his cousin Henry the Lion, and permitted the young duke to exercise almost independent authority over his duchies and in the lands he conquered and colonized east of the Elbe. Frederick was establishing a feudal policy in these arrangements, but unlike Conrad II, the first German emperor to employ such a policy, Frederick hoped to gain a firm claim to feudal suzerainty over his dukes instead of seeking direct feudal relationships with the lesser magnates. As long as Henry the Lion and Frederick cooperated, peace was practically assured in Germany. For twenty-five years the arrangement worked fairly well, although the Saxon nobles were restive under Henry's strict rule. Then his marriage to the daughter of Henry II of England allied Duke Henry with a ruler who was increasingly antagonistic to Frederick's policy toward the popes. Finally, the duke refused to assist Frederick in his most difficult campaign in Italy. The emperor now resolved to crush his overmighty subject, and in 1179 he allowed charges to be brought against Henry the Lion by his discontented vassals. When the duke refused to appear in court, his fiefs were judged to be forfeited, and he was condemned to three years' exile. Saxony and Bavaria were broken up and distributed to Frederick's supporters. This redistribution of fiefs marked an important step in the development of German particularism, for it established the principle that, unlike the kings of France and England, the German monarch could not add forfeited fiefs to the royal domain. The outcome of Frederick's victory also exposed the crucial flaw in any feudal policy followed in Germany, for although Henry the Lion was deprived of his fiefs and even forced into temporary exile in Normandy, he remained the richest man in Germany. The majority of his lands were allodial (that is, his by private rather than feudal right), and Frederick could not touch them. Thus while Henry's fall severely weakened the power of the Guelphs in Germany, his family continued to play an important political role for a generation after his death in 1195.

The case of Henry the Lion shows that Frederick had developed his authority in Germany along feudal lines and that this authority was limited because feudalism did not determine the social, political, and legal structure of the kingdom. The king himself had apparently recognized these limitations and had sought to establish himself on an independent power base within the kingdom. When he succeeded to the throne, he had fairly good control of his own duchy of Swabia, but this territory was isolated in a corner of the kingdom and did not give Frederick the advantages the Île-de-France provided his contemporary Louis VII of France. Frederick decided that he could control Germany only by asserting his rights and powers as emperor and that in other parts of the empire lay the foundations of his monarchy. In Germany, Frederick was isolated, but in the empire, he held a central position, and he acted quickly to extend that power base when he acquired the kingdom of Burgundy by marrying the heiress of its most important county. By 1156 he had consolidated his authority in Burgundy. He had already moved to secure the imperial crown on which his imperial policy rested. This involved Frederick in the complicated political situation in Italy and led to renewed enmity between the papacy and the imperial government.

Conditions in Italy had changed vastly since the days of Henry V. In the cities, the communes, once rural associations transplanted into the cities and directed against the urban lords, had developed into merchant associations directed against the same powers but allied with different interests. The eleventh-century communes had been allied with the papacy against the imperial bishops and other magnates who controlled the towns. After the Concordat of Worms, the papacy no longer had reason to contest the power of the bishops, and thus continued communal opposition to bishops destroyed the alliance between the papacy and communes. In the 1140s the papacy itself was the victim of a communal revolution led by Arnold of Brescia, who attacked the Church's wealth and power. Arnold had been condemned as a heretic, but the papacy could not capture him. To understand the papacy's situation, the history of the reform papacy after the Concordat of Worms must be understood.

Pope Calixtus II achieved his compromise with Henry V in the face of opposition from a group in the papal court. The leader of the opposition was Cardinal Peter Pierleoni, who became a cardinal in 1111 or 1112, the first member of his family since Gregory VI to enter the higher echelons of the Church hierarchy. Peter and his supporters disapproved of the Concordat for complex reasons, not the least of which was that it was the expression of the new French element in the political framework of the Holy See. In order to strengthen his political position in the papal court, Calixtus appointed a Frenchman named Haimeric as chancellor of the Holy See and then supported Haimeric's program of building a party of cardinals to counter the power of the Pierleoni faction. Calixtus also induced the other great

The Medieval Empire, ca. 1190

propapal family in Rome, the Frangipani, into opposition to the Pierleoni. When Calixtus died in 1124, Haimeric was not yet able to elect his man as pope. He demonstrated a hardheaded political sense by bringing Leo Frangipani and an armed band into the electoral meeting and forcing the cardinals to choose his candidate, Honorius II. Haimeric had judged that the Pierleoni faction would not react to his power play, and he judged correctly. In the next six years, he and Honorius built a strong party of cardinals in the Holy See while destroying enemies elsewhere in the Church. When Honorius died in 1130, the Pierleoni faction was prepared for Haimeric's trickery, and the two sides stalemated. Haimeric's candidate, Innocent II (1130–1143), and Peter Pierleoni (who took the name Anaclet II) each received twenty-two votes; the schism was on.

The two parties differed greatly. The Innocentians tended to be French or North Italian and to be younger than the Anacletians, who were mostly from Rome and central or southern Italy. The Innocentians developed from a party that supported the Concordat of Worms, were conciliatory toward the emperor, and considered themselves to be the reform-minded members of the reform papacy, which in their minds had fallen once again under the control of local Roman factions. Witness the power of the Pierleoni. The Anacletians considered themselves successors of the reformers, heirs of Gregory VII, and were supported by the majority of the papal bureaucracy, out of which most of them had risen. In political policy, the Innocentians sought the aid of the French, English, and German monarchies, while the Anacletians turned to the traditional allies of the reform papacy, the Normans of southern Italy. Roger II of Sicily (1127–1154) took the opportunity that the papal schism gave him to raise himself to the kingship. In return for the promise of support, Anaclet II crowned Roger king of Sicily, Apulia, and Capua. In the meantime, Innocent II and Haimeric had enlisted the aid of Abbot Bernard of Clairvaux, who soon brought the kings of France, England, and Germany into Innocent's camp. Nonetheless, Roger's powerful support of Anaclet maintained the schism until Anaclet died in 1137. Within a year, the Anacletian party collapsed, and Innocent took possession of the Roman Church. The papacy was now controlled by men who were conciliatory toward the northern kings, including the emperor. It is not surprising that the first *patricius* (ruler) of the antipapal Roman commune established in 1144 was Anaclet's nephew Jordan Pierleoni.

The victorious party established itself firmly in the papacy and in 1145 elected as pope a monastic son of Bernard of Clairvaux. This pope, Eugene III (1145–1153), faced the full brunt of the communal movement in Rome and often was forced into exile. His successor, Anastasius IV (1153–1154), a very old man who had spent fifty years as a papal city politician, was one of the only older men to join the Innocentians in 1130, and he was able to restore relative peace in the city for a time. He even built a papal residence next to the Pantheon (S. Maria in Rotunda) in the midst of Crescentii territory in Rome, but the palace was completely dismantled after his death. Adrian IV (1154–1159) therefore faced the renewed antipathy of the commune and had trouble maintaining himself in the city. When Frederick Barbarossa made his first Italian expedition in 1154 to 1155, the situation was ripe for an unprecedented alliance between the emperor and Adrian IV.

Each desired the removal of Arnold of Brescia: Adrian because of his attack on the Church and Frederick because of his visionary program of a renovated Senate and Roman People to replace the German emperor. Also, Frederick viewed the Norman kingdom of Sicily as an infringement on his own claims to all of Italy, while Adrian found his nominal vassal so independent and antagonistic that one of his first acts was to excommunicate the new king, William I (1154–1166), son and successor of Roger II. Finally, both pope and emperor opposed the communes of central and northern Italy.

As it turned out, Frederick and Adrian cooperated only to the extent of consigning Arnold of Brescia to the stake as a heretic. On his progress southward through Lombardy, Frederick's brutal repression of towns that did not immediately acknowledge imperial rule alarmed the pope, who was wary of an alliance with a ruler potentially more dangerous than the Norman king in the south or the communes in the north. The old question of papal versus imperial superiority was revived in dramatic fashion when Frederick arrived and was greeted formally by Adrian at Sutri, outside Rome. According to custom, the emperor was obliged to support the pope's stirrup while he alighted from his mount. Frederick would have none of it. The symbolism of such an act implied the submission of emperor to pope as groom to master. Adrian's mettle was equal to the occasion. After a protracted delay filled with last-minute negotiations, Frederick performed the customary ceremonial, muttering loudly for all to hear, "Petrum, non Hadrianum" ("For Saint Peter, not for Adrian"). In this atmosphere Frederick was crowned emperor, and after bludgeoning the Roman mob for an attack on his troops he hastily retired north of the Alps with his by then malaria-ridden army.

Relations between the emperor and the pope were further embittered at the great imperial diet of 1157 held at Besançon in Burgundy. A letter from the pope protesting the mistreatment of a Danish archbishop returning from Rome through Frederick's dominions was presented by Adrian's chancellor, Roland. It was translated aloud by the imperial chancellor for the sake of the nobles who did not understand Latin. The pope reminded Barbarossa that the Roman Church had "most willingly conferred upon you the distinction of the imperial crown," and assured the emperor that he would rejoice if "your excellency had received from our hand even greater *beneficia.*" These were dangerous, because ambiguous, words. In the conservative language of formal charters, the words *confer a benefice* constituted a technical legal phrase meaning "grant a fief" as from a lord to his vassal; while in classical or literary Latin the term *beneficium* retained its general sense of kindness or gift. The imperial chancellor, whose duties in the government included the writing of charters, translated the phrase in its technical sense, thus implying the feudal lordship of pope over emperor. This threw the diet into an uproar. Cardinal Roland made matters even worse by asking, "From whom else, then, does the emperor hold the Empire, if not from the pope?" Frederick had to protect Roland from violence, and although the pope later disavowed any intention to make the imperial crown analogous to a feudal grant, the incident fed Frederick's concern about papal claims to the imperial authority.

Frederick made his position clear in the same year. In 1157 documents issued by the imperial chancery began to refer to the *sacrum imperium* (Holy Empire), borrowing a term from the Roman law, to which Frederick turned more and more for the ideology of his authority. The emperor had contacted the great Roman legal scholars in the north Italian law schools, and four of them had accompanied him to Rome in 1154. In addition to its Roman law meaning, the phrase *sacrum imperium* called forth the biblical foundations of royal authority so important in the ideology of medieval monarchies. When representatives of the Roman senate had asked Barbarossa from whom he held the empire, he had responded "From God alone!"

The year after the Diet of Besançon, Frederick crossed the Alps with the greatest army ever to accompany an emperor on an Italian expedition. In 1158 he held the Diet of Roncaglia, in northern Italy. Here the emperor solemnly claimed all the *regalia* that had slipped from his predecessors' hands either through usurpation or by grants extracted from earlier rulers as the price of support. The *regalia* thus claimed were all based on Roman law: customs and tolls, control of coinage and mints, taxation, appointment of governing officials, and general jurisdiction. This program was a deathblow to the communes' aspirations for independence. Frederick appointed a governor called the *podestà* for each commune and proceeded to collect a large revenue. Most of the communes of Lombardy now put aside their disputes and prepared to resist. Milan was the leader of the anti-imperial communes. It took Frederick three years to subdue Milan; he then punished the Milanese by expelling all the citizens, tearing down the walls, and razing the city to the ground. (That Frederick could do this indicates how small primitive medieval cities were compared with their modern counterparts. The walled city of Milan consisted of no more than twenty acres; nonetheless it was a great metropolis in medieval terms.) By 1161 all resistance was broken, and Frederick organized an extensive imperial domain in Lombardy whose revenues and manpower he could now use to strengthen his position in Germany and to conquer the rest of Italy.

Adrian IV died in 1159. After the events of 1155, he had changed papal policies to meet the renewed vigor of imperial government and claims. Under his aegis, Cardinal Roland arranged a new alliance between the papacy and the Normans in the south. The victory of Innocent II had broken the old policy of alliance established in 1059. Roland's assertions at Besançon had also reflected the papal attempt to re-create the political situation of the late eleventh century. Cardinal Roland was not a naive cleric expressing what he took to be a simple doctrine when he spoke up at Besançon. He was one of Europe's greatest lawyers, formerly professor of law at Bologna. He had also been a student of the great philosopher Peter Abelard. When Adrian died, Roland was the obvious choice to succeed him. He had been the architect of the pope's policy and had demonstrated the capacity to meet the needs of the new situation. He was also the last man in Rome Frederick wanted to see pope. The College of Cardinals elected Roland, but three, holdovers from an earlier era when the proimperial Innocentians had gained control of the Holy See, elected one of their number, Octavian. The ability of Octavian, who took the name Victor IV, to maintain himself against the overwhelming majority of cardinals might seem amazing, but medieval electoral law, enshrined in the decree of 1059, allowed for Octavian's claims. It stated that the election should go to him who had support from the *maior et sanior pars* (greater and wiser part) of the electorate. By *maior,* medieval lawyers meant "greater in quality," and thus an election could theoretically be won by a man supported by one great and wise man. Frederick, of course, recognized Octavian's supporters as that part of the College of Cardinals. The subsequent schism was bitter; upstanding men accused Roland, who took the name Alexander III (1159–1181), of failing to support efforts to bring the contestants together. His actions, they said, implied that he had something to hide about his elevation to the Holy See. Frederick called a council to adjudicate the claims of the two popes; Alexander and his supporters boycotted the council. Most bishops outside Germany backed Alexander, while the kings of France and England gave him tentative support. When Frederick emerged victorious in northern Italy in 1161, Alexander was forced to flee Rome, and during his exile in France (1162–1165), he won the support of Louis VII. Meanwhile, Alexander encouraged rebellion among the Lombard communes, with which the papacy had once again allied itself during the 1150s.

Military success attended Frederick's punitive expedition to Italy in 1166 to 1167, but he was prevented from undertaking an invasion of the kingdom of Sicily when pestilence struck his army. Malaria and other diseases were the common enemies of all armies, especially nonresistant northern armies, that invaded Italy in the Middle Ages. The mosquitoes of the marshes surrounding Ravenna and Rome were the peninsula's last line of defense. After Frederick retired to Germany in 1167, Alexander openly joined the communes to form the Lombard League in 1168. This federation had ample time to organize itself because Frederick was unable to resume his Italian campaigns until 1174. Even then, the emperor received only lukewarm support from his German vassals—among whom Henry the Lion was conspicuously negligent in supporting his lord. After some fruitless siege operations, a full-scale battle was fought at Legnano in 1176; the Italian army dealt Frederick's forces a decisive defeat.

The communes were now exuberant and adamant; Frederick and Alexander III were conciliatory. Within a year the pope and emperor came to terms. Frederick disavowed his most recently created antipope, and by recognizing Alexander ended the schism that had resulted from the double election of 1159. In his moment of triumph Alexander was moderate, perhaps with an eye on the Lombard League. Nothing was said about papal supremacy or about the emperor holding his empire from the pope. Alexander absolved Frederick from excommunication and agreed to recognize all the schismatic bishops and abbots who had supported the imperial side. Frederick was permitted to retain his control over the German Church. The struggle thus terminated in a papal victory: the emperor had been defeated in war and prevented from imposing his antipope on the Church. Frederick's failure was a blow at imperial prestige and a confirmation of papal independence of secular domination.

To mark the end of the schism and emphasize papal leadership of the Church, Alexander called a general council, the Third Lateran Council, in 1179. Most of the canons it enacted concerned reform of the morals and discipline of the clergy, but one of them grew directly out of the recent schism. This was a provision that election of future popes was to be by a two-thirds majority of the cardinals, the will of this majority being valid and final against any minority.

The Lombard League members felt deserted by Alexander and betrayed by a separate peace that did not guarantee their claim to independence. The pope felt justified because the communes were hostile toward their bishops, having gained their autonomy at the expense of episcopal lords as well as by usurping imperial authority. As bishops of Rome, Alexander and his successors struggled for another twenty years against the efforts of the Roman commune (or senate, as the governing body styled itself) to achieve self-government. Frederick and the Lombard League finally came to terms in the Peace of Constance of 1183. By this time it had become clear to the emperor that lenient treatment of the communes would prevent a resumption of their alliance with the papacy. The communes were granted all the essentials of self-government, including the right to elect their own officials, raise taxes, and control the judicial administration. In return, the communes recognized the suzerainty of the emperor. Their magistrates took an oath of loyalty and received their offices by investiture from the emperor or his representative.

For Frederick, only the problem of Sicily remained, and here, after he turned from war to diplomacy, he won his most notable Italian success. In the Norman kingdom, William II (1166–1189) had become involved in an ambitious scheme to conquer Constantinople and was eager for an alliance with Frederick that would aid him in that enterprise while removing the threat of invasion from the north. The alliance was effected by the marriage in 1186 of the emperor's son Henry, who was already the crowned king of both Italy and Germany, with William II's aunt, Constance, who was heiress to the Sicilian throne because William was childless. When the betrothal was negotiated, the pope had not been particularly alarmed, for William was then only thirty-one. He would have to predecease his aunt and also die childless before Constance could inherit the kingdom. Three years after the marriage, these improbable events had occurred. The keystone of papal policy for the past century and a half was destroyed. The empire was united with the kingdom of Sicily, the Papal States were surrounded, and with the alienation of the communes the papacy was deprived of any secular allies in Italy.

Frederick did not live to see his plans come to fruition. In 1187 Latin Christendom was shocked by the news of the fall of Jerusalem. The emperor and three kings (of France, England, and Sicily) led the Third Crusade (1189–1192) to rescue the Holy Land. Frederick Barbarossa, at the head of the greatest crusading army ever assembled, was on the last stage of his march across Asia Minor when he drowned in a small stream. After achieving a remarkable reconstruction of imperial government in Germany and the empire, the old ruler died while on campaign for the military interests of all Christendom.

### Suggestions for Further Reading

**Secondary Works**   For the development of kingship in the early Middle Ages, see F. Kern, *Kingship and Law* (Oxford, 1939); W. A. Chaney, *The Cult of Kingship in Anglo-Saxon England* (Manchester, 1970); and J. M. Wallace-Hadrill, *Early Germanic Kingship in England and on the Continent* (Oxford, 1971). For later development, see the works by Charles Petit-Dutaillis, R. Fawtier, and J. B. Henneman cited at the end of Chapter 8. See also E. H. Kantorowicz, "Kingship Under the Impact of Scientific Jurisprudence," in M. Clagett, G. Post, and R. Reynolds, eds., *Twelfth-Century Europe and the Foundations of Modern Society* (Madison, Wis., 1966), and the excellent book by E. H. Kantorowicz, *The King's Two Bodies* (Princeton, N.J., 1957). On Frederick I Barbarossa, see Peter Munz, *Frederick Barbarossa: A Study in Medieval Politics* (Ithaca, N.Y., 1969). Henry II of England is treated by L. F. Salzman, *Henry II* (London, 1967), and D. M. Stenton, *English Justice from the Norman Conquest to the Great Charter* (Philadelphia, 1964).

**Sources**   On English history in the twelfth century, see the monumental volume *English Historical Documents, 1042–1189,* ed. D. C. Douglas and G. W. Greenaway (New York, 1953). Unfortunately, Suger's biography of Louis VI has not been translated, but for his period, see *Galbert of Bruges: The Murder of Charles the Good, Count of Flanders,* trans. J. B. Ross (New York, 1967). See also *Odo of Deuil: De profectione Ludovici VII in Orientem (The Journey of Louis VII to the East),* trans. V. G. Berry (New York, 1948).

# 15 The Renaissance of the Twelfth Century

The post-Carolingian disintegration of Western and central Europe under-mined but did not extinguish learning and literature. In some of the monas-teries, at the courts of some rulers, and in a few cathedrals of northern France, manuscripts continued to be copied, the rudiments of grammar, rhetoric, and science continued to be taught, and the writing of annals contin-ued, although at a reduced pace. In England, under the patronage of Alfred the Great, the earliest beginnings of a vernacular culture can be seen in the trans-lation of Latin works into Anglo-Saxon and in the compilation of a chronicle in the native tongue. In Germany Otto the Great encouraged a few scholars and kept alive the imperial tradition of patronage for education, the arts, and letters. In Italy urban schools continued to function. But these activities were unimpressive both in quality and in quantity. The few cultural centers were relatively isolated from each other. The little that was achieved depended on only a few individuals, and there was no continuity of interests or activities that might have grown into a more general cultural movement.

Renewed political stability, growing economic prosperity of the European community, ideals of the ecclesiastical reform movement, expanding contact between Europe and the rich Byzantine and Islamic cultures, all achieved in the eleventh century, created the underpinnings for an intellectual and cultural revival—the renaissance of the twelfth century. It was greater than any that preceded it in the Carolingian or Ottonian periods, and it was the foundation of the Renaissance of the fifteenth century. It has also raised all sorts of difficulties of historical interpretation. Some historians have questioned the appropriateness of the term *renaissance,* pointing out that the twelfth-century intellectuals did not consciously seek to return to a classical culture they knew to be different from their own. Instead, twelfth-century thinkers considered their work to be a continuation—not a rebirth—of the ancient tradition. Others have argued that consciously or not the twelfth-century intellectuals renewed the ancient literary tradition, and that is a renaissance. This debate is somewhat arcane, often bordering on the semantic, and it can be left aside. But the question remains: Why did the revival occur at all? In discussions of this issue, the various historiographical traditions conflict, making the twelfth-century renaissance a good vehicle for studying the general problem of historical interpretation. Did the cultural advancement rest on a change in the economic structure of Europe, as economic determinists would argue? Did it result from political stabilization, or the chance association of teachers and students in the eleventh century, or the reform movement in the Church?

## The Intellectual History of the Twelfth-Century Renaissance

In the intellectual development of Europe, the great achievements of the twelfth century were the recovery of knowledge lost since antiquity, the assimilation of the heritage of patristic writings of late antiquity, and the earliest successful efforts to summarize and to treat systematically large fields of knowledge. Besides a rebirth or regeneration of the ancient heritage, the century produced much that was original and creative, either in the reworking of old materials newly mastered or in fields in which there were no models from the past. In both these aspects of revival twelfth-century scholars provided the foundation on which the mature culture of the high Middle Ages rested. Five main areas may be distinguished in which the recovery of ancient knowledge was most impressive: literature, science, law, theology, and philosophy, the last especially in the discipline of logic.

Learning and literature had not disappeared entirely after the Carolingian renaissance. In England, the vernacular culture inaugurated at the court of Alfred was sustained by monastic leaders like Ælfric, the author of homilies and Lives of the Saints written in Old English. In Germany, Hrotsvitha, a nun of the convent at Gandersheim, wrote some mediocre poetry and a half-dozen plays. The plays were modeled on Terence in style, but Terence's glamorous courtesans were replaced by Christian virgins, whose chastity invariably emerged triumphant after various temptations. To the modern reader the most interesting works of the period are those of Liutprand, bishop of Cremona, who wrote a gossipy narrative of the chaotic history of Italy and the lively account, mentioned earlier, of an embassy to Constantinople in the service of Otto I. The classical allusions that adorn the writings of authors who enjoyed imperial patronage have induced historians to talk of an Ottonian "renaissance" of the tenth century, but actually there was no substantial achievement. Classical Latin literature was imperfectly understood, and no lasting literary revival resulted.

Far more important was the work of Gerbert of Aurillac (the future Pope Sylvester II), who taught at Reims and whose great achievement was to reawaken interest in logic. It is interesting that his students were primarily impressed with his knowledge of arithmetic, music, and astronomy, and that Gerbert himself considered rhetoric the preeminent study for which all others were preparatory. In giving rhetoric preeminence, Gerbert followed classical tradition, for he was essentially conservative in his interests. But in reviving the knowledge of late antiquity, Gerbert was also led to study, and later to teach, the art of dialectic, or systematic logic. This was a momentous event in the cultural development of Europe. Gerbert was not satisfied with the superficial manuals of logic used in the Carolingian schools. Instead, he turned to the treatises associated with the name of Boethius. These were Boethius' translations of Porphyry's *Isagoge* and of Aristotle's two elementary treatises on logic, Cicero's *Topics,* plus Boethius' commentaries on all four of these works, and Boethius' own three treatises on the art of argument. This Boethian corpus of logic—later called the Old Logic to distinguish it from the advanced works of Aristotle, recovered in the second half of the twelfth century—constituted the foundation for the revival of philosophy in the eleventh century. Gerbert was the first man since Boethius to master this corpus, and even more important, his achievement led to further advance. Logic became the means by which the enormous mass of revealed truth, the writings of the Church Fathers, and the knowledge inherited from antiquity could be understood and assimilated. It was the most popular study in the eleventh century because it afforded an orderly and systematic approach to knowledge.

The influence of the Old Logic is illustrated by the controversy between Lanfranc (d. 1089), before he became archbishop of Canterbury, and Berengar of Tours (d. 1088) concerning the Real Presence in the Eucharist. Berengar, a grammarian, emphasized the necessity of rational argument. In response to Lanfranc's reproach for introducing dialectical questions into a sacred subject, Berengar summarized the basic position of medieval rationalism: "Recourse to dialectic is recourse to reason, and he who does not avail himself of reason abandons his chief honor since by virtue of reason man was made in the image of God." Berengar did not deny the ultimate authority of revelation in matters of faith. But how, other than by reason, could one resolve the difficulties and seeming inconsistencies to be found in Scripture? Lanfranc was renowned as a dialectician. Against the novel arguments of Berengar, who denied that the bread and wine of the sacrament could become the Lord's body and blood, Lanfranc brought to bear the new logical distinctions between substance and accidents, or essence and external form. Although taking the conservative side in the controversy, Lanfranc's rebuttal demonstrated that the art of dialectic had now become more than merely skill in argument. From this time on, dialectic was concerned with applying the categories and definitions of logical analysis to the increase of knowledge and to the solution of important problems.

The widening scope of logic is illustrated by the treatment given a passage in Porphyry's *Isagoge,* the most famous statement in the whole corpus of the Old Logic:

> As to genera and species, whether they actually exist or are present merely in thought, or if existing whether they are corporeal or incorporeal, and whether they are separate from sensible objects or are really existent only in and with reference to them—I cannot answer here, in an elementary work. 'Tis a lofty topic, one that requires further investigation.

This passage is an allusion to the metaphysical problem of universals, a problem that both Porphyry and Boethius, his commentator, recognized as fundamental but complex. The new logicians of the eleventh century took the lead offered by their sources and began to analyze metaphysical problems that had lain fallow since the early sixth century with only isolated working by men like John Scotus Erigena (in the ninth century). The principal figures in the early stages of the dispute were Roscellinus of Compiègne (d. 1122), who taught at several schools including the cathedral school of Tours; Berengar of Tours; Lanfranc; and Saint Anselm, Lanfranc's successor both as prior of the Norman monastery of Bec and as archbishop of Canterbury.

The problem of universals is simply stated: In Porphyry's terms, do genera and species (which are referred to by words of general signification like *furniture* and *chair* in contrast with *the red chair*) exist in themselves, or are they merely words of convenience denoting an idea in the human mind? In the early stages of the dispute, thinkers tended to take extreme positions. Realists like Lanfranc argued that the words *table* and *chair* named real entities distinct from any particular table or chair. Thus they followed Plato in arguing that universals are real objects. Nominalists like Roscellinus argued that universals are no more than mental abstractions drawn from our observation of individuals classed under a generic word. Thus *table* and *chair* call to mind the common characteristics of tables and chairs, and the only reality these words represent is as names (*nomina*) for the collection of characteristics they represent. Each of these metaphysical theories created difficulties for Christian theological teachings. In the dispute between Berengar and Lanfranc over the elemental reality of the bread and wine of the Eucharist, Berengar's nominalism led him to conclude that the Christ constituted by the Eucharistic transmutation was only an abstraction. Although nominalists accepted the reality of Father, Son, and Holy Spirit, they denied the reality of the Trinity as a single entity of three Persons. Because of this doctrine Roscellinus was condemned as a heretic by a council held at Soissons in 1092.

Realism avoided these problems but created an equally disturbing one. According to the logic of this system, the more general an entity is, the greater reality it has. Thus the generic chair has a greater reality, because it has fewer specific, and therefore limiting, characteristics than a particular chair that is red and located in a corner. For the same reason, furniture has a greater reality than chair. And each entity in this series participates, is subsumed, in the greater reality of the entity above it. This scale, sometimes called the Great Chain of Being in the Middle Ages, ends in God, the highest reality without limitation of any kind and the creator of all lesser reality. But if all reality participates in God and takes its reality from its participation in God, then it becomes impossible to distinguish between God and created reality. This kind of reasoning led to the heretical error of pantheism (everything is God).

Anselm of Canterbury (1035–1109) was a realist who avoided the pantheism implicit in his metaphysics. He was convinced of the priority of faith over reason. As he put it, "I believe so that I may know" (*credo ut intelligam*). He escaped the errors Roscellinus had fallen into by holding that faith leads to knowledge that is rationally grasped and just as firmly known as the lesser things that unaided reason can know. Nominalists overemphasized the three Persons and might lapse into error about the unity of God; extreme realists overemphasized the transcendent reality of one God and might lapse into error about the created universe. Anselm escaped these dangers by accepting faith as the guide to reason.

Nonetheless, Anselm's lasting monuments are some treatises on logic, all of which may not be extant, and a series of theological works in which a powerful logic played the principal part. Anselm created the ontological argument for the existence and nature of God. It is an a priori one, based not on sense experience but on a definition of God from which it follows that God exists. The argument may be paraphrased as follows:

1. The name "God" connotes (even to the fool who would deny God's existence) "a-being-greater-than-which-cannot-be-conceived."
2. Evidently, such a being cannot exist solely in the understanding but must also exist in reality.

      a. for if it is in the understanding, it can be *thought of* as existing in reality, and this is greater;

      b. therefore, if that-greater-than-which-cannot-be-conceived exists only in the understanding, then that-greater-than-which-cannot-be-conceived is the very thing than which a greater *can* be conceived.

      c. but this is self-evidently impossible and self-contradictory.

3. Therefore it is indubitably true that a-being-greater-than-which-cannot-be-conceived must exist both in the understanding and in reality.

It follows that such a being must have all the perfections. A perfection is something-it-is-better-to-be-than-not-to-be, and thus God is whatever it-is-better-to-be-than-not-to-be. Both the arguments for the existence and for the attributes of God rest on a realist metaphysics, since knowledge of true reality is not derived, for Anselm, from sense experience, and the mind cannot reach an understanding of that reality by moving from the particular to the general through a logical argument. Anselm's argument is deceptively simple and was ignored as uninteresting from the late medieval period until recently. Philosophers have again begun to explore its intricacies, just as they have returned to Anselm's logical treatises and are finding them a stimulus to their own work.

The nominalist–realist controversy reached a new stage when Peter Abelard (1070–1142) took up the problem in the early years of the twelfth century. Abelard was the eldest son of a Breton noble, but he apparently showed such intellectual promise as a child that there was little chance he would become a knight. Even before he completed his studies—the *trivium* and *quadrivium* developed by the Carolingian educators of the ninth century —he began to challenge his teachers on philosophical issues. Abelard studied with two great teachers, William of Champeaux, a philosopher at Paris, and Anselm, a theologian at Laon. Unable to gain a position at the cathedral school at Paris because of his attacks on William of Champeaux, the master of the school, and his unorthodox ideas about philosophical issues, Abelard became a free-lance lecturer attached to the church of Sainte-Geneviève. Because of his reputation as a brilliant, unorthodox thinker, Abelard attracted many students to his lectures.

Abelard worked out a moderate realism that avoided the dangers and salvaged the strong points of both nominalism and extreme realism. He accomplished this by demonstrating the logical consequences of some important distinctions, such as the distinction between the word that stands for a thing, the thing itself, and the concept of the thing in the mind. Thus universals are not mere sounds or words, as the nominalists held, nor are they things-in-themselves as extreme realists thought. They are concepts in the mind that have an objective reality derived from a process of mental abstraction. Abelard's philosophy placed universals in a distinct category of reality, so that God was not a universal nor were particulars the only reality.

The intellectuals of the eleventh century exploited the Boethian corpus of treatises, the Old Logic, as the most fruitful of the three disciplines that made up the *trivium*. While interest in logic by no means flagged in the twelfth century, the study of grammar and rhetoric led to a classical renaissance, a revival of interest in the belles-lettres of antiquity that marks the high point of medieval humanism. Medieval humanism was restricted to the Latin classics, except for one or two Greek works, such as Plato's *Timaeus,* that were accessible either in translation or through the commentaries and treatises of Latin authors. The number of authors known and the range of Latin classical literature available were almost as great in the twelfth century as today. In their own writing the humanists of the twelfth century demonstrated wide reading in, understanding of, and enthusiastic devotion to the classics. Their attitude tended to be undiscriminating, as between mediocre and better authors, and they lacked a scholarly or critical appreciation of classical literature as the expression of a society quite different from their own. But to their credit, the medieval humanists were able to recognize the superiority of Virgil and Ovid in poetry and of Cicero in prose.

The two most important centers of humanism in the twelfth century were the cathedral schools at Chartres and Orléans. Chartres emphasized a broad or "general" education based on grammar (that is, literature) and leading to philosophy in its widest or most literary sense. The finest alumnus of the school was John of Salisbury (ca. 1115–1180), who ended his long and varied career as bishop of Chartres. John, the best-educated man of the twelfth century, represented the humanistic reaction to the growing specialization and vocationalism in the schools of his day. Bright young students had a secure future in the service of secular or ecclesiastical government or in teaching in the schools. Students demanded and in many schools teachers provided short cuts through the normal liberal arts curriculum by eliminating subjects that were not "useful" or that did not have a direct bearing on training for a vocation. According to John and the humanists, this sort of education produced ignoramuses who could debate the subtleties of logic or who could use the jargon of learning but who lacked the intellectual maturity and wisdom that were slowly won through assiduous study. John himself knew more logic than most of the teachers of logic, and he was better trained in ancient philosophy than any twelfth-century philosopher. What he objected to was the narrowing of these fields into pedantic and technical disciplines cut off from the totality of human experience as represented by literature and the other disciplines.

In the classrooms the humanists fought for a losing cause, but the influence of the classical revival is evidenced in the abundance and high quality of the literature written in the twelfth century. Some poets of the period, such as Hildebert of Lavardin (d. 1130), imitated ancient models so well that later scholars mistook their work for that of classical poets. In prose writing also, twelfth-century authors affected the forms of classical writings.

Epistolary literature was popular, and Hildebert, Bernard of Clairvaux, Peter the Venerable (abbot of Cluny, 1121–1156), and others left large collections of letters. Many important treatises were written as epistles and as sermons, following another ancient literary form, the oration. More important, the classics provided inspiration and new themes for writers in both Latin and vernacular languages. Twelfth-century humanists filled their works with apt quotation, mythological allusions, and metaphors familiar in classical literature. They also produced more commentaries on classical authors and more treatises on rhetoric and grammar than writers in any other period prior to the fifteenth century. They wrote a clear Latin that was stylistically simpler than the Latin of Cicero, but they used a larger vocabulary and a freer syntax than classical authors. The clarity of twelfth-century prose reflects the humanist emphasis on grammar and rhetoric at the expense of logic.

Scientific knowledge had declined so low in late antiquity and the early Middle Ages that the recovery in this field, begun in the eleventh century, was revolutionary. Before this revolution took place, practically all the science known in the West could be found in the encyclopedic *Etymologies* of Isidore of Seville or in the elementary manuals of Bede, Cassiodorus, and Boethius. The earliest additions to this knowledge were made in the field of medicine at Salerno, where scholars made contact with Arabic learning. By the opening years of the twelfth century, Latin scholars were coming to southern Italy, Sicily, and Spain to seek out the superior Arabic works in mathematics and natural science. Ancient Greek science was recovered through these works in Arabic, since Moslem science was based on Arabic translations of Greek treatises. The Western translators valued equally the Greek treatises and the Arabic commentaries on them, and their translations were necessarily rather free. Many of the translators knew so little Arabic that they depended on trilingual Jews who had Hebrew translations at hand and could explain the texts in Latin. Some of the ancient works thus reached the Latin West by a circuitous route from the original Greek through successive translations into Arabic, Hebrew, and finally Latin. A few works were translated directly from Greek into Latin in the twelfth century, but these were often neglected in favor of translations of the same works from the Arabic, because the latter usually included commentaries. The natural sciences were a living part of Arabic culture, and the treatise-with-commentary from Arabic was often more valuable because "up-to-date" than the treatise alone from the Greek.

Through the work of the translators, the first three sciences of the *quadrivium* (arithmetic, geometry, and astronomy) were transformed from studies on the elementary level into the basic mathematical disciplines that are necessary for advanced scientific work. Adelard of Bath (ca. 1126) translated Euclid's *Geometry* and introduced the Western world to trigonometry from the works of the Arabic mathematician al-Khwarizmi. Robert of Chester (ca. 1145), another Englishman, later translated the same mathematician's basic work, *On the Restoration and Opposition of Numbers*. Arab scholars referred to it

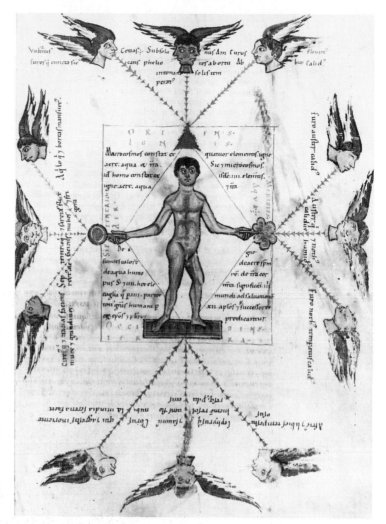

The twelfth-century renaissance produced renewed scientific interest in the world and in man's relation to it. This diagram from a twelfth century manuscript portrays man as a microcosm in which the four elements—earth, water, air, and fire—are combined as they are in the macrocosm. Thus study of man could lead to knowledge of the universe. This point is emphasized by surrounding the figure with depictions of the twelve winds.

as The Book (*Al Gebra*), and from this reference the advanced mathematics of algebra derives its name.

In astronomy the traditional curriculum was vastly enlarged by the translation of the most exhaustive work on the subject in ancient literature, Ptolemy's *Almagest*. About 1160 an unknown scholar at Palermo translated this work directly from Greek to Latin. The Byzantine emperor had made a gift of the Greek manuscript to the king of Sicily. But this translation had little currency in the Middle Ages, and it led to no further exploitation of Greek scientific works preserved at Constantinople. The translation of Ptolemy made at Toledo by Gerard of Cremona (ca. 1175) was preferred, partly because of the prestige of Arabic science and partly because it contained Arabic corrections of Ptolemy's predictions of future locations of planets and stars.

Nowhere was the impact of the contact between Latin Christians and Moslems more obvious than in medicine. The Westerners relied entirely on Arabic transmission of ancient Greek medical treatises and on Arabic commentaries on those works. The most important Greek writer was Galen, a physician at the court of Marcus Aurelius (161–180). This illuminated page from an Arabic translation of Galen's work portrays him (bottom right) along with other notable physicians of antiquity.

Other fields of science were advanced or, as far as Western Europe was concerned, introduced for the first time by the translators. In the twelve years (ca. 1175–1187) Gerard of Cremona stayed at Toledo, the chief center of this work, he translated more than seventy treatises from Arabic into Latin. Many of these were Arabic translations of ancient Greek works. The most important of Gerard's translations were in medicine, including several writings of Galen and Hippocrates. He and other translators introduced the Latin West to physics, optics, mechanics, biology, meteorology, and psychology, including most of Aristotle's scientific treatises. Two other medieval sciences no longer dignified by that title were also expanded by new knowledge gained from Arabic literature and from the Greeks through Arabic translations. These were astrology and alchemy, which medieval scholars thought of as "applied astronomy" and "applied physics," the first surviving into modern times as a pseudoscience and the second becoming one of the foundation stones of modern chemistry.

The reform papacy organized a search for ancient Church law to support its policies and positions. In the 1050s, a reformer produced a compilation of canon law based on the Pseudo-Isidorian Decretals—the *Collection in 74 Titles*—containing legal justification for both the reform and its papal leadership. In the following decades, other, expanded collections appeared. One of the most important was made about 1086 by the nephew of Alexander II, Anselm II of Lucca. These compilations rested on a wide research activity in Italian libraries and showed the influence of new finds of early papal letters. The search for canon law texts produced other discoveries. Early medieval lawyers had relied on the Theodosian Code and on abridgements of Justinian's great compilation, the *Corpus Juris Civilis*. In the last quarter of the eleventh century, scholars found an intact manuscript of the *Corpus Juris* in a Pisan library. This manuscript, called the *Codex Florentinus* (Florentine Book) because the Florentines accepted it as part of a peace settlement in the fourteenth century, is the basis of all modern editions of the *Corpus Juris*. Eleventh-century lawyers immediately recognized its value, for it contained the most elaborate and sophisticated system of jurisprudence produced before the thirteenth century, when modern jurisprudence was in its early development. In many respects, the *Corpus Juris* was the foundation of that jurisprudence.

Roman law had been taught at a few schools in Italy, notably Ravenna, throughout the Middle Ages, but the discovery of the *Corpus Juris* created greatly increased interest in the field. The Ravenna school continued to function, but soon Bologna emerged as the principal center of legal study. It was said that the countess Matilda brought civilists (scholars of Roman law) to Bologna in order to establish a propapal center of legal studies in her territories. If that story is true, Matilda's generosity had little effect on the lawyers. Irnerius, the leading Bolognese civilist in the early twelfth century, traveled in the entourage of Henry V of Germany when the king visited Italy in 1111. Irnerius and his successors were called the Glossators because of their method of explaining legal texts, which was borrowed from biblical exegesis. Their lectures and writings consisted of brief explanatory comments, cross references, emendations to establish a sound text, notes to clarify the meaning of technical terms, and whatever else would aid the reader (or, probably, serve as lecture notes for the professor expounding the text of the *Corpus Juris* in the classroom). Such writings, additional to but closely associated with the text, were inserted either as marginal or as interlinear glosses. In some surviving manuscripts the glosses are more bulky than the legal texts themselves.

The canonists were quick to capitalize on the revival of Roman law. In the late eleventh century, an increasing number of texts from the *Corpus Juris* became part of canon law, including reform-stimulated collections and the compilations of the great lawyer-bishop of Chartres, Ivo. In the 1090s Ivo compiled two large compendiums, the *Decretum* and the *Panormia*. They were independent of the reform movement, although affected by it indirectly. In the twelfth century, then, two canonical traditions coexisted, the Roman reform collections and those based on Ivo's work (called Chartrain collections). The two traditions had much in common but were shaped differently by their ideological underpinnings. In the later 1130s, a Camaldolese monk named Gratian, who taught canon law at Bologna, produced a collection (circulated around 1140) that brought the two traditions together and applied to the law the new methodology developed by Abelard. Gratian's work was the largest, best organized compilation produced up to that time. He called it the *Concordance of Discordant Canons* in order to emphasize its methodological innovations, but it soon became known as the *Decretum,* a name that pointed up its importance as a great compendium. Gratian organized his work topically. The first treatise dealt with the hierarchy and sources of laws, the second with the members of the ecclesiastical hierarchy. To these Gratian added thirty-six hypothetical cases that raised special problems. For example, one part of the first treatise considered legislative power in the Church; the twenty-fifth case involved a conflict between two laws, raising such questions as: Does a later law abrogate an earlier one even though the earlier one has not been specifically repealed? In dealing with each legal doctrine, Gratian arranged the available law texts—conciliar decrees, papal letters, and extracts from the Fathers—to argue both sides of a doctrinal proposition. Then, the Master, as Gratian was called by later lawyers, resolved the conflicts. While Gratian was trying to present canon law in a coherent way, his students wanted to use his treatises as a reference work and basis for study. Gratian's treatises distilled the enormous mass of Chruch law (although they contained over 4000 texts) and thus were analogous to the *Corpus Juris.* Gratian's students divided the first part of the *Decretum* into sections called distinctions; they separated *capitula* (texts) from passages in which Gratian had expressed

Even though Gratian's *Decretum* was a working law book, it occasionally was produced in deluxe editions with miniatures. This illumination adorns part of the first page of a *Decretum* manuscript written at Bologna in the twelfth century. The copyist left wide margins for glossators, who have been at work here, commenting on words and phrases in the text.

his opinion; they added texts that Gratian had omitted; and they renamed the work. Within a short time, the canon law professors were studying Gratian's work as the Roman lawyers studied and glossed the *Corpus Juris*. The first known gloss on the work dates from about 1145. Roland Bandinelli, the future Pope Alexander III, wrote two commentaries on the *Decretum* in the late 1140s when he was teaching canon law at Bologna. Gratian himself taught until his death in the early 1150s. Almost nothing is known about the Master, but he stands as one of the premier figures in the history of European law.

In theology and philosophy, the twelfth-century revival follows a pattern familiar from the development of other disciplines: greater mastery of the sources available, consolidation of the learning of the past, and the organization of each field for systematic study. In biblical studies, the two most important commentaries produced were the *Glossa* attributed to Anselm of Laon (d. 1117) and the *Historia Scholastica* of Peter Comestor (d. 1178), a manual of scriptural history. Each work represented an advance by providing a better commentary on Scripture. In theology, Peter Lombard (d. 1160) was the first to deal with contradictions or divergent statements in the patristic authorities. Peter studied law at Bologna and then theology at Paris, where he became one of the best teachers. His *Four Books of Sentences,* written under the influence of Gratian and Abelard, provided a systematic summary of the faith that also included a critical analysis and harmonization of patristic theology. Peter Lombard's *Sentences* became the standard textbook in theology for the rest of the Middle Ages.

In philosophy, which was not sharply differentiated from theology, the second half of the twelfth century produced no thinker as original or profound as Anselm and Abelard in the first half. The important new work was the translation of the philosophical studies of Aristotle, including the advanced logical treatises that were destined to transform the study of logic. These advanced treatises were the *Prior Analytics,* dealing with the construction of syllogisms; the *Posterior Analytics,* dealing with logical demonstration; the *Topics,* dealing with arguments leading to logical probability; and the *Sophistical Refutations,* dealing with the refutation of false conclusions. These four works were called the New Logic to distinguish them from the Boethian corpus of logical treatises. For philosophy the recovery of the works of Aristotle, translated either directly from the Greek or from Arabic together with Arabic commentaries, was to have as revolutionary an effect as did the rediscovery of the *Corpus Juris Civilis* in the study of law. Humanist critics who complained that logic was driving letters out of the schools and that dialectic had degenerated into quibbling, did not foresee that in the next century Aristotelian logic would be the basis for the greatest medieval achievements in theology and philosophy.

## The Cultural Milieus of the Twelfth-Century Renaissance: Monastery and Town

Benedict of Aniane (751–821) had wanted to isolate the monasteries from society at large in order to concentrate the attention of monks on the *opus Dei* (work of God, prayer). In Benedict's own time, the monasteries had become the center of the Carolingian renaissance organized under the monk Alcuin, who was himself abbot of six monastic communities. Even after the second Benedict's reforms became influential in the Cluniac and other reform movements, monastic schools continued to dominate the educational system of Europe. And aside from their importance as schools, the monasteries were the principal centers of learning in the tenth and eleventh centuries. Supported by the labor of peasants, monastic communities were free from the struggle for survival that trapped most of the medieval population; monks had both the time and wealth to pursue intellectual activities. While the main effort of the monks was directed to the liturgical arts, such activities could and sometimes did engender wider intellectual interests. In many monasteries monks were required to read at least one book a year, usually during Lent. Thus all monks had a reasonably good education, and monasteries maintained fine libraries of classical and patristic works. Although hundreds of manuscripts with the marginal doodlings of bored monks are extant, not all monks found the reading requirement a chore. Most of the great intellectuals of the tenth and eleventh centuries were monks.

The future of the educational system, however, lay in the towns. A few of the influential men of the Carolingian renaissance had been bishops. Men like Theodulf of Orléans and Hincmar of Reims had not permitted their episcopal and archiepiscopal duties to keep them from pursuing their intellectual interests. Those episcopal enemies of Hincmar who compiled the Pseudo-Isidorian Decretals also demonstrated wide learning and intellectual ability. This sparse genealogy of bishop-intellectuals continued through the tenth century, at the end of which stood Gerbert of Aurillac. Gerbert established a school at the cathedral of Reims that continued to exert influence until the late eleventh century. After Gerbert left Reims, however, fame for learning followed his student Fulbert, who became bishop of Chartres (1002–1028). Fulbert was a great teacher, and his school had a more lasting impact on European intellectual life than the one at Reims. After him, Chartres had a series of bishops and *scholastici* (schoolmasters) whose fame attracted large numbers of students. In the late eleventh century, Bishop Ivo of Chartres (1092–1116) was recognized as the leading canon lawyer in Europe; he was a man of wide education and broad interests who played a crucial role in the politics of the Investiture Controversy. During Ivo's pontificate, Chartres became a center of Platonic philosophy and of theology under the brothers Thierry and Bernard.

At Chartres, Reims, Tours, Orléans, Paris, and Laon, scholars like those mentioned revived the learning of antiquity. They took up again the speculative treatises of Augustine and Boethius and looked carefully at Bede and Gregory the Great. In the first stage of this renaissance, scholars engaged in the same kind of imitative work so important during the Carolingian revival. Twentieth-century scholars are discovering that many of the works once attributed to Augustine were actually written by eleventh-century authors. The same is true of other authors' works. Teachers of the period made hundreds of *florilegia* (little flowers), collections of extracts from the writings of the Fathers that became the source for authoritative opinion in discussions of theological questions. These eleventh-century theologians considered themselves, in Bernard of Chartres' saying, "like dwarfs seated on the shoulders of giants; thus we see more things than the ancients." This attitude reveals both the interests and the relative timidity of Bernard and his contemporaries. They focused on the same speculative questions as the Fathers had, concerning the nature of God and the universe, but they deferred to the opinions of the great minds of antiquity. As Peter Abelard charged at the beginning of the twelfth century, this deference too often amounted to mindless compilation of opinion, transcribed verbatim.

By the beginning of the twelfth century, the cathedral schools had replaced the monastic schools as the principal institutions of learning. This was only partially due to the growth in the number and size of the cathedral institutions, however. In the late eleventh century, monasticism experienced another great reform movement that created a series of new orders. The Carthusians, Cistercians, Camaldoli, and Grandmontains were founded in this period, and during the twelfth century, Cluny itself was reformed under the stimulus of these orders. The general history of this new monastic reform is a subject for a later chapter, but the reform had an impact on the role of monasteries in the intellectual renaissance. The new orders excluded all but their own monks from their schools. They also reduced the liturgical element in their communities' lives and emphasized the mystical experience as the goal of prayer, which affected monastic intellectuality because it made the content rather than the form of the liturgy preeminent. The new monasteries produced hundreds of commentaries on the Psalms and stimulated its intellectuals to gloss the other biblical texts on which their spiritualism was based. The result was an intellectuality very different from that developing in the towns at the same time. The new monks made the inner person their principal concern and sought to explore the ways in which a person can achieve the level of spiritual awareness necessary for knowledge (that is, experience) of God. On the one hand, this mystical interest produced works of deep psychological analysis and insight. On the other hand, monastic theology became experiential, designed to raise the mind to a higher spiritual level. Psychology and theology were therefore closely allied. Monastic theologians were not interested in speculation about divine mysteries per se, but were concerned to present those mysteries in a way that would effect a union of intellectuality and the desire for God. Thus the principal vehicle of monastic theology was not the treatise but the sermon, tied closely to the lesson or reading for the day. Scholastic theology, the theology of the urban schools, started from the Bible and ended in philosophic abstraction. Monastic theology began and ended in the Bible, and distrusted its scholastic counterpart because monks thought that true Christian theology could neither wander far from nor fully explain the revealed truth of the Bible. Thus as the two theological traditions developed in the early twelfth century, the likelihood of a clash between them also grew. The clash eventually occurred, and to understand it Peter Abelard's development of the scholastic tradition must first be discussed.

Abelard participated in the main philosophical dispute of his time, but he also made seminal methodological innovations. In a work entitled *Sic et Non (Yes and No)*, written around 1120, he demonstrated the inadequacy of the *florilegium,* as it was then used by men like Anselm of Laon, for significant theological work. Since patristic authorities disagreed about most theological problems, reliance on the *florilegium* produced intellectual nonsense. In *Sic et Non* Abelard listed 158 theological propositions and then cited the authorities affirming and denying each one. He designed the book for student exercises, but its intellectual message was clear. In order to discuss theological issues, citing authorities did not suffice; the students had to apply their own intellectual skills to the question and to the opinions about it. This method had been suggested by Ivo of Chartres (if a preface appended to one of his legal collections was in fact written by him) and by another late–eleventh-century lawyer. The lawyers were well aware of the problems lurking in their sources. But Abelard developed the method and introduced it to the central field of theology. *Sic et Non* forced intellectuals to face the relationship between reason and revelation, or between reason and tradition, and it implied that reason must play a major role in the process by which truth is established. The new intellectuals who had begun the revival of learning by sitting on the comfortable shoulders of giants were being told that the giants were treacherous. They did not like it.

Monastic theologians were disturbed much more deeply than their scholastic colleagues however. While Abelard's new method soon found adherents among the scholars of the cathedral schools and eventually became the hallmark of the scholastic method (which in turn became a principal characteristic of scholastic theology and philosophy), the monastic theologians reacted sharply and almost unanimously to Abelard's method and its implications. Abelard, the monks thought, relied too heavily on the powers of his mind and not enough on God's illumination. Abelard's speculative method could easily lead Christians astray because it explored the unorthodox along with the orthodox and seemed, in its dispassionate approach, to attach equal importance to every doctrine and idea. For the monks, however, God had revealed the true doctrine, and the theologian could not treat it in a speculative, detached manner. Before Abelard, monastic and scholastic theologians had developed their attitudes and their doctrinal systems without too much conflict. Abelard's enormous success as a teacher, and the strident way in which he developed the tendencies of his intellectual milieu, brought about the conflict. It may also be that Abelard's troubles with the leading scholars in the schools, ending in his condemnation by an ecclesiastical synod in 1120, brought him to the attention of monks and made him the representative of the whole school of speculative theologians.

Another element in the clash between the two traditions was the emergence of a monastic theologian who equaled Abelard in intellectual power. Saint Bernard of Clairvaux (1090–1153) was an extraordinary man who made the new Cistercian order of Benedictine monks almost the equal of Cluny, who played a leading role in the reform of Cluny itself, in the artistic and literary culture of his time, and in international politics. He was highly educated, wrote a Latin style marked by its concision and power, and produced some of the key theological and mystical works in Western intellectual and religious history. It was said that he could dictate several letters at a time without losing his place in any of them. During the 1130s, Bernard became increasingly active, on his own and others' initiative, in combating the pernicious effect of Abelard's theology and teaching. Bernard really made a double charge. First, he attacked a number of specific theological positions attributed to Abelard. These positions were the ostensible reason for bringing Abelard before an ecclesiastical council. Second, he wanted to stop Abelard's public teaching because its reliance on unfettered reason endangered the faith of all who came in contact with it.

Thus when Bernard and Abelard met in 1141 to consider Abelard's theological positions, the scholar came to debate the specific issues, and the monk came to condemn Abelard's whole approach. Some contemporaries and many historians have censured the great abbot for fearing to debate Abelard, and Bernard has become one of the symbols of intellectual closed-mindedness. But the condemnation misses the point because it mistakes the issue between Bernard and Abelard. When Abelard realized that Bernard was not going to meet him on his own ground, he broke up the council by appealing to the pope and left immediately for Rome. On the way, he fell ill and stopped at Cluny, where it became clear he would not live long. In the last months of Abelard's life, the abbot of Cluny, who knew Bernard well, effected a reconciliation between the two men, which softened the impact of their ideological conflict.

Notwithstanding the opposition of the monks, Abelard's method was gradually accepted in the schools. About the time Abelard was brought before the council, Gratian produced his great law book organized and argued according to Abelard's principles. Some men held a compromise position and had the effect of blurring the distinction that had been so clear in the confrontation of Bernard and Abelard. Saint Anselm of Canterbury was trained in the schools of Italy, but following the lead of Lanfranc became a monk in Normandy and in 1093 was elected archbishop of Canterbury. Anselm maintained the monastic attitude toward learning, while doing some of the most original and brilliant work in the Western philosophical tradition.

Another twelfth-century theologian, Abelard's contemporary in Paris, was Hugh of Saint-Victor (d. 1141). As a teacher Hugh approved of dialectic and the other arts, but he believed they were merely the necessary first steps in a much grander ascent toward the end of human existence, which is salvation. No one is saved by logical disputation. Or, as he put it, the path to truth is marked by three stages: cogitation (reason applied to the arts and sciences); meditation (the intellect seeking to penetrate beyond knowledge derived from sense experience), and contemplation (the attainment of truth, or knowledge of God, through the union of intellect and love reinforced by grace). Hugh is usually classified as a mystic and an Augustinian. Like most mystics he took a keen interest in physical nature. For him, as for Bernard, the whole of the created universe, in its many and complex parts, was a series of symbols of higher truth. As a thinker in the Augustinian tradition, he recognized the rational character of knowledge at all levels, but insisted that man's unaided reason provided only the starting point in a quest for truth that involved emotion and intuition as well as logic.

## The Rise of the Universities

The intellectual and cultural revival in the twelfth century produced great excitement; increasing numbers of students attended cathedral schools to study with masters of the new knowledge. Academic interest was enhanced by the expansion of bureaucratic organizations, which demanded educated men, as the governmental power of the monarchies and the papacy grew. At individual schools the student population fluctuated, depending on who was teaching there, and since most cathedral schools had one master, his fame determined the success of the institution. In the second half of the twelfth century, Paris and Bologna broke this pattern and became permanent centers of learning. The reason for this new development was the formation of a new scholastic institution, the university.

Even in the early twelfth century, Paris had several masters who competed with one another and who, as a group, maintained the success of the Parisian schools on a more permanent basis than elsewhere in northern Europe. Paris also enjoyed the advantages of being the royal capital and of being centrally located in northern Europe. In the early years of the twelfth century, William of Champeaux, master of the cathedral school, left the school and entered the Parisian monastery of Saint-Victor, where he continued his teaching and where as a result a new school was founded. Under William's successor, Hugh of Saint-Victor, the monastery became an established center of teaching. In the later twelfth century, a master named Adam taught crowds of students so large that he could find no hall to hold them, so he lectured on the Petit-Pont (small bridge) connecting the Île-de-la-Cité (Paris proper in the Middle Ages) with the left bank of the Seine. Hence he was called Adam of Petit-Pont.

Free-lance teachers could be successful in Paris, where the large student population made it possible for lecturers to live on their fees, and by the late twelfth century there were many masters in Paris. Toward the end of the century, they organized a guild (*universitas*). This university of teaching masters had the same basic purposes as the other Parisian universities—of butchers, shoemakers, carters, and so on. The teachers wanted to establish standards of service and competition. At the same time, the guild of teachers could exert more influence than any one teacher and could help individual members negotiate for hall rentals and other services.

It is not known when the University of Paris was founded because its earliest documents, if there were any, are no longer extant. The university is mentioned for the first time in records of the French royal court in 1200. In that year the provost of Paris, a kind of police commandant responsible for keeping the peace in the city, led his men in an attack on a group of German students. One of the students was killed. The university complained to the king, and Philip Augustus reprimanded his provost and confirmed the university's rights and privileges by granting it a royal charter. The king recognized that the university was legally an ecclesiastical institution subject only to ecclesiastical discipline. All masters and students were in clerical orders, although in most cases only minor orders. The chancellor of the bishop of Paris, the episcopal officer traditionally in charge of the cathedral school, granted the *licentiae docendi* (licenses to teach) to the masters of arts and to the doctors of the three higher studies (theology, philosophy, and canon law). The masters and the doctors of the three higher studies constituted the four faculties, each with its own dean. The masters of arts were so numerous that they were organized into four "nations": the French, the Norman, the Picard (including the Low Countries), and the English (including Germany and northern Europe). Thus several conflicts were built into the basic organization of the University of Paris. First, the masters and doctors often disagreed with each other, and the divisions among the masters increased the potential for conflict on the institutional and social level. One has only to think of the situation in the modern Belgian universities, where Flemish- and French-speaking contingents have been feuding for decades, to recognize the problems inherent in the international character of the medieval universities. Second, the faculties often conflicted with the bishop's chancellor, who like modern university boards of regents or trustees sought to control the faculties' activities.

The disturbance of 1200 may have induced some masters to leave Paris and go to England. In any event, there was a university at Oxford in 1209, and it had apparently been founded a few years earlier. The Oxford University first appears on record as a result of another town-gown riot, in which some students got drunk and raped and killed a local girl. The townspeople retaliated by lynching two students. The university appealed to the royal court, which ordered the townspeople to establish scholarships for two poor students. Why the masters who left Paris went to Oxford rather than to a great city like London has always been a mystery. Some historians have suggested

The university at Cambridge was established in 1209 by masters who left Oxford after a particularly vicious town–gown conflict. This first seal of the university, made about 1261, shows the chancellor flanked by the two proctors. The river Cam with its bridge is depicted below the academic officials.

that the masters wanted to be as far from the episcopal authority as possible. Oxford was in a corner of the diocese of Lincoln; the episcopal seat, at Lincoln, was at the opposite end of the diocese. The distance was considerable in the thirteenth century.

The disturbance at Oxford in 1209 may have agitated some masters enough to send them again in search of a new home, for a new university soon appeared at Cambridge. The universities were so mobile because they were made up of people only. They owned no buildings and no library; all the halls were rented. The guilds of masters, like other guilds, eventually acquired guildhalls where they conducted business and where administrative activities concerning students and teachers were centered. European universities still have one building called "the university." The guild's principal business was the establishment of curricular requirements. In the cathedral schools, students just left when they had studied enough. As the number of students and the number of job opportunities for them increased, controls were necessary for determining the ability and level of education of former students.

The universities set a standard course for their students, who were called bachelors because they were generally "celibate" young men in minor clerical orders. Completion of the course (at about the age of thirty) made the student a master of arts, by which he was inducted into the guild of masters and granted the *licentia docendi*. The ceremony, which is the origin of the modern commencement exercises, was similar to the one by which squires were admitted to the community of knights. The student knelt and placed his hands between the hands of the master performing the ceremony and swore to uphold the standards and to obey the rules of the guild. The master then admitted him to the guild, and the new master delivered a lecture, thereby commencing to teach. Many students took the examinations for a license, not in order to teach but because the license was a certificate of competence. Thus the *licentia docendi* was the ancestor of all modern degrees.

When the multiplicity of schools granting *licentiae* made people uncertain about the educational background of those who had them, the papacy took action to provide a solution. The pope granted the title *studium generale* (general school) to certain universities, which guaranteed that their *licentiae* would be recognized throughout Europe. Papal accreditation gave the schools that received it an obvious advantage over others.

Bologna's university had a history partly similar to the one at Paris. Bologna's guild also developed from the teaching activities centered there in the early twelfth century. After the great Roman lawyer Irnerius (d. 1121) settled there, Bologna became the center of legal studies in Europe. When the Bolognese monk Gratian produced his great work on canon law, the school of canonical studies became the major center of such studies. Earlier it had competed with other schools, including one in Paris. As the *Decretum* became the standard reference work in the papal chancery and as it became the principal educational text in the developing north European schools of canon law, Bologna became the greatest law school in Europe. All the great teachers and commentators studied there, although they might eventually teach elsewhere.

The university developed as an organization of students rather than masters because the law students at Bologna were older and more serious than those studying the arts at other schools. Only after becoming masters of arts did students begin studies leading to the doctorate—in theology, medicine, philosophy, or law—which they received at about the age of forty.

In the second half of the twelfth century two universities emerged at the great law school, one consisting of students from Italy (the Cismontane university), and one of students from north of the Alps (the Transmontane university).

The Bologna universities had two purposes: first, they gave the students leverage against the townspeople, who charged what the market would bear for food and lodging. The student guilds could threaten the merchants with boycott or even with a movement of the university. The universities' power eventually won them the right to fix prices and to regulate not only student life but also town–gown relations. Second, they ensured that students received instruction worth the fees they paid professors. In the earliest surviving statutes of the university the professors were subjected to minute and stringent regulations. They were required to begin lecturing with the bell and finish within a minute after the next bell. They could not be absent without permission and had to post bond for their return if they left Bologna. They were required to proceed systematically through the subject matter of the *Corpus Juris* without omitting or postponing difficult sections. If a professor were unable to attract at least five students to a scheduled morning lecture, he was subject to the same fine as if he were absent without leave.

The professors at Bologna had their own organization (college) like the university of masters at Paris but having a more limited function. Admission was gained by passing an examination administered by professors who were already members. The successful candidate for admission was enrolled as the new teacher in the society or college of law teachers as a doctor (*juris doctor,* or J.D.). When other studies were added to the curriculum at Bologna the license to teach created doctors of medicine (M.D.), theology (D.D.), and philosophy (Ph.D.). The student who passed the examination in both canon and Roman law became a doctor of each law (*doctor utriusque juris,* or J.U.D.), after which he was entitled to teach either civil law or canon law.

Bologna became a model for southern universities as Paris was for those in the north. In the early thirteenth century a disturbance at Bologna led some students and masters to migrate to Montpellier in southern France, where an offshoot of the great medical school of Palermo already existed. The law school at Montpellier remained a poor relation of Bologna until about 1295, when brilliant students from France began to go there instead of to Bologna. Petrarch began law studies at Montpellier, but he gave them up to devote himself to classical literature.

The large number of students created problems in Paris, Bologna, and other university centers. Masters often rented rooms in their own houses to students and acted *in loco parentis* to the younger men. As education increasingly became a necessary means to success, wealthy individuals endowed residences for needy scholars, who received free room and board. The educational system became an object for charity, such as the orphanages and hospitals also operated by the Church. In 1258 Robert de Sorbon endowed a hall at Paris that became a model for similar institutions at other universities. Usually a teaching master was placed in charge of the house. In England the colleges, as the halls were called, were so well endowed with property and revenues that they could support other teachers as well as the housemaster and the students. The earliest English colleges, founded around the same time as the Sorbonne in Paris, were Merton and Balliol at Oxford and Peterhouse at Cambridge. By the late thirteenth century, these English institutions had begun to play an important role in the educational life of the universities.

The social importance of the new educational institutions was too great to permit them to be the chance product of a school's fame and prosperity, however, and soon political powers were founding universities. The first one was established by Frederick II of Sicily at Naples in 1224. The king granted the university a charter and was active in attracting masters to it. Saint Thomas Aquinas received his basic university education at Naples. In Germany the emperors and dukes founded universities both for practical and prestige reasons. The first German university was founded at Prague in 1378; the second at Tübingen in 1476. Heidelberg received its charter in 1478. These institutions provided trained people for imperial and ducal government, gave a glitter to the culture of the duchy, and attracted students (and therefore money) to the towns in which they were located. This last factor induced municipalities, first in Italy but soon north of the Alps, to establish teaching chairs with city funds.

Although the majority of medieval universities were founded in the later Middle Ages, the institution itself was the product of the renaissance of the twelfth century. Few institutions of Western civilization have been longer lived, or more stable in their organization, customs, and problems.


## Suggestions for Further Reading

**Secondary Works**   The outstanding work on the twelfth-century renaissance is C. H. Haskins, *The Renaissance of the Twelfth Century* (Cambridge, Mass., 1927). On the background of the renaissance, see the excellent book by R. W. Southern, *The Making of the Middle Ages* (New Haven, Conn., 1953). H. O. Taylor, *The Medieval Mind,* 2 vols., 4th ed. (New York, 1925), and M. D. Chenu, *Nature, Man and Society in the Twelfth Century,* trans. L. Little (Chicago, 1968) are good introductions. E. Gilson, *The Spirit of Medieval Philosophy* (New York, 1936), *Heloise and Abelard* (Chicago, 1951), and *The Mystical Theology of Saint Bernard* (London, 1940) cover many of the intellectual interests of the period. H. Rashdall, *The Universities of Europe in the Middle Ages,* ed. F. M. Powicke and A. B. Emden, 3 vols., rev. ed. (Oxford, 1936) is the standard work; a recent introduction is L. J. Daly, *The Medieval University, 1200–1400* (New York, 1961). A specialized work of interest is M. H. Carré, *Realists and Nominalists* (Oxford, 1946). C. C. J. Webb, *John of Salisbury* (London, 1932), and H. Liebeschutz, *Medieval Humanism in the Life and Writings of John of Salisbury* (London, 1950) deal with the most important philosopher and humanist of the period. On the impact of Abelard, see D. E. Luscombe, *The School of Peter Abelard* (Cambridge, 1969). P. Vinogradoff, *Roman Law in the Middle Ages,* 2nd ed. (Oxford, 1929); R. C. Mortimer, *Western Canon Law* (London, 1953); and S. G. Kuttner, *Harmony from Dissonance: An Interpretation of Medieval*

*Canon Law* (Latrobe, Pa., 1960) treat the revival of legal science. On monastic culture, see J. Leclercq, *The Love of Learning and the Desire for God* (New York, 1961).

**Sources**   *Saint Anselm,* trans. S. N. Deane (Chicago, 1903; reprint ed., La Salle, Ill., 1948) contains the philosopher's *Prologion.* For the story of Abelard's life, see his *Historia Calamitatum (History of My Calamities),* trans. J. T. Muckle (Toronto, 1954), and *The Letters of Abelard and Heloise,* trans. C. K. Scott-Moncrief (New York, 1926). Bernard of Clairvaux's works were translated by S. J. Eales in five volumes (London, 1953). See also *Hugh of Saint-Victor on the Sacraments of the Christian Faith,* trans. R. J. Deferrari (Cambridge, Mass., 1951), and John of Salisbury's works will introduce the reader to many of the intellectual interests of the period. For John, see *The Statesman's Book of John of Salisbury,* trans. J. Dickinson (New York, 1927); *Frivolities of Courtiers and Footprints of Philosophers,* trans. J. B. Pike (Minneapolis, Minn., 1938); *The Metalogicon of John of Salisbury,* trans. D. D. McGarry (Berkeley, Calif., 1955); *The Letters of John of Salisbury,* ed. W. J. Millor and H. E. Butler, 2 vols. (Edinburgh, 1955–); and *John of Salisbury's Memoirs of the Papal Court,* trans. M. Chibnall (Edinburgh, 1956). For the history of the universities, see *University Records and Life,* trans. L. Thorndike (New York, 1944).

# 16 Latin and Vernacular Culture

Before the end of the thirteenth century most medieval writing was in Latin. For the modern student of the early and high Middle Ages, a knowledge of Latin will give access to about 95 percent of the sources of general history in the original language. Latin was the language of religion, learning, government, law, and business. It was also the language in which a large proportion of the literature for enjoyment or entertainment was written.

One obvious difficulty stands in the way of surveying and evaluating medieval Latin literature, a difficulty that does not confront the student of classical Latin. Any diligent reader can read through the whole of the surviving Latin writings of classical antiquity, but the bulk of medieval Latin literature is so great, including both published and still unpublished works, that in a single lifetime no one could read more than a small part of it. This statement remains true even if literature is construed, in a fairly narrow sense, to mean poetry and what is meant today by the terms *fiction* and *nonfiction*—excluding technical or specialized works in science, philosophy, theology, law, and official or unofficial documents and records.

The cultural revival of the twelfth century engendered a great age of vernacular literature. In aristocratic and royal households, the old oral literature of the bards was supplemented by a new written literature based on oral forms but developed far beyond them. In the high and later Middle Ages the use of the vernacular increased rapidly in all fields. From the late twelfth century on, municipal records and chronicles in northern France were written in French. The records of the Anglo-Norman law courts were in the dialect of the Norman judges. As government ceased being equatable with generalship, after the invasions of the Vikings, Magyars, and Moslems ended, aristocrats began to participate in peaceful governance that demanded literacy and education. The vernacular literature originated in their society and in the literate bourgeois society of the growing towns.

## Medieval Latin Literature

Latin composition was taught in the schools, at an elementary level according to the rules of Donatus and other grammarians, and at the university level as part of the liberal arts of grammar and rhetoric. Learning to write was essentially a process of committing to memory the rules of grammar and then observing the rules in practice. Practice, however, tended in fact to outrun principles. The rules of Donatus and Priscian were more concerned with the cases and tenses, the number and gender of words, than they were with word order or what medieval grammarians called "construction" of sentences. Classical grammarians had never developed an adequate Latin syntax—the principles underlying sentence structure, according to which word forms are arranged to show properly their mutual relations within the sentence.

The medieval teachers of grammar took up the problems of syntax in an effort to apply dialectic to their subject and thus make it a science. At the textbook level the best-known work was Alexander of Villa Dei's *Doctrinale* (1199). In his elaborate treatment of syntax he was the first to use extensive excerpts from the Vulgate and from patristic writings as illustrative examples of his rules. The success of the *Doctrinale* was partly due to Alexander's effort to bring grammar into conformity with the best Latin usage of his own day. He decried the subservience of contemporary humanists who imitated classical Latinity. Another reason for the popularity of the *Doctrinale* was that it was written in rhymed verse, so that it could easily be memorized by students. It became the standard textbook of grammar until the Renaissance reaction in favor of classical Latin pushed it into the background in the sixteenth century.

In the northern universities some teachers treated grammar and rhetoric in typically scholastic fashion, as disciplines to be investigated scientifically for their own sake. In addition, the two disciplines had a practical value that was appreciated by students. This practical interest was most highly developed in the Italian universities. Italian grammarians taught the *ars dictaminis,* the art of composing letters and drawing up business and legal documents. One branch of this kind of rhetoric highly developed in the Italian universities was the *ars notaria,* devoted to the execution of legal instruments. These specialized studies derived from the general medieval attitude toward all Latin composition: it should conform to definite rules from which deviation was considered inappropriate. Writing was a craft; poets were not born but made.

Religious works—devotional, didactic, and dogmatic—constituted the largest class of Latin writings in the high Middle Ages. This literature was distinct from scholastic theological writings, and many active churchmen contributed to it. For example, Lothario de Segni wrote a devotional tract on the contemplative life entitled *De Contemptu Mundi* (*On Contempt of the World*) before he became pope as Innocent III (1198–1216). In the same class were a great number of written sermons. The sermon was a favorite vehicle for the experiential theology of the monastic theologians, but it was also used for many other purposes. Abbot Eckbert of Schönau wrote a series of sermons against the Albigensians during the 1160s. Collections of pastoral sermons began to be made in the thirteenth century for use by parish priests. For the edification of the faithful, however, the most popular literary works continued to be Lives of the Saints. With a few exceptions, the high Middle Ages was not as fruitful a period for this kind of writing as the preceding age. But the number of Lives did not abate. The several Lives of Saint Thomas à Becket contain the greatest number of miracle stories connected with the name of any medieval saint. And yet these Lives of Saint Thomas and of other twelfth- and thirteenth-century saints often lack the simplicity, charm, and imaginative quality of earlier saints' Lives or of the contemporary stories about the miracles of the Virgin. More notable than the original Lives being written in the thirteenth century were the compilations of condensed or paraphrased older Lives. The best of these was the *Golden Legend* by James of Voragine (d. 1298), which contained versions of more than two hundred Lives.

The Investiture Controversy impressed contemporaries as a world historical event that demanded explanation and justification. Thus from 1050 on the number of histories and chronicles increased dramatically. The new historical writings were fuller and were composed with greater consideration for style than the Carolingian and post-Carolingian annals. They were also more accurate and critical, for eleventh-century historians often wrote their works in response to or in the interests of political movements and could not be free with their narratives and explanations. Since the reformers and their opponents based many of their arguments on historical precedents, the accuracy of historical narrative became an issue, and early twelfth-century writers often challenged the authenticity of documents. But the new histories reflected politics in more direct ways than in the care historians took with disputable sources. The great chronicler Ekehard of Aura, a German monk who spent much of his time at Henry V's court, rewrote his account of the events from

1101 to 1111 four times, each redaction reflecting changes in the monk's political point of view. Ekehard's revisions were not unique, although in most cases the rewriting was by someone other than the original author. The process of revision brought historiographical issues to the surface and made historians more conscious of their relationship with the story they were telling.

It was conventional to begin a chronicle with the Creation, the Flood, the Incarnation, or some other epoch-making event in sacred history and then to present a summary of events, derived from earlier chronicles, down to the author's own day. At this point the work became original—and important. To reconstruct the narrative of events, the chronicler relied on his own knowledge, on oral reports, and on documents and other contemporary written evidence. Many papal and royal letters are extant only in copies entered in contemporary chronicles and histories.

History writing developed outside of the scholastic tradition of the late eleventh century. History did not become a subject in school curriculum—it was not a formally recognized discipline—until the nineteenth century. In the Middle Ages it was simply one small part of grammar, although grammar, as it was taught in the schools, included both grammar and general literature.

Although the writing of history tended to be a literary enterprise, the best writers were not content to present a well-turned narrative. They inquired into motive and causation and were aware of the complexity of human affairs and the interrelationships between historical events; some of them even attempted to relate historical knowledge to the total framework of human knowledge and divine revelation. The German historian Otto of Freising (d. 1158) not only wrote a detailed and accurate narrative of events but also attempted to show how these events exemplified the Christian philosophy of history as expounded in Augustine's *City of God.* Otto's two most important works, *The Two Cities* and *The Deeds of the Emperor Frederick I,* together cover the period from Adam down to the year 1156. Otto was Frederick's uncle and gained much of his knowledge of events firsthand. The best history written in France was the *Ecclesiastical History* of Ordericus Vitalis (d. 1143), whose work began with the Incarnation and is especially valuable for the history of Normandy and for the relations between the kings of England and France after the Norman Conquest of England in 1066. In England there were more historians of the first rank than in any other country. Ordericus' contemporary William of Malmesbury (d. 1142) and William of Newburgh (fl. 1198) were both monks who wrote general accounts of English history in which they not only recorded but tried to explain historical events. Because he rejected the legends about King Arthur and the Round Table, popularized by Geoffrey of Monmouth's pseudohistorical *History of the Kings of Britain* (1147), Newburgh has been called "the father of historical criticism."

The twelfth century was the golden age of the monastic chronicle. From then until the end of the Middle Ages there was a steady decline in the value of historical works produced by monks. In England the only important exception to this general rule was Matthew Paris (d. 1259), a monk of Saint Albans, a monastery located just north of London that had intimate connections with the royal court. Matthew's four main works, and particularly his *Greater Chronicle,* have earned him the reputation as the best medieval historian.

The Crusades aroused great interest, and most chroniclers included long chapters on the subject. In his *Deeds of the Kings of the English,* William of Malmesbury gave a long derivative account of the First Crusade, with digressions on the Council of Clermont and the topography of the city of Rome. The best-written history of the First Crusade was the *Deeds of God Through the Franks* by Guibert of Nogent (d. 1124), based on an account by an anonymous participant. Of equal importance was the *Historia Hierosolymitana* by Fulcher of Chartres, who brought his chronicle down to the year 1127. On the Second Crusade and its aftermath, an excellent account was written by William, archbishop of Tyre (d. 1185), entitled *History of Deeds Done Across the Sea.* The best histories of the later Crusades were written in the vernacular rather than in Latin.

The first biographies since Carolingian times were written in the twelfth century. In almost every significant bishopric and abbey, biographies of bishops and abbots were produced, and there was renewed interest in an old series of papal lives called the *Liber Pontificalis (Papal Book),* which resulted in its being revised and brought up to date. Royal biographies began to be written, often by counselors and clerks in the service of rulers; they included the previously mentioned work on Frederick Barbarossa by Otto of Freising, and the *Life of Louis VI* by the abbot Suger, another royal counselor. Roger of Howden, an English royal clerk and official, wrote *The Deeds of Henry II and Richard,* which paralleled the work of Otto of Freising. The first truly autobiographical works since Augustine's *Confessions* were produced in the early twelfth century. Guibert of Nogent wrote one revealing his personality and his relationship with contemporary events and society. Peter Abelard's *History of My Calamities* also does this, although with less sensitivity to personal growth and development than Guibert had displayed. Peter's ego stood in the way of such sensitivity. In the thirteenth century, Salimbene (d. 1290) wrote a lively autobiography.

In medieval Latin poetry, the greatest change from the Carolingian period to the high Middle Ages was the abandonment of classical meter based on quantity (long and short syllables) in favor of accentual meter and rhymed versification. Most poetry, like prose, was written on religious themes, and most was rather mediocre. The finest religious poetry was written for liturgical use—the sequence or hymn. The greatest of these were the *Sequences* of Adam of Saint-Victor (d. 1192), as perfect a literary expression of the new emotional piety of the twelfth century, especially of that centered on the Virgin, as the new churches were in architecture. The sequence was sung during the Mass and evolved from musical elaborations called melismas, in which singers set the last syllable of a prayer to a melody. Gradually these melodies were used to introduce new texts, a hymn or commentary on the prayer or psalm just sung; the new texts were called sequences. The two most familiar sequences were written by Franciscans in the thirteenth century, the *Stabat Mater Dolorosa* and the *Dies Irae*. The latter is generally considered to be the greatest hymn, and by some the greatest poem, in the Latin language. The opening stanza is a truly majestic introduction to its mighty theme, the Day of Judgment:

> *Dies irae, dies illa*
> *Solvet saeclum in favilla*
> *Teste David cum Sybilla.*

> [The day of wrath, that dreadful day,
> Shall all the world in ashes lay,
> As David and the Sybils say.][1]

Like Virgil's *Aeneid,* the *Dies Irae* is a supreme example of a poem that cannot be translated without vitiating the beauty and power of the original. No English version exists that has satisfied either the translator or the reader who understands Latin.

Medieval drama also grew out of the liturgy. In the elaborate liturgy developed by the Cluniacs, certain feasts became the province of the nearly professional monk-singers. In syllabic elaborations, within the prayers instead of at their end like the sequences, the singers engaged in dialogues between characters related to the drama of the feast day—for example the three Magi at Christmas; one of the Evangelists, Saint Peter, and Jesus at Easter. These dialogues had evolved from simpler explanatory texts, called tropes, and eventually the trope-dialogues became liturgical dramas in which several characters participated. This development took place during the twelfth century in nonmonastic churches, where the drama functioned as instruction for the laity. During this period the conventions of Christmas and Easter oratorios were formed. Jesus was sung by a baritone; the Evangelist by a tenor; the crowd by a choir of high, boys' voices; and the false witnesses (in the Easter dramas) by two or three high-pitched, nasal voices. Like the ornamentation of the churches, this practice of dramatizing the great liturgical stories was attacked by ecclesiastics like Saint Bernard of Clairvaux, who believed that the dramas dishonored the solemn Mass and distracted the

.

[1] Frederick B. Artz, *The Mind of the Middle Ages,* 3rd ed. (New York: Alfred A. Knopf, 1958), p. 333.

faithful from the true goal of prayer. At the same time, the dramas became too elaborate to be presented in church, and they were then played on the plazas before the churches to give actors and audience more room. By the mid-thirteenth century, dramas had become a regular feature of the celebration of feast days in towns throughout Europe. Each guild was responsible for producing and staging one play. Some of the plays were staged on wagon sets that moved about the town during the day; others were too elaborate to be played on so small a stage and were set up in squares. Scholars have discovered several cycles of plays used in various towns during the later Middle Ages.

The earliest and simplest medieval drama was the mystery play, a dramatization of a story from the Old or the New Testament. In the twelfth century the miracle play became popular; this presented an incident in the life of a saint or of the Virgin, the climax of which was the miraculous intervention by the saint in the daily affairs of human beings. In the later Middle Ages the so-called morality play developed. In this kind of drama the author was free to deal with themes that might be far removed from religion. Most of the morality plays were allegorical dramatizations, very moral and didactic, but some included comic scenes and realistic characterization. The best of the morality plays, and the one that is most familiar to modern audiences, is *Everyman,* a drama that exists in several versions and several languages.

The most novel Latin literature of the Middle Ages was the new secular lyric poetry of the twelfth and thirteenth centuries. This was the Goliardic verse written by students who called themselves disciples of Golias—that is, Goliath the Philistine, who in medieval allegory signified the Devil. Most of this poetry was satirical and humorous and dealt at great length with the pleasures of wine, women, and song. The authors, many of whom later became honored and respected officials in the Church, have been characterized as "lewd fellows of the baser sort," or so they appeared to be in some of their lyrics. It was all in good fun. One of the best Goliardic poems was by the anonymous clerk known as the Archpoet, *The Confessions of Golias* (ca. 1165), from which the following stanza is taken:

> In the public-house to die
> Is my resolution;
> Let wine to my lips be nigh
> At life's dissolution:
> That will make the angels cry,
> With glad elocution,
> "Grant this toper, God on high,
> Grace and absolution!"[2]

[2] J. A. Symonds, trans., *Wine, Women, and Song* (London: Chatto and Windus, 1925), p. 69.

The Goliards were experts at parody, and they occasionally turned their talents to sharply critical and anticlerical satire. A favorite device of theirs was the acrostic. For example, everyone knows that the root of all evil is avarice, and in Latin the Goliards gave this a clever antipapal twist in the acrostic (reading the first letters downward):

*R*adix
*O*mnium
*M*alorum
*A*varicia

Finally, the same group of authors, most of them anonymous, were responsible for a considerable body of satire and parody in prose, directed against peasants, women, monks, and higher clergy—and even the Bible. Among the more popular anticlerical prose satires was the *Gospel According to Saint Mark(s of Silver)*, and of course there were animadversions on the Gospel attributed by the satirists to the "Evangelist" Saint Lucre. This satiric literature grew out of the Latin culture of the twelfth and thirteenth centuries. Every student spent years studying Latin grammar and literary forms, memorizing samples of classical Latin usage, both poetic and prosaic, and when their studies became difficult, or ridiculous, they naturally used their skills to express the mood appropriate to the situation. Goliardic poetry therefore demonstrates how deep the Latin culture of the Middle Ages was. Latin was a natural mode for expressing bawdy as well as spiritual thoughts.

### The Culture of the Noble Classes: Epic and Romance, and the Debut of Polite Society

The intellectual revival took place in communities made safe for learning by the success of the military class, and the cultural revival eventually affected the households and outlooks of that class. The society of the heroic age of feudalism reached its apogee in the first half of the twelfth century. The new age of chivalry—a refined and civilized feudalism grafted onto the customs and conventions, ideas and ideals, inherited from the preceding age— emerged in the second half of the century. That feudal society had reached maturity is illustrated by the literature written for an audience of feudal nobles and expressing their interests and values. The literature of the feudal courts had ancient roots; a heroic literature had been sung by court poets for aristocratic Celtic and Germanic audiences before the migrations, and was passed on to the new aristocracy of medieval Europe. The literature of the premedieval peoples was poetic in form, epic in style, and vernacular in language. It was recited in an alliterative verse heavily laden with formulas that made it easier for poet-singers to compose their works as they sang, using formulaic blocks developed for expressing common ideas, emotions, and narrative elements. The twelfth-century renaissance stimulated the writing down of some of these works, and the written versions exhibit both the general movement toward a literate upper-class culture and some specific developments in intellectual centers.

The early Germanic epics reflect the aristocratic society, the process of Christianization, and a life determined by natural and supernatural forces beyond men's control. Taken as a whole, these northern tales are tragedies in which heroic men meet their assigned fate with indomitable courage. A typical scene is that of the lone warrior holding off an attacking army on a narrow bridge, doomed to perish but bravely fighting on to die a hero's death. Most northern epics portray life on a small canvas; the themes are particular incidents or specific events. If the few surviving poems are typical of the literature as a whole, and if they portray accurately the intellectual and emotional atmosphere in which the early Germanic peoples lived, then the society was somber, moody, and violent. The heroes of these epics lived close to nature, but the bards who sang these epics (accompanying themselves with harps) usually depict the natural environment in a minor key, as it were—grim, unfriendly, and ominous. In *Beowulf* (written down in the mid-eighth century), to take one example, the land is "wild and lonely," ridges are "wind-swept," the stream is a "falling torrent" that plunges into "gloom and shadow" under the "darkening cliff." For the aristocratic audience that listened to these lays, life was essentially a struggle against nature, against human enemies, and against the mysterious forces and marvelous creatures of the supernatural world. The main episodes in *Beowulf* tell how that hero slays first the monster called Grendel, then the mother of Grendel (another monster), and finally a dragon.

In many ways the earliest surviving French epic poetry is similar to the epics of the earlier Teutonic world. A Frankish tradition may lie behind the *chansons de geste* (songs of great deeds) parallel to the Teutonic tradition, although there is no clear evidence. The *chanson de geste,* like the early Germanic epic, is in the vernacular and thus composed for a lay audience. It is essentially tragic in theme and simple in meter, employing assonance rather than rhyme and intended to be recited aloud rather than read. It embodies traces of historical events as preserved and distorted by oral tradition. The same basic virtues of courage and loyalty are glorified, and the central plot revolves around the remarkable feats performed by the hero. Both the Teutonic epics and the *chansons* portray a masculine society whose members behave according to the conventions and values of a tightly knit group. The action is all external; the individual is submerged beneath an idealized portrayal of abstract types, such as the good lord, the faithful man, the treacherous vassal.

The *chansons de geste* also reveal marked differences from the Teutonic epic. They reflect feudal conditions and a more complex society in which Christianity is fully assimilated. The *chansons* deal with a greater number of important characters, giving more attention to the interrelations of these characters, in contrast with the concentration on the central figure in the northern epic. The element of the marvelous remains, but it is not prominent and its quality has changed. Myth and monster are replaced by Christian miracle, but in general the limits of nature are better respected, just as the physical aspect of nature is awesome. The typical heroic battle of the north is fought under lowering skies, but when feudal knights meet the paynims (Moslems), "fair was the day and bright the sun, and all their harness glistens in the light." The feudal heroes are still portrayed from the outside, but they strike the audience as more nearly human in their wider range of emotion and more developed sensibilities. Returning from the wars, at first sight of *la douce France,* the knights of Charlemagne "call to mind their own fiefs, their young maidens and gentle wives, till there is not one that does not weep for pity."

By far the best *chanson,* indeed one of the great monuments of all European literature, is the earliest surviving French epic, the *Song of Roland.* The story dates back in oral tradition at least to the mid-eleventh century (it was sung to the Norman host on the eve of the Battle of Hastings), but in the form that survives, the poem was composed by an anonymous author writing some time between the years 1100 and 1120. The story is based on an obscure incident, the ambush of Charlemagne's rear guard returning over the Pyrenees from his first Spanish campaign. This kernel of history is embellished into a full-scale narrative of four thousand lines in which Charlemagne is the leader of Christendom against the infidel. *Roland* is the earliest of more than thirty epics developing this general subject. The influence of crusading zeal is evident, but the religious ideas are those of the feudal nobles unaffected by the reform movement within the Church. Archbishop Turpin, a prominent actor in the drama, is "a right good knight, for well he knows how to smite with lance and spear." The essence of the tale is the glory that comes to Roland and his loyal companions, despite insuperable odds. Roland as the brave and faithful vassal is the central theme, to which the treacherous vassal, Ganelon, contributes by way of contrast. Although women have their place, subordinate and in the background, there is no hint of a love interest. Roland's dying thoughts are of Durendal (his sword), the many lands he had won by his valor, "sweet France," his liege lord Charlemagne, and, at the very end, the salvation of his soul. So little did Aude the Fair, his betrothed, mean to the hero. As for Aude, she forthwith collapsed and died on receiving news of Roland's death. After the *Song of Roland,* other epics continued to be written; some eighty of them are extant.

At about the same time that *Roland* was being composed in northern

The story of Roland is one of a cycle of stories connected with Charlemagne. Primarily patronized by the French monarchs, the cycle had wide currency and was enjoyed throughout Europe. This north Spanish relief of Roland's battle dates from the second half of the twelfth century. The same wide popularity was won by the Arthurian cycle. The earliest indication that Arthur was becoming a well-known epical character is found on a tympanum in the cathedral of Modina, Italy, dated about 1080.

France, the home of feudalism, William, count of Poitou and duke of Aquitane (1071–1127), wrote a poem from which the following verses are taken:

> I'll make some verses just for fun
> Not about me nor any one,
> Nor deeds that noble knights have done
>         Nor love's ado:
> I made them riding in the sun.
>         (My horse helped, too.)
> When I was born I cannot say.
> I am not sad, I am not gay,
> I am not stiff nor dégagé;
>         What can I do?

> Long since enchanted by a fay
>> Star-touched I grew.
> I have a lady, who or where
> I cannot tell you, but I swear
> She treats me neither ill nor fair.
>> But I'm not blue,
> Just so those Normans stay up there
>> Out of Poitou.
> I have not seen, yet I adore
> This distant love; she sets no store
> By what I think and furthermore
>> ('Tis sad but true)
> Others there are, some three or four,
>> I'm faithful to.[3]

This poem is not typical, but as an extreme example of the new style being cultivated in southern France it serves to introduce the literary revolution that was to replace the epic in the second half of the twelfth century. The new lyric poetry of the south and the new romance of the north (in poetry and prose) are the real beginning of modern literature. Both the lyric and the romance deal with themes that were unknown to the epic tradition and that continue to pervade, if not to dominate, European literature.

In contrast with the epic, the new lyric poetry of southern France dealt with intimate and personal themes. The poet felt free to express a mood, to coin a phrase, or to reveal his inmost thoughts and emotions. He was interested in analyzing the inner life of his characters, especially their emotions, rather than in describing their external actions. More often than not, the lyric poet wrote about himself. The epic was a long and serious poem to be recited or chanted with dignity; the lyric was short and clever, intended to divert, flatter, or even shock the listener. When the lyric was serious, it was passionate or religious; when in a lighter vein, it was gay and often humorous. The poets who introduced this new lyric form were called troubadours in the south (Provençal *trobar,* to find or to invent), and their northern imitators were called trouvères. Not all were the anonymous clerks or wandering, low-born minstrels and jongleurs who made a living by entertaining. Many troubadours were of knightly station, living in the household of their lord, and a few were great nobles like the William of Aquitaine quoted above (grandfather of Eleanor of Aquitaine), who was reputed to have been the first troubadour.

To the earlier ideals of feudalism—courage and loyalty derived from the earlier Germanic tradition, and service to Christendom and charity toward the weak enjoined by the Church—the troubadours added a new set of ideals

[3] "A Song of Nothing," trans. T. G. Bergin, in C. W. Jones, ed., *Medieval Literature in Translation* (New York: David McKay, 1950), p. 668.

that reflected the more sophisticated and refined life of the twelfth century. These new ideals may be summed up in the word *courtoisie,* the courtly ideal. The English word *courtesy* conveys only part of the meaning of this new concept, being restricted in ordinary usage to the sense of politeness. *Courtoisie* in the chivalrous sense employed by the troubadours implies gallantry, gentility, generosity, and the etiquette or mannerisms conventional in the courtly life of a castle where the crudity and roughness of an earlier age had made room for refinement and delicacy.

The *Song of Roland* reflects the attitudes of early twelfth-century aristocratic society toward women. Fair Aude had almost no influence on the formation of Roland's values or of his motives. This is not to say that women played no role in society or politics during the eleventh and early twelfth centuries. It would be easy to point out many women on every level of aristocratic society who participated in politics and who were the principal administrators of their husband's fiefs. But in the social psychology of early medieval aristocrats, women were merely extensions of their husbands, analogous in many ways to the serfs who served as estate managers. In the second half of the twelfth century, clearly visible in the poetry of troubadours like the great Bernart de Ventadorn (1148–1195), a new psychology arose that brought women into the center of the feudal noble's world. The woman became the instructor and arbiter of the man's behavior, his *courtoisie.* The woman still did not participate in the central dramatic action of the new literature, the literature of courtly love or romance, but she was the stimulus to masculine action. For Andreas Capellanus, who enumerated the whole system of courtly love in his treatise *The Art of Courtly Love* (1174–1186), passionate love between man and woman ennobles both—especially the man. And in a society in which marriage was primarily a political union, the love described by the troubadours was an adulterous love. The first of Andreas Capellanus' rules of love is "marriage is no real excuse for not loving." Some other rules indicate the romanticism of Andreas' whole conception: "XIII. When made public love rarely endures." "XV. Every lover regularly turns pale in the presence of his beloved." "XVI. When a lover suddenly catches sight of his beloved his heart palpitates." As the romantic mythology evolved in the courts of highly placed aristocrats, it emphasized the faithfulness of love. The lustfulness of William of Aquitaine's little poem would have received reproach fifty years after it was written. The knight of the new literature went off to his fabulous deeds, his great suffering, for the favor of his lady. If he succeeded in his quest, if he achieved heroic proportions, then he got the favor; the authors and poets were discreet about the favor's character. There was even a mythical "court of love" where cases involving lovers' rights against each other were decided. Andreas Capellanus devoted a chapter to five such cases.

The concept of courtly love was an elaborate artifice, cultivated by the noble class but hardly descriptive of its life. It reflected the refinement of

In the twelfth century, minstrels became a regular feature of aristocratic society. They were also familiar to monks and monastic houses, since most monks came from the upper classes, and many monasteries served as hostelries for travelers, which musicians often were. This capital from a French monastic church is one of a series of reliefs depicting scenes from everyday life.

aristocratic society, and its better treatment of women, in the late twelfth century, but the refinement was a veneer on individuals no less hard-headed nor self-interested than they had been in an earlier age. Historians still disagree about the origins of the new social outlook. Some argue for Moslem influence from Arabic Spain, which was especially strong in southern France. The evidence is not very good, although Arabic romantic literature could have played a role without being the principal foundation. Others have suggested that women created the movement by patronizing the troubadours and trouvères in the long periods when their husbands were absent. The two most important sponsors of the new genre were Eleanor of Aquitaine and her daughter Marie de Champagne. The adulterous character of the new love ideals is attributed to the longings of women who had been pawns in the aristocratic marriage alliances. The problem with this view is that men also patronized the new literature and constituted the largest part of its enthusiastic audience. One of the patrons of the greatest of the romance writers, Chrétien de Troyes (fl. 1160–1190), was Count Philip of Flanders. Some historians have wondered if there was a connection between the rise of women's status in the romance tradition and the tremendous devotion to the Virgin Mary observable in contemporary religious life. Many of the early Gothic cathedrals were devoted to Mary, including Notre-Dame de Paris and Notre-Dame de Chartres. In monastic culture, Mary became the central figure of a cult; she was the principal intermediary between man and God in the person of her Son.

Whatever its origins, the courtly love tradition was the literate vehicle of the noble class and brought other elements of the great twelfth-century revival into the culture of that class. Wolfram von Eschenbach's *Parzival,* for example, builds a story around the most profound religious theme of romance, the quest for the Holy Grail. The romance introduced some of the basic themes of Western literature, including the preoccupation with love. It underlies the modern rules of politeness and etiquette, as well as the idea that marriage ought to be based on love rather than politics. It is perhaps justifiable to say that many ideals of behavior were formed by medieval notions of what was proper.

## Medieval Vernacular Literature

Little of the premedieval and early medieval literary tradition was recorded. The earliest written Gothic was Ulfilas' translation of the Bible. The pagan mythology with which he competed remained outside the literate culture. The first writing down of the old literature occurred in England, where the great poem *Beowulf* was composed. It is possible that like the old German law codes, the recording of the *Beowulf* stories stemmed from the influence of Christianity, which introduced literate Roman culture to the Anglo-Saxons and other Germanic peoples. Ethelbert of Kent had been the first to issue a written law code a few years after he was converted to Christianity in 597. The Germans lagged behind the Anglo-Saxons in conversion, law code writing, and written literature. The earliest surviving German story is the *Hildebrandslied* (ca. 800), of which only fragments remain. Thus the first urge to write down the old stories and myths seems to have been connected with the transition from early Germanic pagan culture, to medieval, Christian culture, and the earliest written works show the imprint of Christianization on the old German lore. The old culture was breaking down, and poets, the preservers of cultural ideals and codes of behavior, may have recorded their lore in order to save the old in the face of the new cultural forms.

The next great age of written vernacular literature began in the eleventh century. In France the *Song of Roland,* mentioned earlier, was written down; it shows that the new medieval culture had produced its own fund of orally transmitted stories. *Roland* had grown as it was transmitted, receiving elements from the ninth, tenth, and eleventh centuries before being frozen in written form around 1100. In Germany the *Nibelungenlied,* composed in writing about 1200, also shows the effects of a long development. The original story incorporated elements of early Germanic mythology in a recounting of the disaster visited on the Burgundians by Aëtius and his Hunnish mercenaries in 436. The Huns destroyed the royal family of the Burgundians and decimated the population. During centuries of oral transmission, the story had become encrusted with later material and appears very anachronistic, giving the old German heroes a chivalrous coating and knightly weapons. The *Nibelungenlied* also exhibits an important facet of the act of writing down the old stories. Its anonymous author showed a keen interest in political problems similar to those of the contemporary German kingdom, which in 1200 was disturbed by competing claimants to the throne. The written form of the ancient poems almost always had a present purpose and certainly reflect present conditions. It is difficult to explain why twelfth-century poets felt compelled to record the old epics. Perhaps the flood of new courtly literature threatened the older stories in the same way that the growth of medieval culture had threatened the culture of early Germanic society centuries earlier. Perhaps the new wave of writing reflected the growing literacy of the upper classes. Perhaps the political consolidation of Europe in the late eleventh century had the double effect of creating a wide audience for literature and a few great courts in which political, economic, and social power was centralized. Thus as the households of the nobility stabilized in the eleventh and twelfth centuries, a widespread milieu was created in which courtly ideals could develop. As political and social power was centralized in the royal and great feudal courts, the courts became both the arbiters of social mores and the patrons of the literature in which those mores were explained. The new literature, both epic and romance, became, then, the vehicle of the great courts' social power and was partially a product of the centralization of government.

In support of this partial explanation of the growth of vernacular literature, many historians have observed that the French monarchy patronized the Charlemagne cycle, of which *Roland* was the first written example, while the Anglo-Norman and Plantagenet court supported the Arthurian cycle. The French kings looked to the Carolingian past for the foundation of their authority, especially against the English kings, who, after the Norman Conquest, were their vassals. The Anglo-Norman kings and their successors sought an independent base for their power in order to counter the Carolingian tradition of their feudal suzerains and to justify their position within England. In the legends about Arthur, who had led the Britons against the Anglo-Saxon invaders in the late fifth century, they found their vehicle, claiming to have an origin even more ancient than that of the Capetians and to have a legitimate authority over the Anglo-Saxons because it was derived from the pre-Anglo-Saxon Britons.

The greatest of the Arthurian writers was Chrétien de Troyes, who wrote under the patronage of Marie de Champagne and Philip of Flanders. (Flanders was traditionally allied with the English, often against the French, because of the close economic relations between the two areas. England supplied the wool that the Flemish wove into their famous cloth.) Chrétien was only the best of many authors, and by the later twelfth century, Arthurian literature had become extremely popular. Caesarius, abbot of Heisterbach, remarked that once when his predecessor was delivering a sermon to the congregation of monks and the monks were dozing off, he suddenly stopped and said, "There was once a king named Arthur." Whereupon everyone snapped awake, eager to hear the story. The tales had a standard pattern. A knight left home to begin a career of adventure, during which he fell in love with a beautiful lady. Eventually he arrived at the court of King Arthur, where he learned that he had not successfully harmonized love and knighthood and that only when he did so would he be accepted into the court. After this fall from grace, the knight wandered for a time seeking adventure and the key to harmonizing his great love for his lady with his need to maintain his knightly virtues. Too much attention to his lover would ruin him as a knight; too much adventure would make him a poor lover. The perfect knight had to do both well. After the hero brought his two apparently contradictory roles into accord, he returned to King Arthur's court, where his achievement was recognized and celebrated. Then he went home to his beautiful lady and lived happily. . . . Typically, the knight was a younger son of a great lord or king making his way on his merits. The lady was heiress of a great kingdom that the young knight won for her and himself.

In the late twelfth century, the Germans began to translate this basically French tradition into their own language. On the one hand, these translations indicate the derivative quality of German secular culture in this period; it was behind the French and Anglo-Norman. On the other hand, the translations were not exact Middle High German reproductions of the originals. Walther von Veldeke's translation of the *Aeneid* was a paraphrase rather than a strict translation, and Gottfried von Strassburg's *Tristan* (ca. 1210) was one version of the old story, not a translation at all. Most impressive was Wolfram von Eschenbach's *Parzival* (ca. 1208), which incorporated materials from Chrétien, among others. Wolfram fashioned them in a new way, however, constructing his work in accordance with the *ordo artificialis* (artificial as opposed to the natural, or chronological, order of a story) of the rhetoricians. He also incorporated many elements of contemporary intellectual activities in his work. The bestiaries, lapidaries, and herbals all contribute lore to the story, as do astronomical studies, canonical and theological developments, and traditional Christian psychological theories. Wolfram was also the first author to create a narrative *persona*. The whole story is organized on the basis of the liturgical calendar, which adds to the symbolic meaning of one of the greatest and most complex pieces of literature in Western civilization. Wolfram's achievement was not an isolated one. A fine group of lyric poets was active in Germany at this time. The greatest of these was Walther von der Vogelweide (d. 1228), whose love poetry and satirical verse are comparable to the best work of the troubadours.

In Italy and Spain the vernacular epic and lyric developed more slowly than they had north of the Alps and Pyrenees, and the quality of the poetry was less distinguished. The one exception was the epic poem *The Cid* (ca. 1140), a collection of legends and stories about the eleventh-century hero of the Christian reconquest of Spain. It is the greatest monument of Spanish medieval literature.

An ancient Celtic poetic tradition had been taken to Ireland by the Britons fleeing the Anglo-Saxons in the fifth and sixth centuries. There it continued to live, producing a collection of stories striking for their imaginativeness. Four of these legends were transmitted in the *Mabinogion,* a compilation probably written down in the eleventh century. Later writers added other stories to the collection, and together they had a great impact on the development of the Arthurian cycle. The famed characters Merlin and the fairy queen Morgan le Fay stem from the Celtic tradition.

The distinguishing characteristic of medieval Irish literature is its imaginative and exuberant quality. The Irish bards used exaggeration as the standard means of expressing emotion or giving emphasis in their lyric poetry and prose narratives. For example, the hero Cu Chulainn is so described:

> A beautiful boy indeed was he: seven toes to each foot he had, and to either hand as many fingers; his eyes were bright with seven pupils apiece . . . on either cheek he had four moles, a blue, a crimson, a green, and a yellow one.

The Scandinavians shared the Germanic oral traditions with the Continental Germans, and this heritage emerged in an independent Icelandic written literature during the late eleventh century. The Icelanders had migrated from Norway in the mid-ninth century to escape the growing royal power of Harald Finehair, and they had established a society in which their ancient conventions and mythology were carefully preserved. They were transmitted in the *Poetic Edda,* a series of elaborate poems written down in the twelfth century (of which only fragments remain); the *Prose Edda,* compiled in the early thirteenth century by Snorri Sturluson (d. 1241); and the *Volsunga-saga,* probably written in the twelfth century. The Icelanders also wrote a series of prose sagas about the immigrants who had come to the island and the community they had founded. These stories tell of the North American explorations of Eric the Red and his son, Lief Ericsson, undertaken around 1000. They and their successors founded settlements on the North American continent, in Greenland, Newfoundland, and around Hudson's Bay. Historians and archeologists are still in the early stages of tracking the Icelandic and Norwegian activities in the New World. The greatest of the sagas was *Njal's Saga* by an anonymous late–thirteenth-century author who looked back to the heroic age of Iceland around 1000 and told of the transformation of the community under the impact of Christianity. *Njal's Saga* stands as one of the great literary masterpieces of the Middle Ages.

In France during the thirteenth century the vernacular romance continued to be popular, but the genre had become fairly stereotyped and little was produced that could rival the best of the twelfth century. The most important work, the *Romance of the Rose,* was more impressive for its quantity than its quality. The first part, four thousand lines long, was left unfinished by William of Lorris (ca. 1237) and was completed thirty years later by Jean de Meun in an incredibly long-winded conclusion of almost eighteen thousand lines. The poem is an allegory of love, an exhaustive recitation of everything that the two authors could think of to say about their subject. The narrative portions are slow moving, and the allegorical presentation substitutes abstract types for characterization. The main interest of the poem lies in the contrast between William of Lorris' part, a conventional allegory of courtly love designed to please a noble audience, and the part by Jean de Meun, who was an educated layman of bourgeois origin. In the latter section Jean presents what amounts to an encyclopedia of bourgeois satire and criticism of the clergy, the nobility, women, rulers, and villeins, together with miscellaneous information and misinformation on dozens of topics. Into the allegory, fantasy, and artificial *courtoisie* of romance, Jean injects a note of realism.

This element of realism had already appeared in a type of literature that was alien to the chivalric romance, the *fabliaux,* brief tales written in rhymed verse for a bourgeois audience. Some of these may originally have been folk tales handed down in oral tradition; others derived from stories preserved from Greco-Roman antiquity in such prose collections as the Latin *Gesta Romanorum.* The *fabliaux* were in some ways the vernacular equivalent of the Goliardic verse, since each subjects to biting satire the interests and values of the feudal nobility, the clergy, and the peasantry. One of the main purposes of the *fabliaux* was to amuse, and the humor is crude and broad. Stock characters appear, as in the romance, but they are characters of a wholly different world. Monks and priests are hypocritical and unscrupulous; the innkeeper usually has a beautiful daughter and a deficiency of common sense; the wealthy merchant is sharp in trade and stupid in all else; and women are usually portrayed as either amoral or simply immoral. In contrast to courtly romance, this literature presents no ideals of conduct, other than the tricks and maneuvers by which the clever rogue outwits "respectable" or conventional people. The hero is often a wandering scholar or a poor but quick-witted commoner.

Sometimes these *fabliaux* point a moral, and this didactic element links them to another popular form of vernacular literature, the fable. The fable or animal story derives both from classical antiquity, which produced the fables attributed to Aesop, and from Germanic folklore. As in the later forms of romance, the allegorical element is prominent; each animal represents a type of human being. The most popular medieval fables were those collectively known as the *Romance of Reynard,* in which Reynard the Fox plays approximately the same role as the heroes of the *fabliaux.*

The center of this bourgeois vernacular literature was the northern French towns, where municipal documents had been written in the vernacular since the late twelfth century. Although the bourgeois literature of all other countries was influenced by that of France, in Italy short stories in prose were especially popular. These were the *novelle,* a kind of up-to-date and vernacular version of the *Gesta Romanorum* in which the greater diversity of subject matter allowed the author greater freedom to create original plots and characters. The earliest collection, *Il Novellino,* dates from the end of the thirteenth century.

The growing amount of vernacular religious literature in the high Middle Ages probably indicates an increasing bourgeois interest in literature as well as an increasing bourgeois piety. In the twelfth century, parts of the New Testament were translated into French by the Waldensians (a heretical sect), and the earliest Lives of the Saints were translated or paraphrased in the vernacular. The *Life of Saint Dominic* and the *Life of Saint Francis,* both in French, were derivative from earlier Latin Lives. Saint Francis and the later Franciscan, Jacopone da Todi (d. 1307) were among the earliest to write poetry in Italian instead of in the literary language of their country, which was still French. Francis' *Canticle of the Sun* is one of the finest expressions of the devotion that inspired the Order of Friars Minor. In England the French of the nobility and the Latin of the clergy almost drove the native tongue out of written literature, but the *Ancren Riwle* (ca. 1210) in Middle English prose compares favorably with any of the contemporary devotional works written in the vernacular on the Continent. It was popular enough to be translated into both French and Latin.

The twelfth century was a turning point for vernacular history, biography, and travel literature. The termination of the Anglo-Saxon Chronicle in England, in 1154, marks the close of the Old English period. Henceforth until the end of the fourteenth century vernacular history in England was written in French, beginning with the mediocre verse of Wace's *Roman de Rou* (ca. 1170), a tedious history commissioned by Henry II to glorify the dukes of Normandy. At about the same time the *Kaiserchronik* was composed, in seventeen thousand verses, relating the history of the medieval empire in German. Neither of these works was as important as the first great history in French prose, *The Conquest of Constantinople* by Villehardouin (ca. 1160–1213), a layman and a participant in the Fourth Crusade.

The best biographies of the thirteenth century were also written in French and by laymen, the first at the beginning of the century in verse and the second at the end in prose. These were the anonymous *History of William the Marshal,* recounting the deeds of the knight whose career was followed earlier, and the *History of Saint Louis* by Jean de Joinville (1224–1317). These works, especially the latter, are full accounts of both the life and times of their subjects, and there are no better guides to the realities, the values, and the ideals of the feudal nobility of the high Middle Ages. Just as popular as the vernacular histories and biographies were the autobiographical works written by travelers, the most familiar of which is Marco Polo's account (ca. 1298) of his travels through the Orient and his residence for seventeen years in China. Although Marco Polo was a Venetian, his work was written in French.

Italian vernacular literature was a product of the thirteenth century, particularly the later part of the century when the complete breakdown of imperial government left Italy to itself. In the complex city-state system produced by the diminution of external influences in the peninsula, a new civic spirit developed in the communes, and the new spirit found expression in literature. At first this literature followed the patterns of French love poetry, but in their independence, the Italians soon became conscious of the need for a new literature. One of the leaders of this movement was the Florentine Dante Alighieri (1265–1321). Dante was an educated layman involved in Florentine politics. In the early fourteenth century, he went into exile when the pope supported an uprising in the city. In the leisure and pain of exile, Dante wrote *The Divine Comedy,* the crowning achievement of medieval literature, if not of medieval civilization. The *Comedy* was based on Virgil's great epic, the *Aeneid,* and on Saint Augustine's *Confessions* (which provided the theological orientation). Dante called his work a comedy to contrast its vernacular style to the high Latin tragedy of Virgil, whose *persona* guided Dante-pilgrim on a journey of the soul toward God. Notwithstanding Virgil's higher style, Dante achieved more than his predecessor both poetically and spiritually because he was Christian. As the builders of the Gothic cathedrals saw the whole world in their creations, so Dante re-created the world of history, natural lore, and theological understanding in his work. The vehicle

P cro fcortcemmo a la rcstra mamella.
cotcce pisli femmo un su lostremo.
per ben ceffar la rena ela fiamella.

Dante's *Divine Comedy* was recognized immediately as a classic and was produced in deluxe, illustrated editions. In this illustration from a fourteenth-century Italian manuscript, Dante and his guide, Virgil, visit the circle of usurers in Hell (Canto XI). The usurers suffer under a rain of fire, huddled on burning sand that gives them no relief.

for presenting this magnificent edifice is a poetry that can only be compared with that of Homer and Virgil for its inventiveness, originality, depth, and power. Wolfram's hero *Parzival* had succeeded in harmonizing body and soul so that the body did not deprive the soul of its salvation. Dante succeeded in harmonizing the material world as he knew it with the spiritual world as men like Saint Thomas Aquinas presented it, and in so doing, created the finest Christian vision of the universe of all time.

### Suggestions for Further Reading

**Secondary Works**   For an introduction to Latin culture, see the book by H. O. Taylor cited at the end of Chapter 15. The basic works on medieval Latin poetry are by F. J. E. Raby: *A History of Christian Latin Poetry from the Beginnings to the Close of the Middle Ages,* 2nd ed. (Oxford, 1953) and *A History of Secular Latin Poetry in the Middle Ages,* 2 vols. (Oxford, 1934). J. W. Thompson, *The History of Historical Writing,* 2 vols. (New York, 1942) is a general work that treats the Middle Ages in detail. R. E. Messenger, *The Medieval Latin Hymn* (Washington, D.C., 1953) is a good work on that subject. A good introduction to the environment and the people who produced Goliardic verse is H. Waddell, *The Wandering Scholars,* 7th ed. (London, 1934). An introduction to the vernacular literature of the Middle Ages may be found in such standard works as W. T. H.

Jackson, *Medieval Literature: A History and a Guide* (New York, 1966); U. T. Holmes, *A History of Old French Literature,* 2nd ed. (New York, 1948); *The Cambridge History of English Literature,* vol. 1, ed. A. W. Ward and A. R. Waller (Cambridge, 1907); R. S. Loomis, *The Development of Arthurian Romance* (London, 1963); J. G. Robertson, *A History of German Literature,* 2nd ed. (London, 1947); and E. H. Wilkins, *A History of Italian Literature* (Cambridge, Mass., 1954). Of the enormous and varied literature that is concerned with Dante, the basic work in English is K. Vossler, *Medieval Culture: An Introduction to Dante and His Times,* 2 vols. (New York, 1929). See also P. Wolff, *Western Languages,* A.D. *100–1500,* trans. F. Partridge (New York, 1971).

**Sources**   For Latin poetry two standard collections are J. A. Symonds, *Wine, Women, and Song* (London, 1884), and H. Waddell, *Medieval Latin Lyrics* (London, 1929). There are numerous easily accessible translations of vernacular poetry, romance, and *fabliaux,* notably in Everyman's Library, where also will be found the best translation of Villehardouin, and in the Modern Library volume edited by R. S. Loomis and L. H. Loomis, *Medieval Romances* (New York, 1957). The poems of the troubadours and trouvères are translated in F. Goldin, *Lyrics of the Troubadours and Trouvères* (Garden City, N.Y., 1973). See also by the same translator, *German and Italian Lyrics of the Middle Ages* (Garden City, N.Y., 1973). There are many translations of *Beowulf* and the *Song of Roland;* for example, *Beowulf,* trans. D. Wright (Harmondsworth, 1957), and *Song of Roland,* trans. R. Harrison (New York, 1970). Wolfram von Eschenbach's *Parzival* was translated by H. M. Mustard and C. E. Passage (New York, 1961). For Icelandic literature, see *Poems of the Vikings,* trans. P. Terry (New York, 1969), which contains the *Elder Edda; Volsunga Saga,* trans. W. Morris (New York, 1962); and *Njal's Saga,* trans. M. Magnusson and H. Palsson (Harmondsworth, 1960). The great Spanish epic was translated by J. G. Markley, *The Epic of the Cid* (New York, 1961). There are many translations of *The Divine Comedy;* for example, J. D. Sinclair's translation in three volumes (Oxford, 1961), which contains both the original Italian and a translation, and an extensive commentary.

# 17  Romanesque
# and Gothic Art

Around the middle of the eleventh century, a French chronicler remarked, "The whole world seems to have shaken off her slumber, cast off her old rags, and clothed herself in a white mantel of new churches." A new era in the history of Western art and architecture had begun, which is significant both for the amount of building and for the new architectural styles it produced. Art historians have termed this new style of building *Romanesque* because it makes use of the rounded arches found in Roman construction. Etymologically the term makes some sense, for while great Romanesque structures do not look like Roman buildings, their architects used construction techniques inherited from antiquity.

In contrast, the word *Gothic,* used for the style that developed from the Romanesque, is a misnomer. The Gothic style has nothing to do with the Goths. In the sixteenth century *Gothic* meant "crude" or "barbaric," and by the early seventeenth century it had come to be used as a technical term referring to medieval structures. *Gothic* is therefore a term descriptive not of the architecture itself but of the taste of early critics. When Racine visited

**413**

the cathedral of Chartres in the seventeenth century he called it "big but a trifle barbarous."

Both the Romanesque and Gothic styles were international and can be illustrated with examples from all over Europe. Although regional variations are sometimes striking, gems of Romanesque construction can be found in Yugoslavia and Sweden, or fine Gothic churches in Hungary and Sweden. It is legitimate, however, to begin the study of Gothic art with French examples, for in the Middle Ages the Gothic was called the French style (*opus francigenum*), since French architects took the lead in the new form of construction and helped to introduce it to other parts of Europe and the Near East.

Medieval art and architecture were not purely religious. The Church possessed the wealth and organization necessary for large-scale and continuing construction, and a strong religious motivation underlay the vast expenditure of labor and resources that went into building churches. But one should not be tricked by the fortunes of survival into forgetting that great resources and skill were also expended on buildings and works of art intended for lay patrons. Churches have survived better than castles, but the remains of a few great castles and town houses show that secular art and construction advanced along with ecclesiastical work.

## The Romanesque Achievement

Romanesque architecture developed in the late eleventh century and had a short life span. It was a transitional style that connected the Roman basilica type building and the Gothic style that developed from about 1140 on. Although the revolutionary advances made by the architects of Gothic buildings are always recognized, the first radical innovations had been made in Romanesque structures. Romanesque buildings were either wholly or predominantly made of stone, which was made possible by the solution of several engineering problems, notably the effective use of stone vaulting for roofs and the buttressing of the thrust created by these heavy roofs.

The great achievement of the Romanesque builders was both technical and aesthetic. The aesthetic problem that challenged the designers of these new churches was to relate the parts of the building to each other, to subordinate all the parts to the whole, and thus to create an organic unity. In the developed Romanesque style, no single part of the building stands by itself, but each contributes to the total impression conveyed by the entire structure. The most important specific problem was to link together the walls by means of vaulting. The old-fashioned basilica type of church had a flat wooden roof that provided a cover but fulfilled almost no aesthetic function; the roof appeared where the walls ended and thus established the proportions of the interior, but beyond that function the roof was simply there.

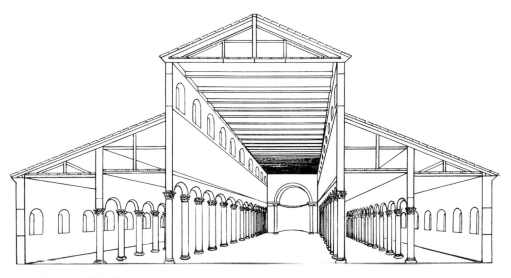

Clerestory (Basilica)

The ground plan of the Romanesque church was derived from that of the basilica church. It had a cruciform plan consisting of nave with aisles on either side, a transept at right angles to the nave to form the cross, and a rounded apse extending beyond the transept. The orientation of the church was west to east, with the altar at the eastern end, just inside the apse. In some of the larger churches a section called the choir extended eastward from the transept before the apse was reached, so that in the largest buildings the choir and apse together were about as long as the nave. In such a building the transept formed a crossing midway between either end of the church. It was also common in the larger buildings to have an ambulatory; that is, a continuation of the aisles beyond the transept, going around the apse or choir and apse. Builders also used a row of windows on an upper level, called a clerestory, to heighten the structure and allow the entrance of light.

The round arch and the round vault were the basic structural elements of the Romanesque style. On the outside, portals and windows were enclosed by arches, the windows often in the form of adjacent double arches so that the wall above the opening was provided with a support running up through the middle. Inside, the aisles and nave were covered by vaulting that supported a very light, sloping roof to shed rain. This vaulting continued the motif of the round arch along the longitudinal axis of the interior. The earlier churches were small enough, and the aisles and nave narrow enough, so that one continuous barrel vault could be employed. In this case the transept was formed by the intersection of another barrel vault, forming a cross vault. The weight of a barrel vault is very great, however, and it creates both downward and outward thrust. The vault rests evenly along the walls on which it is con-

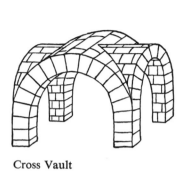

Cross Vault

structed, and to support a barrel vault of great size, the walls must be so massive that no windows can be cut through them. The walls must control the outward thrust as well as support the downward weight of the vault. The walls could be built lighter and higher and the nave and aisles wider, however, if the weight of the vaulting were reduced or concentrated at certain points where buttressing of the wall might contain the thrust. This was accomplished by substituting a series of cross vaults for the one barrel vault.

Cross vaults whose length and width are equal enclose a square space, and the thrust of such a cross vault is concentrated at the four corners. The nave, the aisles, and the transept could be made much larger and higher by covering them with a series of such cross vaults and reinforcing the walls underneath the corners of each successive vault. This reinforcement had to be strong because the resolution of the forces created by the two vaults was at a forty-five degree angle. The Romanesque interior was characterized by the same rhythmic succession of vertical lines along the axis of the structure that marked the interior of a basilica. The difference was that the columns of the smaller and lighter basilica were replaced by the massive compound piers necessary to bear the weight of Romanesque construction. Between these piers the walls were light enough to be pierced by windows, both on the outer walls of the aisles and the clerestory wall supported by the main piers of the nave. The choir, apse, and ambulatory were treated in the same way, except that the rounded end of the church could be covered by a half dome.

The impression made on a modern visitor by the interior of a great Romanesque church differs in many ways from that made on its original patrons. Today the churches have little ornamentation and create the impression of a cool and cavernous retreat, while massive piers and huge vaults produce a monumental and transcendental effect. No part of the interior distracts the observer from the impression created by the whole structure. This is why Romanesque churches have been described by such phrases as "colossal austerity" or "impersonal massiveness." But when they were built, Romanesque churches had interiors rich in gold, silver, and art. The walls were painted with scenes from the Bible, constituting one element of the Church's effort to reach the illiterate masses with its message. Europe's largest church in the

The barrel vault of high Romanesque, as this one in the eleventh-century church of Saint Savin, was an impressive structure that provided painters with an ideal uniform surface. The pillars and side walls had to be enormously thick to contain the thrusts produced by the vault, but adequate light could be admitted through clear windows in the apse and nave end. The paintings of Saint Savin, and the walls too would have been covered with art, are about contemporary with the church building.

twelfth century was, not surprisingly, the Romanesque abbey church at Cluny, and it was extraordinarily ornate. The ubiquitous Saint Bernard of Clairvaux attacked this ornamentation as yet another distraction from the meditation of prayer. The stark impression made by Romanesque churches still standing—Cluny's is not—results not from the criticism of Saint Bernard and his followers, however, but from the vicissitudes of history. In periods of extreme anticlericalism and economic hardship, the gilt and treasures of the churches reentered the economy in various ways. And as time passed tastes changed. Many medieval churches in southern Germany, for example, were transformed into Baroque buildings during the seventeenth and eighteenth centuries. In the nineteenth century many churches were cleansed of their remaining interior wall paintings.

The exterior of the Romanesque church also marked a radical break from the older basilica style. The older churches presented a rather bare appearance, except for the colonnaded porticoes of some of the larger basilicas. In contrast, the Romanesque builders adorned their churches with decorative patterns along the outside walls, usually emphasizing horizontal lines that harmonized with the window and portal arches. The most prominent external feature of the Romanesque style was the addition of one or more towers. Sometimes a single tower was raised above the supporting arches of the transept; more often the façade or front of the structure was provided with two towers, one on either side. The façade, taken as a whole, was dominated by horizontal lines and decorative motifs so that the height of the towers was not emphasized. In the space beneath the arches that surmounted each portal (one for the nave and one for each aisle), sculpture was employed for decorative effect.

In the Romanesque period large-scale or life-size sculpture was used for the first time since later antiquity. The human figure, animals, and natural scenery were rendered in a style designed to bring out the message or symbolic significance of the subject matter. Naturalistic representation, insofar as it might detract from this significance, was avoided. Instead, all unnecessary detail was suppressed, form was exaggerated or distorted to show the salient features, and surfaces were often given a smooth and rounded treatment to emphasize mass. This style developed gradually from the miniature carving and the painting of the tenth and eleventh centuries. It represents the final stage in a slow transformation of classical naturalism, influenced by Germanic and Celtic ornamental and geometrical abstraction, into a new style that was abstract, monumental, and—by directing the observer's attention to the spiritual or symbolic meaning of the subject matter—transcendental.

Romanesque sculpture was strictly subordinated to architecture, both in its physical location and in its purpose. The sculptured figures and scenes were fitted into the building, especially above the portals and along the façade. The elongation of the human body, characteristic of Romanesque style, served to harmonize the sculpture with ornamental columns. Sometimes

The west (royal) portal of Chartres (ca. 1150) was carefully planned and executed. *Below* The tympana represent the beginning (right), end (left, the Ascension), and culmination (center, the Second Coming and Last Judgment) of Christ's mission. *Right* Detail of sculptures from the royal portal that found many imitators in Europe. Along with twenty-one other life-size figures, they represent the human ancestors of Christ.

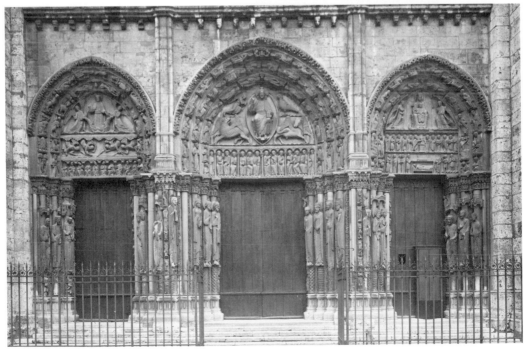

Rich portal and façade sculpture is associated with the Gothic churches, but this tympanum above the west portal to the Romanesque church of Vézelay in Burgundy shows that Romanesque masons were capable of extraordinary work. The artists chose the traditional scene of the Last Judgment and depicted the good and evil souls around the central figure of Christ.

these figures took the place of the columns, standing on the same bases and supporting the same capitals that would have been used for columns. In subject matter, the most common representation was the salvation of the blessed and damnation of the wicked, including the biblical scenes depicting the sufferings of Christ and his plan for redemption.

## Gothic Architecture
## and the Decorative Arts

During the twelfth century several innovations in the art of building transformed the Romanesque into the Gothic style of architecture. The transition was at first gradual, and most of the typically Gothic methods of construction appeared first as particular features of churches that were otherwise Romanesque. This development was combined with, and may have been derived from, the use of the ribbed vault instead of the simple cross vault. The ribbed vault was constructed by connecting the corners of a cross vault by arches that diagonally span the rectangle or square created by the vault. Since the diagonal is longer than the side of a rectangle, the height of the two diagonally constructed arches, the ribs, in the ribbed vault were higher than the arches forming the sides. Romanesque builders introduced the ribbed vault to decrease the weight of the vaulting. In the new structure, the ribs remained very heavy, but the four triangular spaces created by the diagonal arches were filled with light masonry.

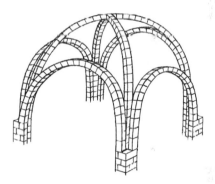

Ribbed Vault: six round arches (diagonal
and on sides) enclosing square area

The effect of this innovation may be seen in Durham Cathedral in England, where the vault undulates down the nave. The paneling of light masonry, however, had two defects. Aesthetically, it was not satisfactory to have the surface of the panels twist from the semicircular plane of the four side arches to the new semicircular plane of the two diagonal arches, which were of greater dimension and revolved around forty-five degrees. Structurally, this kind of masonry tended to be weak because the direction of thrust at any one point was never the same as the thrust at any other point. An understanding of solid geometry and engineering makes this clear to the modern student; medieval builders learned by trial and error. They found a solution to both difficulties by constructing the two diagonal ribs in the form of round arches and the other four ribs along symmetrical curves ending in a point at the greater height of the diagonal arches. What has actually happened is that the two intersecting barrel vaults have been replaced by two vaults that are an extension of a pointed rather than a round arch. Now the panel of masonry between the arches follows a uniform plane, without any change or twisting, so that both structurally and aesthetically the result is satisfactory.

The system of vaulting by ribs and panels, together with the pointed, or ogival, arch or vault implicit in that system, was the essence of Gothic architecture. The more obvious features of the Gothic style all follow logically from this great innovation, for which the Romanesque builders were originally responsible. One of the first large buildings with ribbed vaults and pointed arches was the abbey church of Saint Denis, near Paris, rebuilt by the abbot Suger (d. 1151) in the last ten years of his life. Suger has a special place in the history of architecture because he wrote a treatise about his building program that explained how he felt about the new structure. He tells of his de-

Looking down the nave toward the apse in Amiens Cathedral. The choir screen divides the clergy in their elaborately carved wood stalls from the laity, who, in the Middle Ages, stood on the pavement of the nave, since there were no pews. The vaulting is of the simple cross-vault type.

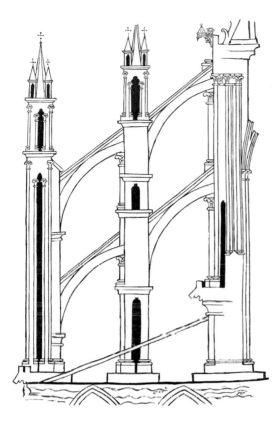

Flying Buttresses. From the Notebooks of Villard de Honnecourt (first half of the thirteenth century)

light in the increased space devoted to stained-glass windows and in the airy height of the new ribbed vaulting. By the end of the century almost all new construction employed the vaulting system based on the pointed arch.

From an engineering point of view, the new style had many advantages. The structure could be built higher, since the height of the pointed arch was not bound by the span it covered. The higher the pointed arch, the greater was the efficiency in buttressing, since the thrust was directed in a more nearly vertical direction as the height increased. Even more important was an innovation in buttressing developed originally by Romanesque builders and employed extensively in Gothic construction. Instead of allowing the whole thrust of the vaulting to descend on the main piers of the nave, half-arch supports were built from the base (and from just above the base) of the rib of the nave vault outward and over the aisle to a pier located outside the building. This was the flying buttress. It contained part of the thrust and brought it to rest where a massive support would not interfere with the walls of the church. This meant that the walls carried no weight but their own and were relieved of the outward pressure exerted by the vaulting above. The walls were reduced in thickness, and thus could be pierced by much larger open-

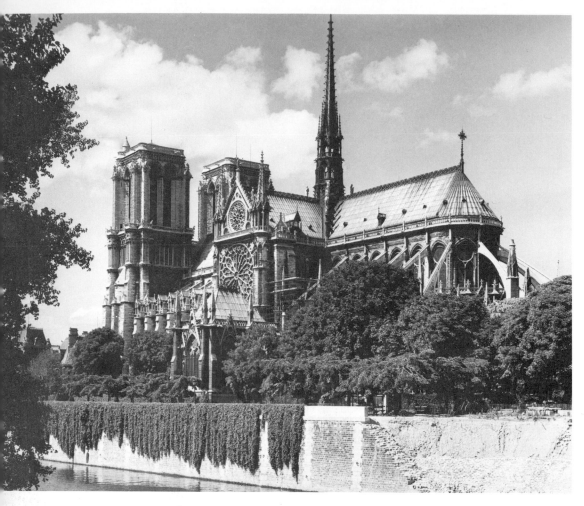

Notre-Dame of Paris from the apse side. By the time this great church was built in the thirteenth century, flying buttresses had become part of the aesthetic as well as the structural aspect of the church building. The builders therefore placed more buttresses around the choir and apse than were necessary for supporting the roof. In thirteenth-century churches, rose windows were used in the transepts as well as in the end wall of the nave, as in this view of the south transept.

ings for windows. The result was a transformation of the interior. The walls of a Gothic church became translucent. Also, and just as important for the general effect of the interior, the flying buttresses made possible a change from massive piers along the nave to a series of thinner columns bearing an arcade.

In the Romanesque interior, massiveness and horizontal lines emphasize the solidity of the structure. In the Gothic interior, almost all the lines are vertical, and weight has been eliminated wherever possible. The proportion of space to mass is exaggerated in the later Gothic cathedrals to the point where the structure appears to be unstable and insecure, conveying an illusion of soaring upward. This illusion of movement is increased by the use of stained-glass windows that flood the interior with multicolored, shimmering light. The central feature of the façade of a Gothic cathedral, viewed from the interior, is the rose window, a circular space that is filled with tracery holding stained glass arranged in a complicated, wheel-like pattern. The northern and southern transept walls are almost wholly cut away, in the developed Gothic style, so that the area before the altar is provided with a maximum of light to correspond with the focus of liturgical interest. Often, as in the cathedral of Notre Dame in Paris, the stained glass of the north window of the transept will be predominantly blue, while the south window catching the sun has been given an extravagant amount of red, yellow, and orange hues.

In the early Gothic period (ca. 1150–1250) many churches were built or begun in which the lightness of Gothic was combined with some of the rugged simplicity of the Romanesque style. The famed Gothic cathedral at Chartres is actually an architectural mixture that contains elements of an earlier Romanesque church, including the elongated sculptures of the west portal. The cathedral of Reims, however, was built in a uniform Gothic style, although like many great churches it never received the spires that would have completed its design. After the thirteenth century, architects began to develop the elaborate articulation and profuse decoration that characterizes the later Gothic style. In England the names Decorated and Perpendicular are accurate descriptive terms for the Gothic building of the fourteenth and fifteenth centuries. Ornamentation and the use of vertical lines are so exaggerated that the total effect is that of architectural ingenuity, a tour de force that displays the builders' skill, rather than an aesthetically satisfying structure. Later Gothic churches exhibit complicated variations of ribbed vaulting, flying buttresses more abundant than strictly necessary for bearing the weight, and a superfluity of decorative patterns in the masonry. Complex curves that suggest the flame of a candle mark the late Gothic style called Flamboyant.

Towns engaged in a rivalry to build the biggest cathedral. The cathedral at Amiens, begun in 1220 and largely completed by 1269, was enormous. Its nave was 141 feet high. The citizens of neighboring Beauvais resolved not to be outdone and began to build their new cathedral in 1247 on an even larger scale. Beginning, as usual, with the choir and apse, they built their vaulting thirteen feet higher than at Amiens, but it came tumbling down almost immediately. In 1272 they began rebuilding the choir, but in 1284 the vaulting collapsed again. Again they rebuilt, introducing additional supporting columns and doubling the number of arches so that the vertical lines were especially pronounced. Although a transept was added, much later, the church as a whole was never finished. The final triumph of the citizens of Beauvais was a choir rising to 157 feet, the height of a modern fifteen-story

Gothic churches gave room to the skills of freemasons, who did the sculpture. By recessing the door in the portal, Gothic architects vastly increased the amount of space that could receive sculpture. As a result, traditional scenes were elaborated, and new themes appeared. The theological importance of the portals, such as these at Reims Cathedral, as entries into the house of God limited thematic material to religious scenes, but elsewhere in the church, stories from popular adventures and romances were often carved into the stone.

building and higher than any Gothic vaulting achieved elsewhere. But the limit had been reached: the choir at Beauvais had to be reinforced with iron rods to hold the structure together.

The sculpture of the Gothic churches continued to be primarily didactic in purpose. The sculptured scenes that adorned the walls and portals were "sermons in stone." According to Suger, "Our poor spirit is so feeble that it is only through sensible realities that it raises itself to the truth." The subject matter remained much the same as in the Romanesque period, ranging from stories and figures from the Old and New Testaments to the details of daily life and common experience.

Sculpture enhanced the outside of the great Gothic churches (the cathedral at Reims has more than two thousand carved figures on its façade), but stained-glass windows dominated the interiors. The stained-glass or painted windows were used in the early Middle Ages, but the earliest extant ones date from the eleventh century. Romanesque churches provided little opportunity for the art to advance. Gothic building techniques, however, permitted the construction of churches with walls of glass, which became the vehicle for display and development of the glaziers. Where dark colors were used for the glass, the walls seem luminescent without being bright. At the great Romanesque church in Vézelay, the windows are small but clear, and they

The classicism of the Gothic style is evident in the comparison of these two representations of the Visitation. *Left*   An early–twelfth-century Romanesque work from the abbey church of Saint Peter of Moissac. *Right*   A Gothic work of the late thirteenth century on the façade of Reims Cathedral. The Gothic is more naturalistic and emphasizes the poses of the figures. The Romanesque is stylized and emphasizes bodily distortion produced by the emotion of the interchange between Mary and the angel.

Gothic builders maximized the downward thrust of the roof and gathered that thrust onto pillars. This structural innovation permitted the architects to virtually eliminate the walls between the pillars; Sainte-Chapelle indicates how far they could go. Built by Louis IX to receive the bits of the True Cross he had gotten from Jerusalem, it is the jewel of Gothic, a translucent structure with few, if any, structural or aesthetic defects.

light the interior of the church more brightly than the huge stained-glass windows light the cathedral at Chartres. In the seventeenth century, modernizing clergymen often replaced Gothic windows with lighter glass so they could read in the choir.

Historians have always wondered who was responsible for the development of the Gothic style. Some have argued that Suger and churchmen like him stood behind the new architecture, telling the masons how they wanted their churches to look. Others have argued that Suger's excitement was simply his reaction to the building his masons had created for him. They also suggest that the reason the first distinctly Gothic church was built at Saint Denis was that the Île-de-France had no architectural style of its own, and therefore Suger had to import his masons from other areas where various elements of Gothic style had been evolving for some time; the masons gathered at Saint Denis created the composite style called Gothic. Both these views present problems. Buildings that stand are not built by committees. In every medieval building project known about in some detail, an architect, called the master mason, designed the building and oversaw its construction. He also did some of the most intricate stonecutting. Many of the great churches were built bit by bit over decades, even centuries, and thus had many architects, but Saint Denis was built in only seven years. Thus its design was relatively unified, the product of one or two master masons. Suger obviously played the role of all architectural patrons. He told his workmen what he wanted; they told him if it could be done and how much they thought it would cost. Suger's treatise makes it clear that he did not simply tell his master mason to build and then go about his own business. However, the abbot's lack of technical skill limited his participation in the project.

The building trades were particularly able to bring styles together from widely separated regions of Europe. While guilds were usually local, limited to the workers or craftsmen in a single town, the stonemasons not only had a rare and highly developed skill but also could not rely on the economy of any one area to support them. Wooden buildings were common and could be built by locals; stone buildings were rare and could be built only by specialists. The masons therefore traveled from site to site, setting up sheds and tents in which to live and work. There were several levels of expertise in the guild. Laborers were usually locals hired for carrying stone and other materials. Within the guild itself, rough masons prepared the basic blocks of stone, and masons squared and finished the blocks, an art that developed significantly in the early twelfth century and is evident in the difference between the stone blocks of Romanesque and Gothic churches. Freemasons, of whom the master mason was one, carved the marvelous façades and portals of the great Gothic churches as well as the animals, plants, and intricate abstract designs along ribs and on the capitals of columns in the interior. In many Gothic churches magnificent stonecarving is hidden in inaccessible nooks near the roofs.

Once it was developed, the Gothic style became predominant throughout Europe. Men like Suger saw in the new churches a model of the universe, a microcosm that was the perfect place for prayer to the Creator of the macrocosm. Suger lavished attention on the geometric proportions of his church as the representation of the universal proportions. Founding his architectural ideology on the work of the Pseudo-Dionysius (supposed by the monks of Saint Denis to be their patron saint, Dionysius the Areopagite), Suger told his readers that the great windows of his church let in light that illuminated the interior, just as God, the Light, illuminated the world itself. Recognizing the symbolic possibilities of the new churches, ecclesiastical writers developed an elaborate system of symbolism, explained by the early–fourteenth-century writer William Durand in his work *On the Symbolism of the Churches*. The whole building represented the body of the Church, and the three parts of the Church building represented the three classes of Church members: the sanctuary symbolized the virgins and the priesthood; the choir stood for the continent, or monks; the nave was the common laity. The four walls represented the teachings of the four Evangelists (portrayed in the stained-glass windows) and the four cardinal virtues (justice, fortitude, temperance, and prudence). The foundation was faith, which is conversant with things unknown; the roof was charity, which covers a multitude of sins. The doors represented obedience in accordance with Matthew 19:17: "If you will enter into life, keep the commandments." The pavement symbolized humility; the pillars, bishops; the roof tiles, soldiers who ward off the enemies of the Church. Finally, the windows were the Holy Scriptures; they let in the light of God and keep out the injurious teachings of heretics and infidels.

Thus the Gothic style was an apt expression of both the deepest and the most superficial religious ideas of high medieval culture in northern Europe: its love of nature carved in the stone; its theological orientation contained in the windows and the literature about the churches; its mysticism revealed in the height, the play of light, and the stark magnificence. In the south, in Italy, the Gothic style never developed. To explain this fact, it is easy to point to the hot sunny climate that made large windows, which admit heat as well as light, less attractive than in the north, but there may also be more interesting reasons. The Italian communities differed significantly from the northern European towns that expressed themselves in Gothic churches. They had survived through the period when northern cities had shrunk to small establishments surrounding the episcopal church, and were therefore economically, socially, and psychologically more independent of the Church than the communities in the north. The Italians had preserved the shreds of an ancient civic tradition and had a more secular, less mystical, communal spirit than the northern communities. Italian churches continued to have large wall surfaces for decoration, and by the end of the thirteenth century Italian painters had developed the technique of fresco painting, in which paint is applied to new plaster while the surface is still wet. It was in this medium that Giotto (1266?–1337) made the great artistic advances in perspective and plasticity that adumbrated the Italian Renaissance styles in which classical models gave new impetus for artistic change.

Sculpture, painting, and stained-glass windows of both the Romanesque and Gothic periods are for the careful modern viewer a source not only of inspiration and aesthetic pleasure but also of information about the medieval world. Works of art portray the clothing, household objects, and activities of social groups. They are the key to the medieval artists' conception of their world. The same movement toward greater realism from Romanesque to Gothic representation can also be found in literature. In literature as in art, details are important clues to meaning. The simple linear figures of the early sculpture at Chartres correspond to the simple delineation of character in the *Song of Roland,* while the harmonious structure and artistic portraiture of *Parzival* and *The Divine Comedy* show the same spirit as an immense Gothic cathedral and its sculpture.

### Suggestions for Further Reading

**Secondary Works**   On architecture, see K. J. Conant, *Early Medieval Church Architecture* (Baltimore, 1942), and T. G. Jackson, *Gothic Architecture,* 2 vols. (Cambridge, 1915). E. Panofsky, *Gothic Architecture and Scholasticism* (Latrobe, Pa., 1951), and O. von Simpson, *The Gothic Cathedral* (New York, 1956) treat the intellectual aspect of Gothic churches. Henry Adams, *Mont-Saint-Michel and Chartres* (Boston, 1922) is an impressionistic survey of medieval art and culture. E. Mâle, *The Gothic Image: Religious Art in France in the Thirteenth Century* (London, 1913) is a classic; see also the more recent A. Martindale, *Gothic Art from the Twelfth to the Fifteenth Century* (London, 1967). Jean Gimpel, *The Cathedral Builders,* trans. C. F. Barnes, Jr. (New York, 1961), and L. F. Salzman, *Building in England down to 1540* (Oxford, 1952) discuss the actual construction of the churches. For a close study of one great cathedral church, see R. Branner, ed., *Chartres Cathedral* (New York, 1969).

**Sources**   The works cited above are profusely illustrated. In addition, see William Durand, *The Symbolism of Churches and Church Ornaments,* 3rd ed. (London, 1906).

# 18 Religious Life and Ecclesiastical Organization

In the high Middle Ages, people understood their world in moral and religious terms, so that the kind of zeal today directed to politics, scientific inquiry, and psychological investigation was directed in the Middle Ages toward questions of religion. The importance of religion in medieval society does not mean medieval society was "religious," as that term is usually understood today, or that the Middle Ages was an "age of faith." Christian orthodoxy, Christian heresy, Judaism, and paganism, all in many forms and varieties, jostled one another in the Latin world. In short, the medieval period was an age of many faiths. But, paradoxically, it was also an age in which many people understood their religion and practiced it casually.

In the modern world, rationalism, materialism, and faith in science as a key to understanding are all powerful rivals to traditional religion. In the Middle Ages it was difficult for a religious skeptic to find an alternative faith. Nevertheless, skeptics were common; in the twelfth century the Count of Soissons called the story of the Resurrection a "fable" and "windy talk," and in the thirteenth century at the University of Paris, an active group of scholars experimented with Arabic science and rational philosophy. But unlike a modern skeptic, a medieval critic could not easily turn to a nonreligious system of values and beliefs. The Count of Soissons was preoccupied with investigating the teachings of Catholics, heretics, and Jews, and the philosophers of Paris were engaged in endless disputation with their more orthodox colleagues. These religious disputes were a sign of the importance of religion, as was the medieval idea that training in theology was a sound background for careers in ecclesiastical and secular administration. The influence of religion pervaded all levels of society and all areas of life in medieval Europe.

But if one could not escape religion, one could take it for granted. The sacraments of the Church formalized the everyday rites of passage—birth, coming of age, marriage, and death—and most people accepted the articles of their faith, whether or not they understood the finer points of dogma. Religion was commonly ceremonial, conventional, and followed when convenient. To the despair of the better educated and more pious clergy, the faith of most people was superstitious and unreflective, saints were more venerated than imitated, and the teachings of the Church were most readily accepted when they did not challenge accepted practices or deeply held values. For example, from the twelfth century on, Church councils regularly anathematized tournaments and those who took part in them, but tournaments continued to flourish. One might compare the importance of the New Testament in medieval Europe with the influence of the Constitution in modern America. Neither society can be understood without reference to these primary texts, and yet members of both societies often ignored or reinterpreted their fundamental documents.

## The Doctrine of Medieval Christendom

Eternal salvation was the goal of Christian life. In the work of the Church, only the worship of God was more important than helping the faithful to attain this goal through the ceremonies and acts by which divine grace, the aid God gives men seeking salvation, might be received. These acts were the sacraments, the means of grace and the visible signs of invisible grace. The administration of the sacraments was the most time-consuming duty of the priest in his relationship with the laity; it was the essence of his care of souls. For centuries, almost all rites performed by the Church were considered sacraments. In the second half of the twelfth century, theologians and canon lawyers worked out a new definition of the sacrament, which differentiated between sacraments that actually conferred grace and those "sacramental" rites that were merely the occasion rather than the cause of grace. The theologians distinguished seven true sacraments from the myriad acts performed by priests. Five were for all Christians, one was reserved for the laity, and one was for priests only.

The first sacrament was baptism. It washed away all sin, including original sin, and constituted the rebirth of the person baptized into a new life of the Spirit and a mystical union with Christ. Baptism usually was administered to an infant by the parish priest, but because it was the essential sacrament, the admission into the state of grace, theologians recognized that in an emergency it could be performed by anyone, even a heretic. This doctrine brought out the principal problems inherent in the theology of the sacraments. The grant of grace was made by God to the recipient of the sacrament. Thus, what was the role of the priest, especially if it was recognized that his role could be performed by another? The theologians answered that the priest functioned as the vehicle, or agent, of God's grant. But in respect to the sacraments for which only the priest could be agent, what happened when the priest was evil? Was the sacrament efficacious? Did evil priests endanger the salvation of their flocks by obstructing the flow of divine grace to them? The eleventh-century reformers had been troubled by this problem, and extremists among them, such as Cardinal Humbert, had argued that no sacrament performed by a bad priest was effective. Others pointed out that if Humbert were correct, God had left thousands of innocent and pious Christians to damnation. In the mid-twelfth century, the great canon lawyer Gratian resolved the problem by differentiating between the actual and the legal state of the priest. As long as the priest was recognized as a member of the priesthood by the ecclesiastical authorities, his sacraments were efficacious regardless of the actual condition of his character.

The problem about the personality of the performer of the sacrament led to one about the condition of the recipient. It was generally agreed that the recipient must have the true faith in order to benefit from the sacrament. In the mid-twelfth century, at least one heretical sect argued that the babies being baptized could not and did not possess the proper spiritual awareness to receive the grace of baptism, and the sect's theologians quoted Mark 16:16 to support their position: "He who believes and is baptized will be saved." Orthodox writers answered this contention by arguing that the child was baptized in the faith of its parents or guardian, who offered it for the sacrament. It should be clear that as the theologians and canonists drew finer distinctions and constructed finer definitions in their sacramental theology, they bared the difficulties implicit in Christian doctrine.

The child began instruction in the Christian faith at about the age of seven, the "age of reason" according to medieval law, and at fourteen, the "age of majority," was ready for the second sacrament, confirmation. Confirmation, the laying on of hands, was performed by a bishop or by a priest delegated by him, and it was usually accompanied by the child's first communion, or Eucharist. The symbolic value of confirmation was not exploited by medieval thinkers, but the sacrament of the Eucharist received an extensive commentary. It was considered the means by which the Christian continued his union with the

Church, the body of Christ. By the later twelfth century, if not earlier, all Christians customarily received the Eucharist once a year, usually at Easter, and the Fourth Lateran Council, held by Innocent III in 1215, made annual communion mandatory.

Although baptism erased previous sin, it could not prevent the newly baptized from sinning again. During the twelfth century, theologians recognized a sacrament in the common practice of asking God's forgiveness for transgressions after baptism, usually through the priest. The sacrament of penance became the vehicle of salvation for the contrite sinner. The penitent confessed his sin to a priest and received absolution. Every priest—whether he were the rector of a country parish or the pope himself—had the power and was obligated by solemn duty to absolve the contrite penitent from the guilt of his sin and from the eternal punishment (damnation) that it entailed. But the sinner did not escape punishment; he was only guaranteed that it would not be eternal. Divine justice being, ultimately, a mystery beyond human comprehension, the priest could only help the sinner to atone for his sin by assigning a temporal punishment or penance to be performed on earth. Penance might take the form of a few extra prayers or additional fasting or almsgiving, or it might be as severe as a long pilgrimage or a substantial contribution to the work of the Church. When King Henry II was absolved from his share of the responsibility for the murder of Archbishop Thomas à Becket, for example, he was required to support two hundred knights for a year in the defense of Jerusalem, establish three new monasteries, allow appeals to be made freely to the papal *curia,* and make restitution to all who had suffered loss by supporting Becket. For the sins of ordinary persons, priests usually assigned penances listed in the penitentials, which were lists of appropriate penances approved by the Church through custom and usage.

Like baptism, the sacrament of penance raised serious problems for theologians and canon lawyers. The power of the priest in this sacrament rested on the so-called Petrine text from Matthew 16:19: "And I will give you the keys of the kingdom of heaven: and whatsoever you shall bind on earth shall be bound in heaven: and whatsoever you shall loose on earth shall be loosed in heaven." All theologians admitted that God—not the priest—remitted sin and that the priest's role was limited to hearing the confession and providing a penitential punishment. But the sacrament was only efficacious if the penitent was truly contrite, and it was clear that only God knows the penitent's mind, and he need not hear the confession to the priest to know it. Thus the theology of the sacrament of penance raised the gravest questions about priestly power, and it did not admit of a simple solution. Gratian discussed the issue at length and then left it to his readers to answer it for themselves.

The priestly power of the keys and of binding and loosing may have been placed in jeopardy by the musings of highly trained theologians and lawyers, but it led a very active life in the Church. Connected with the notion of sin and divine justice was the doctrine of purgatory. The saint might go straight to his reward, but the ordinary Christian expected to pass through an intermediate state after death where further temporal punishment was imposed for sins that had not been expiated by penance performed in mortal life. The canonistic maxim "What man does not punish, God punishes" referred to the temporal punishment in purgatory as well as to the eternal punishment of damnation. The truly penitent might obtain relief from the suffering of purgatory in accordance with a doctrine developed by theologians in the high Middle Ages. As successors of the Apostles, all bishops possessed the power of the keys. A bishop could therefore draw on the inexhaustible "treasury of merit," made up of the virtue of martyrs, saints, and good Christians and of the infinite merits of Jesus, and from this treasury grant an indulgence to the ordinary sinner whose penance would, for all he knew, fall short of satisfying divine justice. The theological doctrine was consistent and clear, but popular credulity sometimes confused the remission of punishment in purgatory (which an indulgence promised) with remission of sin itself (which an indulgence could not grant).

Extreme unction, consisting of prayer and anointment with consecrated oil by a priest, was the sacrament for the dying. These last rites of the Church were usually immediately preceded by confession and absolution, since the efficacy of extreme unction was considered to depend on the recipient's being free from mortal sin. If it was impossible to hear confession, or to determine whether the dying person was in a state of mortal sin, the sacrament was conditionally administered anyway, since it could do no harm and might help.

The sacrament of marriage was reserved for the laity. Celibacy was considered a more nearly perfect state than marriage, but the latter was immeasurably better than a state of unmarried incontinence. Two persons could be married by a civil ceremony, and the resulting marriage was not only a binding contract in terms of local custom but a valid marriage and hence a sacrament according to canon law. But by the end of the twelfth century the Church was taking a stronger stand, insisting that while such marriages were valid they were not proper; marriages ought to be solemnized by the Church with the appropriate religious ceremony. During the Middle Ages, the essence of the sacrament of marriage remained the intention and free consent of the two parties concerned. For example, a marriage that had been celebrated by a priest, even with the birth of children subsequent to that marriage, would have been declared null if it were discovered that one of the parties had formed an earlier marriage based on the mere exchange of spoken consent between himself and a third party.

Ordination to the priesthood was accomplished by the sacrament of Holy Orders, which could be administered only by a bishop. By his ordination, the priest received the spiritual power that set him apart from the laity and the clergy in minor orders: the power to offer the sacrifice of the Mass, to remit

played an important role
the power they had alway
only qualified nominees an
volved him in endless disp
revenues attached to paris
and the patron, and like an
to other persons. The rec
parish work was performe
other complications arisin
churches sometimes led to
endangering or neglecting t
the bishop's responsibility t
tect the incumbents of ch
ecclesiastical superiors.

The register of Archb
thirteenth century, reveals
late October 1256, Eudes k
he was in Caen, where he
dean was there; the number
was running about town g
these defects. Then he visit
rule of silence very well;
young nuns sang the Psalms
to stop. He checked their
much as they owed to other
the cloister was in disrepai
kept rabbit dogs; the bishop
ing to do with religious prac
confess once a month and t
January 1262, Eudes was s
beds and eating meat; he
monks, and incompetent ad
after institution. Eudes was
bishops hardly ever visited
papal affairs, but most spen
ministering their bishoprics
many fronts of religious life

Originally the administra
the bishop alone, assisted l
twelfth and thirteenth cent
permanently to one or mor
was divided into several arcl
direct control. As the deput

sins, and to administer the sacraments. This power was indelible. It could not deteriorate or be deficient in efficacy, nor, as said earlier, did it depend on the priest's moral condition. Only by due process of law, the canon law, could a priest be degraded, and then only by superior ecclesiastical authority. But even the process of degradation did not destroy or withdraw the spiritual power itself; rather, the priest was suspended from the use of the power.

The sacramental system was the heart of the religious life of the regular and secular clergy, but for the great majority of the laity, the sacramental aspect of religion was reserved for special occasions and did not play an important role in daily life. The parish church was as much a social center as it was a place of worship. Except for the great feast days of the Church, such as Christmas and Easter, the importance of saints' days and other festivals varied greatly from one locality to another. The saint to whom a local church had been dedicated, especially if his or her relics were preserved there, tended to be as important in the religious life of the people as the more remote Persons of the Trinity. Elements of the older paganism often survived in the popular mind to influence the meaning of such religious festivals as when the priest and his parishioners honored local saints, prayed for good crops, excommunicated noxious insects, or rendered thanks for abundant harvests. To the common man, illiterate and uneducated, it was easier to ascribe the health of his family or the fertility of his fields to the prayers of his priest or to the intercession by his patron saint than it was to understand the more complex mysteries of the sacraments.

During the eleventh and twelfth centuries a gradual change was completed, whose results might be described as the humanization of Christianity. The shifting emphasis in religion and in religious experience was evident at all levels, from systematic theology down to popular piety and superstition. In theology, for example, the early medieval explanation of the Incarnation and the Crucifixion assigned to human beings a relatively unimportant role. God became Man for the purpose of battling the Devil for the souls of men. Men, in thrall to the Devil, stood by as helpless spectators witnessing a cosmic drama, trembling in the hope that God would win, overawed by the mystery of the Incarnation.

By the middle of the twelfth century this view was considered an inadequate or incomplete account of man's Redemption. Instead of being a mystery beyond understanding, the Incarnation was explained as a supreme act of divine mercy in which God as Man confronted men. An element of mystery remained, but the humanity of Christ was now in the foreground. The incidents of the human life of Jesus—born of a woman, nourished with her milk, suffering weariness, hunger, thirst, and so forth—were the true mysteries, culminating in the ultimate mystery of his suffering on the Cross. Christ was no longer remote and austere, representing some power external to man's immediate experience.

The change
lels the change
the Saints were
or the communi
specific as to tir
places where th
cles were univei
removed them
tectress of the
who, except for

## The Organization
## of the Medieval Church

By the beginnin
Church had ach
—and the lawy
that described a

The basic ur
istrative district
southern Frencl
such as Lincoln
man frontier. T
of the late Rom
and its surround
the most impoi
episcopal seats
nomic and poli
the bishop had
had moved his <
on where he wo
dioceses grew, i
placed on a per

The chief s
confirmation, de
purification of <
episcopal duties
much of the bis
considered pari:
right to nomina
quiesced in this
right to ordain .
duced many lor

responsible for the supervision of parish priests, maintenance of the discipline and morals of both clergy and laity, building and repair of churches, and filling of parish vacancies (that is, making sure that local churches were provided with new priests without undue delay after death, promotion, or some other cause removed the incumbent). The archdeacon held meetings of the clergy under his charge and made visitations periodically to keep informed of local conditions. The archdeacon's court exercised a jurisdiction delegated from the bishop over minor ecclesiastical causes. Since these included both offenses by the clergy and moral lapses on the part of the laity, punishable under canon law, the archidiaconal court was almost universally detested. Some archdeacons were not above accepting bribes from suspected offenders in return for not prosecuting, or even blackmailing, innocent parties—lucrative malpractices that gave all archdeacons an unsavory reputation. Medieval students at the universities amused themselves by debating the mock-serious question: Is it possible for an archdeacon to be saved?

At each level of this diocesan hierarchy, from the parish priest to the bishop, it was possible and often necessary to delegate to a deputy most of the actual functions of office. The bishop, for example, was frequently absent from his diocese on ecclesiastical business or as an important adviser to a king or other secular ruler. Benefices like a parish church or the office of archdeacon were often granted to nonresident clerks for their support while in the service of kings or great lords. Hence deputies with various titles often undertook the daily performance of the duties of many church offices. In the thirteenth century most bishops appointed an official to act in their stead and to preside over the episcopal court for all ecclesiastical causes that had not already been delegated to the jurisdiction of the archdeacons. And nonresident parish priests appointed a vicar to take their place in the care of souls in the parish.

Diocesan administration was further complicated by the existence of the cathedral chapter, the body of clergy that had arisen out of the early medieval bishop's *familia*. The chapter consisted of canons who functioned in the administrative structure of the diocese and performed the daily liturgical services in the cathedral church. This group had been the target of intermittent reform efforts since at least the eighth century, but these efforts were not successful until the eleventh century. Only in England had a tenth-century reform movement done as well, and it succeeded by eliminating the canons altogether, replacing the chapter with a monastic community that provided the liturgical services but took little part in the diocesan administration. On the Continent, the eleventh-century reformers used a device that preserved the original functional character of the cathedral clergy. They brought the canons under a monastic-type rule, so that while they remained priests and episcopal administrators, they lived the common life appropriate to their station. The canons regular, as the new canons were called because they lived by a rule (*regula*), spread throughout Europe as reformers gained control of episcopal sees. In the early twelfth century, a German priest named Norbert (1080–1134) founded an order of canons regular called the Premonstratensian Order because the original house was in Prémontré. The canons of this order were not connected with cathedral churches but performed the care of souls in the parishes.

The effect of the movement to introduce canons regular into cathedral churches was great. Reform legislation stated that the bishop should be elected by the clergy and people of his diocese. In practice, after the Investiture Controversy, the clergy elected and the people acclaimed. Popular opposition could quash an election, but that rarely happened. As the communities of canons regular became established in the cathedrals, the right of election gradually became theirs exclusively. This centralization of the power to elect meant that a distinct group in the diocese could challenge the bishop it had elected. The chapter, as a corporate body, could claim to exercise the episcopal power when the see was vacant, and complicated the administration of episcopal property. Since theoretically all property belonged to the one episcopal church, the bishop and canons tended to become poles in the administrative structure of the diocese. Soon, the canons claimed the right to administer the whole bishopric, not only their share of it, whenever the bishop was away, and of course the bishops often interfered in the chapter's affairs on a variety of grounds. It took very little time for the relationship between bishop and chapter to become complex and problematic, and in the thirteenth century, much ecclesiastical law was written dealing with that relationship.

A bishop was expected not only to make a periodic visitation of his diocese, as Eudes of Rouen did, but also to hold an annual diocesan synod. At the synod, in the presence of the leading clergy of the diocese, the bishop heard the important ecclesiastical cases that had arisen during the year, enacted local legislative measures, and promulgated decrees of general synods and of the pope. This last function was a necessary part of the governance of the Church, since no decree was valid until it had been properly communicated to the clergy and faithful whose lives it regulated.

Archbishops possessed jurisdiction over several dioceses. Some of the archiepiscopal provinces were very large, such as Reims, Mainz, and Canterbury; some were very small. While Canterbury's province comprised eighteen bishoprics, York's had only three. A few archbishops were effective rulers of their provinces, enforcing their jurisdiction by regular visitation of each diocese, by assuming the control of all spiritualities (administration of the sacraments and the revenues arising from pastoral duties) during episcopal vacancies, and by close supervision of their suffragans—that is, bishops under their archiepiscopal authority. Most archbishops, however, exercised little effective control, and were content to express their higher dignity by presiding at infrequent provincial synods of the higher clergy and by consecrating new suffragan bishops.

In the tenth and eleventh centuries, the special relationship between monasteries and the papacy had produced a spate of exemptions for monastic houses throughout Europe. By law, monasteries and houses of canons were subject to episcopal authority, but the communities could escape the subjection by obtaining a papal exemption. By the twelfth century, hundreds of communities were completely exempt from local ecclesiastical authority, and tension developed between monasteries and bishops in many dioceses. From the mid-eleventh until the mid-twelfth century, Cluny was involved in a fierce struggle with the bishop of Mâcon and the archbishop of Lyon. The reform papacy's attack on the old system of lay control over parish churches complicated this relationship between bishops and exempt monasteries. Many lay lords granted their churches to monastic houses. The monasteries often sent monks from their communities to function as pastors in these churches, and a dispute arose over the appropriateness of monks taking on the care of souls. Secular priests, supported by bishops, argued that monastic vows and priesthood were incompatible and that monks could not become parish priests. Monastic writers pointed out that the interests of the faithful would be best served if the holiest men functioned as pastors, and monks were proven to be holy. The real issue was control of the parish churches, and, on the whole, the monks won. The canons regular, who were priests, also gained control of many parishes, but they supported the secular priests in the debates. As a result of the growing participation of monks in normal ecclesiastical governance, an increasing percentage of monks were becoming priests. This movement was also opposed by secular priests, and the old canonical doctrine prohibiting ordinations without titles (that is, without assignment to a church) was revived in the early twelfth century. This doctrine would prevent monasteries from becoming bodies of unemployed priests waiting to enter the hierarchy. Nonetheless, by the middle of the century, men like Saint Bernard of Clairvaux argued that monks were part of the ecclesiastical hierarchy and should participate in episcopal elections and other ecclesiastical affairs.

The movement to regularize the life of priests and to develop extensive monastic orders that were both exempt from local episcopal control and active participants in the pastoral work of the Church, greatly complicated ecclesiastical organization. Monks, nuns, and canons were directly under the authority of the abbot or abbess of their house, or of a prior or prioress if the house were a priory dependent on a mother house. The abbott or abbess was usually elected by the monks or nuns themselves, or, if there was a disagreement, by the *maior et sanior pars* of the community, as in papal and episcopal elections. In a serious dispute in a nonexempt monastery the bishop could intervene to decide the election because he had the right of installation. Other duties of the bishop included surveillance of the spiritual, disciplinary, and financial state of the monastery. In monastic orders, monks, nuns, and canons were also subject to their superiors in the order as well as to their abbot or abbess and to their bishop or the pope. Thus, the organization of the orders often cut across the hierarchy of secular clergy, organized into parishes, archdeaconries, dioceses, and provinces.

The triumph of the Church as an institution that united and provided leadership for all Christendom in the high Middle Ages resulted from three new forces. All three became effective toward the end of the eleventh century. The papacy was reformed and became the leader of the Church and of Christendom. A new monastic revival occurred and infused the whole Church with new vitality. Canon law became a binding force that united the Church under papal leadership. Its success as a legal system throughout Europe enhanced the leadership of the Church in the day-to-day lives of all Latin Christians.

The growth and success of the canon law was closely tied to the history of the papacy in the late twelfth and early thirteenth centuries. The lawyer-monk Gratian seems to have had a connection with those who won control of the Roman Church in the schism of 1130 to 1138, and his great work was used in the papal chancery soon after it appeared around 1140. The number of cases referred or appealed to the Holy See had been growing steadily since the beginning of the eleventh-century reform movement. Saint Bernard complained that Eugenius III (1145–1153) was too involved in legal matters and should turn his attention to his pastoral duties. Under the great lawyer-pope Alexander III (1159–1181), the Roman court was flooded with legal business, as litigants and episcopal judges sought Alexander's advice or decision. Much of the basic law of the Church originated in Alexander's opinions, of which over seven hundred are still extant. These decisions and those of Alexander's predecessors and successors, collected and edited by lawyers throughout Europe, were used to teach and as reference works in lower courts, along with Gratian's *Decretum* and other works. Innocent III (1198–1216) collected his own decisions and sent them to the law school at Bologna for the use of both students and professors. Then Innocent's nephew, Gregory IX (1227–1241), ordered Raymond of Peñafort to make an official collection of all the decisions and decrees issued since the circulation of Gratian's work. This great work, the *Decretales* (Decretals, or papal letters), or the *Liber Extra* (Extra Book) as lawyers called it, became the second element in the developing canonical counterpart of Justinian's *Corpus Juris Civilis*. Lawyers called the canonical corpus the *Corpus Juris Canonici* (corpus of canonical law), and material was added to it until the early fourteenth century.

The reform traditions of the eleventh-century popes were continued throughout the twelfth century. Papal legates went out from the *curia* to represent the pope in all areas of the Church, to hold councils under papal authority, to hear cases referred to the pope but more appropriately tried in the district from which they came, and to collect papal revenues. Most kingdoms had resident legates as well. The archbishops of Canterbury and York vied for the right to be papal legate in England; when York held the position, its usual subordination to Canterbury, the primatial see of the kingdom, was suspended by virtue of the legatine commission. When the volume of legal business became too great for either the *curia* or the regular and special legates to handle, the popes instituted a system of judges-delegate. Cases referred or appealed to the pope would usually be returned to the region from which they originated to be heard by local ecclesiastics considered competent and unbiased by the pope and his advisers. In the letters commissioning the judges-delegate, popes like Alexander III often instructed the judges about the law involved in the case, leaving to them the finding of facts relative to the applicable legal doctrine. Many of these letters contained important legal reforms or innovations and became part of the general canonical tradition.

The most impressive expression of papal authority was the summoning of a general council of the whole Church. In antiquity such councils had been called by emperors. Beginning in the mid-eleventh century the reform papacy had initiated the practice of calling annual councils at Rome during Lent, but these meetings were never presumed to be general or ecumenical, representative of the whole Latin Church. After the Concordat of Worms, Calixtus II called such a universal council to the Lateran in 1123. This council was later recognized as ecumenical, its legislation being universally binding like the canons of the ecumenical councils of antiquity. During the twelfth century, two more Lateran councils were held. The second was summoned by Innocent II in 1139 to reaffirm the unity of the Church after the end of the papal schism. The third was held by Alexander III in 1179 after his conflict with Frederick Barbarossa. Alexander accomplished some important legislative work there. However, the greatest of these councils was the fourth, called to the Lateran in November 1215 by Innocent III. More than four hundred bishops and eight hundred abbots and priors attended, together with proctors of prelates who were absent and representatives of the leading secular rulers. The agenda were prepared by committees of the *curia* and reflected Innocent's wide range of interests. The canons enacted may be grouped under four main headings: doctrine, discipline, reform, and political affairs.

In matters of doctrine the council condemned certain heresies of the day, including that of the Albigensians, and pronounced the theory of transubstantiation—long debated pro and con by theologians—to be a dogma of the Church. Henceforth it was necessary for a Christian to believe that the substance (as opposed to the "accidents," or outward appearance) of the bread and wine, when consecrated in the sacrament of the Eucharist, was changed into the body and blood of Christ.

Many canons affecting discipline, both of the clergy and laity, were enacted. Of the two most important, one prescribed confession, and the performance of penance imposed, at least once each year by all Christians. The other, mentioned earlier, required every Christian to partake of the sacrament of the Eucharist (communion) at least once each year.

Like all councils, the Fourth Lateran dealt at length with reform. The clergy were prohibited from wearing certain apparel and from engaging in unworthy occupations or participating in undignified games or recreational activities of the laity. Bishops were required to preach regularly or provide substitutes to do it for them, and all priests were forbidden to receive fees for administering the sacraments. The most important reform canon prohibited the participation of the clergy in ordeals, which were pronounced to be superstitious. Since the validity of the ordeal depended on divine intercession, which only a priest could be expected to call forth, this canon had a far-reaching effect on the development of English law. The English were already moving away from the old Germanic practices and quickly obeyed the conciliar decree, referring more and more of their criminal cases to juries. Elsewhere, the decree had much less effect. The most that can be said is that it encouraged the secular lawyers and judges of other kingdoms to follow the lead of the English. They did so at their own pace, slowly.

Finally, the work of the council included much that was general or political in purpose. As such, the council culminated the political policies followed by Innocent during his papacy; these policies and the council's political activities will be discussed in Chapter 19.

### The New Piety: Monastic Reforms and Religious Protest in the Twelfth Century

By the late eleventh century, the growth of the Cluniac order and other reform orders, concomitant with the growth of their wealth and power, produced some agitation among monks for a return to the more primitive conditions and the greater isolation that always seemed to serious monks the truer and safer way to God. The liturgical life and the success of Cluny had produced elaborate singing, new prayers, huge ornate churches—in sum, a kind of professionalization of monastic life that in many places deprived it of its original simplicity and homeliness. In the early eleventh century, Romuald (d. 1027) and his disciples led an eremitical movement in Italy. Their goal was escape from the temptations of the world through a life of solitude, intense asceticism, and meditation. The hermit temper of eleventh-century Italy—extreme mortification, fierce hostility toward all things carnal, and passionate craving for salvation—was reminiscent of the desert fathers of Egypt and Syria. North of the Alps, in 1084, Bruno of Cologne resigned as head of the cathedral school of Reims and founded at La Grand Chartreuse (*Carthusia*) in the mountainous wilderness of eastern France south of Cluny, a community somewhat similar to those of Romuald. Here the monks worshiped together in a chapel but lived

Monastic life provided many opportunities for communal prayer and religious instruction. One of the abbot's principal functions was as spiritual guide to his monastic sons, and the sermon was the best instrument of this task. This sketch (ca. 1400) shows Saint Gualbert of Vallombrosa giving a sermon to his monks in the cloister garden.

in isolated cells, combining the eremitic with the cenobitic form of organization. The ideal was severance from the world and seclusion of the brethren from each other, so that they might achieve in manual labor, contemplation, and strict asceticism a higher spiritual life. About 1130 the customs and practices of the community were written down, thus forming a rule for the Carthusian Order. Later in the twelfth century the Carthusians received papal recognition and approval, but the order remained small because its rule was too austere to attract large numbers. The Carthusians were and still are an elite group, justly proud of their unique record of having been "never reformed because never deformed" (*nunquam reformata quia nunquam deformata*).

By far the most important new order in the monastic reform movement of the twelfth century was founded in 1098 by Robert of Molesmes at Cîteaux, in eastern France in the wild country north of Cluny. The purpose of the Cistercians was to restore literally and strictly the observance of the Benedictine rule. The Cistercian ideal was midway between the ascetic extremes of the hermit communities and the relatively lax discipline of the Cluniac houses. After a period of uncertainty and struggle, the success of the monks of Cîteaux led to the foundation of four daughter houses, and eventually these five monasteries multiplied to over seven hundred. Instead of the centralized Cluniac system, in which all houses were priories subject to the abbot of Cluny, the Cistercian foundations were independent monasteries under their own abbots. Each monastery was required to observe the customs and the discipline of Cîteaux. Uniformity was enforced by the rule that each abbot must visit annually the daughter houses of his monastery. For the duration of this visitation the authority of the abbot of the daughter house lapsed to the visiting abbot. The four "primary abbots" of the order (those of the first four daughter houses) jointly visited Cîteaux each year, assuming abbatial authority for the duration of their visitation, to ensure that the mother house of the order adhered to the Benedictine rule and Cistercian customs. Once a year all the abbots of the order gathered at Cîteaux to hold a meeting, or chapter. An erring abbot who obdurately persisted in innovation or departure from the customs of the order was subject to deposition by the abbots in chapter meeting. The Cistercian constitution was a successful combination of local autonomy with control by superior authority that still avoided centralization.

The monastic community at Cîteaux had struggled through its first fifteen years; it was located in a rugged, inaccessible area, and its observances were very strict. In 1112 a young Burgundian noble persuaded several relatives and friends to join him in entering the monastery. Three years later he was directed by the abbot to establish Cîteaux's third daughter house on the lands of the count of Troyes. Setting forth with twelve companions, he journeyed to the austere solitude of Clairvaux (*Clara Vallis*), where he built the new monastery and became its abbot. This young man was Saint Bernard of Clairvaux (1090–1153), who was destined to become the dominant personality of his order, of the Church, and of all Latin Christendom. Bernard combined the qualities of the soldier of Christ with a mystic's love of God and of man. From first to last he was the eager monk and the reluctant but purposeful man of affairs. Only in his cell at Clairvaux could he find contentment and peace; only in the world could he find those battles for the Lord that challenged and satisfied his militant nature. To some of his contemporaries, Bernard's wholehearted piety and rigid orthodoxy were irresistibly attractive. To others, his aggressive self-righteousness was equally repulsive. As a self-appointed guardian of doctrine and morals, Bernard was bound to make enemies. At the same time, he was loved by those who knew him best.

As abbot, Bernard made Clairvaux a model of Cistercian asceticism. Because he had deep affection for the monks in his charge, he subjected them to an uncompromising and severe regime for the good of their souls. The intense life at Clairvaux proved so attractive to aspirant monks that the monastery was always filled to capacity, with more seeking entrance. The only solution to the problem of numbers was to send out a steady stream of monks to establish daughter houses. By the end of Bernard's life more than 160 monasteries had been founded by the monks of Clairvaux and by the monks of the daughter houses of Clairvaux, and a parallel order of nuns had been founded.

His success as a Cistercian abbot and the force of his personality led Bernard to play a dominant role in ecclesiastical affairs. He was prominent in Church councils. He took the lead in criticizing monastic laxity. His influence was decisive in swinging the disputed papal election of 1130 to Innocent II against the antipope Anacletus. He led the attack on what he considered Abelard's rationalistic subversion of the faith. He inspired and influenced the drafting of the original rule of the Knights Templars (1128), and he was both friend and patron of leaders of the monastic reform movement outside the Cistercian Order, notably Norbert, founder of the Premonstratensian Order of canons regular. He was also instrumental in reforming the ancient royal monastery of Saint Denis under Abbot Suger and had an important effect on Cluny through his friendship with Peter the Venerable (abbot, 1121–1156). Bernard's influence over the papacy reached its height when a former monk of Clairvaux was elected Pope Eugenius III (1145–1153). Bernard also made a substantial contribution to religious literature in the form of several hundred sermons, more than five hundred letters dealing with all phases of monastic life and contemporary issues, and several treatises on theology and liturgy. Through these writings Bernard had a profound influence on the development of mysticism, especially in his exposition of the four stages of love as an ascent toward God.

Bernard's earliest participation in secular affairs was as an adviser to the French king. The project most important to him was the Second Crusade (1147–1149), to which he devoted his brilliant gifts as an orator. His success in enlisting thousands for the cause, including Louis VII of France and Conrad III of the empire, was followed by bitter disillusionment when the Crusade failed. His last years were spent largely in rallying the opposition against Arnold of Brescia, the antipapal revolutionary who temporarily ousted Eugenius III and reestablished a "republic" in the city of Rome (1146–1155), but he did not live to see his last enemy defeated and executed by the joint efforts of the pope and emperor. During his active life (ca. 1125–1153), there were few important movements in Latin Christendom in which Bernard did not play some role, and there were few popes or rulers for whom he was not an adviser or critic, friend or foe. His whole public career exemplified the Church Militant, just as his private life was a forceful expression of the monastic ideal.

In the second half of the twelfth century both the relative importance of the monastic orders and the influence of monastic leaders in the life of both the clergy and the laity gradually declined. This is not surprising because the monastic revival was remote from developments that were transforming Europe during this century. Monasticism provided an escape from the world, but the world itself was going through an intellectual awakening and the

The cloister played an important part in the life of the monastery. The main buildings —church, dormitory, refectory—were off it; it served as the avenue for processions, and it was used by monks as a place to walk while thinking or reading. Many cloisters were richly decorated, but this one at the Cistercian house of Fontenay shows the order's predilection for austerity and simplicity.

commercial revolution that made the center of gravity in medieval civilization shift from the manor and the monastery to the city and the cathedral. In religious life there were repercussions of this growth of the cities. The market-place was a concourse for the exchange of ideas as well as goods. As with Arnold of Brescia, urban anticlericalism usually took the form of opposition to the wealth and worldliness of the secular clergy, but sometimes this criticism of the hierarchy drifted into doctrinal disagreement and heresy. In the late twelfth century heretical ideas spread rapidly, particularly in northern Italy and southern France. These two regions were subject to much outside in-

**North Sea**

York ♀
Lincoln ⚕
Cambridge ■
Oxford ■
Malmesbury ⌂  St. Albans ⚕
Winchester ⚕  Canterbury
Amiens ⚕
Beauvais ⚕  Laon ⚕
Bec ⚕  Reims ♀
St. Denis ⌂  Paris ■  Clairvaux ⌂
Avranches ⚕  Chartres ⚕
Orléans ⚕  Troyes ⚕
Tours ♀
Poitiers ⚕
Cîteaux ⌂
Cluny ⌂
Lyon ♀
La Grande Chartreuse ⌂
Toulouse ⚕  Albi ⚕
Montpellier ■
Santiago de Compostella △
Barcelona ⚕
Toledo ♀

Gandersheim ⌂
Magdeburg ♀
Cologne ♀
Worms ⚕
Mainz ♀  Hirsau ⌂
Regensburg ⚕
Freising ⚕
Constance ⚕  Prague ♀
Reichenau ⌂
Salzburg ♀
Bologna ■
Bobbio ⌂
Florence ⚕  Assisi ⚕
Rome ⚕
Monte Cassino ⌂
Naples ⚕  Salerno ⚕
Palermo ⚕

**Atlantic Ocean**

**Mediterranean Sea**

Ecclesiastical and Cultural Centers in the High Middle Ages

fluence, from the eastern and southern Mediterranean world, because they formed the commercial and cultural link between those areas and northern Europe. The cultural mix, the growth of urbanization concomitant with the development of commerce, broke the hold of traditional institutions and opened the way for the development of new subcultures. Much of this subculture manifested itself in heretical movements that began as attacks on the established ecclesiastical hierarchy, the most pervasive and powerful set of institutions in the society. Many urban political movements, aimed at winning freedom for the merchant classes, acquired an anticlerical taint because the principal opponent was often the local bishop.

Anticlerical movements tended to develop either into pietistic sects within the Church, as a kind of silent protest against the worldliness of clergy and laity alike, or into heretical groups that rejected the doctrine and authority of the Church because they rejected the hierarchy as unworthy. Examples of the first kind of movement were the groups of associations in the Lombard communes of northern Italy, known collectively as the *Humiliati*. These groups comprised a loosely organized lay brotherhood of pious workingmen dedicated to a simple life in common, in accordance with their understanding of the Gospel precepts. For the clergy, they advocated a return to apostolic poverty. In 1201 Innocent III recognized the *Humiliati* as a religious order and confirmed their way of life. Some of the more extreme groups of the *Humiliati* broke away from the approved order and joined other "underground" pietistic sects that had heterodox tendencies, such as the Arnoldists (as Arnold of Brescia's later followers were called) and local groups known as Poor Men, who rejected the authority of the Church.

The outstanding example of an anticlerical but orthodox group that developed into a heretical movement was the Waldensians. Around 1173 a wealthy merchant of Lyon, Peter Waldo, founded the organization when he decided to give his worldly goods to the poor and dedicate himself to charitable works and a life of poverty. His followers were a lay society, the Poor Men of Lyon, whose members traveled about preaching to the common people. In their effort to win back the uneducated masses to a life of apostolic simplicity, they translated parts of the New Testament into the vernacular. This activity was tentatively approved by the pope in 1179, on condition that the Poor Men obtain permission to preach from the local bishop. But the ideas of the Waldensians about apostolic poverty and a more spiritual clergy led to conflict with the bishops and diocesan clergy. Friction rapidly developed into open hostility, and the organization was condemned by the pope in 1184, after the Poor Men had developed doctrines and practices that were clearly heretical. They preached that laymen could administer the sacraments, that the Bible alone was authoritative on religious questions, and that the Church possessed no spiritual authority. A later split in the movement brought a few of the Poor Men of Lyon back into the Church in 1205, but Waldensian doctrines continued to spread into Spain, northern France, Germany, and the Low Countries, and, in more extreme form, among the radical "Poor Lombards" of northern Italy. The Waldensian church still exists in parts of Italy.

The most dangerous heretical movement of the later twelfth century was the group of Cathar sects, whose basic theology derived from the third-century Persian philosopher Mani, whose ideas (called Manichaean) had been influenced by Christianity. His teachings, modified by other ethical and religious views, appeared in Asia Minor in late antiquity; in the Balkans in the early Middle Ages; and, by making their way along the trade routes from town to town, in northern Italy and southern France in the eleventh century. The general name given to believers was *Cathari* (the pure). In the Balkans they were called Bogomiles, and in the West they were often known as *Bulgari* (Bulgarians). Their teachings also influenced other groups, such as the Poor Men and the Patarenes in Italy. The *Cathari* were known most generally in the West as Albigensians, from the center of their greatest strength, the town of Albi in Languedoc.

The Albigensian religion was thoroughly dualistic. Instead of one God, there were two gods, a god of light (truth) and a god of darkness (error), the former being the god of the New Testament, the latter the god of the Old Testament. Life on earth, indeed all existence, was a struggle between these gods and their principal forces, spirit and matter. Anything associated with material wealth or worldliness was evil; the Church of orthodox Christians was therefore, to the Albigensians, the Synagogue of Satan. The good life for human beings was a gradual purification from matter (that is, evil). Hence, the Albigensians condemned marriage, procreation, and eating meat and eggs. They abhorred war and physical violence, the veneration of relics, the use of pictorial representations (especially the cross), the wearing of vestments, and the employment of anything material in worship. Because they refused to take oaths, they were subversive to a society that rested on the oath of vassal to feudal lord. They also opposed political authority as being worldly and there-fore evil. All these tenets and teachings represent the extreme doctrine, and in practice, the Albigensians recognized the needs of human nature and human society.

The Albigensians were divided into the few *perfecti* (the perfect), who as clergy were expected to adhere to the rigid asceticism of the religion, and the great mass of followers, called believers. The main duties of the believers were to venerate the *perfecti* and prepare to become *perfecti* themselves. This was accomplished by receiving the only sacrament allowed, the *consolamentum* (consolation). Because the sacrament, ideally and properly, should be admin-istered only once for an individual, it was often postponed until the recipient was about to die. If the newly consecrated *perfectus* showed evidence of not being able to live up to the ascetic discipline of his new calling, his friends could still ensure the salvation of his soul through a ceremonial death by suffocation, called the *endura*. Believers who did not receive the *consolamen-tum* were still taught that such places as purgatory and hell were false Chris-tian myths. The only "hell" conceivable was the imprisonment of the soul in a material body, life in this world. This teaching, joined to the belief that procreation was a more serious wrong than either intercourse or homosexual-ity, probably underlay the Albigensians' reputation for licentiousness.

Southern France at the end of the twelfth century was a pleasant and prosperous land, the center of a flourishing Provençal civilization. Wealthy towns, castles, and courts were prominent in this home of the troubadours. Christianity was very old in this area; but the orthodox faith had become little more than external form. In this tolerant and cosmopolitan society, Jews and

Moslems traded and debated without hindrance. The nobles and the wealthy bourgeoisie were attracted to the Albigensian heresy, some because of its tenets and others because they were eager to plunder the Church—the Albigensian program included the confiscation of the lands and wealth of the orthodox clergy. But few of the important lords actually joined the Albigensian movement. Most were content to tolerate or protect the heretics within their lands, without committing themselves on the religious issue.

Under Innocent III and his successors a long and bloody war (1209–1229), the so-called Albigensian Crusade, finally stamped out the movement, but other peaceful efforts had been made before. Saint Bernard had traveled through southern France preaching against the new heretics and had gone to Cologne in Germany for the same purpose, but the monks were not appropriate soldiers in the Church's new struggle. The secular clergy was not numerous enough to meet the crisis in many areas where heresy was rampant, and many clerics even joined the heretics. By the beginning of the thirteenth century ecclesiastical rulers recognized the situation as extremely serious; a powerful independent religious organization existed in southern France, and heretical communities dotted Europe.

The last great religious reform movement of the Middle Ages originated as a response to this crisis. Members of the new orders were to add their strength to the regular hierarchy of the Church. They settled in the cities and involved themselves in the active care of souls. They met the challenge of anticlericalism by setting an example of poverty and piety. They were remarkably successful and not only brought many heretics back into the Church but also captured and directed the new piety in the Christian communities. This new piety reached back to the New Testament for its inspiration and reinvigorated the life of the Church.

The first of these new orders was founded by one of the most remarkable personalities of the Middle Ages, Saint Francis of Assisi (1181–1226). Francis was the son of a fairly prosperous Italian merchant. After a wayward youth, he experienced a conversion, renounced the life in store for him, and dedicated himself to complete poverty and service to the poor. Like the early Christian hermits, Francis enjoyed the life of a solitary apart from human society and delighted in preaching the word of God to birds and beasts—who, according to report, found his preaching eminently worth hearing. But Francis' real calling was service to "Lady Poverty," a task to which he turned with the same devotion that a knight-errant gave his lady. Serving the poor took him to the towns where they abounded, and most of his life was spent preaching the Gospel while living in complete poverty among the common people.

Francis' magnetism, simplicity, humility, and charm attracted many followers. He drew up a brief and simple rule for them consisting of quotations from the Gospels. Each quotation illuminated an aspect of the life of Christ and the twelve Apostles, the *vita apostolica* that was the model for Francis' way of life. In 1210 he sought approval for his work from Pope Innocent III.

Innocent, a man of extraordinary administrative and political ability who raised the institutionalized Church to the pinnacle of its power, hesitated, perhaps a bit doubtful about the orthodoxy or even the sanity of his beggarly but cheerful petitioner. Finally, he allowed Francis to continue his work and to govern his followers as an authorized religious order. Innocent's ability to recognize the potential or at least the special place of Francis' new ideas about the religious life, so different from traditional monasticism, confirms the pope's genius and breadth of vision. Francis, for his part, demonstrated his compelling humility by calling his followers the Order of Friars Minor (Lesser Brothers). Under him and for a few years after his death, the order remained much as he had planned, a group of itinerant preachers who affected a simplicity to match the simplicity of the people to whom they preached, and who owned nothing either as individuals or as a corporate group.

The success of the Franciscans and the consequent rapid growth of the order necessitated a more elaborate rule and a better organization than Francis had wanted. In 1223 the new rule was authorized by Innocent III's successor, Honorius III (1216–1227), against Francis' wishes. Many of those joining the order were former students and teachers attracted by the emphasis Francis placed on returning to the original documents of Christian faith and taking a new look at how Christ wanted Christians to live. To these men, the founder's ideal of preaching in simple biblical terms without reference to the long and honored tradition of Christian exegesis made little sense, and was close to impossible. As more and more intellectuals entered the order, they exerted tremendous pressure for raising the intellectual level of the friars. When the first Franciscan mission arrived in England in 1226, it went first to London and then to Oxford. Soon all the universities had Orders of Friars Minor attached to them.

Concomitant with this change, the original ideal of total corporate and individual poverty was undermined. In the older monastic orders, monks owned nothing, but communities were often very wealthy. Francis had broken with this tradition, but as his order became increasingly involved in the day-to-day care of souls and in the scholastic milieu of the universities, the Franciscan houses found material wealth to be necessary. The urban houses needed living quarters, food, and a church in which to preach and perform the sacraments. The holiness of the friars attracted large numbers of faithful, who turned to them for performance of all the sacraments usually performed by secular parish priests. This resulted in much tension between the friars and the secular clergy, and in many dioceses, friars were excluded from churches; they had to build their own. By the end of the thirteenth century, the Franciscans had devised an elaborate edifice of doctrine justifying its disposition of considerable wealth through agents and patrons who "owned" everything but administered it in trust for the friars. Francis' simplicity had been subverted by an intricate, often sophistical, set of legal doctrines. The order became divided between those who wanted to preserve the purity of Francis' vision and life style and those who accepted the mission of the order as it had developed and the compromises that that development entailed. The bitter conflict continued for generations, during which the Franciscans were reformed several times. The Capuchins resulted from one such reform.

The second new order was founded by Francis's contemporary, Saint Dominic (1170–1221), a Spanish priest who had undertaken an unsuccessful mission to win back heretics in southern France. Convinced that the best way to fight heresy was to combat ignorance among the orthodox clergy and laity, Dominic founded an order whose special task was to study theology and preach. This purpose could not be fulfilled by retiring from the world. As Dominic told his followers, "Henceforth the world is your home: go forth into the whole world, teach and preach." In 1216 the order was sanctioned by Honorius III and given the name Friars Preachers. The Dominicans were mendicant like the Franciscans, and like the latter they too relaxed the early rules against possession of property. Some Dominicans spent so much time studying and teaching that the only preaching for which they could take credit, indirectly, was through their students who went out as "hounds of the lord" (*domini canes,* a pun on the name *dominicani,* Dominicans) to keep sheep from straying from the flock.

Many intelligent and well-educated men joined Dominic's order, attracted by the idea that their learning, their intellectual profession, could have a use in the world. One of these men was the great canon lawyer Raymond of Peñafort, who wrote a constitution for the Dominicans, based on that of the order of Augustinian canons but improving on it significantly. The constitutional fabric of the new order consisted in a system of elected officials and representatives. Each house had an elected conventual prior who served for a term. All the conventual priors plus another elected friar from each house met annually in a provincial chapter meeting. The provincial chapter elected a provincial prior and four administrators to govern the province during the ensuing year. Every three years a general chapter was held, which was attended by the provincial priors and special representatives elected by each province. This chapter elected a master general for the whole order to serve for life. Raymond's constitution became one of the models for the organization of religious groups in the Church and stands with the Benedictine rule and the Constitution of the United States as one of the great constitutional documents produced by Western civilization.

The Franciscan and Dominican orders engendered similar movements among women. The Dominican sisters have engaged in teaching and hospital work since their foundation. Their Franciscan counterparts were organized by a friend of Francis named Clare. Under Francis' guidance, the Poor Clares lived a more cloistered life than the Franciscans, but they were active among leper colonies and in hospital work. As the Friars Minor became involved in the care of souls and in the intellectual life of the Church, the order became increasingly removed from the popular lay piety in which it had originated.

The Poor Clares, the female counterparts of the Franciscans, were more cloistered than the friars. This manuscript illumination shows them in choir singing their offices (Psalms). The Franciscans were too active to participate in such communal prayers often and usually said their offices wherever they found themselves at the proper time.

The Dominican sisters and the Poor Clares remained close to that piety and gave women the opportunity to enter religious life while practicing the good works so dear to good Christian laymen since the beginning of the Christian movement. Thus the feminine counterparts of the two mendicant orders remained a link between the laity and the ecclesiastical hierarchy.

Both the two major orders of friars and smaller orders founded during the thirteenth century possessed a privileged position in the Church. Earlier monastic orders had received papal exemptions after they were well established as local institutions. The new orders were founded under direct papal aegis. During the thirteenth century, the popes used the friars for all kinds of missions and other business, and the friars were often considered, and often were, papal representatives. Thus they were caught in the middle of the developing conflict between the papal and episcopal powers. The growth of the papacy threatened the local authority of bishops, who pointed out that the pope, the bishop of Rome, was really only one of them. As the tension increased between lower secular clergy and friars, the bishops joined their subordinates in opposition to the friars as representatives of the pope. Many bishops refused to permit friars to enter or to preach in their dioceses, claiming that, as governors of their dioceses, they had the right to exclude the friars. The friars in turn sought papal privileges permitting them to enter and preach wherever they wished. To understand all the elements of this complex conflict, the growth of papal power both within and without the Church must first be considered. This subject is part of the wider story of European politics at the beginning of the thirteenth century, to which the next chapter is devoted.

## Suggestions for Further Reading

**Secondary Works**  M. W. Baldwin, *The Mediaeval Church* (Ithaca, N.Y., 1953); R. W. Southern, *Western Society and the Church in the Middle Ages* (Harmondsworth, 1970); and J. B. Russell, *A History of Medieval Christianity: Prophecy and Order* (New York, 1968) are general introductions to the medieval Church. A specialized work of great value for the student of general history is C. R. Cheney, *From Becket to Langton* (Manchester, 1956). See also R. Brentano, *Two Churches: England and Italy in the Thirteenth Century* (Princeton, N.J., 1968). On the constitutional law of the Church, see S. Chodorow, *Christian Political Theory and Church Politics in the Mid-Twelfth Century* (Berkeley and Los Angeles, 1972). The various heretical movements of the twelfth century are treated in J. B. Russell, *Dissent and Reform in the Early Middle Ages* (Berkeley and Los Angeles, 1965); E. S. Dawson, *Forerunners of Saint Francis* (New York, 1926); and W. L. Wakefield and A. P. Evans, *Heresies of the High Middle Ages* (New York, 1969). On the general reaction of the Church to heretics, see the monumental work of H. C. Lea, *A History of the Inquisition of the Middle Ages,* 3 vols. (New York, 1888), written from a Protestant point of view; E. Vacandard, *The Inquisition* (New York, 1918), a less critical treatment; and A. C. Shannon, *The Popes and Heresy in the Thirteenth Century* (New York, 1955). For the history of the Franciscan Order, see P. Sabatier, *The Life of Saint Francis of Assisi* (London, 1894); J. Moorman, *A History of the Franciscan Order* (Oxford, 1968); and R. Brooke, *Early Franciscan Government* (Cambridge, 1959). On the Dominicans, see P. Mandonnet, *Saint Dominic and His Work* (London, 1944); R. F. Bennett, *The Early Dominicans* (Cambridge, 1937); and the first volume of W. A. Hinnebusch, *History of the Dominican Order* (New York, 1966). F. M. Powicke, "The Christian Life," in *The Legacy of the Middle Ages,* ed. C. G. Crump and E. F. Jacob (Oxford, 1932) is an outstanding essay.

**Sources**  *The Register of Eudes of Rouen,* ed. J. F. O'Sullivan, and trans. S. M. Brown (New York, 1965) gives a clear picture of episcopal work. For the Dominicans, see F. C. Lehner, *Saint Dominic: Biographical Documents* (Washington, D.C., 1964). For the Franciscans, see *The Lives of Saint Francis of Assisi by Thomas of Celano,* trans. A. G. F. Howell (London, 1908); *The Writings of Saint Francis of Assisi,* ed. P. Robinson (Philadelphia, 1906); and *The Little Flowers of Saint Francis and Other Franciscan Writings,* trans. S. Hughes (New York, 1964).

# V THE THIRTEENTH CENTURY

# 19 The Politics of the Western States in the Early Thirteenth Century

At the death of Frederick I (1190) the strength of his government in both Germany and Italy seemed secure. In the following generation Innocent III brought the medieval papacy to the height of its power. As long as empire and papacy could support each other, as they had done so effectively in the time of Charlemagne or the Ottonian emperors, these two powers, which transcended local, tribal, or national loyalties, could easily dominate the politics of Europe. At the end of the twelfth century England was ruled by a nonresident monarch who had little time for his island kingdom and could not have conceived of making a nationalistic appeal to his subjects. The French monarch had not yet made the major territorial gains that changed his kingdom from a collection of principalities into a country with some sense of national unity. The complex history of four "states"—the papacy, the empire, England, and France—during the thirteenth century illustrates how political preeminence shifted from the supranational governments to the national monarchies.

**461**

# Innocent III and the
# Papal Monarchy

A modern state can collect taxes, legislate, enforce judicial decisions through a bureaucracy and police power, field armies, and hold the loyalty of its citizens. In the twelfth century the papacy could do all these things. Moreover, the pope had a territorial base in the Papal States in Italy, and various European rulers owed him homage as vassals. It is true that many Christians who acknowledged the leadership of the papacy were also subjects of secular kings and owed allegiance to feudal lords, but since the nationalistic idea of exclusive political loyalties had not yet developed, the pope may properly be compared with other monarchs.

Under Innocent III (1198–1216) the medieval papacy achieved its greatest prestige, leadership capacity, and power. Innocent III was the most powerful pope of the Middle Ages, but his position rested on a century and a half of earlier development. Ever since the days of Leo IX (1049–1054) and Gregory VII (1073–1085) the popes had pressed their claims, with varying fortunes and through many vicissitudes, to supremacy over the Church, freedom of the Church from secular intervention, and the superiority of the spiritual authority over the secular. Innocent came closest to realizing these claims. During his pontificate Latin Christendom came closest to being united under one supreme head, and the papacy emerged as a monarchy that possessed the machinery and the moral force sufficient not only to govern the spiritual work and the organization of the Church, but also to arbitrate, intervene in, and control the affairs of secular rulers.

Innocent's first achievement was to solve a problem that had vexed almost all the twelfth-century popes—security in Rome and control of the Papal States. A pope who could not dominate the Roman nobility could hardly aspire to rule Christendom. Innocent worked out a compromise that withdrew the papacy from active participation in the strictly local affairs of city government, thus freeing the Holy See from local factional strife. Toward the Papal States Innocent could not afford to be conciliatory. By armed force, or the threat of force, he revived the full temporal authority of the papacy over the duchy of Spoleto and the march of Ancona. Control of the Papal States was especially important because of the political situation in the empire and in the kingdom of Sicily.

Frederick Barbarossa's son, the emperor Henry VI (1190–1197), had united Sicily to the empire by his marriage to Constance, heiress of the Sicilian throne. This turn of events deprived the papacy of its Norman allies to the south and replaced them with the Hohenstaufen enemy. To make matters worse, part of the Papal States had fallen under imperial control. Henry had isolated Rome and secured his communications between the southern kingdom and the empire. Then, fortunately for the papacy, Henry died suddenly, and a fierce struggle for the throne broke out in both Germany and Sicily. Constance appealed to Innocent for help in preserving the Sicilian throne for her three-year-old son, Frederick, against the ambitions of the Norman nobility. Shortly before she died, in 1198, Constance recognized the pope as feudal lord of the kingdom and renounced the extraordinary powers over the Sicilian Church formerly exercised by the king. In return, Frederick became a papal ward and was recognized as heir to the kingdom.

In Germany civil war was raging between the adherents of the late emperor's brother, Philip of Swabia, who was the Hohenstaufen candidate, and the candidate of the Guelph party, Otto of Brunswick, son of Henry the Lion. Innocent asserted his right to decide between them, basing the claim on his duty to judge the fitness of a candidate before performing the coronation of the emperor. From Otto IV, his choice, Innocent obtained an almost complete renunciation of the royal control of the German Church that had been secured by the Concordat of Worms (1122). However, as soon as he was crowned emperor in 1209, Otto disregarded his promises and resumed as imperial a policy as that of any Hohenstaufen, including an invasion of southern Italy to reunite Sicily with the empire. Innocent absolved Otto's vassals from their fealty, stirred up rebellion in Germany, and promoted the candidacy of Frederick II, king of Sicily. His young ward promised never to reunite Sicily with the empire and confirmed all the concessions that Otto had made before being crowned emperor. Philip Augustus of France helped Innocent obtain the support of the German nobility. In retaliation Otto IV invaded France in a campaign timed to coincide with an attack by John of England, but the effort ended in a disastrous defeat for the Anglo-German alliance at the Battle of Bouvines in 1214. Otto's support in Germany deteriorated rapidly, and Frederick was confirmed as emperor-elect.

In his relations with the empire, Innocent had seemingly won a resounding triumph after many tribulations. His protégé and vassal had secured the imperial throne; Sicily, a papal fief, was to be separated forever from the empire; the German Church was freed from royal control and subordinate to full papal jurisdiction; and the Papal States were once more subject to the pope's authority.

In his relations with other secular rulers, Innocent was almost as successful. He negotiated a truce between Philip Augustus of France and Richard I of England. In the later quarrel between Philip and John he intervened vigorously, although unsuccessfully, to prevent war. This dispute was feudal— between lord and vassal in terms of feudal law—and the pope found it difficult to justify the intervention he wanted to make. While claiming no jurisdiction over a purely feudal matter, Innocent enunciated an important principle that canon lawyers later employed to justify the indirect power of the pope. Whenever war is threatened there is an imminent danger of commission of sin by Christians. It is the pope's duty, Innocent argued, to intervene in any temporal affair where sin is concerned (*ratione peccati*) and to pass judgment as the Vicar of Christ.

Innocent III was perhaps the greatest pope of the Middle Ages. From the family of the counts of Segni, he moved rapidly up the hierarchy of the Holy See to become pope at the age of thirty-seven. Among Innocent's most important activities was the rebuilding of the Papal States after the imperial threat had ended with the death of Henry VI (1197). This thirteenth-century fresco portrait is in one of the most important ecclesiastical centers of the Papal States, the church of Subiaco.

The papal claim to supreme jurisdiction over all moral, spiritual, or ecclesiastical causes led Innocent to intervene in the internal affairs of most of the kingdoms and principalities of Europe. Philip Augustus proved least tractable, but even he lost a long conflict with Innocent. Philip had made a second marriage with the Danish princess Ingeborg in 1193. But for reasons that are not entirely clear, the day after their marriage Philip put Ingeborg away, and, as soon as it could be arranged, he obtained an annulment from a council of French bishops. Ingeborg resolutely appealed to the papacy, but to no avail until Innocent became pope in 1198 and supported her cause. Twenty years after their nuptials—during which Philip remarried, raised a family, suffered an interdict on his realm decreed by Innocent, and went through the empty forms of public reconciliation that gave the lady no solace—Philip finally restored Ingeborg to her full rights as wife and queen. Since marriage was both a personal and a political act, ecclesiastical control over the marriage bed often had immense political consequences.

Conflict between John and Innocent arose from a disputed election to the archbishopric of Canterbury in 1206. Representatives were sent to Rome by all three contending parties—the cathedral chapter, the suffragan bishops, and the king. Innocent quashed all previous proceedings in the case and persuaded the representatives of the chapter to elect his own candidate, Stephen Langton, an English cardinal and formerly a professor of theology at Paris. John refused to recognize the election, and Innocent retaliated in 1208 by putting England under an interdict. A year and a half later John was excommunicated and threatened with deposition, and Innocent negotiated with Philip Augustus with a view to replacing John with a Capetian. Under this pressure John finally capitulated and, in 1213, recognized the pope as his feudal lord from whom he and his successors were to hold England as a papal fief. John's submission is a striking example of the supreme jurisdiction, the "plenitude of power" (*plenitudo potestatis*) in the canon law phrase, that the pope claimed to wield directly in all spiritual causes and indirectly in all temporal matters.

Innocent also used the spiritual weapons of the interdict and excommunication in his relations with the rulers of Castile, León, Navarre, and Norway. By the end of his pontificate Innocent was acknowledged as feudal lord of the kingdoms of Sicily, Portugal, Aragón, and England in the west, and of Bulgaria and Armenia in the east, while Hungary, Bohemia, and Poland recognized the pope's superiority and right to intervene or arbitrate in their internal affairs. It should be remembered, however, that normally both parties gained from a feudal relationship. John of England, for example, was in desperate straits when he became a papal vassal and thereby gained the neutrality of the English Church as well as his strongest supporter in his new lord, Innocent.

One of Innocent's most cherished goals was to organize a successful Crusade, a project he initiated as soon as he became pope. Conditions seemed favorable, for the response among the nobility was warm, and no ruler was ready to compete with papal leadership. Yet the Fourth Crusade, launched in 1202, became a grotesque perversion of the crusading ideal. From the very beginning Innocent lost control. The Venetians persuaded the Crusaders to conquer the Adriatic port of Zara for them, in payment for transportation provided by the Venetian fleet. Innocent excommunicated the whole army for attacking a Christian city. Undaunted, the Venetians and the leaders of the Crusade then concluded an alliance with a claimant to the Byzantine throne, promising to restore him in Constantinople in return for money, supplies, and troops to use against Egypt. Although the treaty looked to the eventual conquest of the Holy Land and promised the reunion of the Greek and Latin churches under Rome, Innocent prohibited this further diversion from the Crusade. The pope's instinct was sound, for the only result of the whole venture was the conquest of Constantinople and the establishment of a Latin empire under the French leaders. The former Byzantine Empire was irreparably weakened, as the French carved it up into petty feudal principalities. Economic interests and political ambitions had distorted the Fourth Crusade into a travesty, but Innocent eventually accepted the conquest, and in 1215 he extracted a promise from Frederick II to lead another Crusade.

Against the heretics of southern France Innocent had greater success, although with ultimate results that he had not foreseen. When the local bishops failed to extirpate heresy in this region, papal legates were entrusted with the task. They were authorized to call on secular rulers for assistance. When they did so, a war broke out, and Innocent caused a crusade to be preached in northern France against the southern heretics. Land-greedy French nobles joined the Albigensian Crusade, which rapidly got out of control. Until Innocent's death, the situation remained fluid and confused. The pope's objective was to win back heretics; the lay leaders of the "crusade" followed their own ambitions. This mixture of religious and purely selfish motives produced extreme ferocity on both sides, from which the economy and culture of Languedoc were never fully to recover.

The policies enacted at the Fourth Lateran Council under Innocent III had political as well as religious consequences. For example, the council established the requirement that every Christian must confess to his parish priest once a year. This provision made confession a continuing reminder of the dependency of the laity on the clergy. Another decree required the priest to elevate the Host with his back to the congregation, separating clergy and laity in a subtle way and making the congregation more observers than participants in the mysteries of the Mass. The council also took action against non-Christians. It reaffirmed the authority of secular rulers to confiscate the property of heretics and put into effect a series of provisions against the Jews: Jews were still barred from holding public office, and they were forbidden to appear in public during Holy Week. The canon with the most far-reaching consequences provided that whenever Jews and Moslems appeared in public in Christian lands, they had to wear distinctive clothing so that Christians could recognize them. Innocent did not desire that Jews should suffer active persecution, and in fact he ordered Christians (and particularly Crusaders) not to molest Jews or their families, but legislation requiring non-Christians to wear unusual clothing or a badge made pogroms both easier to accomplish and more likely.

Finally, Innocent proclaimed and the council approved a new Crusade, the Fifth, which Frederick II agreed to lead. It was at the council that Otto IV was deposed in favor of Frederick II, and Raymond VI of Toulouse was excommunicated as a heretic and replaced by Simon de Montfort, the leader of

The Fourth Lateran Council of 1215 ordered Jews and Moslems to wear distinctive clothing or a distinguishing sign when they appeared in public. This fourteenth-century wall painting in Tarragona Cathedral depicts a Jew with the sign of his religion on his chest. Church law regulated the activities of Jews and the interaction between Christians and Jews and therefore sought to make Jews easily identifiable.

Innocent's Albigensian Crusade. The English barons in rebellion against John, now a papal vassal, were condemned, while the suspension of Archbishop Stephen Langton, who supported the rebels, was confirmed.

Of all the events of the pontificate of Innocent III, the Fourth Lateran Council best illustrates the papal monarchy of the high Middle Ages in action. In the spiritual life of Europe, in the organization of the Church, in the temporal affairs of the Western kingdoms, and in the struggle against non-Christian peoples at home and abroad, the papal monarchy was the supreme authority and the directive force.

## Frederick II

The reign of Frederick II (1215–1250) was a turning point in the history of both Germany and Italy. Some historians believe that if Henry VI had not died prematurely, in 1197, he might have succeeded in carrying out the Hohenstaufen policy originally conceived by Frederick I. This policy sought to create a strong German monarchy as the basis of imperial power, this monarchy being served by a large corps of royal officials who exploited and enlarged the crown lands and who preserved and administered the regalian rights; maintain imperial authority in Burgundy; enforce imperial authority in northern Italy in accordance with the Peace of Constance (1183); and bring the kingdom of Sicily into the empire, realizing the dreams of the German emperors since Otto the Great.

When Frederick II assumed the throne the political situation throughout the empire had deteriorated seriously as the result of a struggle for power in Sicily during his own minority and the struggle between Philip of Swabia and Otto IV of Brunswick for the imperial crown. In Germany both Philip and Otto had made grants of crown lands and regalian rights in their efforts to win supporters. After Philip's death, the Hohenstaufen officials refused to recognize Otto IV and treated their offices and lands as private possessions. For eighteen years no effective royal jurisdiction had been exercised in Germany. Although the nobles accepted Frederick after Otto's defeat at Bouvines in 1214, the balance of power was already shifting from the monarchy to the greater territorial princes. In Italy in this period (1197–1215), the Lombard communes established their autonomy, and the Norman monarchy in Sicily collapsed.

Young Frederick and his advisers had to decide where to concentrate their efforts to restore the empire. The situation was complicated by the fact that Frederick had won papal support for the imperial throne at a high price, a promise that he would abdicate the Sicilian throne in favor of his son Henry, so that the kingdom of Sicily and the empire would never be united. Innocent III died before Frederick could have been expected to complete arrangements to this end. The next pope, Honorius III (1216–1227), was agreeable to a postponement of the Sicilian question if Frederick would fulfill his Crusader's vow taken when he was crowned king of the Romans and recognized as emperor-elect in 1215.

By 1220 Frederick's policy had become clear. It was almost a reversal of the traditional Hohenstaufen policy. Sicily and Italy were given priority, the German monarchy was subordinated to his Italian policy, and Burgundy was almost ignored. Frederick had no intention of carrying out his promise to separate Sicily from the empire. His son Henry, already crowned king of Sicily, was elected and crowned king of the Romans in 1220. Nevertheless, in the same year Honorius III willingly officiated at Frederick's formal coronation as emperor. Papal–imperial relations were strained, but the pope wanted, above all else, to sponsor a Crusade led by the highest secular authority in Latin Christendom, and no conflict could break out as long as Frederick would fulfill this desire.

Frederick, however, was determined to secure his position at home before going off to the Holy Land. From Germany Frederick wanted recognition of his authority, recognition of the succession of his son, and support for his program of restoring his power in Italy. Beyond that, for the time being at least, he was willing to let Germany go its own way without any effort to increase his powers, or even to exercise them fully. On three occasions he conceded extensive privileges to the ecclesiastical and lay princes. To gain the support of the magnates for his own election, he issued the Golden Bull of Eger (1213), which confirmed the *status quo* in Germany, including the powers acquired by the nobility since 1197. By his Confederation with the Ecclesiastical Princes (1220), he won the support of the bishops for the election of his son by making ecclesiastical lands practically exempt from royal administration. And later, his Constitution in Favor of the Princes (1231) made the greater lay lords virtually independent within their own territories. In return for these grants, the German nobility put no obstacle in the way of Frederick's Italian policy and from time to time supplied troops for his armies.

After 1220 Frederick practically ignored Germany, and only once after that date did he personally intervene, briefly, in German affairs. Frederick's Mediterranean tastes were repelled by the gloomy forests, rude towns, and long winters of his lands beyond the Alps. He was born and brought up in the kingdom of Sicily, and he always thought of himself as first and foremost the heir of the Norman rulers of the south. The highest value he placed on his imperial title was that as ruler of Germany he could protect his Italian kingdoms against attack from the north.

Frederick's first task in Italy was to restore the Norman monarchy of Sicily. In complete contrast with his treatment of Germany, Frederick considered all the powers and privileges acquired by the Sicilian nobility since 1197 illegal usurpations, and he set out to recover them for the crown. By 1224 he had largely accomplished this goal. Meanwhile, Honorius III was patiently waiting for the emperor to proceed with the Crusade. The break between Frederick and the pope was precipitated by the emperor's determination to restore imperial authority in northern Italy. Now the old papal fears of being crushed between a strong power to the north and one to the south were revived. Honorius sought to mediate the impending quarrel and to salvage the Crusade by arranging for Frederick's marriage in 1225 to the heiress of the kingdom of Jerusalem. But to no avail.

Frederick's position at this juncture was not wholly unreasonable. The pope had accepted earlier delays in the Crusade. Also, in contrast with Henry VI and Otto IV, both of whom had claimed the direct rule of the Papal States, Frederick restored central Italy to papal rule and was willing to respect the pope's temporal authority over that area. Before leaving the peninsula, therefore, Frederick wanted to establish a strong imperial administration in the north. In Lombardy the communes had long since exceeded the limits of autonomy granted by the Peace of Constance (1183), which had given them a restricted right of self-government in return for tribute to the imperial government, and Frederick seized this as the excuse for revoking the settlement and declaring the whole of northern Italy to be directly subject to the emperor. This meant war. Under the leadership of Milan, the Lombard

League was revived, but hostilities had not yet begun when Honorius died. By this time the custom had developed that when the cardinals could not agree on whom they wanted as the new pope, they simply elected the oldest of their colleagues—so that the papacy should not remain vacant and also to provide an interim of several months, or perhaps a few years, during which the cardinals could reconcile their differences and be ready to elect a successor with the required two-thirds majority. Such a stalemate in the College of Cardinals seems to have been why Gregory IX (1227–1241), at the age of eighty, was elected. He was very able and, as it turned out, very long-lived. He survived most of the cardinals who had elected him, and, after Innocent III and before Boniface VIII, he was perhaps the most vigorous of all the thirteenth-century popes. His contribution to the development of canon law has already been discussed. He was also instrumental in the foundation of the mendicant orders, particularly the Franciscans, and in the establishment of the Inquisition.

With respect to Frederick's projected Crusade, Gregory IX would brook no delay and presented the emperor with the simple alternatives of immediately fulfilling his Crusader's vow or being excommunicated. Under this prodding Frederick sailed in 1227, on a date previously agreed on with Honorius. But his fleet was ridden with sickness, and the emperor himself fell ill and returned to port. Gregory was furious at what appeared to be a stratagem to evade a solemn obligation; he excommunicated Frederick forthwith. Pope and emperor were divided not only by policy but by personality. Each was imperious and uncompromising, each was shrewd, aggressive, and jealous of his own prerogatives. Their personal relations help to explain the bitterness of the rupture between papacy and empire that followed.

Frederick, ignoring Gregory's excommunication, recouped his forces and sailed to the Holy Land in 1228. Gregory took notice of this by excommunicating the emperor again for presuming to lead a Crusade while excommunicated. Frederick replied by denouncing the pope for worldliness and political ambition. Then he proceeded to negotiate an advantageous treaty with the sultan that gave Frederick Jerusalem and other cities without a fight. Still excommunicated, he then had himself crowned king of Jerusalem. To Gregory, all these events were a travesty of the crusading ideal. The pope launched an attack on the kingdom of Sicily, excommunicated the emperor a third time for dealing with the infidel, and tried to stir up rebellion in Germany and Italy. Frederick returned from the Holy Land in a vengeful spirit. He easily routed the papal army and put an end to Gregory's meddling in southern Italy, but by the Peace of San Germano (1230), he deliberately left the pope's rule of the Papal States unimpaired.

Frederick now turned to the task of strengthening his government in Sicily. His goal was to create a centralized state, whose main outlines were revealed in 1231 by the Constitutions of Melfi, and then to extend this centralized sys-

Was this seal of Frederick II used on letters to Gregory IX? It celebrates the emperor's campaign of 1228, in which he negotiated a peace with the Moslems and crowned himself king of Jerusalem. Gregory had excommunicated Frederick for not having gone on the Crusade earlier, then again for going while under excommunication, and, finally, for again negotiating with the infidel.

tcm to northern Italy—and, possibly, to central Italy, Germany, and Burgundy, although his ultimate plans will never be known. By the Constitutions of Melfi the privileges of both clergy and nobility were severely curtailed, and all rights of local jurisdiction were so circumscribed that the royal bureaucracy was given a monopoly of governmental power. The kingdom of Sicily under Frederick II was little less than a modern absolute monarchy. Legislation was by royal fiat, the royal courts had jurisdiction over almost all criminal and civil matters (even heresy was defined as a crime against the state), and the whole administrative system was controlled by the will of the king. The kingdom as a whole profited from this strong and arbitrary government. Unruly barons were kept in their place. Taxes were high, but they fell on all classes in accordance with their capacity to pay. Frederick carefully fostered the economic welfare of his realm. The production, export, and import of economically important commodities were controlled, internal customs were abolished, and duties on foreign trade were regulated to encourage commerce.

Frederick was now ready to impose this system on northern Italy, by force if necessary. Gregory IX was equally resolved to prevent any such thing. Unexpected help for Gregory came from Germany, where the emperor's son

Henry rebelled in 1234. The Lombard League threw its weight on the rebel's side. Frederick crushed this rebellion, deposed Henry in favor of another son, Conrad, and returned to Italy determined to destroy the Lombard League. Hostilities reached a climax in an imperial victory at the Battle of Cortenuova in 1237. At first it seemed that Cortenuova meant a complete reversal of all that the Battle of Legnano had won for the communes. The Lombard League fell apart, most of the towns submitted, and a strong imperial party was built up in the north. Many of the nobility saw their chance to gain power in the emperor's service and at the expense of the communes.

Frederick's victory on the battlefield did not end the war, however. Instead of accepting terms, the emperor insisted on unconditional surrender. This intransigence drove the remaining towns into a resistance born of desperation. Gregory IX intervened aggressively, asserting his right to reestablish peace as mediator between the two sides. When the emperor refused, Gregory sent agents into Lombardy to organize the anti-imperial forces, and Frederick was excommunicated again. In the field, Frederick's military operations against Brescia and Milan failed, and he finally turned to an attack on the Papal States. At this point Gregory died, and two years passed before the new pope, Innocent IV (1243–1254), was elected.

Meanwhile, Frederick's conquest of the Papal States continued. The cost of war, however, was beginning to drain his resources, and he was eager to come to terms. Innocent IV renewed Gregory's demand to mediate the quarrel between Frederick and the communes. Frederick refused because he would not admit the pope's claim to define imperial rights in northern Italy. Then, in the midst of further negotiations, Innocent IV fled from Rome to France, where he called a general council at Lyon in 1245. The strife between the papacy and empire had now reached the point where a negotiated peace was impossible. The Council of Lyon declared the emperor guilty of sacrilege and an enemy of the faith, while Innocent deposed and excommunicated him. The pope appealed to the public opinion and conscience of all Europe for support, but the Crusade he preached against Frederick failed to interest more than a few adventurers.

The war dragged on for five more years without definite result. Savage fighting characterized hostilities in Lombardy, where the communes were irrevocably alienated from the empire. Just as the tide seemed to be turning in the emperor's favor, Frederick died. Neither side won the war; indeed, both lost it. Frederick had failed to reestablish imperial control in northern Italy and had overtaxed the resources of his kingdom of Sicily in the effort. In Germany and Burgundy this failure resulted in the further development of particularism—the breakdown of central authority in favor of the territorial princes, who were from then on practically independent under the vague suzerainty of the emperor. As for the papacy, what it gained from the defeat of the Hohenstaufen was more than counterbalanced by what it lost in prestige. Pressed to the point where extreme measures seemed necessary for survival, both Gregory IX and Innocent IV employed every resource at their disposal, including the use of excommunication and the Crusade as instruments of an essentially political and secular policy. It is difficult for the modern historian to judge just what else these popes should have done, but there is no doubt that most contemporaries agreed with Louis IX of France, who turned a deaf ear to the popes' call for a Crusade against a ruler who was at least nominally Christian and who had not been properly and convincingly convicted of heresy.

Frederick II's unsuccessful struggles brought disastrous consequences to both imperial and papal authority, but it would be a mistake to suppose that Italy and Germany as a whole were adversely affected to the same degree. Towns continued to grow in wealth and power, despite the temporary calamities that afflicted the Lombard communes. In Germany the rural society of nobility and peasantry was no less prosperous and peaceful than before the civil wars that followed Henry VI's death. What did come to an end in Italy was the predominance of the kingdom of Sicily.

During the reign of Frederick II the leading cultural center in southern Europe was the court of the emperor at Palermo. Frederick was not only a patron but also a participant. His interests dominated the scholars and writers who were attracted to his court, and he himself produced an important scientific treatise on falconry entitled *The Art of Hunting with Birds,* which is still considered an excellent introduction to that sport as well as a good handbook of ornithology. Frederick reveals himself as a keen observer of nature. This interest is further illustrated by the zoo he collected, including such exotic animals as elephants, giraffes, lions, and other African and Asian specimens. The emperor's curiosity led him to make many experiments whose imaginative quality caught the fancy of contemporary chroniclers and led them to embellish and exaggerate the marvels of nature that the emperor investigated. For example, he had some children reared in isolation from human speech in an effort to learn what language Adam and Eve spoke. In another experiment he had several convicted criminals disemboweled in order to ascertain the functions of the internal organs of the body. The main scientific achievements of the court of Palermo were, however, the work of scholars and translators of Arabic and Greek texts, such as Michael Scot and the mathematician Leonard Fibonacci of Pisa. The cosmopolitan character of the court is illustrated by the presence of scholars from Moslem Africa and the Greek-speaking East.

Frederick II's intellectual interests and his political struggle with the papacy combined to make him notorious to his and later generations. He was *Stupor Mundi* (the wonder of the world), a colossus of impertinence, curiosity, and skepticism. Although not overtly anti-Christian, his tolerance of Jews and Moslems and his seeming belief that Christianity did not monopolize the truth were attitudes that gave rise to the charge that he was an enemy of the faith. To his bitterest critics, he was Antichrist: he defied the pope; he consorted with infidels; and he behaved more like a sultan than a consecrated Christian ruler. Frederick was the only medieval emperor Dante consigned to hell in his *Divine Comedy*. Some, however, praised him in equally exaggerated terms as a near divinity. The cleric Nicholas of Bari wrote in a eulogy: "Let us praise him along with the angel Gabriel. Hear us say: Ave, lord emperor, full of the grace of God, the Lord is with thee. . . . Blessed art thou amongst kings, that is, over all kings."

## The Growth of Royal Power in France

During the reign of Louis VII (1137–1180), the French monarchy was rivaled by the great lords of the kingdom and overshadowed by both Henry II of England and the emperor Frederick I. With the accession of Philip II Augustus (1180–1223) the situation changed rapidly. By the end of Philip's reign, the crown had become the greatest single power in France, and France had become the most powerful kingdom in northern Europe. Philip II created one of the strongest monarchies in medieval European history.

The French king commanded greater resources than the English king, although, as will be seen, he did not attain the same degree of direct control over his subjects as his English counterpart. In France the growth of royal power rested on two accomplishments: the enlargement of the royal domain, or the territory directly under the rule of the king; and the development of a larger and more effective government at both the central and local levels. In both the territorial and the governmental sense, before the reign of Philip Augustus the king was *primus inter pares,* first in dignity but not in power among the lords of France. After Philip Augustus the French king was not only first in prestige but in power as well, and his power was based on the solid realities of more territory, more officials and more subjects, and more wealth under his control than any other French lord could claim.

It would be difficult to imagine less promising beginnings than those of the reign of Philip II. Philip succeeded to the throne as a youth of fifteen, unhealthy and unimpressive physically, and lacking in most of the conventional virtues of knight or lord. He was neither bold nor dashing; instead, he was patient and avoided mistakes, while quick to turn to his own advantage the mistakes of others. However, he possessed a keen practical intelligence and a capacity both to formulate and to execute long-range plans. He was superbly endowed with a cunning, tenacity, and unscrupulous opportunism that enabled him to wring the last advantage out of every situation confronting him. By the end of his reign he had even acquired some measure of popularity among his subjects.

Philip's dominating ambition was to enlarge his royal domain and increase his power. When his reign began the domain hardly extended beyond the country immediately surrounding Paris and Orléans, while the paramount influence at his court was exercised by his mother's relatives of the house of Champagne and Blois. Philip's first important step toward independence was his marriage to an heiress connected with the house of Flanders, whose dowry was the county of Artois. This marriage was opposed by Philip's relatives, and in the ensuing quarrel Philip was able to involve Champagne and Flanders in a fight that he ended only when his relatives and in-laws agreed to his annexation in 1185 of the county of Vermandois. This was a valuable addition to the royal domain because it connected the older Capetian lands with Artois on the Channel coast.

During these years Henry II of England, Philip's greatest vassal and the long-time foe of his father, refrained from intervening—perhaps with the hope that Philip would exercise similar restraint when the time came to divide the great Plantagenet inheritance among Henry's sons. Any such hope was dispelled by the greed and ambition of the younger Plantagenets, who were already conspiring against their father. Philip played on their jealousies, and when the final revolt of Richard and John came, in 1189, Philip actively promoted the downfall of the old king. Friction between Richard and Philip grew into open hostility while both kings participated in the Third Crusade. Underlying their relationship was a mutual suspicion, in each case well-founded, that the one coveted the lands and lordships of the other.

Philip's heart was not in the Crusade, and on the plea of ill health he returned to France in 1191 convinced that Richard would be as great a danger to him as Henry II had been to his father. To weaken Richard wherever he could, Philip seized some territory on the border of Normandy, stirred up dissension among Richard's vassals in Aquitaine, and intrigued with Richard's brother John. When news came that Richard was held prisoner by the emperor Henry VI, Philip did all he could to prevent his release and encouraged John to seize the English crown. Richard's return from Germany, of course, meant war. From 1194 until 1199 the fighting slowly went against Philip, and it was a lucky stroke for him when Richard was killed by a crossbowman's bolt during a minor siege operation.

In the contest between John and the supporters of Arthur of Brittany for the succession to the English crown, Philip favored Arthur but refrained from active intervention. He did not have long to wait, however. John provided the occasion for Philip's next move by suddenly marrying the daughter of the count of Angoulême, whose hand was already pledged to John's vassal, the count of La Marche. When the latter appealed for justice to Philip, his lord's lord, John was summoned to Paris to answer charges. John refused to recognize the validity of this summons, and his French fiefs were declared forfeited.

In the war that followed, Philip reduced Normandy without much difficulty and incorporated it into the royal domain in 1204. By the end of the following year all of John's other lands north of the Loire—Maine, Anjou, Brittany, and Touraine—were under Philip's control, and many of the barons of Poitou had submitted. All these territories, except Brittany, came under direct royal control. In Brittany, John's lordship was extinguished, and the count now held directly from Philip. South of the Loire the only part of Aquitaine that John could rely on was Gascony in the southwest. The Gascons were not particularly pro-English, but they did not want to jeopardize their lucrative wine trade with England, and they preferred a weak duke or a king far removed to a strong king near home. John used Gascony as his base for an attempted reconquest of his French lands, but after reoccupying part of Poitou in 1206, he could do no more because of his struggle with Innocent III and the opposition of many of his barons.

Meanwhile, the aggrandizement of the French monarchy had begun to alarm the lords of the Low Countries, including the count of Flanders, and Philip's support of the Hohenstaufen candidate for the imperial crown antagonized the Guelph party in Germany. Otto IV, the Guelph emperor and John's nephew, revived the traditional alliance between his house and that of the Plantagenets. After several years of negotiations, during which Otto and John won the support of most of the lords of the Rhineland and the Low Countries, Western Europe was divided into two great international coalitions. One was based on the alliance between the Plantagenets and the Guelphs, and the other included the supporters of the Capetians and the Hohenstaufens.

The forces of John and Otto were ready to move in the summer of 1214. The English army coordinated its attack from Gascony in the southwest with an invasion of German, English, and Flemish troops from the northeast, with the intention of crushing Philip's forces between two arms of a great pincers movement. This strategy was well conceived but its execution left something to be desired. John failed to press home his initial advantage in Poitou and Anjou, and this gave Philip his opportunity. Whether it was by a brilliant stroke of well-planned strategy or merely by a desperate gamble forced on him by circumstances, Philip correctly gauged the situation in leaving the defense of the southwest to his son Louis with only eight hundred knights. Philip then hastened north with the bulk of his army. At Bouvines in Flanders the French feudal levy, backed up by footmen supplied by the towns of the royal domain, met and defeated Otto's Anglo-Flemish-German army. The Battle of Bouvines was the French king's greatest hour. Unhorsed in the fight, and saved only by the stout defense of his personal bodyguard, Philip Augustus emerged from the ordeal a hero. The battle ended Otto's rule as emperor, it rendered hopeless John's effort to regain his French lands, and it established the French monarchy as the greatest European power of the thirteenth century.

On his return from the great victory, Philip Augustus was greeted with wild rejoicing. After Bouvines he abstained from any further battlefield heroics and entrusted the fighting of the Albigensian Crusade to his son Louis. By temperament wholly unsuited to the hardships and skills of fighting, Philip had gained more by war and diplomacy in ten years than all of his more bellicose contemporaries put together. The royal domain had more than tripled in size, and the royal revenues increased incredibly. If the figures of chroniclers can be believed, and they are probably accurate as to order of magnitude if not to actual figures, Louis VII left his son an annual income of £ 60,000, which Philip Augustus increased to £ 438,000 a year.

Besides the power he gained through conquest or held through feudal contracts, a medieval monarch had other rights and obligations as an anointed king. For example, the king was specially obligated to defend the Church and had always exercised a greater influence in ecclesiastical affairs than any of the great lords of the kingdom. He was also obligated to maintain peace, protect the poor and the weak, and do justice to all. These duties and the rights they implied were not clearly defined but were universally recognized. In terms of practical politics this meant that the king could intervene in local affairs to provide royal protection or to extend the power of the royal courts of justice. The result was often an extension of royal jurisdiction beyond the usual limits of feudal relations. Under a powerful king, when local government under feudal lords broke down, or failed to fulfill its purpose, the king might send his royal officials to redress grievances and correct abuses.

Under Philip Augustus such use of royal officials outside the royal domain and Normandy was infrequent because Philip's main problem was to govern effectively the vastly enlarged territories now under his direct rule. The royal domain he had inherited was divided into small districts under the administration of *prévôts,* who farmed the royal revenues. This meant that each *prévôt* paid in to the central government a fixed sum of money each year and then recouped himself and tried to make a profit by collecting the royal taxes, tolls, profits of justice, feudal dues, and other revenues owing to the king from his district. As the middleman in this scheme, the *prévôt* might cheat both the king and his subjects, and each *prévôt* aspired to make his office hereditary. This system was not efficient, nor did it serve the king very well because the interests of the *prévôts* were more like those of a local lord than of a royal official.

Throughout the newly conquered territories and wherever feasible in the older royal domain Philip established new and larger territories for local government, each under the administration of a new official called a *bailli.* Farming the revenues was replaced by fixed salaries, and local interests or connections were circumvented by the rule that no *bailli* should remain in one district for more than a few years. Like the *bailli* himself, subordinate officials were appointed by the king and held their office at the king's pleasure. This put an end to the threat that a hereditary officialdom might encroach on royal authority. Most of the new officials were recruited from the ranks of the lesser nobility or the bourgeoisie. Their loyalty was thus assured by the fact that their status and income were dependent on serving the king well. When large acquisitions to the royal domain were made later, in the south of France, much the same system was extended to that area also. The main differences were that the local governor was called a seneschal, rather than *bailli,* and that the seneschals were usually nobles of some rank and power and were entrusted with more important military commands than their northern counterparts. This modification in the scheme was necessary because the greater distance from the central government required a more powerful royal official on the spot, and because in the more turbulent south, the military aspect of local government was more prominent.

Philip Augustus had established the monarchy so securely that Louis VIII (1223–1226) was the first Capetian to succeed to the throne without having been crowned during his father's lifetime. Louis had been active in the government for several years before his accession, and his reign was little more than a continuation of Philip II's policy. He completed the conquest of Poitou and intervened successfully in the south of France against the Albigensian heretics. The final success of his southern policy was the annexation of the greater part of Languedoc to the royal domain. This was accomplished by the marriage of Louis' third son to the heiress of the count of Toulouse, and their subsequent deaths without heirs, so that their lands escheated to the crown in 1271. The royal domain now extended from the Channel to the Mediterranean.

The later ideal of a unified and indivisible kingdom had not yet developed in thirteenth-century France. On his death Louis VIII left a will to be executed by his eldest son Louis IX directing that when his sons came of age, his second son should be given Artois; his third son, Alphonse, who married the heiress of Toulouse, should have Poitou; and his youngest son, Charles, who later became king of the Two Sicilies and founder of the Angevin royal house of Naples, was to have Anjou. This royal policy of family fiefs, or appanages, has been criticized by historians who can look back on the difficulties it later created for the monarchy, but this was something Louis VIII could scarcely have foreseen. During the thirteenth century this system worked well, providing strong and friendly rulers for large areas in France that were still beyond the strength of the royal government to rule directly. For example, Alphonse of Poitou was not only completely loyal to his brother but also extended to his two great counties many of the methods of administration employed by the royal government. When he died the absorption of Poitou and Toulouse into the royal domain was simplified by the transitional period of his rule. It was only after appanages had remained in the hands of a collateral branch of the royal house for several generations that these great fiefs became a menace to the crown. By that time ties of family loyalty had weakened, and the political situation in France had deteriorated from the relative stability of the thirteenth century.

When Louis VIII died at an early age, he left the throne to a boy of twelve. He also left a redoubtable widow, Blanche, daughter of Alphonso the Noble of Castile and granddaughter of Henry II of England. Blanche of Castile headed a stormy regency until her son Louis IX (1226–1270) came of age in 1234. During this regency Blanche had to meet and quell the only serious reaction against the growing powers of the government during the whole century. The royal officials stood by her; she had the support of most of the towns; and the papacy was a helpful ally. But even more decisive was the fact that the greater royal vassals who participated in the confused and at times half-hearted revolt had no program and were unable to unite in the kind of alliance the English barons achieved in forcing Magna Carta on John in 1215. France was a large and conglomerate kingdom in which wide regional differences in language, culture, economic life, and social and political institutions endured. It was therefore difficult to find common interests that could unite all the nobles. Although Henry III of England intervened in 1230 to support the rebellion and reconquer his lost fiefs, the English campaign only demonstrated Henry's ineffectiveness, and Blanche was able to stifle the ambitions of the rebellious lords, some by force and others by conciliation.

By shrewdly taking advantage of the rights that feudal customs and the traditions of kingship provided, Philip Augustus and his son had established the French monarchy so firmly that it easily surmounted the troubles of Louis IX's minority, in striking contrast to the disintegration of royal power in Germany following the death of Henry VI. In England, however, the ability of the barons to form a community of interest that could check the monarchy led to the eventual strengthening of English government and produced a constitutional government that is usually taken for granted but that is, historically, a rare and unlikely form of governmental organization.

## England Under the Sons of Henry II

Henry II died in 1189, an embittered old man. Yet as far as England was concerned, his rule had been the strongest of any monarch of his time, and his reforms and innovations provided a solid foundation for the constitutional development of England during several centuries. The system of government he bequeathed his successors continued to grow stronger even under unfavorable circumstances. Richard was for all practical purposes an absentee ruler. John was the most unpopular monarch ever to rule England. Henry III, succeeding to the crown as a boy of nine, gave England its first regency. Later, he tried ineffectually to impose his weak and vacillating will on his realm.

Eleanor of Aquitaine was buried with Richard I, her favorite son. Their tombs in Fontevrault Abbey are adorned with lifelike sculptures.

And yet when Edward I became king in 1272, the English monarchy was flourishing as never before, despite major political crises in each of the three preceding reigns. Viewed as a whole, the history of England in the thirteenth century poses the question whether the royal government gained strength in spite of the limitations placed on it or because of them.

Richard I (1189–1199) had already taken the cross when he became king. Before departing for the Holy Land he visited England for four months, to receive his crown and arrange for the government in his absence. After he returned from the Third Crusade he was in England two more months; he spent the rest of his reign on the Continent. Richard had grown up in France, had made his mark as duke of Aquitaine, and was the least English of all medieval kings of England. Although he chose good officials, he cared little for the art of government, and even less for England. His consuming interest was warfare; for recreation he dabbled with poetry and music. He was a popular king because he was an able leader in war. His barons respected him on the battlefield, and he was indefatigable in defending his dominions against his greatest enemy, who was also his feudal lord, the French king.

In his initial arrangement for the government in his absence, Richard made the mistake of dividing authority between two justiciars and his brother John, a situation that invited a struggle for power. One justiciar was William Marshal, whose rise to eminence was followed earlier and who now achieved the pinnacle of aristocratic power. The other was William Longchamp, the chancellor, who had risen from humble origins and was in Richard's service before he became king. In the three-cornered struggle that followed, Long-champ's unscrupulous methods won him a temporary supremacy, while John was cast in the anomalous role of leading the opposition against Longchamp's tyranny. In 1191 most of the bishops and barons, together with John and his personal supporters, deposed Longchamp by a formal judgment of the *curia regis* acting in the king's absence. This crisis reinforced a rudimentary notion of the right of the baronage to act collectively in defense of its rights.

In 1193 the government was once more firmly in the hands of Richard's supporters under the leadership of Hubert Walter, one of the most capable administrators to serve any medieval king. As archbishop of Canterbury, papal legate, and justiciar, Hubert Walter combined the supreme ecclesiastical and secular authority of the realm. Itinerant justices increased their activity, local officials were appointed to keep the peace, the power of the sheriffs was curbed, and the central government became more efficient.

The main task of Richard's government in England was to raise money to support his several ventures and to pay off the king's ransom. While returning from the Crusade, Richard was captured in Austria by his enemies, who turned him over to the emperor (1192–1194). In spite of occasional and local resistance, the money was raised. Almost every medieval form of taxation was employed: an extraordinary feudal aid (owed by any vassal to ransom his lord, but in this case collected from subvassals as well under the guise of scutage), an income tax, a tax on personal property, a land tax, and a variety of other methods, such as tallages, extortionate fines, and forced loans. After Richard's return in 1194, tremendous sums of money were extracted from England to pay for castle building in Normandy and to defray the expenses of reconquering territories lost to Philip Augustus. The war went well, but in the midst of it Richard was mortally wounded in a minor skirmish.

John's reign (1199–1216) got off to a bad start. The succession was disputed by supporters of his nephew Arthur, son of his older brother Geoffrey, late count of Brittany. The unexplained death of this nephew while in John's custody gave rise to unpleasant rumors. Even more important, the loss of Normandy in 1204 and of most of his other Continental fiefs was a severe blow to John's prestige and power. His futile efforts to recover his Continental possessions became a continuing drain on his resources.

The next great crisis of John's reign was his quarrel with Innocent III over the election of Stephen Langton as archbishop of Canterbury in 1206. England was placed under an interdict in 1208, and John was excommunicated in 1209, but not until 1213 did he capitulate. That he could resist for five years under such circumstances was proof of the strength of the royal government. John was supported by most of the barons and bishops on this issue, and his final surrender did not in fact weaken his position. By becoming the vassal of the pope John now gained a powerful ally who could restrain his greatest foreign enemy, Philip Augustus. But meanwhile enemies were gathering at home.

These were the growing number of barons who objected to the desperate means by which John tried to raise funds for his campaign to recover his lost French lands. They were bold enough to speak out against the often arbitrary methods John employed in governing England and in exploiting his position as feudal lord. Stephen Langton, as archbishop and papal legate, tried to mediate between king and barons. By his insistence that John should observe the laws and customs of the realm—and especially to refrain from punishing his enemies without giving them a trial by due process of law—Stephen succeeded in introducing some broader principles into the demands of the dissident barons. The signal for a general uprising was the conspicuous failure of John's campaign to defeat Philip Augustus in the summer of 1214. John returned to England to raise money for another campaign and found instead a rebellion.

After fruitless negotiations the barons formally defied the king and renounced their homage. John was forced to submit. The king met the rebels at Runnymede in June 1215, and peace was preserved temporarily when he set his seal to a document containing their demands. From this draft the chancery clerks drew up a better worded and slightly modified version that is known as Magna Carta—the Great Charter.

The core of Magna Carta is the set of feudal grievances of the dissident barons, and the charter is essentially a statement of feudal laws and customs that the king bound himself to observe. This statement was detailed and specific; the document is a bill of particulars, not a "constitution" of principles. The barons were particularly insistent on limiting the financial exactions of the king as feudal lord. By defining the amount to be paid for reliefs, by restricting the king's rights with respect to the feudal incidents of wardship and marriage, and by requiring that no scutages or extraordinary aids be imposed without the counsel of all the barons and prelates properly assembled, the charter restricted the financial resources of the monarchy. But Magna Carta was more than a baronial attack on the king. In one clause the liberties of the Church in England were guaranteed; in others the rights and privileges of the boroughs and of the merchants were set forth; and the clauses dealing with administrative and judicial matters benefited all freemen of England. For

Does this thirteenth-century manuscript portrait of the first four Plantagenet kings attempt to convey their characters? Henry II (top left) strikes a judicial pose. By the thirteenth century, his legal reforms had been accepted even by those whose judicial rights they had curtailed. Richard I (top right) presents the image of the great warrior. A knight who became a hero during the Third Crusade, he returned to England to rebuild his empire. John (bottom left) pressed administrative reforms and appears, from the attitude of his crown, to have had a rakish reputation. Henry III (bottom right), an unimaginative king, was constantly in financial trouble. Is that a treasure chest on his lap?

example, almost all the judicial reforms of Henry II were recognized to be important elements in the government and in the laws and customs of the realm. Most important of all the clauses was the thirty-ninth, which enshrined the principle of due process of law: no freeman was to be proceeded against except by legal judgment of his peers or by the law of the land.

After the theory of the divine right of kings had flowered in the seventeenth century, the greatest importance of Magna Carta appeared to be its recognition that the king was under the law, that his rule was not arbitrary but limited. Since the principle of royal responsibility was generally accepted in medieval Europe—it appears, for instance, in the coronation oath of Henry I in 1100—the contemporary significance of Magna Carta lay in the existence of a community that could produce such a document and make it effective. The only means of enforcement available was a recognition of the legitimacy of civil war; a committee of twenty-five barons was given a right of resistance by force if John should transgress any of his promises. These barons were already preparing for war when John appealed to his feudal suzerain Innocent III, who annulled the charter as an illegal and immoral invasion of royal governance. Civil war broke out, and the barons appealed to Louis, son of Philip Augustus, offering him the crown in return for military assistance. Hence as a peace treaty, Magna Carta had little actual effect on the course of events under John. Its significance lay in the future and in the amended version of 1225, which was confirmed again and again in the next three centuries as a statement of the fundamental laws and customs of the realm.

French troops commanded by Prince Louis successfully invaded England in 1216, but John's death shortly after the outbreak of the war saved the situation for the government. Already some of the barons had deserted to the royalist side; now most of them came over to the government. Since Henry III (1216–1272) was a minor, a regency was established under the influence of two of the older barons, William Marshal and Hubert de Burgh, and of the papal legate. Resistance broke down quickly when the regency, as an act of good faith, immediately reissued Magna Carta, omitting all controversial clauses with the promise to reconsider them when peace had been restored. This promise was kept (in 1217 and again in 1225). The goal of the regency was to restore the monarchy on the basis of consultation and cooperation with the baronage. This balance of power was maintained until Henry came of age in 1227 and even afterward until Hubert de Burgh was dismissed from his office of justiciar in 1232 (William Marshal died in 1219). Then Henry III tried unsuccessfully to assert his full control over royal administration and royal policy.

The important point was not the tyranny of John or the weakness of Henry III. What Magna Carta demonstrated went beyond the personality of monarchs to the concept of the community of the realm, a concept midway between the theory of individual contractual rights as determining the relationship between ruler and subject and the modern theory of the state. According to this concept, the ruler is both obligated and empowered to act for the common welfare. To meet this great responsibility, the ruler must possess and exercise the full range of royal authority, undiminished and unshared with anyone. At the same time, subjects possess and exercise rights beyond the reach of royal governance and thus should be consulted on all questions that concern their rights within the community.

This was a legal concept, and it worked both to limit the monarchy and to strengthen it. An arbitrary and tyrannical king could find himself embroiled in endless civil war, but an extremely effective form of government was produced when a king added to the power of monarchy both the majesty of the law and the support of the active political members of the community, who supported the government because they were a part of it. In the thirteenth century, it was difficult to imagine a government without a king, but kings were most effective when they governed under the law rather than against it.

**Suggestions for Further Reading**

**Secondary Works**    Three biographies of Innocent III are S. R. Packard, *Europe and the Church Under Innocent III* (New York, 1927); C. Edwards, *Innocent III: Church Defender* (Baton Rouge, La., 1951); and J. M. Powell, ed., *Innocent III: Vicar of Christ or Lord of the World?* (Boston, 1963), a collection of articles that focuses on Innocent's goals. A comprehensive study of Frederick II is E. H. Kantorowicz, *Frederick II* (London, 1931). It may be supplemented by T. C. Van Cleve, *The Emperor Frederick II of Hohenstaufen: Immutator Mundi* (Oxford, 1972). See also C. C. Bayley, *The Formation of the German College of Electors in the Thirteenth Century* (Toronto, 1949), and the work of G. Barraclough cited at the end of Chapter 8. On the development of French government, see the work of R. Fawtier cited at the end of Chapter 8; C. T. Wood, *The French Appanages and the French Monarchy* (Cambridge, Mass., 1966); J. R. Strayer and C. H. Taylor, *Studies in Early French Taxation* (Cambridge, Mass., 1939); and T. N. Bisson, *Assemblies and Representation in Languedoc in the Thirteenth Century* (Princeton, N.J., 1964). For England, see the general work of A. L. Poole, *From Domesday Book to Magna Carta*, 2nd ed. (Oxford, 1955); W. L. Warren, *King John* (London, 1961); J. C. Holt, *Magna Carta* (Cambridge, 1965); and F. M. Powicke, *Stephen Langton* (Oxford, 1928).

**Sources**    For sources on Innocent III, see B. Tierney, *The Crisis of Church and State, 1050–1300* (Englewood Cliffs, N.J., 1964). *English Historical Documents,* ed. D. C. Douglas and G. W. Greenaway, vol. 2 (New York, 1953), and C. Stephenson and F. G. Marcham, *Sources of English Constitutional History* (New York, 1937) are important. See also *The Art of Falconry, Being the De Arte Venandi cum Avibus of Frederick II,* trans. C. Wood and F. M. Fyfe (Stanford, Calif., 1943).

# 20  The Dominance of the Western Monarchies

In the second half of the thirteenth century the French and English kings consolidated their power and created effective ways of unifying their subjects, while both the emperor and the pope struggled to hold on to their past glories. In Italy the papacy finally succeeded in defeating its imperial rivals, but by the end of the century it was clear that the Church had lost its ability to influence affairs as a supranational political power.

## The Disintegration of the Empire, 1250–1308

After the death of Frederick II (1250), the imperial cause in Italy rapidly deteriorated, and the papacy finally triumphed over the last of the Hohenstaufen. Conrad IV (1250–1254), who had been governing Germany for his father, hurried south to continue the struggle but died before he could achieve any notable results. Conrad's half brother Manfred then assumed control of the imperial, or Ghibelline, forces in Italy as regent for Conrad's infant son, Conradin, who remained in Germany. For several years Manfred's effective

486

authority was confined to the kingdom of Sicily, but after defeating a papal army in 1258 he turned to the task of reviving imperial power in northern Italy.

Meanwhile the popes were desperately seeking foreign aid. Innocent IV had excommunicated the whole Hohenstaufen family as a "viper brood" of oppressors of the Church and had begun negotiations with France and England. Innocent's successor had reached an agreement with Henry III of England according to which Henry's son Edmund was to be granted the Sicilian throne in return for Henry's underwriting of papal debts incurred in the wars against the Hohenstaufen. This plan failed, and Henry's commitment to the pope touched off a new baronial rebellion in 1258 in England. Louis IX of France at first turned a deaf ear to papal appeals. Finally Clement IV (1265–1268), alarmed at the growth of Manfred's power in Italy and supported by the ambitions of Louis' brother Charles of Anjou, was able to convince the French king that a friendly power in Sicily was necessary for the peace of Christendom and for a successful Crusade. Accordingly, in 1265 Charles of Anjou was granted the kingdom of Sicily to hold as a papal fief. In return, Charles agreed to keep the kingdom of Sicily independent of the empire forever, to make a substantial payment against papal debts, and to render an annual tribute in recognition of papal lordship.

Charles of Anjou led a French army into Italy and, after defeating and killing Manfred in the Battle of Benevento (1266), found the situation remarkably easy to control. The kingdom of Sicily submitted with little resistance, the Ghibellines throughout the peninsula were discredited, and the Guelph factions took over most of the Italian cities. In Tuscany and Lombardy Charles was hailed as a liberator. The only serious threat to the new Angevin kingdom of Sicily lay in the supporters of the youthful Conradin, who was persuaded to invade Italy and assert his hereditary claims. The Ghibellines rose in Lombardy and in Sicily, but the issue was quickly decided in favor of the Angevins when Charles defeated, captured, and executed Conradin in 1268. Many Ghibelline nobles in the kingdom of Sicily suffered confiscation of their lands and were replaced by a new French nobility, who had already taken over most of the important government offices. A dangerous situation was brewing.

Oblivious to the resentment of his new subjects, Charles of Anjou now turned eagerly to dreams of a Mediterranean empire. Already count of Provence through his wife, he was also the dominant influence in Italian politics. His kingdom of Sicily was strategically located as a base for the conquest of the southern Balkans, Constantinople, and the Holy Land. To prepare the way, Charles arranged several marriage alliances for his children and bought the claims of one of the pretenders to the kingdom of Jerusalem. For ten years Charles' plans were blocked by the popes, especially Gregory X (1271–1276), who had no use for an adventurer whose ambitions could only interfere with that pope's desire for a grand Crusade by a united Christendom.

Gregory undermined Charles' influence in northern Italy and entered into negotiations with the Byzantine emperor, who promised the reunion of the Greek and Latin churches under papal supremacy. Gregory then forbade Charles of Anjou to attack Constantinople. But opposition in Constantinople prevented the emperor from fulfilling his promise, and Charles' fortunes took a turn for the better when he finally secured the election of his own nominee as Pope Martin IV (1281–1285). Martin obliged his patron by excommunicating all Greeks who opposed reunion of the Churches and by lifting the papal ban against attacking Constantinople.

At this point the Angevin cause suffered a complete reversal. A bloody anti-French riot erupted in Palermo on Easter Monday 1282, just as the church bells were ringing for Vespers. By the following morning all the French who had not escaped from the city were dead. The revolt, the so-called Sicilian Vespers, spread throughout the island. The natives' resentment against excessive taxation and foreign rule led to the slaughter of several thousand French. The throne was offered to Peter of Aragón, who was married to Manfred's daughter. The Sicilian war dragged on for twenty years—Philip III's "crusade" against Aragón in 1285 was an incident in the struggle—but in the end, Aragonese sea power was decisive. Charles of Anjou (1265–1285) withdrew to the mainland, where his descendants ruled the kingdom of Naples, while Peter of Aragón (1282–1285) and his descendants ruled a separate kingdom of Sicily. The two kingdoms were not reunited until 1435 when Alfonso the Magnanimous, already king of Sicily, succeeded to the throne of Naples and became king of the Two Sicilies.

In central and northern Italy, the waning influence of Charles of Anjou was the signal for a Ghibelline revival. Party strife provided opportunities for tyrants to seize power in many cities, and a few of these lords built up fairly extensive dominions, including several cities and stretching across many miles of the countryside. Some towns, striving to preserve their freedom and autonomy, joined together in leagues. Neither such leagues nor the city-states of the tyrants were very stable. Guelphs and Ghibellines struggled for power, and these internal divisions led to appeals for outside help, which embroiled most of the Italian cities in constantly shifting alliances and nearly endless, although usually inconsequential, warfare. By the end of the thirteenth century no power was strong enough to impose peace on the cities and princes of central and northern Italy.

In Germany, immediately after Frederick II's death the princes achieved the almost complete independence for which they had striven for generations. From about 1250 on, after a long period in which power had shifted gradually from the monarchy to the great magnates, Germany was ruled by the princes. There was no longer any chance that the central theme of German history would be the history of the monarchy. Even if Frederick's policy had succeeded, this development probably would have occurred because of his concessions to the German nobles and prelates. Frederick's failure made it inevitable. Papal policy speeded the process. Perhaps the greatest single reason for Frederick's weakness in the last years of his reign was the growth in Germany of an anti-imperial party encouraged by the popes. In 1246, after Innocent IV had excommunicated and deposed Frederick at the Council of Lyon, the papal party elected an antiking, Henry Raspe. German prelates were required to recognize Henry under pain of excommunication, and the popes did not hesitate to employ the full force of ecclesiastical discipline to crush the Hohenstaufen north of the Alps. On Henry Raspe's death, William of Holland was elected king of the Romans in 1247; he was little more than the puppet of the ecclesiastical princes.

After the premature death of William of Holland in 1256 the lay princes joined the prelates in asserting their right to elect the king, as against the hereditary claims of Conradin. The princes agreed that a foreigner was to be preferred to any German lord who might revive the strength of the central government, but they were divided on the question of whom to elect. One group chose Richard of Cornwall, brother of Henry III of England; another group elected Alfonso X of Castile. The result was highly gratifying to the German princes. Since neither could make good his claim to the throne, both Richard and Alfonso sought to gain supporters by granting rights and revenues to princes who were not yet committed or who could be won over. The Great Interregnum, as the period from 1254 to 1273 is called, caused the virtual collapse of all central authority.

The anarchy of these years should not be exaggerated. Peace was fairly well preserved, and the functions of government were carried on within the several states. Regional agreements to keep the peace, the *Landfrieden,* effectively maintained order in some areas, while the autonomous and privileged free cities of the empire formed leagues for the same purpose. Despite the confused political situation, towns and trade continued to grow, and the eastward expansion of Germany continued unabated. This expansion resulted in the growth of larger territorial states in the eastern parts—notably Austria, Bohemia, and Brandenburg. The shift in power from the emperor to the princes in the thirteenth century was thus paralleled by a shift in the balance from the older western principalities of the Rhineland to the newer principalities of the east.

It was Gregory X (1271–1276) who took the initiative in bringing the Interregnum to a close following the death of Richard of Cornwall in 1272. Gregory had reason to fear the ambitions of Charles of Anjou, and he was eager to launch a grand Crusade. To counterbalance the threat from Charles and to unite Christendom, Gregory secured from Alfonso of Castile a renunciation of his claims to the empire, defeated Charles' plan to have his nephew Philip III of France elected, and used papal influence in Germany to obtain the unanimous election of a new emperor, Count Rudolf of Habsburg. He was acceptable mainly because he did not appear powerful enough to enforce imperial authority. Rudolf of Habsburg (1273–1291) had a keen eye for realities; he ignored or even renounced imperial rights that were beyond his strength to maintain. Thus he confirmed the temporal rule of the popes in the Papal States, abandoned Italy entirely, and refused to protect the western border of the empire against French encroachments. He did not interfere in the affairs of greater lords, either within their states or in their relations with each other, but he did suppress the maraudings of petty knights and barons, thus gaining the support of the free cities.

Rudolf's one major venture in German politics turned out to be a resounding success, but it was a success for the Habsburg family, not for imperial power. This was his war against the king of Bohemia, in which Rudolf was supported by the magnates because Bohemia had grown into the largest territorial state in the empire. From this war Rudolf acquired Austria and at one stroke became one of the most powerful princes of Germany. The Habsburg lands now stretched from scattered holdings in Alsace, southern Germany, and Switzerland into the Danube valley all the way to the eastern frontier. From having been a western German power of the second rank, the Habsburgs became an eastern dynasty of the first rank.

Fear of Habsburg aggrandizement and of Rudolf's efforts to reestablish the hereditary principle of succession led the princes to pass over Rudolf's son, Albert of Austria, and elect another weak ruler, Adolf of Nassau (1292–1298). Adolf followed the example of his predecessor in using his office to enhance his family's territorial position, but with less notable success. Albert of Austria organized an opposition party that deposed Adolf, who had grown too strong, and elected Albert (1298–1308) in the hope that he would maintain the *status quo*. These events were complicated by the absence of a strong central authority in Germany, which made intervention from outside an irresistible temptation. Edward I of England tried to build up an alliance of German lords, led by Adolf of Nassau, against France. The French king countered that move by supporting Albert of Austria and subsidizing enough princes to swing the election to Albert. After gaining office, however, Albert broke with the French and made peace with the pope, and consequently French influence helped defeat Albert's effort to pass on the imperial title to his son. The attempt of the Habsburgs to replace the Hohenstaufen dynasty with a new hereditary dynasty thus failed. The course of German history in the later Middle Ages and well into modern times was fixed. Germany remained a congeries of territorial states lacking any effective central government. The empire became a shadow, a dream, an ideal—but no longer a reality.

## England Under Henry III and Edward I

Henry III (1216–1272) was well-educated, a connoisseur of the arts, a devout Christian (and a credulous opponent of the Jews), but above all an ineffective king. He alienated himself from his English barons by his reliance on his friends and relatives from France, and he ruined the finances of the monarchy with his grandiose and unsuccessful attempts to reconquer French territory and to advance the fortunes of his son Edmund in Sicily by paying off the debts the papacy had incurred in its war against the Hohenstaufen. The stage was set for a constitutional crisis.

By 1258 Henry was hopelessly in debt and had to turn to his barons for help. His appeal was greeted with a demand for reforms and for greater baronial participation both in the administrative work of the government and in the formulation of royal policy. The barons' program, beginning with the Provisions of Oxford (1258), put the government under the joint direction of the king and a baronial council. Abuses of local government were investigated, most of the sheriffs were replaced by new men, and inquiries were made into alienations of royal rights that might deprive the king of revenues. In foreign policy, the barons pushed forward a general settlement and the establishment of peace with France by the Treaty of Paris (1259). The constructive work of the first few years of reform was impressive, and Henry grudgingly agreed with most of the demands. The great difference between the baronial action of 1215 and that of 1258 and 1264 was that the primary goal of Magna Carta was to *limit* the government, while the primary goal of the Provisions of Oxford and the other enactments preceding the Barons' War was to *participate* in the government.

Never convinced of the desirability of sharing power, Henry bided his time and began to gather support as the barons developed rifts in their ranks. Eventually only a small group of barons, led by the king's brother-in-law Simon de Montfort, son of the leader of the Albigensian Crusade, continued to press for full execution of the baronial program. After much acrimonious debate and a brief resort to arms, the leaders of the conflicting parties agreed to submit their differences to the arbitration of Louis IX of France, who was asked to pass judgment on the Provisions of Oxford and disputes growing out of them. Convinced by his office of the prerogatives of monarchy, Louis took less than a week to decide and declare in his Mise of Amiens (1264) that the Provisions were null and void, an illegal invasion of royal rights. Simon and his followers were shocked. All along they had been acting in the king's name, and on every issue they had gained the king's acquiescence, however grudgingly granted. This meant war.

The Barons' War was settled by two major battles. At Lewes, in 1264, Simon de Montfort was victorious. During the next fifteen months he continued to rule in the king's name, held parliaments, and gained considerable popular support. Then the royalist forces were rallied under the lord Edward, son and heir of Henry III, and at the Battle of Evesham (1265) Simon was killed, his army defeated, and his cause destroyed. The outcome, however, was not simply a royalist reaction. It took more than a year of fighting before Edward could pursue and catch all the rebels. By that time passions had cooled, and a papal legate, Cardinal Ottobuono, arrived to take the lead in reestablishing peace.

Ottobuono's influence is seen in the Dictum of Kenilworth (1266). By this royalist proclamation the king was recognized to have full control over the royal government, former rebels were allowed to redeem their confiscated lands by paying the king up to one-half their value, and the laws and customs of the realm were confirmed as they had existed "before the time of this disturbance." Then, in 1267, most of the constructive reforms of the preceding nine years were incorporated into the Statute of Marlborough, which also contained a clause confirming Magna Carta. The work of Simon de Montfort and the barons had not been wholly in vain. Furthermore, these years provided an education in kingship for the lord Edward, who as king never forgot the lessons he had learned. Chief of these was the necessity for cooperation with the community of the realm—the barons and their followers of lesser status—if the monarchy itself was to be strong.

The general pacification following the Barons' War proceeded so well that in 1270 Edward could depart on his long-planned Crusade. He was returning from this venture when he received the news of his father's death. In England the royal council proclaimed Edward king in his absence, took oaths of allegiance, and kept the administration running in orderly fashion until Edward returned in 1274. It was the first time that an English king was recognized to have succeeded from the day of his predecessor's death, rather than from the day of his own coronation.

Edward I (1272–1307) was both a chivalrous leader and a ruler jealous of his rights and sometimes unscrupulous in maintaining them. In spite of his brutal wars in Wales and Scotland and his expulsion of the English Jews, he has often been called England's greatest medieval king. He was a Crusader; he personally led his troops in battle; he made foreign conquests. And for most of his reign he ruled well at home, strengthening the laws, reforming the government, maintaining the peace, protecting the Church.

On his arrival in England, Edward launched a series of inquests into almost every aspect of local government. Because the information was gathered hundred by hundred, within each county, the results were recorded and preserved on what are called the Hundred Rolls. These records were used by Edward to reform abuses and to regain illegally alienated or usurped royal lands and rights. The most important result of these inquests of 1274 to 1275 was a long series of judicial proceedings in which the lords of franchises were summoned to the royal courts by writs of *quo warranto*. These writs required each lord to prove "by what warrant" or authority he held his franchise. If the lord could produce a royal charter granting the franchise to him or one of his ancestors, he received a confirmation of his grant and was quit. However, most lords based their rights of jurisdiction on prescription, that is, long usage, and could not defend themselves with documentary evidence. To meet this situation, Edward directed his justices to confirm all franchises that had been continuously exercised since the accession of Richard in 1189. The king wanted to establish the principle that all private jurisdiction was a delegation from the crown, so that the royal government could supervise, intervene, and correct abuses within franchises just as it did in the local administration of counties and hundreds.

During the thirteenth century the central courts emerged as three separate and distinct tribunals, each with its own personnel, records, and jurisdiction: the Court of Common Pleas, where civil disputes were adjudicated; the Court of Exchequer, whose common law jurisdiction grew out of pleas involving debts to the crown; and the Court of King's Bench, concerned primarily with pleas of the crown or criminal cases and other cases in which the king was an interested party. The king remained the fount of justice. He exercised his residual and all-inclusive jurisdiction in his council. The royal council consisted of the highest officials, plus the judges and others (bishops, barons, servants or friends, clerk or lay) whom the king was pleased to appoint. The council corrected errors on appeal from other courts and determined cases referred to it because of their difficulty or importance or because they did not fall under the common law. As a contemporary writer put it, echoing Justinian, in the council "judicial doubts are determined and new remedies created for new wrongs, and . . . justice is done to every one according to his deserts." *Every one* did not include the Jews, who were dispossessed and expelled from the kingdom or the Italian bankers forced into bankruptcy by Edward's failure to pay his debts. Nonetheless, in the council justice was done to some malfactors of such rank and power as to overawe a local jury. The council also provided administrative supervision of the whole government and advised the king on policy matters. Its decisions, whether legal or administrative, were often promulgated by the king as one form of legislation. Its functions were undifferentiated, but in modern terminology the royal council was the executive, legislative, and judicial heart of the government.

Edward's reign marks a stage in the growth of the common law equal in importance to the work of Henry II. Unlike his predecessor, Edward was not an innovator. The importance of Henry II's reforms lay in the area of procedure—the regular and frequent use of writs, juries, and itinerant justices as essential elements in the legal machinery—while the importance of the statutes of Edward I lay in reconciling contradictions or eliminating inconsistencies in the laws. Edward I has been called the "English Justinian" because, like the Roman emperor, he was a great legislator. But the superficial brilliance of Edward's reign obscured the fact that on his death the king left a government deeply in debt and committed to foreign wars that eventually failed, after huge costs in men and money.

In foreign affairs Edward had two main objectives: to extend his control over the British Isles and to protect his Continental fiefs. Wales presented an immediate problem. When Llywelyn ap Gruffyd, lord of the Welsh princes, refused to do homage, Edward launched an invasion. This was by no means the first effort to conquer Wales. English kings had claimed the overlordship of Wales since before the Norman Conquest, and this claim had been formalized during the twelfth century by the feudal bond of homage uniting the more important Welsh princes to the king, as vassals to lord. Disputes between the king, the Welsh princes, and aggressive Anglo-Norman lords continued, however. While Henry III was distracted by his other problems, Llywelyn ap Gruffyd reconquered most of the southern and eastern parts and, in 1258, created for himself the title of Prince of Wales.

Edward's invasion was carefully organized and ably supported by the Marcher (frontier) lords. Llywelyn was forced to submit, renew his homage, and relinquish most of his power although not his title. Then once more the Welsh suddenly rebelled against the new order, Llywelyn taking the lead. Edward had previously treated Llywelyn as a contumacious vassal who nonetheless deserved respect for his dignity and rights. Now, taken by surprise and furious, Edward threw all his resources into crushing the rebellion, dealing with Llywelyn and the Welsh simply as rebels whose revolt forfeited any consideration of rights. Llywelyn was killed in 1283, and his brother David was captured; their heads were chopped off and exposed on lances on the Tower of London. By the Statute of Rhuddlan (1284), Edward introduced an English type of administration throughout most of Wales. Welsh civil laws were preserved and administered in the old local districts by Welsh officials. English criminal law was introduced to preserve order under sheriffs who were the English administrators of the larger shires into which Wales was now divided.

The conquest of Wales proved to be a great burden on England. The campaigns of 1276 to 1277 and 1282 to 1284 required large armies made up not only of the feudal host but also of even greater numbers of mercenary soldiers and laborers. Edward conquered because he consolidated each gain by erecting a castle. In twenty-five years of castle building after 1277, Edward spent £80,000, an unprecedented drain on the treasury. Raising taxes became the most prominent single feature of Edward's domestic policy in the later years of his reign—a policy that had important constitutional results. Meanwhile, the title of Prince of Wales had lapsed with Llywelyn's death. Edward's queen, Eleanor of Castile, had accompanied her husband on the great campaign and in 1284 gave birth to a son in the new castle of Caernarvon. This son, Edward of Caernarvon, became heir apparent on the death of an older brother and— after two more rebellions in Wales had been suppressed at great expense— was created Prince of Wales in 1301. This gesture of conciliation was accepted by the Welsh. Except for a few unimportant incidents, the problem of Wales was solved.

Ireland presented a quite different situation. Henry II had made his son John lord of Ireland in 1177. Although John failed as a youth to promote English interests in the half-conquered island, as king he was successful (his

The castle built by Edward I at Caernarvon in Wales. The extraordinary expense of such stone fortresses severely taxed the resources of the English kingdom.

only success abroad) in expanding the area under English control and in strengthening the royal administration. After John, a round of petty wars of the Irish kinglets and English lords, both between each other and among themselves, disturbed the island. The appointment of Edward as lord of Ireland in 1254 brought no great change. The English area, called the Pale, continued to grow slowly, and the economic prosperity of the towns accentuated the difference between the more advanced occupied territory and the still primitive Gaelic lands, beyond the Pale, held by "the wild Irish," as the English called them. The natives found the peace and order brought by English domination not worth the loss of independence and of freedom to fight out their differences. During the reign of Edward I the most significant development was the introduction by the king's justiciars of English political institutions, notably an Irish parliament modeled closely on the English assembly.

Relations with Scotland were of a different order from those with Wales and Ireland. Scotland was a kingdom over which the king of England claimed rights of overlordship that had been acknowledged on several occasions. The king of Scots held lands in England for which he did homage as a matter of course. In 1290 the Scottish throne fell vacant, and the question of the succession awakened old rivalries. More than a dozen claimants appeared, and they all appealed to Edward I to decide among them. This Edward was glad to do, since he could now claim that it was a recognition of his position as superior lord and since it gave him an opportunity to define his rights over Scotland, especially the right to hear appeals from vassals of the Scottish king.

The "great cause" of 1291 to 1292 proved to be a prolonged debate about rules of succession and about the nature of a medieval kingdom. Going back for three generations, the male line of the royal family was extinct. Of the claimants, the nearest kin were John Baliol and Robert Bruce. Edward decided in favor of John Baliol, who did not last long as king because his council was dominated by anti-English magnates who entered into an alliance with the king of France. In 1296 Edward retaliated by invading Scotland, deposing Baliol, and annexing Scotland to England, but this action was followed by a widespread rebellion. Edward returned north, but was unable to subdue the rebels until 1304. A form of government was drawn up to provide a joint Scottish-English administration under Edward's control. Then Robert Bruce (grandson of the claimant of 1291) murdered the only other strong contender to the throne and had himself crowned king of Scotland in 1306. Edward organized a merciless suppression of Bruce's supporters, but before the aging monarch could complete the task he died. Edward II could not endure the grinding effort that had taxed his father's strength. Bruce, a fugitive with only a small group of friends, returned to lead a successful movement for Scottish independence.

Edward's aggressive policies toward the non-English peoples of the British Isles, and his expensive conflict with France over the great English fief of Gascony forced him to cooperate with his barons. A group of barons took advantage of the king's desperate need for money and his absence in Flanders to force Edward in 1297 to agree to a solemn Confirmation of the Charters (Magna Carta and the Charter of the Forest) and to agree that he would not impose unaccustomed levies or collect taxes without the consent of his magnates. By accepting the necessity of some restraints, Edward avoided the direct conflict with the barons that had weakened John and Henry III.

## The French Monarchy in the Thirteenth Century

When Louis IX came of age in 1234, the monarchy was as strong as it had been at the death of his father eight years earlier. The young king had been carefully raised by his mother, Blanche of Castile. He was pious and ascetic, an ardent persecutor of heretics and Jews. Louis showed a careful respect for his mother even after he came of age, but he was also a good husband to Margaret of Provence and a good father to his six children. He embraced the ideals of chivalry and demonstrated a high respect for his own and others' rights. His sense of justice and fairness according to the accepted rules of the knightly class made him a successful leader of the French nobility. He admitted the legitimacy of the nobility's claims to share in the power and authority of the realm, but as the Mise of Amiens shows, he was also jealous of intrusions by the nobility into the rights, authority, and prerogatives of the monarchy. Louis was a conscientious king, conscientious in fulfilling the obligations he believed given to him by God, who placed him on the throne.

A medieval king who was serious about governing his realm soon began to encroach on the rights claimed by the great feudatories. The process was much like that by which the United States government has widened its activities and jurisdiction at the expense of the state governments, always doing so in the interests of efficiency or because the state governments have failed to accomplish some task. Thus the trend toward centralization begun by Philip Augustus continued at a fast pace during his grandson's reign. It was aided by the conquests and arrangements, made by Philip and Louis VIII, that brought the great duchies and counties, and their governments, under royal control. Now, Louis IX began the process of bringing all of France under his good government, of making the monarchy more absolutist than any other monarchy in Europe, for the good of the country. The ecclesiastical doctrine of the divinely ordained king functioning as the vicar of God on earth led logically to the seriousness of purpose and the political doctrine of absolutism that Louis was beginning to create for the French monarchy.

Louis successfully suppressed the private warfare endemic among the nobility and helped create a period of peace and prosperity that lasted from 1245 until his death in 1270. The king brought unruly or unjust barons to his justice and sharply repelled any who suggested that he was overstepping his authority in doing so. He set the currency aright and returned his kingdom to a gold coinage that helped French merchants achieve a new level of prosperity at home and abroad. He wrote a set of instructions for his son Philip (the future Philip III) in which he outlined his principles of good government: never deny justice to anyone for any reason; always support the poor against the rich until the truth of the matter is made plain, then do justice; do not favor your own case when you are involved until the nature of the case is clear; surrender whatever you discover you hold unjustly; seek the advice of honest men and encourage them to speak the truth, even if it goes against your own wishes and ideas. Louis himself put these principles into practice, and the people venerated him for it. In 1247 he sent royal representatives called *enquêteurs* throughout the realm to receive complaints about and to check on the activities of the royal officials responsible for local administration—the *baillis, prévôts,* foresters, and seneschals. In 1254 and 1256, the

Louis IX was canonized by Boniface VIII in 1297 as part of the settlement of the first dispute between the pope and Louis' grandson Philip IV the Fair. This statue of the king was sculpted in the early fourteenth century and emphasizes his serene goodness.

king issued new instructions for these officials based on the information gathered by the *enquêteurs*. In the 1250s and 1260s, Louis extended his inquests to the seigneurial courts and administration. As in England, he opened the royal courts to all freemen.

Louis developed the institutions of royal government designed to carry out the functions of government as he conceived them. Under his authority, the *Parlement* at Paris, the royal court responsible for both giving justice and guiding the administration of royal government, became a permanent body of professionals, mostly lawyers. The *Parlement* had developed from the council of earlier kings, which had included a few specialists who helped the king with day-to-day financial and judicial administration. Princes of the royal family, great nobles, high churchmen and abbots, and any others the king wished to keep with him were also members of the council. Under Louis IX the council continued to function, but the more important administrative duties were performed by the *Parlement,* which met in regular sessions of varying length during the year. The principal work of the *Parlement* was judicial, and its officials were recruited from the lesser nobility, the bourgeoisie, and the lower clergy. These were substantial people, but they had no hope of exercising power or participating in national affairs outside the royal administration. They were thus loyal and able servants of royal power who owed their advancement to a combination of ability and royal generosity.

Unlike the English royal government, the French had no specialized financial bureaucracy until the fourteenth century. During Louis IX's reign the *baillis* and seneschals rendered their accounts three times a year in Paris at the Temple, the seat of the Knights Templar. This knightly order had been organized to provide protection for pilgrims to the Holy Land, but they now performed myriad functions, especially financial, in Western Europe. During the thirteenth century they kept the French monarchy's revenues and administered its expenditures. In the early fourteenth century an independent royal financial administration called the *Chambre des Comptes* (Chamber of Accounts) was organized and became a sister institution to the *Parlement*. Both had permanent staffs of professional civil servants who prepared their work, but they existed as functioning departments only when in session.

In his relations with other monarchs Louis showed similar forbearance in the interests of peace. Often provoked by the efforts of Henry III to regain the lost English fiefs, Louis could easily have converted his victories on the battlefields into conquests of territory. Instead he chose to negotiate the Treaty of Paris in 1259. By this settlement Louis relinquished several disputed districts on the borders of Gascony and confirmed Henry in his possession of the duchy of Aquitaine, for which he received Henry's homage. In return, Henry renounced all claims to the former Plantagenet provinces lost by John—Normandy, Maine, Anjou, and Poitou. Although criticized for this generosity, Louis was pleased with the outcome. His suzerainty over Aquitaine was acknowledged; his direct lordship over the four northern provinces recognized; and a former enemy had become his vassal. The previous year Louis had settled his inherited dispute with Aragón, in the Treaty of Corbeil (1258). French claims to lands south of the Pyrenees (descending from the Carolingian Spanish March) were extinguished, and in return the king of Aragón gave up all claims to Languedoc except the city of Montpellier, for which he did homage.

Louis was no pacifist, however. He felt that one important purpose of maintaining peace among Christian rulers was to free the resources of Christendom to make war on the infidel. He was more enthusiastic for the Holy War than any ruler of his age, leading one ill-fated expedition to Egypt and the Holy Land from 1248 to 1254 and another to Tunis, where he died as a Crusader in 1270.

The prestige of the medieval French monarchy reached its zenith under Louis IX. By the end of the reign royal power stood higher than ever before. The monarchy was not only respected, it was popular. Louis had made a great effort to govern effectively and had tended toward authoritarianism, but no charge of grasping power, nor of courting popular approval, can be brought against him. He stood for peace and justice, as every other feudal ruler should have—and often did. How can his remarkable success be explained? Louis' personal popularity cannot be left out of account, but the most important reason for the continued growth of royal power under Louis was that the aggressive new monarchy built by Philip Augustus had been put on a leash. Without permitting his officials to invade the rights of others, Louis insisted on exercising his own rights as king. Since these rights were often difficult to define in practice, although admitted by all in theory, the royal government was able to resolve most conflicts over rights in favor of the king. At the same time, Louis' subjects had confidence that the king would protect them against violence and oppression either from the feudal lords or from the officials of his government. Even before he was canonized as Saint Louis in 1298, Frenchmen venerated this king, and in succeeding years opposition to the crown was almost always accompanied by a demand for a return to conditions as they were in the days of Saint Louis.

During the later years of his father's reign, Philip, Louis' eldest son, had been associated in the governance of the realm. He was regent during the last two years, when Louis was on his second Crusade. When he succeeded in 1270, Philip III was thus well prepared to govern, but since Philip lacked his father's ability and character, the history of his reign presents a medley of successes and failures in which the failures predominated. Philip continued the domestic policies of Louis but was not able to develop them or the institutions that carried them out any further than they were when he succeeded to the throne. But Philip was successful in adding much territory to the royal domain. He made claim to Toulouse and Poitou in 1271 after the death of his uncle Alphonse. Then he married his son and heir Philip to the heiress of both the vast county of Champagne and the kingdom of Navarre. When Philip IV became king, he ruled these areas through his wife, but when his son and heir Louis X succeeded in 1314, he ruled them by hereditary right and incorporated them into the royal domain. The county of Champagne, second in value only to the duchy of Normandy, remained permanently in the hands of the crown.

In foreign affairs Philip III was a great failure. Under the influence of his uncle Charles of Anjou, Philip allowed himself to be a candidate for the imperial throne in 1272. Unsuccessful in that venture, Philip next intervened in favor of his nephews during the disputed succession to the throne of Castile, again in vain. The capstone of his ill-fated involvement in Spanish affairs occurred in 1285. After the uprising of the Sicilian Vespers in 1282, Charles had engaged in a war against Peter of Aragón, who had become king of Sicily through the request of the leaders of the rebellion. Since Peter was married to the heiress of the last Hohenstaufen king of Sicily, the papacy vehemently denounced the Sicilian rebels and their allies. Peter was excommunicated and his throne declared vacant. Philip was invited by the pope and urged by his uncle to conquer the vacated throne for one of his sons. But the "crusade" against Aragón, in 1285, was a dismal failure despite elaborate preparations and the large number of troops raised for the expedition. Philip's army had penetrated halfway to Barcelona when an Aragonese naval victory cut off French supplies, and the king was forced to turn back. Philip died shortly after recrossing the Pyrenees.

Philip IV the Fair (1285–1314) was an enigmatic king. He led a powerful royal government run by a group of highly trained lawyers, who earned a reputation for efficiency and unscrupulousness. He was handsome and self-effacing; an enemy characterized him as "the handsomest man in the world, who could do nothing but stare speechless at people." But to friends and supporters, he was king of such majesty that he was the worthy successor of Saint Louis, whom Philip venerated. Some of his southern subjects dubbed him "King Owl" because of the attention he devoted to administrative detail and of the belief that he stood somewhere above the impressive machinery of his government watching everything with fearfully penetrating eyes.

Regardless of his personal qualities, which historians, like his contemporaries, have found difficult to evaluate, there is no question that under Philip the monarchy took every opportunity to increase its power. His lawyer-administrators propagandized that "the king of France is emperor within his kingdom," and Philip was determined to realize that doctrine in practice. He pursued this goal by promoting institutional development in the royal government, asserting royal authority over all competing powers within the realm, and pursuing an aggressive foreign policy in which Spain was ignored so that the count of Flanders, the king of England, and the pope could be defeated.

The development of central government in France and England presents an instructive contrast. In England, where the king's jurisdiction over the whole realm was unquestioned after 1066, the earliest specialization of function within the royal court was for the collection and auditing of royal revenues. In France almost all the ordinary revenues came from the royal domain alone; as for the realm as a whole, the most important problems of the government concerned jurisdiction, not revenue. The earliest specialization of function in the French royal court was therefore the development of the *Parlement* of Paris during the thirteenth century.

Under Philip the Fair the *Parlement* usually met once a year for a term lasting three or four months. In addition to the professional judges, clerks, notaries, and other permanent members of its staff, for important or extraordinary cases the king might appoint other royal officials, or great nobles and prelates, to afforce the court. The volume of business had grown so large that specialization within the *Parlement* was necessary. The main tribunal was called the *Chambre des Plaids*. In it alone pleadings were heard and judgment pronounced. For cases involving the written (Roman) law of the south of France, it was assisted by a special bureau called the *Auditoire du Droit Écrit.* Two other offices of the *Parlement* relieved the main tribunal of part of the judicial work. These were the *Chambre des Requêtes,* which received petitions and exercised what would later be called the gracious, or equitable, jurisdiction of the crown; and the *Chambre des Enquêtes,* which was responsible for judicial inquests preliminary to the initiation of suits and for supervision of the local administration of royal justice in the bailiwicks and *sénéchaussées.*

Other special departments of the central government emerge clearly in the reign of Philip the Fair, for it is from that time that most of the earliest records of their activities have survived. When the king wanted advice on problems of royal policy, he summoned the more important officials of the government, plus whichever nobles, prelates, and others he desired. Such a meeting was called a great council. For day-to-day business of the government, Philip relied on a smaller and permanent body, the secret council (*conseil étroit*), consisting of the officials of the royal household who were always with the king wherever he traveled. These were the professional civil servants, like Guillaume de Nogaret and Pierre Flote, who might also hold high offices in the government in addition to being members of the household.

Royal finances under Philip the Fair were transferred from the control of the Templars to royal officials who were organized into the *Chambre des Comptes,* mentioned earlier. The secretariat of the central government was burdened with far more work than ever before. The chancery was responsible for most of the formal or public documents and correspondence, while the chamber was the household secretariat in charge of business and correspondence within the government or intimately connected with the king's private business.

The first serious crisis of the reign grew out of Philip's relations with his royal vassal Edward I, duke of Aquitaine and king of England. As overlord of Scotland, Edward had always insisted on his right to hear and adjudicate appeals from the Scottish king's vassals, but he resented the French government's encouragement of his own French vassals to appeal their disputes to the *Parlement* of Paris. Relations were also embittered by jurisdictional disputes between Philip and Edward in areas along the Gascon border. Matters were brought to a head when some Gascon and English ships routed a Norman fleet off Brittany and went on to the coast of Poitou, where they sacked the town of La Rochelle. Each side accused the other of piracy. Although this was but the latest of a long series of such incidents between sailors, Philip chose to make an issue out of it. A French army occupied parts of Gascony to ensure compensation for damages suffered by Philip's subjects. Edward was cited to appear before the *Parlement.* When he refused, the duchy of Aquitaine was declared forfeit. The war over this action lasted from 1294 until 1303, although hostilities were interrupted by frequent and lengthy truces during which negotiations took place.

Before peace was restored, both Scotland and Flanders had been drawn into the conflict, the former in alliance with France and the count of Flanders as Edward's ally. The Flemish situation was further complicated by a revolt against the count and an appeal to Philip, the count's lord. The French invaded Flanders in 1297, and the county was subjected to French control until an uprising in favor of the count drove out the garrisons occupying several towns. Philip then assembled a large army that was met and routed by the Flemings at Courtrai in 1302. Although Philip recovered from this defeat, and even annexed a few towns, after the Battle of Courtrai Flemish resistance was strong enough to forestall the future efforts of French kings to subjugate the county.

The foreign policy of Philip the Fair was far too expensive for the ordinary revenues of the government to support, and the government employed various expedients to raise more money. Frenchmen were taxed as never before: Feudal aids were collected from the nobility; towns were regularly tallaged; vassals who did not fight in person paid scutage at a high rate; a sales tax was imposed on basic commodities like salt and wine; and extraordinary aids or grants were demanded because of the national emergency. Most of these last mentioned taxes were negotiated in local meetings with those who had to pay them. There were three classes, called estates, of taxpayers: the nobility, the townspeople, and the clergy. Philip's need for money led to desperate measures. He devalued the currency, realizing an immediate gain for the government but each time raising such a protest that he had to restore it. In 1306 he expelled the Jews from France, seizing their property and taking over the collection of debts owed to them. Then he acted to resolve the problem created by the crown's debts; he attacked the Knights Templar. While acting as the royal financial bureau, the order had lent the monarchy huge sums. Philip dissolved the debt by attacking the order for heresy and a series of trumped-up charges of iniquitous behavior. By 1312 the king had won the support of the pope, who condemned and dissolved the order at the first session of the Council of Vienne, held that year. Royal debts to the Templars were cancelled, and money on deposit with them was seized for the crown. The extensive fiefs held by the Templars were transferred to the Hospitallers, who paid dearly for the right to enter them.

That the papacy should have aided Philip to resolve his financial problems in 1312 represented a sharp reversal of the earlier relations between the two powers. In his pursuit of money, Philip had asserted, in 1296, his right to tax the French churches, and his claim had created a conflict with the papacy. Taxation of the clergy was not new, but it had been infrequent, reserved for a special purpose, such as the support of a Crusade. The king who wished to invoke the tax was expected to obtain papal approval beforehand. Now Philip asserted the right to tax the clergy whenever it was necessary for the defense of the realm. Edward, his enemy, also asserted this "doctrine of necessity" to tax the English clergy. Pope Boniface VIII (1294–1303) reacted sharply to the actions of both kings, but the pope's dispute with Philip attained a greater historical importance than the one with Edward.

Boniface had come to power in unfortunate circumstances. When Nicholas IV died in 1292, the cardinals could not agree on any candidate, partially because the leading candidate, Benedict Gaetani, a very able lawyer-administrator, was very unpopular with his associates. After a two year hiatus, the College of Cardinals finally agreed on the election of a compromise candidate from outside, way outside, the papal court. This was a hermit named Peter Murrone, who lived in a cave on Mount Vesuvius and who now became pope as Celestine V. Completely unprepared for the governance of the complex and powerful papal administration, Celestine abdicated after only five months, doubtful of his chance for salvation as a result of the experience of being Christendom's spiritual leader. The College of Cardinals now were ready for Benedict Gaetani; papal government had drifted badly for more than two years. But the new pope, who took the name Boniface, could be challenged on several grounds. Celestine was the only pope in the Church's history to abdicate, and it was not clear that he could legally do so. Boniface's enemies soon charged him with forcing the poor Celestine from office and added all kinds of other charges of misbehavior as time passed. It did not help that Boniface was a dedicated nepotist, had an acid tongue and a sharp temper, and lost two bitter disputes with Philip the Fair.

The first dispute concerned Philip's, and Edward's, claim to an independent right to tax the clergy of their realms. Boniface reacted to the assertion by issuing the bull *Clericis laicos* (1296), in which he carefully but forcefully restated the canon law on the subject. Because the clergy were especially privileged, both in their persons and in their property, secular rulers were prohibited from taxing the clergy without authorization from the papacy. To prevent all future unauthorized taxation, the bull provided that any ruler who presumed to levy such taxes was, by that act, to be automatically excommunicated. The reaction in France and England was equally forceful. Philip, with the support of the majority of the clergy, forbade the export of money from his realm; this effectively cut off all papal revenues from France. Edward I withdrew royal protection from all clergy who did not pay taxes; this in effect outlawed them and put them at the mercy of any marauding thief or covetous lord who would take their goods or seize their property. While Philip struck directly at the pope, Edward struck at the English clergy, whom he knew to be divided on the issue. Opposition was so strong that Boniface in 1297 declared that *Clericis laicos* did not apply to emergency taxation for defense of a kingdom and that the king could decide when such an emergency existed.

Boniface thus lost the first struggle. The second began when Philip the Fair arrested a French bishop who was accused of treason. When the bishop

This detail from a fifteenth-century fresco shows Celestine V putting down his tiara, symbolic of his abdication after five disastrous months as pope. The character of the portrait shows the sympathy many had with the simple hermit and their feeling that it was not he but the complexity and worldliness of the papal court that was responsible for his failure.

appealed to Rome for trial, the question of jurisdiction was raised. This brought forth from Boniface some of the most extreme statements ever made officially concerning the supremacy of the pope. In 1301 he reinstituted *Clericis laicos* and issued the bull *Ausculta fili*. This bull asserted the superiority of the pope over kings and the right of the pope to intervene in temporal affairs when the ruler was impious and wicked. Then followed a long list of charges against Philip's government and the summons of a synod of bishops to consider these charges and other alleged abuses. Philip's officials stirred up public opinion in France by publishing falsified copies of *Ausculta fili,* in which Boniface was misrepresented as claiming direct temporal authority over France. The height of the propaganda war was reached when Philip called a

Boniface VIII was a highly competent lawyer and proven hand at the subtleties of papal governmental administration. This fourteenth-century illumination from a Bolognese manuscript shows him as judge, with clerks and cardinals surrounding him in consistory. Boniface's predecessors had sometimes pressed claims to review cases decided in secular courts and often regarded themselves as the highest judge in Christendom. Boniface repeated those claims in extreme language. Many pious Christians were repelled by scenes like this one, with the pope surrounded by litigants and immersed in the affairs of the world.

meeting of representatives from the three estates in 1302. This was the first Estates General, considered by the king and its members as representing the whole realm, and called by the king to enhance his popular support against the pope. Each estate sent a letter of protest to Boniface.

At this point the French suffered the defeat at Courtrai, which momentarily weakened Philip so that he could not prevent French clergy from attending the council Boniface had summoned to Rome. At the council, Boniface promulgated a new bull against the king, *Unam sanctam* (1302). The circumstances and the rhetoric of this bull made it especially important in the history of the Church–state relations. In fact, it was a restatement of doctrines enunciated by Innocent III and Innocent IV now put in language that made it seem Boniface was claiming more than any of his predecessors. It ended with the resounding statement, "Furthermore, we declare, state, define, and proclaim that it is altogether necessary to salvation for every human creature to be subject to the Roman pontiff," a thoroughly conventional but strikingly stated idea. Boniface's general argument was that because every Christian's highest goal was salvation and because the Church, organized under papal leadership, was ordained to lead Christians to that goal, the pope had a supreme authority to intervene in the affairs of secular communities whenever the achievement of salvation was threatened. Boniface made no claim to direct authority over temporal affairs.

The reaction in France was swift. Philip's advisers, led by the lawyer Guillaume de Nogaret, drew up an indictment against Boniface charging that his election had been illegal, that he had murdered Celestine V, and that he was guilty of heresy, simony, adultery, schism, and the keeping of a private demon as a pet and a sorcerer as an adviser. It was an imaginative document. Philip's council then called for a trial of the pope by a general council of the Church, and Nogaret set out with an armed force to arrest Boniface and bring him to France to stand trial. In Italy the pope's enemies within the Church, principally the Colonna family, joined the French force. They caught Boniface by surprise in his family residence at Anagni and held him prisoner for several days. Boniface was more than eighty years old, and Nogaret judged that he could not carry the pope to France through the territory of outraged Italians. He therefore released him and returned to France. Boniface died within a month, after returning to Rome.

The episode indicates the results of thirteenth-century political developments. The supranational authority of the emperor had been crucially weakened and had collapsed by the middle of the century. No one ruler could hold together under an effective government the widely separated and culturally differentiated territories that made up the medieval empire. When historians speak of the success of Frederick Barbarossa or Henry VI, they recognize that the success was qualified and the unity more apparent than real. The empire had always had several governments; the emperors had struggled for control of them severally. The imperial government had been a real force for so long because its principal opponent had been like itself, an edifice on ethereal foundations. The papacy held claim to tremendous authority but wielded little effective power. In the twelfth and early thirteenth centuries, it had been a successful political authority because there was little to resist it in Europe. None of the kings was strong enough nor were their governments developed enough to challenge the power of the papacy to collect revenues, summon councils, or exercise effective authority in secular affairs. Henry II's attempt to assert royal rights, bringing on his dispute with Thomas à Becket, demonstrated that even a strong twelfth-century king faced too much opposition and shared his power too widely with other interests in his realm to challenge the Church effectively or permanently. But the slow, steady growth of royal power—the marshaling of the kingdom's major social and political forces under royal authority in England and the gathering of the great principalities under royal control in France—had created powers able to challenge papal authority. Saint Louis had been an obedient son of the Church, but he had continued the construction of a monarchy, on foundations laid by his grandfather Philip Augustus, that would reach a stage of development at which conflict with papal authority became inevitable. Boniface's failure was his inability to recognize that conditions had changed and that the royal opponent he faced was different from the imperial opponent his predecessors had confronted. But while he may be faulted for lack of perception, he cannot be criticized for engaging in the struggle. His alternative was to surrender an authority won by two centuries of hard effort by the heroic figures of the medieval Church. Yet, while the French and English kings arrived at approximately the same point, they founded their success on very different institutions.

## The Growth of Representative Institutions

Medieval government was never recognized to be absolute. Justice and the law, whose origin was custom, usually had precedence over royal or governmental power, and the king guided the affairs of the realm with the counsel and aid of the kingdom's great men. Although the political situation of the kingdom usually prevented the king from overstepping the recognized bounds of his authority, no established institutions, no constitutional framework, existed to serve the same function. The king was required to take counsel with the great men, but the degree to which their advice affected the royal will depended on circumstances, and since the king usually operated his government on revenues received from crown lands and rights, control of royal government through control of the purse was not possible. It was in the thirteenth century that constitutionally recognized institutions began to make the theory of royal government according to law a reality. The development took generations, was intermittent and complex, and did not occur in the same way or at the same pace in every region. In some areas, such as France, it hardly occurred at all.

The basic institutional ingredients for constitutionalism were products of the political, cultural, and economic revival of the twelfth century. First, the evolution of royal government brought the kings, especially in England and Germany, into conflict with the feudal nobility who had assumed control of much governmental authority in the previous two centuries. This development affected the character of the royal councils because by the late twelfth century their meetings brought together the king and his growing body of administrators with a group increasingly aware of its cohesiveness and distinctiveness relative to royal power. During the Magna Carta crisis the English barons articulated their new consciousness as the "community of the realm." Second, the growth of royal government outstripped the growth of royal revenues and placed the king increasingly in need of donations from various groups of his subjects. By the time of John's reign in England, the king was forced to ask the barons and others for money every few years. Requests for revenue previously had been tied to projects like the defense of the realm or an aggressive war the king thought would be attractive to those with money to pay for it. In the thirteenth century the English kings engaged in an extraordinary number of these projects, and they were particularly unsuccessful. Such are fertile grounds for taxpayers' revolts. Third, the economic revival and concomitant growth of the towns produced a charter movement that reached its peak about the turn of the thirteenth century. Older feudal forms of taxation struck at the commercial system in ways that hindered it—for example, by taxing raw materials and charging heavy fees for entering towns —and the merchants sought independent control of their economy and obligations to the central government. They received that independence through royal charters of incorporation, which gave them local governmental autonomy and permitted them to collect taxes for the king in whatever way they saw fit. As town governments developed at the beginning of the thirteenth century, awareness of corporateness was brought to the fore in wealthy communities soon to be asked for contributions to the royal coffers. The corporateness of these communities provided a model of political and legal organization that could be represented before the king, which made the obtaining of consent to special taxes easier than it had been when the king had to deal individually with each person of means. Another model of such organization was the Church, which provided the fourth ingredient of constitutional government, a legal theory on which it could be based.

Within the Church, the development of the theoretical foundations of representative institutions was one of the long-term results of the eleventh-century reform movement. As the reformed cathedral chapters began enlarging their claims to participate in episcopal government, ecclesiastical lawyers turned to the rejuvenated Roman law to find a legal doctrine that justified the chapters' demands. They found their instrument in a doctrine governing co-heirs or co-guardians, according to which when more than one person inherited or had guardianship over something, nothing could be done to or with that thing without the consent of all because *Quod omnes tangit ab omnibus approbetur* (what touches all ought to be approved by all). This principle had become part of canon law in the fifth century when Celestine I (422–432) and Leo I the Great (440–461) paraphrased it while arguing that bishops ought not to be elevated without the consent of those they were to govern. Late twelfth- and early thirteenth-century lawyers revived the Roman formulation and applied it widely to the relationship between bishop and cathedral chapter.

The bishops fought vigorously against the assertions of the chapters, but when King John asked for extraordinary contributions from his bishops, in preparation for one of his Continental campaigns, the bishops replied that they could not grant the king's request until they had conferred with their chapters because *Quod omnes tangit. . . .* The bishops had found a double-edged weapon in their legal doctrine because in protecting their interests against the king they had laid them open to the chapters. In addition, John's bad reputation was earned partially because he was so capable at manipulating the institutions that might produce revenue, and he was quick to recognize the counterdevice to be used in this situation. Toward the end of his reign, he summoned bishops and knights from the shires, demanding that they come with *plena potestas* (full power) to act on behalf of the communities and institutions from which they came. This doctrine too derived from canon law, in which some papal legates were recognized to have full power to act on behalf of the pope.

The earliest parliaments, under John and Henry III, were extensions of the great council of the king. They brought together knights elected to represent the shires, bishops, great barons, and members of merchant guilds selected by the town governments as their representatives—all who might help the king raise moneys—and in the friction caused by royal demands these parliaments produced the legal doctrines and political ideas that underlie the development of constitutional government in England. Kings in Spain and Hungary were using the same devices for their purposes; Pope Innocent III had summoned large meetings in the Papal States as early as 1207; and Frederick II held an assembly in 1232. But on the Continent, change and events disturbed constitutional development. Only England was stable enough to provide the milieu for a continuous, although slow and uneven, evolution of parliamentary institutions.

English parliaments were great occasions, and those attending them took advantage of the opportunity they afforded to transact all manner of business with the king. The representatives brought judicial business and petitions with them, and study of the records of thirteenth- and early–fourteenth-century parliaments shows that in volume, most business was judicial. This does not mean that parliaments were courts, but they met coincidentally with the royal court. In 1307, for example, the majority of business was done after the commons, as the knights of the shires and the bourgeois representatives were called, went home. But the coincidence provided the impetus for development of the institution and of its work during the fourteenth century. The king's summons delineated the groups that were to participate: barons, prelates, knights of the shires, and burgesses from the towns (first summoned by Simon de Montfort in 1265 during the Barons' War). These groups further defined themselves by their relations with the king and his council at the meetings. In the fourteenth century the commons elected a speaker to deal with the king

An illustration of Edward I in Parliament from an early–sixteenth-century book. On the king's right is Alexander III of Scotland. On his left is Llywelyn ap Gruffyd of Wales. The smaller crowned figure below Llywelyn may be the future Edward II. The nobles and bishops sit on benches in the hall. Parliaments were held in conjunction with the great festivals, principally Pentecost but also Easter and Christmas, when the king held court and wore his crown.

and to present petitions to the king and council. Thus, the coincidence of judicial and political functions had produced a parliamentary request for legislation by the king and led to the establishment of a cohesive, self-conscious commons in the developing institution. Early in its history, the English parliament had been forced to become representative of the realm, receiving its character from the conjunction of the king's demands and the ideas that had made the barons of 1215 consider themselves the community of the realm. Now that the commons was organizing itself, parliament, made up of commons and lords, became representative of the whole kingdom. The post-medieval future held more refinement and the shift of power from king to parliament that produced the modern English constitution.

The differences between English developments and those in France, England's greatest Continental rival, are difficult to explain. But some main points can be singled out. Although the French monarchy developed an effective central authority much later than its English counterpart, in one respect twelfth-century France was more stable politically than contemporary England. The twelfth-century English kings held great power, but no really effective secondary level of political organization existed that could save the country from anarchy if the king failed to exercise his authority. The history of Stephen's reign (1135–1152) demonstrated the result of his predecessors' success in reducing the power of the great feudatories. The twelfth-century French kings had only a nominal authority over the great lords who actually controlled the country. Thus political stability was not as endangered by weakness in the monarchy as it was in England. The differences in the two kingdoms had another consequence. The English king competed with the greater and lesser nobility, churches, and myriad interests in the towns as he struggled to define and develop his authority, and the resolution of one conflict did not have a decisive effect on the others. In France this same conflict took place, but it was primarily contended by the great feudatories. The king gained effective political and administrative control over the Île-de-France at the same time as his greatest vassals were consolidating their authority in their counties and duchies. Thus whereas the English kings struggled for control of a great kingdom and by the thirteenth century still confronted a politically particularized realm, the French monarchs for the most part limited their government to the ancient county of Paris and faced a small number of powerful lords who had successfully thwarted the development of royal power but who had done much of the work of organization and institutional development that the monarchy would have had to do had it possessed effective power. Since the history of war, marriage, and accident that brought the great feudal principalities under the control of the French kings during the thirteenth century gave them national authority without the sort of institutional compromises forced on the English kings, they were able to build up their governmental administration without restraints. In addition, the success of the French monarchy had been at the expense of the English, who spent enormous resources in a futile struggle to recover their lost Continental fiefs. The constitutional principles and institutions developed in thirteenth-century England arose out of the repeated need of the kings to extricate themselves from the consequences of such failures. The English kings appealed to the principal socioeconomic groups for aid, which transformed them into powerful political interests.

When Philip the Fair summoned the Estates General in 1302, he did so for specifically political reasons, and he arranged the meetings so that little friction arose between himself and the estates. He was organizing the kingdom against the unacceptable assertions of the pope. In his preoccupation with financial problems, Philip did not call the kind of meetings held by Edward I. It may be that he did not have the power Edward had over local districts like the shires and towns, so that he did not bother to summon those he could not hope to control. It may be that Philip's financial problems stemmed from the arrangement of his domainal affairs and that he therefore sought to solve them by making changes in his financial administration. Certainly, his attack on the Templars, Jews, and Italian bankers (he expelled the latter from France in 1311, bankrupting them in the process), his reorganization of revenue collection and disbursement, and the emphasis he placed on efficient and professional administration indicate that he considered his problems in that light. In any case, the French monarchy needed much less aid from its subjects than the English king, and it emerged from the thirteenth century unfettered by the constitutional institutions taking shape in England.

### Suggestions for Further Reading

**Secondary Works**   The work of G. Barraclough cited at the end of Chapter 8 treats German history in the later thirteenth century. For England, see the two outstanding studies by F. M. Powicke, *The Thirteenth Century,* 2nd ed. (Oxford, 1962) and *King Henry III and the Lord Edward,* 2 vols. (Oxford, 1947). In addition, see T. F. T. Plucknett, *The Legislation of Edward I* (Oxford, 1949); R. F. Treharne, *The Baronial Plan of Reform* (Manchester, 1932); and D. W. Sutherland, *Quo Warranto Proceedings in the Reign of Edward I, 1278–1294* (Oxford, 1963). For France, see the relevant works cited at the end of Chapter 19, as well as F. J. Pegues, *The Lawyers of the Last Capetians* (Princeton, N.J., 1962). The growth of constitutional government is surveyed in G. L. Haskins, *The Growth of English Representative Government* (Philadelphia, 1948); P. Spufford, *Origins of the English Parliament* (London, 1967); A. Marongui, *Medieval Parliaments: A Comparative Study* (London, 1968), which focuses on Italy; and the work of T. N. Bisson cited at the end of Chapter 19.

**Sources**   The works cited at the end of Chapter 19 are important. See also *The Life of Saint Louis by John of Joinville,* trans. R. Hague (New York, 1955).

# 21 The Medieval Synthesis of Thought and Learning

The intellectual life of the thirteenth century was a continuation of the twelfth-century renaissance. Twelfth-century scholars had dispensed with the manuals and compendiums of the early Middle Ages and returned to the original works of classical and patristic authors. The body of these works already possessed by the Western community at the end of the eleventh century was then expanded by the discovery of ancient Greek philosophy and science and of the *Corpus Juris Civilis* of Justinian. The recovery of ancient knowledge occupied much of the time and effort of teachers and translators in the twelfth century. Thirteenth-century translators continued this work, seeking better texts and making improved translations. They also discovered treatises previously unknown in the West.

Twelfth-century scholars began mastering the content of the ancient sources and restating it in commentaries that interpreted and clarified the major texts, and their work continued into the thirteenth century. The two most important commentaries on the works of Aristotle were written by Albertus Magnus and Thomas Aquinas. These two men, and many others, continued another twelfth-century activity, the systematic representation of the body of knowledge in each of the main fields. Gratian's *Decretum* in canon law, Justinian's *Corpus Juris* in Roman law, Peter Lombard's *Sentences* in theology, and other works in various fields were great syntheses used throughout the twelfth and thirteenth centuries as basic texts in the schools, where lectures in the respective subjects consisted of commentaries on them. Every professor of theology began his career with a commentary on the *Sentences* and every law professor with similar treatments of the *Decretum* or *Corpus Juris*. Philosophers commented on the works of Aristotle, medical professors on the works of Galen and Hippocrates. In law, the basic texts remained valuable until modern times (Gratian's *Decretum* was replaced by a modern code in 1907), and the thirteenth-century lawyers simply made additions to the basic corpus. The large canon law collection authorized by Gregory IX and issued in 1234 has already been mentioned. Later collections were added to the *Corpus Juris Canonici* in 1298 and 1314 with some still later additions made in the form of new editions of the last part. In Roman law, the later civilists, as the Roman lawyers were called, added new material in the form of *Novellae* (Novels, or new laws). In theology and philosophy, however, thirteenth-century professors produced new syntheses to replace the work of Peter Lombard and to bring the new corpus of Aristotelian philosophy into harmony with Christian thought. Peter's work had reflected the early scholastic mastery of logic and of the patristic sources of Christian thought, but it did not deal with the enormous collection of natural philosophy (science) available to Western scholars once they had mastered Aristotle's work. Thomas Aquinas undertook to harmonize the two great traditions, and he produced two large works containing his solution to the problem.

### The Patristic Heritage and the Reception of Aristotle

In the Middle Ages, theology was the "queen of the sciences," the highest form of intellectual activity, which brought together the unaided rational understanding of the universe provided by philosophy and the revealed truth about the universe provided by Christian tradition. Thus in medieval thought there was no sharp distinction between the *scientia* of philosophy and the *sacra doctrina* of theology. The two fields overlapped so much that in practice most medieval writers ignored the formal distinction, even though they were often interested in defining the limits claimed for each field. The interdependence of the two subjects was reflected in the university curriculum. Theology students usually spent most of their first year studying philosophy, and it would be difficult to find writers who specialized in one field to the exclusion of the other.

The most important works in both subjects grew directly out of classroom lectures, and the interests, content, and method of both were so much influenced by the Schoolmen that medieval philosophy and theology are usually referred to as "scholasticism," or scholastic philosophy and theology. In the

Stonemasons cut scenes from all aspects of life into the façades of cathedrals, and it is particularly fitting that representations of the liberal arts were carved into the royal portal of Chartres, where one of medieval Europe's most famous schools had its seat. Music (left) holds a psaltery (stringed instrument with a shallow sound box) while striking a tuned bell with a hammer. Below the figure of Music is Pythagoras, who formulated the theory of musical intervals and connected them with the structural principles of the universe. Grammar (right) is symbolized by a teacher of two young boys. Elementary students studied Latin for several years before progressing to the study of other liberal arts. Below the figure of Grammar is probably Donatus, the ancient grammarian most favored in the Middle Ages.

earlier discussions of Abelard and his contemporaries, the origins of the scholastic tradition were traced. By the thirteenth century, the scholastic method was associated with two types of treatises, the *summa* and the Question. The *summa* was a work that dealt with a specific subject exhaustively and systematically. The subject was developed in a series of propositions, each one treated by analyzing the arguments for and against it and by setting out a resolution of the conflicting arguments that either proved or denied the proposition. The Questions were generally collections of unrelated problems that interested the author, without any systematic development or treatment of a whole subject, as the *Questions* of Stephen Langton, a famous theology teacher at Paris before becoming archbishop of Canterbury (1209). Some authors' Questions were didactic and expository rather than analytical, and this form could be and was used for a variety of purposes. Lawyers, for example, used it extensively to treat hypothetical cases raising special problems of jurisprudence. Both the *summa* and the Question gave writers the opportunity to develop highly refined distinctions and arguments because they concentrated attention on narrow, well-defined problems.

The teaching activities of the scholastics induced them to organize as well as analyze the sources of knowledge. The Bible remained the foundation of theological studies, but it was transmitted in several versions that differed from one another in the order of books and the chapter divisions within books. Toward the end of the twelfth century, Stephen Langton, recognizing the problems in teaching and scholarship created by the multivarious biblical traditions, worked out an order of books and a division of books into chapters that was adopted by the theological teachers at Paris. The modern Catholic and Protestant versions of the Bible are based on Langton's plan. Scholars in canon law introduced divisions into Gratian's treatises. Many of the modern forms of ancient literature were developed in the high Middle Ages to make teaching and analysis easier.

The full impact of the newly recovered Aristotelian philosophical and scientific works began to be felt in the opening decades of the thirteenth century. New and better translations superseded versions already available through the efforts of the twelfth-century translators. At the beginning of the thirteenth century, the leading teachers at centers like the University of Paris recognized the inadequacy of the older translations, usually made from the Arabic, and they based their studies of Aristotle on new versions rendered directly from the original Greek. The establishment of the Latin Empire in Constantinople (1204–1261) provided the opportunity for Western scholars to study the sources. The leader of this new school of translators was William of Moerbeke (fl. ca. 1260), a Flemish Dominican who became bishop of Corinth and who collaborated with the Paris teachers.

Thirteenth-century scholars also received the whole corpus of Aristotelian philosophy. In addition to the New Logic, Aristotle's *Physics* and some of his treatises on natural science were available before 1200. About the turn of the century the *Metaphysics* was translated from the Arabic, together with Arabic commentaries; and in the thirteenth century the rest of Aristotle's writings were translated from the Greek, notably the *Ethics, Politics, Rhetoric,* and *Poetics.* The whole of this Aristotelian philosophy was digested and assimilated in Western thought by the numerous and extensive commentaries of the scholastics. These commentaries, including commentaries on Arabic commentaries, were the necessary preliminary to the creative phase of scholastic thought. The *summa* was based on the commentary.

The reception of Aristotle raised problems for the thirteenth-century scholastics that their predecessors, who were familiar only with the Old Logic and the New Logic, did not have to face. Logic is neutral; metaphysics borders on, and at points is even based on, doctrine. And the metaphysics of Aristotle was pagan. Most philosophers of the two faiths related to Christianity, such as the Moslem Avicenna (d. 1036) and the Jew Maimonides

(d. 1204), had already confronted the problem created by the differences between Aristotle and orthodoxy. Some had simply ignored, and others had explained away, the elements of Aristotelian philosophy that contradicted Jewish-Christian-Moslem revelation. Now, in the thirteenth century, Christian philosophers were confronted with the problem in an especially difficult form.

The *Metaphysics* of Aristotle arrived in Latin Christendom accompanied by the commentary by Averroës. Averroës did not have a great influence in the Moslem world, but his commentary on Aristotle was so influential in certain Christian circles that it led to the major intellectual heresy of the thirteenth century, called Averroism, together with its corollary, Siger of Brabant's theory of double truth. The dangers of unmitigated Aristotelianism were recognized by a provincial council at Paris, in 1210, which prohibited the study of Aristotle's natural philosophy and specifically condemned Averroës' commentaries. In 1215 Aristotle's *Metaphysics* was banned, and in 1231 the pope renewed the prohibition and appointed a commission of scholars to review the works of Aristotle and of his commentators and to purge them of error. But these prohibitions and efforts at censorship came to nothing, and in fact they illustrate the degree of academic freedom enjoyed in a medieval university. What actually happened was that the professors at Paris continued to expound Aristotle, and the papal commission never got around to its work of expurgation. In 1255 the University of Paris openly prescribed the whole of Aristotle as required reading.

The problem of Aristotle was solved, not by prohibitions and censorship, but by a continuing intellectual debate. In the end it was not the Averroists who won, but the Franciscans and, especially, the Dominicans at Paris, who, to sum up a long job briefly, "baptized" Aristotle and his Arabic commentators. The first scholar to make use of Aristotle's physics, metaphysics, and natural science in a systematic treatise designed to harmonize Aristotelian philosophy with Christian theology was the Englishman Alexander of Hales (d. 1245). He was also the first Franciscan to be a professor of theology at Paris. Albertus Magnus (1193–1280) was even more important in the development of scholasticism, for he was the first to master the whole corpus of Aristotle. Born in Swabia of noble parentage, he became a Dominican in 1223 and taught in Dominican schools in Germany from 1228 until 1245, when he spent three years teaching at Paris. From 1248 until 1254 he taught at Cologne, after which he was successively the provincial governor of the Dominican Order in Germany and bishop of Regensburg until 1262, when he retired to the Dominican convent at Cologne. During this active and varied career he wrote twenty-one massive volumes, most of them devoted to commentaries on Aristotle's works and to theological treatises based on Aristotelian philosophy. His main interest lay in the natural philosophy of Aristotle and the problem of reconciliation between Aristotelian philosophy and Christian revelation. Above all he was the expositor and interpreter of Aristotle for

Many notable medieval intellectuals not only pursued active teaching and scholarly careers but also entered the hierarchy of the Church. Robert Grosseteste continued his intellectual pursuits after he became bishop of Lincoln, as did Bonaventura after he became Governor General of the Franciscans. Albertus Magnus (right), teacher of Thomas Aquinas, became bishop of the important see of Regensburg after teaching at Cologne and Paris, and he retired at the end of his life to continue his teaching and writing.

the Christian West. And yet, despite his monumental achievement, Albertus Magnus is best known in the history of Western thought as the teacher of a philosopher and theologian who was even greater than himself. His pupil was Thomas Aquinas.

### Thomas Aquinas

Saint Thomas Aquinas (1225–1274) was born in southern Italy near Monte Cassino, where he was sent to school as a boy. After a few years at the schools in Naples, Thomas joined the Dominican Order in 1244 and went to study under Albertus Magnus at Cologne and Paris. In 1252 he was lecturing at Paris, and he later taught briefly at Rome, Bologna, and Naples. In 1268 he returned to Paris at the height of his career as a teacher and scholar; four years later he left, having been directed to establish a Dominican university at Naples. He died before he was fifty years old.

Thomas' written works total eighteen folio volumes. These include commentaries on most of the books of the Old and New Testaments, on the *Sentences,* and on thirteen works of Aristotle; about twenty short treatises and as many "academic disputations" on theological and philosophical topics; and a number of miscellaneous works ranging from sermons to part of a handbook for princes. The two works on which his reputation rests are the

*Summa Theologica* and the *Summa contra Gentiles.* The first is the greatest monument of scholasticism. Together they represent an orderly and encyclopedic summary of Christian thought, the first based on revelation and the second designed to show how far unaided human reason could buttress the Christian faith. In each, Thomas makes use of Aristotelian logic to incorporate and harmonize Aristotelian philosophy with Christian theology and philosophy.

Thomas' method represents the ultimate refinement of the scholastic organization, analysis, and synthesis of knowledge. He built a vast ideological structure concerning the nature of God, man, and the universe, a systematic exposition in which each of the broader topics is taken up in logical order, just as each statement in the detailed analysis follows logically on the preceding statement. The *Summa Theologica* consists of three Parts (the second Part is actually divided into two, the *Prima Secundae* and the *Secunda Secundae*). Each of these consists of a number of Questions, or general topics, totaling more than six hundred for the whole treatise. Each Question is broken down into Articles, or specific queries, beginning with "Whether. . . ." For example, in the *Summa Theologica, Prima Secundae,* Question 94 is entitled "Concerning Natural Law," and the fifth Article under this Question is headed, "Whether natural law can be changed?" The bulk of the *Summa* consists of the arguments systematically marshaled *pro* and *contra* in the Articles. Taking the same example (which would be referred to briefly as *S. Theol.,* Ia 2ae, XCIV, 5), Thomas first enumerates three objections or arguments *contra,* one drawn from Scripture, another in the form of a syllogism, and the last a logical inference from a statement quoted from Isidore of Seville, all three seeming to lead to the conclusion that natural law is subject to change. The second part of the Article contains Thomas' own answer, supported both by authority and by his own argument. The third and final part of the Article consists of Thomas' refutations of the objections with which the Article began. It has been estimated that the *Summa Theologica* contains more than ten thousand objections to the more than six hundred conclusions in the Articles, each objection being refuted. In the refutations Thomas frequently cites the authority of revelation, the Fathers, or Aristotle, but the main burden of the argument is invariably borne by logical analysis.

Even more important than his method was Thomas' attitude toward the role of reason. It is sometimes said that Thomas occupied a middle ground between the rationalistic Averroists and the traditional Augustinians. The Averroists believed that human reason could establish truth even though contradictory to faith; the Augustinians were skeptical of the usefulness of reason in comprehending the supernatural world revealed in the Scriptures. Both Averroists and Augustinians were agreed, therefore, that reason was futile as a means of understanding the higher truths of the faith. Thomas disagreed with both. He would not admit that between faith and reason there could be any real contradiction, as long as rational inquiry was properly conducted. Where the two seemed to conflict, faith provided guidance for human reason to reject error and reach a correct conclusion. According to Thomas, human reason could not by itself comprehend the whole of the Christian universe, but when aided by revelation, reason could establish more certainly what a person already accepts by faith. The basis of this Thomistic rationalism was the premise that revelation and reason, which both come from God, must be in accord. If faith leads to a conclusion that defies rational explanation, the seeming incompatibility exists because of a failure of human reason.

The role of reason, then, is to make deductions from the first principles laid down by faith, as well as to acquire knowledge from the data of sense experience. Reason, for Thomas, is a connecting link between the natural and the supernatural parts of the universe, even though access to knowledge of the latter is made possible by revelation. It would be fruitless for man to attempt to prove or disprove the first principles of revelation; the undemonstrable cannot be demonstrated. But by proceeding from the articles of faith, reason can vastly enlarge the body of certain knowledge that man can rationally comprehend.

The actual content of the Articles in the *Summa Theologica* and the *Summa contra Gentiles* can be divided into two main parts. First, there are conclusions logically deduced from premises that are undemonstrable, that is, articles of faith. If the premises are accepted, the conclusions are guaranteed by the application of Aristotelian logic. For the dissenter who does not grant the premises, the necessity of these conclusions has not been demonstrated philosophically, nor can it be. But Thomas' faith in reason is sufficient for him to hold that articles of faith can be rationally proved to be not impossible. For example, it is by faith alone that man can believe that the world, created in time, is not eternal; and this belief cannot be demonstrated. But natural reason can demonstrate that this belief is logical, possible, and even probable. And objections to Christian doctrine can be shown by reason to have failed to demonstrate the contrary. Thomistic rationalism is thus a weapon in defense of faith as well as a means of deducing knowledge from premises provided by faith. Finally, these conclusions illustrate the kind of knowledge to which man would not have rational access but for the guidance of faith.

The second group of Articles, in the content of the two *Summae,* contain conclusions that are based only on natural reason. These conclusions are demonstrably necessary, without regard for the premises of faith, but of course in these Articles there can be no attempt to deal with doctrine. They deal rather with the visible world of sense experience and with some of the problems of the nature of man and of natural theology. The existence of a deity, for Thomas, would fall under the last heading; the existence or nature of the Trinity would not. Where man and nature are the subject of discussion, Aristotelian physics and metaphysics predominate. Where God and the supernatural are discussed, revelation and Christian teaching predominate.

Thomas agreed with Aristotle that the universe is orderly and rational. But for Thomas, the guarantee of that rationality could only be in the divine order and in the reason in God's mind, both reflected in the universe as comprehensible to human reason. Thus in harmonizing Aristotle's philosophy with Christian doctrine it is the Aristotelian element that must be fitted into the Christian system, not the other way around. This is why Aristotle is never used, in the two *Summae,* in large blocks but rather in bits. Particular statements from Aristotle are taken out of context and put into a new Thomistic context.

To summarize Thomas' view of the Christian universe, part is cognizable by unaided natural reason, and it is connected in logical probability with the second part, which must, ultimately, be accepted on faith. But if revelation be granted as providing valid premises or first principles, this second part also can be shown to be no less rational than the first part. The two parts of the Thomistic universe are nature and supernature. The conclusions concerning nature can be demonstrated to be true; nature can be demonstrated to be consonant with supernature as revealed, in the sense that by arguments from natural reason no revealed truth can be demonstrated to be false and all revealed truths can be demonstrated to be not impossible. The Christian universe is thus coherent: its parts fit together logically if faith is accepted, and if faith is not accepted it still cannot be shown that the two do not fit together logically. Hence Thomas saw the universe as one and rational.

The achievement of Saint Thomas, canonized in 1323, earned him the title of the Angelic Doctor, but in his own lifetime and immediately after his death there was considerable opposition to his supremely confident rationalism. Traditional-minded Augustinians, the great majority of the Franciscans, and many Dominicans and secular clergy were hostile to the general plan and purpose of his work, while certain specific doctrines and philosophical arguments were condemned as being in error. These attacks were focused on the *Summa Theologica,* and since this work was a product of Thomas' last years (1267–1272) and was left incomplete, Thomas never answered his critics. In the long run, however, his ideas triumphed. The cogency and clarity of Thomas' exposition in the *Summa Theologica* made it, with Augustine's *City of God,* one of the two medieval works most influential in the history of Western thought.

## Mysticism and Science: Bonaventura and Grosseteste

The alternative to Thomistic rationalism was presented by a group of Franciscan scholars whose theology was more traditional and Augustinian, and whose philosophical interests led them to make considerable advances in natural science. Their thought was derived largely from Saint Bernard of Clairvaux, and unlike Thomas Aquinas, they preferred to reaffirm the priority of faith over reason rather than to reconcile them. Thomas' contemporary John of Fidanza, better known as Saint Bonaventura (1221–1274), best represents their point of view. Bonaventura was born of a nonnoble Italian family, and his career parallels Thomas' in many respects. After joining the Franciscans, Bonaventura went to Paris in 1242 to study with Alexander of Hales, and he began his own teaching career there in 1248. Like Thomas, Bonaventura was a brilliant student who had an accelerated academic career. The two men knew each other well at Paris. While Thomas remained a teacher all his life, however, Bonaventura entered the mainstream of ecclesiastical life, rising to be Governor General of the Franciscan Order and a cardinal. In the image of Saint Bernard, Bonaventura was a mystic whose spiritual authority placed him near the center of worldly affairs.

Bonaventura placed man's goodness of will and love before man's intellect in the quest for union with God. It followed therefore that the total Christian universe could not be comprehended by the human mind. The natural intellect was a tool of fallen man, and only the visible world of physical nature could be the province of human reason. Supernature, or the mystery of the divine order, was cognizable only by a supernatural agency. Just as nature requires supernature to complete the Christian universe, natural reason requires supernatural aid in apprehending this universe, including God, with any certitude. Such apprehension is possible only by divine illumination; that is, knowledge implanted by divine grace, not captured by unaided reason.

"In everything," said Bonaventura, "that is perceived through sense experience, God lies concealed." The supernatural is hidden from view by the natural. While human cognition can see nature unaided, when fortified by grace it can see through nature to supernature and to God. Nature is dual. It is both literal and symbolic—it truly is what sense perception tells us, but it is also something more. Physical nature consists of an almost infinite variety of symbols hinting at the full significance of the supernatural. But how is knowledge of the supernatural to be acquired? Bonaventura's answer is best given in his own words: "If you ask how these things may be known, interrogate grace and not doctrine, desire and not knowledge, the groaning of prayer and not study, God and not man—not the light of reason but the fire of yearning, all aflame and tending toward God with devotion and glowing affection."

For Bonaventura as for all Augustinians, the emotions have cognitive value. Love and intuition play a part in the search for understanding revealed truth, and faith is more useful than reason in establishing the certainty of human knowledge of the total universe. Bonaventura believed the supernatural was all-important, and finite nature was a limited manifestation of true, supernatural reality that could be consigned to mere natural reason and Aristotelian logic, or any other useful activity of the human intellect, such as observation or experiment. This was not to disparage reason, but simply to recognize its proper role. Furthermore, Bonaventura's Augustinianism did not amount to an oversimple rejection of Aristotle. For example, he was able to reconcile the Augustinian theory of divine illumination with the Aristotelian theory of knowledge, according to which the mind abstracts ideas from the data of sense experience and stores them in the memory. In effect what Bonaventura did was to put one on top of the other, fitting illumination and abstraction together in man's mind. Man, standing halfway between God and created nature, uses illumination in seeking knowledge of supernature above, and abstraction when confronted with natural objects below.

This interest in philosophy gave to Bonaventura's mysticism a quality of intellectual discipline quite lacking in Bernard. In his essay *On Leading the Arts back to Theology* Bonaventura expounded the relationship between secular knowledge and revelation, showing how the former subserves understanding of the latter. Bonaventura's two systematic theological treatises were his commentary on Peter Lombard's *Sentences* and his *Breviloquium,* a compendium of Christian doctrine. His best-known work, and the one that best portrays his mysticism, is aptly entitled *The Itinerary of the Mind to God.* It is both a description of and an exhortation to the ascent toward God, which is salvation. All human faculties are needed for this search for man's supreme good and final end. While the mind unaided begins the journey, and reason uplifted by grace can contemplate the divine mystery, what Bonaventura calls the final "passing over into God" is an experience of which love and yearning are the necessary but insufficient human causes and God's grace is the sufficient cause.

The separation between faith and reason in Bonaventura's thought was developed by mystics of the later Middle Ages, especially the Spiritual Franciscans, into a kind of skepticism—a doubt not in faith but in the usefulness of reason, a doubt that corresponded with their disinterest both in reason and in nature. Reason, according to them, cannot be trusted in the realms of the supernatural. Therefore the Christian must rely on faith alone; any effort to harmonize Aristotle and Christian theology is a waste of time. The later mystics were convinced of the undemonstrable nature of dogma and the primacy of will over intellect in the quest for salvation.

Another group was very much interested in nature, and they developed Bonaventura's Augustinian position in the opposite direction. While they agreed that reason was not useful in dogmatic theology, they also argued that doctrine was of little use in understanding nature. This was the attitude of the majority of the Franciscan scholars. Typical of this group (but not himself a Franciscan) was Bonaventura's older contemporary Robert Grosseteste (1168–1253), who as chancellor of Oxford University and its most influential teacher founded a school of scientific thought that included such men as the Franciscans Roger Bacon (d. 1292) and Duns Scotus (d. 1308).

In his criticism of Aristotle and of Arabic scientific works, Grosseteste became the first in Western Europe to elaborate a systematic theory of experimental science. His major contribution was methodological, specifically the development of an intellectual procedure by which knowledge of observed facts could lead by abstraction to a statement of the principles that explain the observed facts. This is the inductive method, working from fact to theory, as opposed to Thomas Aquinas' deductive method of working from general principles to a statement of the particular and logical consequences. Modern science is rooted in Grosseteste's assumption that it is necessary to proceed inductively from effects to causes before it is possible, with accuracy, to apply knowledge of cause to explain the nature of effects. In his own work, Grosseteste employed controlled experiments that could be repeated if necessary. For example, he sought to explain the nature of the rainbow by studying the properties of refraction in a glass lens. In addition to experiment, Grosseteste insisted on the application of mathematics to scientific procedures both in describing phenomena and in correlating the results of experiment and observation. The thirteenth-century scientific work at Oxford, Paris, and elsewhere, in which Franciscans were prominent and Grosseteste was the earliest leader, resulted in the first major advance beyond the science of the Greeks and the Arabs.

Like Bonaventura, Grosseteste was also a busy churchman and theologian. He was bishop of Lincoln during the last eighteen years of his life, and he ardently championed episcopal rights against interference by the archbishop of Canterbury and the papal *curia*. He was active in English politics, and, although a patron of the Friars Minor, he was friend and counselor to politicians like Simon de Montfort, who distrusted Franciscans as agents of the papacy. Grosseteste also had an interest in systematic theology; his commentary on the corpus of writings attributed to an anonymous fifth-century writer erroneously called Dionysius the Areopagite was a popular source of ideas for the mystics of the later Middle Ages. The originality or creative thought so evident in his scientific speculation does not characterize Grosseteste's religious writings, however.

Although the great advance in medieval science came with the new criticism of Aristotle and the Arabs, older scientific or pseudoscientific interests continued to be pursued. Before the end of the twelfth century most scholars were preoccupied with finding the moral or symbolic meaning, or else the magical or astrological properties, in the objects and events of physical nature. Such was the motivation of Alexander of Neckham (1157–1217), who compiled a lengthy encyclopedia of facts and fables, for the most part culled from literature but also based in part on firsthand knowledge or observation. This work, *On the Nature of Things,* contains the earliest reference to the mariner's compass. Later encyclopedias were produced by several compilers, including Albertus Magnus and his pupils. They were devoted less to drawing moral lessons from the facts of nature than to presenting an accurate description of natural phenomena. All these works were largely dependent on Greek and Arabic sources.

Vincent of Beauvais (d. 1264) was the most industrious compiler. He put together three massive encyclopedias "containing," as he wrote in his introduction, "whatever has been made or done or said in the visible or invisible world from the beginning until the end, and also of things to come." The resulting work, which Vincent called the *Speculum Majus* (*Great Mirror*), was divided into a Mirror of Nature, a Mirror of Doctrine, and a Mirror of History. They are uniformly derivative and mediocre but full of information for those interested in the allusions and symbolism of medieval art and literature. Natural philosophy and science are not included in the Mirror of Nature, which is mainly concerned with systematic theology. Instead they form a section of the Mirror of Doctrine. In Vincent's view, knowledge of the arts and sciences should serve man's welfare, and because his highest welfare is salvation, all this knowledge comes under the heading of doctrine, which leads man to salvation.

Far more important work than that of the encyclopedists was accomplished in particular fields of science. The thirteenth century witnessed the triumph of the Ptolemaic system of astronomy against an effort to revive

This illumination portrays the cooperation between the astronomer and the mathematician. The mathematician makes his calculations while the astronomer uses an astrolabe to measure the angles and altitudes of the stars, providing data to prove the theory. Behind the astronomer, a clerk records the readings.

Monks often led the way in the development of new technology. Advanced agricultural techniques, animal husbandry, and manufacture were the result of the need of monastic communities to produce large amounts of food, to live off land avoided by others, and to serve their widespread estates. This illumination shows Richard of Wallingford, abbot of the abbey of Saint Albans in England, constructing a scientific instrument, probably an astrolabe, using compass and square.

Aristotle's less accurate system. Dissatisfaction with some aspects of both systems led to the earliest independent hypotheses concerning the motion of heavenly bodies. For example, a Franciscan scholar, François de Meyronnes, raised the possibility of the earth's revolving rather than the stars being borne around the heavens on revolving spheres. Astronomical observation and calculation were improved by the use of better astrolabes, quadrants, and armillary spheres. With such instruments the correct latitude of Paris was determined in 1290 by a student of Roger Bacon. The most accurate set of calculations of the movement of planets and stars before the work of Tycho Brahe in the sixteenth century was completed about 1270, at the order of King Alfonso X the Wise of Spain. These *Alfonsine Tables* were in general use throughout the West by the end of the century.

Biology was a chief interest of medieval scientists. Botany was important primarily for medical reasons, and zoology for providing the material from which to draw moral lessons. In the thirteenth century scholars began to treat these fields as important areas for investigation based on observation and accurate description. The best work in botany was done by Albertus Magnus and by Rufinus (ca. 1287), who catalogued and classified plants as well as giving their healing properties. In zoology the outstanding work was written by the emperor Frederick II (1215–1250). *The Art of Hunting with Birds* not only remains an excellent introduction to the subject of falconry but also contains extensive descriptions of the anatomy and habits of birds, based on Aristotelian and Arabic writings and on the observations of the emperor himself. Where his own experience differed from what he read, Frederick did not hesitate to brand the authors of earlier books on the subject as liars.

Knowledge of human anatomy was almost wholly based on the treatises of Galen (ca. 200) and the Moslem Avicenna (d. 1036), but it is probable that at the medical school of Salerno dissection of animal and human bodies had been done in the twelfth century. In the thirteenth century human dissection was definitely practiced at Bologna, in connection with post-mortem examination to establish the cause of death for legal purposes. The earliest surviving formal report of a post-mortem was written by Bartholomew of Varignana (ca. 1302).

Much of the newly recovered ancient and Arabic science and much of the recent progress in scientific knowledge began to appear in textbooks and students' manuals before the end of the thirteenth century. One of the most popular writers was John of Sacrobosco (ca. 1240), whose textbooks in mathematics and astronomy were widely used in the high and later Middle Ages. In his *Sphere,* Sacrobosco presented a convincing empirical argument that the world must be round. If a sailor on a boat sailing out to sea watches a landmark on the coast, he will see it disappear under the horizon, but if he then climbs the mast, he can see the landmark again; also, stars at night rise in the east earlier than in the west, but this could not be true if the earth were flat. Hence the world is round. In his other works he helped popularize the use of Arabic (that is, Hindu) numerals, first introduced to the Latin West by Leonard of Pisa, a mathematician patronized by Frederick II, in his *Liber Abaci* (ca. 1202). The *Sphere* of Sacrobosco continued to be so popular that after the invention of printing it went through sixty-five editions before 1647.

## Suggestions for Further Reading

**Secondary Works**   See the works cited at the end of Chapter 15 for an introduction to thought in the thirteenth century. F. Van Steenberghen, *Aristotle in the West* (Louvain, 1955) treats the reception of Aristotle, and the medieval Platonic tradition is dealt with in R. Klibansky, *The Continuity of the Platonic Tradition During the Middle Ages: Outline of a Corpus Platonicum Medii Aevi* (London, 1939). For the history of philosophy in the thirteenth century, see F. Van Steenberghen, *The Philosophical Movement in the Thirteenth Century* (Edinburgh, 1955); E. Gilson, *The Elements of Christian Philosophy* (New York, 1960) and *The Spirit of Medieval Philosophy* (London, 1936); and J. Pieper, *Scholasticism: Personalities and Problems of Medieval Philosophy* (New York, 1960). E. Gilson, *The Christian Philosophy of Saint Thomas Aquinas* (New York, 1956), which contains a catalogue by I. T. Eschmann of all of Saint Thomas' philosophical writings; V. J. Bourke, *Aquinas' Search for Wisdom* (Milwaukee, Wis., 1965); and M. D. Chenu, *Toward Understanding Saint Thomas* (Chicago, 1964) are excellent introductions. M. Grabmann, *Thomas Aquinas* (New York, 1928) is also important. See also F. J. Roensch, *The Early Thomistic School* (Dubuque, Ia., 1964). On Saint Bonaventura, see E. Gilson, *The Philosophy of Saint Bonaventure* (London, 1938). D. E. Sharp, *Franciscan Philosophy at Oxford* (Oxford, 1930) is a good general introduction. The history of medieval science is surveyed in A. C. Crombie, *Medieval and Early Modern Science,* 2 vols. (Cambridge, Mass., 1959), and E. Grant, *Physical Science in the Middle Ages* (New York, 1970); more detailed treatments are A. C. Crombie, *Robert Grosseteste and the Origins of Experimental Science, 1100–1700* (Oxford, 1953), and S. C. Easton, *Roger Bacon and His Search for a Universal Science* (New York, 1952).

**Sources**  Translations of Saint Thomas' writings are numerous. See *The Basic Writings of Aquinas,* 2 vols., ed. A. Pegis (New York, 1945); *The Pocket Aquinas,* ed. V. J. Bourke (New York, 1960); and *The Political Ideas of Saint Thomas Aquinas,* ed. D. Bigongiari (New York, 1963). *The Works of Saint Bonaventure,* 5 vols., trans. J. de Vinck (Paterson, N.J., 1960–72); *Saint Bonaventure's De Reductione Artium ad Theologiam,* trans. E. T. Healy (New York, 1935); and *Saint Bonaventure's Itinerarium mentis in Deum,* trans. P. Boehner (New York, 1956) are good sources. See also *The Opus Majus of Roger Bacon,* 2 vols., trans. R. B. Burke (Philadelphia, 1928).

# 22 The Growth of Secular Culture

Medieval civilization reached its highest point in the thirteenth century. The centralizing tendencies of feudalism and medieval monarchy worked together to produce strong kingdoms in most of Europe and the best and most effective governments of the medieval period. The Church reached a high point in its evolution; its claims to moral and juridical superiority coincided with the development of a powerful bureaucracy that could administer the authority it claimed. The church-building movement gained speed; universities were established throughout Europe; towns grew rapidly and became productive centers rather than just conduits for the flow of goods. Yet, in this same period European society was changing. The development of territorial states, based on the new monarchies and on the communes of Italy, absorbed the feudal principalities and fiefs and transformed the political life of Europe. Feudalism itself evolved as a result of the changing economic system as well as of the new politics. While feudal nobles were still powerful at the end of the thirteenth century, their role had changed subtly but significantly. Finally, the influence of the Church was being undermined at the same time that it reached the pinnacle of its power. When Boniface VIII confronted Philip the Fair and Edward I, he presided over a Church that was no longer the arbiter of political and economic life.

## Economic Conditions in the High Middle Ages

The growth of the towns in the eleventh and twelfth centuries had resulted in the movement toward mercantile freedom and urban political development discussed in part in Chapter 11. The earliest impulse for bourgeois freedom came from the needs and demands of the merchants who associated themselves in organizations called guilds. The merchant guild grew naturally out of the efforts of the merchants to survive in a hostile world where robbery on the highways and waterways could ruin them and where exactions levied by feudal lords whenever they crossed a bridge or passed a boundary could cut deeply into their profits. The merchants discovered they could resist these losses and exactions if they worked in concert, pooling their resources to pay for security or to control the movement and sale of goods so that uncooperative feudal lords would lose the profits of tolls and customs. The liberties obtained by these merchant guilds consisted of specific privileges and exemptions, rather than any general or abstract freedom. Merchants, in other words, were peasants, unfree and ignoble except for specified privileges. They never became the social or legal equals of the nobility, whose freedom was qualified only by the restrictions or obligations specified by custom.

The earliest bourgeois liberties were almost entirely economic and social, rather than political. Outside of Italy self-government in medieval towns was, with few exceptions, a development of the late twelfth and the thirteenth centuries. Typical of the eleventh and twelfth centuries was the recognition by charter, the legal instrument by which proprietary rights were granted in the feudal world, of certain basic rights and privileges that made possible the economic activity of the new mercantile class and its urban dependents. Bourgeois liberties varied from region to region and within regions from town to town, according to the charters secured by the collective action of the merchants, but some of the liberties, although not universal, have come to typify urban life in the Middle Ages. In many towns the inhabitants were guaranteed a free status—the bonds of serfdom did not reach into the town. Any inhabitant who could prove residence for a year and a day within the town was accepted by the territorial lord of the region as being free in person. Any villein who could escape from his manor and "go underground" within a chartered town for a year could thus free himself from the servile obligations and the status of a serf attached to the soil.

Freedom to enter into binding contracts covering the purchase and sale of urban property and the commodities exchanged in commerce was just as important for the bourgeoisie as freedom of person and freedom of movement. The earliest charters of liberties to medieval towns therefore granted the right to buy, sell, or lease land within the town, exemption from the labor services owed by peasants, the substitution therefor of fixed money rents due to the lord of the town, and finally the right to sue and be sued only in the urban court, in which disputes were adjudicated according to the customs of the

Town governments regulated the weights and measures used in trade within their jurisdiction, and the rules governing sales and shipments could become complex. Like stonemasons, glaziers often recorded scenes from everyday life in their works. This detail from a stained-glass window in the cathedral of Tournai shows the city office where barrels and sacks containing goods (and signed with the marks of their merchant owners) are weighed according to the standard weights.

town. The overall effect of these early town charters was to create within the feudal world jurisdictional immunities of a wholly new sort. In such privileged towns the customs and procedures of the feudal and manorial courts of the region were ignored in favor of the special needs of the bourgeoisie engaged in commerce. In the urban courts a new corpus of law evolved, later called the *ius mercatorum* (law merchant). This law provided speedy remedies, actions on debt and contract not covered by feudal custom, and the enforcement of rights over real property and chattels that were alienable (that is, subject to purchase and sale) without the restrictions of feudal or manorial custom. Finally, the most typical of all bourgeois liberties was the right to hold a perpetual market; that is, the right to buy and sell goods at any time and under the terms and conditions established for such trade by the merchants of the town themselves. The resident merchants, moreover, were usually granted monopolistic control over the trade within the town and sometimes within a part or the whole of the region subject to the lord who granted the charter.

Lords who first granted these bourgeois liberties found that rights given up by charter were more than paid for by the profits accruing therefrom. The merchants paid large sums of money to induce lords to grant town charters; tolls and customs collected by the lord grew as a result of larger trade; and the profits of the lord's neighboring manors increased because of the growing market for agricultural products created by growing towns. In the early twelfth century the more enlightened lords, led by the kings of England and of France, founded new urban settlements with the same privileges as those granted to the merchants of older towns. Sometimes these new towns were laid out where no previous settlement had existed, as Henry I's foundation of Newcastle-on-Tyne. In other cases, a rural village was granted a charter in the hope that it would develop into a full-fledged urban and commercial center, as did the little town of Lorris in northern France. Louis VI's charter to Lorris and that of Henry I to Newcastle became models according to which liberties were granted widely to both old and new towns in France and England. In Germany the greater lords promoted trade and urban development more effectively than the kings. The duke of Zähringen, for example, provided his newly established town of Freiburg (in southern Germany, between the head-waters of the Danube and the upper Rhine) with the charter of liberties that became the model for urban colonization eastward. Where these new foundations or older settlements were favorably situated with respect to trade routes and local markets, they often flourished. Otherwise, the grant of privileges to artificially created mercantile settlements only stimulated the peasants of neighboring rural communities to aspire to the same degree of freedom.

Commerce continued to prosper and expand during the thirteenth century, although the rate of expansion was slower than it had been earlier. The towns, however, continued to grow rapidly, at a rate that would seem to have out-stripped the rate of commercial expansion. The foundation for this rapid growth was a new activity in the economic life of the towns, the manufacture of goods. Early medieval manufacture had been domestic, done by urban and country dwellers primarily for their own use or for a small-scale commerce. Some products were made by cooperation between individuals and the operators of special machines, such as mills or iron forges. Typically, buyers brought their wheat to the mill and paid the miller for the use of his machinery and his skill in operating it; the wheat and flour remained in the buyer's control. Other types of manufacturing activity were organized on a retail handicraft model in which the maker of the goods, such as shoes or household articles, owned the raw materials and sold the merchandise in the market. This kind of craft industry has continued to predominate in many areas of manufacture until very recent times. It is a small volume, local activity.

Large-scale industrial enterprise was not possible until after the commercial revolution was well under way, and merchants rather than craftsmen were its organizers. Merchants had access to raw materials not obtainable locally, they could buy them in larger quantities at lower prices, and they could secure raw materials of better quality in distant markets. Just as important, the great merchant could sell in large quantities in foreign markets at prices that might be higher because of greater demand. Both in buying raw material and in selling finished goods the great merchant could take advantage of market conditions, of improving credit facilities, and of the efficiency of

In the late Middle Ages, craftsmen made rapid progress in the design and manufacture of machines. The first mechanical clock was built around 1340, but it had been preceded by all kinds of devices designed to keep accurate time—water clocks, sand clocks, and many failures in the building of mechanical clocks. In these illuminations from a guild book of Nuremburg (fourteenth century), a pewterer turns a jug on a lathe, and a locksmith works at his bench. The new technology introduced by such late-medieval craftsmen was the basis of the later industrialization of Europe.

transactions of greater volume. As far as manufacture was concerned, he used what is called a putting-out system. He would secure raw material from the market, which might be remote (wool from northern England), transport it to his warehouse (in Flanders or Florence), put out the material to craftsmen who sold the merchants their skilled labor and the use of their equipment (spinning, weaving, and dyeing), after which the merchant would take the finished product (woolen cloth) and sell it in the most favorable market (northern Germany). Between the sheepraiser and the ultimate retail consumer there were many operations, all controlled by a merchant, as in this example, or by several merchants, each specializing in one particular operation, such as exporting the wool or dealing in finished cloth. The craftsmen at no stage owned either raw material or product; the manufacture was for a wholesale transaction or what has been called wholesale handicraft.

Craftsmen engaged in large-scale manufacture were essentially wage earners with little control over their own economic welfare. To protect themselves against the extremes of exploitation by the merchants, they began to organize themselves into guilds patterned on the craft guilds of the retail handicraft sector. In the thirteenth century tension developed between merchants' and craftsmen's guilds in the cities, and many urban riots in the second half of the century stemmed from this hostility.

The entrance of merchants into the industrial field in connection with their large-scale and long-distance trade was one of three significant commercial advances in the high Middle Ages. The second was the development of the fair. Beginning in a few localities as early as the eleventh century, their number and importance grew until the thirteenth century, the golden age of the medieval fair. What the weekly village market or the daily town market were for local and retail trade, the annual or semiannual fair was for wholesale and long-distance trade. Every region with a substantial population had its fair and many countryside districts had smaller fairs—like the modern state and county fairs. A few of the greatest fairs were truly international institutions. Their success depended on a favorable geographical location, where two or more important trade routes crossed or converged. The most famous were those held east of Paris in the county of Champagne, a region from which navigable streams and land routes spread out in all directions. The fairs of Champagne were held at six different times at one or another of four different towns, from early spring to late autumn of each year. The counts of Champagne, like other enlightened feudal rulers, encouraged and protected the fairs because tolls and taxes collected there were a considerable source of revenue.

This revenue included the fees and fines collected in a special court held during the fair. Since the fair usually lasted no more than several days—even the largest ended after a fortnight or three weeks—merchants needed speedy justice in the settlement of their disputes. This was provided by the informal procedure of a court administering the law merchant, in England called the Court of Piepowder because merchants could come into court with the dust of the fair still on their feet (*pieds poudrés,* dusty feet). Here also merchants could have their contracts, bills of exchange, agreements, and other documents authenticated by the seal of the clerk of the fair.

The third important commercial development in the thirteenth century involved financial methods. The origins of modern credit operations lie in the transactions of the great merchants, especially the buying and selling of large quantities of goods at the fairs. Rather than take the risk of carrying with them the huge sums of money necessary to purchase goods, merchants preferred to take the smaller risk of trusting each other. The seller would accept from the buyer a written and sealed promise to pay in the future. Since most merchants were both buyers and sellers of goods, they were both creditors and debtors to other merchants. Many of these debts and credits canceled out, or nearly so. It was found expedient therefore to settle accounts by the exchange of actual money at infrequent intervals, after the net sums due or owed were determined during the last day of an annual fair. Money-changers supplied the currency for these clearinghouses at the fairs. The money-changers also developed methods for safekeeping the money of others held on deposit, from which they would pay out, on order of the depositor, sums owed to a third party. This was one precursor of the modern check.

The bill of exchange was a convenient device by which credit did the work of money. It was a promise to pay, a negotiable piece of "commercial paper" allowing merchants to settle accounts and transfer payments without going through clearinghouses or money-changers. In its simplest form, supposing merchant A owes B 100 shillings, and C owes D 100 shillings: A sends B a promise to pay 100 shillings, which B sells to C for that amount; C then sends the promise (to pay off his debt) to D, and D recovers the 100 shillings from A, who originally promised to pay it. The real convenience of this kind of credit is obvious if, in this example, A and D are merchants of one town and B and C are merchants of another town. No money has to be shipped from either town, but both A and C have paid off their debts in the same amount.

Despite the importance of industrial and commercial developments, the total economy of Europe in the thirteenth century remained predominantly rural and agricultural. Traditional ways of working and living on the manor, and the techniques of agricultural exploitation, did not greatly change. Impressed by these facts, historians have often emphasized the static nature of medieval European society as a whole. But a closer investigation of rural economic conditions has revealed several changes, two of which were highly significant. The first consisted of divergent tendencies away from traditional manorial management. In some parts of Europe, notably England, manorial lords turned their energies to farming for profit. They enlarged their manorial demesnes and exacted full labor services from their peasants, or even increased these services. The earlier trend toward leasing the demesne to peasants and commuting services into cash rents, a practice that caught lords between rising prices and fixed money income, was reversed. The period from around 1200 to 1340 in England was the great age of "demesne farming" to increase production and improve farming methods in order to take advantage of rising prices. When the manorial economy of subsistence gave way to farming for the market, the peasants suffered greater exploitation, but they were in no position to offer effective resistance. When leases expired, lords canceled them; lords won most of the disputes concerning the amount of labor services owed by the peasants; and lords were usually able to encroach on the peasants' customary rights of common in meadows, woods, waste, and pasture. Finally, it should be added that the actual situation varied from manor to manor. Not all lords were willing to commute services in the twelfth century, and by no means did every lord require services in the thirteenth. Many lords reserved the right to require either services or cash rent, from year to year, as they saw fit. A sure sign of the interest of English lords in the various means by which manorial income might be increased was the appearance,

As business became more complex, so did contractual agreements, and businessmen often had to seek arbitration to resolve misunderstandings. Since feudal courts usually took a long time to settle disputes and might rely on such incivilities as trial by battle or ordeal to decide the matter, merchants sought arbitration within their own community, and towns established courts in which modern commercial law began to develop. This illumination shows merchants making a deal (top) and seeking to settle a disagreement about it in a rational and peaceful way (bottom).

toward the end of the thirteenth century, of the earliest treatises concerning estate management. Such was the little work *On Husbandry* by Walter of Henley.

If demesne farming was the growing practice in some areas, the reverse tendency characterized the rural economy in other areas, notably many parts of France, the Low Countries, and on the eastern frontier. French lords were willing to lease their demesnes and to commute services. It has been conjectured that the reason was the relatively greater importance to French lords of their political activities. The seigniory in France was primarily a unit of local government. In England royal officials in shires and hundreds had come to predominate in local government, so that the English manor was increasingly an economic rather than a jurisdictional unit. In any case, the French nobility did not develop the economic interests that characterized their English counterparts. French lords gradually relinquished the various services and payments in kind in return for annual rents from the peasantry. The predominance of peasant rentals in the Low Countries and on the eastern frontier was probably a consequence of the premium on labor in those parts. Great efforts were expended in draining the low country in Flanders and clearing forests in the east, and this labor could be attracted only by offering favorable terms and conditions, allowing the peasants themselves to take advantage of the growing market in agricultural products.

The other important rural development in the thirteenth century was the extension of the eastern frontier beyond central Germany. In the north it reached the Vistula by about 1200 and was extended all the way around the Baltic shores and into Latvia and Estonia by the end of the century. The resistance put up by the Slavic Pomeranians, the Baltic Prussians and Letts, and the Finnish Livs and Esths was broken during the middle years of the thirteenth century by the Knights of the Teutonic Order, a military crusading order that abandoned the Holy Land in favor of converting the heathen peoples of the north when the king of Poland invited it to conquer the Baltic area. In the wake of the Teutonic Knights came immigrants from the Low Countries and Germany to settle towns and villages under the lordship of the Knights and of a small number of the German nobility. By the end of the century this area had begun to flourish as a center of production and trade. Food was exported westward, and German merchants began to replace Scandinavians in the trade in the Baltic and farther east in Russia. This thrust into northeastern Europe constituted the final medieval expansion of Latin Christendom.

## The Transformation of Feudal Society

Although they continued to be the predominant social class, the feudal nobles in most of Europe declined in power during the thirteenth century. There were many reasons for this decline. In the heyday of feudalism, during the eleventh and early twelfth centuries, the feudal nobility controlled nearly all the wealth in Europe, and as long as agricultural production continued to be almost the only form of wealth, the nobility maintained its economic preeminence. Until the twelfth century, nobles were lenders rather than borrowers of money. The expense of crusading was the first cause, chronologically, of the reversal of this pattern; the second was the economic changes discussed in the preceding section. The growth of commerce and commercial centers produced a class of people whose wealth was fluid and impressive in amount, although it did not equal the landed wealth of the nobility until modern times. But the fluid money wealth of the merchants possessed many advantages over the wealth of the nobility. Money wealth was easily transferred, moving through the economic cycle and giving advantages to many throughout the society. It was a wealth that could be separated from its owner and that was therefore not restricted by personal rights and obligations fixed by customary law. Thus while the king might get forty days service from his tenants-in-chief and sub-vassals, he could field an army for months if he could raise the money to do so. The growth of commerce produced the liquid wealth that permitted rulers to escape the restrictions of traditional society by giving them an alternative to the feudal levy.

Henry II of England encouraged a trend toward the commutation of feudal obligations by the payment of money. Both king and feudal lords were anxious to make use of the new arrangement. The king wanted a ready army of knights to take advantage of opportunities and to react to crises as they arose and to pursue the relentless project of rebuilding the monarchy after the Anarchy. The feudal lords were interested in pursuing new economic activities, developing their estates as economically viable units in a commercial system in which prices were rising and agricultural surplus could realize a good profit. The nobility did not want to relinquish their traditional military role, but during Henry's reign more and more lords paid the scutage, as the payment in lieu of service was called, instead of serving the king. This development continued under Henry's successors, and the kings increasingly relied on mercenary armies, made up primarily of knights-errant.

The rising power of the kings enhanced whatever tendencies the scutage system had of diminishing the role of the baronage in government. During the thirteenth century, royal courts encroached on the traditional jurisdictional spheres of the baronial courts, reducing them to a minor part of the kingdom's judicial system. In addition, successful assertions of royal power like Henry II of England's Inquest of Sheriffs (1170) and Louis IX of France's *Enquêtes* (1247) extended the crown's influence and made it possible for the kings to enforce royal rights relative to the barons. Finally, the special relationship between the king and the towns in the European kingdoms not only placed the bulk of the kingdom's fluid wealth at the king's disposal but also made him increasingly independent of the feudal nobility. In the early twelfth century, Henry IV of Germany had tried, unsuccessfully, to found his monarchy on the urban communities. By the end of the thirteenth century, however, the prospects for success of such a policy were greatly increased.

The relative importance of the military elite during the thirteenth century was also diminished as a result of changes in the art of warfare. In the late twelfth century, wooden and earthwork castles were replaced by great stone structures. This development had several effects. Since the enormous cost of stone castles could be borne only by a few, the feudal class became more heterogeneous in terms of military power as well as in wealth and station. The stone castles were virtually siegeproof, and those who could wall themselves in safely did not often sally forth to risk their lives and their positions. Thus mounted fighting gave way to siege warfare, which made the knight less valuable than the engineer and the sapper. The appearance of new weapons in the later thirteenth century also devalued the knightly warriors. The crossbow threw a bolt with great force that rendered the chain mail of the knight obsolete, but the crossbow had a short range and was difficult to load. It posed

These sketches from late-medieval manuscripts illustrate the advantages of the longbow over the crossbow. Whereas loading the crossbow was difficult and time-consuming, the longbow could be rapid-fired, which gave the bowman's enemy no time to recover or take cover. In addition, the short span of the crossbow did not give the bolt much directional stability; thus while the bolt flew with tremendous force, its accuracy was adequate only at short range. Finally, the longbow was inexpensive, while the crossbow required considerable manufacturing skill and expenditure.

little danger. Then, Edward I of England, in his campaigns against the Welsh and Scots, introduced a related weapon, the longbow. The longbow, wielded by English commoners who used the weapon in hunting and sport, developed tremendous power over great distances and could be refired at a very rapid rate. To protect themselves from longbowmen, knights had to wear heavy plate armor that immobilized them and significantly diminished the effectiveness of every traditional tactic other than the charge. When cannon and pikes were introduced in the early fifteenth century, even this tactic became largely useless.

The result of these developments was the emergence of territorial states with definite boundaries, states that were still not unified or sovereign like the modern nation-state but were definite geographical areas within which the central power of king or duke or archbishop or commune was recognized and enforced. Some areas, such as England, had already reached this stage early in the thirteenth century; in other areas the competing feudal jurisdictions continued to be a serious obstacle to such centralizing tendencies until late in the Middle Ages.

The generalizations can best be illustrated by the attitude of feudal lords of the middle rank, those barons who were not counts or dukes or kings but who were possessed of baronies that numbered from a dozen to several dozen fiefs held by about the same number of vassals. Such a baron in the year 1100 thought of his barony as being his "honor." The honor consisted not only of his own demesne manors and all the fiefs held by his vassals but also of all his rights of jurisdiction and his rights as feudal lord of his vassals. These rights the baron exercised effectively over all his vassals and their scattered fiefs from the center of his barony, his feudal, or honorial, court. The cohesive bond of the honor was the set of personal relationships between lord and vassals, symbolized by the act of homage performed by each vassal when he received his fief. The court often acted as a unit, and the vassals thought of themselves as peers or equal participants in the affairs of the honor, but the honorial court never became a corporate body with rights or functions of its own. It was the baron's court, not the peers'. The ties uniting the baron as lord to each vassal individually were stronger than the interests that might on occasion bring vassals together in opposition to their lord. Thus the strongest bonds of feudal society may be described as both individualistic and vertical; that is, between lord and vassal, superior and inferior, as individuals.

By the year 1300 the baron possessed of a barony of similar size had quite a different attitude. His barony would probably consist of many more fiefs of much smaller size, so that his vassals were not so important, individually, to his own interests. His feudal court no longer met so often nor did it do so much business because his vassals had discovered that a better brand of justice, less encumbered by feudal custom, was available in royal courts. Since the baron's right of private warfare had been restricted by the peace enforced by kings or Church or higher lords, the old relationship between baron and vassals as comrades in arms had all but disappeared. The relationship was no longer really feudal; the lord looked on his vassals as tenants of fiefs from which he derived revenues. The lord had become, to use the modern term, a landlord.

With the vertical ties between lord and vassal thus attenuated, and with the decline of feudal jurisdiction, lords who had once devoted most of their energy to governing their baronies became more involved in the activities of the growing central government. This involvement, in turn, made it easier for the lords to recognize and act on their mutual interests against the royal government. The lower nobility also became less concerned with their relationships with their immediate lords and increasingly active in royal government, from which they received justice and whatever advancement they might achieve. Gradually the feudal world was becoming stratified into classes whose horizontal ties, the interests binding together groups of the same social status and economic condition, superseded the older vertical ties. In central Europe, and to a lesser degree in France, where the central authority of king or prince was slow in developing, such tendencies toward horizontal social organizations led to the formation of estates. An estate was a class defined in terms of similar social status, economic interests, and political position. The growth of self-conscious estates reflected the breakdown of the feudal organization of society, even though feudal institutions survived until the French Revolution and later.

The tendency of the feudal lords to enter the money economy increased as prices rose during the late twelfth and the thirteenth centuries. The lords had taken their income in kind and in services, but the process of conversion to a money economy in the relationship between king and lords also affected the lower-level relationship between lord and peasants. In many areas during the second half of the twelfth century, services and rents in kind were commuted into money rents, which produced immediate monetary gain for the nobility but was disadvantageous in the long run. The conversion of services to money rents did not free rents from custom, permitting them to rise in response to the inflationary trends. Thus while the lords could not violate custom by pushing rents up as prices rose, they could reconvert the rents to services and produce when conditions made that the best course of action. In the thirteenth century, rents sometimes were reconverted into services and kind, so that the lords would reap the benefits of rising prices in the agricultural market. In addition, greater lords and ecclesiastical institutions that faced the same problems began to enlarge their land holdings, increasing their income, while lesser, lower and middle-rank, lords and institutions sold land to pay off their debts. This process of consolidation continued throughout the thirteenth century and undermined the broad base of the feudal class. It also put pressure on the traditional legal system, since the law did not recognize the right to sell land. In 1225 the English royal court finally declared that the sale of land, already a widespread practice in rural districts as it had been in the cities, was a legally valid act. This new rule, adopted elsewhere in Europe during the thirteenth century, reflected the fact that feudalism, the centralization of control over the landed wealth of the community, was breaking down and being replaced by a decentralized money economy on which there were as yet few social and political controls.

The breakdown of feudalism was also accelerated by causes inherent to the institution. Subinfeudation, the act by which a vassal created vassals, could be used to increase the money income of lords. Instead of enfeoffing vassals for military service, lords enfeoffed for money rents valued at some part of the military service due from the fief. A vassal might hold a fief for a twentieth part of a knight's service or for a fixed rent that bore no relation to the system of military obligations. As prices rose, a piece of land's productivity also rose in value, and lords were induced to rent out more and more land, realizing in that way the greater returns possible from their fiefs. Old rents were fixed by custom; new rents could be fixed to reflect the current market value of production. This development led to the breaking up of old fiefs into smaller farms and estates that produced sufficient income, and rent, to support both leasor and leasee. The tendency toward more, smaller fiefs and the replacement of personal service by money payments, which is best illustrated by subinfeudation and its consequences, was also promoted by the feudal laws of inheritance. Primogeniture (inheritance of the whole fief by the oldest surviving son) usually preserved the integrity of the fief. But what if no son were born or survived? In most regions feudal custom provided that on the failure of male heirs the fief descended to the surviving daughters equally as co-heiresses. Feudal families were large, so this did not happen frequently, but when it did happen there were often many co-heiresses among whom the fief was partitioned. A great fief could suddenly become a collection of rather insignificant fiefs. Other feudal customs provided that the widow should retain part of her late husband's fief as her dower to possess during her lifetime, or that a younger son could be enfeoffed of part of the father's fief during the father's life, or even permanently if the oldest son consented, or that a daughter should be enfeoffed with a "marriage portion" of her father's fief, which meant that she and her heirs would deprive the oldest son of that portion of the inheritance. These and many other customs tended to reduce the size of fiefs, either temporarily or permanently, although occasionally they might work to increase their size. But despite the bewildering complexity of feudal law, the main generalization is clear: historically the tendency was in the direction of more fiefs, smaller fiefs, and the conversion of services into money payments.

The result was that, below the level of the kingdoms and greater principalities, the old feudal lordships—fiefs, honors, baronies—became less important as political units. The old personal relationships and the jurisdictional powers of lords over vassals were giving way to new and impersonal relationships that were proprietary and economic. These relationships might lead to endless disputes concerning rights and duties between the parties involved, thus providing an opportunity for the greater rulers with their more effective governments—the king of England, the count of Flanders, the archbishop of Cologne—to intervene and control the feudal society within the area of their jurisdiction. This transformation of feudal society was gradual, and to the modern historian its course is almost imperceptible. But when the feudal world of the twelfth century is contrasted with the structure of society and the concentration of political authority evident in the fourteenth century, it is clear that the intervening period was one of profound change.

## The Secularization of Medieval Institutions and Values

The influence of both the Church and many of the doctrines it promoted began to decline in the high Middle Ages. With a gradual and uneven progress, secular institutions and values have become increasingly important ever since. The process of secularization could be illustrated in almost every aspect of thirteenth-century life. It should be kept in mind that *secularization* is a relative term and that at no time was medieval civilization as secular as the modern world.

The Church had developed a set of ethical principles to govern the economic relations among men. In the thirteenth century, the rapid development of the economy undermined some of these principles, while making others almost impossible to apply. The Church taught that people engaged in commerce should avoid the sin of avarice. The theologians and canon lawyers developed the doctrine of the just price, according to which the price of goods should be set by the marketplace. The concern of the theologians was the same as that of the authors of modern antitrust and fair-trade legislation: they insisted that merchants not raise prices by collusion or by holding back goods from the market. The just price theory thus did not hamper economic activity by forcing a merchant to sell below market value, but it did prevent the seller from being unfair and thus uncharitable to the buyer. The seller who sold goods above the just price was required to give the extra profit to charity. The theory might have worked in a stable, local, and small-scale market, where the cost of materials and labor were known or easily determined, where the risks of commerce were low, where the free-market system could be watched effectively, and where social and economic pressure could be applied against swindlers. But in the complex commercial system developed in the twelfth and thirteenth centuries, it was unfeasible. Establishing the just price of goods produced by a complicated manufacturing process and transported over long distances was difficult, and the merchants themselves were left to regulate prices.

The ecclesiastical doctrine on usury was founded not only on the desire to reduce the incidence of avarice but also on biblical texts. The Book of Deuteronomy forbade the Jews from charging interest on loans to other Jews, and the Christians had followed this doctrine. Analysis of the prohibition produced a rationale based on the virtue of charity and the sin of avarice. He who had money to lend to those in need should lend it as an act of charity. Otherwise he would be taking avaricious advantage of another's poverty. Today usury means exorbitant interest; in the early Middle Ages any interest at all was called usury, and even the lowest interest rate was considered morally exorbitant. But the facts were rapidly outstripping the moral teachings of the Church. Most of the men who sought loans were not charity-fed paupers but businessmen and manorial lords who needed capital for commercial or agricultural enterprise, or nobles who were living beyond their means to keep up the proper appearances. The most important borrowers of all were governments. When political policy or military exigencies required castle building along frontiers or the fortification of towns, such projects could not be financed out of ordinary revenues. The only recourse was to borrow money against future income, and this could be done only by paying interest. Even the papal government, while deploring usury, found it necessary to borrow heavily and pay interest. The teaching of the Church on usury broke down

In the small-market economy, governmental control could be effective. This drawing from a thirteenth-century manuscript served as a warning to tradesmen. On the left, a baker puts a short-weight loaf in the oven. On the right, he is carted through town with the loaf around his neck. Public humiliation was a major part of the system of punishment in the Middle Ages. That this form of punishment for minor, but antisocial, crimes persisted is demonstrated by the pillory stocks so often found in seventeenth-century New England towns.

before the elaborate and sometimes devious exceptions developed by the canonists to allow interest under certain conditions. For example, if the lender were risking the loss of his money, a moderate interest charge was not to be considered usury. Like the history of the just price, the history of usury exemplifies the gradual triumph of secular over religious values.

In even more dramatic fashion political developments illustrate the growing secularization of society in the thirteenth century. The Church took the lead in trying to establish orderly and peaceful conditions during the turbulent early days of feudalism. Dramatic struggles, such as those between Gregory VII and the emperor Henry IV or between Archbishop Thomas à Beckett and Henry II of England, should not obscure the fact that in general the Church supported strong rulers who could keep their vassals under control. The Church not only taught the virtue of obedience to secular rulers, most secular governments were largely staffed by churchmen—clerks in lower positions and prelates in the higher offices. In the coronation service kings were consecrated with holy oil, a symbol of divine sanction for just rule. Partly because of Church support, royal governments grew more powerful. The king's peace supplanted the Peace of God.

About the year 1200, most Europeans would have found it difficult to decide where their primary allegiance was placed. Was it to the local political unit, the barony or the town; or was it to the greater unit, the kingdom or feudal principality; or was it to the totality of Latin Christendom? Opinion would certainly have been divided, but most people would have felt their greatest emotional attachment directed toward the universal Christian commonwealth and their greatest material interests bound up with the locality in which they lived. The intermediate unit of kingdom or duchy (or even the county in some regions) would have been last in the division of loyalties. By the end of the thirteenth century this situation was largely altered. The sense of belonging to a local community or of being a member of Christendom persisted, but the balance of men's allegiance had shifted to the kings and greater lords who governed territorial principalities.

This change took place at different times and in different ways in different regions. In England and France the monarchies triumphed, but in northern Italy the struggle for power was won by the communes as they expanded into territorial city-states. The main goal of the governments of the thirteenth century was to eliminate divided loyalties within the territories under their jurisdiction. This did not mean the destruction of competing jurisdictions, such as the seignorial rights and privileges of the lay nobles or of the Church, but rather the definition and limitation of those jurisdictions so that the central government was recognized as supreme over all subordinate authority. The characteristic expression of this supremacy was the power of the government to determine and settle all jurisdictional disputes within its territory. The central government did not directly take over the functions of feudal or ecclesiastical courts, nor did it abolish local seigniorial administration. But it did insist on drawing the line between its own jurisdiction and that of lords and prelates. In doing so, the government usually resolved disputes in its own favor and always claimed that subordinate jurisdiction was exercised as a delegated power subject to supervision and correction by the central authority.

This growth of lay governments in the high Middle Ages undermined the influence of the Church in many ways. As their powers grew, their activities increased. This meant that governments had to recruit increasing numbers of officials and "civil servants" to assess and collect taxes, preside over and staff courts, maintain peace, keep jails, investigate complaints, and eliminate abuses of local jurisdiction. Government service became a new career open to the talented, as joining the clergy always had been. By the end of the thirteenth century government "clerks" were no longer always clerics. Laymen trained in the legal profession found easy access to important posts, and the minor officialdom of government attracted increasing numbers of ambitious but uneducated laity.

Contemporaries objected—then even as today—to the evils of bureaucracy, not only to the number of officials but also to the way they operated. Older and more casual methods were replaced by the impersonal and ruthless efficiency of royal agents whose own profit lay in promoting the power of their masters. Specialization of function marked the expansion of administrative and judicial work. Different departments or bureaus of the central government were responsible for different activities; orders to local officials were sent out and reports received. Government by discussion gave way to government by writing. Records were kept carefully, and the official memory of the government was preserved in those duplicates and triplicates of communications and correspondence that characterize every bureaucracy. The size and power of medieval central government should not be exaggerated, but the growth of such governments in the thirteenth century was impressive to contemporaries and is still impressive today.

It is paradoxical that the age in which the secular governments began to challenge the ecclesiastical government in power and organization should have been the same age in which Church government achieved its greatest authority. Beginning with Innocent III (1198–1216), the popes of the thirteenth century were the best in the Middle Ages. They were, on the whole, well-trained lawyers who had spent many years in papal administration before being elected to the papacy. They developed the administrative capacity and efficiency of the ecclesiastical government and presided over a Church in which provincial and diocesan synods, episcopal visitation of monasteries and other ecclesiastical institutions, and the enforcement of ecclesiastical reform on the parish level became regular activities. In its spiritual and ecclesiastical functions the Church of the thirteenth century came nearer to realizing its ideals than in any previous period. But the achievement of the Church's leadership of Christendom involved it deeply in lay affairs; it secularized the Church. In the tenth and eleventh centuries, lay lords and kings had secularized the Church by making control of it one of the foundations of their strength. In the twelfth and thirteenth centuries, the Church freed itself from these impositions and asserted its moral superiority in Europe. The victory brought the Church into the secular sphere on an equal footing with the lay powers, and often in the thirteenth century the popes and other powerful ecclesiastics competed with the lay powers on purely secular issues without obvious or credible spiritual or moral overtones. Dante, among others, criticized the Church for its embroilment in politics and worldly affairs, feeling that such things should be left to secular rulers. The papal *curia* headed the most advanced bureaucracy in Europe, and contemporaries were impressed with the papacy's imposition of heavy taxes on the clergy to support the political or secular goals of papal policy in Italy and elsewhere. Thus when in 1296 Philip the Fair placed an embargo on the export of bullion from France, he not only put the papacy in a serious financial squeeze but also touched a nerve in the moral consciousness of many people who had been dismayed by the activities of the highest priest in Christendom. At the same time, the limited territorial and armed power of the papacy forced it to rely on such ecclesiastical weapons as excommunication and the interdict in the pursuit of its policies, so that during the thirteenth century, the moral effect of these penalties declined significantly.

As power shifted from the Church to the secular governments, the claims of papal apologists grew and their arguments became increasingly extreme. Papal supporters couched their arguments in well-worn terms of competing jurisdictions within Christendom as a whole, the *respublica Christiana,* at a time when the unity of that entity was being fractured both in theory and in reality. In the period when the kings and greater lords were weak, the idea of a Christendom unified under the joint rulership of the emperor and pope had a certain verisimilitude. It had been argued that all kings were subject to the emperor, and under the emperor Henry VI (1190–1196) it appeared that the subordination might become a reality. Canonists had mused about the existence of imperial power outside the Church, implying that they took seriously the notion that the Church and legitimate secular political authority were conterminous. But the rise of the Western monarchies destroyed such dreams, and lawyers in the service of the French monarchy, for example, spelled out the notion of royal supremacy within the territorial limits of the French realm, best summarized by the formula "The king is emperor within his kingdom." This doctrine already had been expressed by a Spanish canonist at the beginning of the thirteenth century. French and English lawyers adopted another canonical doctrine during the 1290s to justify their kings' claims to a power to tax the clergy. According to this doctrine of necessity, the king might exercise emergency powers in the defense of national welfare. Thus the king might protect the community as a whole at the expense of groups or interests within the community, which was defined as the body under royal jurisdiction. Papal political writers met these views with theories supporting the claims of papal universal jurisdiction. Perhaps the most popular treatise advocating the papalist position was the *Summa de Potestate Ecclesiastica* (ca. 1325) by Augustinus Triumphus. Augustinus marshaled all the arguments of his predecessors, presenting them, in true scholastic fashion, in a systematic way beginning with first principles and ending with the logical conclusion that the pope held the highest authority in the world and was the arbiter of all other powers.

Arguments of this sort underlay Boniface VIII's extreme statements in the bull *Unam Sanctam;* they did not reflect political, social, or even attitudinal realities any better than Boniface's assertions had. By the end of the thirteenth century, people were looking to the secular governments for services, protection, and justice, and reacted angrily when papal and other ecclesiastical powers interfered with those governments' activities. In economics and politics, the developments of the thirteenth century had produced difficulties in the application of ethical attitudes and doctrines expounded by the Church and had created a new pragmatism. It was an age of transition in which the ideas and institutions of traditional medieval society persisted in conflict with ideas and institutional developments of a new commercial and secular society.

**Suggestions for Further Reading**

**Secondary Works**  On the economy of the twelfth and thirteenth centuries, see the works cited at the end of the Introduction and of Chapter 11. In addition, see R. S. Lopez, *The Commercial Revolution of the Middle Ages* (Englewood Cliffs, N.J., 1971), and G. Luzzatte, *An Economic History of Italy (to 1500)* (New York, 1961). J. W. Baldwin, *Medieval Theories of the Just Price* (Philadelphia, 1959); J. T. Noonan, *The Scholastic Analysis of Usury* (Cambridge, Mass., 1957); and B. N. Nelson, *The Idea of Usury* (Princeton, N.J., 1949) treat specific economic problems. On late feudalism, see B. Lyon, *From Fief to Indenture* (Cambridge, Mass., 1957). See also the articles collected by C. L. Tipton, *Nationalism in the Middle Ages* (New York, 1972).

**Sources**  A collection of commercial documents is in I. W. Raymonds and R. S. Lopez, eds., *Medieval Trade in the Mediterranean World* (New York, 1955). *Walter of Henley's Husbandry,* trans. E. Lamond (London, 1890), and *Walter of Henley and Other Treatises on Estate Management and Accounting,* ed. and trans. D. Oschinsky (Oxford, 1971) are good sources for estate management in the thirteenth century.

# 23 Spain,
# the Mediterranean,
# and the East

In the high and later Middle Ages developments on the periphery of Latin Christendom were as portentous for the modern world as the course of events in Western and central Europe. The Spanish and Portuguese kingdoms were consolidated under strong and adventurous rulers who played a major role in discovering the New World and in opening that older "new world" of the East to Europeans, both of which movements led to the expansion of European civilization around the globe. The initial momentum of Iberian expansion came from the *Reconquista,* the expulsion of the Moslems. In the eastern Mediterranean the struggle between Cross and Crescent went the other way. After the fall of Jerusalem in 1187, Christendom was on the defensive. By the end of the Middle Ages the Moslems had destroyed the Latin states in Syria, and Islam was firmly planted in Europe.

It would be a mistake to emphasize the religious aspect of the Eastern contests between the rising and declining powers of the Moslem world. Neither the Holy War nor the *jihad* aroused much enthusiasm on either side. The decline of the Seljuk Turks gave a reprieve to the Latin kingdom of

Jerusalem. The rise of the Mameluk Turks within Islam resulted from struggles that hardly affected the Christian principalities. Only after defeating new conquerors from farther Asia did the Mameluks end the life of the Latin kingdom, and this was a mere mopping-up operation. The later expansion of the Ottoman Turks into Europe was not inspired by religious zeal against Christendom: the Byzantine Empire was easier to conquer than the Mameluk Sultanate.

Meanwhile the steppes of central Asia had, early in the thirteenth century, produced one more wave of conquerors, the Mongols under Genghis Khan. In the Near East their coming brought few permanent results, but to the north and east they settled down to live on the tribute of the inhabitants of the Russian plains. The Mongol domination hastened the decline of Kiev and was the main impetus for the rise of the principality of Moscow. By the end of the Middle Ages Moscow was the center of a new Russian nation whose life depended on successful resistance against invaders from both East and West. With the fall of Constantinople in 1453, Moscow also became the center of Orthodox Christianity, the heir of Byzantine civilization.

The Mongols struck terror everywhere, but they also raised the hopes of Western Christians who nursed the illusion that Genghis Khan and his successors either were Christian or could be converted, and would form an alliance against the Moslems. Emissaries traveled between the court of the Great Khan and the courts of Innocent IV and Saint Louis. But these first efforts at diplomatic intercourse between the West and the farther East produced little beyond the fascinating accounts written by several of the ambassadors, notably those of John of Pian de Carpine and William of Rubruck. The character of the negotiations provides some light relief in an essentially dismal chapter of European history. For example, in 1246 Pian de Carpine brought to the Great Khan a letter from Innocent IV in which the pope stipulated acceptance of Christianity as a basis for further negotiation. The Khan sent back a letter ordering the pope forthwith to come in person to outer Mongolia, together with all the rulers of Western Europe, so they could all do homage to the Khan—as the basis for further negotiation. It is not surprising that the hoped-for grand alliance against Islam never materialized.

## Medieval Spain: The Christian Reconquest

The Christian expansion in Spain during the late eleventh century slowed significantly in the twelfth century. The push to the south had been led chiefly by Alfonso VI of Castile (1065–1109), who also united the kingdom of León with Castile. The Moslems had countered the Christian advances by accepting the lordship of the North African Almoravides (1086–1146), who successfully organized a united resistance in Andalusia, the Moslem part of the peninsula. After Alfonso VI's death, the Christian kingdoms in the north revived old rivalries, and a period of shifting alliances, wars, and dynastic struggles ensued. In the last year of his life, Alfonso had attempted to unite Aragón and Castile by marrying one of his daughters to the heir of the Aragonese throne. This plan failed when widespread rebellion broke out after the king died. By the mid-twelfth century, another of Alfonso's sons-in-law had established an independent kingdom of Portugal; Castile had temporarily absorbed León; Navarre was involved in French affairs; and Aragón had been united by means of a marriage alliance to the old Carolingian county of Barcelona (Catalonia), which had close cultural, economic, and political connections with southern France. In this complex situation Christians and Moslems entered into a confusing series of alliances that kept the attention of the Christian kingdoms from concentrating on reconquest.

In 1146 a new Moslem power from Africa took over the organization of resistance against the Christians from the Almoravides, who had largely failed to accomplish the task and whose dominions were splintered into about thirty principalities. The new lords were the Almohades, who held the Castilian king Alfonso VIII (1158–1214) in check until the last years of his reign. Alfonso's weakness stemmed from his own political problems. León had successfully broken from Castile and had raised its own king. The combined kingdom of Aragón and Catalonia was deeply involved in the affairs of southern France, where Peter II of Aragón (1196–1213) was a leader of the Albigensian defense against the Crusaders. The Almohades dealt Alfonso's armies a very serious defeat in 1195, but unsuccessful as he was, Alfonso maintained his leadership of the reconquest. As Alfonso's position deteriorated in the last years of the twelfth century and the first decade of the thirteenth, Innocent III proclaimed a Crusade in Spain. The pope's call brought Crusaders from across the Pyrenees, and in 1212 a conglomerate Christian army, under Castilian leadership, moved against the Almohades. The Christians defeated the Moslems decisively at Las Navas de Tolosa, a battle from which the Almohades never fully recovered. The next year, Peter II of Aragón died defending the Albigensian cause, and under his son James I (1213–1276), Aragón-Catalonia reentered the history of the reconquest.

In the thirteenth century the reconquest was carried forward under James I of Aragón, called the Conqueror, and Ferdinand III of Castile (1217–1252), grandson of Alfonso VIII. Their efforts were made easier by the disintegration of the Almohades' dominion into a half-dozen warring states. Ferdinand III occupied Córdoba in 1236 and Seville in 1248. His forces reached the southeastern coast at Murcia and Cartagena by 1243, and his son reached the southwestern coast at Cádiz in 1262. Between these two coastal regions lay the Moslem kingdom of Granada, by 1270 the only remaining Moslem principality. Meanwhile, James I began creating a Mediterranean empire by conquering the Balearic Islands (1229–1235). At the same time, he moved south along the coast to Valencia. He took the city in 1238 and began the organiza-

Spain in the Later Middle Ages

tion of a Christian kingdom of Valencia, which became with Aragón and Catalonia a constituent part of his expanded kingdom. James' plans are indicated by the marriage he arranged for his heir Peter with Constance, daughter of Manfred of Sicily. This was Peter III of Aragón (1276–1285), who became king of Sicily after the Sicilian Vespers (1282) had expelled Charles of Anjou and the French.

The Aragonese kings maintained the ancient principle of divided inheritance, and thus James I apportioned his kingdom between his sons. Peter III received the mainland kingdom, and his younger brother was granted the new kingdom of Majorca (the Balearics). After Peter III became king of Sicily, he tried to hold Aragón and Sicily together, but his effort failed. A separate Aragonese dynasty ruled Sicily from 1296 until the fifteenth century. Majorca was reunited with Aragón in 1349, about the time the island of Sardinia was conquered from Genoa. Sicily was not firmly reunited with Aragón until the reign of Alfonso V the Magnanimous (1416–1458), who added the kingdom of Naples to his empire in 1435. This was the height of Aragonese territorial expansion in the Mediterranean. After the death of Alfonso the Magnanimous, one son, John II, took over Aragón and Sicily, while Alfonso's illegitimate son, Ferrante (1458–1494), became king of Naples.

On the other side of the Iberian Peninsula, Portugal also expanded southward during the thirteenth century. In 1267 a treaty between Castile and Portugal partitioned the territory the two kingdoms had conquered. Within the next three years, Portugal attained its present southern coastline. After 1270 the only real threat from the Moslems lay in the possibility of another influx of African reinforcements. In the fourteenth century this threat materialized, but the result was a decisive victory for Castilian forces at the

Battle of the River Salado in 1340. After that, for a century and a half the *Reconquista* stopped until Ferdinand and Isabella completed the conquest of Granada in 1492.

Within the Spanish kingdoms, political, economic, and cultural development varied greatly. During the twelfth and thirteenth centuries, each of the kingdoms had developed parliamentary institutions (*cortes*) that functioned much like the parliaments in thirteenth-century England. The demands of conquest placed the kings in a financial position that gave the *cortes* the opportunity to establish precedents and make demands. Each of the old districts had an independent *cortes;* in Aragón this regionalism had a far-reaching effect. The old kingdom of Aragón was a highly feudalized region dominated by military landlords. Its *cortes* was principally comprised of feudal nobles. In the 1280s, taking advantage of the preoccupation of Peter III and his son Alfonso III (1285–1291) with Sicily and the Balearics, the Aragonese *cortes* won concessions from the kings. Peter IV (1336–1387) waged a costly civil war against the Aragonese and Valencian nobility to win back these concessions. Castile suffered the same kind of division; although Castile and León were united after 1230, the two regions maintained separate *cortes* and governmental institutions. This persistence of regionalism lasted into early modern times and qualified the success of monarchs like Ferdinand and Isabella who appeared to have united Spain under their royal government.

Aragón suffered most from the old divisions. While Aragón was a region of landed estates and military aristocrats, Catalonia was part of the southern French commercial civilization. The *cortes* in Catalonia was a merchant body, and Catalan interests had urged, supported, and gained most from the Mediterranean conquests of James I and his successors. Valencia brought the two regions into a kind of cooperative conflict. The Aragonese provided the main forces for conquering Valencia, but when James began to organize a new kingdom there, it was the Catalans, moving into the coastal cities, who controlled the new government.

The thirteenth-century expansion engendered a wide activity in developing governmental and legal institutions for the newly conquered districts. Ferdinand III's successor in Castile, Alfonso X the Wise (1252–1284), who unwisely devoted his resources to obtaining the imperial crown (1254–1273), was a man of many talents, notably in literature and jurisprudence. Under him, the Moslems and Christians in Castile lived in rare harmony, and the Jews, in language, religion, and culture intermediary between the two major groups, flourished. During Alfonso's reign, northern Europeans went to Castile to study Arabic and Hebrew science, and Spaniards, particularly Jews who had mastered Arabic, Hebrew, and Latin (along with one or more vernacular languages), went north at the behest of bishops and great lords. The bishop of Lincoln, Robert Grosseteste (who had been the first chancellor of the university at Oxford), brought together a committee of Sephardic (southern)

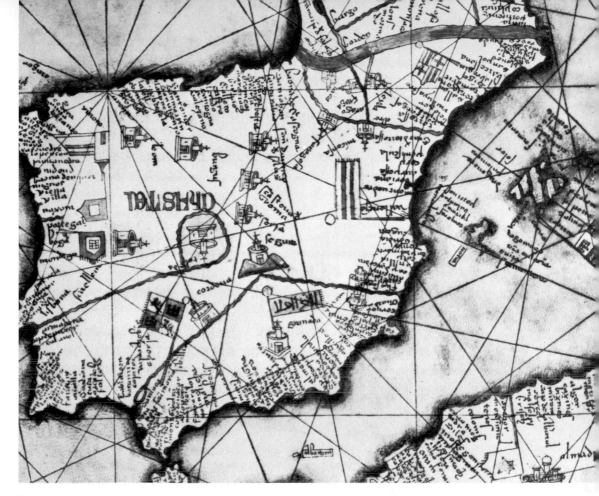

Iresques of Majorca, a Jewish cartographer, drew this map of the Iberian Peninsula in 1375. The cluster of town names along the coasts indicates the connection of such mapmaking with coastal merchant activity. The merchants knew so little about the interior that they imagined Toledo, the capital of Castile and part of the trading network, as linked to the sea by a river. Granada has an Arabic banner, signifying that it remained unconquered at this time.

Jews at Lincoln for some major scientific translating projects. Alfonso X himself participated in such activities, but his outstanding achievement was the production of a great legal code, the *Siete Partidas,* in which Castilian customs were set forth and adapted to the principles of Roman and canon law. James I of Aragón had also drafted a code of law for his conquered territories, but the Aragonese nobles who had carved out new estates successfully resisted imposition of the code, seeking instead to bring their own customary law to the new lands. The Catalans also wanted to preserve their old laws, even though James' code was advantageous for their commercial activities.

Both Castile and Aragón were disturbed by dynastic struggles in the late thirteenth and the fourteenth centuries. After Alfonso X's death, a fierce struggle erupted in Castile between the king's younger sons and the sons of his eldest son. In six of the nine reigns separating Alfonso X from Isabella (1474–1504), Castile was troubled by civil wars and court intrigues over disputed successions to the crown. In the other three reigns the heirs were minors, so the struggles revolved around control of the regency. Aragón suffered similar strife, but the tradition of dividing the kingdom among the king's sons diluted the conflicts while placing them on a much larger stage than in Castile. In the fifteenth century, under Alfonso the Magnanimous' son John II, Aragón suffered a severe civil war brought on when the Catalans revolted for independence. John II's throne tottered, but he purchased French help by ceding his claims to Roussillon, and the Catalans were finally defeated in 1472. Meanwhile, John had negotiated his greatest triumph—the marriage of his son Ferdinand with Isabella of Castile.

The constant civil strife in Castile and the prolonged revolt of the Catalans form the background for the reign of Isabella of Castile and Ferdinand of Aragón (1479–1516). The Catholic Kings, as they styled themselves, established the strong monarchy on which was based the predominance of Spain in sixteenth-century Europe. The power they attained and the methods they used make their reign a turning point in Spanish history. The territorial expansion of Spain in the Iberian Peninsula was completed by the conquest of Granada (1481–1492), the retrocession of Roussillon from France in 1494, and the conquest in 1512 of the part of Navarre lying south of the Pyrenees. Within the realm the Catholic Kings enforced a unity hitherto unknown. Catalan separatism was crushed, nobles were everywhere held in check, and Moslems and Jews were given the choice of conversion or exile. The ensuing flight of the Sephardic Jews was a blow from which Spanish economic and cultural life suffered for two centuries. To enforce unity of faith as the basis of national unity Ferdinand and Isabella gained control of the Inquisition in Spain, making it virtually a department of state. Political opponents often found themselves convicted of heresy.

The degree of unification, or of "absolutism" as the reign is frequently characterized, should not be exaggerated. The force of local custom and the strength of regional institutions and privileges remained important. Centralization was almost wholly administrative. In contrast with England, where administrative institutions were employed by royal officials to enforce a common law for the whole realm, in Spain the royal governors presided over local tribunals that enforced local custom. The *cortes* of each of the original kingdoms or principalities—Castile, Old Aragón, Valencia, and Catalonia—continued to legislate and to grant taxes for its region.

The diversity of Spanish political interests is illustrated by the projects that engaged the attention of the two Catholic Kings. Isabella, inheriting the Castilian interest in Moslem Africa and the Castilian competition with Portugal, patronized Columbus. Colonization of the New World owed much to the institutions and to the methods worked out in the Castilian settlement of the areas taken over during the *Reconquista*. Ferdinand, meanwhile, devoted his energies to Europe. Inheriting Sicily along with Aragón, he opposed French designs on the kingdom of Naples and during the subsequent Italian wars ended by becoming its king. Ferdinand brought Spain even more directly into European politics by arranging the marriage alliance between his daughter Joanna and Philip, son of the emperor, a marriage that ultimately united Spain with the Habsburg dominions in the empire and in the Low Countries.

## The East from the Fall of Jerusalem to the Fall of Constantinople

On July 4, 1187, the greatest army ever assembled by the kingdom of Jerusalem was annihilated in the Battle of Hattin. The whole history of the kingdom had been one of recurrent crises and catastrophes, but this one was the worst. The immediate cause of the defeat was division among Jerusalem's defenders, which led to a miscalculation about when and where to fight. The Latin kingdom had never had a sufficient indigenous fighting force and was dependent on Crusaders from the West. Just a few years earlier, William Marshal had spent a few seasons there. Now the motley Western army, motley in leadership as well as in the rank and file, made the mistake of going to the enemy, led by the general Saladin, instead of making him come to them. Saladin crushed the Christians at the time and place of his choosing; the bottom dropped out of the Moslem slave markets in Syria. Three months later Jerusalem fell; within the year all of the kingdom except the port of Tyre, a few isolated castles, and the northern counties was in Saladin's hands. The Latins sent another desperate appeal for succor to the West.

In 1100 the Crusaders had established a Latin kingdom based in Jerusalem that had suzerainty over the counties of Antioch and Tripoli on the coast and Edessa to the north. The kingdom had been carefully founded on an idealized model of the north European feudal kingdoms from which most of the Crusaders came. During the twelfth century, Crusaders had joined the original settlers, carving out baronies and fiefs within the territories controlled by the Westerners. The Moslems had prepared immediately to counterattack, but for many years after 1100, they were too disorganized to make an effective assault on the Christians. The most able Turkish leader, Zengi, spent most of his time gaining mastery over the other Syrian Moslem rulers and in this task he relied on the neutrality, and sometimes even the military help, of certain of the Christian lords. The Crusaders had their own domestic quarrels, and they were not above employing Turkish allies against their Christian enemies. Power politics explains more than either the Holy War or the *jihad* about the relations of the Latin kingdom with Moslem states from 1100 to 1144. In the latter year Zengi had grown powerful enough to conquer Edessa.

Apud me oracio deo uite mee: di
cam deo susceptor meus es.

The conflict between Christians and Moslems in the late twelfth century is represented by a one-to-one joust between the hero of Christendom, Richard I the Lion-Hearted, pictured as the victor, and the enemy of Christ, Saladin, who has the visage of Satan.

The fall of Edessa was recognized as a great threat to the Crusaders, since that county protected the northern flank of the kingdom. The reaction in Europe was immediate: the pope preached a new Crusade, Saint Bernard became its leading spirit, and both Louis VII of France and Conrad III of the empire took the cross. The Second Crusade (1147–1149) was inconclusive, and in some ways the net result was even harmful. The armies of Louis and Conrad were each defeated before they reached the Holy Land; the recovery of Edessa was abandoned in favor of a foolish and fruitless siege of Damascus; and the Moslems learned once and for all that the "Franks" (as all Western Europeans were called in the East) could be defeated in pitched battle. Even more significant for the future, it was now apparent that there was a split between the older Crusaders and the new. The inhabitants of Outremer had settled down in the Levant, become accustomed to the ways of the East, and learned to value their higher standard of living. The newcomers were fired by zeal to crush the infidel. The consequence was further division and dissension among the Franks.

After the Second Crusade the Moslems grew stronger under Saladin, whose strength was based on Egypt. He had spent his early years in unifying Moslem Syria and then had turned to the conquest of the kingdom of Jerusalem in 1187. The fall of Jerusalem was the occasion for the Third Crusade (1189–1192), a failure although led by Europe's three greatest monarchs. The emperor Frederick I Barbarossa died before he reached the Holy Land. Philip II Augustus of France reached the coast of Palestine, where he took part in the first phase of operations, the siege of Acre. Falling ill, and with no heart for crusading anyway, Philip returned to France. Richard I of England spent two years fighting against Saladin. The conquest of Acre and other coastal cities was made possible by naval power supplied mainly by Venice, Genoa, and Pisa—and it was the Italian merchants who gained most from the Crusade, through trading privileges in return for naval assistance. In the end, Richard was able to negotiate a treaty under which the coastal cities were returned to the kingdom, the Moslems retained the interior, and Christian pilgrims were allowed to visit Jerusalem. After the Third Crusade it was apparent to Western rulers that a united Moslem Syria could not be defeated without a major effort.

After the death of Saladin in 1193 Moslem unity broke down rapidly in a struggle for power among Saladin's brothers and sons. Conditions were ideal for a new Crusade. The emperor, Henry VI, took the cross and even sent troops on ahead to prepare the way, but he died before he could depart for the Holy Land. Crusading by emperors and kings, as in 1147 and 1189, had not been very successful, and Innocent III was not displeased that Henry VI's plans had come to naught. It was rumored that the emperor was less interested in redeeming the Holy Land than he was in conquering the Byzantine Empire and the kingdom of Jerusalem for his own rule. Innocent decided to sponsor a Crusade by lesser men in the hope that higher politics could be kept from diverting the Crusade from its real purpose. The original proposal for a new expedition came from some barons of northern France and the Low Countries, including Baldwin, count of Flanders. They asked for and immediately received papal blessings from Innocent, who then strove, but with little success, to control or at least influence the decisions of the leaders.

These barons were certainly motivated by a love of adventure, and some of them by political ambition as well, and it is doubtful that many above the rank and file were moved by any pious desire to liberate the Holy Land. Some of the main results of the Fourth "Crusade" (1202–1204) have already been discussed in Chapter 19: the agreement with Venice, the conquest of Zara, Innocent's excommunication of the whole army, and the conquest of Constantinople in 1204. The immediate instigator of this diversion of the Crusade to Constantinople was Alexius, whose father Isaac Angelus had been deposed in a palace revolution. The Crusaders agreed to restore Alexius and his father in return for substantial payments toward their indebtedness to the Venetians for transport and in return for supplies and troops to use in the reconquest of Jerusalem. An additional feature of the agreement was the reunion of the Greek and Latin churches under papal supremacy. Most of the rank and file of the Crusaders welcomed the attack on Constantinople. Western Europeans generally believed that the Byzantines were faithless allies and probably heretics, and that Constantinople should be forced to do its share in the task of freeing the Holy Land. Innocent heard of the plan and vainly prohibited the Venetians and Crusaders from attacking any Christians unless they were overtly opponents of the Crusade.

The combined sea and land attack on Constantinople was inconclusive, but it frightened the usurper into flight from the throne. The way was now open for the restoration of Isaac and his son Alexius. At this point the Crusaders suddenly realized that Alexius was in no position to keep his side of the bargain until he had consolidated his power both in Constantinople and throughout the Byzantine Empire. As the Crusaders impatiently waited for the promised money, supplies, and troops, friction developed not only between the Latins and the Greeks but also between different Greek factions. Isaac and Alexius were again deposed, the one imprisoned and the other murdered. Now, whatever had been their earlier intentions, the Crusaders and Venetians agreed to take Constantinople for themselves. The city was put to the sack. The Crusaders elected Baldwin of Flanders as emperor, divided the spoils of the city, and proceeded to conquer the European provinces of the empire. The Venetians, meanwhile, took over many of the islands and most of the trading ports as their share of the loot. This Latin Empire of Constantinople endured from 1204 until 1261, when the throne of a much diminished Byzantine Empire was regained by Michael VIII Palaeologus, a descendant of Alexius and ruler of the so-called empire of Nicaea—the unconquered part of the empire consisting mainly of the provinces in Asia Minor.

The Fifth Crusade (1217–1221) was the one Innocent had proclaimed at the Fourth Lateran Council of 1215, and the one in which Frederick II was expected to participate after taking the cross in the same year. The expectation was not fulfilled, and that was one reason for the failure of this Crusade. For some time experienced Crusaders were convinced that the key to victory in Palestine was Egypt. Egypt was both a source of reserve strength for the Moslems and a base for turning the southern flank of Moslem Syria. Hence the military effort of the Fifth Crusade was directed against Egypt's chief port of Damietta, which was taken, and then against Cairo. The Franks of Outremer were appalled by these plans, realizing the futility of any attempt to penetrate inland beyond the range of Western seapower. As they foresaw, the crusading army—whose leaders not only miscalculated the strength of their foe but also expected reinforcement from Frederick II at any moment— was caught between a Moslem army and a flooding Nile. Disaster was averted only by the fact that Damietta was securely in Christian hands and could thus be traded to the infidel in return for the safe retreat of the invading force. For the failure of the Fifth Crusade the papal legate in charge blamed Frederick II; the Franks of Outremer blamed the fatuous strategy of the legate. Meanwhile, the Moslems were vastly relieved to be able to resume normal trading relations with the Italian merchants who, like the Moslems, deplored any interference with their lucrative commerce.

Frederick II finally did fulfill his Crusader's vow, although under somewhat bizarre circumstances. The emperor secured possession of Jerusalem in 1229 by treaty with the infidel and then crowned himself king—since he was excommunicated no prelate would officiate at the coronation. Jerusalem was placed under an interdict for his impious act. Frederick's success by negotia-

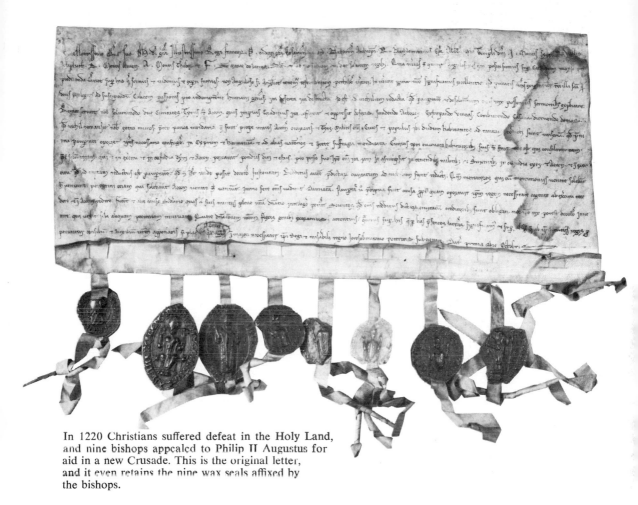

In 1220 Christians suffered defeat in the Holy Land, and nine bishops appealed to Philip II Augustus for aid in a new Crusade. This is the original letter, and it even retains the nine wax seals affixed by the bishops.

tion, where his predecessors had failed in warfare, was the measure of Moslem division and weakness after the death of Saladin. The Moslems were unable even to take advantage of the civil wars among the Christians, which began as a reaction against Frederick's attempt to curtail the privileges of the barons in the Latin kingdom and to transform it into a centralized state on the model of his kingdom of Sicily. The struggle against Frederick's absentee absolutism degenerated into a simple struggle for power among the lords of Outremer. Christian lords and Moslem potentates alike shifted their loyalties as circumstances of the moment dictated. A few Crusaders from Western Europe arrived at intervals, but they were simply absorbed into the local political turmoil. The surprising fact is that in this period, from Frederick's departure in 1229 until the arrival of Saint Louis in 1248, the Latin states not only survived but were enlarged.

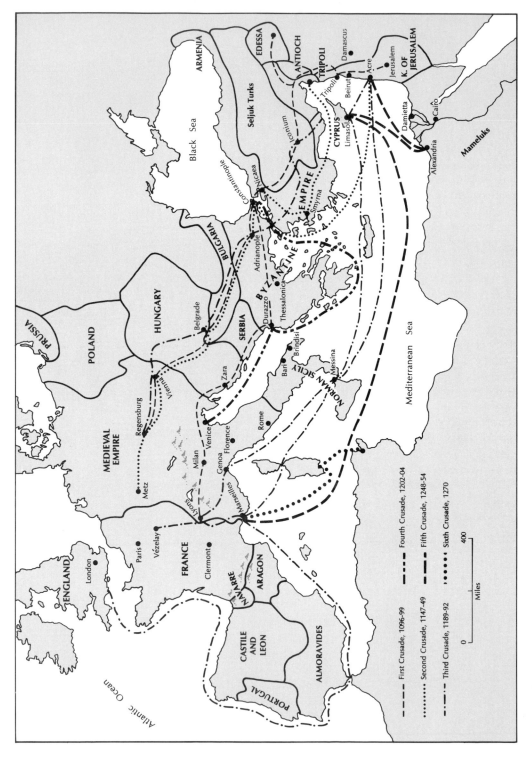

The Crusades

ARMENIA

Black Sea

Seljuk Turks

EDESSA

ANTIOCH

Damascus

TRIPOLI

Iconium

Tripoli

Beirut

Acre

Jerusalem

K. OF
JERUSALEM

CYPRUS

Limasol

Damietta

Cairo

Alexandria

Mameluks

Smyrna

Nicaea

Constantinople

BYZANTINE EMPIRE

BULGARIA

Adrianople

Thessalonica

HUNGARY

Belgrade

Durazzo

SERBIA

POLAND

PRUSSIA

Zara

Bari

Brindisi

NORMAN SICILY

Messina

Vienna

Regensburg

MEDIEVAL
EMPIRE

Venice

Milan

Rome

Florence

Genoa

Mediterranean Sea

Lyons

Metz

Marseilles

Vézelay

Paris

FRANCE

Clermont

NAVARRE

ARAGON

ENGLAND

London

CASTILE
AND
LEON

PORTUGAL

ALMORAVIDES

Atlantic Ocean

First Crusade, 1096–99

Second Crusade, 1147–49

Third Crusade, 1189–92

Fourth Crusade, 1202–04

Fifth Crusade, 1248–54

Sixth Crusade, 1270

400

Miles

0

The major event of the years following Frederick's Crusade was the capture of Jerusalem once more by the Moslems in 1244. This called forth the last major Crusade, Louis' first expedition (1248–1254). It followed the same course as the Fifth Crusade, the easy capture of Damietta and an invasion of Egypt ending in disaster. The army extricated itself only by surrendering Damietta and paying a huge ransom. Louis stayed on in the kingdom of Jerusalem for four years, but his efforts did little to strengthen the Latin principalities or to end their petty struggles. Louis' second expedition was diverted to Tunisia; his death while there (in 1270) sealed the failure of the Crusade. Saint Louis was the last of the real Crusaders, although expeditions continued to go out to the Levant from time to time.

Between Louis' first and second Crusades, Islam itself suffered a severe shock—the invasion of the Mongols, who captured Baghdad and destroyed the caliphate. The Mongol conquest was not permanent however. The Mameluk Turk Baybars led a successful counterattack from the sultanate he had established in Egypt during Saint Louis' first Crusade, and soon the Abbasid caliphs were reestablished in Cairo, although real power was held by the sultan. This sultanate, which controlled Egypt, Syria, and the Islamic east, lasted until 1517, when the Ottoman Turks finally destroyed it and took the caliphate for themselves. After 1291 the only Christian outpost in the Levant was the island of Cyprus.

The thirteenth century was also the crucial turning point in the history of the Byzantine Empire. The Latin Empire of Constantinople was actually nothing but a congeries of loosely knit feudal principalities incapable of united action. The restoration of the Palaeologi in 1261 did not restore Byzantine power. Many of the Frankish states held out against the Greeks, some of them until the end of the fourteenth century. The Byzantine state, for centuries the bulwark of Christendom against invasion from the East, had been irreparably weakened. Its Balkan provinces had largely been absorbed first by the kingdom of Bulgaria and later by the kingdom of Serbia, which reached its height under Stephen Dushan (1331–1355). Stephen's kingdom extended from the Danube to the Aegean. But an even greater threat to the Byzantine state rose in the East. For a decade or two it appeared that the Mongols would be that threat. However, the combination of Mameluk resistance and internal difficulties in their own sprawling empire kept the Mongols from establishing more than temporary control of part of Asia Minor.

It was one of the peoples displaced from their homeland in central Asia during the Mongol expansion that finally destroyed the Byzantine Empire— the Ottoman Turks. Appearing first in Asia Minor as mercenary troops, by the opening years of the fourteenth century they had built their own independent state and had expanded at the expense of both the Greeks and the independent Moslem states. They entered Europe in 1354 as the allies of the Byzantine Empire, now threatened by the expanding kingdom of Serbia. The Ottomans ended the threat from Serbia and crushed the kingdom of Bulgaria as well.

The orders of religious knights, such as the Templars and the Hospitallers, were established to protect pilgrims traveling to and in the Holy Land. To accomplish this, they built powerful castles like this one in Lebanon, the *Krak des Chevaliers,* which guarded the northern approach to Palestine. Many of these fortresses withstood the Moslems long after the rest of the Holy Land had fallen to them.

But then they settled down and held their conquests as an independent Ottoman state. By the end of the fourteenth century they had subjugated most of the Balkans and Greece and had resumed the conquest of the rest of Asia Minor.

At this point, with almost all its provinces lost, Constantinople got a respite. The Ottomans were proceeding methodically with the reduction of Asia Minor when there suddenly appeared a new invasion from central Asia, under Tamerlane. In 1401 Tamerlane overran Syria; the next year his army swept through Asia Minor, where it met the Ottoman Turks in the great Battle of Ankara. It took the Ottomans a generation to recover from the loss of manpower suffered in this crushing defeat. And yet the Ottoman Empire did not collapse. Tamerlane's interests turned to China, and when he died three years later his empire disintegrated. The emperor at Constantinople was too weak to take full advantage of this last opportunity to stop the Ottoman rise. A few provinces were reconquered but were soon lost again, and under

Murad II (1421–1451) the Ottoman Empire was pulled firmly together for a new phase of expansion. Murad's enemies included Venice, Albania, a much diminished Serbia, Hungary, and Poland. These states were reinforced by some Western troops under papal sponsorship of a Crusade against the Turk. The decisive battle was fought at Varna (1444) in Bulgaria. When the Ottomans won, they were free to complete their reconquest of Greece and the Balkans, and to turn finally to another attack on Constantinople.

If the so-called Crusade of Varna had come a generation earlier, when the Turks were weak, rather than as a response to growing Turkish strength, the course of Eastern European history might have been different. As it was, the final siege and capture of Constantinople was a fairly easy task for Mohammed II the Conqueror (1451–1481), who justified his sobriquet by further conquests in Europe and in Asia. Serbia and Albania were subjugated; Venetian control of the Aegean islands was restricted; Armenia was overrun; and the Crimea came under Ottoman rule.

The fall of Constantinople was thus only an incident in the rise of the Ottoman Empire, an incident that did not materially alter the balance of political power in the East. Nor did it have much effect on the economic life of the area, for the Italians—even the Venetians to some extent—were soon able to resume their normal trading relations with the markets and ports of the Levant. But as a symbol of the rise of Moslem power in the East, as a symbol of the threat to the Christian West, the fall of Constantinople created a sensation. For half a century after 1453 each pope proclaimed a Crusade against the Turk, but the secular rulers were too much concerned with their own affairs to worry about the Turkish peril. In the centuries-long struggle between Christendom and Islam, the offensive had long since shifted to the Moslems, and the fall of Constantinople did not change that fact. The fall of Jerusalem in 1187 and the Battle of Varna in 1444 were more significant, as turning points in the general course of European expansion, than was the fall of Constantinople. The future of European expansion lay with the policy of the monarchs of Spain and Portugal—with the discovery of new worlds, not with the resumption of the Holy War against the infidel. Europe was reorienting itself.

## Eastern Europe: The Golden Horde and the Rise of the Principality of Moscow

On the whole, historians of Western Europe pay little attention to a development that Westerners in the thirteenth century thought was a major threat to the very existence of their culture: the sudden and ominous rise of the Mongol empire of Genghis Khan (1167–1227). The Great Khan's empire was far larger than the ancient empires of Alexander the Great or of Rome, and it was considered the most serious threat ever to rise on Europe's frontier. Yet,

566 SPAIN, THE MEDITERRANEAN, AND THE EAST

as quickly as the threat materialized, it vanished, leaving as its most enduring monument the establishment of the principality of Moscow.

In the twelfth century the Mongols lived in the northern parts of east-central Asia. They were one of a half-dozen nomad tribes, each consisting of several independent or semi-independent clans, that inhabited the steppes of central Asia. The earliest years of the rule of Genghis Khan are reminiscent of Clovis the Frank. By success in a local feud, by assassination or betrayal, by diplomatic agreement adhered to as long as it was profitable—in fact, by any means fair or foul—Genghis Khan clawed his way upward in the politics of the steppes until in 1206 he was recognized as supreme ruler of all the Mongol clans and several of the neighboring tribes. At this point in his career he defined the policies that were to remain basic in the Mongol empire as it grew. The clan and tribal organization of subject people was recognized and confirmed, thus preserving the semblance of local autonomy. The central government demanded little, but what it demanded was categorically required of all subjects: tribute, military service from all adult males, and unqualified submission to the criminal, property, and commercial laws laid down by the will of the Khan. On the one hand, Genghis Khan offered to his subject clans their fair share of the booty of conquered enemies. On the other hand, subjects who did not entirely submit to his will in all things were in danger of complete destruction of their lives and property.

The system worked remarkably well—under a leader like Genghis Khan, that is. The hardened nomads of the central Asian plains needed a leader to fear and respect. They admired the Khan's brilliantly conceived and daring campaigns as much as they loved the booty of conquest. During their conquests, they won a reputation for extreme brutality. The Mongol camp after a victory in the field was a sadist's delight. Terror was their ally. They usually outnumbered their enemies in any given battle, and they always struck swiftly, depending on the speed and endurance of their tough little horses to carry them far into enemy territory before an adequate defense could be organized. Their campaigns probably killed more people than any war prior to the twentieth century.

After 1206 Mongol power expanded in every direction. The Chin empire of northern China put up the best and longest resistance, and the Mongols did not completely control it until 1226, a year before Genghis' death. Meanwhile, the Mongols conquered Korea, overran various tribal states in central and eastern Asia, such as that of the Tartars, and invaded the far-flung dominions of the Moslem Khwarismian Turks, the largest and most powerful kingdom in the Middle East. This Khwarismian campaign (1219–1222) was the Mongols' finest hour. At the city of Bokhara the Turkish garrison resisted stoutly; all who survived were butchered. At Samarkand the Turks surrendered their city without a fight and offered to join the Mongols; they were all put to death. As Genghis told them, they were obviously unreliable if they would desert their master, and he had no use for treacherous

The Asian armies of the khans that invaded Eastern Europe, Russia, and the Moslem lands from the late twelfth through the fourteenth century were based on mounted bowmen. These light-armored warriors rode small, swift horses that allowed them much maneuverability. The Asians' greatest advantage was the speed with which they struck and retreated and the fear they inspired as stories of their ferocity spread.

soldiers. Some cities were spared, but not the city of Bamian, where the Turks put up a magnificent stand. The Khan's grandson was among those slain. For this unpardonable error of judgment, no living creature—two- or four-legged —was allowed to survive.

An incident of the Khwarismian campaign led to the first appearance of the Mongols in Europe. With a Mongol army in hot pursuit, the Khwarismian ruler fled westward, only to die on a little island in the Caspian Sea in 1220. The frustrated Mongols decided to scout out the area before returning to central Asia. They sacked several towns south of the Caspian and then moved northward into Georgia, between the Caspian and the Black seas. Here in 1221 they defeated the Georgians and moved farther northward into the plains of southern Russia, between the Volga and the Don. Pressing westward across the Don, the Mongols were met by a combined army of most of the Russian princes from as far as Kiev. At the Battle of the Kalka River (1223), north of the Black Sea, these Russians were routed. The Mongols, who were now about a thousand miles away from where they had planned to be, contented themselves with pillaging the Crimea before returning eastward to the Siberian steppes.

The return of the Mongols to Asia, and the death of Genghis Khan in 1227, gave Eastern Europe a respite. After the death of each khan a great assembly of the leading Mongols was held to select a new khan and to divide the empire among the relatives of the succeeding ruler. All this took time, since the assembly was held in the original homeland of the Mongols, and it was a leisurely affair. In 1237 the Mongols reappeared in Eastern Europe. Led by Batu, grandson of Genghis Khan, the Tartars (as Westerners called the Mongols) swarmed all over Russia. Most cities were sacked and laid waste, whether they resisted or submitted. At Kiev, the leading city and seat of Russia's strongest principality, the destruction of life and property was almost complete. From Kiev the Mongols raided far into Poland, Silesia, and Hungary, and in 1242 a Mongol reconnaissance even reached the shores of the Adriatic.

At this point, by a stroke of luck for the Europeans, the great khan died, and Batu hurried eastward to attend the assembly where a successor would be chosen. Mongol garrisons were left at strategic points in Russia, but the threat to central Europe had passed. When Batu returned to Russia, he and his successors established the khanate of the Golden Horde (Russian *Zolotaya Orda,* the word *orda* (horde) means "a tribal group of Mongolian nomads"), as one of the half-dozen khanates into which the Mongol empire was divided under the supreme rule of the great khan. The fact that Kublai Khan (1257–1294), the last truly great Mongol ruler, spent most of his reign in China meant that the western khanates were practically free to pursue an independent course. The Golden Horde continued to dominate most of central, southern, and eastern Russia until well into the fifteenth century.

In the twelfth and thirteenth centuries, several Russian principalities had competed with Kiev for hegemony. The Golden Horde put an end to their competition. Each state was required to produce its quota of tribute. Occasional marauding expeditions by the Mongols kept the principalities in line and made sure that the tribute was paid on time. The influence of the Mongol domination on the development of Russia is a question of great controversy among historians. Perhaps the safest conclusion is that the "Tartar yoke" did not fundamentally alter the nature of Russian religious, social, and even local political institutions, or culture. The Russians were not "Mongolized," but two centuries of subordination leaves its mark on a nation's development. The later rise of the principality of Moscow owed something to the Mongol methods of conquering and organizing subject peoples. Beyond that, the initial shock of the Mongol invasion disrupted the economic life of Russia for at least a generation, and the continuing payment of tribute to the Mongols was a nonproductive drain on the income and wealth of the Russian peoples.

A special position among Russian principalities was occupied by Novgorod in the northwest. The terrain of this state protected it from Mongol conquest; its extensive commerce made it wealthy; and its republican form of government guaranteed the control of policy by a mercantile oligarchy that elected the prince. The greatest of Novgorod's princes was Alexander Nevsky, who not only led the resistance against the Mongols but also defended Russia against encroachment from the West. In 1240 at the Battle of the Neva River he defeated the Swedish effort to expand eastward. Two years later at the Battle of Lake Peipus he defeated a similar effort by the Knights of the Teutonic Order. The expansion of the Knights was thus limited to Prussia and the Baltic lands west of Lake Peipus. His prestige high, Alexander then was appointed Grand Prince of Vladimir (1246–1263), and in this position he became the chief spokesman for all the Russian princes in their relations with the Golden Horde. The Tartars, who were never expert in administrative or financial affairs, were satisfied to deal with their subjects through the Grand Prince as their deputy. The first Russian Grand Prince to use this authority effectively was Ivan I of Moscow (1328–1341).

The principality of Moscow had recovered from the Mongol inundation rather better than other areas, primarily because it was favorably situated to profit from the river trade in the heart of Great Russia. The princes of Moscow in the thirteenth century, among whom was a son of Alexander Nevsky, eschewed higher politics and contented themselves with building up their own local power until Ivan I felt strong enough to make the office of Grand Prince an instrument of further aggrandizement. Ivan was granted permission by the Tartars to be the sole tribute-collector for all the Russian states, and he also secured the succession of his own son to the office of Grand Prince. The princes of Moscow built their power on this office and on the support of the Church, whose metropolitan held the see of Moscow and whose teachings promoted the unity of Slavic Christendom. In disputes with other princes, the rulers of Moscow could rely on the support of the Church, whose power was enhanced by the Tartar policy exempting the clergy and their property from tribute. If a dispute among princes concerned the amount of tribute to be collected, the Grand Prince of Moscow could rely on the military assistance of the Tartars. Rather than suffer such a catastrophe, the other princes gradually recognized the superior authority of the ruler of Moscow to adjudicate disputes among them.

The first efforts by Russian princes to free themselves from the "Tartar yoke" began in the second half of the fourteenth century. Up to this time the princes of Moscow had been thoroughly subservient to the Golden Horde, for obvious reasons. But in 1380 Grand Prince Dimitri of the Don (1359–1389) put Moscow at the head of a grand coalition of princes and defeated the Tartars in a great battle on the Don River. Although the Golden Horde suppressed this revolt within three years, the battle was important in the growth

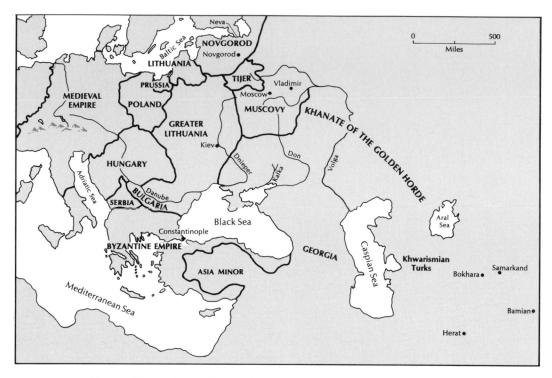

Eastern Europe in the Later Middle Ages

of Russian nationalism, and it indicated that Muscovite leadership was necessary for ultimate victory against the Tartars. That the princes of Moscow retained the office of Grand Prince after 1380 was the happy result of a series of crises that weakened the Golden Horde. Civil wars were followed by subjection of the Horde to Tamerlane at the end of the century. In the fifteenth century, the history of the Tartars in Russia is a complicated story of intrigues for power, civil wars, and an inevitable decline. It was the weakness of the Tartars rather than Russian strength that led to the gradual reduction of tribute, and then to the final repudiation of all Tartar rule in 1480, exactly one century after the Battle of the Don.

The rise of Moscow after 1380 was by no means sure and certain. As the "Tartar yoke" grew lighter, civil strife among the boyars, or greater nobles, increased. Even more ominous, a new power loomed in the west. The kingdom of Lithuania, dynastically united with the kingdom of Poland, expanded eastward and southward into Russia during the fifteenth century. Not until the reign of Ivan III the Great (1462–1505) was it clear that a strong Russian state could be built on the principality of Moscow. Ivan III consolidated the piecemeal conquests of his predecessors, threw back the Lithuanians, and forced the other princes to recognize his superiority. To his title of Grand Prince he added the more resounding title of Autocrat of all the Russias.

The Orthodox Church in Russia was centered in Moscow, and in the battle against the Lithuanians, the Grand Prince could enlist the support of the metropolitan to defeat what the Church considered an invasion from the West; the Lithuanians were Latin Christians. After the fall of Constantinople, the metropolitan of Moscow claimed to be head of the Greek Orthodox Church. Thus when Ivan III began to build his power, he did it from the "Third Rome," the mother of the Eastern churches, and this link with religious authority greatly enhanced his own image, now analogous to the old Byzantine emperors.

### Suggestions for Further Reading

**Secondary Works** The works of Altamira and Chaytor cited at the end of Chapter 13 are relevant to medieval Spain. See also the important work of R. I. Burns, *The Crusader Kingdom of Valencia: Reconstruction on a Thirteenth-Century Frontier* (Cambridge, Mass., 1967), and K. M. Setton, *Catalan Domination of Athens, 1311–1388* (Cambridge, Mass., 1948). On the East and the later Crusades, see A. S. Atiya, *The Crusades in the Later Middle Ages* (London, 1938); E. Bradford, *The Great Betrayal* (London, 1967), which treats the Fourth Crusade; D. J. Geanakoplos, *Emperor Michael Palaeologus and the West, 1258–1282* (Cambridge, 1959); S. Runciman, *The Fall of Constantinople, 1453* (Cambridge, 1965); and the excellent study of the Eastern Empire in transition by S. Vryonis, *The Decline of Medieval Hellenism in Asia Minor and the Process of Islamization from the Eleventh through the Fifteenth Century* (Berkeley and Los Angeles, 1971). S. Runciman, *A History of the First Bulgarian Empire* (London, 1930), and F. Nowak, *Medieval Slavdom and the Rise of Russia* (New York, 1930) are good studies of Eastern Europe and Russia; more detailed accounts are G. Vernadsky, *Ancient Russia* (New Haven, Conn., 1943), *Kievan Russia* (New Haven, Conn., 1948), and *The Mongols and Russia* (New Haven, Conn., 1953).

**Sources** *The Chronicle of James I, King of Aragon,* trans. J. Forster, 2 vols. (London, 1883) is the Conqueror's own account of the *Reconquista* during the thirteenth century. On the Crusades, see the sources cited at the end of Chapter 13, and on the Fourth Crusade, see *Villehardouin: Chronicle of the Fourth Crusade,* trans. F. Marzials (London, 1908), and *The Conquest of Constantinople: Robert of Clari,* trans. E. H. McNeal (New York, 1936). The work of John of Joinville on Louis IX, cited at the end of Chapter 20, contains a history of the king's Crusades.

# VI THE FOURTEENTH AND FIFTEENTH CENTURIES

# 24 England and France in the Later Middle Ages

In the later Middle Ages, Europeans confronted difficulties and disorders more serious than those of any period since the disintegration of the Carolingian empire. During the fourteenth and fifteenth centuries many institutions and values characteristic of medieval civilization were transformed, and new conditions appeared that marked the transition to modern times. It was not an especially happy or optimistic age.

Economic conditions had a great deal to do with the troubles that Europeans experienced in the period. The increase in wealth and population that had been fairly steady since the eleventh century was not maintained after the generation of Dante, Boniface VIII, Philip the Fair, and Edward I. Some of the achievements of that age had to be paid for at a price that later generations found burdensome. For example, the growth of the national monarchies entailed expenses of government and of foreign policy that presupposed the ability and willingness of subjects to pay high taxes. The failures of the late thirteenth century had repercussions from which Europe suffered during the fourteenth and fifteenth centuries, notably the failure of the Church to maintain its moral and spiritual leadership of a united Christendom. These generalizations apply to the period as a whole and to Europe as a whole.

In Western Europe the most dramatic event of the later Middle Ages was the conflict between France and England called the Hundred Years' War. The causes of this war were not new. Some of the issues dated back to the Norman Conquest, but none of them was beyond amicable settlement. The results of the Hundred Years' War permanently affected the future of Europe. Both nations, whose internal affairs had been complicated for centuries by the English position in southwestern France, were now free to develop independently, and this "national disentanglement" ushered in a new phase of European nationalism. Another result was the recuperation of the French monarchy from a state of almost chronic crisis. By the end of the fifteenth century the kings of France possessed more power than any of their predecessors. In England failure in war produced an acute crisis from which the monarchy had to recover or else suffer eclipse. The result was the strong monarchy of the Tudors. In each country the monarchy not only survived the disorders of the later Middle Ages but became the center and basis of the national state in modern times.

## The Hundred Years' War:
## The First Phase

In France and England the predominant position of the monarchy under Philip the Fair and Edward I was achieved primarily at the expense of the papacy and the nobility. Against the papacy both monarchs were supported by their nobility and even by the majority of their clergy. In the fourteenth century the nobles of each country made strenuous efforts to redress the balance of power in their own favor.

The fourteenth-century kings depended as much on the nobility as on the recently developed bureaucracies. The nobles and the Church, whose greatest personages were among the king's tenants-in-chief, controlled by far the largest share of the wealth, and thus any successful program of taxation depended on their cooperation. The nobles still formed the core of the royal army, which was no longer the feudal host of old but an army of mercenary soldiers whom the nobles were commissioned to recruit, train, provision, and lead in the name of the king. The nobility took every opportunity to enhance its power. In the fourteenth and fifteenth centuries, however, aristocratic opposition to the monarchies was almost invariably opportunistic and irresponsible. In England the barons of 1215, 1258, and 1297 had been motivated by some notion of constitutional principles, even if not very articulate and scarcely going beyond the belief that government should be limited by law. It is difficult to see in the aristocratic revolts after Edward I's reign anything more than a struggle for power and an effort by the nobles to seize control of the royal administration for their personal benefit.

The reaction against the growing power of the monarchy in England built up quickly under Edward II (1307–1327). The situation called for a forceful ruler. The government was burdened with huge debts; the Scots were far from subdued; and the nobles were restless and resentful. But Edward II was weak-willed and frivolous, idle and incompetent. It was a medieval king's business to govern, but this king left the government to civil servants and personal favorites. A group of the barons, called the Lords Ordainers, forced Edward to accept the Ordinances of 1311, which severely curtailed the governmental powers of the royal household and required the approval of the magnates in parliament for appointment of the greater officers of state and for important policy decisions. Edward hoped to regain some power by a successful campaign against the Scots, but the disastrous defeat of his army at Bannockburn in 1314 ensured Scottish independence and discredited both the king and the barons of England. Although the barons now dominated the government; their incompetence and selfishness were so obvious that a moderate royalist party was able to restore the king to power in 1322. At the parliament held at York that year Edward enacted a statute declaring null and void the Ordinances of 1311 and any similar future provisions, but also recognizing that important legislation should be enacted by the king in parliament with the consent of those summoned and present "as it hath been hitherto accustomed." After this royalist restoration, the king again fell under the influence of favorites, and the tragicomedy of his reign was climaxed when Queen Isabella ran off with her paramour, Mortimer, and then returned to lead a successful rebellion against her husband. For the first time since the days of the Anglo-Saxons, an anointed king was deposed.

Edward III (1327–1377) succeeded as a minor, while Isabella and Mortimer controlled the throne to their own advantage. In 1330 the young king was able to throw off their tutelage in a *coup d'état* that cost Mortimer his life and Isabella her freedom. The early years of Edward III were auspicious. He revived the royal household as the center of government and temporarily appeased the barons by yielding on minor issues. On major issues he made promises that he later failed to keep. Personally Edward III was popular with the nobles, whose interests and tastes he shared. He gave England the solace of a victory over the Scots, at Halidon Hill in 1333, although the battle led to no permanent results. But the campaigns of the early 1330s made Edward recognize that foreign adventures could distract his nobles from domestic grievances that had disrupted his father's reign.

The basic conditions for war between France and England had existed since 1204, when Philip Augustus conquered Normandy. The Treaty of Paris (1259) had brought peace but had not removed the sources of conflict. War had broken out sporadically under both Edward I and Edward II, but neither they nor the French kings were in a position to carry through a major campaign. The main grievance of the English was the continuing pressure by French kings to assert their authority over Gascony—the greater part of the old duchy of Aquitaine—in much the same manner that the English kings asserted their rights over Scotland. Added to this were the French support of the Scots against England and the English support of the Flemings against France, plus the interminable squabbles of sailors on both sides of the Channel. These sailors were little more than pirates whose misdeeds both monarchs could disown when convenient. The only undeniable difference of national interests lay in the English dependence on Flanders as the major market for English wool production and the necessity of protecting and preserving that market, as against the French determination to dominate if not absorb Flanders because of its lucrative trade and industry. But it would be a distortion to portray the Hundred Years' War as growing out of any real economic necessity on the part of either country. The problem of Gascony alone was sufficient reason for war, as soon as a king of either nation desired war.

Edward III and his contemporary Philip VI of Valois (1328–1350) were both eager to go to war. Philip was a man of about the same romantic and chivalrous mettle as Edward, and he too recognized the usefulness of foreign adventure for preventing aristocratic discontent at home. Philip precipitated hostilities in 1337 by declaring Gascony forfeit because of a defect in Edward's oath of homage. But the first action took place in Flanders, which was always vital to English military planning. In friendly hands it provided a secure flank that made possible an attack from the north in combination with an invasion directed toward Paris from Gascony. The count of Flanders remained loyal to his lord, Philip VI, but the working classes and some of the merchants wanted to throw off French control. In 1339 their spokesman, Jacques van Artevelde, negotiated an alliance with Edward III by which Edward agreed to provide military aid and to guarantee a steady supply of English wool for Flemish looms. In return, the Flemings recognized Edward as lawful king of France. Thus an essentially old-fashioned feudal war over conflicting jurisdictions became a dynastic war of conquest.

Edward's claim to the French crown descended through his mother, Isabella, daughter of Philip the Fair. Philip VI was the son of Philip the Fair's younger brother. Hence Edward was a nephew of the last three kings of France, while Philip was their cousin; Edward was a grandson of Philip the Fair, while Philip was a grandson of Philip III, the father of Philip the Fair. No matter how the lawyers figured these relationships, Edward Plantagenet stood one degree nearer the throne of France than Philip of Valois. But Edward's claim had two fatal flaws. First, it descended through a female. The daughters of the last three kings had all been excluded from the succession, and French lawyers argued that one who could not inherit a claim could not transmit that claim. Second, and much more serious, Edward was king of England, and the French royal council would not accept the duke of Aquitaine and hereditary enemy of the Capetians as ruler of France. Thus the house of Valois replaced the house of Capet.

The military side of the Hundred Years' War can be summarized in the statement that the English won most of the battles and the French won the war. The end result reflected the fact that the kings of England during he period had at their disposal approximately one-third of the resources in manpower and wealth at the disposal of the French kings. During the first phase of the war (1337–1360) the English army applied brilliantly the new weapons and tactics that they had learned to use during the battles against Welshmen and Scots in the preceding half-century. Chief among the new weapons was the longbow and the pike, which was not new but which the English used in ways new to the French.

The first great English victory illustrates the tactical advances they had made. In the summer of 1346 the English were retreating after a fruitless expedition aimed at Paris, when they were overtaken by a superior French force at Crécy. Edward dismounted his knights and took up a defensive position on a slope protected on one flank by a stream and on the other by a rise of ground. His archers were ranged on the flanks of each of the three divisions of his army. The French army began arriving toward mid-afternoon, but rather than wait to organize his attack properly, Philip threw his cavalry against the English in piecemeal fashion, as each major contingent arrived. The English archers slaughtered each succeeding wave of charging horsemen. The few French knights who got through the rain of arrows found their mounts gutted on the ends of anchored pikes or sharpened logs, making it impossible to escape being killed or captured by the English knights and men-at-arms. The French far outnumbered the English, but because the French cavalry was committed only one part at a time, the numerical advantage at any given point in the battle was with the English.

Before the French had recovered from the defeat at Crécy, Edward was able to take the port of Calais (1347) and thus secure a base on the coast for future operations. However, the Black Death (1348–1349) intervened, and it was several years before either side could put a large force in the field again. When hostilities were resumed France had a new king who was even less able than Philip VI. This was John the Good (1350–1364), whose sobriquet referred not to his merit or virtue but expressed the sense of the phrase "good fellow." In 1356 John caught an army led by Edward, the Black Prince, heir to the English crown, near Poitiers. The whole story of Crécy was repeated, except that most of the French knights dismounted and advanced over broken country for a mile before engaging the waiting English army. Some knights survived the hail of arrows, but they were so exhausted from marching in full armor that they were no match for the outnumbered English knights and pikemen. The Battle of Poitiers was another resounding defeat for the French, climaxed by the capture of King John himself.

France suffered greatly during these wars, and the war was harder on noncombatants than on the soldiers. To the usual ravages of medieval war, in which armies lived off the countryside to the detriment of the peasants, were added the terrors of the Black Death and a new emphasis by the English leaders on systematic destruction. The English were unable to field large armies of conquest, but they regularly sent out raiding armies that destroyed everything in their path. The list of ecclesiastical buildings alone destroyed during the whole Hundred Years' War, compiled by a late–nineteenth-century French historian, fills two large folio volumes. The uncounted villages and farmhouses destroyed would require many times that space. After the defeat at Poitiers, the prestige of the French monarchy and the nobility sank to a new low. But the need for more money and for labor services to rebuild or shore up the defensive strongholds of the monarchy and nobles was now acute. Accordingly, the Dauphin, the captured king's eldest son, whose appanage was the county surrounding Vienne called the Dauphiné, commanded the peasants to work on the castles and for the townspeople to contribute money. This demand led to a great peasant rebellion, the *Jacquerie,* in 1358. It was a bloody, antinoble uprising in which hundreds of nobles and members of their families died and their houses were burned. In Paris a revolutionary communal movement led by Étienne Marcel extracted privileges from and forced reforms on the government of the Dauphin. Marcel, who was a wealthy cloth merchant and a rabble-rousing demagogue, certainly had political ambitions for himself, but his reforms were also designed to strengthen the inefficient and wasteful royal government. The Dauphin, thoroughly terrified, lived out the storm of unrest and finally suppressed the revolutionists, but he also adopted their program for a stronger government. Meanwhile, his father enjoyed his pleasant and honorable captivity in England.

At this low point in French fortunes the first phase of the Hundred Years' War ended by the Treaty of Brétigny-Calais (1360). A huge ransom was fixed for King John. John ceded to Edward all the Gascon lands in dispute. In addition, Edward acquired Calais and Ponthieu, the county in which Crécy was situated, and the two monarchs agreed that when these conditions had been fulfilled—the ransom paid and the territories actually transferred—they would make a simultaneous renunciation. Edward was to renounce his claim to the French crown; John was to renounce his suzerainty over all the lands Edward held in France. If carried out, the Treaty of Brétigny-Calais would have effected a general pacification, and Edward would have traded a nebulous claim to the throne for full sovereignty over more than one-third of France. Actually neither side was eager to fulfill the terms. Edward took advantage of the failure of the French to pay the ransom to try to negotiate a revision of terms that would be still more favorable to the English. The French welcomed this or any other delay as an excuse to postpone carrying out the original terms. When one of the French hostages held by the English escaped from custody, King John, chivalrous to the last, felt honor bound to return to captivity. He died in London in 1364, and the Treaty of Brétigny-Calais became a dead letter.

## England to the Accession of Henry Tudor

Success in war made Edward III a popular king. The nobles profited from the booty and ransoms of the French campaigns. For a time at least, the war was welcomed by the middle and lower classes. The Flemish wool market was preserved for the merchants; soldiering and pillage in France had far greater appeal for many peasants than did the drudgery of field work at home. The cost of war was borne willingly as long as conquests in France held out prospects of ultimate victory. But after the Treaty of Brétigny-Calais these prospects dimmed. War was resumed in 1369, and by the end of the reign of Edward III only Calais and the region around Bordeaux in the southwest remained under English control. Ever since the Black Death had struck England in 1349, the country had been suffering from economic dislocation, and to this was now added a veterans' problem. Soldiers returning from overseas were usually unskilled except in the use of arms. Most of them were former peasants who did not relish a return to their former status. Some veterans became outlaws, pillaging the English countryside in the fashion they had learned in France. Others hired themselves out to ambitious lords who needed armed retainers to advance their power in the counties or to support them against other nobles.

Under these unsettled conditions, opposition to the monarchy increased during the last decades of the reign of Edward III. This resistance was focused in parliament, for a meeting of that body brought together most of the nobles, and it was only their opposition, or opposition of a significant faction of them, that could be dangerous. Thus parliament, which Edward I had shaped as an agency of royal power, became under his successors a means of resisting royal power. The financial straits of the government forced Edward III to convoke parliament frequently in order to obtain money for his wars. He tried other means of raising taxes, but the parliamentary subsidy was the most profitable and encountered the least resistance. By the end of the reign the standard form of taxation had become the grant by parliament of one-fifteenth of the value of the movable goods or personal property from the inhabitants of the counties and one-tenth from those who lived in boroughs.

During the reign of Edward III the Commons in Parliament gained certain powers and rights that became a real limitation on the king. Chief of these was the Commons' control of direct taxation. The king had other ways of raising taxes than by parliamentary grant, but the Commons remonstrated over every arbitrary levy or tax granted by a nonparliamentary group, and at the same time were liberal in consenting to taxes granted in Parliament, so that finally the king gave up trying to raise money in any other way than by the consent of the Commons and the Lords in Parliament. From this effective, if not exclusive, control of taxation grew the Commons' later right to withhold taxes until the fulfillment of specified conditions. This right in turn led ultimately to the principles that redress of grievances must precede supply,

Edward III was a heroic king who led his country to victory over the French in the first phase of the Hundred Years' War. This gilt-bronze effigy of him in Westminster Abbey (by John Orchard) captures a different aspect of his character—the wise judge, protector of his people, God's vicar.

and that money bills must originate in the Commons. The Commons also claimed, and sometimes made good, the right to appropriate taxes for specified uses and to audit public accounts to determine whether the money had been spent as directed. In the sphere of legislation, the right of the Commons to assent to all statutes grew out of the regular practice of initiating legislation by means of a single petition that included all petitions of a general nature presented by the knights and burgesses. The "common petition" would then be formally approved by all the Commons and sent to the Lords for their assent before being presented to the council for the king's acceptance or rejection.

The last major gain of the Commons was the right to impeach the king's ministers for misconduct. By the procedure of impeachment, the Commons collectively brought charges against the minister before the Lords, who pronounced the minister innocent or guilty. This was a powerful weapon to use against the king—and also, as it turned out, a powerful weapon that the king did not hesitate to use against his opponents. This use of impeachment as a political weapon illustrates the nature of most of the gains by Parliament and, particularly, those made by the Commons. The institutional development of Parliament resulted mainly from its value to the king and to the lords in their political struggles. Most of the knights and burgesses were under the patronage or influence of lords, and they followed the lead of their patrons. The Commons were the agents of a struggle for power. It was no love of democracy or desire for limited monarchy that sent the Commons before the bar of the Lords to impeach a minister. It was merely another episode in which a faction of the nobles had gained control of Parliament and felt strong enough to destroy its enemies.

In Edward III's later years, the nobility was badly splintered, and this situation did not improve when Edward was succeeded by a minor. The Black Prince, Edward's heir, had predeceased his father, and his son Richard II (1377–1399) took the throne. Richard became the focal point of a vicious competition among his uncles to control the regency government. The preoccupation with internecine struggles among those who should have been governing made the royal government ineffective, and local aristocrats usurped control of local administration. The administrative and judicial institutions became corrupted by bribery and undue influence of men concerned primarily with their own interests. The corruption of the government came at the end of a quarter of a century of economic and social dislocation caused by the recurrent epidemics of bubonic plague and the attempts of the government to prevent the rise of wages and prices. The epidemics greatly reduced the labor force, which led to the rise of labor costs that hurt the great wool producers—the nobility—and wool exporters—the merchants. These groups induced the royal government to issue controls that hurt the peasants and the lower classes in the cities. When the government became ineffective in curbing the more extreme excesses of the nobles and merchants, the discontent broke out in 1381 in a full-scale rebellion called the Peasants' Revolt. The two most conspicuous symbols of upper-class exploitation of the peasants, the archbishop of Canterbury and the royal treasurer, were murdered, and there was widespread destruction of property, especially of the houses of wealthy aristocrats. The rebellious mobs called on the young king to take control of the government and to protect the downtrodden from the selfish rule of the regency and the nobles. The fifteen-year-old Richard played a heroic role in bringing the movement to a temporary halt, going into the midst of the mob that marched on London in order to hear complaints and promise redress. Once the momentum of the movement diminished, the aristocracy united with other propertied classes in brutally suppressing the rebels.

After these events Richard II can scarcely be blamed for deciding, once he came of age, that the country needed a strong monarch who could preserve order and curb the ambitions of the bungling magnates who had jockeyed for power during his minority. But he went too far. He alienated most of the

The main body of rebels in the Peasants' Revolt of 1381 marched on London from Kent, picking up supporters as it went. When Richard II rode into the mob to hear its grievances and to promise redress, Wat Tyler, one of the principal rebel leaders, raised his sword against the king, but the mayor of London moved to intervene.

nobles and lost the support of the middle classes. When Richard confiscated the duchy of Lancaster, disinheriting his cousin Henry, it was clear that no property was safe with a king on the throne who held himself above the law. Henry of Lancaster raised a baronial rebellion to reclaim his inheritance and to claim the crown for himself. Richard was no match for the arms of Lancaster. The king was captured and a Parliament was summoned in his name. Claiming to represent the estates of the realm, this assembly received Richard's abdication and approved his deposition. Then Henry of Lancaster claimed the crown by conquest, by inheritance, and by the acceptance of the estates of the realm. A new Parliament was summoned, consisting of the members of the old, and the "liberty royal" of Henry IV (1399–1413) was solemnly affirmed. This elaborate attempt to legalize a *coup d'état* was followed by parliamentary acts recognizing the right of Henry's heirs to succeed to the throne. But no amount of legal fiction and constitutional theory could remove "the nemesis of Lancaster," the fatal flaw in the usurper's title wrested by force.

The Lancastrian period (1399–1461) has been called an age of "premature constitutional monarchy," but the realities of English politics were not radically altered. If Parliament seems more prominent, it is because Parliament was useful in sanctioning the measures of whichever faction happened at the moment to be in control. The usefulness of Parliament guaranteed its survival in the fourteenth and fifteenth centuries. By making it their means of trying to control or limit the king, the nobles made it an indispensable part of the machinery of government. Because of their need for parliamentary support, no Lancastrian king tried to enact laws or raise taxes without the approval of Parliament. Furthermore, all important political decisions, although arrived at earlier by king or nobles, were made public in and thus made formally by Parliament, as the best means of securing widespread support for royal policy or for an attack on royal power. The institutional development of Parliament continued in the fifteenth century, but the institution itself remained essentially the tool of contending groups: the king and his supporters, or one or another faction of magnates ambitious for more power.

In 1399 Henry Bolingbroke confronted the captured Richard II in White Tower (the oldest part of the Tower of London) and forced him to abdicate. It was a solemn scene, carefully staged to make it credible as a legal act by the royal prisoner. This contemporary painting captures the solemnity, picturing the tower room hung with rich tapestries between stained-glass windows.

The real center of government was not Parliament but the royal council. Since the Lancastrians owed their crown to the support of the nobles and needed their cooperation to stay on the throne, the nobles usually dominated the council rather than the professional civil servants who had done the will of the Plantagenet kings.

Henry IV kept hold of his throne by suppressing several rebellions and by reducing governmental expenses to retain the support of the middle classes. This cautious policy was jettisoned by his son and successor, Henry V (1413–1422). Conditions in France, where strife among the nobility had degenerated into anarchy and civil war, were ideal for a renewal of the Hundred Years' War. Henry V revived Edward III's claim to the French throne and proclaimed to the French that he was coming to restore peace and prosperity to his realm of France.

The campaign of 1415 was climaxed by a brilliant victory at Agincourt, where the English won their third great battle of the Hundred Years' War using the same tactics as at Crécy and Poitiers. The reduction and occupation of Normandy followed in the next few years, and in 1420 Henry won his greatest triumph, the Treaty of Troyes. This treaty provided for the marriage of Henry V and Catherine, daughter of the insane French king Charles VI, together with the recognition of Henry as heir to the French crown and regent during the life of his father-in-law. Within two years most of France north of the Loire had fallen to the English, but the task of conquering and occupying all of France was beyond the resources of any fifteenth-century English king. Fortunately for his later reputation, Henry V died prematurely at the height of his power. Having spent most of his time in foreign ventures, Henry had done practically nothing toward reestablishing an effective central government in England firmly under royal control. The circumstances after his death made that less likely than ever.

Henry VI (1422–1461) was a nine-month-old baby when he inherited the throne. He later lapsed into mental incompetence (1453–1455) from which he probably never fully recovered. During his minority England was governed by a regency of his relatives, who were divided into two major factions. Both council and Parliament were dominated alternately by one or the other group of magnates. On the Continent, English expansion actually continued slowly until by 1428 the English regent for France, John, duke of Bedford, penetrated as far south as Orléans. This success was the measure of French weakness and Bedford's personal ability, rather than the result of a concerted English effort. Parliament was weary of the cost of war. The regents in England were jealous of Bedford and fearful lest he exploit military success to gain power in England. The French recovery began in 1429, under Joan of Arc, and proceeded rapidly after the death of Bedford in 1435. By 1453, when the Hundred Years' War ended, only Calais was left to English rule.

The war abroad was followed by the Wars of the Roses at home, a civil conflict that continued intermittently for thirty years (1455–1485). The contending sides were the Yorkists (whose emblem was a white rose) and the Lancastrians (whose emblem was a red rose). Insofar as it was a dynastic contest, the Lancastrian king, Henry VI, derived his claim to the throne through his father and grandfather from a younger son of Edward III, while the dukes of York based their claim to the throne on descent from an older son of Edward III through the female line. But aside from dynastic legalities, the war was actually nothing more than a struggle for power, involving no political principles or constitutional issues. The fighting did not seriously affect more than a small minority of Englishmen. There was little pillaging, such as France had endured so long, and the daily life of the middle and lower classes was not seriously disturbed.

In one way England gained from the civil strife. The ranks of the factious nobility were depleted. The gap between the great nobles and the gentry of the fifteenth century was much greater than it had been in the age of Edward I. The number of great lords had diminished, and their wealth had increased. Each lord retained armed servants, often veterans of the French wars, who wore the livery (distinctive colors or uniforms) of their lord and who helped settle the constant private feuds and quarrels in which the magnates engaged. In addition, the normal course of law enforcement was perverted in favor of powerful lords by a system called maintenance, which usually consisted of bribery or intimidation of local officials, courts, and juries. Livery and maintenance were the great abuses of the age. Law-abiding gentry and merchants, whose voices could occasionally be heard through their representatives in Parliament, desired above all else "abundant governance," that is, the strong rule of a king who could restore order, repress the ambitions and quarrels of the nobles, and enforce the law.

The Wars of the Roses came to a temporary halt when Edward of York defeated Henry VI. As Edward IV (1461–1483) he gave England the "abundant governance" that the Lancastrians had failed to provide. But the reign was disturbed by occasional uprisings in favor of Henry VI, who even regained the crown for a few months in 1471. That temporary success cost Henry his life, and in the following years judicial murders and acts of attainder eliminated other great nobles whose fate was sealed by their royal blood. On the death of Edward IV, the last grisly act of the times was played out. Edward's young son succeeded as Edward V (1483), but the duke of Gloucester (Edward IV's brother) usurped the throne as Richard III (1483–1485), and the boy-king with his younger brother disappeared into the Tower, where both were probably murdered. A dutiful Parliament recognized the succession of Richard III, just as it had sanctioned the titles and ratified the acts of Edward IV, Henry VI in 1471, Edward IV again in 1471, and Edward V.

The long tale of intrigue, treachery, and assassination finally ended at

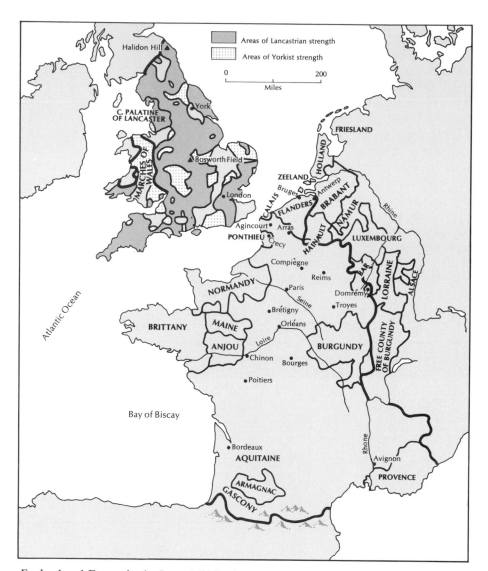

England and France in the Later Middle Ages

Bosworth Field in 1485, when Richard III was defeated and killed by Henry Tudor. Henry VII (1485–1509) was the grandson of Catherine, Henry V's widow, and a Welsh lord named Owen Tudor. On his mother's side he was descended from Edward III. Many others stood nearer the throne, but none had Henry Tudor's courage and ability. He strengthened his flimsy hereditary rights by marrying a daughter of Edward IV, uniting in his children both Yorkist and Lancastrian claims.

The accession of Henry VII established the Tudor dynasty, which brought England more than a century of relative peace and prosperity. But it took several years to convince contemporaries that Henry's success was not simply another violent episode in the civil wars. Little was discernible that anyone could recognize as new. The foundations of Tudor policy had been laid by Edward IV: "abundant governance," the encouragement of commerce and industry, royal control of the council, and economy in government. Henry VII's task was lightened by the decimation of the nobility during the preceding thirty years and by the nearly universal desire for orderly government. The Wars of the Roses had discredited the nobility, and the Tudor monarchy was the beneficiary of the nobles' incompetence.

## France: Charles V to Louis XI

Charles V the Wise (1364–1380) served his apprenticeship in royal rule during the years following Poitiers, when his father was a prisoner of the English. As Dauphin he joined with the nobility in suppressing the great *Jacquerie* of 1358, while he accepted some of the reforms demanded by a revolutionary movement in Paris in the same year. These reforms later became the basis of a more efficient royal administration and system of collecting taxes. More difficult to control were the troopers, who were released from service in the English and French armies after the Treaty of Brétigny-Calais. These "free companies" of mercenary soldiers fought under a captain who hired out his services in time of war. When peace came, the companies were without pay, so they swarmed throughout France pillaging the countryside, putting villages to ransom or to flames, and capturing castles from which they could systematically loot the towns and highways of a region. Charles solved this problem by meddling in the disputed succession to the throne of Castile. Charles' general, Bertrand Du Guesclin, rounded up most of the mercenaries and led them south of the Pyrenees. This venture was inconclusive because the Black Prince immediately intervened to preserve English interests in Castile, but Charles' main object was accomplished: ridding France of the "free companies."

Du Guesclin was put in command of the army when the Hundred Years' War was renewed in 1369. The French harried English supply lines, cut off small raiding or scouting parties, struck swiftly at vulnerable points, and always retreated before any major English army. These harassing tactics paid off splendidly. The English exhausted themselves sending large raiding parties to pillage the land. The French finally wore them down and forced the English to relinquish all of their occupied territories except Calais and the area around Bordeaux.

Charles V aided the French recovery by carrying through several reforms in the royal government. The soldiers were paid more regularly, and more emphasis was placed on the infantry, whose training and discipline were improved. Castles were repaired and properly garrisoned so that English raiding parties found it difficult to seize fortified bases for their operations. The collection of taxes was made more efficient by the institution of new tax districts under collectors responsible to the central government. Under Charles V the monarchy gained the consent of various regional meetings of estates to continue to collect the emergency taxes imposed originally for the ransom of King John. These included the hearth tax and several indirect taxes on merchandise, notably the salt tax. Theoretically these taxes were temporary and subject to consent by the taxpayers' representatives at meetings of the estates, but in practice the king won the right to impose taxes to meet a national emergency. This meant that the French monarchy could count on a permanent revenue far larger than any other European government's.

Despite these reforms, the task of completing the expulsion of the English was beyond French resources. Discontent broke out into occasional rebellion during the last years of Charles' reign, and on his death the throne descended to a minor. Fortunately for France, England was equally exhausted and also burdened with a royal minority. The new French king was Charles VI the Mad (1380–1422), who earned his sobriquet by succumbing to an attack of madness in 1392 and, except for a few lucid intervals, remaining insane until his death. A struggle for power ensued, but the constitutional results of this struggle in France were almost diametrically opposite to the results of the contemporary struggle in England under Richard II. In England Parliament was the main tool of contending factions. In France, there was no institution of the central government in which the struggle could be focused. The Estates General met rarely, and the *Parlement* of Paris was wholly a law court whose judges did not play an influential role in higher politics. The French nobility had no intention of destroying or limiting the central government: their purpose was to seize control of the government in the name of Charles VI.

After a few years the factions in the regency united around two men —Philip the Bold, duke of Burgundy (the king's uncle) and Louis, duke of Orléans (the king's brother). Both men held large appanages of the crown, and it became clear that while the appanage system had worked well during the thirteenth century, when the kings were effective rulers, it was a disaster when a man like Charles VI reigned. The appanages gave the cadet branches of the royal house an independence that made the competition for control of the royal government a long-lasting and harmful struggle. During Philip the Bold's lifetime, the struggle remained peaceful, but Philip's son John the Fearless made the feud virtually irreconcilable by having Louis of Orléans murdered in 1407.

The count of Armagnac, Louis' son's father-in-law, now took over the leadership of the Orleanist party (henceforth called the Armagnacs), and during the next twelve years intermittent civil war disturbed France. These

Relations between the French monarchy and the duke of Burgundy were strained but not broken in 1419 when Duke John the Fearless met Charles VII for a conference on the bridge at Montereau. After fruitless negotiations, as the Dauphin was leaving, one of his men rushed at the duke and buried an ax in his head. Charles VII has never been proved responsible for the murder, but he bore the guilt of it for the rest of his reign. A manuscript illuminator who painted the gory event seems to imply that the Dauphin had planned the crime.

struggles formed the background for Henry V of England's invasion in 1415. The Burgundians went over to the English, although John the Fearless continued to negotiate with the Armagnacs. Then in 1419 John was assassinated, and his son Philip the Good (1419–1467) affirmed his allegiance to the English invaders. The Treaty of Troyes, negotiated in 1420, served the interests of the Burgundians as well as those of Henry V. The Dauphin Charles VII retreated to the south and became the figurehead of a shadow government. The crisis came in 1428 when the Burgundians and English besieged Orléans; if the city fell, the south would be open to the invaders and their allies.

At this point Joan of Arc appeared. Joan had been born at Domrémy, a village situated near the border of France and Lorraine in a region that had suffered greatly from the civil war between Armagnacs and Burgundians. She and her family had experienced the plundering of Burgundian raids and the temporary exile these raids forced on a defenseless peasantry. As she grew up she imbibed the inarticulate resentment of the common people against the dis-orders and misfortunes associated with the English occupation, the abase-ment of the monarchy, and the Burgundian ascendancy in northern France. In Joan's case, however, the resentment was not wholly inarticulate. As an adolescent, she began to hear voices and to have visions. She was sure that they were the voices of angels, and finally she became convinced that she had been chosen as an instrument of divine will. All this is known from Joan's statements at her trial. Few historians doubt that Joan honestly and sincerely believed what she said. Her contemporaries put it more simply. To them the question was: Did the Maid come from God or from the Devil? As one chronicler put it, "God only knows."

Whether divinely inspired or not, Joan's program was straightforward and politically realistic. The king must receive his crown, and to accomplish this and restore his kingdom to him the English must be driven out and their Burgundian allies must be reduced to obedience. Joan resolved to carry out this program shortly after news of the siege of Orléans reached her region. Morale in Armagnac-controlled France had hit a new low. It seemed to many that only by a miracle could the royalist cause be saved. Joan convinced the local military governor of her mission, and he gave her arms, armor, and an escort to the court of Charles VII at Chinon. After some hesitation Charles also was convinced that the Maid was sent by heaven to drive the English out of France. Although Charles and his advisers had some misgivings about this girl who cut her hair like a boy and wore the clothes of a man, she was allowed to ride off with troops that had been assembled for the relief of Orléans. The English forces were depleted and weary, and the presence of Joan sent a thrill through the French ranks. Although legend has it otherwise, Joan did not actually lead the troops. More important, she rallied their sag-ging morale, and with a sure instinct she repeatedly made her dramatic appearance at just the critical juncture of a battle or skirmish to swing the victory to French arms. The siege of Orléans was raised ten days after Joan's arrival, and she got the credit. Thus inspired, the French troops reduced all the other English outposts on the Loire, and the way was cleared for a drive northward toward Paris.

At this juncture Joan once more intervened to determine the course of events. She insisted, and the royal advisers finally agreed, that Charles should be crowned at Reims. From a military point of view the project seemed hazardous, for Reims was deep within enemy-occupied territory. Actually, however, Charles' army drove through to Reims without difficulty. Town after town shifted allegiance and opened its gates to the royalist forces. A simple coronation service took place in July 1429, with only three peers of France—and Joan—in attendance. Now once more, after seven years of devastation and defeat, the kingdom had a solemnly anointed king, and Frenchmen rallied to the support of their monarchy. Many towns deserted the English or Burgundian cause without a fight. But in the military sphere Joan's earlier success did not continue. An assault on Paris failed, and efforts to capture towns where adequate English garrisons were stationed were also unsuccessful. The Anglo-Burgundian forces even resumed the offensive. In the defense of the royalist town of Compiègne, during a sortie to break up the besieging forces, Joan was captured by the Burgundians in May 1430.

What happened next can be understood only in terms of contemporary ideas and values. The code of war at this time was a latter-day chivalry that prescribed "honorable" treatment of prisoners of war who were noble, but that permitted the most brutal treatment of mercenary soldiers who fell into enemy hands and of peasants who dwelt in enemy territory. Charles VII has been severely criticized for not rescuing Joan of Arc from her Burgundian captors. It is possible that this could have been done, but all the values and attitudes of the age were against it. Joan was neither the squire nor the personal retainer nor the valet of the king. No compulsion of honor required Charles to come to her aid. She was a phenomenon unknown to contemporary standards of proper conduct. Even worse for her personal welfare, she seemed at this point to have served her purpose. No success had come her way since the coronation at Reims, and Charles did not demean himself to come to the peasant girl's rescue. Joan was handed over to the English, who in turn handed her over to the Inquisition for trial as a heretic and a witch. It was an easy matter to convict an illiterate girl—she told the tribunal that she thought she was nineteen but was not sure. When she faltered and seemed to recant, but then persisted in her earlier statements about her visions, she was convicted as a relapsed heretic so that she could be burned at the stake by the English.

Meanwhile, French recovery proceeded rapidly. All across northern France national resistance mounted, guerrilla fighting broke out in isolated regions, and the English were unable to collect taxes and maintain order. At court Charles VII's Armagnac advisers were replaced by more nationally minded officials who were ready to patch up the quarrel with Burgundy and who favored an energetic prosecution of the war. At the Congress of Arras in 1435, Duke Philip the Good broke with his English allies, papal legates condemned the Treaty of Troyes as invalid, and the Burgundians recognized Charles VII as king. Negotiations for peace with the English now bogged down, and in the same year the duke of Bedford, England's best general, died. In 1436 Paris fell. With the reoccupation of the capital all of France except Normandy, Maine, and part of Gascony was once more united under one king, Charles VII the Well-Served (1422–1461).

These developments were the work of an able group of ministers whose efforts gave Charles VII his sobriquet. Weary of the ambitions and quarrels of the nobles, Burgundian and Armagnac alike, Charles replaced as many councilors and officials as he dared with new men whose bourgeois origins were some guarantee of dependence on royal favor. These ministers now turned to the restoration of the royal administration and the strengthening of the central government. The task was not difficult, for the prestige of the monarchy stood high. Public opinion associated peace, order, and the expulsion of the foreigner with the monarchy. The king was the beneficiary of the successful conclusion of the Hundred Years' War in 1453, when only Calais remained in English hands. The war taxes were continued on a permanent basis, although occasionally the government found it expedient to gain the consent and approval of local or even national meetings of the estates. Conditions justified a permanent army, for in addition to war against the English, the government had to wage unceasing campaigns against bands of unemployed mercenary soldiers who roamed the country. The desolation of France actually strengthened the monarchy. Although already burdened with heavy taxation, the people gladly paid extra taxes for a royal army to protect them from the pillaging of these lawless bands.

Charles VII was succeeded by the fascinating and very able Louis XI (1461–1483), who completed the reconstruction of the French monarchy. Louis' goal was to build what may be called, with some exaggeration, an absolute state. He had no taste for chivalry, and he considered the feudal privileges of his nobles simply as obstacles. He shrank from warfare, preferring to use his consummate skill in diplomacy and bribery to achieve his ends. He filled the offices of government with low-born men and constantly traveled the length and breadth of his kingdom supervising the minutest affairs. Parsimonious and pious in the extreme, he dressed shabbily and treated the Virgin and the saints like allies to be won by diplomatic maneuvers and timely offerings. Louis was the antithesis of the Valois ideal of kingship; he was bourgeois in sympathies, and the bourgeoisie profited from his strong rule more than any other class.

One reason for Louis' attitude was the aristocratic reaction that took place in the opening years of his reign. The nobles leagued together in an effort to regain the powers in the central government from which Charles VII had systematically excluded them. The coalition of great nobles was led by Duke Philip the Good of Burgundy, whose own ambitions went beyond resistance to the crown. He sought to establish an independent "middle kingdom" between France and Germany. Although Louis XI weathered the storm of aristocratic reaction, by promising much and parting with little, a danger from Burgundy remained. Philip's successor was the even more ambitious Duke Charles the Rash (1467–1477). Louis carefully avoided committing French troops to battle, but he stirred up Duke Charles' enemies in Alsace and Lorraine. The crowning achievement of his diplomacy was to bring the Swiss into conflict with Burgundy. Twice the Swiss pikemen met and defeated the Burgundian cavalry, and in the second battle Charles was killed. Rejoicing over the death of his cousin, Louis XI moved swiftly to declare the French fiefs of the duchy escheated to the crown, although this disinherited Charles' daughter Mary of Burgundy. Mary's later marriage to Maximilian of Habsburg brought to that dynasty her claims to these fiefs, which led to the great Habsburg–Valois struggles of the sixteenth century. Louis' good fortune persisted, however. Before the end of the reign the duchy of Anjou and the counties of Maine, Bar, and Provence also escheated to the crown. Only Flanders and Brittany remained outside the royal domain.

When Louis XI died, the foundations of the strong monarchy of early modern France had been established: a centralized royal administration, a judicial system that reflected provincial diversity but that was under royal control, a kingdom almost entirely under the direct rule of the king, and a system of government in which the nobility were subordinate and the bourgeoisie prominent. Even more than Henry Tudor of England, Louis XI typified the "new monarchy" based on medieval institutions, but relatively free from medieval limitations, that marked the close of the Middle Ages.

The court of Duke Philip the Good of Burgundy was one of the richest and most important centers of fifteenth-century Europe. In this illumination the duke and his son receive a presentation copy of the *Chroniques de Hainault* from its publisher, Simon Nockart. The duke sought to create an independent state between Germany and France, and he exhibited his claim to royal status by patronizing many notable artists and poets. The literature emanating from his court helped to establish the northern French dialect as the literary language of France, and artists like the van Eycks had a profound influence on artistic currents both north and south of the Alps.

## Suggestions for Further Reading

**Secondary Works**   The best one-volume study of the Hundred Years' War is E. Perroy, *The Hundred Years' War* (London, 1951). See also H. Lucas, *The Low Countries and the Hundred Years' War* (Ann Arbor, Mich., 1929). D. Hay, *Europe in the Fourteenth and Fifteenth Centuries* (London, 1966); D. Waley, *Later Medieval Europe* (New York, 1964); and the classic J. Huizinga, *The Waning of the Middle Ages* (New York, 1949) treat the later Middle Ages in general. On specific aspects of English and French involvement in the war, considered from the standpoint of the history of each country, see H. J. Hewitt, *The Organization of War Under Edward III* (Manchester, 1966), and J. B. Henneman, *Royal Taxation in Fourteenth Century France: The Development of War Financing, 1322–1356* (Princeton, N.J., 1971). Two standard works on England (with ample bibliographies) are M. McKisack, *The Fourteenth Century* (Oxford, 1959), and E. F. Jacob, *The Fifteenth Century* (Oxford, 1961). On France, see P. S. Lewis, *Later Medieval France: The Polity* (New York, 1967); R. Vaughan, *Philip the Bold: The Formation of the Burgundian State* (London, 1962); and the relevant works cited at the end of Chapter 20. See also the biography of Louis XI by P. M. Kendall, *Louis Eleventh* (New York, 1971). On Joan of Arc, see S. Stolpe, *The Maid of Orléans* (London, 1956), and R. Pernoud, *Joan of Arc,* trans. E. Hyams (New York, 1966), which is a documentary history.

**Sources**   The principal account of the Hundred Years' War is *Sir John Froissart: The Chronicles of England, France and Spain* (New York, 1961). This edition is a condensation; the complete work is six volumes. The best approach to Joan of Arc is through these original sources: the record of her trial by the English, *Trial of Jeanne d'Arc,* trans. W. P. Barret (London, 1931), and R. Pernoud, *The Retrial of Joan of Arc* (New York, 1955).

# 25 The Church in the Later Middle Ages

The history of the Church in the two centuries before the Reformation may be divided into four periods. The first three are: the Avignon papacy (1305–1378), the Great Schism (1378–1409), and the Age of the Councils (1409–1447). The failure of the conciliar movement marked the end of the medieval Church as an effective international or universal force in Western society. In the fourth period (after 1447), the history of the Church can best be understood in terms of the politics of the various European countries.

The vitality and leadership once provided by the Church declined in the later Middle Ages. Part of the reason for this decline was the vigor and growth of secular governments, especially those of the Western monarchies. But the malady went deeper than simple competition from secular institutions. Within the clergy the capacity for reform was waning. No new religious order founded in the fourteenth and fifteenth centuries had anywhere near the importance or influence of the Cistercians in the twelfth century or of the Franciscans and Dominicans in the thirteenth.

In the fourteenth century a new wave of anticlericalism assailed the Church. The Black Death engendered a surge of religious hysteria and seemed to many a divine punishment for the wickedness of society. As a pillar of society and as the organization supposed to have the power to intercede with God, the Church bore the brunt of the feelings aroused by the epidemics. There seemed to be a greater and greater distance between the values and ideals of the Christian community and the realities of the opulent Church. The papal court at Avignon had become one of the richest and most splendid in Christendom and now became the target of severe criticism. The fourteenth-century disasters of war and pestilence turned the few critical voices of the early years of the century into a great chorus in its later part. When the Church became divided against itself, the great achievements of the universal Church of the Middle Ages were largely lost, and from the Great Schism and the Age of Councils, there emerged an ecclesiastical organization that maintained the medieval tradition of extensive ecclesiastical government but that held a mere shadow of the authority possessed by the medieval Church.

## The Avignon Papacy and the Great Schism

After the brief pontificate of Benedict XI (1303–1304), the cardinals chose an outsider, a man acceptable to Philip the Fair and not committed to any of the factions in the College of Cardinals. This was the Gascon archbishop of Bordeaux, who became Clement V (1305–1314). Clement possibly intended to go to Rome, but he kept postponing his trip. The situation in Italy offered little to attract a French pope: Guelphs and Ghibellines had reduced most of central and northern Italy to anarchy; the Papal States were torn by the feuds of noble families; with the appearance of the emperor Henry VII in Italy the city of Rome became a battlefield for the imperial and papal forces. Meanwhile, urgent business detained Clement on the other side of the Alps: negotiations for peace between Edward I and Philip the Fair; the accusations against Boniface VIII that had never been terminated; Philip's attack on the Templars; and the Council of Vienne in 1312.

Clement was timid, sedulously avoiding any conflict such as had brought Boniface VIII to his inglorious end. But it would be an exaggeration to portray Clement simply as a subservient tool of the French monarchy. Papal residence at Avignon actually resulted from Clement's desire to be free from Philip's pressure and at the same time to live in surroundings more congenial than strife-ridden Rome. The imperial city of Avignon was French in everything except political allegiance. Situated on the east bank of the Rhone, it lay within a county of Provence that belonged to the papacy. Nevertheless, Clement filled vacancies in the College of Cardinals with French prelates, and by the end of his pontificate the majority were quite content to elect another French pope and remain in Avignon.

Avignon was a well-situated papal city that allowed the fourteenth-century popes to be close to the French sources of their income and far from the factional struggles in Rome. The Avignon court became one of Europe's most sumptuous. Popes and cardinals patronized the arts and did some monumental building. The papal palace, the most extensive structure, was the fortified center of Europe's largest government.

Continued residence at Avignon invited criticism. If absenteeism was a vice, it was all the more vicious for a pope. If Saint Peter had faced the dangers of pagan Rome, even at the price of martyrdom, why should his successor shrink from the perils of Christian Rome? The Avignon popes sensed their responsibility but could not bring themselves to live up to it. Three times, at the last minute, they called off plans to return to Italy because the situation was too dangerous. The price of security came high. The popes at Avignon could no longer speak with the authority and prestige that for centuries had been associated with the Holy City.

Furthermore, the popes were criticized, unfairly, for being little more than "chaplains of the French king." This charge had a basis in the fact that all the Avignon popes were French, as were most of their cardinals. The popes were remarkably independent, however, especially during the brief reigns of the sons of Philip the Fair (1314–1328) and during the reign of John the Good (1350–1364). On several occasions they intervened to reestablish peace between France and England when it was definitely against French interests to do so. Finally, when the situation in Italy was at last favorable for a return of the papacy, the strongest French king of the period, Charles V, was unable to prevent the pope from resuming his residence in Rome.

On the whole the Avignon popes were able men although not outstanding religious leaders. Their talents lay in the fields of administration, law, and finance, and the Avignon papacy marked the culmination of the centralization of the medieval Church. The characteristic feature of this centralization, which critics then and now single out for special condemnation, was the system of financial extortion. The main author of this system was John XXII (1316–1334), who was almost constantly engaged in political or ecclesiastical struggles. He was convinced that the Church could not be independent of temporal rulers unless the papacy were wealthy enough to meet them on equal terms. The other characteristic feature of papal centralization was the increasing control of all ecclesiastical business by the papal *curia.* Here too the justification was the necessity of papal supremacy over the clergy if the Church were to be free from secular control. The result was the rapid growth of offices and officials, a bureaucratic proliferation at Avignon that made the *curia* of Innocent III seem primitive.

At the center of the papal government, as of any other medieval government, was the household. The pope's household differed mainly in being larger and more elaborate than the others. Counting such minor officials as the keeper of the papal plate, the keeper of the papal zoo, physicians and barbers, and all the others, it had more than three hundred, perhaps more than four hundred, members.

The College of Cardinals was the Senate of Christendom, as some contemporaries thought. The pope consulted the cardinals on major decisions and rarely acted on an important matter without their collective advice and approval. Although their most important function as a college was to elect a new pope, the cardinals, individually, were active in every phase of papal government, whether as legates representing the pope at courts of secular rulers or as officials in the several departments of the government at Avignon. In addition, each cardinal, as a "prince of the Church," maintained a household on a princely scale.

The papal government at Avignon was divided into four main branches: the chancery, the *camera apostolica,* the Datary, and a hierarchy of judicial tribunals. The papal *curia,* just as in the case of the *curia* of a king or emperor, originally transacted whatever business was at hand, without separate offices or specialized officials. The earliest department to be differentiated from the *curia* as a whole was the chancery. By the fourteenth century it consisted of seven offices whose main business was the dispatch of various kinds of routine administrative correspondence. The chancery also received petitions, examined the qualifications of candidates for benefices, and had official custody of the records of the *curia*.

The financial business of the *curia* was transacted in the *camera apostolica,* which emerged as a separate department in the thirteenth century. Its administrative head was the treasurer, and its policymaking head was the chamberlain. Since finance and policy, or politics, were inseparable (for example, negotiating with a secular ruler for a new collection of clerical taxes, or for the appointment of a bishop and the payment of fees in connection therewith), the chamberlain became the equivalent of a papal prime minister, the most trusted councilor of the pope. Most instructions to papal legates and correspondence of a confidential nature went through the chamberlain. He had his own secretarial staff, and most of the officials in the papal *curia* were responsible to him. The papal mint was under his control, and legal disputes concerning papal revenues were determined in the court of an auditor under his jurisdiction.

The chamberlain also supervised the work of a host of tax collectors and other agents, ran the extensive courier system, and was responsible for the receipt and auditing of revenues. Some of the older papal revenues were declining, such as the taxes and rents collected from the Papal States, and to make up for these losses and to increase the total income, collection of extraordinary taxes from the clergy was intensified, and other revenues were collected more rigorously. Revenues paid by the clergy were of various kinds. For example, bishops and abbots appointed or provided by the pope paid annual income taxes, in addition to a multitude of fees and gratuities charged at the time of appointment, plus a tax called "common services," payable from the first year's revenues of the see or abbey, a tax that corresponded with the annates paid by the lesser clergy from benefices reserved for papal appointment. In many dioceses (although not in France or England), on the death of a prelate provided by the pope, the papal *curia* exercised the right of *spolia* (confiscation of the personal property of the deceased) and then collected the revenues of the benefice as long as it was vacant. Because so many revenues were collectible from clergy who were provided by the pope, papal provisions were extended steadily until by the end of the fourteenth century all episcopal and most monastic benefices, and a multitude of lesser positions, were reserved for papal nomination. These reservations were also made to produce revenue by the practice of selling "expectancies" to hopeful candidates for the right to be considered for provision to benefices when they became vacant.

In the first half of the fourteenth century the Datary became a separate department of the papal *curia,* taking over several functions previously the responsibility of the chancery. Its main business consisted of the receipt of and action on petitions that did not require judicial determination by one of the tribunals. Where no dispute between parties was involved, and in cases that did not concern matters of conscience, the Datary disposed of appointments to benefices, dispensations from provisions of the canon law (especially in routine cases of marriage irregularities), and the granting of papal approval to the disposition of ecclesiastical property or offices among the clergy.

The judicial branch of the *curia* was composed of several tribunals, the highest being a full meeting of pope and cardinals in the Consistory. Cases were usually referred from the Consistory to local judges-delegate or to some other court of the *curia* for preliminary investigation. Any number, or even all, of the cardinals could constitute a court for a particular case. Such special courts usually delegated their functions to auditors for most of the litigation, after which the case was usually referred back to the pope for judgment based on the recommendation of the lower tribunal. The more routine side of papal jurisdiction was administered by the *Rota,* where the litigant could secure final judgment without reference of his case to the pope or cardinals. Cases were normally initiated through a petition submitted in the chancery, or else by reference from the Consistory. The judges of the *Rota* were a panel of auditors from which several were appointed to hear each case, but judgment was pronounced by all the auditors (or a majority) after a review of the evidence and arguments. Finally, cases could at any stage be referred to a special tribunal, the *Audientia,* which pronounced on technical legal points and investigated the authenticity of documentary evidence. It can be seen, therefore, that litigation at the papal *curia* could be complicated, lengthy, and expensive. The judicial machinery was ideal for defendants who sought to delay the due process of law. Even in the twentieth century, cases can take decades to work their way through the papal judicial system.

The Penitentiary, organized in 1338, was a department whose primary responsibility was giving penance to members of the papal court. The head of the department, the Grand Penitentiary, was the pope's confessor. In addition, this department maintained a large body of clerics who heard the confessions of the thousands of visitors to Avignon, and was thus made up of men who spoke many languages. Its jurisdiction ranged from the relaxation of excommunication or interdict to the granting of dispensations.

The operation of this vast machinery of papal government absorbed most of the time and energy of the popes. Critics who thought the clergy were too wealthy and worldly denounced the papacy for setting a bad example. Papal provisions were the main target for much of this criticism. When a benefice was reserved for papal provision, not only did the local patron lose his right (often lucrative) of nomination, but frequently a nonresident was appointed to the benefice, with most of the revenues drained away to foreign

The ecclesiastical and political struggles created by the Great Schism had counterparts in writings and even cartoons. In this drawing the antipope, crowned by an agent of the Devil, crowns in turn an emperor who is accompanied by a lion and a leopard, symbols of pride and avarice.

parts, while an underpaid vicar attended to the duties of the parish or other benefice. Also encouraged by papal provisions was pluralism, the holding of more than one benefice by papal dispensation, a practice that compounded all the abuses of absenteeism. The multiplication of fees for all the services offered by the papal *curia,* and payable at every stage of litigation in papal courts, led to the charge of simony at the see of Saint Peter.

Criticism came from diverse quarters. The Avignon regime suffered a desertion of the intellectuals, led by Petrarch (d. 1374), who coined the phrase "Babylonian captivity" to castigate all the evils of the *curia* at Avignon. Saint Catherine of Siena (d. 1380) bombarded the popes and the rulers of Europe with indignant letters demanding the return of the papacy to Rome. Earlier, the disputes between John XXII and the emperor Lewis IV the Bavarian (1314–1347)—which merely continued old arguments about the superiority of spiritual or secular authority—brought forth bitter denunciations of the papacy as an institution subverted by political ambition and ill-gotten wealth. A dispute within the Franciscan Order over the ownership of

Rome suffered severe decline without the papacy: buildings fell into disrepair; sheep grazed in the square of Saint Peter's; the pilgrim traffic became a trickle, which seriously affected Rome's economy. Many poems and letters were written urging the popes to return to the Holy City, and this drawing accompanied one such eulogy to Rome. It shows Lady Roma as a widow mourning the loss of the pope. The round church in the foreground is the Pantheon (S. Maria in Rotunda), and the round structure next to Roma is the Colosseum. In the Middle Ages, the Colosseum was always pictured with a domed top because of a muddled description of it in an early–twelfth-century pilgrim's guide to the city.

property led some friars to generalize their views into the theory of apostolic poverty applying to all the clergy. According to this theory, Christ and the Apostles possessed no property, and therefore the clergy and above all the pope as vicar of Christ should relinquish all earthly possessions. This conclusion stupified John XXII, who in 1323 denounced the whole theory as heretical. Antipapal feeling was turned to the profit of secular rulers. The most notable example comes from England, where Edward III was able to redress the balance of ecclesiastical control in favor of the crown. The Statute of Provisors (1351) formally prohibited papal provisions but left the king free to negotiate compromises on particular appointments, and the Statute of Praemunire (1353) prohibited appeals from English courts to the papal *curia* in cases where, by English interpretation, the jurisdiction of royal courts was competent.

Pressure on the popes to return to Rome mounted. The Romans, deprived of their profits of the tourist trade to the Holy City, and with injured pride, clamored for the return of the pontiff. Meanwhile, conditions in Rome were much improved during the pontificate of Innocent VI (1352–1362), and Avignon, disturbed by companies of mercenaries idled after the Treaty of Brétigny-Calais (1360), lost its appeal as a haven. Urban V (1362–1370) actually brought the *curia* back to Rome, but after three years of vain efforts to reestablish papal authority he returned to Avignon. Gregory XI (1370–1378) tried it again, and he too finally decided to return to Avignon, but before he could actually depart, he died.

The sixteen cardinals (eleven French, four Italian, and one Spanish) who were with Gregory XI in Rome met immediately in conclave to elect a new pope. After a brief stalemate because the French cardinals could not agree, a compromise candidate favored by the Italian cardinals was elected with the necessary two-thirds majority. This was the archbishop of Bari, who had served the papal *curia* and the cardinals successfully in various important administrative capacities, although he had not been elevated to the rank of cardinal himself. Since he was not then in Rome, messengers were sent to inform the archbishop before public announcement was made. Meanwhile, unaware that the election had already taken place, a tumultuous mob gathered outside the conclave, shouting for a Roman, or at least an Italian, to be elected pope. When some of the demonstrators broke into the conclave, threatening physical violence, most of the cardinals fled in terror. Order was restored, and on the next day the archbishop arrived. The remaining cardinals confirmed his election, he assumed the papal name of Urban VI, and ten days later he was crowned on Easter Sunday before an enthusiastic crowd.

Urban VI (1378–1389) had been an exemplary and efficient, if somewhat colorless, prelate, an able servant of the Church as it existed in Avignon. Now, much to everybody's surprise (especially the cardinals'), the new pope suddenly became a reformer, determined to root out the worldliness of the clergy, and to begin at the top with the papal *curia* and the cardinals. The latter bitterly resisted Urban's efforts to reduce their personal revenues, eliminate corrupt practices, and put a bridle on their influence. Goaded by their resistance, Urban became arbitrary and violent, according to his enemies. (Even his supporters admitted he was tactless and unusually suspicious.) At this point the French cardinals fled to Anagni, where they declared Urban's election invalid because it was forced on them by the Roman mob. Following the logic of this pronouncement, they later elected a new pope, Clement VII (1378–1394), with whom they returned to Avignon.

Thus began the Great Schism, during which Europe was divided in obedience between the Roman and the Avignon line of popes. The abuses of the "Babylonian captivity" were multiplied by two. The additional scandal of schism was charged against both popes, while each hurled anathema at the other. Charles V of France supported the French cardinals and their pope, Clement VII of Avignon. In what was really nothing more than a political alignment, the French allies—Scotland, Navarre, Castile, Aragón, and various German princes under French influence—fell into line in support of the Avignon papacy. The enemies of France recognized the Roman line: England (with Gascony), Flanders, Portugal, the emperor and most of the German princes, together with Bohemia and Hungary. Italy was divided, and the Italian states were divided and fickle.

## The Age of the Councils

The immediate problem created by the Schism was: Which of the rival popes was the true pope? With Europe so evenly divided, and with no clear legal theory by which one or the other pope could be preferred, the conflict between Avignon and Rome did not rise above the level of personalities and power politics. Each pope excommunicated the other, together with their respective supporters. Each pope was willing to accept the other's abdication on lenient terms but refused to consider the judgment of any secular prince or ecclesiastical body. Canon law and the tradition of the Church provided no clear basis for arguing that there was any higher jurisdiction than that of a true pope— and neither pope was prepared to admit that his election was not canonical. Thus Christians could not be certain that sacraments performed by their priests, whose allegiance might be to the wrong pope, were efficacious. Who exercised the power of the keys granted by Christ? The deadlock called for an urgent resolution. It was not just a matter of politics and finances, of the exercise of papal and other jurisdictional authority. It was a matter of spiritual life and death.

The members of the Roman Church were unable to work out a solution. When Urban VI died, the Roman cardinals elected Boniface IX (1389–1404), and when Clement VII died, the cardinals at Avignon elected Benedict XIII (1394–1423). When it became clear that the alignment of European monarchies and lesser states would not throw the decision to either side, the French urged that both popes abdicate so that a reunited College of Cardinals might elevate a compromise candidate. The Romans seemed to accept this solution, since when Innocent VII (1404–1406) and Gregory XII (1406–1415) were elected, each promised to abdicate if the act would end the Schism. However, Benedict XIII steadfastly refused to step down, even when the French withdrew support from him between 1398 and 1403.

As the Schism continued, more and more intellectuals urged a new way to resolve it, by calling a general council of the Church to judge the popes. A long tradition of legal discussion had dealt with this possibility, and the professors at the University of Paris took the lead in bringing it to bear on the present situation. Ironically, the tradition was based on a text in Gratian's *Decretum* that derived from the writings of Cardinal Humbert of Silva-Candida, the extreme papalist of the eleventh century. Humbert had stated that the pope could be judged by no one, *unless he deviated from the faith*. But, asked the lawyers of the twelfth and thirteenth centuries, who could judge whether the pope had deviated from the faith? And did deviation from the faith include heinous crimes? As commentary on the passage built up in the thirteenth century, many urged that only a council of the whole Church could judge the pope and that many crimes might be construed as included under the general phrase "deviation from the faith." The general council would be representative of that body about which Jesus had said in Matthew 16:18: ". . . the gates of hell shall not prevail against it." If hell prevailed in the papacy, then the promise could only be realized in the body of the Church, which would operate in the council. When around the beginning of the fifteenth century the professors at Paris revived this venerable tradition, they found general theories but no details of how to put the principles into effect. Who is authorized to call a council? Who presides? What is the relationship between the authority of the council and that of the pope? If the council has greater authority, as is implied in the doctrine that it can judge the pope, then in what sense is the pope head of the Church? The Schism had engendered a general debate about basic constitutional issues. The conciliarists argued that a council must be called to deal with the Schism, and in 1408 the cardinals on both sides agreed to participate in a general council the next year at Pisa.

More than five hundred prelates met in the Council of Pisa to end the Schism, suppress heresy, and reform the Church. Both popes were deposed as "schismatics and notorious heretics, guilty of perjury and the sources of open scandal to the Church." The cardinals present at Pisa were commissioned to elect a new pope: Alexander V (1409–1410). Gregory XII and Benedict XIII promptly denounced the council and excommunicated Alexander V. The result was a triple schism. The situation was unchanged when Alexander died and was succeeded by John XXIII (1410–1415).[1] John's character was reprehensible, and his interests were almost wholly confined to defeating the reforms promulgated by the Council of Pisa and to defending the Papal States against invasion by the king of Naples.

The failure of the Council of Pisa led to demands for a new council. In accordance with medieval precedent, John XXIII, as the pope recognized by

---

[1] Later popes recognized the validity of the election of Alexander V by taking his name and recognizing his number in their series. John XXIII was elected in the same manner as Alexander V, but he was later deposed by another council. When John XXIII (1958–1963) took the name and number of the fifteenth-century pope, he rejected the validity of the earlier pontificate. Modern papal lists omit both Alexander V and the first John XXIII.

the conciliar party, was the proper authority to summon the new council. When he procrastinated, the conciliarists appealed to the emperor Sigismund on the precedent of the general councils of antiquity convened by the Roman emperors. At this time, John XXIII was in a difficult situation. Rome had fallen in 1413 to the king of Naples, who also occupied much of the Papal States. Any hope of recovering these losses depended on the support of Sigismund, whose troops were then in northern Italy. John XXIII therefore reluctantly approved the principle of calling a new council, and Sigismund forthwith issued an imperial summons to all prelates and princes to attend or send representatives to a new general council at Constance. There was nothing for John to do but issue his own summons to the same effect.

Sigismund's motives in calling the Council of Constance (1414–1418) were mixed. He probably approved of strengthening the Church by reform and by the suppression of heresy. Also, it enhanced imperial prestige to assume the initiative in business that affected all of Christendom, and to hold the council within the empire. The summons to lay rulers as well as the clergy was well calculated to commit the former to support the acts of the council. The council itself was a leisurely, although magnificent, affair. Its organization was novel. Instead of voting by head, the traditional method that would have favored John XXIII because of the numerous Italian clergy present, the council was organized into five nations after the pattern of medieval universities. Each nation—Italian, German, English, French, and Spanish—had one vote in the formal casting of ballots.

The main agenda were the same as at Pisa. The Schism was finally healed by the deposition of all three popes. After much futile maneuvering, including a brief flight from Constance disguised as a stable boy, John XXIII accepted and ratified the action of the council. With more grace and acumen Gregory XII anticipated the action by first formally summoning the council as true pope and then notifying it of his voluntary abdication—thus preserving the legal fiction of papal independence and supremacy over a general council. Benedict XIII obstinately held out and hurled anathemas at all and sundry from his castle in Spain until his death in 1423. Even then this Avignonese-Aragonese line was not ended. In a comic-opera denouement, three of his cardinals elected an antipope who finally abdicated in 1429, while the fourth cardinal created a schism within the schismatic line by electing a rival antipope of whom little beyond his name is known. Meanwhile, in 1417 at the Council of Constance the cardinals, afforced by representatives of each of the five nations, elected Martin V (1417–1431), and for all practical purposes the Great Schism was ended.

The suppression of heresy was more readily handled but with less enduring results. The main problem was John Huss, whose followers in Bohemia not only accepted his religious views but used them as a rallying point for anti-imperial Czech nationalism. Huss received an imperial safe-conduct guaran-

THE AGE OF THE COUNCILS

teeing his journey to Constance, a hearing before the whole council, and a safe return to Bohemia. Shortly after his arrival, his enemies persuaded the council that for an accused heretic an imperial safe-conduct could not prevail against the due process of canon law. Accordingly, Huss was thrown into prison to await trial. Huss wanted to debate; the fathers of the council wanted only to hear from him "yes" or "no" as each charge was read to him, so that an opportunity to abjure was provided the accused before they gave judgment. Thus he was accused of denying transubstantiation, a doctrine on which his teaching was in fact orthodox. The charges were worded so that he could neither affirm the teaching attributed to him, nor could he "recant" the alleged teaching without admitting that he was unorthodox before he "recanted." Nor would the council allow him to explain his position. Finally, when he refused to give up his view of the Church—as a congregation of all the faithful under Christ, with no true authority vested in Peter or in Peter's successors—unless it was proved false, Huss was condemned as an obdurate heretic. However, the Czech movement he led did not collapse after he was burned at the stake—the punishment for obdurate heresy.

In the matter of reform, the conciliarists won two signal victories, on paper. In the decree *Sacrosancta* the Council of Constance affirmed that a general council represented the whole Church, held its power directly from Christ, and must be obeyed by all men including the pope in matters pertaining to the faith, the abolition of schism, and reform. Having formally stated the doctrine of conciliar supremacy, the council promulgated the decree *Frequens* as a fundamental law of the Church. This decree required the convocation of another general council in five years, the meeting of future councils at regular intervals, and the automatic meeting of a council in the event of a future schism. On specific matters, however, it was a different matter. The council spent two years working, in various committees, on the reform of abuses connected mainly with papal revenues and papal provisions. Everyone was ready to reform whatever did not affect his own selfish interests. In the end, Martin V was presented with a bill of particulars that he formally accepted— but then did not bother to enforce.

As a cardinal, Martin had supported the conciliar movement, but as pope he worked without stint for papal supremacy and resisted all reforms that diminished papal power. His policy was moderate but tenacious. In 1423 Martin summoned but would not preside over the council required by the decree *Frequens*. Held at Pavia, it was ill-attended, and under the astute guidance of papal legates it accomplished little beyond reiterating the condemnations of the Council of Constance against heretics. Martin was unable, however, to prevent the council from proclaiming the place of meeting of the next council, scheduled to be held in 1431. This was Basel. By that time the conciliar movement had so languished that Martin would have ignored the convention except for the conviction among a growing number of German princes that a

Bronze doors of Saint Peter's by Filarete depict scenes from the life of Pope Eugenius IV, who came into conflict with the Council of Basel and was forced to withdraw his repeated decrees of dissolution. *Right* The pope and Sigismund enter Rome, with Sigismund performing the role of *strator* (squire) in a symbolic act of subordination. *Opposite page* The pope crowns Sigismund in Saint Peter's.

new council was necessary to deal again with the Hussite movement in Bohemia. Reluctantly, Martin made arrangements on February 1 for a papal legate to convene the council; on February 20 he died of apoplexy.

The legate reached Basel at the appointed time, but nobody else had arrived. For three months the legate waited, and the "attendance" grew to one bishop, two abbots, and a few delegates from the University of Paris. Then the Hussites scored some notable victories, and the council was soon filled with prelates from all over Europe concerned by the spread of heresy. Meanwhile, Eugenius IV (1431–1447) had dissolved the council, and when he learned of its renewed vigor, he repeated his order of dissolution. The council refused to obey, desiring to deal with the Hussites in its own way, by negotiation. It also issued a decree denying anyone but the council itself the right to dissolve or transfer a council. The conciliarists' greatest moment came when Eugenius was forced to withdraw his bulls of dissolution and confirm the acts of the council.

Eugenius continued, however, to maneuver for a reestablishment of papal authority and began to make headway when radical members of the council advanced extreme decrees that would have stripped the papacy of virtually all its power. Moderates began to support the pope, and in 1437 the conflict reached a climax. The council summoned the pope to answer charges of misconduct; Eugenius responded by transferring the council to Ferrara, so that, he alleged, it could meet with representatives of the Greek Orthodox Church

and with the Eastern emperor himself. The critical situation in the Byzantine Empire, under pressure from the Ottoman Turks, played into Eugenius' hands by making him the linchpin in a new move to heal the schism between the Orthodox and Catholic churches. The moderate conciliarists met in Ferrara in 1438, and the negotiations there and at Florence, to which the council was transferred in 1439, resulted in an agreement between Eugenius and the Eastern emperor. It was an agreement the emperor could not keep.

With the desertion of the moderates to Ferrara-Florence, the Council of Basel fell under the control of extremists who rapidly lost much of the council's former support and prestige. Their deposition of Eugenius as a heretic struck most people as irresponsible and foolhardy. A more serious error was their election of an antipope, Felix V (1439–1449). The conciliar movement was discredited as leading to a new schism. Earlier reforms were now ignored by Eugenius with impunity. In a final and tragicomic display of futility, the Council of Basel proceeded to quarrel with Felix over *his* papal prerogatives. It was merely to clean up loose ends that, after the death of Eugenius, Nicholas V condescended to negotiate a settlement with the council, now removed to Lausanne. Felix abdicated with some relief, the council voted its own dissolution in one expiring assertion of independence, and the conciliar movement was at an end.

To understand the failure of the conciliar movement one more factor must be noticed. This was the gradual alienation of secular rulers from the reform program. During the closing months of the Council of Constance, when it became clear that no general program of reform could be agreed on by the whole council, Martin V had negotiated a series of treaties or concordats (1418) in which the interests of secular rulers were scrupulously observed. This policy was carried forward by Eugenius IV, who by making concessions to the rulers was able to win their support for papal supremacy. Without secular support the conciliar movement was bound to fail. In 1438 Charles VII of France issued the Pragmatic Sanction of Bourges, under which many of the reforms of the Council of Basel were accepted as binding in France, and many papal rights over revenues and appointments were declared to be vested in the French crown. Although these so-called Gallican Liberties were never fully enforced, the Pragmatic Sanction became the basis for negotiations with the papacy. The result was that control over the French clergy and ecclesiastical revenues was divided between the king and the pope, in return for royal recognition of papal supremacy over the Church. A similar division of control over the German Church was effected by the legislation of the Diet of Mainz in 1439, modeled on the Pragmatic Sanction of Bourges, and by the later Concordat of Vienna of 1448. Other concordats were negotiated during the fifteenth century.

The popes, then, were not unqualified victors in the struggle. Defeat of the conciliar movement had been won at the price of sharing papal authority with secular rulers. The unity of the Church had been preserved, and constitutional reform of the Church had been curbed, but a long step had been taken toward the nationalization of the churches, a main feature of the Protestant Reformation. More than that, the papacy suffered a loss in prestige. The problems of the Great Schism and the Age of the Councils were primarily political. Their solution crowded into the background the spiritual mission of the supreme pontiff. Control of the clergy north of the Alps, security in Rome, the Papal States, and Italy—these objectives seemed more pressing than the solution of problems that were primarily religious in nature. The reformers of the conciliar movement and even the secular rulers had a better record than the popes in dealing with heresy, the discipline and morals of the clergy, promotion of learning in the universities, the support of charitable organizations, and other nonpolitical matters that had always been the concern of the medieval Church under the leadership of the popes.

## Suggestions for Further Reading

**Secondary Works**   On the Avignon papacy, see G. Mollat, *The Popes at Avignon, 1305–1378* (Edinburgh, 1963). A. C. Flick, *The Decline of the Medieval Church*, 2 vols. (New York, 1930), and L. E. Binns, *The Decline and Fall of the Medieval Papacy* (London, 1934) are more general studies. G. Barraclough, *Papal Provisions* (Oxford, 1935), and W. E. Lunt, *Papal Revenues in the Middle Ages* (New

York, 1934) treat the practice of papal government. On the Great Schism, see W. Ullmann, *Origins of the Great Schism* (London, 1948). B. Tierney, *Foundations of the Conciliar Theory* (Cambridge, 1955) and *Origins of Papal Infallibility* (Leiden, 1972), and M. J. Wilks, *The Problem of Sovereignty in the Later Middle Ages* (Cambridge, 1963) survey the background of the conciliar movement, while E. F. Jacob, *Essays in the Conciliar Epoch,* 3rd ed. (Manchester, 1963), and J. Gill, *The Council of Florence* (Cambridge, 1959) discuss the conciliar movement itself. On the heresies in the later Middle Ages, see G. Leff, *Heresy in the Later Middle Ages,* 2 vols. (Manchester, 1967); M. Spinka, *John Hus and the Czech Reform* (Chicago, 1941); H. Kaminsky, *A History of the Hussite Revolution* (Berkeley and Los Angeles, 1967); and K. B. McFarlane, *John Wycliffe and the Beginnings of English Nonconformity* (London, 1952).

**Sources**   The best approach to the councils is through the sources: L. R. Loomis, *The Council of Constance* (New York, 1961); Aeneas Piccolominus (Pope Pius II), *De Gestis Concilii Basiliensis,* trans. D. Hay and W. H. Smith (Oxford, 1967); and M. Spinka, *John Hus at the Council of Constance* (New York, 1966). For other sources from the period, see M. Spinka, *Advocates of Reform* (Philadelphia, 1953).

# 26 Italy and Germany in the Later Middle Ages

On a hot afternoon in June 1312, Henry VII of Luxembourg was solemnly crowned emperor of the Holy Roman Empire. The ceremony took place in the Lateran palace because Henry's German troops had been unable to dislodge his Italian enemies from the half of Rome that included Saint Peter's Basilica, where an imperial coronation ought properly to have taken place. Papal legates officiated because the pope refused to leave Avignon. After the ceremony, the open-air coronation banquet was broken up by enemy archers shooting down on the guests from the heights of the Aventine. The whole incident was symbolic of the degradation of the medieval empire and the hopeless involvement of imperial dreams with Italian partisan politics.

Henry VII, to whom Dante had appealed for the reestablishment of universal peace through a revival of the empire, has been called "the last of the medieval emperors." The phrase is appropriate. He was the last emperor to make a determined effort to control Italy, and although his successors as Kings of the Romans (the official title of the German king) are conventionally called emperors, few of them bothered to receive that title officially through an imperial coronation. After Henry VII the connection between Italy and Germany, originally established by Otto I the Great in 962, was for all practical purposes at an end, although Lewis IV the Bavarian tried to maintain it. Thus the history of Italy and Germany during the later Middle Ages follows the general pattern of "national disentanglement" that characterizes the later medieval history of France and England. There were few other parallels, however. The tendency of local political units to become autonomous continued unabated in central Europe. This tendency was in direct contrast with the growing centralization of the Western monarchies.

In the fourteenth century, Italy became dominated by despots and Germany by the princes. Nonetheless, both north and south of the Alps, the constitutional structure of the various territorial states was so diverse that few generalizations hold for all of them. The main difference between conditions in Germany and Italy was that the balance of political and economic power in the north was still held by the greater nobles, an essentially rural class based on agricultural wealth, while in Italy power was shifting rapidly to the urban bourgeoisie, whose wealth lay in commercial, industrial, and financial enterprise rather than in land, and to the lesser nobility, whose power remained a landed power but who were becoming part of the city-state society.

### The Age of the Despots: City-States in Italy and the Renaissance Papacy

In the early fourteenth century most of northern and central Italy consisted of independent towns. The imperial government had never been particularly effective in northern Italy and in the later thirteenth century had lost whatever effectiveness it had. Also, the withdrawal of the papacy to Avignon, followed by the Great Schism, eliminated the only power capable of preserving some unity and order in central Italy. The Papal States disintegrated into a congeries of towns and petty principalities, each striving with varying degrees of success to throw off papal rule. Only in the south, where town life lagged behind, were larger territorial units preserved in the kingdom of Naples and the kingdom of Sicily. And there frequent civil wars stirred up by the feudal barons kept the central governments weak.

The internal organization of most of the towns of Tuscany and Lombardy was republican in form and oligarchical in fact. Participation in the government was restricted almost entirely to the upper classes. The most striking feature of political life was incessant factional strife, and although the party labels, Ghibelline and Guelph, were still used, neither stood for any clear set of political principles or any definite program. All parties and factions sought control of the town government and the independence of the town from outside authority.

Two new factors entered Italian politics during the fourteenth century. One was the *popolo minuto* (lower economic classes). The other was the despot. Political strife in towns where industry thrived often took the form of a class struggle. Sometimes it was the frightened upper and middle classes, sometimes the lower classes in their moment of victory, who adopted some form of tyranny or despotism—the one to maintain order, the other to preserve newly won liberties. The despot was theoretically above faction. Hence he was often an outsider called in to impose peace impartially on all groups. Actually, of course, the despots were more concerned for their own power than for the welfare of the town, so they usually acted in the interests of the dominant group.

The despots had diverse origins. Some were nobles of the surrounding countryside, others were officials like the *podestà* of a neighboring town, others were *condottieri*—captains of mercenary troops. Some were elected by constitutional methods and then seized dictatorial and hereditary power. Others usurped their authority with the connivance of a faction in the town. Very few of the despots had a completely legitimate right to all the governmental powers they exercised. Many of them adopted resounding titles with a specious ring of legitimacy, such as Captain of the People, to compensate for their dubious origins. For the same reason some of the despots held splendid courts and patronized the arts and letters, while most of them sought to win support from their subjects and to increase their power by territorial conquests. The political methods of the despots ranged from wars and marriage alliances to assassination, betrayal, and calculated dissimulation. Methods that were once the exception became in the Renaissance the accepted means by which petty rulers clawed their way to the top and greater rulers were unseated from power.

Not all the Italian city-states were ruled by despots, nor was the political power of all the rulers petty and local. By the end of the fourteenth century five states had become dominant: Venice and Milan in the north; Florence and the Papal States in central Italy; and the kingdom of Naples in the south. Of these only Milan conformed with the typical pattern of despotism. Here the Visconti dynasty was established early in the fourteenth century and continued in power until the middle of the fifteenth. Milanese power and territorial expansion reached their height under Gian Galeazzo Visconti (1385–1402), who married a daughter of the French king, purchased the title of duke from the emperor, and aspired to become king of Italy by conquest. Under Gian Galeazzo, Milan controlled most of Lombardy and pushed eastward toward Venice and southeastward into the Papal States and Tuscany.

Venice was the least typical of the Italian city-states. Its constitution was a model of oligarchy, its commerce stretched throughout the eastern Mediterranean and into the Black Sea, and its fleets regularly visited northern Europe. Until the fifteenth century Venice was more of a world power than an Italian city-state. The state was rigidly controlled by the greater merchants. Executive authority was originally vested in an elected doge. After the failure of a con-

Jacopo de Barbari's woodcut (1500) of Venice, the great commercial city. The importance of the sea in the city's life is emphasized by the way it crowds the shore, by the ships in the foreground, and by the amount of open water.

spiracy aimed at establishing a despotism, in 1310, the Great Council instituted the Council of Ten. Together with the doge and six councilors, the Council of Ten was the supreme authority. Other than the provision for annual election of its members by the Great Council, the Ten's powers were hardly limited at all. As a sort of committee of public safety, the Council of Ten moved with speed and secrecy against suspected enemies of the state, domestic or foreign. The government's policy was aimed primarily at the advancement of Venetian commerce. The government regulated trade minutely, built and owned all shipping, and organized the great fleets into convoys protected by swift naval vessels. Commercial rivalry with other Italian ports frequently led to armed reprisals and petty wars, but in 1376 an all-out war with Genoa began. It lasted until the Genoese forces besieging Venice were annihilated on the island of Chioggia in 1380, the first major military operation in which cannon and gunpowder played an important role. The Genoese never fully recovered from this disaster.

After defeating Genoa, Venice confronted the threat of Milanese expansion by adopting a *terra firma* policy, that is, the conquest of the lands to its west in order to safeguard its trade routes north over the Alps and to ensure a food supply for its population. At the height of its expansion, the Venetian empire included a large hinterland to the west and north of the city, plus areas on the eastern shores of the Adriatic, more than a dozen islands in the eastern Mediterranean, including Crete, and many trading stations in the cities of the Levant. But this territorial expansion committed Venice to participation in the politics of the Italian mainland and coincided with the slow decline of its commerce and of the importance of Mediterranean commerce in the total economy of Europe. By the middle of the sixteenth century, Venice was no longer a world power.

Like Venice, Florence also resisted despotism in the fourteenth century, both within the republic and beyond its frontiers. But although Florentines made much of their republican institutions and championed the resistance of smaller states to Milanese aggression, Florence was in many ways a typical Renaissance city-state, both in its internal development and in its foreign policy. In contrast with Venetian constitutional stability, power in Florence shifted from party to party until the rise of the Medici in the fifteenth century. The main reason for the instability was the complexity of Florentine society, which reflected the highly developed and often divergent economic interests in the state. Florence was the leading industrial and financial power in Italy as well as a rival to Venice in commerce. Also, a class of nobles lived in Florence whose wealth lay in the countryside beyond the city. Class conflict was thus complicated and endemic in Florentine politics. The gravest crisis occurred in 1378, when the *popolo minuto* revolted—the famous Ciompi uprising. On several occasions the Florentines had invited a foreign despot to bring peace, but that plan never worked because the situation was too complex for an outsider to control, and Florence was too strong to be held down by force alone.

Political stability finally came to Florence with the rise of the Medici family, the most powerful bankers not only in Italy but in all of Europe. The Medici had been associated with lower-class elements in Florentine politics ever since the Ciompi uprising, but they were acceptable to the wealthy merchants and bankers. Cosimo de' Medici was the real ruler of Florence from 1434 until his death in 1464, although he preserved republican institutions and rarely held office himself. He controlled the elected officials like a modern political "boss," and manipulated Florentine policy by exerting his influence behind the scenes. Carefully avoiding the name and the appearance of a despot, he lived a simple life but on state occasions held a magnificent "court." Success earned him the extravagant title of *Pater Patriae* (father of his country) toward the end of his long political career.

The character of Cosimo de' Medici's power had been determined by the struggles between republican Florence and the despotically ruled cities surrounding it. The greatest challenge had come from the Gian Galeazzo Visconti of Milan at the end of the fourteenth century, when Florence stood almost alone against Milanese expansion to the south. The confrontation between Visconti despotism and Florentine republicanism, enshrined dramatically in the struggle, engendered a new civic humanism in Florence that linked the city with ancient civic traditions of republican Rome, whose citizens had, according to revisionist Florentine historiography, founded Florence. This intellectual development strengthened the spirit and structure of republican institutions in Florence and helped form the framework within which the Medici would wield their power.

The expansion of Milanese power ended as a significant threat when Gian Galeazzo died in 1402. Gian's successors inherited his title but not his ability. The Visconti empire almost collapsed. Some towns recovered their independence; Venice conquered the eastern Milanese lands; and the popes worked hard to restore their authority in the Papal States, both against the Milanese domination in the north and against the petty independent despots of the central States. Florence, having conquered Pisa in 1410 and thus gained an outlet to the sea, now supported the *status quo* and peace, refusing to take advantage of the weakness of the Visconti. Then, in addition to the scramble for territory and power in central and northern Italy, a new threat of conquest arose from the south. Ladislas, king of Naples—flaunting his motto, *Aut Caesar aut nullus* (either Caesar or nothing)—set out to conquer and found a united kingdom of all of Italy. Only Florence stood between him and conquest of the north when he died prematurely in 1414. "Death was the best friend of the Florentines," Machiavelli later observed.

The threat from Naples was replaced by a new threat from Milan, and Florence once more took the lead in resisting aggression. When the last of the Visconti died in 1447, Cosimo de' Medici sponsored the rise of Francesco Sforza in Milan. Sforza had been a *condottiere* in the hire of both the Visconti and their enemies. Because of the gratitude of the other states whose territories had been protected from Visconti aggression, Cosimo was the leading spirit behind the general pacification of Italy by the Peace of Lodi in 1455. By this settlement, Venice, Milan, Florence, the papacy, and the kingdom of Naples all guaranteed each other's territorial security and that of their allied city-states. The peace of Italy was assured for another generation, and a balance of power became the guiding principle in relations between the city-states of Italy as it was later between the nation-states of Europe.

The Peace of Lodi was a triumph for the papacy, since it guaranteed the integrity of the Papal States. After defeating the conciliar attack on papal supremacy, the popes were free to turn to other problems. In calling the conference that led to the Peace of Lodi, Nicholas V (1447–1455) hoped the restoration of peace in Italy would make possible a Crusade against the Ottoman Turks, who had just completed the conquest of Constantinople. Papal sponsorship of a Crusade became one of the goals of the Renaissance popes. But their other interests were more characteristic. Nicholas V, a Humanist himself, adorned the papal court with scholars and men of letters, after the fashion of the Renaissance despots. An avid collector of manuscripts, Nicholas founded the Vatican Library, of which his personal collection of several thousand volumes became the nucleus. Calixtus III (1455–1458) had no use for Humanism or Humanists; he filled the offices of the papal government with his own relatives. Among others, he appointed his nephew Roderigo Borgia to the cardinalate. Aeneas Sylvius Piccolomini, as Pius II (1458–1464), united in his person all the characteristics of the Renaissance papacy. A leading Humanist, his court attracted and rewarded other Humanists as well as relatives from his native Siena. He died during his last vain effort to organize a Crusade, having taken the cross himself. Paul II (1464–1471), a Venetian, actually launched a Crusade to recapture some of the Aegean islands from the Turks, but the expedition was not well supported and ended in disaster. Otherwise Paul II is chiefly remembered for closing the Roman Academy, a center of Humanistic studies, and for his patronage of horse racing.

Sixtus IV (1471–1484) was a man of very different mettle. He set out to enforce papal authority throughout the Papal States, and his methods were typical of Renaissance despotism. As usual, Florence stood in the way of any change in the *status quo*. Cosimo's son Piero had succeeded to his father's position; on his death Piero passed on the control of Florence to his two sons, Lorenzo and Giuliano. Sixtus IV lent his support to a group of conspirators headed by the Pazzi, a banking family and rivals of the Medici. The so-called Pazzi conspiracy (1478) was designed to eliminate their competitors in Florence by the simple expedient of assassination—at High Mass on Easter Sunday and by the hand of a priest. Giuliano was killed, but Lorenzo survived to continue and strengthen the Medicean rule of Florence.

Sixtus IV had already attempted to upset the balance of power by forming an alliance with Naples against Florence. Moving swiftly to cement his relations with Milan and Venice, and making a dramatic personal appeal to the king of Naples, Lorenzo de' Medici prevented the outbreak of a major war in Italy and preserved the precarious Peace of Lodi. His success in this critical hour, his patronage of the arts and letters, and his rule of Florence in the interests of peace and prosperity for Florentines—and incidentally, also, for all Italians—earned him the title of Lorenzo the Magnificent (1469–1492).

After Lorenzo's death the balance of power in Italy broke down rapidly. Innocent VIII (1484–1492) meddled ineffectively in the affairs of other

Sixtus IV engineered the assassination attempt on Lorenzo de' Medici and his brother Giuliano. But he also patronized the arts and Humanistic scholarship and built the Sistine Chapel, named for him. This painting shows him appointing the scholar Platina, best known for his biographies of the popes, prefect of the papal library.

Italian states. His successor, Alexander VI (1492–1503), the cardinal Roderigo Borgia, sought to create a central Italian state for his son Cesare Borgia, made famous by Machiavelli. Milan bore the brunt of this threat, intensified by a new claim by the king of Naples to the Milanese duchy, and in 1493 Ludovico Sforza of Milan appealed to Charles VIII of France (1483–1498) for help. The French king responded by asserting the Angevin claims to the kingdom of Naples and later to the duchy of Milan itself. In 1494 Charles invaded Italy; the invasion transformed the politics of the peninsula and became a turning point in Italian political history. For the first time since the early fourteenth century, an outside nation exerted its influence through armed intervention. The balance-of-power politics of the fifteenth century were replaced by alignment for and against the outsiders, and in town after town, this issue became the crucial one. At the same time, French involvement in the peninsula soon made Italy a focal point for the conflict developing in northern Europe between the Valois and the Habsburgs. The Habsburgs became heirs of the Aragonese claims to Naples when Joanna, heiress

Cesare Borgia was immortalized by Machiavelli as the archetypal Renaissance prince who had tried to create a universal Italian state. His portrait shows him holding a document of diplomacy, which, with the judicious use of force, was his most powerful weapon.

of Ferdinand and Isabella, married the Habsburg heir, Philip. Imperial claims to northern Italy, not pursued for more than a century, were now revived as an added impetus to Habsburg intervention in the peninsula. The politics of sixteenth-century Italy thus were part of and reflected European-wide conflicts; the Italians no longer controlled their own destinies.

## The Age of the Princes:
## Germany Under the Luxembourgs
## and Habsburgs

From the accession of Rudolf of Habsburg in 1273 until the death of Albert of Austria in 1308, each ruler had tried unsuccessfully to restore the rights of the German crown and to reestablish the hereditary principle of succession. To this end they had built up their own hereditary lands as the basis of a revived monarchy. The princes' opposition to this policy was climaxed by the deposition of Adolf of Nassau (1298) and the murder of Albert of Austria.

Henry VII of Luxembourg (1309–1313) abandoned the policy. Unable to oppose the princes, he tried unsuccessfully to revive the Hohenstaufen policy of basing his power on control of Italy. After Henry VII the king no longer possessed effective authority, and the dignity of the crown provided little more than an opportunity for dynastic aggrandizement.

At his accession, Henry VII was head of the small western house of Luxembourg. Before the end of his reign, he had established his son John on the throne of the kingdom of Bohemia, thus transforming the Luxembourgs into an eastern dynasty rivaling the Habsburgs. When Henry died prematurely, King John of Bohemia was only sixteen, and the Luxembourg party of the German magnates swung their support in the electoral college to the strongest anti-Habsburg prince, Lewis, duke of Bavaria. The supporters of Lewis and of Frederick of Habsburg were about equally divided. A disputed election was followed by civil war from 1314 to 1322, when Lewis IV the Bavarian won the throne by defeating Frederick in battle.

The reign of Lewis the Bavarian was little more than an ignoble scramble for territory and power among the magnates. Lewis himself took the lead in the land grab. Without any regard for the unity of Germany or the regalian rights of his office, Lewis used the waning powers of the crown primarily as the means of promoting the dynastic interests of his family. Meanwhile, John XXII (1316–1334) had become pope and refused to recognize either of the rival candidates. John asserted the right of the papacy to judge a disputed imperial election and denied that the fortunes of battle gave Lewis any superior right over Frederick. Summoned by the pope to renounce his prerogative until papal recognition of his title, Lewis refused. The pope excommunicated Lewis; the final phase of the medieval contest between the pope and the emperor began. It was a war of words in which all the old theories were revived and given more extreme expression than ever before.

Most of the German magnates supported Lewis, but only because they could gain more substantial concessions from the emperor than from a pope who could grant no lands or regalian rights in return for support. The princes thought they saw in the struggle an opportunity to enhance their own electoral powers at the expense of the papacy. They issued the Declaration of Rense in 1338, in which they asserted that whomever they chose as King of the Romans was, by that election, qualified to assume the title of king and to exercise the imperial authority without confirmation by the pope. In the same year Lewis promulgated the imperial ordinance *Licet juris* at the Diet of Frankfort. This ordinance confirmed the Declaration of Rense and further stated that election by the German electors was sufficient authority for the ruler so chosen to assume the titles of both king and emperor without papal approval. The ordinance further provided that those who resisted the imperial authority of Lewis should suffer confiscation of their imperial fiefs and of all privileges granted by Lewis and his predecessors.

Lewis then bungled badly, alienating the princes by entering into new negotiations with the pope and losing the support of Bohemia by allying with the English against the French, with whom the Luxembourgs had close ties. In 1346 the princes acted on the papal theory that the office of emperor was vacant and proceeded to elect a more satisfactory ruler—without, of course, admitting that this contradicted the Declaration of Rense. The pope had already agreed secretly to recognize the new emperor-elect if he would request papal confirmation before exercising the authority of the King of the Romans—without admitting that this agreement in any way limited the papal authority asserted by John XXII. And the candidate who made this agreement and who was in due course elected, Charles of Luxembourg, heir of King John of Bohemia, promised to wait for papal approval before being crowned king or emperor—without admitting that his coronation was in any way necessary for the valid exercise of royal authority in Germany. The whole business was a complicated series of subterfuges for political gains.

Civil war broke out immediately after the election of 1346, but within a year both King John of Bohemia and Lewis the Bavarian were dead, and Charles IV (1347–1378) was accepted by the majority of the princes and towns as emperor. Charles IV devoted most of his time and effort to strengthening his rule in Bohemia and expanding the kingdom. But he did not wholly neglect the German monarchy and the imperial dignity. He pacified the greater princes, including the Habsburgs and the successors and supporters of Lewis the Bavarian, by confirming them in the possession of all their lands and privileges. By tacit agreement each prince had a free hand to pursue his own dynastic ambitions. Beyond that Charles used his prestige and influence (there being nothing else to use, for lack of a royal administration or army) to preserve the peace. These efforts usually resulted in *Landfrieden,* or regional agreements among the magnates to keep the peace, which had begun to be an important part of German public law during the Great Interregnum. Pacification of Germany was important to Charles. He was determined to receive the imperial crown and could not risk disturbance or rebellion at home while he journeyed to Rome for his coronation. Charles scrupulously adhered to his agreement with the pope before his election in 1346 to refrain from exercising any authority in Italy without papal authorization, and to enter and leave Rome on the same day of his coronation, Easter Sunday 1355. Aside from gaining the imperial crown, to fortify his position in Germany, Charles had no interest in Italy beyond selling imperial titles to ambitious Ghibellines and gathering whatever taxes he could extract from the northern towns.

Back in Germany Charles turned to the task of excluding the papacy from German affairs as he had accepted exclusion from Italian affairs. After discussion in the diet, he promulgated the Golden Bull in 1356. This act confirmed the ordinance *Licet juris,* but while *Licet* denied papal authority in imperial elections, the Golden Bull simply ignored the pope. Otherwise, the

The table of contents from one of the seven known official copies of the Golden Bull of 1356. This copy is called the Mainz copy because it came from the archives of the archbishop of Mainz. The seal belongs to the Bohemian copy. Its obverse shows Charles IV in majesty, with scepter and globe, between the arms of the empire and of Bohemia. Its reverse shows "aurea Roma," the seat of empire.

document regularized and legalized the *status quo*. Because of divided successions in several princely houses, disputes over electoral rights had become a source of conflict among the greater nobles. Therefore, the Golden Bull provided that henceforth only seven princes were to be electors: the archbishops of Mainz, Trier, and Cologne; the count Palatine of the Rhine; the duke of Saxony; the margrave of Brandenburg; and the king of Bohemia. These great ecclesiastical and lay princes were confirmed in their regalian rights, so that each was practically independent of the emperor. In the electoral college a majority vote was defined as being legally a unanimous vote; royal and imperial authority were stated to be effective immediately on election; the count Palatine and the duke of Saxony were named regents during a vacancy in the throne; and provisions for a speedy election after the death of an emperor were set forth—including rations of bread and water for the electors if they took more than thirty days to reach a vote. Although the pope was not mentioned, these provisions nullified papal claims to adjudicate a disputed elec-

This copy of the Golden Bull was made in the court atelier of Wenceslas IV (ca. 1400). It is an extremely fine example of late-medieval illumination. In the bottom margin, Wenceslas' initial is illuminated to show him with his bath attendants.

tion, to confirm an election before the exercise of royal authority, and to govern the empire during a vacancy.

The Golden Bull was the last important public act of any medieval emperor, and it was one of the most effective. The Golden Bull did not increase but merely recognized the existing independence of the electoral princes, and it was in fact the only important deterrent to the general process of German decentralization. The electoral principalities were declared indivisible, and henceforth succession to the lay electorates was by primogeniture alone. The other principalities, not covered by the act, continued to be subdivided. Thus between the electoral states and the others the difference in size and power grew steadily. As the magnates of the middle and lesser ranks declined in power, the relative strength of the class of knights (or lowest nobles) and of the towns increased. Also, the towns holding privileges granted by the emperors, the free cities of the empire, often leagued together for mutual protection against the ambitions and avarice of the nobles.

The history of Germany in the later Middle Ages is the history of more than a hundred principalities. The emperors were no longer important, after Charles IV, and even he paid more attention to his kingdom of Bohemia than to Germany. Charles was succeeded by his son Wenceslas (1378–1400), whom the electors finally deposed after he lapsed into a prolonged drunken stupor. The next emperor was Rupert, count Palatine of the Rhine (1400–1410), whose ineffective reign was brought to a close by an early death. The second son of Charles IV, Sigismund (1410–1437), was more able, but he dissipated his energies in attempting too much with too little, both in resources and in personal capacity. At one point in the conciliar movement it appeared that Sigismund might reassert imperial leadership in a disunited Christendom, but he failed to play any significant role in the struggle between the popes and the councils. One reason for this failure was the rebellion confronting him in the kingdom of Bohemia, which he inherited after his brother Wenceslas' death in 1419. Here the Hussites stirred up a national resistance against German domination until internal divisions among them weakened the movement.

Anticipating his own death without an heir, Sigismund arranged the marriage of his daughter with Albert of Austria, which brought to the Habsburg dynasty the Luxembourg lands, including the kingdoms of Hungary and Bohemia, together with the strongest claim on the imperial title. Albert II (1438–1439) was duly elected, and the Habsburgs continued on the throne of the Holy Roman Empire for three more centuries. The change of dynasty, however, brought no change in imperial policy or power. Having resisted mounting pressure to concede the title of king to Duke Charles the Rash of Burgundy, Frederick III (1440–1493) negotiated the marriage of Charles' heiress, Mary of Burgundy, with his son Maximilian. Thus Maximilian (1493–1519) acquired the Burgundian inheritance and laid the basis for the predominance of the Habsburgs in Europe during the sixteenth century.

More than any other part of Europe, Germany suffered, under the Luxembourgs and Habsburgs, that "lack of governance" that afflicted England during the fifteenth century. Besides the seven electors, less than two dozen princes of the empire ruled territorial states of any substantial size. Only a few of these states were compact blocks of land under an effective central administration. The rest of Germany was a confusing conglomeration of tiny principalities, free cities, and fiefs held by knights who admitted no superior authority under the emperor. Constant subdivision of territories, wars and rebellions, and the transfer of lands through marriage or sale contributed to the general instability. Each petty prince sought only the aggrandizement of his own family possessions and power, without much regard for the legal rights of others or for the welfare of his subjects. The "Age of the Princes" was also

Central and Eastern Europe in the Later Middle Ages, ca. 1490–1494

the age of the robber barons. Private warfare between these petty princes and imperial knights could not be suppressed. The burghers of the towns found some protection in their leagues, but the mass of peasantry—who ultimately footed the bill for this anarchy—simply suffered exploitation or contributed to the general confusion by their sporadic and futile revolts.

## Central Europe and Scandinavia in the Later Middle Ages

In all of European history, the most striking political success achieved by peasants belongs to the hardy inhabitants of the three Forest Cantons of Uri, Schweiz, and Unterwalden on the northern slopes of the Alps. From their struggle to wrest independence from their Habsburg overlords grew the modern state of Switzerland. The Swiss valleys offered little to the farmers and shepherds who eked out a subsistence living, but their strategic location made them important in the control of trade and communications between Italy and Germany. The Saint Gothard Pass was opened in 1231, and at that time the emperor, Frederick II, granted privileges to the peasants of the Cantons because the other passes were controlled by his enemies. The Forest Cantons relied on their imperial privileges against the Habsburgs until, when Rudolf of Habsburg was emperor, they formed a confederation in 1291 for the maintenance of peace and mutual assistance against foreign intervention. Later Swiss popular histories depict the Habsburgs as cruel tyrants intent on crushing the freedom and draining the wealth of the liberty-loving mountaineers. Actually, the Habsburgs' main interest in the Forest Cantons was the encouragement of trade so that heavy taxes could be levied on the goods of German and Italian merchants using the Saint Gothard Pass.

For a while the Habsburgs were able to reassert their direct rule of the area, but under Henry VII of Luxembourg the Cantons were once more freed from all external authority except that of the imperial government. On Henry's death the Habsburgs decided to recover their rights by force. In 1315 the invading Austrian army was met in the mountain pass at Morgarten and decisively beaten. This was the first great victory of the Swiss infantry over the feudal cavalry of Europe. Following this victory, the emperor Lewis the Bavarian confirmed the Cantons in their privileges, and the Habsburg duke could do no more than conclude a truce that, in effect, recognized the independence of the Forest Cantons.

After Morgarten, the original confederation grew with the addition of neighboring districts, beginning with Lucerne in 1332. Each canton or town retained its own institutions and local self-government, while agreeing to maintain the peace and assist other cantons against enemies outside the confederation. Relations between the cantons and towns were complicated by the fact that new members frequently had to make exceptions to their adherence to the confederation or risk open rebellion. When the city of Berne joined, for example, its terms of alliance reserved the right of neutrality in any war against the Habsburgs, unless the Habsburgs attacked Berne. Meanwhile the confederation had grown aggressive. Incessant conflict marked the relations of the cantons with their neighbors, some of whom were forced to submit and join the confederation on dictated terms. The Habsburgs and other south German lords whose territorial rights were infringed by these developments now determined to crush the Swiss. In 1386 and again two years later full-scale war led to decisive victories by the burghers and peasants over the knightly armies of their feudal neighbors. In these campaigns the Swiss infantry, armed with crossbows and long pikes, proved their effectiveness in attack as well as in the defense of prepared positions. The threat of Austrian conquest led to a greater consolidation of the Swiss cantons. The military obligations of the several members were defined more precisely, and the power of the canton governments was ensured by placing limitations on the jurisdiction of ecclesiastical courts; but the confederation continued to exist without any central or federal government.

Security came with the Perpetual Peace of 1474, negotiated between the Swiss and the Habsburgs with French help. The Perpetual Peace lasted until 1499, when Maximilian once more tried but failed to subdue the Swiss. The confederation continued to grow throughout the period: by the end of the fifteenth century it consisted of thirteen confederate cantons, a dozen allied cantons, towns, and smaller districts, and about two dozen subject territories and bailiwicks. The local institutions of the allied and subject territories were respected, but participation in policy and control of revenues were restricted to the thirteen member cantons. The strongest aspect of the confederation was its military organization. The fame of the Swiss infantry spread far, and the most important Swiss export was mercenary soldiery, which could be found in the armies of all the major European rulers, including the papacy.

The Swiss demonstrated that under special circumstances a larger territorial unit could be built up by the confederation of small and contiguous areas. In northern Germany the Hanseatic League was the most successful of several efforts by towns to form similar confederations. However, the Hanseatic towns were not able to achieve a permanent union because they were allied primarily for economic purposes, and they were spread out over northern Europe.

In Scandinavia the nobles were the preponderant class at the beginning of the fourteenth century. They controlled the Church, whose prelates were recruited from their ranks, and they effectively limited their kings by continual opposition and occasional rebellion. The royal houses of the three kingdoms were closely related by marriage, as were many of the noble families, and little sense of national tradition existed in any of the kingdoms. German princes dabbled in Scandinavian politics, and in the endless northern wars the Hanseatic League threw its weight on whichever side would protect its monopoly of trade. The League's treatment of Scandinavia as a backward area for economic exploitation was an important factor in the tardy development of the kingdoms of Denmark, Norway, and Sweden in the later Middle Ages.

Toward the end of the fourteenth century a determined effort to unite the three kingdoms was made by Queen Margaret of Norway, daughter of the king of Denmark. Margaret's efforts for union and a strong monarchy under Danish predominance failed, however, and the three northern kingdoms continued to be troubled by frequent political upheavals. The nobility continued to be the predominant power, but peasants' uprisings and the ambitions of a slowly rising mercantile class in the towns contributed to the general instability. Nowhere in Europe were the medieval foundations of modern nation-states less impressive. Sporadic efforts in the fifteenth century to reunite Sweden and Denmark and Norway failed. The only beneficiaries of these efforts were the nobles. No one in the year 1500 could have predicted that Sweden was to become an important power in early modern Europe, or that Norway would lapse even further into the somnolence that characterized its existence under the tutelage of Denmark until the nineteenth century.

To the east of Germany were four states whose fortunes influenced the general course of European history. In the north were the territories won by the Teutonic Knights; south of these were the kingdom of Poland with the principality of Lithuania to its east; then the kingdom of Hungary with its Slavic vassal-states; and finally the kingdom of Serbia in the Balkans at the far south. During the later Middle Ages the eastward expansion of Germany in these areas was checked and in some cases thrown back by Slavic resistance. By the occupation of Estonia in 1326 the Teutonic Knights ruled the whole Baltic coast with its hinterland from the Oder River in eastern Germany all the way to Lake Peipus, on the confines of the territory ruled by the Grand Prince of Moscow. As each area was subdued, German merchants and nobles moved in to monopolize the trade and the landed wealth of the territory. Only in Prussia did a substantial German population follow the Knights; elsewhere the German occupation brought only an upper class to exploit the native population. But the eastward movement of German merchants was not confined to following the sword and the cross (the Baltic peoples were heathen and were converted and organized into a German-dominated Church). By peaceful penetration large numbers of Germans settled in Polish towns as well, where they formed the bulk of a small middle class of tradesmen.

The German expansion cut off both Poland and Lithuania from access to the Baltic and threatened further territorial losses to each state. Under native heathen princes, Lithuania in the fourteenth century expanded rapidly toward the southeast, stretching all the way to the Black Sea. The height of Lithuanian power was attained under Jagiello (1377–1434), to whom the Polish nobles looked for protection against the aggressive Teutonic Knights. Poland during this period had no strong central power to resist the encroachments of its neighbors. The nobles promoted a dynastic revolution in 1386, offering Jagiello the Polish crown and the hand of the princess Jadwiga, in return for the conversion of himself and his people to Latin Christianity. It was also expected that Jagiello would repel the Teutonic Knights. While it lasted, this dynastic union made the kingdom of Poland and Lithuania the largest state in Europe, in area if not in strength. But no real union took place. Lithuania almost always, even under Jagiello, had its own Grand Prince. Neither Poland nor Lithuania possessed what a Western ruler would have recognized as a central government. The king of Poland and the Grand Prince of Lithuania exercised over their privileged nobles even less authority than was wielded by the emperor over his German princes and nobles.

On the battlefield Jagiello acquitted himself well on behalf of his Polish supporters, although he was in no hurry to do so. It was only after further acquisitions of Polish territory by the Teutonic Knights that he finally raised a huge and motley army of Poles, Lithuanians, Russians, Tartars, Czechs, and still-heathen Balts and invaded Prussia. At Tannenberg in 1410 Jagiello's horde overran the German army and then occupied most of Prussia. Only the great headquarters fortress of Marienburg on the lower Vistula held out. But neither Jagiello's army nor his government were capable of a sustained military effort. Troubles at home diverted the king's attention, and by the Peace of Thorn (1411) the Teutonic Knights were left in possession of their lands except Samogitia, which gave Lithuania access to the Baltic.

The power of the Knights was broken, but their oppressive rule continued to alienate both the native and the German population of Prussia. After Jagiello's successor in Lithuania, Casimir IV (1434–1492), became king of Poland (1447–1492) as well, a coalition of nobles and towns known as the Prussian League appealed to Casimir for help in their revolt against the Knights. Hostilities dragged out for years until by the second Peace of Thorn (1466) West Prussia was restored to Poland. East Prussia was thus severed from territorial connection with Germany, and it was to be held by the Grand Master of the Teutonic Knights as a fief of the Polish crown. By the end of the Middle Ages, German expansion eastward had thus been brought to a halt and partially thrown back.

The kingdom of Hungary in the fourteenth and fifteenth centuries was, like all its neighbors, torn by dynastic struggles for the throne. These conflicts involved claims by the kings or princes of Lithuania, Poland, Bohemia, Luxembourg, Naples, and even Anjou in France. One reason the emperor Sigismund was so ineffective in Germany was his constant embroilment as king of Hungary (1387–1437) in the politics of Italy and the Balkans. Sigismund led a disastrous expedition against the Turks, the so-called Crusade of Nicopolis (1396), from which the badly mauled knights straggled back to their homes throughout Western and central Europe. Meanwhile the Turks had destroyed the kingdom of Serbia (1389). For the rest of the Middle Ages, Hungary replaced the Byzantine Empire as the eastern bastion of Europe, and under Matthias Corvinus (1458–1490) the Magyars firmly blocked the Danube valley against Ottoman expansion.

## Suggestions for Further Reading

The work by Denys Hay cited at the end of Chapter 24 is a good source for the general history of the late medieval period. See also the recent survey by E. Rice, *The Foundations of Early Modern Europe, 1460–1559* (New York, 1971). For late medieval Germany, see the work of Barraclough cited at the end of Chapter 8; that of Bayley cited at the end of Chapter 19; and F. L. Carsten, *Princes and Parliaments in Germany* (Oxford, 1959). D. P. Waley, *The Papal State in the Thirteenth Century* (London, 1961); P. Partner, *The Lands of Saint Peter: The Papal State in the Middle Ages and the Early Renaissance* (Berkeley and Los Angeles, 1972) and *The Papal State Under Martin V* (London, 1958); W. F. Butler, *The Lombard Communes* (New York, 1906); J. A. Symonds, *The Renaissance in Italy*, vol. 1, *The Age of the Despots* (London, 1926); and F. Schevill, *A History of Florence* (New York, 1936) are useful. For more detailed studies of Italian politics in the period, see W. M. Bowsky, *Henry VII in Italy: The Conflict of Empire and City-State* (Lincoln, Neb., 1960), and G. A. Brucker, *Florentine Politics and Society, 1343–1378* (Princeton, N.J., 1962). The surveys by O. Halecki, *Borderlands of Civilization: A History of East Central Europe* (New York, 1952) and *A History of Poland* (New York, 1956); P. W. Knoll, *The Rise of the Polish Monarchy: Piast Poland in East Central Europe, 1320–1370* (Chicago, 1972); F. J. Heymann, *John Zizka and the Hussite Revolution* (Princeton, N.J., 1955); and F. L. Carsten, *The Origin of Prussia* (Oxford, 1954) are good treatments of central Europe. On Scandinavia, see K. Larsen, *A History of Norway* (Princeton, N.J., 1948); J. H. S. Birch, *Denmark in History* (London, 1938); A. S. Stomberg, *Sweden* (New York, 1931); and I. Andersen, *A History of Sweden* (London, 1956). On Switzerland, see E. Bonjour, H. S. Offler, and G. R. Potter, *A Short History of Switzerland* (Oxford, 1952).

# 27 Social and Economic Changes in the Later Middle Ages

Two causes stand out for social and economic changes in the late fourteenth century: the Hundred Years' War and the Black Death. The plague, which had a wider effect on the European Continent, would seem to have had the greater impact of the two. Yet historians have not been satisfied to point to the recurrent epidemics and their drastic demographic effects as the source of the changes. They have asked whether the plague itself might have resulted from overpopulation. If this were true, then the European situation in the fourteenth century might have conformed almost perfectly to the Malthusian pattern according to which overpopulation would spread the food resources of Europe too thin and weaken the population, making it susceptible to disease. Certainly there is evidence that Italy at least was overpopulated in the decade prior to the plague; a Florentine chronicler reported that 17,000 paupers lived in his city in 1330. Yet, recent studies have shown that the population in some European regions was declining for a century before the plague struck in 1348, so that while overpopulation may have been a problem in the 1340s, it was in the process of curing itself by less catastrophic means than the plague. In addition, the plague hit some cities very hard late in the fourteenth century, after earlier epidemics had depleted the population by half or more and when resources were unquestionably sufficient for the existing population. Thus although the plague had an enormous demographic impact—the populations of some areas did not reach their late–thirteenth-century level again until the twentieth century—it is obvious that the simple Malthusian interpretation of its role will not suffice. The incredible mortality figures were produced by a combination of factors—demographic, sanitary, and the nature of the disease itself.

Other factors contributed to the economic disruption in the fourteenth century. The decline of population before and as a result of the plague reduced the labor force and the demand for goods and slowed the growth of late medieval industrial activities. The Hundred Years' War disrupted the commercial network throughout France and caused widespread destruction that diverted capital from economic enterprise to rebuilding. The scorched-earth policies of both sides during the war deprived many areas of the product contributions they normally made to the commercial system and put those areas into a tight economic situation that lengthened the effect of the destruction. At the same time, the wars endangered those who had accumulated large amounts of capital. Governments were in constant need of money and borrowed heavily from merchant-bankers who paid in that way for trading monopolies in the kingdoms. This system of finance might have worked in the interests of both parties if the wars had not continued so long. The long-term drain on governmental resources, however, made the borrowers unable to repay their debts and led to the bankruptcy of the great financial powers that had lent the money. These bankruptcies affected not only the commercial system but also the agricultural communities that had emerged from their early medieval isolation to participate in the international trade system developing in the thirteenth century.

These economic disasters changed the optimistic mood of the thirteenth and the first half of the fourteenth centuries to a pessimistic mood in the second half of the fourteenth century. Some historians have found that one reason the population was falling, in all classes, was that young people, uncertain about whether they could support a family, were not marrying or were delaying marriage until their economic situation improved. Since older couples produced fewer children than young ones, family size tended to decline. The same caution influenced the various interest groups and social classes in Europe. Lords secured legislation favorable to landowners. The bourgeoisie protected their monopolies with charters from rulers or with guild regulations. Peasants and urban lower classes sought to sell their labor or production at higher prices. Since the lower classes were often prevented by restrictive legislation and old servitudes from taking advantage of whatever economic strength they possessed, the tension between the classes increased.

## Agrarian and Urban Unrest

The economic position of the nobility was based on control of land, and land continued to be the most important form of wealth. The nobility, enjoying a rising standard of living in the twelfth and thirteenth centuries, exploited their landed wealth for the money income it would provide. The two ways of extracting profits from the land were by renting part or all of the manor to peasants, and by exploiting the manor directly by employing peasant labor on the demesne, that part of the manor reserved for the lord's own occupation. In an age of rising prices the latter method was generally more successful. Then in the fourteenth century prices of agricultural products began to decline. This situation was aggravated by the fact that prices of non-agricultural commodities tended to hold firm or even to increase. Thus the landholding class was caught between lower prices for what was sold and steady or higher prices for what was bought.

Except in circumstances especially favorable for direct exploitation—as when a manor was very productive and located near a good market—many lords had been willing to convert their manorial rights into money income. The demesnes were let out to the peasants, whose services were commuted for money payments to the lords. From the lords' point of view this system was satisfactory if rents held up, but in the fourteenth century, the peasants were squeezed between high rents and declining prices. The old bonds that held the manorial population together had been dissolved by the new cash nexus between landlord and tenant, and this gave a relatively greater freedom of movement to the peasants. Hence lords found it difficult to hold their tenants to their contractual obligations. Some peasants moved to more prosperous regions where they found opportunity to work for wages, others went to the towns to hire out their labor. Manorial lords were therefore under increasing pressure to lower rents. In some cases the manorial population declined to the point where tenements were actually deserted. To keep their land in production, some lords turned to hiring labor for wages. This system had the advantage of flexibility. Instead of adapting the operations of a manor to the labor supply on hand, lords could hire as much labor as was needed at a particular time, for example during spring plowing or for harvesting. These generalizations apply to many regions north of the Pyrenees and the Alps, but the economic picture of rural Europe in the fourteenth century was extremely complex, and exceptional conditions were found everywhere: exceptionally prosperous and exceptionally depressed localities, depending mainly on fluctuations in local production and prices.

Then in 1348 the Black Death struck Europe, having moved slowly westward along the trade routes from the Far East. All the wars of the Middle Ages did not cause as many casualties as the first onslaught and the successive waves of bubonic plague during the second half of the fourteenth century. The disease was spread by fleas infected by plague-stricken rats. In an age wholly ignorant of sanitation there was no defense against what seemed to be the wrath of God: to the destruction of life was added the horror and uncertainty in which men lived. The economic results must therefore be measured not only by the loss of population but also by the disruption of normal existence. People fled from stricken areas, deserting their work and spreading the plague to new regions. Some people squandered their money in one last fling; others abandoned their wealth and worldly goods in a last desperate effort to earn salvation by a life of asceticism and penance before death overtook them. The mortality has been variously estimated, ranging from one-fifth to one-third of the total population, but in some places it was more than one-half. More important was the incidence of mortality: death struck most heavily in the centers of greatest urban and rural population, that is, where economic life was most advanced. Some backward and isolated regions escaped the plague altogether.

The immediate results of the Black Death were deceptive. The mortality produced a labor shortage and a sudden increase in the income per capita. Wages and prices rose together. The result was an apparent prosperity. Peasants migrated to the towns to replace urban workers who had died, and the shortage of rural labor made possible not only higher wages for peasants but also the purchase of freedom from the manorial obligations of serfdom. For a few years everyone had more money and prices increased sharply. Then the reaction set in. Prosperity had been based on inflation, not on an expanding market. Production of agricultural and industrial commodities was soon able to meet the now diminished demand, and employers sought to cut their costs by rolling back wages to the level of 1348. Where the power of the state was strong enough to be effective, this effort took the form of maximum wage laws. In England, the Statute of Laborers (1351) and later statutes required laborers to accept customary wages (those prevailing before the plague) and also fixed the prices of food and other basic necessities at the 1348 level. It was very difficult to enforce such legislation, but, for the most part, the peasants were prevented from taking full advantage of the labor shortage resulting from the Black Death.

Despite the legislation, rural wages tended to rise. Under these circumstances manorial lords clung tenaciously to the customary labor services of the peasants, since it was too costly to hire workers to exploit the manorial demesne. However, the process of commutation and leasing the demesne for rent was not arrested entirely. Lords who had already commuted services for a money rent found it no longer profitable to exploit the demesne with hired labor; they leased their demesnes and collected rents from their whole manors. In either case—whether it was to the lord's advantage to enforce customary services or to convert his whole manor into rent-paying tenancies—the interests of the peasants and their lords clashed. Peasants agitated for the commutation of services into cash rents, since they could make more money as wage-earning laborers. This agitation grew into a general demand for the abolition of all manorial obligations, as lords tried to compensate for their declining incomes by enforcing their rights over the manorial commons, such as the meadows, fisheries, pastures, and woods, and to enforce the customary payments for use of mills, ovens, and other "appurtenances."

The lot of the urban working class was no better than that of the peasantry. Individual employers, the craft guilds, and town governments all tightened up regulations and laws designed to keep wages low and to protect the static or declining market from outside competition. The Black Death struck impartially at both employer and worker, but after the plague finally had passed, artisans found it more difficult than ever to gain admittance into the craft guilds. The economic and social gulf between masters and workers widened as economic conditions steadily deteriorated. Europe as a whole was confronted with the problem of overproduction. New opportunities to acquire fortunes by taking risks in an expanding market were extremely rare. Under these conditions the efforts of merchants and manufacturers to cut the costs of production (including wages) sometimes actually depressed the urban working class below the level of subsistence enjoyed by the peasants of the country.

The workers and peasants had no legal means for improving their lot. Many peasants were still unfree and subject to the jurisdiction of their lord's manorial court. Those who were free from the customary services were restive under legislation that favored the propertied classes by fixing wages and prices. In the towns discontent was even greater because urban workers were not protected by the customary rules that regulated the services and obligations of the manorial population. The result of these economic grievances was a series of revolts and uprisings during the second half of the fourteenth century. The Peasants' Revolt in England in 1381, the sporadic risings of the *Jacquerie* in France, and the Ciompi rising in Florence in 1378 have already been mentioned. Strife was frequent in towns of the Low Countries. These movements were by no means confined to the exploited urban and rural proletariat. Free peasants and some of the lesser nobles often participated in and sometimes led the uprisings, while the independent artisans and small shopkeepers of the towns, who resented the restrictions imposed by guild regulations, gave their support to revolutionary movements. The great merchants and the masters of the craft guilds controlled the urban governments in the interests of their guild organizations, just as the nobility dominated the lawmaking and the law-enforcing authorities in the country as a whole. The common cause that united all dissident groups was the absence of economic opportunity. The movements of the later fourteenth century were symptoms of a contracting economy in both town and country. The Peasants' Revolt was widely supported by townsmen in depressed areas in eastern and southern England, and the *Jacquerie* united with a radical movement in Paris led by Étienne Marcel, who was by no means a proletarian—actually, he was an influential member of the merchants' guild of the city.

The violent uprisings were aimed blindly at the existing order. Not only serfdom and the regulations restricting manufacture and trade, but the dominant classes were themselves attacked without much purpose, although often with brutal and destructive results. Manor houses were burned down, shops and town residences wrecked, and sometimes people were killed. Most of the movements were also strongly anticlerical because the Church was the greatest landlord and the most powerful single vested interest in maintaining the economic and social *status quo*. Peace and order, in almost every instance, were restored with even more violence and brutality, often with great loss of life among the lower classes. Few peasants or urban workers were better off as the result of revolt.

Rural economic conditions slowly improved during the middle years of the fifteenth century in Western Europe. In France and England by the end of the Middle Ages the great majority of peasants held their land in return for rents and subject to the payment of the customary heriot, or fee recognizing the lord's superior rights when the tenancy changed hands or passed to the heir. In France especially, and elsewhere in smaller degree, the nobles clung to certain seignorial rights fixed in terms of cash payments, such as tallage, tolls, and fees for use of the lord's share of meadows or commons. On the whole, the peasants were not as well off as their ancestors of the twelfth and thirteenth centuries, but they were more secure and a little more prosperous than their parents and grandparents, who had lived during the ravages of plague, famine, and the Hundred Years' War.

In central Europe economic recovery in the country lagged behind that of the towns. Declining incomes for both lords and peasants led to sporadic outbursts of violence from the latter during the fifteenth century, repressed with equal violence by the lords. In western Germany conditions generally resembled those of France, but in central and eastern Germany the earlier tendency toward emancipation of peasants was reversed. Lords exacted labor services and enforced manorial obligations to the full. The eastward movement began to slow down during the fourteenth century, and the defeat of the Teutonic Knights in the early fifteenth century closed the Baltic area to any further expansion. Peasants, therefore, ceased to benefit from the competition for labor on the frontier. However, the situation in central Europe was extremely complex, varying from region to region even more than in Western Europe. The main general difference between Western and central Europe, as far as the urban and rural lower classes were concerned, was the relatively depressed condition of the majority of German peasants at a time when German towns were in a relatively thriving condition. This is illustrated by the fact that few class conflicts in the towns actually erupted into violence.

## Commerce, Finance, and Industry:
## The Origins of Capitalism

One of the most striking features of the economic history of the later Middle Ages was the amassing of huge private fortunes by a few enterprising individuals or families. In the expanding economy of the twelfth and thirteenth centuries income and wealth were far more evenly distributed among members of the same social class than they were during the later period of diminishing opportunity and contracting markets. Not only was the gulf between rich and poor growing wider, but within the merchant and industrial class inequalities were increasing. In Venice, for example, during the last quarter of the fourteenth century about two-thirds of the merchant oligarchy possessed from 1200 to 12,000 ducats, one-third had more than 12,000, and seven great merchants possessed fortunes of over 140,000 ducats. In Basel one-quarter of the citizens possessed less than ten florins of taxable wealth in 1424, and by 1453 the number had grown to one-third of the citizens. In contrast, one-twentieth of the citizens owned half of the city's wealth.

While the majority of merchants suffered from the economic decline, a small number were able to accumulate amazing profits. Those who did so either diversified their interests or entered the field of "public" finance, or did both. With their wealth of experience as well as of money, the Italians were the most conspicuously successful. Among the remarkably prosperous businessmen were the Medici family of Florence and Jacques Cœur of France. The Medici got their start in the wool trade and soon branched out into cloth, silks, spices, furs, and other luxury goods. Throughout Europe they had branches and agents who bought and sold at their direction. At the very time that the Florentine population was declining and the textile industry was stagnant, the Medici were rapidly becoming the wealthiest family in Europe. They were able to dominate Florence for three generations. Meanwhile, the Medici diverted capital into the field of banking. Their extensive trading involved many separate credit operations, and their profits gave them funds to lend at interest to others. The success of the Medici bank attracted deposits from merchants with surplus capital, and by the time of Cosimo de' Medici (1434–1464) the Medici bank was the largest in Europe. The Medici acted as fiscal agents for the papacy, advancing loans and collecting ecclesiastical taxes. They also lent to secular governments, a risky enterprise that had involved earlier Florentine banking houses in failure when Edward III of England repudiated his debts in 1345. On a smaller scale merchant-bankers in Italy and elsewhere supplied princes all over Europe with credit.

Jacques Cœur of Bourges (1395–1456) got his start by supplying luxury articles to the court of the French king, Charles VII. This contact led to his appointment as director of the mint, a position from which he advanced in the service of the government until he finally had control of all finances and fiscal policy. His enterprises included extensive trade with the Levant, and he

Jacques Cœur's house in Bourges, built between 1442 and 1453, was worthy of his success and central position in the administration of the finances of the French crown.

invested in factories, mills, and mines. Aided by privileges and financial support from the government, he built a fleet of ships and dreamed of replacing the Italians and Aragonese in the control of Mediterranean trade. In his rapid rise, and—having incurred the king's displeasure as well as the enmity of his many noble debtors—in his spectacular fall from favor, the career of Jacques Cœur illustrates the possibilities and the dangers of public finance in the fifteenth century. More typical of the successful French bourgeoisie of the period were the merchants who made their fortunes from the war. Through illicit speculation, disposal of war booty, and the sale of food at inflated prices in famine-struck areas, many tradesmen of modest means made huge profits. But the risks of commerce were so great that this activity did not lead to a real commercial revival. After taking their profits, most of these ancestors of the modern black-market profiteers withdrew from business and invested their money in land. Within another generation many of them had entered the nobility.

Commerce in northern Europe had a different character. There was less emphasis on luxury trade, and few great fortunes were suddenly made. Banking played a role, but no great banking houses like those in Italy developed. Hence practically no great merchant princes like the Medici or Jacques Cœur rose to prominence. Rigid regulation of local trade by the merchant guilds left little room for individual initiative. The rising importance of craft guilds introduced a new factor, and in the fourteenth century German and Flemish towns were often disturbed by class conflict. But in Germany, at least, the greater merchants and their guilds reestablished themselves in control at the expense of the masters of the craft guilds. Since this was also the period when the imperial free cities were gaining independence from their lords, except for token allegiance to the emperor, the greater merchant families ruled in political as well as in economic matters, and since the guilds were practically closed to outsiders, the ruling families were a self-perpetuating oligarchy or patriciate. Earlier tendencies toward wider participation in the political and economic life of the towns were arrested, as the patricians made determined efforts to exclude competitors from their dwindling markets. The general decline in trade and industry that affected all of Europe thus had important social and political effects in the cities.

Northern commerce had enjoyed a vigorous growth in the early fourteenth century, however. The Champagne fairs declined at the end of the thirteenth

The spread of educational institutions, especially commercial schools, was necessitated by the advances of late-medieval merchants in developing complex forms of business. International business and elaborate trade networks could not be maintained without adequate records. This early–fourteenth-century trade book, recording sales of Flemish cloth, was kept by a merchant of Nuremberg.

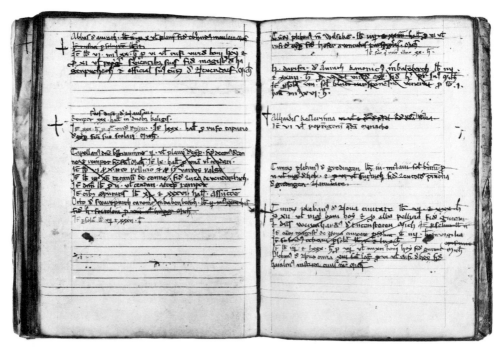

The importance of the cloth trade to the economy and culture of Bruges is made plain by the enormous Cloth Hall built by the city's merchants. Such buildings often dwarfed even the central churches of the northern towns in which merchants dominated town life. The hall of Bruges was begun in 1248, and the history of the belfry demonstrates the continued prosperity of the city throughout the later Middle Ages. The base of the tower was built between 1282 and 1296; the central section in 1395; and the octagonal top in 1482.

century, and the growing use of the sea route from Italy to Flanders made Bruges the new emporium for international exchange of goods between northern and southern Europe. The trade routes over the Alps into southern Germany carried a steadily increasing traffic that brought prosperity to many towns. The backward regions of Scandinavia were opened to exploitation. And the eastward expansion of the Teutonic Knights led to a flourishing Baltic trade. In the later Middle Ages cheap Baltic grains helped keep grain prices depressed throughout northern Europe.

From an early time the German merchants had found that cooperation in foreign parts served their interests better than competition. In England, for example, the Germans had a trading station in London and had secured common privileges from the crown by the end of the twelfth century. By the end of the thirteenth century similar stations were scattered from Lisbon in Portugal to Novgorod in Russia. Merchants from a score of German towns participated in their business and shared their privileges. The association of these merchants in foreign parts was the origin of the later association of the towns from which they came, the Hanseatic League.

Like the ecclesiastics who built the Gothic churches, the late-medieval merchants adorned the buildings in which they performed their lives' work. This relief depicting the weighing of goods was done by Adam Krafft for the façade of the public weighing house in Nuremberg.

The Hanseatic League grew up originally for economic reasons alone, primarily to increase and protect the Hansards' commerce and to secure a monopoly of trade where possible. The towns of the League combined their military and naval power to sweep pirates from the North and Baltic seas and to protect their merchants traveling inland by river or road. These purposes did not at first involve the merchants or their towns in any very systematic organization. During the fourteenth century the earlier occasional cooperation of several towns to meet exigencies was transformed into a permanent federation of towns with a central diet, or assembly, capable of formulating a common policy. At the same time the League grew until at its height about seventy towns belonged. These included towns in the Baltic region, Scandinavia, and the Low Countries as well as in Germany. Each town was assessed for its share of taxes, ships, and manpower in support of the League's policies. The basic reason for this stronger federation of the fourteenth century was the decline in trade, which made firm action necessary to protect the Hanseatic commercial interests from foreign competition. Hence the League was largest and most powerful after the main German commercial expansion came to an end.

In order to protect their trade the Hansards used both diplomacy and force. The critical struggle came from 1367 to 1370, when the League fought its first war. The king of Denmark was trying to restore royal authority and to extend his power into Sweden. The Danish conquest of Scania, in southern

Sweden, was a direct blow at the League because while under Swedish control the Hanseatic merchants enjoyed exclusive control of the great herring fisheries, the most important single economic asset of northern Europe at that time. Beyond that, the Danish king attacked the Hanseatic town of Wisby, on the island of Gotland, the key town in all the Baltic trade, and he raised and enforced the collection of tolls on shipping through the straits between the Baltic and the North seas. In its first effective united action, the Hanseatic League defeated Denmark and imposed the Treaty of Stralsund (1370) granting the League extensive privileges and maintaining the supremacy of Hanseatic merchants throughout Scandinavia.

The Hanseatic League declined slowly, yet inevitably. No method, short of economic reprisals or war, could force towns to remain in the League or even to abide by League policies. Divergent regional interests tended to separate the eastern, central, and western towns. Danzig and the Baltic towns desired unrestrained access to the markets of England and the Low Countries through the straits, while the central group wanted to preserve the older overland routes through northern Germany. The western towns were not interested in the special difficulties of the Baltic and were reluctant to contribute ships and money for the suppression of piracy in eastern waters. Even more serious was the rise of English and Dutch trade in northern waters. The English threat was staved off until after the Middle Ages, but the Dutch slowly increased their trade in Scandinavia and the Baltic area until the Hanseatic predominance was broken, and Antwerp in Brabant replaced Bruges in Flanders as the most important western terminus of the northern and northeastern trade.

The generally declining European economy of the later Middle Ages showed a few signs of strength or growth, most of them connected with technological improvements in industry. In the manufacture of woolen cloth, the invention and introduction of the spinning wheel and the fulling mill (to clean and shrink cloth) reduced the amount of labor required while increasing production. The water-driven fulling mill, appearing in the twelfth century and widely adopted by the fourteenth, was the first substitution of mechanical power for human effort in the textile industry. By its use, triphammers replaced human feet in the fulling process. The results were far-reaching. To take advantage of the fulling mill the industry had to be at least partially dispersed into hitherto backward areas where the fall of streams provided power. In the older urban textile centers this resulted in unemployment and unrest among the working classes, but regions where water power was abundant, especially in England and Italy, benefited from the greater efficiency of the mill.

The infant woolen industry in England also possessed the advantage of cheap raw material. The Flemish merchant paid not only the cost of transporting the wool from England to Flanders but also the export duties levied by the English government. In contrast, his English competitor had low transportation costs and a great tax advantage. English wool consumed in English looms was not taxed, the duty on exported cloth was low, and the duty on cloth imported from abroad was high. Thus encouraged by fiscal policy, the infant industry slowly grew, and by the middle of the fourteenth century English textiles had captured the home market, while by the middle of the fifteenth, England exported more woolen cloth than raw wool. The growth of English textiles was by no means even or easy, but by the end of the Middle Ages English woolens had outdistanced those of both Flanders and Italy in European markets. The Yorkist and Tudor kings reaped the profits of their predecessors' policy of fostering the woolen industry, for customs duties on exported cloth were an important revenue for the new monarchy.

Another strong sector of the later medieval economy of Europe was the mining and metallurgical industry. Here again technological improvements played an important role. New methods of extracting metals and the application of water power—for pumping out mines, operating bellows in blast furnaces, and crushing the ore—reduced costs and increased production, including the production of metal from low-grade ores hitherto unusable. Central and southern Germany led the way in iron, copper, and silver mining and extraction. The growth of mining and metallurgy was accelerated after around 1450, to become one of the important industries of the sixteenth century as well as the basis of new fortunes made by enterprising investors.

A final word is necessary concerning the medieval economy as a whole. If attention is shifted from particular persons, events, or developments to the general nature of business methods, it is clear that much of medieval industry and commerce—and the financial operations that supported them—was capitalistic both in spirit and in method. The question of when capitalism began is largely a quibble, since the answer will depend on the definition of the term. Characteristic features of modern capitalism were certainly present and in some regions conspicuous during the Middle Ages. These include the accumulation of capital in the form of money or goods, the extensive use of credit in both manufacturing and commercial transactions, and the separation of management from ownership. Such typically capitalistic attitudes and practices as large-scale and long-range planning, the assumption of calculated risks, the subordination of other considerations to the profit motive, and the treatment of labor merely as a factor in the production and distribution of goods for market—all these were present if not prevalent in the fourteenth and fifteenth centuries, and had appeared even earlier. Medieval capitalism had not yet achieved the refinements of modern techniques of industrial organization. Mass markets, joint stock companies, exchanges for the sale of stocks and bonds, and other features or agencies of modern capitalism had not yet developed. But on a small scale, and within the limits of a society whose population and purchasing power were no longer expanding, it is clear that the capitalistic economy of modern times was already beginning to develop long before the end of the fifteenth century.

## The Decay of Feudalism:
## The "New Chivalry"

A popular chronicler, writing in the fifteenth century, paused in his task of narrating chivalrous deeds to describe briefly the orders, or estates, of society. His account is conventionally hierarchical. God, he wrote, created the common people to labor in the fields and to supply the goods of life through trade, the clergy for worship and the works of religion, and the nobles to cultivate virtue and maintain justice. The nobles, according to this account, protect the Church, defend the faith, shelter the people from oppression, oppose tyranny and violence, maintain the peace, and support the common weal. The virtues of the nobility are honor, truth, courage, largesse, and integrity. This is a typical view; it is also a beautiful illustration of that triumph of fiction over fact especially characteristic of the period's ideas and values. Contemporary chroniclers do not provide the historian with very reliable evidence about the classes of society and the changes in their condition.

The character of the dominant class, the aristocracy, was transformed during the later Middle Ages. Some of the developments that were undermining the "classical" feudal institutions of the twelfth and thirteenth centuries have already been discussed. These forces continued to have their effect, and by the end of the fourteenth century a strictly feudal society no longer existed in most of Europe.

Later medieval society still contained feudal elements. Some particular elements or aspects of feudalism survived well beyond the Middle Ages. For example, the modern law of real property in English-speaking countries derives partly from feudal custom. But these survivals obviously do not explain the nature of modern society. Less obviously, the continuity of feudal institutions in the later Middle Ages does not reveal the real nature of the society of that period. Lords still had vassals, but their relations had changed. Fiefs and feudal incidents, feudal jurisdictions and feudal privileges still existed, but their nature had changed and their effectiveness had been circumscribed. In two ways feudal institutions were no longer the real framework of later medieval society. First, the obligations of the noble to the lord from whom he held his fief were not as important as his obligations to the territorial ruler. Within the aristocracy the vassal–lord relationship was less immediate and binding than the subject–ruler relationship. Second, the economic position of the aristocracy was not assured merely by the possession of landed wealth. Nobles who could not make their manors pay a profit in an age of uncertain markets, declining agricultural prices, and depreciated currency were no longer able to maintain their status. Some lesser nobles declined substantially in their economic and social condition, so that their manor houses were dubbed *châteaux de la misère,* and their noble status was little more than a legal fiction.

Other nobles held their own or even advanced in economic status or political power. For convenience, the several developments affecting the status of nobles in the later Middle Ages may be classified as military, political, and economic. The feudal levy of vassals gradually disappeared in many regions. Some reasons for this development are clear enough. The infantry became the dominant branch in the English forces of the Hundred Years' War and in the Swiss forces that defeated Duke Charles the Rash of Burgundy and the Habsburgs. But even the French armies, which continued to be predominantly cavalry until well into the fifteenth century, no longer consisted primarily of the feudal levy of vassals doing knights' service. The cavalrymen were often royal vassals, or vassals of royal vassals fighting for their immediate lords in the service of the king—but they fought when needed, as long as needed, and for pay. Warfare had become part of the money economy. Poorer vassals could not equip themselves properly for cavalry fighting, and rulers did not want their service. It was more efficient to commute their military obligations into money payments with which to hire the services of well-equipped and trained mercenaries. Often as not, such cavalrymen were in fact nobles. But now their service was performed as the result of an indenture between the ruler and themselves, without regard to the tenure of a fief or the general obligations of vassalage.

The indenture of the later Middle Ages was not essentially new. It grew out of a practice, going back at least to the early twelfth century, by which lords occasionally granted their vassals annual sums of money in lieu of fiefs. Originally these money-fiefs often carried the same obligations of vassal to lord as ordinary fiefs. But it was a simple matter to change the terms of the charters creating such money-fiefs into written contracts for specific military service in return for a stipulated salary. Such a contract was an indenture. It often included, or took the form of, a commission authorizing the noble to recruit a company of troops. As their captain, the noble would train, provision, and lead them in battle at a stipulated rate of pay to be supplied by the ruler.

Thus military service and feudal institutions often had no significant connection. Lords both great and petty entered into agreements to raise and lead troops for pay, and the size of such contingents of mercenaries bore no relation to the fiefs held by these nobles. In the Hundred Years' War some very minor lords accumulated fortunes from the booty and ransoms they and their men collected. Also, it was possible to rise to a higher position in the government by successful leadership of mercenary companies. The aristocracy continued to play a leading role in warfare, but no longer as the feudal host of an earlier age.

The political role of the aristocracy also declined during the thirteenth century, when the Western monarchies were building governments that employed professional civil servants and no longer needed to depend so much on the cooperation of the nobles. In central Europe no central government was strong enough to subordinate the nobility, but the tendency toward disintegration or particularism resulted in the multiplication of petty principalities. The power of the nobles as a whole, as an estate, increased; but the power of individual nobles declined as the territories and populations that the majority of nobles ruled grew smaller. Two different trends are therefore apparent. In the Western monarchies the aristocracy struggled to regain its lost political power; in central Europe the aristocracy was jealous to preserve its rights of local political autonomy against any assertion of authority by the emperor or by the greater princes of the empire or, in Italy, by the pope. Despite these divergent tendencies and the special conditions that prevailed in Italy, the basic fact for all of Europe is that in the later Middle Ages the political activity of the aristocracy can no longer be described adequately by the feudal phrase "aid and counsel," according to which the vassal owes his lord advice and material assistance in the formulation and execution of political policies.

In the political sphere, as in the military, the aristocracy of the later Middle Ages was no longer feudal in the same way as the barons of the twelfth and thirteenth centuries. Those barons had pursued essentially feudal goals and acted in accordance with feudal custom governing the relations between vassals and lords. For all the crudity and violence of the earlier age, the feudal rules were still observed well enough so that a breach of accepted standards of conduct was scandalous. In the later period it would be difficult to find any standards by which nobles vied with each other and with rulers to increase their power. Partly this can be explained by the fact that the political stakes were far higher. The twelfth-century lord generally fought only for his fief— either to defend it against attack or to enlarge it at the expense of his immediate neighbors. In the fifteenth century the English and French nobles were struggling for control of an entire nation. In the difference may be seen the decline of feudalism as a political system.

In the economic sphere the confusion of ideals and realities in the decadent feudal society of the later Middle Ages is a striking feature. Just as the noble was ideally supposed to maintain the peace and repress tyranny, but often spent his time fighting civil wars or oppressing the weak and defenseless, he was also supposed to promote the general welfare of the people, but actually devoted his energies to exploiting or simply robbing whatever poor peasants or wealthy merchants came within his reach. The robber barons of Germany are appropriately so called. In Western Europe simple lawlessness was not quite so easy, but exploitation was at least as great as the law would allow, and usually a little more so. The economic tendencies of the later Middle Ages generally worked against the interests of the landowning aristocracy and to the benefit of the peasantry. The more aggressive nobles recouped themselves with the spoils of war or the spoils of political office, but some found more peaceful ways of preserving or even improving their economic status.

Deep-rooted prejudice against the occupations of the lower-classes prevented all but a tiny minority of the aristocracy from diverting their resources into commercial enterprise. Of the few who did, most were Italians of the lesser nobility. The trend was actually the other way around. Prospering commoners who were engaged in trade or industry bought their way by marriage into the ranks of the aristocracy. More typical were nobles who followed the lead of the greater ecclesiastical landowning corporations and turned to large-scale or commercial agriculture. Rather than extract services from unwilling peasants or collect rents that tended to decline with every change in tenancy, these lords expelled their peasants and consolidated their manorial fields in favor of production for market, using hired labor. This system worked best where little labor was required, or where conditions were well suited for a single crop that could be produced more economically in a particular region. Thus in northern England some lords converted their manors into sheep farms for growing wool exclusively, while in eastern Germany lords often found it profitable to limit production to a single grain crop for market. Nobles who were so engaged made their profits by careful management of hired labor and equally careful attention to current prices in various markets. They were essentially rural businessmen, no longer members of the feudal nobility holding fiefs merely to support their service to their lords.

As the realities of feudal society gave way to a new social order, in its military, political, and economic aspects, the ideals and values of feudalism were asserted more strongly than ever. People seemed unwilling to recognize the changes that were shaping a new Europe. The age that witnessed the triumph of the foot soldier over the mounted knight, the rise of both peasants and townsmen to a greater share in the total wealth of Europe, and the advent of strong monarchies in the West and power politics in all regions, was also the age in which the ideals of chivalry were expressed most extravagantly. The vogue of the "new chivalry" reached its climax in the foundation of several knightly orders. Edward III, for example, founded the Order of the Garter; John the Good of France established the Order of the Star; and Duke Philip the Good instituted the Order of the Golden Fleece. The overt aims of these orders may be indicated by a contemporary explanation of the high purpose of the Order of the Golden Fleece:

> Not at all for play or pastime,
> But to the end that praise be given
> First to God above all,
> And also glory and high renown to good men.[1]

[1] J. Huizinga, *The Waning of the Middle Ages* (London: Edward Arnold Ltd., 1948), p. 75.

Actually, these orders were sponsored by the courts almost exclusively for courtiers, noble politicians, and foreign nobles whose political support was coveted. They had an elaborate and artificial ceremonial, complete with special offices, titles, and chivalrous vows, and they were very popular with the aristocracy, or at least with those who had social and political ambitions. In contrast with the Knights Templar, Hospitallers, and Teutonic Knights of earlier times, these latter-day orders of chivalry performed no military, social, or economic function of immediate practical value. They provided a kind of organized social world for the nobles who made good in the later Middle Ages.

### Suggestions for Further Reading

For the economic developments of the later Middle Ages, see the general works cited at the end of the Introduction. J. W. Thompson, *Economic and Social History of the Later Middle Ages* (New York, 1931); E. E. Power and M. M. Postan, eds., *Studies in English Trade in the Fifteenth Century* (London, 1933); E. E. Power, *The Wool Trade in English History* (New York, 1941); H. Zimmern, *The Hansa Towns* (New York, 1889); and P. Dollinger, *The German Hansa,* trans. D. S. Ault and S. H. Steinberg (Stanford, Calif., 1970) are also good studies. Among more recent works of smaller scope but great value are David Herlihy, *Pisa in the Early Renaissance: A Study of Urban Growth* (New Haven, Conn., 1958); S. L. Thrupp, *The Merchant Class of Medieval London, 1300–1500* (Chicago, 1948); Iris Origo, *The Merchant of Prato* (New York, 1957); Raymond de Roover, *Money Banking and Credit in Medieval Bruges* (Cambridge, Mass., 1948) and *The Rise and Decline of the Medici Bank, 1397–1494* (Cambridge, Mass., 1963); A. R. Bridbury, *England and the Salt Trade in the Later Middle Ages* (Oxford, 1955); and A. B. Kerr, *Jacques Cœur* (New York, 1928). On later medieval agriculture and rural life, see H. S. Bennett, *Life on the English Manor* (Cambridge, 1937); G. C. Homans, *English Villagers of the Thirteenth Century* (Cambridge, Mass., 1940), a sociological study; E. A. Kosminsky, *Studies in the Agrarian History of England in the Thirteenth Century* (Oxford, 1956); R. H. Hilton, *A Medieval Society: The West Midlands at the End of the Thirteenth Century* (New York, 1966); and J. Z. Titow, *English Rural Society, 1200–1350* (New York, 1969), which contains documents as well as commentary. For France, see the classic of M. Bloch and the study by G. Duby, both cited at the end of Chapter 11.

# 28 Cultural Developments in the Later Middle Ages

The intellectual and artistic history of the Middle Ages is one of much fluctuation in activity and many changes in taste, interest, and emphasis. This constant change of course characterized other periods as well, and thus it is always difficult to argue that an epochal change has taken place. It has been seen that this is a problem in dealing with the transition from the Roman to the medieval period, but the massive Germanic invasions gave a natural impetus to talk of epochal change. Nonetheless, while seventh-century society differed greatly from fourth- or fifth-century society and while the invasions had something to do with this change, the same can be said about any two eras separated by two or more centuries. If the transition problem is difficult to pinpoint in the beginnings of the Middle Ages, it is much more difficult at its end, for that transformation took place in the minds of men, not in social, economic, or political change. Social and economic change continued along lines established in the later Middle Ages toward greater commercialism, urbanism, and nationalism. Even the terrible disruption caused by the Black Death had been anticipated in earlier demographic and economic changes.

Thus discussion of the dawn of a new era in the fifteenth century has focused on intellectual and artistic changes wrought by a small group of men centered first in Italy but then spreading their influence north of the Alps.

The importance of these men, primarily the Humanists but also the new-style artists, has been a subject of much debate. In the nineteenth century, Jacob Burckhardt and Jules Michelet saw in them the creators of the modern age, the geniuses who broke with the weighty tradition of medieval abstractness, mysticism, and intellectual aridness to rediscover the classical world's love of nature, realism, and secular, rational perspective. These historians were presenting ideas derived from the fifteenth-century writers themslves, for the Humanists had come to look on the vast period separating them from the ancients as a dark age. The age was not as dark as the Humanists wanted to believe, however, and modern scholars, having achieved an appreciation of medieval civilization, have been debating whether they should nevertheless accept the fifteenth-century judgment that a new age was born then. The division of opinion on this issue reflects the judgments of historians about what elements in civilization are crucially important. The problem is one of definition and identity. What is medieval civilization, and how much and what kind of changes must occur before that civilization is recognized as having been transformed into a different one? Modern historians have maintained the view that a new era began in the fifteenth and sixteenth centuries, while questioning the importance of individual changes in that period.

## The Intellectual Background of the Italian Renaissance

In most regions of Europe, educational opportunity and institutions expanded in the later Middle Ages. Elementary education was still carried on in the households of noble and successful bourgeois families. Poor boys—when they were lucky—received the basics from parish priests. In larger towns, teachers were sometimes hired by chapels founded and maintained by guilds or other lay associations. These schools, which became widespread in the later fourteenth and the fifteenth centuries, were not established institutions. The grammar schools, the secondary level of education where the *trivium* was taught to boys between the ages of about ten and sixteen or seventeen, were run by the cathedral churches, as they had been in the high Middle Ages, and by the town councils and lay religious associations. Thus in the first decades of the fifteenth century, the educational system below the university level had a less ecclesiastical but not less religious look than it had earlier. Most schools were founded to produce better educated clergy, but many students did not intend to become clergy, and a significant number of the merchants appear to have received their education in such schools. The Florentine chronicler Giovanni Villani reports that in the 1340s the four grammar schools in the city taught between 550 and 600 boys each year and that another 1000 to 1200 went to commercial schools, which taught the basics of arithmetic needed by those who wanted to go into the service of merchants and bankers. These commercial schools were free from Church control and were found in the north as well as the south. The city fathers of Hamburg and Lubeck had established such institutions.

The number of universities also increased in this period, not to meet a new or growing student demand but for political and economic reasons. Many local governments established universities as an expression of their political independence, and some of them tried to force students from their principalities to attend the local institutions. Louvain's city council founded a university in 1425 in the hope that it would revitalize the town's economy. The older international universities remained strong but lost students and became more regional in their student bodies if not in their intellectual impact.

The curriculum in the schools and universities remained traditional. Most of the textbooks had been standard since the twelfth century: the *Sentences* of Peter Lombard, the *Decretum* of Gratian, the *Corpus Juris* in civil law, and, along with the late classical grammars, others compiled in the twelfth century. The reaction against Thomism in the generation immediately following Thomas Aquinas received a strong impetus from the work of Duns Scotus (1265?–1308) and William Ockham (1270?–1349). Duns Scotus was a Franciscan who taught at Oxford and subjected Thomistic epistomology to a careful critical analysis. The fineness and subtlety of his distinctions earned him the title "The Subtle Doctor."

Duns Scotus accepted, while desiring to improve, the basically rationalistic metaphysics of medieval scholasticism. His most important successor, William of Ockham, another English Franciscan, went beyond constructive criticism to a position that was basically antirationalistic. The two spheres of reason and revelation, which Aquinas sought to join, Ockham now rent asunder. Christian dogma, he insisted, must be accepted on faith only, because it could not be demonstrated by reason. This position implied the converse: that the sphere of natural truth should be open to rational investigation unimpeded by metaphysical or theological considerations. In the same spirit, Ockham argued that the simpler of two hypotheses or principles should always be preferred in offering an explanation of natural phenomena. It followed that all discussion of universals was simply irrelevant because knowledge thereof added nothing to knowledge of particulars or individual things, of which unaided reason can attain a direct apprehension. Ockham's nominalism condemned the metaphysical speculation so popular among the earlier realists as useless and misleading. It also consigned the data of revelation to a doubtful, if not needless, category as far as human knowledge of the natural world is concerned. It is in this sense that Ockham has been called one of the founders of modern science. In his own and the next generation at the University of Paris some important contributions were made by Ockham's followers, such as Jean Buridan (d. 1358) and Nicholas Oresme (d. 1382), who advanced beyond Aristotle's theory of motion and even proposed the heliocentric theory in the field of celestial mechanics. These and similar efforts, however, did not lead to any general development of scientific enquiry in the fifteenth century, although the work of Nicholas of Cusa (d. 1464) and others kept the University of Paris in the forefront of later medieval science.

Ockham's ideas received widespread support in the later medieval universities, and nominalism can even be said to have predominated during this period. Thomism remained strong at some places, such as Cologne, however, and several of the leading thinkers of the period were, like the Thomists, realists in their metaphysics. During the later fourteenth and the fifteenth centuries, university faculties therefore divided into schools sharply opposed to each other.

The trend of Ockham's philosophical and theological thought, its emphasis on the separation of reason and faith, was reflected in parallel, but not derivative, religious movements. Lay piety and mysticism grew significantly. The wide appeal of mysticism in the later Middle Ages gave rise to a voluminous and popular devotional literature. The *Imitation of Christ,* attributed to Thomas à Kempis (1380–1471), was the outstanding work, and a score of important treatises and a hundred mediocre ones of a similar nature were also produced. All these works, in greater or lesser degree, appeal to the emotions rather than to the intellect. They provided a program of salvation emphasizing inner spirituality, faith, and love above reason and good works. They were not, with a few exceptions, unorthodox. But by minimizing the role of the clergy and of the sacramental system they helped create a climate of religious experience that was favorable to the Protestant reformers of the sixteenth century. Martin Luther was profoundly moved by the anonymous fifteenth-century work *German Theology,* a typical tract of the times.

Most of the new religious organizations of the later Middle Ages found their inspiration in mysticism, especially those whose work or teaching tended toward extreme expressions of piety. Best known and most influential were the Brethren of the Common Life, founded by Gerard Groot (d. 1384), a popular lay preacher in the Low Countries and a follower of Jan van Ruysbroek, who in turn was a disciple of Eckhart (d. 1327), a German Dominican whose mystical preaching and writing had a powerful impact. The teachings of Groot and the Brethren, at first suspected for heretical tendencies, soon became the finest example of the new devotion (*devotio moderna*). Like the mendicant friars, they were dedicated to preaching and charitable work among the poor and the downtrodden, but they were not mendicants. The majority of Brethren were laymen, and although they lived in common, they took no monastic vows. Their most lasting contribution was in education. Among the intellectual leaders of northern Europe who went to their schools or attended classes in schools where Brethren taught were Nicholas of Cusa, Thomas à Kempis, Rudolf Agricola (1443–1485), who was the first important German Humanist, Erasmus of Rotterdam, and Martin Luther.

Closely related to popular mysticism were many other communal movements, more or less organized, such as the lay brotherhood of the Beghards and the sisterhood of the Beguines, the Brethren of the Free Spirit, the Friends of God, and the Flagellants. Some of these groups were so extreme that they lapsed into heretical beliefs or practices. These movements were important symptoms of unrest and dissatisfaction with the established order and with the teachings of the Church.

On a higher intellectual level, but expressing the same dissatisfaction, were the movements led by John Wycliffe (1325?–1384) in England and John Huss (1369–1415) in Bohemia. Both Wycliffe and Huss criticized contemporary ecclesiastical abuses. In theology Wycliffe was influenced strongly by Ockham in emphasizing the priority of faith over reason. He also stressed the priority of the Scriptures over *Traditio,* the traditional customs and teachings of the Church. Many of Wycliffe's views verged on heresy without quite being heretical, but his stand on apostolic poverty and his denial of transubstantiation definitely placed him outside the orthodox fold. Even after he was condemned for heresy, however, Wycliffe was secure in his person and died peacefully. For this good fortune he had to thank his supporters at the court of Richard II and the fact that his attack on the papacy and on ecclesiastical wealth and privilege was popular with the English aristocracy. His was one of the early voices of English nationalism. Wycliffe's ideas were developed further and spread throughout England by his followers, or by those who claimed to speak in his name and who called themselves Lollards. Because Lollardy emphasized a program of economic and social reform together with an attack on ecclesiastical abuses, and associated itself with the Peasants' Revolt of 1381, the movement was ruthlessly suppressed.

Wycliffe's teachings were preserved, by a curious circumstance, not in England but in far-off Bohemia. The courts of the two countries were in close communication because of the marriage of Richard II with Anne of Bohemia, who was the half-sister of Wenceslas and the sister of Sigismund, both kings of Bohemia and emperors. Czech students who went to England in the entourage of Queen Anne brought the works of Wycliffe back to the University of Prague. Wycliffe's ideas were congenial to the developing Czech movement of lay preaching that became centered in a special chapel, the Bethlehem Chapel (founded in 1391), in Prague. John Huss, one of the principal preachers at the chapel and the rector of the university, made Wycliffe's theology an element in the growing tension between Czechs and Germans both inside and outside the university. The Hussite movement gained strength in the early fifteenth century, which resulted in the expulsion of the Germans from the university—they went to Leipzig and founded a new university there—and in Huss' condemnation and burning at Constance.

Many late-medieval heretical groups aimed sharp criticism, often wickedly humorous, at monastic institutions. This drawing stems from Hussite propaganda charging that monks and nuns fell a bit short of their vows of celibacy.

Both Wycliffe and Huss were important figures in the growing vernacular culture. They preached in their native languages and urged the translation of the Bible into the vernacular. In fact, the fourteenth century was an important period in the development of the vernacular languages and literatures of Europe generally. One of the variety of dialects spoken in each of the major European languages, with the exception of German, established its preeminence as the literary language of the nation.

In Italy, Dante (1265–1321), Francesco Petrarch (1304–1374), and Giovanni Boccaccio (1313–1375) established Tuscan as the literary language of the peninsula. In France the long tradition of the *langue d'oïl* (the courtly romances and *fabliaux* of the twelfth and thirteenth centuries) became the basis for the predominance of this language over the southern *langue d'oc*. Two main factors played a role in this victory of the northern language: the thirteenth-century Albigensian Crusade and the subsequent assertion of royal power in the south made the *langue d'oïl* the political and legal language of the whole kingdom; and the brilliance of the court of Burgundy in the fifteenth century produced literary works of great popularity and impact. In Spain, Castilian became the vehicle of Iberian literary production. The Castilians had been the principal heirs of the peninsula's rich mixture of cultures, which enriched their language. In the fifteenth century the kingdom of Castile also became the center of a school of writers who copied the French and Italian modes. Finally, several fourteenth-century English writers produced works of lasting literary and linguistic importance. William Langland (1330?–1395) wrote an allegorical poem, *The Vision of William Concerning Piers Plowman,* that presented not only the traditional religious themes of salvation but also a critical view of contemporary society. In the same period, many English mystical writers wrote in their native tongue. The most important English vernacular author of the period was Geoffrey Chaucer (1343?–1400), whose *Canterbury Tales* are the greatest literary monument in Middle English. This work had much to do with the growing predominance in the early modern period of the English of London as the national form of the language. The spread of literacy in the fourteenth century is demonstrated not only by the increasing amount of vernacular literature but by the widespread movement to translate the Bible into the vernacular languages. The culture and religion of the towns was becoming a literate culture.

The rise of vernacular literatures would seem to have been an expression of the growing definition of political entities in the later Middle Ages and to have been itself a factor increasing the isolation of regions from one another. But the rise of the vernacular literatures did not reflect the decline of the international Latin culture of Europe, but the growing literacy of the people who were not intellectuals. And the vernacular writers borrowed from one another across linguistic boundaries. Chaucer adopted material from Boccaccio and translated the *Roman de la Rose* into English. The French romances were translated into German, English, and Spanish. Italians borrowed French material for their work. Thus, the expanding vernacular culture did not increase the cultural division between regions to the degree one might suppose.

In art the same communication between areas had important effects. The Gothic style had developed steadily, becoming more and more elaborate with each new building, and the late Gothic style spread throughout Europe, including Italy, during the fourteenth century. But as architecture became increasingly ornate, painting and sculpture became increasingly realistic. Portrait painting developed in northern Europe in the later fourteenth century, and under the patronage of the duke of Burgundy, Hubert van Eyck (1366–1426) and his more talented brother Jan van Eyck (1385?–1441) led a movement toward realistic painting that emphasized detail. The aim of the painter became the presentation of the world as it is. Italian painters like the Florentine Giotto (1266–1337) and the Sienese Simone Martini (1283–1344) had already begun to develop a more realistic style, but the Flemish painters went much further and won the admiration of fifteenth-century Italians. The Flemish also invented oil painting, to replace egg tempera, giving painters the ability to work on large canvases and to develop better techniques of representation.

Giotto was recognized as the greatest painter of his age: the bishop of Florence commissioned him to build the campanile of the cathedral there; the Franciscans had him paint frescoes in their central church of Saint Francis at Assisi. In the gesture of a great artist, Giotto responded to a papal emissary's request for a sample of his work by drawing a perfect circle in a single stroke and handing it to the inquirer. His masterpieces are in Padua, from which this fresco, the *Pietà,* comes. His weighty figures express profound emotion, and he was the first painter to use perspective effectively.

Another northern invention that had an enormous cultural impact was printing. From the 1430s on, several people were experimenting with printing methods. Among them, Johann Gutenberg (1397–1468) appears to have been the first to perfect movable type, which might be set and reset for the printing of many books. In 1453 Gutenberg produced a large Bible (the forty-two-line Bible), the first printed book in Europe. The new invention met the great demand for books that accompanied the increase of literacy. By the 1480s, printing presses had been established in major cities throughout

A page from the forty-two-line Bible printed by Gutenberg in 1453. Many attempts had been made to develop a working press, and Gutenberg's achievement thus met a felt need. As a result of the invention of movable type, printing quickly spread throughout Europe.

Europe, and the production of these presses is revealing. By 1500, ninety-four Vulgate Bibles, more than thirty vernacular Bibles, ninety-nine editions of Thomas à Kempis, and all sorts of grammars and school books had been printed. By the end of the century, the printing center was Venice, where in 1490 the first great scholar-printer, Manutius Aldus (1447–1515), established his business. His editions of classical works won widespread acceptance throughout Europe and helped to establish the Roman type (based on Carolingian Minuscule) used by the Italians as the principal typeface.

In this active intellectual and artistic life a new force arose during the fifteenth century—Florence. Influenced by northern intellectual and artistic movements, using northern inventions like oil paints and the press, the Florentines and their followers in other Italian states transformed the intellectual and artistic outlook and styles of Europe. The Renaissance in fifteenth-century Italy spread to Spain and northern Europe in the sixteenth and seventeenth centuries.

## The Origins of the Italian Renaissance

During the Middle Ages, there were many renaissances, periods when scholars and artists revived classical forms of language, literature, and representation. The Carolingian renaissance had been perhaps the first important movement of this kind. The Ottonian revival had been more of a recovery of the Carolingian renaissance than a rebirth of classical culture. Then in the twelfth century, the greatest medieval renaissance had occurred, carrying into the thirteenth century and visible in the revival of Latin letters, realism in Gothic sculpture, and the efforts in both Romanesque and Gothic architecture to follow Roman practices of constructing large buildings by the use of vaulting. In all these movements, the scholars and artists involved considered themselves the continuators of classical culture. Bernard of Chartres, the twelfth-century teacher of arts, saw himself and his contemporaries as sitting on the shoulders of the giants of classical civilization. His vision was better than theirs, he thought, because their work had placed him in a position to progress along their common route. In political thought, this same idea was expressed by men who saw the medieval empire and papacy as the successors of Rome, both secular and spiritual. Like the authority of the popes, that of the emperors was, with some unfortunate hiatuses, continuously existent from ancient through their own times.

These ideas influenced the character of the medieval renaissances. At first the scholars attempted to reproduce classical models, as in the poetry of the twelfth-century bishop Hildebert of Lavardin (d. 1130). Yet the classical artistic and literary forms eventually were assimilated into contemporary styles because people had no consciousness that the classical forms were distinct from their own. They only saw them as models. Thus the occasional classicality of Gothic sculpture gave way to an absorption of the classical in the medieval style. In literature the ancient epistolary art became a contemporary literary form that imitated generally, not specifically, the classical models. These renaissances were like the monastic reform movements that constantly returned to the Benedictine rule for inspiration but not for creating the new monasticism in the perfect image of the old. A sense of progress was expressed in Bernard of Chartres' statement and in the emphasis of medieval historical thinking on man's progression toward salvation. But the renaissance that began in fourteenth-century Italy was based on a different perspective and attained a different character.

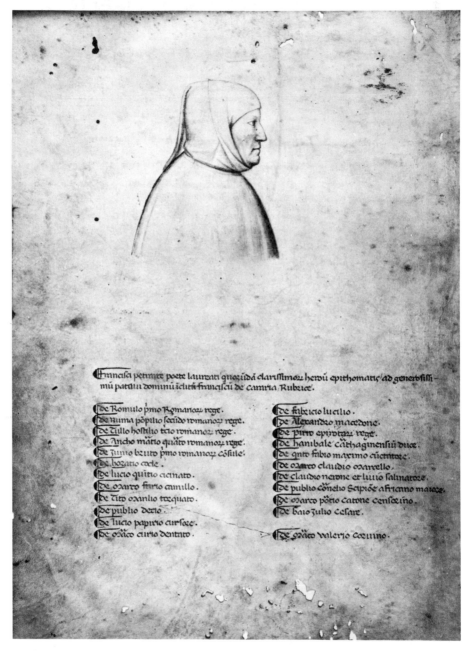

A sketched portrait of Petrarch, done by a friend in a manuscript of the scholar's last work. This excellent portrait as well as much of Petrarch's personal library and letters, with some things written in his own hand, which have been preserved, contribute to the sense of the man Petrarch.

The first man to attempt a new revival was Francesco Petrarch. Petrarch had attended law school at Montpellier but had quit legal studies to devote himself to Cicero and other Latin authors. He was the first to recognize the vast era separating himself from the ancient writers he admired and to argue that medieval intellectuals and artists had not preserved classical culture as they thought. Petrarch coined the term *Gothic* to describe the achievements of the long period between the fourteenth century and the age of Constantine and to emphasize that it was an era in which culture had been barbarian and non-Latin. In his long epic poem *Africa* he tried to re-create classical style, and he sought to rediscover classical work lost for ten centuries. The core of his program was the recognition that he and his contemporaries were definitively separated from the classical age and that they might re-create it but could not continue it, as his predecessors and most of his contemporaries believed. Petrarch therefore had a historical perspective significantly different from the traditional medieval view that saw history as a continuum from the Fall of Man to the Last Judgment.

Other intellectuals shared Petrarch's views and his enthusiasm for the classical world. Giovanni Boccaccio compiled a new and much improved work on classical mythology, *On the Genealogy of the Pagan Gods,* that replaced a twelfth-century collection. In Florence, Boccaccio became the center of a small group of Humanists—a term that meant classicist, a person enamored with classical culture. But a danger was present in this new trend. The Humanists of the fourteenth century began to isolate themselves from the contemporary world in order to devote themselves wholly to the study of classical civilization. Petrarch, who still held the old medieval views about the excellence of the Roman Empire and of its founder, Julius Caesar, criticized Cicero for becoming involved in worldly affairs and for opposing Caesar. The man of culture could not pursue truth and beauty while busy with politics, business, or even the ordinary role of husband and father. Cicero's example showed what might happen if he did so. This tendency in Florentine Humanism began to change in the late fourteenth century. In 1375 Coluccio Salutati (1331–1406), a leading Humanist, became chancellor of the Florentine republic and with his circle began to develop a link between service to the state and Humanistic scholarship. The rise of republican Florence in the struggle against the conquests of Gian Galeazzo Visconti of Milan found expression in the rediscovery of the Roman Republic and in an attack on the medieval legend that Florence had been founded by Julius Caesar and was an expression of the empire. The involvement of the Humanists in civic affairs was intensified by the crisis of 1401 to 1402, when Florence stood alone against Visconti. The city was saved by Gian Galeazzo's death in 1402, but the impression made by the confrontation of the republic against the tyrant had a profound effect on the Humanists, who became propagandists for their city. The greatest of these Humanists, Leonardo Bruni (1369–1444), who followed Salutati in the chancellorship, wrote a long history of Florence linking its founding and its civic greatness with republican Rome.

It has been argued that the crisis of 1401 to 1402 played a crucial role in the development of Humanist culture by saving it from the isolation and social peculiarity into which it seemed to have been falling during the fourteenth century. Certainly, the transformation did not take place at once in the first years of the fifteenth century and can be seen developing, along with the confrontation with Milan, during the last decades of the previous century. The Humanists were also reaffirmed in their social and political role in the 1420s and the 1440s by further confrontations with tyrants. These political events made the Humanists and their culture a prominent part of Florentine civic life and solidified the connection between the city's leading families and figures and its intellectuals; it engendered a form of Humanism now often called civic Humanism. The movement also affected artists like Masaccio (1402–1429) and Brunelleschi (1377–1446), both of whom studied the ancient monuments so that they might re-create them in their own work. The civic Humanists made the active life a part of their ethos and concomitantly made their intellectual and educational interests part of their active life. The leaders of society looked to the Humanists for the education in classical studies that would prepare them for public life. Only in the twentieth century, under the impact of a burgeoning science, have the educational ideals developed by the fifteenth-century Florentines and exported to all Europe begun to give way.

Did the Middle Ages end in Italy in the fifteenth century and elsewhere in Europe in the sixteenth or seventeenth centuries? It can be argued that medieval institutions, religion, society, and economy had been changing for centuries and continued to change in a continuum that was not broken by a few intellectuals and artists in fifteenth-century Italy. It can be argued that almost all the ideas and ideals of the Humanists were anticipated in the Middle Ages and that what originality they possessed cannot justify calling their period a new historical age. All these things are true; some medieval institutions and ideas still exist—the university is one example. Yet the Humanists did create something new that has had a profound effect on Europeans and on those they conquered or colonized in the postmedieval centuries. They created a historical consciousness that broke with the old view of history as a continuous development toward a goal, and they recognized the past as definitively distinct from the present. Medieval scholars and artists, considering the classical period but an earlier stage of their own era, took from it what they wanted and what appealed to them. The Humanists looked on the past as lost and sought to re-create it as a whole, as they found it. This task led to a critical appreciation of the sources and the apparent shape and characteristics of classical civilization. The Humanists' approach to history made them aware of their own perspective and of the problems of their subjectivity. This same problem of awareness characterized artists of the period, who began to see

Masaccio's fresco *The Expulsion from Eden*. Masaccio was associated with the Florentine Humanists and sought to recapture the classical style, which emphasized realism and emotional intensity. The fresco (ca. 1425) is in Brancacci Chapel of Santa Maria del Carmine, Florence.

painting and sculpture as the product of their personal vision of reality, of their perspective. The later development of the Humanists' consciousness of history and the world would astonish and probably dismay them, but during the succeeding centuries, their idea of the way man and the world interact pervaded European culture.

Humanist ideas of history and society did not take hold in Europe simply because they were a compelling way to perceive the world. Late–fifteenth- and early–sixteenth-century events and developments disrupted the social, economic, and political fabric of medieval civilization, producing the kind of situation-in-flux that forms a fertile bed for new ideas and a new consciousness.

Conventionally, the year 1500 is used to mark the end of the Middle Ages and the beginning of the early modern period of European history. That uneventful year appears to be a chronological midpoint for a series of events that resulted in fundamental changes in European society and in an extraordinary growth of European wealth and power. Between 1488 and 1522 Díaz sailed around the Cape of Good Hope, Columbus discovered America, Magellan's expedition circumnavigated the globe. These and other explorations opened a new era in the history of European expansionism, the era of great colonial empires. Since the late eleventh century, European conquest had been at the expense of Arab states, principally those of the Levant and of Spain. This expansion had resulted in the enlargement of the Spanish Christian kingdoms, in the establishment of some European states in the eastern Mediterranean, and in the placement of trading colonies in Eastern cities. But no European power had established a colonial empire. In the sixteenth century, the European nations did create such empires, bringing into their control new sources of wealth and power unknown in the Middle Ages.

The new imperialism enriched the nations of Europe and gave impetus to the growth of commerce and the commercial classes. The urbanization of the Western economy, as opposed to Western culture, began in the sixteenth century. The new imperialism also had an important political effect. The power of medieval monarchies had been limited, in theory by the doctrine that the ruler is under the law and under God, in practice by the limited funds kings had at their disposal. In the later Middle Ages, almost every monarch in Europe had been forced to turn to representative assemblies for financial aid and, as a result, had faced the prospect of constitutional limitation of his power. The new wealth of the colonies benefited the kings as much as the merchants. The royal governments patented the overseas expeditions and received enormous fees and tax revenues from the new trade. Thus in the early modern age kings were able again, as they had been in the early Middle Ages, to support their policies and activities from their own income, able to govern without the aid of parliaments, *cortes,* or estates. The early modern age was an age of absolutism in government.

Other events of the years around 1500 had far-reaching effects. Erasmus published the first Greek edition of the New Testament in 1516, two years after Machiavelli's *Prince* appeared and a year before Martin Luther nailed his Ninety-Five Theses to the door of his church in Wittenberg. Machiavelli's work responded to the confusing political world of fifteenth-century Italy, freed from the hierarchical structure and the values of medieval kingdoms. Machiavelli developed a political theory to deal with the new kind of political authority.

Erasmus' work evinced the Humanist attitude toward the literature of classical times. The Greek New Testament was a classical work rediscovered, which would become the basis for a new biblical criticism sensitive to the language and meaning of the original authors and ultimately to the historical context in which they wrote. Luther's theological positions also were consistent with the Humanist perspective. He claimed to be reasserting the doctrines of the Fathers, which, he argued, had been abandoned by the Church. But Luther also followed the long line of medieval churchmen and monks who had criticized the Church of their times, often on the same grounds as he, and the far-reaching results of his reformation were more a function of the contemporary political situation than of the force or character of his argument.

In fact, none of the events of Luther's lifetime surprise the medievalist: they all have medieval precursors and causes. And yet the profound changes in intellectual attitudes, in institutions, in economic and social life that resulted from these events justify the treatment of the Middle Ages as a distinct civilization.

### Suggestions for Further Reading

**Secondary Works**   On late medieval intellectual history, see E. A. Moody, *The Logic of William of Ockham* (New York, 1935); S. C. Tornay, *Ockham: Studies and Selections* (La Salle, Ill., 1938); L. Thorndike, *Science and Thought in the Fifteenth Century* (New York, 1929); and G. Sarton, *The Appreciation of Ancient and Medieval Science During the Renaissance* (Philadelphia, 1955). For later medieval mysticism, J. M. Clark, *The Great German Mystics: Eckhart, Tauler, and Suso* (Oxford, 1949), and A. Hyma, *The Youth of Erasmus* (Ann Arbor, Mich., 1930) contain good accounts. H. B. Workman, *John Wyclif*, 2 vols. (Oxford, 1926) is the basic modern work, while K. B. McFarlane, *John Wycliffe and the Beginnings of English Nonconformity* (London, 1952) is an interesting essay. Of equal interest is Montague Summers, *The History of Witchcraft and Demonology*, 2nd ed. (New York, 1956). The great classic on late medieval culture is J. Huizinga, *The Waning of the Middle Ages* (New York, 1949). On literature, see E. K. Chambers, *English Literature at the Close of the Middle Ages* (London, 1951); E. F. Chaney, *François Villon in His Environment* (Oxford, 1946); H. S. Bennett, *Chaucer and the Fifteenth Century* (Oxford, 1947); E. H. Wilkins, *Studies in the Life and Works of Petrarch* (Cambridge, Mass., 1955); and E. Hutton, *Giovanni Boccaccio, A Biographical Study* (London, 1910). J. Evans, *English Art, 1307–1461* (Oxford, 1949); B. Berenson, *Italian Painters of the Renaissance*, rev. ed. (New York, 1957); M. Meiss, *Giotto and Assisi* (New York, 1960), *Painting in Florence and Siena After the Black Death* (Princeton, N.J., 1951), and *French Painting in the Time of Jean de Berry: The Late XIV Century and the Patronage of the Duke*, 2 vols. (New York, 1967); and E. Panofsky, *Early Netherlandish Painting: Its Origins and Character* (Cambridge, Mass., 1953) are good sources for the art of the later Middle Ages. On the origins of printing, see G. P. Winship, *Printing in the Fifteenth Century* (Philadelphia, 1940), and P. Butler, *The Origin of Printing in Europe* (Chicago, 1940). J. Burckhardt, *The Civilization of the Renaissance in Italy* (New York, 1954) is a classic study of the early history of Humanism and the Italian Renaissance. A good, brief survey is W. F. Ferguson, *The Renaissance* (New York, 1940); see also the work of E. Rice cited at the end of Chapter 26. Some more recent works of great value are H. Baron, *The Crisis of the Early Italian Renaissance,* 2 vols. (Princeton, N.J., 1955); W. F. Ferguson, *The Renaissance in Historical Thought* (Boston, 1948); G. C. Sellery, *The Renaissance* (Madison, Wis., 1950); P. O. Kristeller, *The Classics and Renaissance Thought* (Cambridge, Mass., 1955); and Denys Hay, *The Italian Renaissance in Its Historical Background* (Cambridge, 1961). Besides the basic work of Berenson cited above, see E. Panofsky, *Studies in Iconology: Humanistic Themes in the Art of the Renaissance* (Oxford, 1939), and R. Wittkower, *Architectural Principles in the Age of Humanism* (London, 1949), while A. C. Krey, *Florence, A City that Art Built* (Minneapolis, Minn., 1936) is an interesting introduction to several aspects of art and life in the period.

**Sources** Useful general collections are F. Schevill, ed., *The First Century of Italian Humanism* (New York, 1928); J. B. Ross and M. M. McLaughlin, *The Portable Renaissance Reader* (New York, 1953); and E. Cassirer et al., eds., *The Renaissance Philosophy of Man* (Chicago, 1948). The following works are a selection of the more interesting of the translated sources for the later Middle Ages: J. H. Robinson and H. W. Rolfe, *Petrarch,* 2nd ed. (New York, 1914); *Petrarch: Sonnets & Songs,* trans. A. M. Armi (New York, 1946); *The Decameron of Boccaccio,* trans. John Payne (Modern Library and other editions); *The Imitation of Christ* (many editions); *Theologia Germanica,* trans. T. S. Kepler (Cleveland, 1952); *The Revelations of . . . Julian of Norwich,* ed. R. Hudleston (London, 1952); *The Book of Margery Kempe,* trans. W. Butler-Bowden (London, 1936); T. Morrison, *The Portable Chaucer* (New York, 1949); Froissart and Commines (both in several editions); an abridged edition of the *Memoirs of a Renaissance Pope: The Commentaries of Pius II,* ed. and trans. F. A. Gragg and L. C. Gabel (New York, 1959); and *I Laugh Through Tears: The Ballades of François Villon,* trans. G. P. Cuttino (New York, 1955), the most recent effort to convey the thought and feeling of Villon to modern readers.

# The Medieval Popes[1]

Sylvester I, 314–335
Mark, 336
Julius I, 337–352
Liberius, 352–366
(Felix II, 355–365)
Damasus I, 366–384
Siricius, 384–399
Anastasius I, 399–401
Innocent I, 401–417
Zosimus, 417–418
Boniface I, 418–422
Celestine I, 422–432
Sixtus III, 432–440
Leo I the Great, 440–461

Hilary, 461–468
Simplicius, 468–483
Felix III, 483–492
Gelasius I, 492–496
Anastasius II, 496–498
Symmachus, 498–514
Hormisdas, 514–523
John I, 523–526
Felix IV, 526–530
Boniface II, 530–532
John II, 533–535
Agapitus I, 535–536
Silverius, 536–537
Vigilius, 537–555

[1] This list is based on Angelo Mercati, "The New List of the Popes," *Medieval Studies* 9 (1947): 71–80, which reprints with corrections the list in the *Annuario Pontificio* for 1947. Names and dates in parentheses are those of antipopes.

Pelagius I, 555–561

John III, 561–574

Benedict I, 575–579

Pelagius II, 579–590

Gregory I the Great, 590–604

Sabinianus, 604–606

Boniface III, 607

Boniface IV, 608–615

Deusdedit, 615–618[2]

Boniface V, 619–625

Honorius I, 625–638

Severinus, 640

John IV, 640–642

Theodore I, 642–649

Martin I, 649–655

Eugenius I, 654–657[3]

Vitalian, 657–672

Adeodatus II, 672–676

Donus, 676–678

Agatho, 678–681

Leo II, 682–683

Benedict II, 684–685

John V, 685–686

Conon, 686–687

Sergius I, 687–701

John VI, 701–705

John VII, 705–707

Sisinnius, 708

Constantine, 708–715

Gregory II, 715–731

Gregory III, 731–741

Zacharias, 741–752

Stephen II, 752–757[4]

Paul I, 757–767

Stephen III, 768–772

Adrian I, 772–795

Leo III, 795–816

Stephen IV, 816–817

Paschal I, 817–824

Eugenius II, 824–827

Valentine, 827

Gregory IV, 827–844

Sergius II, 844–847

Leo IV, 847–855

Benedict III, 855–858

Nicholas I the Great, 858–867

Adrian II, 867–872

John VIII, 872–882

Marinus I, 882–884

Adrian III, 884–885

Stephen V, 885–891

Formosus, 891–896

Boniface VI, 896

Stephen VI, 896–897

Romanus, 897

Theodore II, 897

John IX, 898–900

Benedict IV, 900–903

Leo V, 903

(Christopher, 903–904)

Sergius III, 904–911

Anastasius III, 911–913

Lando, 913–914

John X, 914–928

Leo VI, 928

Stephen VII, 928–931

John XI, 931–935

Leo VII, 936–939

Stephen VIII, 939–942

Marinus II, 942–946

---

[2] Also known as Adeodatus I.

[3] Martin I was exiled, and Eugenius I was crowned pope before Martin's death.

[4] On later lists known as Stephen III because a priest by the name of Stephen was elected to succeed Zacharias but died three days after election and without being consecrated. The numeration of all Stephens on this list follows the medieval usage, which omits the unconsecrated "successor" of Zacharias.

Agapitus II, 946–955
John XII, 955–964[5]
Leo VIII, 963–965
Benedict V, 964–966
John XIII, 965–972
Benedict VI, 973–974
(Boniface VII, 974 and 984–985)
Benedict VII, 974–983
John XIV, 983–984
John XV, 985–996
Gregory V, 996–999
(John XVI, 997–998)
Sylvester II, 999–1003
John XVII, 1003
John XVIII, 1004–1009
Sergius IV, 1009–1012
Benedict VIII, 1012–1024
John XIX, 1024–1032
Benedict IX, 1032–1044
Sylvester III, 1045
Benedict IX, 1045
    [for the second time]
Gregory VI, 1045–1046
Clement II, 1046–1047
Benedict IX, 1047–1048
    [for the third time]
Damasus II, 1048
Leo IX, 1049–1054
Victor II, 1055–1057
Stephen IX, 1057–1058
(Benedict X, 1058–1059)
Nicholas II, 1059–1061
Alexander II, 1061–1073
Gregory VII, 1073–1085
(Clement III, 1080 and 1084–1100)
Victor III, 1086–1087

Urban II, 1088–1099
Paschal II, 1099–1118
(Theodoric, 1100)
(Albert, 1102)
(Sylvester IV, 1105–1111)
Gelasius II, 1118–1119
(Gregory VIII, 1118–1121)
Calixtus II, 1119–1124
Honorius II, 1124–1130
Innocent II, 1130–1143
(Anacletus II, 1130–1138)
Celestine II, 1143–1144
Lucius II, 1144–1145
Eugenius III, 1145–1153
Anastasius IV, 1153–1154
Adrian IV, 1154–1159
Alexander III, 1159–1181
(Victor IV, 1159–1164)
(Paschal III, 1164–1168)
(Calixtus III, 1168–1178)
(Innocent III, 1179–1180)
Lucius III, 1181–1185
Urban III, 1185–1187
Gregory VIII, 1187
Clement III, 1187–1191
Celestine III, 1191–1198
Innocent III, 1198–1216
Honorius III, 1216–1227
Gregory IX, 1227–1241
Celestine IV, 1241
Innocent IV, 1243–1254
Alexander IV, 1254–1261
Urban IV, 1261–1264
Clement IV, 1265–1268
Gregory X, 1271–1276
Innocent V, 1276

[5] John XII was deposed at a Roman council in 963 where Leo VIII was elected, under the influence of Otto I, the emperor. On the death of John XII, Benedict V was elected by John's supporters and was promptly deposed at another council held by Leo VIII and Otto I. Under these circumstances either Leo VIII or Benedict V may be considered an antipope.

Adrian V, 1276
John XXI, 1276–1277[6]
Nicholas III, 1277–1280
Martin IV, 1281–1285[7]
Honorius IV, 1285–1287
Nicholas IV, 1288–1292
Celestine V, 1294
Boniface VIII, 1294–1303
Benedict XI, 1303–1304
Clement V, 1305–1314
John XXII, 1316–1334
Benedict XII, 1334–1342
Clement VI, 1342–1352
Innocent VI, 1352–1362
Urban V, 1362–1370
Gregory XI, 1370–1378
Urban VI, 1378–1389
    Clement VII, 1378–1394[8]

Boniface IX, 1389–1404
    Benedict XIII, 1394–1423[8]
Innocent VII, 1404–1406
Gregory XII, 1406–1415
    (Alexander V, 1409–1410)[9]
    (John XXIII, 1410–1415)[9]
Martin V, 1417–1431
    (Clement VIII, 1423–1429)[8]
    (Benedict XIV, 1425–1430?)[8]
Eugenius IV, 1431–1447
(Felix V, 1439–1449)
Nicholas V, 1447–1455
Calixtus III, 1455–1458
Pius II, 1458–1464
Paul II, 1464–1471
Sixtus IV, 1471–1484
Innocent VIII, 1484–1492
Alexander VI, 1492–1503

[6] Although he was the twentieth pope of this name (or the nineteenth if John XVI be excluded), by an error of enumeration this pope has always been called John XXI.
[7] Numbered "IV" because Marinus I and Marinus II were also considered as "Martin."
[8] Of the Avignon line.
[9] Elected at the Council of Pisa.

# Genealogical Tables

## THE MEROVINGIANS

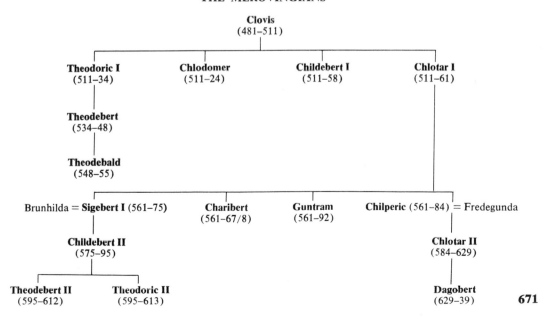

**Clovis**
(481–511)

**Theodoric I**
(511–34)

**Chlodomer**
(511–24)

**Childebert I**
(511–58)

**Chlotar I**
(511–61)

**Theodebert**
(534–48)

**Theodebald**
(548–55)

Brunhilda = **Sigebert I** (561–75)

**Charibert**
(561–67/8)

**Guntram**
(561–92)

**Chilperic** (561–84) = Fredegunda

**Childebert II**
(575–95)

**Chlotar II**
(584–629)

**Theodebert II**
(595–612)

**Theodoric II**
(595–613)

**Dagobert**
(629–39)

## THE CAROLINGIANS

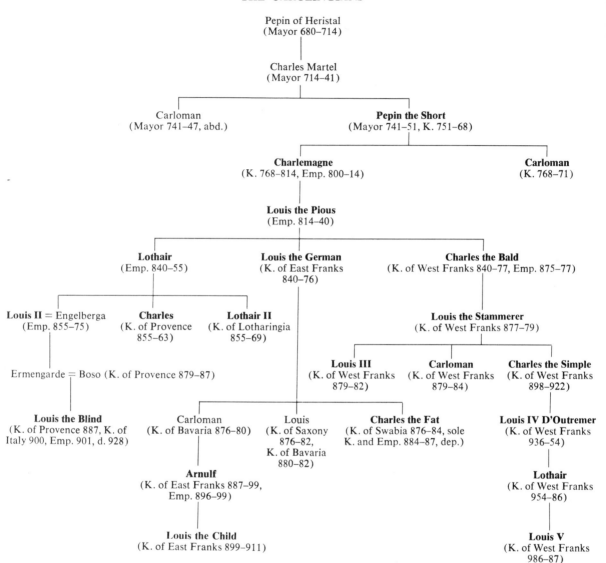

Pepin of Heristal
(Mayor 680–714)

Charles Martel
(Mayor 714–41)

Carloman
(Mayor 741–47, abd.)

**Pepin the Short**
(Mayor 741–51, K. 751–68)

**Charlemagne**
(K. 768–814, Emp. 800–14)

**Carloman**
(K. 768–71)

Louis the Pious
(Emp. 814–40)

**Lothair**
(Emp. 840–55)

**Louis the German**
(K. of East Franks
840–76)

**Charles the Bald**
(K. of West Franks 840–77, Emp. 875–77)

Louis II = Engelberga
(Emp. 855–75)

**Charles**
(K. of Provence
855–63)

**Lothair II**
(K. of Lotharingia
855–69)

**Louis the Stammerer**
(K. of West Franks 877–79)

Ermengarde = Boso (K. of Provence 879–87)

**Louis III**
(K. of West Franks
879–82)

**Carloman**
(K. of West Franks
879–84)

**Charles the Simple**
(K. of West Franks
898–922)

**Louis the Blind**
(K. of Provence 887, K. of
Italy 900, Emp. 901, d. 928)

Carloman
(K. of Bavaria 876–80)

Louis
(K. of Saxony
876–82,
K. of Bavaria
880–82)

**Charles the Fat**
(K. of Swabia 876–84, sole
K. and Emp. 884–87, dep.)

**Louis IV D'Outremer**
(K. of West Franks
936–54)

**Arnulf**
(K. of East Franks 887–99,
Emp. 896–99)

**Lothair**
(K. of West Franks
954–86)

**Louis the Child**
(K. of East Franks 899–911)

**Louis V**
(K. of West Franks
986–87)

## THE SAXON, SALIAN, AND HOHENSTAUFEN DYNASTIES

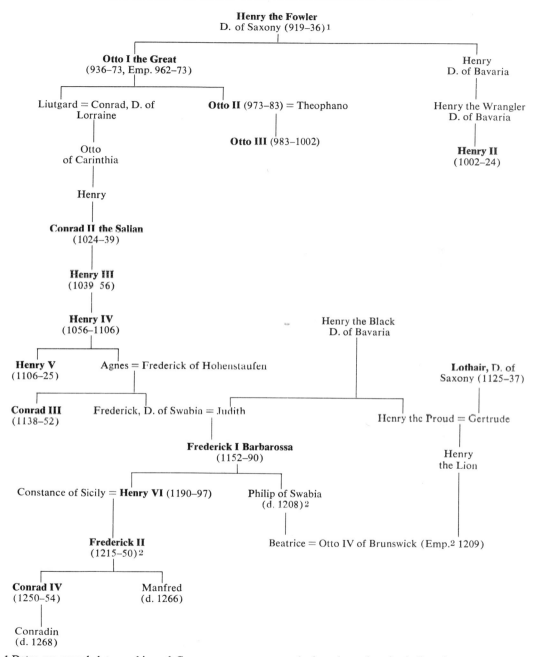

**Henry the Fowler**
D. of Saxony (919–36)[1]

**Otto I the Great**
(936–73, Emp. 962–73)

Henry
D. of Bavaria

Liutgard = Conrad, D. of
Lorraine

**Otto II** (973–83) = Theophano

Henry the Wrangler
D. of Bavaria

Otto
of Carinthia

**Otto III** (983–1002)

**Henry II**
(1002–24)

Henry

**Conrad II the Salian**
(1024–39)

**Henry III**
(1039–56)

**Henry IV**
(1056–1106)

Henry the Black
D. of Bavaria

**Henry V**
(1106–25)

Agnes = Frederick of Hohenstaufen

**Lothair**, D. of
Saxony (1125–37)

**Conrad III**
(1138–52)

Frederick, D. of Swabia = Judith

Henry the Proud = Gertrude

**Frederick I Barbarossa**
(1152–90)

Henry
the Lion

Constance of Sicily = **Henry VI** (1190–97)

Philip of Swabia
(d. 1208)[2]

**Frederick II**
(1215–50)[2]

Beatrice = Otto IV of Brunswick (Emp.[2] 1209)

**Conrad IV**
(1250–54)

Manfred
(d. 1266)

Conradin
(d. 1268)

[1] Dates are regnal dates as king of Germany or emperor, or both, unless otherwise indicated.
[2] For the claims of Philip of Swabia, Otto IV of Brunswick, and Frederick II during the period 1198–1215, see pp. 462–63, 466, 468.

## THE CAPETIAN DYNASTY

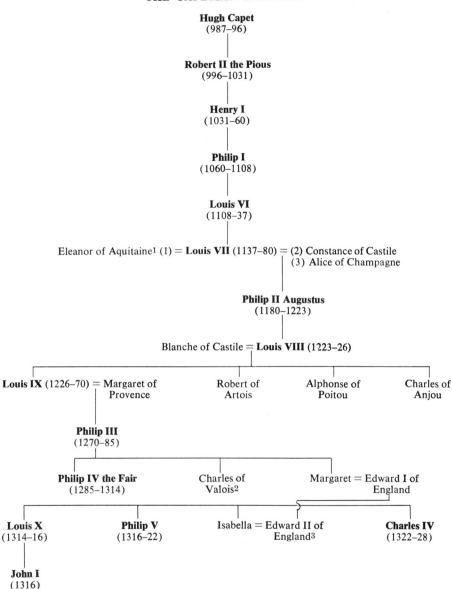

**Hugh Capet**
(987–96)

**Robert II the Pious**
(996–1031)

**Henry I**
(1031–60)

**Philip I**
(1060–1108)

**Louis VI**
(1108–37)

Eleanor of Aquitaine[1] (1) = **Louis VII** (1137–80) = (2) Constance of Castile
(3) Alice of Champagne

**Philip II Augustus**
(1180–1223)

Blanche of Castile = **Louis VIII** (1223–26)

**Louis IX** (1226–70) = Margaret of Provence     Robert of Artois     Alphonse of Poitou     Charles of Anjou

**Philip III**
(1270–85)

**Philip IV the Fair**
(1285–1314)     Charles of Valois[2]     Margaret = Edward I of England

**Louis X**
(1314–16)     **Philip V**
(1316–22)     Isabella = Edward II of England[3]     **Charles IV**
(1322–28)

**John I**
(1316)

[1] Eleanor of Aquitaine late married Henry of Anjou, who became Henry II of England in 1154; see the genealogy of the Norman and Plantagenet kings.
[2] Philip VI of Valois was the son of Charles of Valois; see the genealogy of the Valois kings.
[3] The union of Edward II of England and Isabella produced Edward III of England; see the genealogy of the Norman and Plantagenet kings.

# NORMAN AND PLANTAGENET RULERS OF ENGLAND

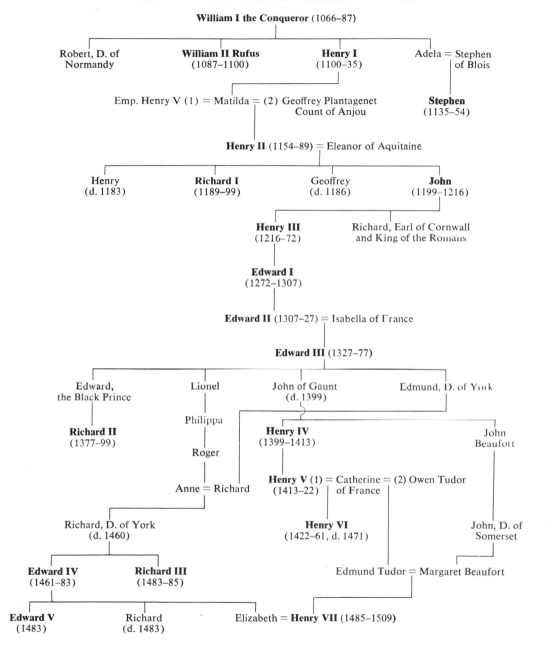

**William I the Conqueror** (1066–87)

Robert, D. of Normandy

**William II Rufus** (1087–1100)

**Henry I** (1100–35)

Adela = Stephen of Blois

Emp. Henry V (1) = Matilda = (2) Geoffrey Plantagenet Count of Anjou

**Stephen** (1135–54)

**Henry II** (1154–89) = Eleanor of Aquitaine

Henry (d. 1183)

**Richard I** (1189–99)

Geoffrey (d. 1186)

**John** (1199–1216)

**Henry III** (1216–72)

Richard, Earl of Cornwall and King of the Romans

**Edward I** (1272–1307)

**Edward II** (1307–27) = Isabella of France

**Edward III** (1327–77)

Edward, the Black Prince

Lionel

John of Gaunt (d. 1399)

Edmund, D. of York

**Richard II** (1377–99)

Philippa

**Henry IV** (1399–1413)

John Beaufort

Roger

**Henry V** (1) = Catherine = (2) Owen Tudor (1413–22) of France

Anne = Richard

Richard, D. of York (d. 1460)

**Henry VI** (1422–61, d. 1471)

John, D. of Somerset

**Edward IV** (1461–83)

**Richard III** (1483–85)

Edmund Tudor = Margaret Beaufort

**Edward V** (1483)

Richard (d. 1483)

Elizabeth = **Henry VII** (1485–1509)

## GERMANY UNDER THE LUXEMBOURGS AND HABSBURGS

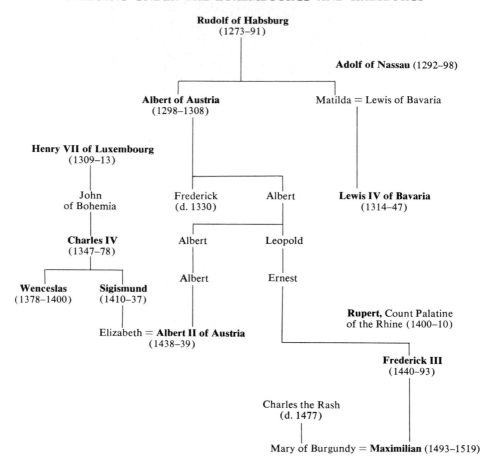

**Rudolf of Habsburg**
(1273–91)

**Adolf of Nassau** (1292–98)

**Albert of Austria**
(1298–1308)

Matilda = Lewis of Bavaria

**Henry VII of Luxembourg**
(1309–13)

John
of Bohemia

Frederick
(d. 1330)

Albert

**Lewis IV of Bavaria**
(1314–47)

**Charles IV**
(1347–78)

Albert

Leopold

**Wenceslas**
(1378–1400)

**Sigismund**
(1410–37)

Albert

Ernest

**Rupert,** Count Palatine
of the Rhine (1400–10)

Elizabeth = **Albert II of Austria**
(1438–39)

**Frederick III**
(1440–93)

Charles the Rash
(d. 1477)

Mary of Burgundy = **Maximilian** (1493–1519)

## THE VALOIS KINGS OF FRANCE

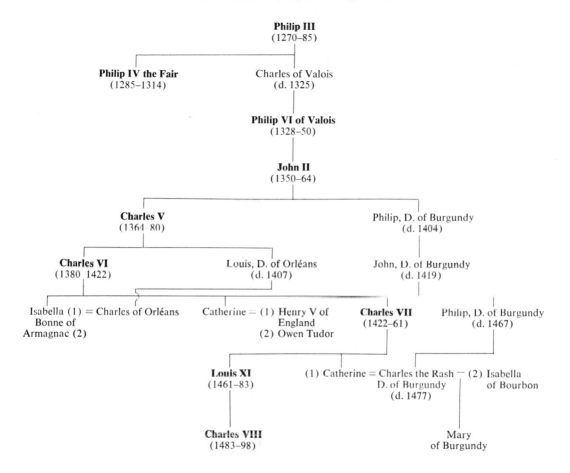

**Philip III**
(1270–85)

**Philip IV the Fair**
(1285–1314)

Charles of Valois
(d. 1325)

**Philip VI of Valois**
(1328–50)

**John II**
(1350–64)

**Charles V**
(1364–80)

Philip, D. of Burgundy
(d. 1404)

**Charles VI**
(1380–1422)

Louis, D. of Orléans
(d. 1407)

John, D. of Burgundy
(d. 1419)

Isabella (1) = Charles of Orléans
Bonne of
Armagnac (2)

Catherine = (1) Henry V of
England
(2) Owen Tudor

**Charles VII**
(1422–61)

Philip, D. of Burgundy
(d. 1467)

**Louis XI**
(1461–83)

(1) Catherine = Charles the Rash — (2) Isabella
D. of Burgundy           of Bourbon
(d. 1477)

**Charles VIII**
(1483–98)

Mary
of Burgundy

# Index